The LNICST series publishes ICST's conferences, symposia and workshops.
LNICST reports state-of-the-art results in areas related to the scope of the Institute.
The type of material published includes

- Proceedings (published in time for the respective event)
- Other edited monographs (such as project reports or invited volumes)

LNICST topics span the following areas:

- General Computer Science
- E-Economy
- E-Medicine
- Knowledge Management
- Multimedia
- Operations, Management and Policy
- Social Informatics
- Systems

Wei Liang · Sun-Yuan Kung · Meikang Qiu
Editors

Security and Privacy in Communication Networks

21st EAI International Conference, SecureComm 2025
Xiangtan, China, July 4–6, 2025
Proceedings, Part IV

 Springer

Editors
Wei Liang [ID]
Hunan University of Science and Technology
Xiangtan, China

Sun-Yuan Kung [ID]
Princeton University
Princeton, NJ, USA

Meikang Qiu [ID]
Augusta University
Augusta, GA, USA

ISSN 1867-8211   ISSN 1867-822X (electronic)
Lecture Notes of the Institute for Computer Sciences, Social Informatics
and Telecommunications Engineering
ISBN 978-3-032-23455-1   ISBN 978-3-032-23456-8 (eBook)
https://doi.org/10.1007/978-3-032-23456-8

Preface

We are excited to present the proceedings of the 21st EAI International Conference on Security and Privacy in Communication Networks (SecureComm 2025), held from 4 July 2025 to 6 July 2025 in Xiangtan, China under the sponsorship of the European Alliance for Innovation (EAI). This year's conference brought together leading researchers, practitioners, and academics to explore the forefront of security and privacy challenges in communication networks.

Over the past two decades, SecureComm has become a premier forum for discussing innovations and advancements in secure communications and information systems. This year, it continued this tradition by featuring a diverse collection of cutting-edge research, thought-provoking keynote addresses, and insightful panel discussions, all tailored to address the ever-evolving landscape of cybersecurity and privacy.

This year's submissions reached a record number in the history of the SecureComm conference. A total of 341 manuscripts were received, and all submissions went through an extensive single-blind review process with at least 3 reviews by Technical Program Committee (TPC) members with relevant subject matter expertise. Eventually only 119 submissions were accepted. The acceptance rate was 35%. Authors of accepted papers presented their work and took questions from the audience. The 2025 edition highlighted key topics including five major areas: Distributed and Network Security, ML/AI Security, CyberSecurity, Cryptography and Authentication, and Security and Optimization. We gave special attention to emerging areas such as LLM Security, Quantum Security, and CPU and Chip design-related security, confirming the conference's commitment to addressing contemporary and future challenges.

We extend our heartfelt gratitude to the authors for their invaluable contributions, the TPC members and reviewers for their dedication to ensuring a rigorous selection process, and the keynote speakers for sharing their expertise. We are also deeply appreciative of the conference organizers, sponsors, and volunteers whose efforts made this event possible.

We extend our heartfelt gratitude to the Program Committee members and external reviewers for generously volunteering their time to review and discuss the conference papers. Special thanks go to the General Chair and Program Chairs for their outstanding leadership, and to the Host, Local, Publicity, and Publication Chairs for their dedicated efforts to ensure the success of SecureComm 2025. Finally, we would like to express our appreciation to all the authors for contributing their invaluable work to SecureComm 2025.

We hope these proceedings will serve as valuable resources for researchers, educators, practitioners, and policymakers, fostering innovation and collaboration to advance the state of the art in communication security and privacy.

We hope you enjoyed the conference at Xiangtan!

Wei Liang
Sun-Yuan Kung
Meikang Qiu

Organization

Steering Committee

Peng Liu   Pennsylvania State University, USA
Sencun Zhu   Pennsylvania State University, USA
Xiapu Luo   Hong Kong Polytechnic University, China

Organizing Committee

General Chair

Meikang Qiu   Augusta University, USA

General Co-chairs

Dafang Zhang   Hunan University, China
Keqin Li   State University of New York at New Paltz, USA

TPC Chair and Co-chairs

Wei Liang   Hunan University of Science and Technology
                         China
Sun-Yuan Kung   Princeton University, USA
Kuan-Ching Li   Hunan University of Science and Technology,
                         China
Naixue Xiong   Hunan University of Science and Technology,
                         China

Host Chairs

Yan Zhang   University of Oslo, Norway
Jin Wang   Hunan University of Science and Technology,
                         China
Gérard Memmi   Télécom Paris, France
Kun Xie   Hunan University, China
Jing Long   Hunan Normal University, China

Publicity and Social Media Chair

Songwen Pei   University of Shanghai for Science and Technology, China

Web Chair

Yunhe Feng   University of North Texas, USA

Workshops Chair and Posters and Demos Track Chair

Jihe Wang   Northwestern Polytechnical University, China

Sponsorship and Exhibits Chairs

Yongxing Zhu   Chinese Academy of Sciences, China
Qinhong Jiang   Hong Kong Polytechnic University, China

Publications Chairs

Zhihui Lu   Fudan University, China
Xiang Li   Nankai University, China

Local Chair and Tutorials Chair

Xiangwei Meng   Hunan University of Science and Technology, China

Local Chairs

Lijun Xiao   Hunan University of Science and Technology, China
Shiwen Zhang   Hunan University of Science and Technology, China
Xuchong Liu   Hunan Police Academy, China
Zulong Diao   Hunan University of Science and Technology, China

Technical Program Committee

Abhinav Mehta	Amazon, USA
Abubakar Sadiq Sani	University of Greenwich, UK
Antreas Dionysiou	University of Cyprus, Cyprus
Azadeh Tabiban	University of Manitoba, Canada
Bo Chen	Michigan Technological University, USA
Bo Luo	University of Kansas, USA
Bowen Zhao	Xidian University, China
Chenxi Qiu	University of North Texas, USA
Chenxiong Qian	University of Hong Kong, China
Chunhua Su	University of Aizu, Japan
David Arroyo	Spanish National Research Council, Spain
Debiao He	Wuhan University, China
Ding Wang	Nankai University, China
Dong Zhong	University of Tennessee, USA
Ehab Al-Shaer	Carnegie Mellon University, USA
Fan Sang	Georgia Institute of Technology, USA
Furkan Alaca	Queen's University, Canada
Georgios Kavallieratos	Norwegian University of Science and Technology, Norway
Guangquan Xu	Tianjin University, China
Guillaume Hiet	CentraleSupélec, France
Haibing Lu	Santa Clara University, USA
Haibo Wang	University of Kentucky, USA
Han Qiu	Tsinghua University, China
Hongxin Hu	University at Buffalo, USA
Irdin Pekaric	University of Liechtenstein, Liechtenstein
Jacques Traore	Orange Innovation, France
Jihe Wang	Northwestern Polytechnical University, China
Jingqiang Lin	University of Science and Technology of China, China
Jinguang Han	Southeast University, China
Jinjin Liang	Qi An Xin Group, China
Keting Jia	Tsinghua University, China
Keyu Man	Meta, USA
Lei Xue	Sun Yat-sen University, China
Lei Zhang	East China Normal University, China
Lu Zhou	Nanjing University of Aeronautics and Astronautics, China
Martin Andreoni	Technology Innovation Institute, United Arab Emirates

Contents

Cryptography and Authentication

Security and Optimization

Cryptography and Authentication

Optimized Entanglement Routing for Enhanced Quantum Key Distribution Performance in Quantum Networks

Hongding Zhang[1]($\boxtimes$), Sheng Huo[2], Ping Jiang[2], and Xiaoyan Chen[3]

[1] School of Computer Science and Engineering, Hunan University of Science and Technology, Xiangtan, China
`hdzhang@mail.hnust.edu.cn`
[2] Zhuzhou CRRC Times Electriz Co., Ltd., Zhuzhou, China
`{huosheng,jiangping}@csrzic.com`
[3] School of Software Engineering, Xiamen University of Technology, Xiamen, China
`cxy@xmut.edu.cn`

Abstract. In quantum networks supporting Quantum Key Distribution (QKD), establishing reliable end-to-end entanglement is essential for secure communication. This requires selecting optimal entanglement paths. However, resource shortages and potential congestion in the network limit QKD performance. In this work, we achieve efficient entanglement path selection by balancing link load and formally formulate the load optimization problem. We propose the Utilization-based Entanglement Routing Algorithm (UERA), which dynamically selects resource-abundant paths to alleviate congestion caused by high resource demand on bottleneck links, thereby enhancing network throughput. Extensive simulations show that UERA effectively reduces congestion and improves network throughput by 7.3% compared to conventional methods.

Keywords: Quantum networks · Entanglement routing

1 Introduction

In the era of digital transformation, information security remains one of the most critical challenges across all technological applications [10]. Over the decades, conventional cryptographic techniques have evolved to safeguard network communications. A prominent example is the Rivest-Shamir-Adleman (RSA) public-key cryptosystem, which has served as a cornerstone for secure key exchange and identity authentication in modern protocols, relying on the computational hardness assumption of the Integer Factorization Problem (IFP) [6]. However, the rapid advancement of quantum information technology has introduced unprecedented threats. Quantum algorithms such as Shor's algorithm have demonstrated

This work is supported by the Natural Science Foundation of Fujian Province, China (Grant No. 2023J011460).

W. Liang et al. (Eds.): SecureComm 2025, LNICST 690, pp. 3–17, 2026.
https://doi.org/10.1007/978-3-032-23456-8_1

exponential speedup in integer factorization, posing a severe risk to existing security infrastructures [22]. This breakthrough fundamentally undermines the computational assumptions that underpin RSA and similar classical cryptosystems.

Among the solutions to counter quantum threats, Quantum Key Distribution (QKD) has emerged as one of the most promising approaches. QKD enables communication parties to share secure cryptographic keys through quantum entanglement mechanisms, with its absolute security theoretically guaranteed by fundamental quantum principles - particularly the no-cloning theorem, which ensures that any eavesdropping attempt would inevitably disturb the entangled system and thus be detectable [6]. This technology provides a foundational security layer for various sensitive services. However, as communication distances and network scales expand, point-to-point QKD implementation through direct quantum channel connections becomes increasingly impractical. In more realistic scenarios, users would need to be interconnected via a quantum data network, where end-to-end quantum entanglement could be established with the assistance of quantum repeaters.

To realize such long-distance entanglement distribution, a multi-hop paradigm is typically adopted. Specifically, quantum repeaters generate link-level entanglement pairs (or entanglement links) between adjacent nodes along the path, then couple them through entanglement swapping operations. This process ultimately extends the entanglement into an end-to-end (E2E) connection. Selecting optimal entanglement swapping paths is essential for quantum networks. However, the scarcity of resources in quantum networks presents a critical challenge for entanglement routing design. Due to the limitations of physical hardware and entanglement preparation techniques, each quantum node's quantum memory can only store a limited number of qubits. This means that the number of entanglement pairs available for the routing process on each link at any given time is restricted [23]. In contrast, entanglement-related quantum operations require substantial amounts of entanglement pairs. Therefore, developing efficient entanglement routing strategies is crucial for optimizing entanglement resource utilization and ultimately enhancing quantum key distribution performance.

In this work, we propose a Utilization-based Entanglement Routing Algorithm (UERA) designed to establish as many entanglement connections as possible. We introduce link utilization as the primary evaluation metric for path selection and transform the routing selection into a network workload optimization process, maximizing resource efficiency by fully utilizing each link in the network. The main contributions of this paper are summarized as follows:

- We transform the path selection problem under limited resource competition into a network workload optimization problem and provide a formal formulation of the problem. The objective is to improve the entanglement efficiency of the network by balancing the network workload.
- We propose a Utilization-based Entanglement Routing Algorithm (UERA), which prioritizes allocating requests to paths with lower workloads, thereby

mitigating the load growth on bottleneck links and accommodating more entanglement demands.
- Through extensive simulations, we validated the effectiveness of the proposed algorithm. Performance evaluations indicate that our approach exceeds baseline routing schemes in fulfilling more entanglement requests.

The remainder of this paper is organized as follows: In Sect. 2 and Sect. 3, we introduce the related work and the quantum network model respectively. Section 4 provides the detailed design of UERA. Finally, performance analysis is conducted in Sect. 5, and conclusions are drawn in Sect. 6.

2   Related Work

To design ideal large-scale quantum networks, numerous studies have been conducted to address the problem of entanglement routing. Some of these routing frameworks start by focusing on specific network topologies. For instance, Pirandola [20] discusses the issue of multipath routing in diamond-shaped topologies. Schoute et al. [25] propose an efficient routing scheme for ring-shaped quantum network architectures, while Vardoyan et al. [27] use Markov chains to model quantum repeater systems in star-shaped topologies. Additionally, Pant et al. [19] apply a greedy approach to guide routing decisions in grid topologies. However, these designs face significant limitations in practical deployment, as real-world quantum devices are likely to be arranged in arbitrary network topologies.

More research has been conducted on quantum networks in general topologies, focusing on the entanglement between multiple quantum users. Shi et al. [26] employed an extended Dijkstra algorithm to identify the initial entanglement path between source and destination pairs with the highest success probability. In cases of path establishment failure, adjacent nodes would collect information to attempt reconnection. However, this method lacks sufficient flexibility in path selection, leading to suboptimal performance in online path recovery. Zhao et al. [33] proposed an approach that addresses the failure of partial entanglement links by setting up redundant links, supported by corresponding theoretical analysis. Experimental results demonstrate that resource redundancy significantly improves network throughput. Zeng et al. [31] emphasized the importance of the number of serviceable users in a network. Their method divides the routing problem into two phases: the first aims to maximize the number of quantum user pairs that can be serviced by the network, while the second focuses on establishing more entanglement connections between the selected quantum user pairs. Studies [1,24] employ reinforcement learning strategies to learn and optimize routing decisions in quantum entanglement networks.

Furthermore, several studies [9,34] have incorporated purification techniques into the routing design framework to address the issue of decoherence in entanglement connections. Li et al. [9] proposed an iterative search-based routing design that identifies the optimal entanglement path by examining and updating

Fig. 1. Illustration of entanglement swapping.

the solution with the minimum entanglement cost, which includes both routing paths and purification decisions. Zhao et al. [34] were the first to quantify the E2E fidelity of entanglement connections established through multiple entanglement links with given fidelity levels. They introduced a critical link purification scheme, which selects the entanglement link that maximizes the improvement in E2E fidelity for purification, thereby enhancing purification efficiency.

The aforementioned studies primarily focus on path selection in entanglement routing, aiming to maximize the number of entanglement requests between user pairs. However, the limited entanglement resources in quantum networks cannot accommodate large-scale requests in multi-user routing scenarios, inevitably leading to network congestion. When further investigating and addressing the challenges of entanglement routing, we need to concentrate on efficiently allocating entanglement resources to accommodate simultaneous entanglement distribution requests among multiple Source-Destination (S-D) pairs. This remains a crucial challenge in entanglement routing design. Accordingly, this paper proposes an entanglement routing scheme aimed at effectively alleviating network congestion.

3   Quantum Network Model

1)*E2E Entanglement:* Quantum entanglement is a unique physical phenomenon where a set of qubits share a correlated state, such that the quantum state of each qubit cannot be described independently of the others [15]. When two quantum nodes each hold one qubit from an entangled pair, they can overcome distance limitations and transfer quantum information through quantum teleportation [3, 21]. In this paper, we consider the most common form of entanglement, namely Bell-pair entanglement, with the typical Bell state represented as $\frac{|00\rangle + |11\rangle}{\sqrt{2}}$. Using various entanglement generation devices within the quantum network, two quantum nodes can repeatedly attempt to generate physical entanglement. Successfully generated entangled pairs are stored in the quantum memory of the nodes as available resources and can be used to establish entanglement connections or perform operations such as entanglement purification [18]. However, the probability of successfully generating entanglement between two quantum nodes decreases exponentially with increasing physical distance [12], making it difficult for remote quantum nodes to directly obtain entangled pairs. Therefore, for entanglement-based quantum networks, a quantum technol-

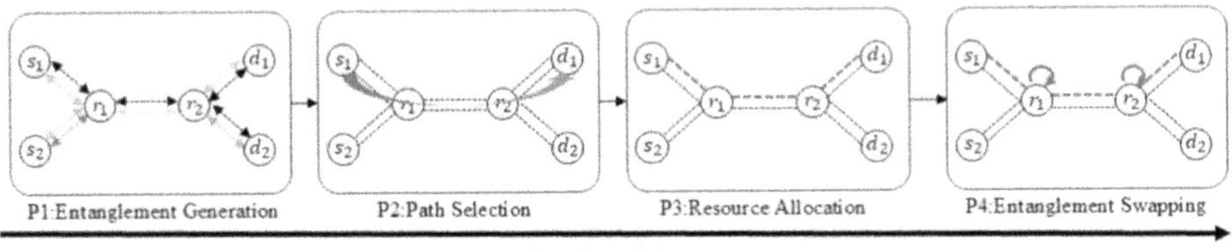

Fig. 2. Four phases in a time slot.

ogy capable of extending the distribution of entanglement over long distances is required.

Entanglement swapping is an effective technique for extending the distance of entanglement distribution, as illustrated in Fig. 1. Initially, Alice and Bob each share a Bell pair with an adjacent intermediate quantum node, Carol. Carol then performs a joint Bell-state measurement on the two Bell pairs [35]. As a result, Alice's qubit becomes entangled with Bob's, and Carol's qubits are released. Thus, Alice and Bob establish long-distance entanglement via the relay node. With the help of entanglement swapping, E2E entanglement connections between any communication nodes can be achieved by "merging" short-distance entangled pairs along a selected path.

2) *Centralized Controller:* Quantum networks must be integrated with classical networks to collaboratively meet the remote communication needs of quantum users. Due to the inherent fragility of quantum states, entanglement links or connections can only be maintained for a short duration [29]. This necessitates efficient entanglement distribution to complete the entire communication process before decoherence fully occurs. To achieve this, we introduce a classical centralized controller to manage and schedule the quantum network. This controller possesses all essential information about the quantum network, including network topology and entanglement resources, which are reported and updated by the quantum nodes. Additionally, the centralized controller is responsible for calculating the routing paths and resource allocation schemes for each S-D pair, and it communicates this information to all quantum nodes via the classical network.

Under the management of a centralized controller, the network's operational time is divided into a series of equally long time slots. In this context, a time slot refers to the fixed duration reserved by the quantum network to execute a single round of information transmission, during which the centralized controller periodically collects information and issues instructions. As shown in Fig. 2, the entanglement routing process within a time slot is summarized into four stages. At the beginning of each time slot, entanglement sources generate and distribute Bell pairs to adjacent quantum nodes, where they are stored in quantum memory for further operations. Simultaneously, the centralized controller collects routing requests and network state information via the classical network. Based on these inputs, the controller determines the entanglement swapping path for each S-D pair and allocates the necessary link-level entanglement resources along the selected path. If sufficient resources are unavailable, the request is discarded. Finally, nodes execute entanglement swapping according to the controller's scheduling, establishing end-to-end entanglement. It is important to note that, to ensure operational consistency, all quantum nodes in the network must first perform precise time synchronization [4].

4   Our Proposed UERA

We abstract a quantum network as an undirected graph $G = (V, E, C)$, where V represents the set of nodes, E represents the set of edges, and C represents the capacities of all edges. Each node $v \in V$ represents a quantum node, and each edge $e \in E$ represents the physical quantum link connecting two adjacent nodes. Each edge $e \in E$ has a capacity $c_e \in C$, which indicates the maximum number of entangled pairs the link can provide per time slot. Consistent with many previous works [7,9,11,31], we assume that the quantum network operates on a time slot cycle under the scheduling of a central controller (Table 1).

Table 1. NOTATION LIST

Notation	Description
V	The set of quantum nodes.
E	The set of quantum links.
C	The set of all link capacities.
s_i	The Source node of ith SD pair.
d_i	The Destination node of ith SD pair.
c_e	The capacity of quantum link e.
u_e	The utilization rate of link e.
$x_{(s_i,d_i),k}$	Binary variable indicates whether the ith SD pair selects the kth candidate path.
$P_{(s_i,d_i),k}$	The set of edges traversed by the kth path from s_i to d_i.

4.1   Problem Formulation

In this section, we discuss how to address the path selection problem during the entanglement routing process, which involves determining an effective entanglement exchange path for any given source-destination request. Considering the complexities of entanglement routing, such as the instability of the entanglement process, single-link failures, and limited entanglement resources, UERA aims to distribute user requests as evenly as possible across different links or paths. This ensures that each link retains more available resources to handle various contingencies. The number of remaining entangled pairs on a link is directly related to the number of quantum operations that can be performed. Therefore, we use a metric called link utilization to assess the resource redundancy of each link in the network, and we base routing decisions on this indicator. Link utilization is defined as the ratio of the number of entangled pairs in use on a link at a given time to the total capacity of the link. The formula for calculating this is as follows:

$$u_e = \frac{\sum\limits_{(s_i,d_i)} \sum\limits_{e \in P_{(s_i,d_i),k}} x_{(s_i,d_i),k}}{c_e}, \forall i, \forall e \in E. \tag{1}$$

Maximizing the utilization of all links in the network can enhance its resilience. In the following, we will transform the path selection problem into a constrained feasibility problem and outline its constraints:

$$\min u_e^{\max}. \tag{2}$$

Subject to:

$$u_e \leq u_e^{\max}, \forall e \in E. \tag{3}$$

$$0 \leq u_e \leq 1, \forall e \in E. \tag{4}$$

$$\sum_{k \in K} x_{(s_i,d_i),k} = 1, \forall i. \tag{5}$$

The objective in (2) is to minimize the maximum link utilization across all links. Constraints (3) and (4) ensure that the utilization of all edges does not exceed 1, thereby maintaining a congestion-free state. Constraint (5) stipulates that each entanglement request can ultimately select only one path to attempt to establish entanglement.

4.2   Path Selection

It can be discerned through analysis that (2) constitutes a mixed integer linear programming(MILP) problem. The prerequisite for solving this problem is to calculate a set of candidate paths for each entanglement request. However, fully computing all possible paths can incur substantial computational overhead. For instance, in a complete graph with $|\varepsilon|$ edges, there could be up to $|\varepsilon|!$ paths between a pair of quantum user nodes if relay nodes are allowed to be reused, which results in an unacceptable level of computational complexity [31]. To address this challenge, we restricted the candidate path set based on path length and selected the K shortest paths between user node pairs using Yen's algorithm [30]. Given that each edge must provide an entangled pair to facilitate the establishment of path-level entanglement(i.e., entanglement connection), prioritizing shorter paths is beneficial for resource conservation, allowing the network to serve more quantum user pairs. Moreover, shorter paths generally increase the probability of successful entanglement establishment and enhance entanglement stability [8].

Algorithm 1. Utilization-based Entanglement Routing Algorithm (UERA)

Input: Quantum network $G = (V, E, C)$, request set $\mathcal{R}$
Output: Entanglement paths for all requests
1: Sort all requests in increasing order of length
2: **for** each request $r \in \mathcal{R}$ **do**
3:     Find the K shortest paths as *candidate_paths*
4:     $best\_util = \infty$
5:     $best\_path =$ **None**
6:     **for** each *path* $\in$ *candidate_paths* **do**
7:         Pre-allocate request r along *path*
8:         Compute maximum utilization *max_util* on *path*
9:         **if** $max\_util > 1$ **then**
10:             **break**
11:         **end if**
12:         **if** $max\_util < best\_util$ **then**
13:             $best\_util = max\_util$
14:             $best\_path = path$
15:         **end if**
16:     **end for**
17:     **if** $best\_path \neq$ **None then**
18:         Assign the optimal path *best_path* to request r
19:         Update the utilization of each edge in *best_path*
20:     **end if**
21: **end for**

In lines 6–16, each candidate path undergoes a preliminary allocation for the request, and the current utilization of every edge along the path is computed. We assess each path based on the maximum utilization observed among its constituent edges, which serves as an indicator of the most congested edge along that path. To mitigate congestion, every edge must offer sufficient entanglement resources to satisfy the demands of any end-to-end entanglement connection traversing it. Consequently, any path that includes an edge with a utilization exceeding 1 is excluded from consideration. Ultimately, UERA selects the candidate path that yields the lowest maximum utilization after allocation. This strategy helps prevent any single edge from becoming a bottleneck prematurely, thereby increasing the likelihood that a greater number of requests can be successfully accommodated. It should be noted that if none of the candidate paths can provide the requisite resources for a given request, the entanglement request will have to be dropped. Once an optimal path is selected for a given request, UERA formally allocates the necessary resources and updates the utilization of each edge along that path (lines 17–20).

4.3   Complexity Analysis

UERA first employs Yen's algorithm to compute a set of K candidate paths for each source-destination request pair. The complexity of Yen's algorithm for

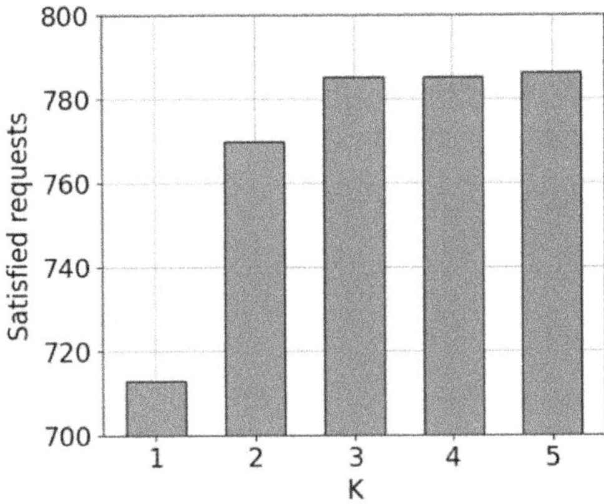

Fig. 3. Effect of the candidate path set size K.

a single request is $O(K \cdot V \cdot (E + VlogV))$, where V and E are the number of nodes and edges in the network, respectively. Given R routing requests, the total complexity for generating all candidate paths becomes $O(R \cdot K \cdot V \cdot (E + VlogV))$. Following a distance-prioritized strategy, UERA sorts all requests in ascending order of their hop count, as shorter paths are more likely to succeed in establishing entanglement. This sorting step has a time complexity of $O(RlogR)$. Finally, UERA iterates over the K candidate paths of each request to select the optimal one, with a time complexity of $O(R \cdot K)$. Therefore, the total time complexity of the UERA algorithm is $O(R \cdot K \cdot V \cdot (E + VlogV)) + O(RlogR) + O(R \cdot K)$.

5   Performance Analysis

5.1   Evaluation Setup

This section evaluates the effectiveness of the proposed entanglement routing method through comprehensive simulations using a custom quantum network simulator. The simulations are based on randomly generated quantum networks that include a defined number of quantum nodes and quantum links connecting these nodes, as well as controlled parameters for quantum link capacity. The simulated requests in the network are generated from randomly selected source-destination pairs. To ensure fairness in the experiments, all given parameter settings are run 100 times, and average results are reported.

Default Parameters: By default, the network consists of 100 quantum nodes and 200 quantum links. The average capacity of all quantum links is 20 (with individual capacities independently uniformly distributed between $[16, 25]$). In each time slot, there are 600 end-to-end entanglement requests waiting to be created.

Comparison Schemes: We compare UERA with two baseline routing schemes. One approach is the minimum hops algorithm (denoted as MinHops),

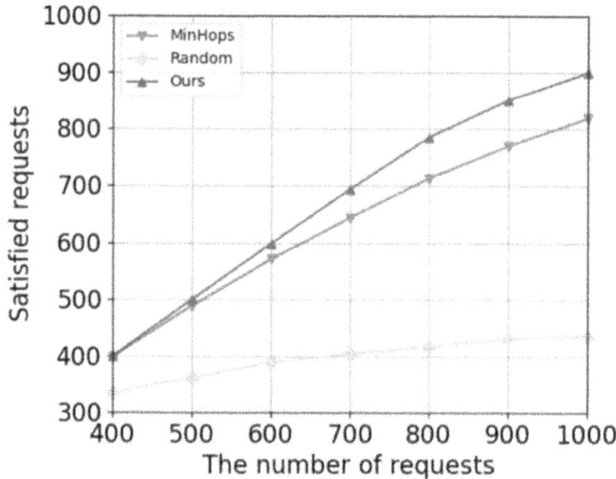

Fig. 4. Effect of the requests scale.

which always selects the path with the shortest hop count between the S-D pair. The other is the random selection algorithm (denoted as Random), which randomly selects a path from all simple paths between the S-D pair that contain no duplicate nodes.

Performance Metrics: We evaluate the performance of different routing schemes based on the number of entanglement requests that can be satisfied within each time slot. A higher number of established E2E connections indicates better performance of the algorithm in terms of service provision and alleviating network congestion.

5.2   Evaluation Results

Effect of Candidate Path Set Size: To examine the impact of the candidate path set size K on routing algorithm performance, we varied K from 1 to 5 and analyzed the performance of UERA, as shown in Fig. 3. The throughput comparison between $K = 1$ (where UERA reduces to MinHops) and $K = 2$ demonstrates UERA's effectiveness in improving entanglement routing efficiency by enabling better path allocation. At $K = 3$, UERA reaches near-optimal efficiency, and further increasing the candidate path set size has little effect on performance. Therefore, in the following experiments, we set $K = 3$ for all simulations and report the corresponding results.

Effect of Requests Scale: Fig. 4 illustrates the number of entanglement requests that different routing algorithms can satisfy under varying scales of requests. The Random routing algorithm suffers from severe resource contention and network congestion, limiting its ability to establish only a small number of low-consumption requests. As the network scales up, the performance gap between the MinHops approach and UERA continues to widen. We attribute

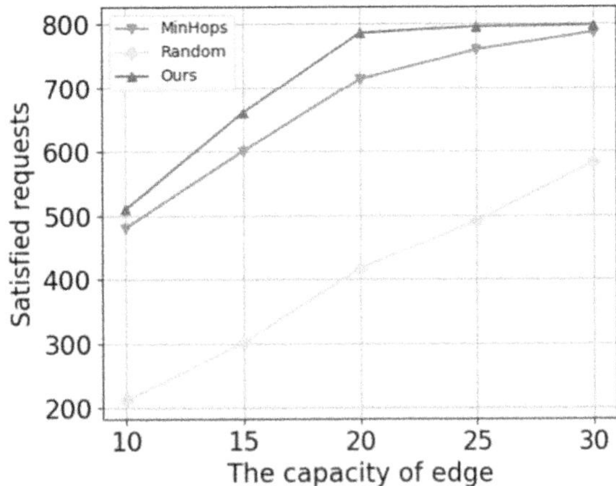

Fig. 5. Effect of the edge capacity.

UERA's strong performance in handling large-scale requests to its workload-balancing strategy. While all schemes experience some degree of performance decline as the number of requests increases, UERA maintains a relatively high entanglement satisfaction rate. In our simulations, UERA outperforms the best alternative scheme by 7.3%.

Effect of Edge Capacity: As shown in Fig. 5, we varied the average capacity of the links and compared the proposed UERA with other baseline schemes. As the average capacity of the links increased from 10 to 30, more quantum resources became available to meet larger numbers of entanglement requests. This indicates that link capacity bottlenecks are consistently a critical factor limiting end-to-end entanglement connections. Consequently, resource contention and congestion are inevitable on certain links, highlighting that fine management of limited link resources can significantly enhance network performance. In contrast, our approach manages routing decisions by consistently selecting less congested paths, effectively mitigating capacity bottlenecks and overcoming challenges in the entanglement routing process. As a result, UERA demonstrates significant advantages in the same network environment.

Effect of Network Density: To evaluate the adaptability of different routing schemes to varying levels of network connectivity, we tested the performance of all algorithms under different numbers of links, as shown in Fig. 6. With a fixed number of requests, all algorithms exhibited improved performance as network connectivity increased. Notably, UERA demonstrated a significant increase in throughput as the number of links grew. We attribute this to the expanded link availability, which allows UERA to select optimal paths from a more diverse candidate set, thereby enhancing end-to-end entanglement efficiency.

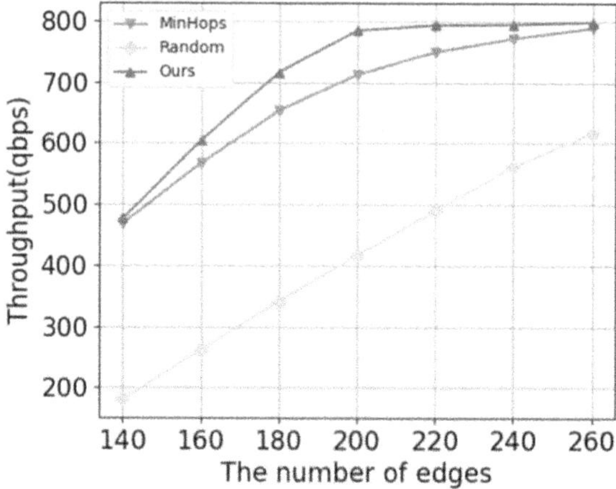

Fig. 6. Effect of the network density.

5.3 Engineering Applications

Quantum networks have transitioned from theory to practical implementation, demonstrating unmatched advantages in various applications. One prominent application is Quantum Key Distribution (QKD). Supported by unique quantum properties, the transmission of quantum state information can completely prevent third-party eavesdropping. This is something that traditional network protocols cannot achieve [14,28]. Therefore, QKD networks based on trusted relays have been widely applied in scenarios such as commercial data protection, government information encryption, and communications in the defense industry [2,5,13,16,17,32], as illustrated in Fig. 7.

However, the key assumption of these networks is that every relay must be trusted, which poses certain limitations in practical applications. Looking ahead, quantum relay-based QKD networks are envisioned to provide the ultimate solution for secure communications, allowing key distribution over any distance with near-absolute security. One of the critical challenges in such networks is optimizing key distribution paths. Factors like request distribution and the entanglement capacity of links can significantly affect the efficiency of end-to-end entanglement distribution, potentially introducing security risks in various fields of communication. To address this problem, we adopt a data-driven approach, where the network's central controller collects device and resource status information to guide the routing algorithm in making decisions. Specifically, load-balancing path selection strategies help maintain a sufficient number of available entangled pairs on each link during a given time slot. Furthermore, we design a purification and resource allocation method to effectively ensure the stability of entanglement, thus enhancing the quality of key distribution. Ultimately, UERA enables the network to generate more end-to-end entanglement with fidelity guarantees, establishing more secure key-sharing channels. This makes network adaptable to different security application scenarios and user needs, which is of significant importance for the future applications of QKD.

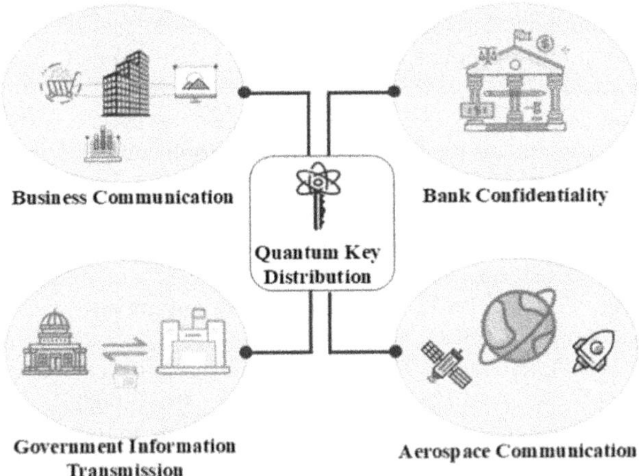

Fig. 7. The application scenarios of quantum network.

6   Conclusion and Future Work

In this paper, we propose a multi-entanglement routing protocol called UERA, designed to accommodate large-scale dynamic QKD requests in quantum communication networks. To enhance the utilization of quantum resources, UERA evenly selects paths for all entanglement connections by balancing link workloads, thereby alleviating the increasing workload on bottleneck links. Through extensive simulations, our method significantly increases the number of satisfiable entanglement requests compared to existing path selection algorithm, while effectively mitigating network congestion.

In this work, we focus primarily on the impact of limited network resources on the performance of quantum networks. However, the fabrication technologies for key quantum hardware components, such as quantum repeaters and quantum memories, are still immature. Due to factors such as quantum decoherence and imperfect entanglement swapping, achieving reliable long-distance entanglement remains a significant challenge. In future work, we plan to incorporate entanglement quality considerations into UERA. Specifically, we aim to introduce entanglement purification mechanisms into the entanglement routing design to meet the quality requirements of quantum network applications.

References

1. Abreu, D., Abelém, A.: qRL: reinforcement learning routing for quantum entanglement networks. In: 2024 IEEE Symposium on Computers and Communications (ISCC), pp. 1–6. IEEE (2024)
2. Avesani, M., et al.: Deployment-ready quantum key distribution over a classical network infrastructure in Padua. J. Lightwave Technol. **40**(6), 1658–1663 (2022)
3. Bouwmeester, D., Pan, J.W., Mattle, K., Eibl, M., Weinfurter, H., Zeilinger, A.: Experimental quantum teleportation. Nature **390**(6660), 575–579 (1997)

4. Brand, S., Coopmans, T., Elkouss, D.: Efficient computation of the waiting time and fidelity in quantum repeater chains. IEEE J. Sel. Areas Commun. **38**(3), 619–639 (2020)

5. Cai, J., Liang, W., Li, X., Li, K., Gui, Z., Khan, M.K.: GTxChain: a secure IOT smart blockchain architecture based on graph neural network. IEEE Internet Things J. **10**(24), 21502–21515 (2023)

6. Cao, Y., Zhao, Y., Wang, Q., Zhang, J., Ng, S.X., Hanzo, L.: The evolution of quantum key distribution networks: On the road to the qinternet. IEEE Commun. Surv. Tutorials **24**(2), 839–894 (2022)

7. Dai, W., Peng, T., Win, M.Z.: Optimal remote entanglement distribution. IEEE J. Sel. Areas Commun. **38**(3), 540–556 (2020)

8. Ford, L.R., Jr., Fulkerson, D.R.: A suggested computation for maximal multi-commodity network flows. Manage. Sci. **5**(1), 97–101 (1958)

9. Li, J., et al.: Fidelity-guaranteed entanglement routing in quantum networks. IEEE Trans. Commun. **70**(10), 6748–6763 (2022)

10. Li, Y., Liang, W., Xie, K., Zhang, D., Li, K., Xiong, N.N.: EventMon: real-time event-based streaming network monitoring data recovery. IEEE Trans. Dependable Secure Comput. **22**(3), 2413–2429 (2024)

11. Li, Z., et al.: Swapping-based entanglement routing design for congestion mitigation in quantum networks. IEEE Trans. Netw. Serv. Manage. **20**(4), 3999–4012 (2023)

12. Li, Z., et al.: Entanglement-assisted quantum networks: mechanics, enabling technologies, challenges, and research directions. IEEE Commun. Surv. Tutorials **25**(4), 2133–2189 (2023)

13. Liang, W., Liu, Y., Yang, C., Xie, S., Li, K., Susilo, W.: On identity, transaction, and smart contract privacy on permissioned and permissionless blockchain: a comprehensive survey. ACM Comput. Surv. **56**(12), 1–35 (2024)

14. Lin, C., He, Y.X., Xiong, N.: An energy-efficient dynamic power management in wireless sensor networks. In: 2006 Fifth International Symposium on Parallel and Distributed Computing, pp. 148–154. IEEE (2006)

15. Lloyd, S., Shapiro, J.H., Wong, F.N., Kumar, P., Shahriar, S.M., Yuen, H.P.: Infrastructure for the quantum internet. ACM SIGCOMM Comput. Commun. Rev. **34**(5), 9–20 (2004)

16. Long, J., Liang, W., Li, K.C., Wei, Y., Marino, M.D.: A regularized cross-layer ladder network for intrusion detection in industrial internet of things. IEEE Trans. Industr. Inf. **19**(2), 1747–1755 (2022)

17. Meng, X., Liang, W., Xu, Z., Li, K., Khan, M.K., Kui, X.: An anonymous authenticated group key agreement scheme for transfer learning edge services systems. ACM Trans. Sensor Netw. **20**(3), 1–23 (2024)

18. Pan, J.W., Simon, C., Brukner, Č, Zeilinger, A.: Entanglement purification for quantum communication. Nature **410**(6832), 1067–1070 (2001)

19. Pant, M., et al.: Routing entanglement in the quantum internet. NPJ Quant. Inf. **5**(1), 25 (2019)

20. Pirandola, S.: End-to-end capacities of a quantum communication network. Commun. Phys. **2**(1), 51 (2019)

21. Pirandola, S., Eisert, J., Weedbrook, C., Furusawa, A., Braunstein, S.L.: Advances in quantum teleportation. Nat. Photonics **9**(10), 641–652 (2015)

22. Politi, A., Matthews, J.C., O'Brien, J.L.: Shor's quantum factoring algorithm on a photonic chip. Science **325**(5945), 1221 (2009)

23. Qiao, C., Zhao, Y., Zhao, G., Xu, H.: Quantum data networking for distributed quantum computing: Opportunities and challenges. In: IEEE INFOCOM 2022-IEEE Conference on Computer Communications Workshops (INFOCOM WKSHPS), pp. 1–6. IEEE (2022)
24. Roik, J., Bartkiewicz, K., Černoch, A., Lemr, K.: Routing in quantum communication networks using reinforcement machine learning. Quantum Inf. Process. **23**(3), 89 (2024)
25. Schoute, E., Mancinska, L., Islam, T., Kerenidis, I., Wehner, S.: Shortcuts to quantum network routing (2016). arXiv preprint arXiv:1610.05238
26. Shi, S., Qian, C.: Concurrent entanglement routing for quantum networks: model and designs. In: Proceedings of the Annual Conference of the ACM Special Interest Group on Data Communication on the Applications, Technologies, Architectures, and Protocols for Computer Communication, pp. 62–75 (2020)
27. Vardoyan, G., Guha, S., Nain, P., Towsley, D.: On the stochastic analysis of a quantum entanglement switch. ACM SIGMETRICS Perform. Eval. Rev. **47**(2), 27–29 (2019)
28. Wang, Z., Li, T., Xiong, N., Pan, Y.: A novel dynamic network data replication scheme based on historical access record and proactive deletion. J. Supercomput. **62**, 227–250 (2012)
29. Yang, L., Zhao, Y., Huang, L., Qiao, C.: Asynchronous entanglement provisioning and routing for distributed quantum computing. In: IEEE INFOCOM 2023-IEEE Conference on Computer Communications, pp. 1–10. IEEE (2023)
30. Yen, J.Y.: An algorithm for finding shortest routes from all source nodes to a given destination in general networks. Q. Appl. Math. **27**(4), 526–530 (1970)
31. Zeng, Y., Zhang, J., Liu, J., Liu, Z., Yang, Y.: Multi-entanglement routing design over quantum networks. In: IEEE INFOCOM 2022-IEEE Conference on Computer Communications, pp. 510–519. IEEE (2022)
32. Zhang, S., Yan, Z., Liang, W., Li, K.C., Dobre, C.: BAKA: biometric authentication and key agreement scheme based on fuzzy extractor for wireless body area networks. IEEE Internet Things J. **11**(3), 5118–5128 (2023)
33. Zhao, Y., Qiao, C.: Redundant entanglement provisioning and selection for throughput maximization in quantum networks. In: IEEE INFOCOM 2021-IEEE Conference on Computer Communications, pp. 1–10. IEEE (2021)
34. Zhao, Y., Zhao, G., Qiao, C.: E2E fidelity aware routing and purification for throughput maximization in quantum networks. In: IEEE INFOCOM 2022-IEEE Conference on Computer Communications, pp. 480–489. IEEE (2022)
35. Zukowski, M., Zeilinger, A., Horne, M., Ekert, A.: "Event-ready-detectors" bell experiment via entanglement swapping. Phys. Rev. Lett. **71**(26), 4287 (1993)

Att-SFI: Attestable Software Sandboxing
with Control Flow Integrity

Wei Li[1,2], Wei Feng[1], Yu Qin[1(✉)], and Zeyu Gu[3]

[1] Institute of Software, Chinese Academy of Sciences, Beijing, China
{liwei2018,fengwei2009,qinyu}@iscas.ac.cn
[2] University of Chinese Academy of Sciences, Beijing, China
[3] Xiaomi Corporation, Beijing, China
guzeyu@xiaomi.com

Abstract. Software Fault Isolation (SFI) is an effective sandboxing technique that prevents potentially vulnerable code from impacting the rest of the system. SFI requires an effective Control Flow Integrity (CFI) mechanism to ensure the proper enforcement of isolation. However, existing SFI schemes often use coarse-grained CFI or assume sufficient CFI protection, lacking effective implementation and thorough evaluation of CFI. SFIs relying on hardware-assisted CFI are also constrained by platform-specific limitations. We propose an architecture-neutral SFI with fine-grained CFI, achieving run-time security for sandboxed programs at a 21.9% performance overhead, suitable for high-security scenarios such as confidential computing in IoT and cloud environments. Our approach enhances the isolation of confidential workloads while enabling attestable run-time security guarantees.

Keywords: CFI · SFI · Remote attestation · Software security · System security · Run-time security

1 Introduction

Software Fault Isolation (SFI) [24] provides memory integrity protection for systems running software and various software components. SFI typically ensures that all virtual addresses in instructions remain within the isolated domain by inspecting and rewriting binaries and by performing run-time sanitization and checks on external calls, so that sandboxed programs cannot access data or code outside the isolated domain through unauthorized interfaces. SFI is commonly used in scenarios that require local execution of untrusted binaries, such as the web browser [19] and IoT [18]. Moreover, with the advent of confidential computing [11], SFI can also be applied to Trusted Execution Environments (TEE) to enhance the isolation of TEE applications and environments [21]; this is particularly meaningful for system-level TEEs [3,6,10], where further isolation of workloads and complex system components is warranted.

© ICST Institute for Computer Sciences, Social Informatics and Telecommunications Engineering 2026
Published by Springer Nature Switzerland AG 2026. All Rights Reserved
W. Liang et al. (Eds.): SecureComm 2025, LNICST 690, pp. 18–37, 2026.
https://doi.org/10.1007/978-3-032-23456-8_2

The effective implementation of SFI mandates rigorous Control Flow Integrity (CFI) to prevent bypassing address masks or checks through unintended control flow transfers. Notably, architectures like x86-64, with variable-length instructions, offer adversaries greater flexibility in constructing attack gadgets compared to ARM64, which features fixed-length encoding (with thumb encoding disabled) and reduced gadget complexity [19].

However, most SFIs do not consider fine-grained CFI and only use coarse-grained CFI to enforce that control flow jump addresses stay within the sandbox [19,22,24,26]. This aims to mitigate sandbox bypass attacks by untrusted code but does not address the security needs of the sandboxed program itself. For example, it does not protect against third-party adversaries that exploit memory vulnerabilities within a sandboxed program to steal secrets from within the sandbox. Given the increasing demand for high security and privacy protection, especially in IoT and cloud computing environments, such as in confidential computing scenarios, it is meaningful to consider additional isolation protections for confidential workloads [21].

Moreover, SFIs that only guarantee coarse-grained CFI have not fully considered the security of sandbox interfaces. They typically assume that the sandbox runtime interfaces are well-designed and that access control prevents exploitation [22]. However, the effectiveness of this design is closely tied to the specific implementation. Coarse-grained CFI cannot detect abuse or attacks targeting the SFI runtime interfaces. Such abuse can impact the performance or availability of the sandbox, and when vulnerabilities exist in these interfaces, the isolation is compromised. In contrast, fine-grained CFI monitors specific control flow transfer addresses, enabling it to detect abuse and mitigate such attacks, at the cost of a certain performance overhead.

We propose Att-SFI, an attestable software sandbox that enhances existing Software Fault Isolation (SFI) solutions with fine-grained Control Flow Integrity (CFI). Att-SFI instruments trampolines at critical control flow transfers to record the exact addresses of run-time control flows. These records are subsequently verified by the sandbox runtime and can be included in the remote attestation report upon request by the relying party. We use Att-SFI to provide context-sensitive CFI for sandboxed programs and discuss the necessary granularity of CFI required to ensure the effectiveness of SFI. Our prototype shows that Att-SFI introduces about 21.9% overhead over standard SFI, which is considered moderate given the introduction of high-security fine-grained CFI. Our contributions are as follows:

- We introduce, for the first time, a software sandbox with software-based context-sensitive fine-grained CFI, ensuring that SFI provides the expected memory integrity across different architectures while protecting the control flow of sandboxed programs.
- The proposed Att-SFI can be further integrated with other isolation environments, especially in TEE-based scenarios within IoT or cloud computing, providing run-time attestation for sandboxed programs and enhancing the security capabilities of the isolation environment.

– We provide a prototype implementation in a cloud computing environment on the ARM64 architecture, and the experimental results demonstrate that the proposed solution incurs an acceptable performance overhead.

2   Background

2.1   SFI

SFI implements control flow and data flow isolation between software components, allowing communication only through limited interfaces. While providing a lightweight isolation mechanism, SFI avoids the overhead of context switches associated with hardware isolation, and its software-based implementation offers strong flexibility. There are significant differences in the details of various SFI solutions. Instruction rewriting is a common method for achieving control flow and data flow isolation in SFI [22], relying on code segment write protection (W⊕X), which is supported by modern processors. Guard pages are used at both ends of the sandbox address domain to prevent escape due to overflow or displacement addressing. SFI schemes [22] also employ static verifiers to inspect compiled programs, reducing trust in complex compiler frameworks and minimizing the Trusted Computing Base (TCB). For example, LFI [26] is a lightweight software sandbox implemented on ARM64 and x86-64 architectures, utilizing the 32-bit addressing mode in 64-bit systems, achieving better performance than other works. As a representative SFI scheme, its implementation consists of three components: a compiler capable of instruction rewriting, a static validator, and a sandbox runtime.

```
Memory access (original):        Memory access (sandboxed):
   ldr    x0, [x1]                  ldr    x0, [x21, w1, uxtw]
----------------------------     ----------------------------
Indirect branch (original):      Indirect branch (sandboxed):
                                    add    x18, x21, w0, uxtw
   blr    x0                        blr    x18
----------------------------     ----------------------------
Function return (original):      Function return (sandboxed):
   ldp    x29, x30, [sp], #16       ldp    x29, x22, [sp], #16
                                    add    x30, x21, w22, uxtw
   ret                              ret
```

Fig. 1. Instruction rewiring examples of SFI for address masking.

The rewritten instructions include address masking for any addressing operations. For example, in the implementation of LFI on ARM64, as shown in Fig. 1, specific registers are reserved to add address masking to the addressing operations of original memory access instructions, indirect jump instructions, function return instructions, etc. Here, x18 and x21 are reserved registers for LFI, where x18 always contains an address within the sandbox address domain, and x21 always has the sandbox base address, with its lower 32 bits set to 0. For target registers used for addressing in these instructions, such as x1, x0, and x30 in Fig. 1, the target values are first masked before use, and then these registers are set to the masked values.

Combined with guard pages, this type of rewriting can enforce that control flow and data flow addresses are within the 4GiB sandbox range. However, due to the lack of fine-grained CFI, adversaries can still exploit vulnerabilities to violate the control flow graph of the sandboxed program, for instance, by overflowing and overwriting the x29 and x22 addresses stored on the stack. The security of the sandboxed program is typically not a concern in most SFI solutions, but in practice, the sandbox runtime often needs to provide interfaces to ensure the program works properly, such as redirected system calls and inter-component communication. Coarse-grained CFI cannot guarantee that adversaries will not abuse these interfaces for lateral movement.

2.2 CFI and Attestation

CFI is used to monitor or prevent program control flow hijacking. Common techniques include Data Execution Prevention (DEP), Address Space Layout Randomization (ASLR), stack canaries, instrumentation for dynamic checks of control flow addresses, such as using CFI labels [21] or shadow stacks [9]. Fine-grained CFI typically references a program's Control Flow Graph (CFG), which can be extracted either statically from different encoding levels or at run time.

Control Flow Attestation (CFA) [5] combines CFI with remote attestation [13]. In addition to protecting control flow, it can provide run-time attestation of a program's security, assist with provenance analysis [23], and offer further attack detection capabilities [5]. CFA uses control flow as the run-time measurement of the program, using control flow logs as the quote that are provided to the verifier for verification. CFA focuses on how to extract and prevent tampering with control flow logs while ensuring their expressiveness.

It is worth mentioning that any SFI implicitly assumes a CFI prerequisite, which requires that control flow does not break out of the sandbox. On platforms with variable-length instructions like x86-64, alignment constraints are often applied to avoid more gadgets, or other fine-grained hardware-assisted CFI, such as Intel CET [20], are leveraged to ensure the completeness of address masking.

2.3 Confidential Computing and TEE

Confidential computing aims to protect the confidentiality and integrity of data in use, providing hardware-based isolation for workloads via TEE and using remote attestation to prove its trustworthiness. Current mainstream hardware architectures for TEE can be divided into process-level TEE and system-level

TEE, as known as non-priviledged TEE and priviledged TEE [16], with the key difference being whether the TEE includes a trusted OS. Intel SGX is a representative example of process-level TEE, isolating the trusted and untrusted parts of an application at the thread level. This requires modification of the source code or the introduction of a libOS to ensure compatibility with existing programs. System-level TEE [3,6,10], which includes a trusted OS, is compatible with the programming models of existing programs. Its TCB is larger than that of process-level TEE, but due to its compatibility, it is the primary development direction for TEE. Most of these TEEs provide memory encryption, isolation, and remote attestation to prevent privileged adversaries, including host OSes and hypervisors.

Confidential computing platforms use standard remote attestation procedures, such as IETF RATS [13], to prove the trustworthiness of TEEs externally. A relying party, typically a remote user, obtains an attestation report from the verifier, which verifies the quote provided by the attester through a challenge-response process. This report helps assess the trustworthiness and security of the attester. The quote contains hardware-level evidence, such as the platform's identity and the integrity measurements of the TEE before its initializing, but it does not include run-time measurements of the TEE application. Some solutions [15,23] address the lack of run-time measurement evidence for TEEs by introducing CFA. However, these solutions lack proper isolation design between the introduced inline monitors and the target programs, and they also introduce significant performance overhead.

In this case, the advantage of our method is its ability to provide and prove the CFI of isolated programs, safeguarding the run-time security of TEE applications in IoT devices or cloud computing. For example, when confidential workloads are released and run as sandboxed programs, Att-SFI not only prevents them from affecting other TEE components but also provides run-time security guarantees for the sandboxed application, which are included in the remote attestation report of the TEE.

3 Threat Model

Our approach follows the same threat model as existing SFI solutions. For instance, we assume that an attacker could exploit memory vulnerabilities in the sandboxed program through external inputs, such as network-based attacks, potentially using stack buffer overflows to execute Return-Oriented Programming (ROP) attacks.

One subtle distinction, however, is that existing SFI solutions do not consider the impact of such attacks on the security of the sandboxed program itself. In contrast, our approach takes into account the run-time security of the sandboxed program. This introduces a nuanced difference in the threat model: our approach requires the sandboxed program to be recognized, typically released by a specific developer, for which run-time security protection is meaningful. As a result, not just any code (including code directly released by an attacker) can become a sandboxed program. However, this does not affect the attacker's ability to exploit memory vulnerabilities within the sandboxed program.

4 Design and Implementation

The high-level strategy of our solution is to instrument the sandboxed program to monitor the actual addresses of control flow instructions at run-time. To achieve this, we first need to identify which control flow instructions require our attention. Following most modern SFI, the program must be verified by an SFI static verifier before execution, and we assume that the target environment has data execution protection and can prevent tampering with program code. All direct address jumps can be statically verified and are difficult for adversaries to exploit. For example, branch instructions that include direct addresses. However, instructions with indirect addresses, such as call, branch, and ret instructions that use register values as target addresses, cannot be statically verified. Therefore, we need to instrument the program to capture the actual addresses of these instructions at run-time. Moreover, to ensure context-sensitive CFI, call instructions that contain direct addresses also need to be monitored, and backward control flow edges should be verified using a shadow stack.

Two new designs of Att-SFI that differentiate it from traditional SFI will be discussed in detail: the instrumentation of trampoline for the target instructions, and the verification of control flow integrity of the sandboxed program.

4.1 Trampoline Instrumentation

Our design is based on software instrumentation and does not rely on specific SFI or hardware architectures. A trusted trampoline is instrumented into the sandboxed program at compile-time to capture the program's run-time control flow transfers, recording the control flow logs in the form of $<$ *source, destination* $>$ to a reserved memory region within the sandbox, known as the control flow log (cflog) buffer.

The instructions instrumented with the trampoline include three types: call, ret, and indirect branch. There is no need to differentiate between instruction types in the control flow logs. The run-time verifier identifies the type of each control flow based on its source address, enabling the shadow stack to match call and ret instructions.

Figure 2 illustrates the difference before and after instrumentation using a ret instruction as an example, showing both the LLVM IR and assembly levels. Before the function returns, the trampoline captures the value in the register x30 at run time and passes it as the parameter x0 to the `<traceret>` function. In the `<traceret>` function, x30 points to the address of the `bl 1f834 <traceret>` + 4, which will be used as the source address for this control flow transfer. The cflog for this transfer is recorded as $<$ x30, x0 $>$ and written to the cflog buffer. A more specific example is provided in Appendix A.

<table>
<tr><td valign="top">

```
LLVM IR (original):
  store i8 1, ptr %0, align 1



  ret void
- - - - - - - - - - - - - - - - - - - - -
Assembly (original):




  mov    w8, #0x1
  strb   w8, [x21, w0, uxtw]







  ret
```

</td><td valign="top">

```
LLVM IR (instrumented):
  store i8 1, ptr %p, align 1
  %0 = call ptr @llvm.returnaddress(i32 0)
  call void @traceret(ptr %0)
  ret void
- - - - - - - - - - - - - - - - - - - - - - - - - - - - - - - - - -
Assembly (instrumented):
  stp    x29, x30, [sp, #-16]!
  mov    x29, sp
  mov    w8, #0x1
  strb   w8, [x21, w0, uxtw]
  mov    x0, x30
  bl     1f834 <traceret>
  ldp    x29, x22, [sp], #16
  add    x30, x21, w22, uxtw
  ret
```

</td></tr>
</table>

Fig. 2. Instrumentation of the trampoline in Att-SFI.

Since the trampoline is designed to be clear and easy to verify, we assume that it correctly performs its function without introducing new attack surfaces. Additionally, to comply with SFI, the instrumented trampoline is also protected by instruction rewriting and address masking. However, this raises challenges regarding the integrity of the cflogs, as the cflog buffer must reside within the sandbox's address domain, allowing it to be accessed by instructions outside the trampoline within the sandbox. To address this, we use an additional reserved register, the "buffer address register," to record the memory address of the cflog buffer. The buffer address register can only be used by the trampoline, preventing adversaries from tampering with or discarding generated cflogs to hide their attack activities. Further discussion of this design can be found in Sect. 5.1 and Sect. 6.

When the cflog buffer is full, the trampoline dumps it into memory outside the sandbox through an interface provided by the sandbox runtime. The runtime can also dump the control flow logs and perform cflog verification at any time, such as when a remote attestation request is received.

The implementation of Att-SFI does not violate the security model of SFI. In the compiler pipeline, the instrumentation of the trampoline takes effect before the instruction rewriting. We achieve this process by writing an LLVM IR pass. The trampoline is instrumented as a function call, marked as non-inlined, before the target instructions (call, ret, indirect branch), passing the destination address of the target instruction as a parameter. The trampoline uses its own return address to determine the source address of the target instruction. The $<source, destination>$ address pair is recorded in the cflog buffer. During the execution of the sandboxed program, the trampoline records the cflogs via the buffer address register. Once the log is full, the trampoline notifies the runtime through an interface provided by the runtime to dump the cflogs and reset the cflog buffer.

4.2   Control Flow Verification

Static Verifier. The verification scope of the SFI static verifier is extended. In addition to ensuring that instruction rewriting and checking of reserved registers are correctly implemented, the static verifier also ensures that instrumentation is properly executed. Using a static verifier helps avoid reliance on complex compilers, reduces the TCB, and ensures that direct control flow transfers contain valid destination addresses.

The static verifier of Att-SFI performs a simple linear verification on the binary files generated by the compiler. In addition to the properties required by SFI, it also verifies the following: (1) trampoline calls are properly instrumented before all target instructions, and (2) trampoline binary instructions are properly linked as expected. Since the trampoline procedure is simple (less than 30 assembly instructions on ARM64), this static verification is easy to implement.

Run-Time Verifier. The run-time verifier in the sandbox runtime performs verification of the cflogs. Specifically, it determines the legality of the $< source, destination >$ pair in the log based on the instruction addresses in the sandboxed program's text segmentation. The verifier identifies the type of the control flow transfer using the source address in the cflog. When it is a call or ret instruction, the verifier matches and further verifies the call/ret pairs using the shadow stack. This ensures that the sandboxed program has context-sensitive CFI. Specifically, the runtime extends three functionalities:

1. Measurement of the binary. When the runtime loads the sandboxed program, it measures the loaded binary of it. Unlike the static verifier, this process hashes the sandboxed program to generate a static measurement, which is included as evidence in the remote attestation report.
2. Cflog buffer. Before the sandboxed program executes, the runtime allocates a cflog buffer at a random location within its memory address space and sets the "buffer address register", such as the x25 on ARM64. Att-SFI introduces a runtime call that allows the trampoline to refresh the cflog buffer and get its address. The cflog buffer has little impact on the sandboxed program, occupying only about 2MiB within the 4GiB sandbox memory.
3. Remote attestation. At any time, such as when a remote attestation request is received, the runtime includes the cflog verification results as evidence in the remote attestation report, with the static measurement as well.

For indirect branches, the actual address is verified against the expected control flow address, which is pre-extracted. For example, for a jump table, the valid destination addresses can be obtained from the target address label array within the indirectbr instruction in LLVM IR. Att-SFI retrieves the virtual address of these labels representing basic blocks in the text segment using the LLVM blockaddress constant. For calls/rets, the run-time verifier maintains a shadow stack to check if the function call context matches. Specifically, the run-time verifier sequentially reads the instructions and pushes the $cflog_{call}$ $< src_{call}, dest_{call} >$ onto the stack. When meeting a $cflog_{ret}$ $< src_{ret}, dest_{ret} >$, it checks from the top of the stack downward to find a $cflog_{call}$ that its src_{call} is the instruction immediately preceding $dest_{ret}$, and that $dest_{call}$ and src_{ret} are within the same function. If the matched $cflog_{call}$ is not at the top of the stack, all logs from that $cflog_{call}$ to the top of the stack must belong to the same function and be interfaces provided by the runtime.

Typically, asynchronous cflog verification minimizes the performance impact on the sandboxed program. For example, before the program finishes or before receiving a remote attestation request, the logs are cached in memory. This approach works well for simple, short-running programs. However, for complex, long-running programs, a method for quickly caching a huge number of cflogs is required. We address this by performing quick synchronous verification of the buffer during each dump to avoid this issue. In fact, the design of our run-time verifier is limited to demonstrating the effectiveness of the scheme. The verifier performs simple forward verification, using the shadow stack to match call/ret pairs to achieve context-sensitive CFI. As with most CFA works discussed in [5], the design of a perfect run-time verifier is beyond the scope of our work.

5   Evaluation

We conducted a systematic evaluation of Att-SFI to demonstrate its effectiveness in achieving an optimal balance between introduced security properties and performance overhead. Table 1 presents the assessed security properties along with their associated performance overheads. For comparative analysis, we selected four representative approaches in related areas. Occlum [21] and SGXMonitor [23] implement SFI and CFA respectively within isolation environments. BLAST [25] implements SFI to isolate the CFA inline monitor. LFI [26] represents the state-of-the-art SFI solution and serves as the foundation for our Att-SFI prototype. The performance data in Table 1 originates from respective academic publications and should only be interpreted as qualitative magnitude references due to methodological differences in test cases, environments, and statistical analysis approaches.

Table 1. The magnitude of performance overhead induced by different properties.

Scheme	SFI	CFA	Both
Occlum [21]	36.6%	—	36.6%
SGXMonitor [23]	—	3.9x	3.9x
BLAST [25]	15% *	50% *	67%
LFI [26]	6.4%	—	6.4%
Att-SFI	6.5%	21.9%	31.4%

*Estimated based on graphical data and indirect evidence.

As Table 1 shows, security and performance often exhibit a trade-off. Especially, introducing software-based CFA always incurs significant overhead: SGX-

Monitor [23] achieves fine-grained basic block level CFA at the highest cost. BLAST [25] optimizes CFA through WPP [14], custom aggressive inlining, and parallel log submission but still maintains high overhead. Furthermore, their SFI implementations are suboptimal. Att-SFI, however, strikes the best balance between security and performance. The detailed analyses of the security properties and the performance evaluations are also provided.

5.1 Security Analysis

The goal of Att-SFI is to implement fine-grained CFI for sandboxed programs while maintaining full compatibility with SFI, in order to monitor control flow hijacking attacks that could lead to the leakage of secrets within the sandbox or the abuse of the sandbox runtime interfaces. This section analyzes the effectiveness of Att-SFI in achieving this goal.

According to our threat model, an attacker can launch a ROP attack within the sandboxed program. This involves the legitimacy of the destination of a ret somewhere. In Att-SFI's design, this would lead to a $cflog < src_{ret}, dest_{ret} >$ with an invalid destination, where $dest_{ret}$ cannot pass shadow stack verification. Att-SFI ensures the completeness of its CFI by guaranteeing that all control flow hijacks result in unexpected cflog entries.

Since the logging of $dest_{ret}$ happens before the sandboxed program is compromised, the attacker, once in control of the sandbox, can only attempt to tamper with the cflog, otherwise the attack will be detected. Att-SFI protects the integrity of the cflog based on its design. Specifically, Att-SFI hides the virtual address of the cflog buffer using the reserved buffer address register. Only the trampoline can use this register for control flow logging. As a result, the attacker cannot directly obtain the cflog buffer's address from the runtime interface or the buffer address register. Due to the randomness of the cflog buffer allocation, it would be hard for the attacker to organize enough gadgets to calculate its address. Additionally, operations such as traversing memory would lead to abnormal states in the sandboxed program, making the attack easier to detect, for example, by high CPU usage or unusually increased executing time.

In fact, allocating the cflog buffer outside the sandbox and allowing only the trampoline to access this address is technically feasible. If that, when the trampoline uses the buffer address register as a parameter for register-indirect addressing, no SFI address masking is applied. This allows the trampoline to bypass SFI's data flow protection when accessing the cflog buffer outside the sandbox. Also, the attacker cannot directly exploit the reserved buffer address register to carry out a sandbox breakout attack. However, to fully comply with SFI's security model, Att-SFI adopts a domain-internal cflog buffer design.

Att-SFI does not monitor direct control flow transfers other than calls at run time. This results in Att-SFI providing function-level CFI instead of basic block level. Att-SFI statically verifies direct control flow addresses, such as verifying all candidate addresses for direct branches, rather than capturing the actual control flow at run time. This makes Att-SFI's CFI not path-sensitive but significantly reduces the performance overhead. Att-SFI also does not consider non-control data attacks.

5.2   Performance Evaluation

We extend the state-of-the-art SFI scheme, LFI [26], and implement our Att-SFI prototype. We tested Att-SFI using the SPEC CPU2017 benchmark suite. For comparison, we selected 14 benchmarks, and the compilation and running options, and data statistics were kept consistent with LFI. This includes using the single-copy SPECrate benchmarks, running the native version in the LFI environment, compiling with the O3 optimization level (except for the *lbm_r*), and enabling LTO, among other settings. The tests were conducted on an ARM64 server with Kunpeng-920 (2.5GHz, 32 cores and 64 threads), simulating a cloud computing environment in a QEMU-KVM virtual machine. The software environment was Ubuntu 24.04, with LLVM version 19.1.14. Our primary evaluation focused on the additional overhead introduced by Att-SFI due to the inclusion of CFI security properties, and we also compared these results with the overhead introduced by LFI over the native.

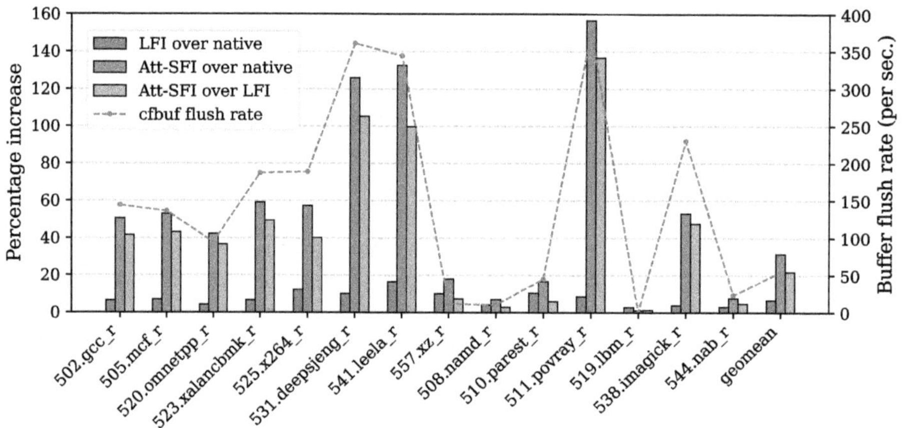

Fig. 3. Performance overhead of Att-SFI.

Run-Time Overhead. Figure 3 shows the time overhead comparison between native, LFI [26], and Att-SFI across different benchmarks, as well as their geomeans. Table 2 presents more detailed data. We measured that LFI introduces a 6.5% additional overhead compared to native, which is consistent with the result in LFI's publication. Att-SFI, on the other hand, introduces a higher overhead, with a 31.4% increase compared to native and a 21.9% increase compared to LFI. The higher overhead of fine-grained CFI, compared to SFI, is within our expected range, as its instrumentation involves longer instruction sequences than SFI.

Specifically, Att-SFI introduces more than 50% overhead on three benchmarks: 136.7% for provray_r, 105.2% for *deepsjeng_r*, and 99.8% for *leela_r*. The high overhead benchmarks for LFI, on the other hand, are primarily *leela_r*, *x264_r*, and *parest_r*. This indicates that the sources of overhead for Att-SFI and LFI are not the same. Due to differences in instrumentation targets, the additional overhead of Att-SFI is primarily correlated with the frequency of function calls, whereas LFI's overhead mainly stems from the frequency of memory accesses.

Table 2. Overhead on SPEC CPU 2017 benchmarks.

Benchmark	Native	SFI				Att-SFI			
	Time (sec.)	Time (sec.)	Binaries size(kB)	Time overhead	Time (sec.)	Binaries size(kB)	Time overhead	Flush rate
gcc_r	734	781	14,474	6.4%	1,106	16,817	41.5%	144.1
mcf_r	753	805	229	6.8%	1,151	232	43.1%	135.9
omnetpp_r	1,496	1,558	4,600	4.2%	2,128	5,173	36.6%	94.4
xalancbmk_r	450	480	8,525	6.5%	716	10,018	49.4%	187.0
x264_r	232	260	1,984	12.1%	365	2,281	40.1%	188.6
deepsjeng_r	365	402	302	10.0%	825	308	105.2%	360.9
leela_r	582	677	1,790	16.4%	1,352	1,869	99.8%	344.2
xz_r	741	816	306	10.1%	875	314	7.2%	11.9
namd_r	402	418	1,292	4.0%	430	1,359	2.8%	9.9
parest_r	1,112	1,226	4,800	10.3%	1,298	5,369	5.8%	45.1
povray_r	645	699	2,428	8.4%	1,655	2,601	136.7%	377.2
lbm_r(-O2)	484	506	227	2.8%	512	229	1.2%	0.02
imagick_r	523	542	2,021	3.8%	800	2,593	47.5%	230.0
nab_r	635	654	312	2.9%	684	316	4.7%	23.6
Arith. mean	—	—	—	7.5%	—	—	44.4%	153.8
geomean	—	—	—	6.5%	—	—	21.9%	54.4

The buffer flush rate refers to the number of times the cflog buffer is flushed per second due to being filled, with the buffer size set to 2 MiB, which we determined to be the optimal value through experimentation. This data represents the rate at which different benchmarks generate logs, and the overhead of Att-SFI is positively correlated with the buffer flush rate. In our experiment, the geomean of the buffer flush rate was 54.4. Since each control flow log is 8 bytes, this implies that approximately 14 million logs are generated per second, occupying about 109 MiB of storage. This means that the runtime verifier must operate at a same level rate, or it will lead to an increasing storage occupation over time.

In the best-case scenario, *lbm_r* incurs an overhead of 1.2%, *namd_r* has 2.8%, and *nab_r* has 4.7%. In particular, the data used for *lbm_r* comes from O2 optimization instead of O3. When using O3, Att-SFI exhibits a -1.7% overhead compared to LFI. Our experiments reveal that Att-SFI instrumented function calls avoid aggressive inlining optimizations in some functions with O3, and in *lbm_r*, code bloat caused by aggressive inlining negatively impacts LFI performance.

Code Size and Memory. We measured the binary size of both LFI and Att-SFI, which is especially important in resource-constrained scenarios such as IoT. In our experiments, compared to LFI, Att-SFI led to a geomean increase in binary size of 3.6% and an arithmetic mean increase of 8.4%. The best and worst cases both occurred in *imagick_r*, where the executable *imagevalidate* saw an increase of 0.3% from 229kB, while the *imagick* saw a 31.9% increase from 1.8MB. The size increase does not have a direct correlation with the binary's original size. The largest binary increased by 16.2% from 14.5MB, while the three binaries with the highest increases had the following sizes: 1.8MB (31.9%), 803kB (27.2%), and 8.5MB (17.5%).

In terms of memory usage, in addition to the binary segments loaded into memory, each sandboxed program in Att-SFI requires an additional 4 MiB of memory. This happens when the cflog buffer is full, and the runtime copies it outside the sandbox for verification. Furthermore, as mentioned earlier, if the verification rate of the cflogs is lower than their generation rate, there will be a backlog of cflogs in memory, leading to continuous memory usage growth. Discarding unverified logs that exceed the expected size can alleviate this issue but would reduce the security of CFI, as it could allow certain control flow violations to go undetected.

6   Discussion

Integration with System-Level TEE. Att-SFI leverages system-level TEE compatibility for seamless integration without modifications. Although experiments were conducted in a simulated environment, this does not compromise the validity of our results. Incorporating CFI verification into TEE remote attestation reports is straightforward due to the hardware-assisted attestation in modern TEEs (e.g., Intel TDX [10], AMD SEV [3], ARM CCA [6]) allow customized guest report data. Unlike SGXMonitor [23] and BLAST [25], which rely on network/inter-process communication for cflog transmission, Att-SFI performs verification within the sandbox runtime through SFI's intra-process isolation. This approach eliminates additional network latency, IPC overhead, and potential TEE security model violations associated with cross-component interactions.

Reasons and Limitations of Instrumentation Using LLVM. Some SFI works [8,26] have pointed out the limitations of directly using LLVM for SFI. For instance, LLVM cannot perform instruction rewriting at both the frontend and backend for assembly sources. Additionally, the solution may be tied to specific versions of LLVM, and rapid updates and complex compilation architectures can lead to maintenance challenges. These limitations are present in not only SFI but also CFI. Att-SFI cannot instrument instructions that are located within the assembly source code. The advantage of using LLVM for instrumentation at the IR level is that it achieves architecture neutrality. For instance, in the Att-SFI implementation built upon the LFI software sandbox, when LFI adds support for a new architecture (such as the recently supported RISC-V), Att-SFI only needs few modifications to the runtime call. Another limitation of LLVM IR-level instrumentation is that Att-SFI relies on the source code of the sandboxed program. However, this is a common limitation of many SFI tools, including LFI, on which Att-SFI is based. In future work, we will consider implementing binary-level instrumentation to support projects that involve assembly source code with indirect control flow transfers on mainstream architectures.

Side-Channel Attacks. Att-SFI is not designed to directly defend against side-channel attacks, but it is important to discuss the new attack surface introduced by our solution and the mitigations. For adversaries capable of inferring which memory locations have been written to (such as via cache-timing attacks), the writing to the cflog buffer in Att-SFI could potentially expose control flow information of the sandboxed program. This is because different control flow paths might result in different frequencies of buffer writes. However, this information is difficult to exploit for guessing the actual control flow path of the program, as Att-SFI does not generate cflogs for direct branches. Introducing random delays during the writing of cflog buffer can mitigate this, but it comes with additional performance overhead.

Cflog Buffer Inside Sandbox vs. Outside Sandbox. Att-SFI uses a cflog buffer within the sandbox address domain and hides it through a reserved buffer address register. This design results in a lack of "strong isolation" between the sandboxed program and the cflog buffer. Once an adversary learns the buffer's address, they could tamper with the buffer's contents after hijacking the control flow, and bypass the CFI monitoring. The reason for adopting this design is that we strictly adhere to the principle of not breaking the original SFI model. Allowing a well-verified trampoline to use unmasked sandbox-external addresses would achieve strong isolation of the cflog buffer, but it would break the original SFI design and introduce additional security assumptions. Even when using sandbox-internal addresses, it remains hard for an adversary to organize gadgets to guess the right address of the cflog buffer. Moreover, simply overwriting all possible memory locations roughly would still allow us to detect the attack effectively.

Optimization of Cflogs. The cflogs in Att-SFI are compact, with each entry is only 8 bytes. However, long-running complex programs still generate a large number of logs, as the buffer flush rate shown in our experiments. Currently, we used a motivating example of run-time verification, and designing a complete run-time verifier for more precise attack detection [5] would lead to higher overhead. Asynchronous verification can help avoid this overhead, but if the verifier cannot process logs at line speed, the accumulated logs will lead to significant memory consumption. Therefore, for complex programs long-running in the sandbox, further optimization of cflog storage needs to be considered. We tested asynchronous file storage of the cflogs, but compression is still necessary to avoid high storage usage. In our future work, we will consider optimizing instrumentation targets to generate fewer cflog entries.

7   Related Work

SFI. Our solution is closely related to SFI. Google Native Client (NaCl) [19] applies SFI for running untrusted code in browsers. It uses instruction rewriting for software sandboxing on 64-bit ARM and x86 architectures, with coarse-grained CFI through alignment constraints. WebAssembly [12] enhances CFI through structured control flow, type signatures, and other methods in its software sandbox. ARMor [28] introduces fine-grained CFI in SFI by distinguishing control stacks from data stacks and assigning unique identifiers to indirect jump targets, but prioritizes strict security design and lacks practicality evaluation. Bin et al. [27] have used program analysis and CFI to eliminate redundant SFI protections for performance optimization. LFI [26] uses the 32-bit addressing mode in 64-bit architectures to implement a high-performance, lightweight software sandbox. On the x86-64 architecture, LFI requires alignment constraints or other hardware CFI to ensure SFI address masking. All of these SFI solutions' security models do not guarantee the run-time security of the sandboxed program itself. Att-SFI provides context-sensitive fine-grained CFI, preventing sandbox breaches without the need for alignment constraints or hardware-assisted CFI, while also ensuring the attestable runtime security of the sandboxed program.

CFI and CFA. CFI effectively prevents or monitors code reuse attacks by checking whether the program's control flow deviates from its Control Flow Graph (CFG). Work [1] was first proposed to enforce control flow integrity checks through instrumentation, particularly focusing on forward and backward edge CFI. Att-SFI is designed for run-time CFI monitoring rather than preventing, while the validation takes place outside the sandbox after the cflogs being collected. This is more like the Control Flow Attestation (CFA), such as C-Flat [2], the earliest CFA scheme proposed for IoT devices based on ARM Trustzone, verifying the control flow on a remote verifier, allowing run-time security to be attested. Att-SFI also records the control flows as cflogs and allows the run-time verifier to detect more types of attacks from the expressive cflogs [5]. It also allows the provenance analysis [23].

Hardware CFI features are provided on different architectures for better performance. ARMv8.5-A provides BTI (Branch Target Identification) [7], which, through the insertion of landing pad instructions, can achieve similar functionality to run-time checks in Att-SFI. Similarly, Intel CET [20] not only features IBT (Indirect Branch Tracking) but also implements hardware-assisted shadow stacks. These hardware-assisted CFIs introduce little performance overhead. For instance, CFA+ [4] based on ARM BTI focuses on the same instructions as Att-SFI, call, ret, and indirect branches, introducing less than 3% overhead in SPEC CPU2006. CFA+ ensures context-awareness by assigning a unique ID to each function call and XOR-masking the return address (x30 register) of the current function before and after each function call. This approach avoids the high overhead associated with control flow logging and shadow stacks. However, the static assignment of IDs in programs with simple CFGs, such as programs on IoT devices with deterministic paths, makes it possible for an adversary to pre-compute the masking value at run time and bypass it during exploitations. CFA+ also relies on SAT solvers to calculate the iterated XOR-ed state register and report the actual control flow in remote attestation, but it requires significant additional computation and does not effectively resolve collisions. In contrast, Att-SFI provides more expressive cflogs and more complete context-sensitive CFI without relying on specific hardware architectures.

CFI in Isolated Environment. Providing run-time security for programs in isolated environments is a crucial capability of our solution. Occlum [21] implements SFI using Intel MPX [17] inside the TEE, and provides coarse-grained CFI via custom *cfi_labels* instruction instrumentation in Intel SGX enclaves. While Occlum implements remote attestation based on SGX, it does not include run-time security attestation for SFI-isolated processes. In contrast, Att-SFI provides both architecture-neutral SFI and fine-grained CFI for sandboxed programs, along with remote attestation for run-time security. SGXMonitor [23] also offers CFA within SGX enclaves, providing context-insensitive basic block level CFI. However, this approach results in extremely high overhead, ranging from several times to hundreds of times, which is much more than Att-SFI.

8   Conclusion

Traditional SFI schemes do not account for the run-time security of sandboxed programs and rely on coarse-grained CFI to prevent sandbox bypass attacks. We propose Att-SFI, which is the first to introduce fine-grained CFI and run-time attestation for sandboxed programs into SFI, without depending on specific hardware features. Att-SFI inherits the efficient isolation benefits of SFI while also addressing the run-time security of sandboxed programs, making it highly applicable to today's popular cloud computing and confidential computing scenarios. Experimental results show that the Att-SFI introduces a reasonable performance overhead on top of existing SFI solutions.

Acknowledgments. This study was funded by the National Key Research and development Program of China (2022YFB4501500, 2022YFB4501501) and Xiaomi Young Scholars' Key Research Program via Open Competition (2024).

A Motivating Demonstration for Effectiveness

The following example demonstrates the effectiveness of our approach in providing CFI protection. Consider the code running within a software sandbox, where the `vulnerable_function` contains a stack overflow vulnerability. By using standard input, the attacker can write data exceeding the length of the buffer array, thus modifying the function's return address:

```c
void vulnerable_function() {
    char buffer[8];
    read(STDIN_FILENO, buffer, 24);
}
void secret_function() {
    printf("Secret function executed!\n");
    exit(-1);
}
int main() {
    ...
    vulnerable_function();
    printf("Correctly returned.\n");
    return 0;
}
```

Figure 4 shows a portion of the assembly code instrumented by Att-SFI. In this example, the location of the `traceret` differs from that in Fig. 2, because the LLVM intrinsic function `llvm.returnaddress` retrieves the invalidated x30 value, which may not accurately reflect the function's actual return address. We modified the LLVM backend to instrument `traceret` after the function's epilogue, ensuring that it captures the correct return address. Importantly, this issue can be addressed without compromising the architecture-neutral nature of Att-SFI. Specifically, `llvm.returnaddress` could be implemented in a way such as reading the return address from the stack, as in its x86-64 implementation.

Figure 5 shows a part of the cflogs both without and with the hijacked return address of `vulnerable_function`. The destinations and sources of the cflogs are in little-endian format and have an offset of 0x15000 from the dumped static assembly code.

In Fig. 5, the normal return destination address of `vulnerable_function` (0x025508) matches its source address (0x025504) when the function is called. However, the abnormal return destination address of `vulnerable_function` (0x02543c) violates this requirement, and thus, it will be detected by the sandbox's run-time verifier.

```
0000000000103e0 <vulnerable_function>:
   103e0:    sub     x22, sp, #0x20
   103e4:    add     sp, x21, w22, uxtw
   103e8:    stp     x29, x30, [sp, #16]      ; Push return address
   ......                                     ; Overflow happens here
   10410:    ldp     x29, x22, [sp, #16]      ; Pop return address
   10414:    add     x30, x21, w22, uxtw
   10418:    add     x22, sp, #0x20
   1041c:    add     sp, x21, w22, uxtw
   10420:    mov     x27, x0                  ; Save x0 and x30
   10424:    mov     x26, x30
   10428:    mov     x0, x30                  ; Pass x30 as argument
   1042c:    bl      10628 <traceret>
   10430:    add     x30, x21, w26, uxtw      ; Restore x0 and x30
   10434:    mov     x0, x27
   10438:    ret

000000000001043c <secret_function>:
   ......

0000000000010478 <main>:
   ......
```

Fig. 4. Assembly code instrumented by Att-SFI.

```
Cflogs without control flow hijacking:
Destination     | Source
--------------- |-----------------
e0 53 02 00     | 04 55 02 00      // call to vulnerable_function()
1c e6 02 00     | 00 54 02 00      // call to read()
08 55 02 00     | 30 54 02 00      // ret from vulnerable_function()
ac 61 02 00     | 10 55 02 00      // call to printf() in main()
9c 5a 02 00     | 44 55 02 00      // ret from main()

Cflogs with control flow hijacking:
Destination     | Source
--------------- |-----------------
e0 53 02 00     | 04 55 02 00      // call to vulnerable_function()
1c e6 02 00     | 00 54 02 00      // call to read()
3c 54 02 00     | 30 54 02 00      // ret to manipulated destination
ac 61 02 00     | 54 54 02 00      // call to printf() in secret_function()
4c 5f 02 00     | 70 54 02 00      // call to exit()
```

Fig. 5. Cflogs without and with control flow hijacking.

References

1. Abadi, M., Budiu, M., Erlingsson, U., Ligatti, J.: Control-flow integrity principles, implementations, and applications. ACM Trans. Inf. Syst. Secur. **13**(1) (2009)
2. Abera, T., et al.: C-flat: control-flow attestation for embedded systems software. In: Proceedings of the 2016 ACM SIGSAC Conference on Computer and Communications Security, CCS 2016, pp. 743–754. Association for Computing Machinery, New York, NY, USA (2016)

3. AMD: AMD SEV-SNP: strengthening VM isolation with integrity protection and more (2020). https://www.amd.com/content/dam/amd/en/documents/epyc-business-docs/white-papers/SEV-SNP-strengthening-vm-isolation-with-integrity-protection-and-more.pdf

4. Ammar, M., Abdelraoof, A., Vlasceanu, S.: On bridging the gap between control flow integrity and attestation schemes. In: 33rd USENIX Security Symposium (USENIX Security 2024), pp. 6633–6650. USENIX Association, Philadelphia, PA (2024)

5. Ammar, M., Caulfield, A., De Oliveira Nunes, I.: SoK: integrity, attestation, and auditing of program execution. In: 2025 IEEE Symposium on Security and Privacy (SP), p. 77. IEEE Computer Society, Los Alamitos, CA, USA (2025). https://doi.org/10.1109/SP61157.2025.00077

6. ARM: ARM confidential compute architecture (2021). https://www.arm.com/architecture/security-features/arm-confidential-compute-architecture

7. ARM: Learn the architecture - providing protection for complex software (2023). https://developer.arm.com/documentation/102433/0200

8. Bai, M., Pan, R., Parmer, G.: Omniwasm: efficient, granular fault isolation and control-flow integrity for arm microcontrollers. In: 2024 IEEE 30th Real-Time and Embedded Technology and Applications Symposium (RTAS), pp. 239–251 (2024). https://doi.org/10.1109/RTAS61025.2024.00027

9. Burow, N., Zhang, X., Payer, M.: SoK: shining light on shadow stacks. In: 2019 IEEE Symposium on Security and Privacy (SP), pp. 985–999 (2019). https://doi.org/10.1109/SP.2019.00076

10. Cheng, P.C., et al.: Intel TDX demystified: a top-down approach. ACM Comput. Surv. **56**(9) (2024). https://doi.org/10.1145/3652597

11. Confidential Computing Consortium: A technical analysis of confidential computing (2022). https://confidentialcomputing.io/resources/white-papers-reports

12. Webassembly core specification. W3C recommendation, World Wide Web Consortium (W3C) (2022). https://www.w3.org/TR/wasm-core-2/

13. IETF: Remote attestation procedures (RATS) (2023). https://datatracker.ietf.org/wg/rats/about

14. Larus, J.R.: Whole program paths. In: Proceedings of the ACM SIGPLAN 1999 Conference on Programming Language Design and Implementation, PLDI 1999, pp. 259–269. Association for Computing Machinery, New York, NY, USA (1999)

15. Morbitzer, M., Kopf, B., Zieris, P.: Guarantee: introducing control-flow attestation for trusted execution environments. In: 2023 IEEE 16th International Conference on Cloud Computing (CLOUD), pp. 547–553 (2023)

16. Munoz, A., Rios, R., Roman, R., Lopez, J.: A survey on the (in)security of trusted execution environments. Comput. Secur. **129**, 103180 (2023). https://doi.org/10.1016/j.cose.2023.103180

17. Oleksenko, O., Kuvaiskii, D., Bhatotia, P., Felber, P., Fetzer, C.: Intel MPX explained: an empirical study of intel MPX and software-based bounds checking approaches (2017). https://arxiv.org/abs/1702.00719

18. Peach, G., Pan, R., Wu, Z., Parmer, G., Haster, C., Cherkasova, L.: eWASM: practical software fault isolation for reliable embedded devices. IEEE Trans. Comput. Aided Des. Integr. Circuits Syst. **39**(11), 3492–3505 (2020). https://doi.org/10.1109/TCAD.2020.3012647

19. Sehr, D., et al.: Adapting software fault isolation to contemporary CPU architectures. In: USENIX Security Symposium (2010)

20. Shanbhogue, V., Gupta, D., Sahita, R.: Security analysis of processor instruction set architecture for enforcing control-flow integrity. In: Proceedings of the 8th International Workshop on Hardware and Architectural Support for Security and Privacy. HASP 2019. Association for Computing Machinery, New York, NY, USA (2019). https://doi.org/10.1145/3337167.3337175
21. Shen, Y., et al.: Occlum: secure and efficient multitasking inside a single enclave of intel SGX. In: Proceedings of the Twenty-Fifth International Conference on Architectural Support for Programming Languages and Operating Systems, ASPLOS 2020, pp. 955–970. Association for Computing Machinery, New York, NY, USA (2020)
22. Tan, G.: Principles and implementation techniques of software-based fault isolation. Found. Trends Priv. Secur. $\mathbf{1}$(3), 137–198 (2017). https://doi.org/10.1561/3300000013
23. Toffalini, F., Payer, M., Zhou, J., Cavallaro, L.: Designing a provenance analysis for SGX enclaves. In: Proceedings of the 38th Annual Computer Security Applications Conference, ACSAC 2022, pp. 102–116. Association for Computing Machinery, New York, NY, USA (2022)
24. Wahbe, R., Lucco, S., Anderson, T.E., Graham, S.L.: Efficient software-based fault isolation. In: Proceedings of the Fourteenth ACM Symposium on Operating Systems Principles - SOSP 1993 (1993)
25. Yadav, N., Ganapathy, V.: Whole-program control-flow path attestation. In: Proceedings of the 2023 ACM SIGSAC Conference on Computer and Communications Security, CCS 2023, pp. 2680–2694. Association for Computing Machinery, New York, NY, USA (2023)
26. Yedidia, Z.: Lightweight fault isolation: Practical, efficient, and secure software sandboxing. In: Proceedings of the 29th ACM International Conference on Architectural Support for Programming Languages and Operating Systems, ASPLOS 2024, vol. 2, pp. 649–665. Association for Computing Machinery, New York, NY, USA (2024). https://doi.org/10.1145/3620665.3640408
27. Zeng, B., Tan, G., Morrisett, G.: Combining control-flow integrity and static analysis for efficient and validated data sandboxing. In: Proceedings of the 18th ACM Conference on Computer and Communications Security, CCS 2011, pp. 29–40. Association for Computing Machinery, New York, NY, USA (2011). https://doi.org/10.1145/2046707.2046713
28. Zhao, L., Li, G., De Sutter, B., Regehr, J.: Armor: fully verified software fault isolation. In: Proceedings of the Ninth ACM International Conference on Embedded Software, EMSOFT 2011, pp. 289–298. Association for Computing Machinery, New York, NY, USA (2011). https://doi.org/10.1145/2038642.2038687

A Blockchain-Based Four-Factor Authentication and Key Agreement Protocol for Wireless Medical Sensor Networks

Bo Gong[(✉)], Zhongqing Wu, Ying Wang, and Jianbo Xu

School of Computer Science and Engineering, Hunan University of Science and Technology, Xiangtan, China
2741075@qq.com, {1050060,jbxu}@hnust.edu.cn

Abstract. In recent years, the Internet of Things (IoT) technology has propelled the widespread application of Wireless Medical Sensor Networks (WMSNs) in the healthcare field. WMSNs integrate various technologies to establish a remote diagnosis platform. However, the physiological data transmitted by WMSNs is highly sensitive, imposing stringent requirements on security and reliability. Currently, the mainstream three-factor authentication protocols have vulnerabilities. The reliance on third-party institutions brings risks of single-point failures and Distributed Denial of Service (DDoS) attacks, and there is also insufficient defense against physical layer threats. To address these issues, this study proposes a blockchain-enhanced four-factor authentication protocol. This protocol leverages blockchain technology to achieve decentralized authentication. Physical Unclonable Functions (PUFs) are employed to mitigate the security risks of sensor nodes and smart cards, while fuzzy extractors are utilized to safeguard the security of biometric templates. Through formal verification using the AVISPA tool and multi-dimensional informal analysis, it has been confirmed that this protocol can resist a variety of known attacks. Comparative analysis reveals that the proposed protocol not only attains a higher security level but also incurs the lowest communication overhead, making it highly suitable for the resource-constrained environment of WMSNs.

Keywords: Authentication · Blockchain · Physical unclonable functions (PUFs) · Security · Wireless Medical Sensor Networks (WMSNs)

1 Introduction

As the core of next-generation information infrastructure, Internet of Things (IoT) technology has been deeply integrated into various fields, such as industrial automation, smart agriculture, and more. In the medical field, the coordinated development of Wireless Sensor Network (WSN) and 5G technology

W. Liang et al. (Eds.): SecureComm 2025, LNICST 690, pp. 38–55, 2026.
https://doi.org/10.1007/978-3-032-23456-8_3

has accelerated the application of real-time health monitoring systems. These systems integrate high-precision sensors to collect vital signs and utilize Bluetooth Low Energy (BLE) and 5G technology for high-speed data transmission, establishing a remote diagnostic framework. This not only supports personalized healthcare but also helps alleviate the uneven distribution of medical resources [17]. During the COVID-19 pandemic, remote diagnostic systems reduced physical contact between medical staff and patients, lowering the risk of nosocomial infections, improving diagnostic efficiency, and optimizing resource allocation and the patient experience [9]. According to the prediction of Shanmugam et al., the global smart healthcare market is expected to grow at a compound annual growth rate (CAGR) of 21.3%, expanding from \$72.5 billion in 2020 to \$188.2 billion in 2025 [21].

WMSN has revolutionized the traditional medical model, improving diagnostic efficiency and optimizing medical resource allocation through device interconnection. However, this open architecture brings security risks. On one hand, the physiological data it collects is sensitive, and when transmitted via public channels, it is vulnerable to man-in-the-middle attacks and data tampering. On the other hand, there are loopholes in the remote identity authentication of medical staff, allowing unauthorized individuals to potentially access the system by forging credentials. Therefore, building a reliable authentication framework is crucial for ensuring the secure operation of smart healthcare systems.

In recent years, researchers have explored the three-factor authentication scheme [18], which improves the traditional two-factor authentication [7] by incorporating biometric elements. It uses fuzzy extractors to process biometric features, enhancing the security and reliability of the authentication system. However, the existing three-factor authentication framework still has security vulnerabilities, especially in terms of sensor node capture, smart card theft, and single-point-of-failure attacks. To address the security risks of smart cards, this study proposes integrating PUF circuits into the smart card chip architecture [4], establishing a security barrier at the hardware level to prevent identity theft. In addition, considering that the traditional three-factor authentication's reliance on third-party institutions can easily lead to single-point-of-failure and privacy leakage, this study introduces blockchain technology to build a decentralized authentication network [19]. By combining smart contracts, it achieves decentralized identity verification and secure session key negotiation, providing a more reliable authentication solution for Wireless Medical Sensor Network.

Therefore, based on the aforementioned considerations, this paper proposes a blockchain-based four-factor authentication and key agreement protocol to address the identified security challenges. The primary contributions of this research can be summarized as follows:

- This paper proposes a blockchain-based four-factor identity authentication scheme to achieve secure communication between Medical Professionals and Sensor Nodes.
- Blockchain technology and smart contracts are utilized to construct a decentralized authentication network, replacing the traditional Trusted Authority

(TA) authentication model. This design reduces single-point-of-failure risks and eliminates privacy concerns associated with centralized architectures.

- The protocol has undergone rigorous security validation using the AVISPA tool for formal analysis, complemented by detailed informal security assessments. These analyses confirm that the protocol satisfies critical security requirements, including session key security and forward secrecy.
- Compared with existing solutions, the proposed protocol has lower communication overhead and relatively low computational overhead.

This article is organized as follows. Section 2 discusses related works, Sect. 3 introduces the necessary background and preparation, Sect. 4 elaborates on the details of the proposed protocol, Sect. 5 provides a comprehensive security analysis, Sect. 6 evaluates the protocol's security functionality and performance, and Sect. 7 concludes the paper.

2 Related Works

Over the past few years, numerous researchers have proposed their own schemes to address security communication in WMSN. In 2016, Amin et al. [1] addressed the gap in prior privacy-preserving protocols, which rarely considered user anonymity, by developing an authentication protocol for mobile users to maintain anonymity in WSN. They employed BAN logic and AVISPA attacks to conduct a formal security analysis of their scheme. Unfortunately, in 2017, Jiang et al. [11] conducted a detailed analysis of Amin et al.'s scheme and identified vulnerabilities, including susceptibility to desynchronization attacks, stolen mobile device attacks, and sensor node exposure. Based on these findings, Jiang et al. proposed an end-to-end identity authentication and key agreement protocol based on quadratic residues, claiming that their scheme could withstand desynchronization attacks and stolen mobile device attacks. In 2018, Challa et al. [3] introduced a three-factor authentication scheme based on elliptic curve cryptography (ECC), incorporating fuzzy extractors to encrypt user biometric features. Their scheme aimed to resist attacks such as smart card stolen and insider privilege attacks. In 2019, Li et al. [16] pointed out that Amin et al.'s scheme lacked forward secrecy and was vulnerable to DDoS attacks. To enhance forward secrecy in WSN, Li et al. employed error-correcting codes and fuzzy extractors for biometric recognition, combined with ECC to achieve forward secrecy.

In 2021, To address physical-layer security and server centralization issues in WMSN, Wang et al. [22] designed a lightweight authentication and key agreement (AKP) scheme for medical IoT systems based on blockchain and PUF. Wang et al. claimed that their scheme could mitigate potential network and physical security threats, such as sensor node capture and single-point-of-failure attacks, while preserving user anonymity. However, in 2022, Yu et al. [23] identified security vulnerabilities in Wang et al.'s [22] scheme, including susceptibility to man-in-the-middle attacks and session key leakage, as well as a lack of mutual authentication. To address these flaws, Yu et al. proposed a robust revised authentication protocol based on blockchain and PUF. Unfortunately, in 2024, Kang et al. [12] discovered that Yu et al.'s revised protocol was vulnerable to sensor node capture attacks and exposed critical information. Kang et al. subsequently proposed an enhanced protocol that reduced security risks by limiting data interactions with smart contracts. In 2024, Miao et al. [20] introduced a blockchain-based three-factor privacy-preserving authentication protocol, incorporating Chebyshev chaotic mapping to enhance security during user login and authentication. However, their scheme only utilized blockchain as a database for storing identities and data, requiring registration with a trusted center, and thus remained susceptible to single-point-of-failure attacks. In 2025, Lee et al. [14] addressed the vulnerabilities of WSN systems to sensor node spoofing attacks and mobile device impersonation attacks by proposing a lightweight authentication scheme that provided user anonymity. However, their scheme lacked resistance to DDoS attacks and single-point-of-failure attacks.

3   Preliminaries

In this section, we will provide an overview of the blockchain technology, smart contracts, fuzzy extractors, PUF, network model, and attack model adopted in our proposed scheme.

3.1   Network Model

Our network model, illustrated in Fig. 1, comprises three primary entities: sensor nodes (SN), gateway nodes (GWN), and medical professionals (MP). It is assumed that all entities are equipped with PUF technology, which will be detailed in subsequent sections.

- **Sensor Nodes (SN)**: As the terminals for collecting medical data, SN perform two core functions:
    - **Physiological Data Acquisition**: SN monitor patients' vital signs (e.g., heart rate, blood oxygen, and body temperature) in real time, converting analog signals into encrypted medical data packets using analog - to - digital conversion techniques.
    - **Secure Communication Hub**: SN store dynamic communication credentials and encryption parameters issued by the GWN. After completing registration with the GWN, they establish a temporary session key with the MP using a lightweight key agreement protocol.
- **Gateway Node (GWN) Architecture**: To address the limitations of centralized architectures, our proposal introduces a blockchain - enhanced GWN framework. This design abandons the traditional single trusted third - party model, instead deploying a cluster of smart contracts on the Ethereum Virtual Machine (EVM). These smart contracts autonomously execute device registration and session key negotiation requests. Node access control is realized through PoW consensus mechanism to ensure network credibility.

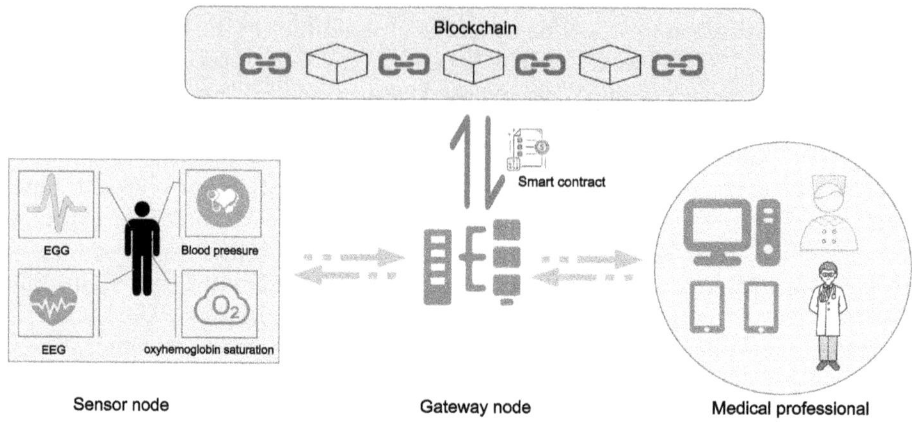

Fig. 1. Network model of the proposed protocol.

- **Medical Professionals (MP)**: MP are responsible for diagnosing medical data transmitted by SN. Prior to initiating communication, MP must provide their credentials, including passwords and biometric information, to register with the GWN. Upon successful registration, MP can establish a session with SN and negotiate a session key for secure communication.

3.2   Blockchain and Smart Contracts

In our proposed WMSN architecture, blockchain technology is employed to ensure a decentralized structure, data integrity, and transparency. Smart contracts are utilized to automate access control mechanisms, thereby enabling fine-grained management of data permissions. This architecture protects the privacy of medical participants while leveraging the self-executing logic of smart contracts to enforce security policies.

3.3   Fuzzy Extractor

Fuzzy extraction [5] is a cryptographic technique used to process biometric data, such as fingerprints, iris patterns, facial recognition, and palm prints. It involves two primary operations:

Gen(): After the user inputs the biometric information Bio, the Gen function will generate a random string α and a random auxiliary string β. $Gen(Bio) = \{\alpha, \beta\}$

Rep(): After inputting a biometric information Bio_{new} into the algorithm, by leveraging the random auxiliary string β, if $Rep(Bio_{new}, \beta) \leq t$ (where t represents the size of a given interval), the random string α will be output.

3.4 Physical Unclonable Function

PUF are employed in authorized devices to securely store sensitive parameters through the challenge-response pair (CRP) mechanism [8]. As a digital representation of a device's inherent physical characteristics, PUF exhibit both uniqueness and irreproducibility. Uniqueness: Each integrated circuit (IC) instance has statistically unique PUF responses. Irreproducibility: It is impossible to replicate or reverse-engineer the PUF characteristics of a device. PUF provide robust security against attacks, as an attacker cannot derive the internal physical mechanisms of a PUF from known CRPs. Additionally, session keys are dynamically generated using CRPs, eliminating the risk of static key storage. Even if an attacker obtains challenge data, they cannot forge legitimate responses. These properties enable our system to construct unique hardware-based identities for each communication entity, offering robust protection against sensor node capture attacks.

3.5 Attack Model

Our attack model is based on the Dolev-Yao threat model [6]. The adversary's capabilities are defined as follows:

- The attacker can eavesdrop, modify, intercept, and replay information transmitted over public channels.
- The attacker may perform differential power analysis [13] to illegally obtain legitimate users' devices and extract stored information.
- The attacker can physically capture sensor nodes to retrieve internal key parameters.
- The attacker is unable to compute hash function collisions within a polynomial time frame.
- If an attacker gains access to critical parameters stored in medical devices or sensor nodes, they may launch attacks such as replay attacks, sensor node impersonation, or compromise forward secrecy.

4 Proposed Protocol

In this section, we present a detailed description of our blockchain-based multi-factor authentication protocol for WMSN. The protocol comprises four phases: initialization phase, registration phase, login and mutual authentication phase, and password update phase. Table 1 defines the notations used throughout this protocol.

Table 1. Notations

Notation	Description
$SN/GWN/MP/MD$	Sensor node/Gateway node/Medical Professional/Mobile device
ID_i/ID_j	Identity of MP / Identity of SN
SC/IV	Smart contract / Identities verification table
hID_i/hID_j	The anonymous identity of MP and SN
PW_i	Password of MP
C_i/R_i	Challenge - response of MP
C_j/R_j	Challenge - response of SN
R_u	Random nonce of MP
$\text{Gen}(\cdot), \text{Rep}(\cdot)$	Fuzzy extractors
BIO_i	Biometric
$h(\cdot)$	Cryptographic hash function
R_{MP}/R_{SN}	Random number generated by MP and SN
T_1, T_2, T_3, T_4	Timestamps
$\oplus$	XOR operation
$\parallel$	Concatenate operation
S_K	Mutually established session key among MP and SN

4.1   Initialization Phase

The system administrator initializes the blockchain platform. Our framework adopts a Proof-of-Work (PoW) consensus mechanism, though public blockchain platforms like Ethereum may also be utilized for cost efficiency, robustness against single-point-of-failure attacks, and resilience to DDoS attacks. Additionally, the administrator deploys smart contracts to automate the registration and authentication processes for SN and MP.

4.2   Registration Phase

The registration phase consists of two sub-processes: SN registration phase and MP registration phase, both conducted over secure channels.

SN Registration Phase. At this stage, the SN needs to be registered through the SC and then negotiate a common key with the GWN. In the protocol we proposed, the identity information ID_j of the SN is already stored in the blockchain. The specific operation steps are as follows:

Step 1. The SN generates a challenge C_j, through the PUF, calculates the response $R_j = \text{PUF}(C_j)$, calculate $hID_j = h(ID_j \| R_j)$, and then send the information $\{ID_j, R_j, hID_j\}$ to the GWN.

Step 2. After receiving the information $\{ID_j, R_j, hID_j\}$, the GWN uses the SC deployed on the blockchain to initiate the Sensor Node Registration

(SNR) function. Check the uniqueness of the identity ID_j of this SN through the Identity Verification Table (IV). If $ID_j \notin IV$, then the GWN selects a random value R_g, and calculates $X_j = h(R_g||hID_j)$. Otherwise, the SC rejects this session. Finally, the SC returns X_j to the SN through a private channel via the GWN. The GWN saves R_g in the local database.

Step 3. After receiving X_j, the SN saves it in the secure memory.

MP Registration Phase. Every medical professional is required to register on-site, and after the first registration, they will be issued a smart card, and it is ensured that ID_i is unique. The detailed steps are as follows.

Step 1. The MP chooses a unique ID_i, PW_i and BIO_i, generates a challenge C_i, MP calculates $R_i = \text{PUF}(C_i)$, $Gen(BIO_i) = \{\alpha_i, \beta_i\}$, $hID_i = h(ID_i||\alpha_i)$ and $hPW_i = h(PW_i||R_i)$. After that, the MP sends the information $\{hID_i, hPW_i, ID_i, R_i\}$ to the GWN.

Step 2. After receiving the message, the GWN retrieves the Medical Professional Registration (MPR) function deployed on the SC. The SC checks whether the identity ID_i of the MP exists through the IV. If it does not exist, then the GWN selects a random value R_u, calculates $X_i = h(R_u||hID_i||hPW_i)$, $Q_i = h(R_i||hID_i) \oplus X_i$, $W_i = h(X_i, hPW_i)$. After that, the SC stores $\{W_i, Q_i\}$ in the smart card and sends it to the MP. The GWN saves R_u in the local database.

4.3 Login and Mutual Authentication Phase

With the assistance of blockchain technology and smart contracts, the MP requests access to the data of the SN through the GWN. After mutual authentication, a common session key is established between the SN and the MP. All communications in this stage are transmitted through a public channel, and this stage is shown in Fig. 2. The specific steps are as follows:

Step 1. The MP first inserts the smart card, and then enters ID_i, PW_i and the biometric feature BIO_i stored in the MD. After that, the MD calculates $Rep(BIO_i, \beta_i) = \alpha_i$, $R_i = \text{PUF}(C_i)$, $hID_i = h(ID_i||\alpha_i)$ and $hPW_i = h(PW_i||R_i)$. After that, calculate $X_i = h(R_i||hID_i) \oplus Q_i$, $W_i = h(X_i, hPW_i)$, and verify whether W_i^* is equal to W_i. If they are equal, it indicates that the MP has successfully logged in to the MD. If not, the MD rejects this service.

Step 2. The MP selects a random value R_{MP} and a timestamp T_1, and calculates $P_1 = h(X_i||hID_i||T_1) \oplus R_{MP}$ and $M_2 = h(X_i||hID_i||T_1||R_{MP})$. After that, the MP sends the message $\{M_1, M_2, hID_i, T_1\}$ to the GWN through the MD via the public channel.

Step 3. After receiving the message sent from the MP, the GWN first checks the freshness of T_1. If it is unreasonable, the GWN will reject this session. If it is reasonable, the GWN will call the MPAuth function to establish a transaction with the SC. The SC will first confirm the validity of the GWN address, and then check the number of requests from the MP and the SN. We can set a threshold for failed requests. If the threshold is exceeded, the SC will suspend the authentication of this MP and SN for a period of time. If it is reasonable, the SC calculates $X_i = h(R_u||hID_i)$,$R_{MP} = h(X_i||hID_i||T_1) \oplus M_1$ and $M_2{}^* = h(X_i||hID_i||T_1||R_{MP})$, and verifies whether M_2^* is equal to M_2. If they are equal, it means that the SC has completed the verification of the legitimacy of the MP. If not, the SC will increment the failure count of the counter set for this MP by one. After that, the SC selects a random value R_{GWN} and a timestamp T_2, calculates $M_3 = (R_{GWN}||R_{MP}) \oplus h(hID_i||X_j||T_2)$ and $M_4 = h(R_{GWN}||R_{MP}||hID_i||X_j||T_2)$. After that, the SC sends the message $\{M_3, M_4, hID_i, T_2\}$ to the SN via the public channel.

Step 4. After receiving the message, the SN first checks the freshness of T_2. If it is reasonable, the SN calculates $(R_{GWN}||R_{MP}) = M_3 \oplus h(hID_i||X_j||T_2)$,$M_4{}^* = h(R_{GWN}||R_{MP}||hID_i||X_j||T_2)$, and verifies whether M_4^* is equal to M_4. If they are equal, the SN selects a random value R_{SN} and a timestamp T_3, calculates session key $S_K = h(R_{MP}||R_{SN})$,$M_5 = R_{SN} \oplus h(R_{MP}||hID_j||T_3||X_j)$,$M_6 = h(R_{MP}||R_{SN}||T_3||X_j)$ and $M_7 = h(S_K||R_{MP}||R_{SN}||hID_i||hID_j)$. After that, the SN sends the message $\{M_5, M_6, M_7, T_3\}$ to the GWN via the public channel.

Step 5. After receiving the message sent from the SN, the GWN first checks the freshness of T_3. If it is reasonable, the GWN will call the SNAuth function to establish a transaction with the SC. The SC will first confirm the validity of the GWN address. If it is reasonable, the SC then calculates $R_{SN} = M_5 \oplus h(R_{MP}||hID_j||T_3||X_j)$ and $M_6{}^* = h(R_{MP}||R_{SN}||T_3||X_j)$, and determines whether M_6^* is equal to M_6. If they are equal, the SC selects a timestamp T_4, calculates $M_8 = (R_{SN}||hID_j) \oplus h(R_{MP}||X_i||hID_i||T_4)$. After that, the SC sends the message $\{M_8, M_7, T_3\}$ to the MP via the public channel.

Step 6. After receiving the message, the MP first checks the freshness of T_4. If it is reasonable, the MP calculates $(R_{SN}||hID_j) = M_8 \oplus h(R_{MP}||X_i||hID_i||T_4)$, $S_K = h(R_{MP}||R_{SN})$, $M_7{}^* = h(S_K||R_{MP}||R_{SN}||hID_i||hID_j)$, and verifies whether M_7^* is equal to M_7. If they are equal, the MP can use S_K as the session key for communication with the SN.

4.4   Password Update Phase

The MP can change the password through the smart card on the local legal server. The specific steps are as follows:

Step 1. The MP inserts the smart card into the local legal server, and then verifies the correctness of the smart card, the password, the biometric feature, and the PUF.

Step 2. The MP enters the new password PW_i^{new}, using this new password, and then calculates $hPW_i{}^{new} = h(PW_i{}^{new}||R_i)$, $X_i{}^{new} = h(R_u||hID_i||hPW_i{}^{new})$, $Q_i{}^{new} = h(R_i||hID_i) \oplus X_i{}^{new}$ and $W_i{}^{new} = h(X_i{}^{new}, hPW_i{}^{new})$. Finally, store $\{W_i{}^{new}, Q_i{}^{new}\}$ in the smart card.

5   Security Analysis

In this section, we first conduct a formal security analysis using the widely recognized AVISPA tool to evaluate whether our protocol can withstand attacks targeting session key security. Following this, we provide a non-formal security analysis to demonstrate the protocol's resilience against common attack vectors.

5.1   Formal Security Analysis Using AVISPA

AVISPA is a widely accepted tool for formal security evaluations [2], enabling users to define protocol specifications and security properties using its High-Level Protocol Specification Language (HLPSL). The tool converts HLPSL scripts into intermediate forms (IF) for further processing by its backend tools, which include: On-the-fly Model-Checker (OFMC), Constraint-Logic-based Attack Searcher (CL-AtSe), SAT-based Model-Checker (SATMC), Tree Automata based on Automatic Approximations for the Analysis of Security Protocols (TA4SP). For our proposed protocol, we selected OFMC and CL-AtSe to assess its resistance to attacks defined in Sect. 3.5. As shown in Figs. 3 and 4, the analysis results under these back-end confirm that our protocol is secure against the identified threats.

5.2   Informal Analysis

This section offers a detailed non-formal security analysis of our protocol, addressing its resilience against various attack vectors.

Smart Card Stolen Attack. Even if an attacker successfully steals a smart card, it is difficult for them to quickly obtain the user information stored in the card. This is because all the information stored in the smart card is encrypted using a hash function, which keeps the user's identity identifier ID_i and password PW_i in an anonymous state, greatly increasing the difficulty for the attacker to crack the correct identity and password. At the same time, the attacker is unable to generate specific information because the generation of this information requires the use of a PUF, and the attacker does not have the corresponding PUF device. Since the attacker cannot generate the correct W_i and Q_i, they will not be able to pass the authentication and successfully log in to the GWN. It can be seen that the protocol we have designed has strong resistance against smart card stolen attacks, and can effectively protect system security and user information privacy.

Confidentiality. Since the MP, SN, and GWN transmit messages to each other through a public channel, it is extremely necessary to ensure the confidentiality of the personal privacy data of the participating entities. In our protocol, the transmitted messages are all encrypted using XOR operations or hash functions. Therefore, our protocol is capable of providing confidentiality for the personal privacy information of the participating entities.

Fig. 2. Authentication and key agreement phase.

Privileged Insider Attack. In practical real-life applications, an MP may use the same password to register in different systems. If a privileged insider within a certain system obtains the MP's password through illegal means, they may attempt to use this password to access other systems. However, in the protocol we proposed, the password entered by the MP is encrypted. Therefore, even if someone has the initial password, they will not be able to log in correctly. Thus, our protocol is capable of resisting attacks from privileged insiders.

Replay Attack. An attacker may intercept the messages transmitted among the three entities in the public channel and then launch a replay attack. However, in our protocol, the messages transmitted in the public channel are all encrypted using hash functions. Moreover, each message contains a timestamp. By verifying

```
% OFMC
% Version of 2006/02/13
SUMMARY
  SAFE
DETAILS
  BOUNDED_NUMBER_OF_SESSIONS
PROTOCOL
  /home/span/span/testsuite/results/my_protocol.if
GOAL
  as_specified
BACKEND
  OFMC
COMMENTS
STATISTICS
  parseTime: 0.00s
  searchTime: 5.76s
  visitedNodes: 1168 nodes
  depth: 9 plies
```

Fig. 3. OFMC back-end result.

```
SUMMARY
  SAFE

DETAILS
  BOUNDED_NUMBER_OF_SESSIONS
  TYPED_MODEL

PROTOCOL
  /home/span/span/testsuite/results/my_protocol.if

GOAL
  As Specified

BACKEND
  CL-AtSe

STATISTICS

  Analysed   : 0 states
  Reachable  : 0 states
  Translation: 0.05 seconds
  Computation: 0.00 seconds
```

Fig. 4. CL-AtSe back-end result.

the freshness of the timestamp and the hash value, the legitimacy of the message can be detected. Therefore, our protocol is able to resist replay attacks.

Man-In-The-Middle (MITM) Attack. An attacker may attempt to disrupt the establishment of a session key between the two parties by intercepting, resending, modifying, or deleting messages. In our protocol, we utilize a PUF to generate response challenges, and all messages are protected using hash functions and XOR operations to safeguard the privacy data of the participating entities. The session key consists of fresh random values respectively selected by the MP and the SN. Without knowledge of these values, the attacker is unable to disrupt the communication. Therefore, our protocol is capable of resisting man-in-the-middle attacks.

DDoS Attack. In the authentication phase of our protocol, a failure calculator is introduced for each participating entity, and a threshold value is set. If the number of failures reaches this threshold, the corresponding part will stop responding to requests for an extended period of time. Therefore, our protocol is able to withstand DDoS attacks.

Sensor Node Capturing Attack. Generally speaking, sensor nodes are prone to being physically captured by attackers. Nevertheless, our proposed protocol has introduced a PUF. When an attacker tries to break into the sensor node to retrieve the internally stored messages, since the attacker is unable to calculate the response challenge from the PUF, for instance, if relevant calculations in the protocol involve operations like those based on the PUF output in formulas such as certain verification processes related to $R_i = \text{PUF}(C_i)$ (where C_i is the generated challenge), our protocol can effectively resist the attacks of sensor node capture.

Session Key Agreement. When the MP initiates a session request and successfully completes the session eventually, a session key will be negotiated between the MP and the SN for subsequent message transmission. In our protocol, the session key depends on the random values selected by the MP and the SN, say R_{MP} and R_{SN}, and they each safeguard the security of the randomly chosen values they have selected. For example, the session key $S_K = h(R_{MP}\|R_{SN})$ (where h represents a hash function and $\|$ represents concatenation). When it is detected that an attacker is attempting to crack the session key, the stability and security of the session can be ensured by quickly modifying the random values of the key.

User Anonymity. Attackers attempt to capture all messages transmitted over the public channel and then try to crack the identity identifier ID_i of the Mobile Node (MP). However, in the protocol we designed, ID_i is encrypted, specifically, $hID_i = h(ID_i\|\alpha_i)$. To obtain$ID_i$ by cracking hID_i, attackers must know the biometric features of the MP. However, this is unachievable for attackers. Since biometric features are unique to users, and the protocol does not expose such information during transmission, attackers have no way to acquire it. Therefore, our protocol can effectively guarantee user anonymity and prevent attackers from obtaining users' true identity information through message analysis.

Sensor Node Anonymity. If attackers attempt to crack the identity identifier ID_j of the sensor node, in the protocol we designed, ID_j is protected by hID_j. Specifically, $hID_j = h(ID_j\|PUF(C_j))$, where C_j represents the challenge issued to the sensor chip. To successfully crack hID_j and obtain ID_j, attackers must acquire the response generated by the sensor chip in response to the challenge. However, due to the uniqueness of the PUF, the PUF response of each sensor chip is unique and difficult to replicate or predict. It is nearly impossible for attackers to obtain the required challenge response. Therefore, our protocol can effectively guarantee user anonymity and prevent attackers from obtaining the true identity information of sensor node users through illegal means.

Password Update. To effectively prevent serious hazards caused by password leakage, our protocol incorporates a password modification function. With this function, the MP can independently change its password. This effectively circumvents potential unknown losses and significantly enhances the security of the system as well as the protection of user data.

Four-Factor Security. Attackers may attempt a simulated attack by taking advantage of any one of the four factors. However, even if attackers manage to obtain the identity information and password of the MP, and even get hold of the smart card storing identity features, they still won't succeed. This is because attackers are unable to find a compatible card reader device, thus failing to obtain the correct response value of the PUF [10]. Precisely for this reason, our protocol can meet the strict requirements of four-factor security, effectively safeguarding the security of the system.

6   Performance Analysis

In this section, we compare our proposed protocol with competing schemes [12,14,15,22,23] in terms of security performance, computational overhead, and communication overhead.

6.1   Security Comparison

We summarize the security performance comparison between our proposed scheme and competing protocols in Table 2. Our protocol demonstrates robustness against various attacks, including single-point-of-failure (SPOF) attacks, spoofing attacks, sensor node physical capture attacks, replay attacks, and MITM attacks. In contrast: Scheme [14,15] are vulnerable to DDoS attacks and SPOF failures. Scheme [22] cannot resist session key leakage attacks and lacks mutual authentication. Additionally, our protocol ensures anonymity for both users and sensor nodes while maintaining a high level of security. Therefore, our protocol is better suited for resource-constrained WMSN environments.

6.2   Computation Overhead

Since the scheme we proposed only employs XOR operations and hash functions, for the sake of fairness, the comparison schemes we use also only adopt XOR operations and hash functions. We use T_h to represent the execution time of the hash operation. Since the time taken for an XOR operation is much smaller compared to that of a hash function, in practical comparisons, we only measured the time of the hash function. Our experimental environment is as follows: The processor is an AMD Ryzen 5 5600 6-Core Processor with a frequency of 4.60 GHz, the memory is 32GB, and the operating system is Windows 10 64-bit. We measured that the average execution time of the SHA-256 algorithm for 100,000 times is 0.001 ms. Our scheme executes a total of 25 hash operations during the identity authentication and key negotiation phase, and the total computation time is 0.025 ms. Although our computational overhead is slightly higher than the schemes proposed by Wang et al.'s scheme [22] and Lee et al.'s scheme [15], it has a much lower computational overhead compared to other relevant schemes, and provides higher security. In Table 3, we summarize the comparison of the computational overheads between the scheme proposed in this paper and other comparative protocols.

Table 2. Security Comparison

Feature	Li et al. [15]	Wang et al. [22]	Yu et al. [23]	Kang et al. [12]	Lee et al. [14]	ours
User anonymity	✓	✓	✓	✓	✓	✓
Sensor anonymity	✓	✓	✓	✓	✓	✓
Privileged inside attack	✓	✓	✓	✓	✓	✓
Perfect forward secrecy	✓	✓	✓	✓	✓	✓
Stolen Verifier attack	✓	✓	✓	✓	✓	✓
Session key disclosure attack	✓	×	✓	✓	✓	✓
Mutual authentication	✓	×	✓	✓	✓	✓
Sensor node capture attack	✓	✓	✓	✓	✓	✓
Replay attack	✓	✓	✓	✓	✓	✓
Impersonation attack	✓	✓	✓	✓	✓	✓
DDoS attack	×	✓	✓	✓	×	✓
Man-in-the-middle attack	✓	✓	✓	✓	✓	✓
SPOF and bottleneck	×	✓	✓	✓	×	✓
Smart card stolen attack	✓	×	×	×	×	✓
Four-factor security	×	×	×	×	×	✓
Password change	✓	×	✓	✓	✓	✓

Table 3. Computation Cost Comparison

Scheme	MP	GWN	SN	Total
Li et al. [15]	$10T_h$	$9T_h$	$7T_h$	$26T_h$
Wang et al. [22]	$6T_h$	$4T_h$	$3T_h$	$13T_h$
Yu et al. [23]	$9T_h$	$9T_h$	$7T_h$	$25T_h$
Kang et al. [12]	$11T_h$	$12T_h$	$9T_h$	$32T_h$
Lee et al. [14]	$9T_h$	$8T_h$	$3T_h$	$20T_h$
Ours	$10T_h$	$9T_h$	$6T_h$	$25T_h$

Table 4. Communication Cost Comparison

Scheme	MP	GWN/SC	SN	Total costs
Li et al. [15]	1024 bits	576 bits	544 bits	2144 bits
Wang et al. [22]	608 bits	992 bits	448 bits	2048 bits
Yu et al. [23]	448 bits	1088 bits	576 bits	2112 bits
Kang et al. [12]	512 bits	1216 bits	512 bits	2240 bits
Lee et al. [14]	731 bits	1056 bits	192 bits	1979 bits
Ours	512 bits	864 bits	512 bits	1888 bits

6.3   Communication Overheade

In order to compare the communication overheads of various schemes more accurately, we make the following assumptions: The size of the message generated by the hash function is 160 bits, the length of the identity identifierIDof the MP is 160 bits, the size of the identity identifierIDof the SN is 32 bits, the size of the ran-

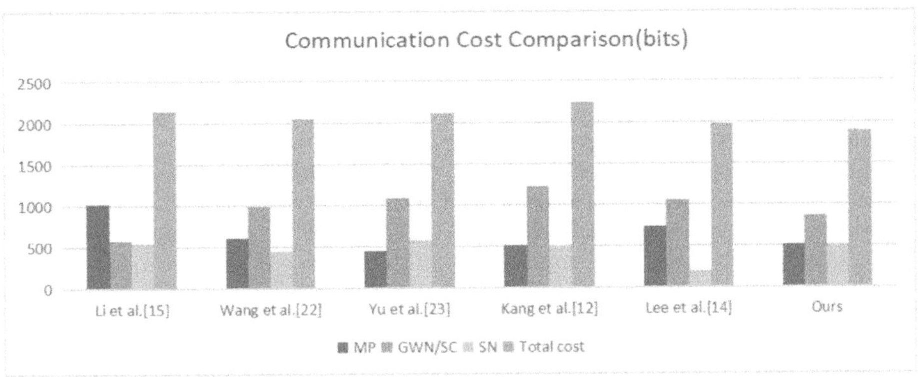

Fig. 5. Communication Cost Comparison.

dom value is set to 160 bits, the size of the timestamp is 32 bits, and the size of the challenge of the PUF is 32 bits. In the scheme proposed in this paper, the message sent by the MP to the GWN is $\{M_1, M_2, hID_i, T_1\}$, and its length is calculated as $160 + 160 + 160 + 32 = 512$bits. The GWN conducts two message transmission operations. The message of the first transmission is $\{M_3, M_4, hID_i, T_2\}$, and the message of the second transmission is $\{M_7, M_8, T_4\}$. The total length of these two transmitted messages is $(160 + 160 + 160 + 32) + (160 + 160 + 32) = 864$ bits. The Sensor Node (SN) only conducts one message transmission, and the length of the sent message $\{M_7, M_6, M_5, T_3\}$ is $160 + 160 + 160 + 32 = 512$ bits. Overall, the total communication overhead of our proposed scheme is $512 + 864 + 512 = 1888$ bits, which is the lowest among the compared schemes. This fully demonstrates that our scheme has significant advantages in the WMSN system with limited resources. In Table 4 and Fig. 5, we comprehensively summarize the detailed comparison of the communication overheads between the scheme proposed in this paper and other comparative protocols.

7   Conclusion

This study introduces a blockchain-enhanced four-factor identity authentication framework, which systematically addresses the key security issues in traditional three-factor authentication systems. The security of the scheme is proven by using the AVISPA security tool and conducting a detailed informal security analysis. In addition, the performance analysis shows that this protocol reduces communication overhead and computational overhead, making it more suitable for the WMSN systems with limited resources.

References

1. Amin, R., Islam, S.K.H., Biswas, G.P., Khan, M.K., Leng, L., Kumar, N.: Design of an anonymity-preserving three-factor authenticated key exchange protocol for wireless sensor networks. Comput. Netw. **101**, 42–62 (2016)

2. Armando, A., et al.: The AVISPA tool for the automated validation of internet security protocols and applications. In: Etessami, K., Rajamani, S.K. (eds.) Computer Aided Verification. CAV 2005. LNCS, vol. 3576, pp. 281–285. Springer, Heidelberg (2005). https://doi.org/10.1007/11513988_27

3. Challa, S., et al.: An efficient ECC-based provably secure three-factor user authentication and key agreement protocol for wireless healthcare sensor networks. Comput. Elect. Eng. **69**, 534–554 (2018). https://doi.org/10.1016/j.compeleceng.2017.08.003, https://www.sciencedirect.com/science/article/pii/S0045790616302622

4. Das, A.K., Kalam, S., Sahar, N., Sinha, D.: UCFL: user categorization using fuzzy logic towards PUF based two-phase authentication of fog assisted IOT devices. Comput. Secur. **97**, p. 101938 (2020). https://doi.org/10.1016/j.cose.2020.101938, https://www.sciencedirect.com/science/article/pii/S0167404820302145

5. Dodis, Y., Reyzin, L., Smith, A.: Fuzzy extractors: how to generate strong keys from biometrics and other noisy data. In: Cachin, C., Camenisch, J.L. (eds.) Advances in Cryptology - EUROCRYPT 2004, pp. 523–540. Springer, Berlin Heidelberg, Berlin, Heidelberg (2004)

6. Dolev, D., Yao, A.: On the security of public key protocols. IEEE Trans. Inf. Theory **29**(2), 198–208 (1983). https://doi.org/10.1109/TIT.1983.1056650

7. Farash, M.S., Turkanović, M., Kumari, S., Hölbl, M.: An efficient user authentication and key agreement scheme for heterogeneous wireless sensor network tailored for the internet of things environment. Ad Hoc Netw. **36**, 152–176 (2016). https://doi.org/10.1016/j.adhoc.2015.05.014, https://www.sciencedirect.com/science/article/pii/S1570870515001195

8. Gao, Y., Al-Sarawi, S.F., Abbott, D.: Physical unclonable functions. Nat. Elect. **3**(2), 81–91 (2020). https://doi.org/10.1038/s41928-020-0372-5

9. Ghubaish, A., Salman, T., Zolanvari, M., Unal, D., Al-Ali, A., Jain, R.: Recent advances in the internet-of-medical-things (IOMT) systems security. IEEE Internet Things J. **8**(11), 8707–8718 (2021). https://doi.org/10.1109/JIOT.2020.3045653

10. Guo, P., Liang, W., Xu, S.: A privacy preserving four-factor authentication protocol for internet of medical things. Comput. Secur. **137** (2024). https://doi.org/10.1016/j.cose.2023.103632

11. Jiang, Q., Ma, J., Yang, C., Ma, X., Shen, J., Chaudhry, S.A.: Efficient end-to-end authentication protocol for wearable health monitoring systems. Comput. Elect. Eng. **63**, 182–195 (2017). https://doi.org/10.1016/j.compeleceng.2017.03.016, https://www.sciencedirect.com/science/article/pii/S0045790617305128

12. Kang, T., Woo, N., Ryu, J.: Enhanced lightweight medical sensor networks authentication scheme based on blockchain. IEEE Access **12**, 35612–35629 (2024). https://doi.org/10.1109/ACCESS.2024.3373879

13. Kocher, P., Jaffe, J., Jun, B.: Differential power analysis. In: Wiener, M. (ed.) Advances in Cryptology – CRYPTO' 99, pp. 388–397. Springer, Berlin Heidelberg, Berlin, Heidelberg (1999)

14. Lee, H.J., Kook, S., Kim, K., Ryu, J., Lee, Y., Won, D.: LAMT: Lightweight and anonymous authentication scheme for medical internet of things services. Sensors **25**(3), 821 (2025). https://doi.org/10.3390/s25030821

15. Li, J., Su, Z., Guo, D., Choo, K.K.R., Ji, Y.: PSL-MMAAKA: provably secure and lightweight mutual authentication and key agreement protocol for fully public channels in internet of medical things. IEEE Internet Things J. **8**(17), 13183–13195 (2021). https://doi.org/10.1109/JIOT.2021.3055827
16. Li, X., Peng, J., Obaidat, M.S., Wu, F., Khan, M.K., Chen, C.: A secure three-factor user authentication protocol with forward secrecy for wireless medical sensor network systems. IEEE Syst. J. **14**(1), 39–50 (2020). https://doi.org/10.1109/JSYST.2019.2899580
17. Li, X., Dai, H.N., Wang, Q., Imran, M., Li, D., Imran, M.A.: Securing internet of medical things with friendly-jamming schemes. Comput. Commun. **160**, 431–442 (2020)
18. Li, Y., Tian, Y.: A lightweight and secure three-factor authentication protocol with adaptive privacy-preserving property for wireless sensor networks. IEEE Syst. J. **16**(4), 6197–6208 (2022). https://doi.org/10.1109/JSYST.2022.3152561
19. Liao, Z., Pang, X., Zhang, J., Xiong, B., Wang, J.: Blockchain on security and forensics management in edge computing for IOT: a comprehensive survey. IEEE Trans. Netw. Serv. Manage. **19**(2), 1159–1175 (2022). https://doi.org/10.1109/TNSM.2021.3122147
20. Miao, J., Wang, Z., Wu, Z., Ning, X., Tiwari, P.: A blockchain-enabled privacy-preserving authentication management protocol for internet of medical things. Expert Syst. Appl. **237**(1), 121329 (2024). https://doi.org/10.1016/j.eswa.2023.121329
21. Shanmugam, B., Azam, S.: Risk assessment of heterogeneous IoMT devices: a review. Technologies **11**(1), p. 31 (2023). https://doi.org/10.3390/technologies11010031, https://www.mdpi.com/2227-7080/11/1/31
22. Wang, W., et al.: Blockchain and PUF-based lightweight authentication protocol for wireless medical sensor networks. IEEE Internet Things J. **9**(11), 8883–8891 (2022). https://doi.org/10.1109/JIOT.2021.3117762
23. Yu, S., Park, Y.: A robust authentication protocol for wireless medical sensor networks using blockchain and physically unclonable functions. IEEE Internet Things J. **9**(20), 20214–20228 (2022). https://doi.org/10.1109/JIOT.2022.3171791

A Re-authentication Scheme Based on Blockchain and Reinforcement Learning

Zixuan Chen[1], Chuncao Li[1], Pengjie Zeng[4], Lian Zhou[1], Yuanyuan Ai[1],
Jin Wang[1,2], and Xiaoliang Wang[1,2,3(✉)]

[1] School of Computer Science and Engineering, Hunan University of Science and
Technology, Xiangtan 411100, China
fengwxl@163.com
[2] Sanya Research Institute, Hunan University of Science and Technology,
Sanya 572024, China
[3] Hunan Key Laboratory for Service Computing and Novel Software Technology,
Xiangtan 411100, China
[4] Central South University, Changsha 410000, China

Abstract. In recent years, with the development of Internet of Things
(IoT) technology, Internet of Vehicles (IoV) has become a key trend
in the automotive industry. However, challenges remain, especially in
the authentication of new vehicles and roadside units (RSUs), including
data privacy, security, and interruptions caused by high vehicle speed
or RSU confirmation delays across blocks. To address this, we propose a method based on blockchain and reinforcement learning (RL).
Leveraging the decentralized, distributed, and tamper-proof nature of
blockchain, a nearby vehicle moving in the same direction as the disconnected one is selected as a relay mining node to complete the interrupted
authentication process. By modeling ledger grouping and scheduling with
a Markov decision process, we establish a feasible system model to solve
the disconnection issue. Simulation results demonstrate that the proposed solution effectively handles vehicle authentication interruptions,
significantly improves verification efficiency, and ensures privacy and
security throughout the process.

Keywords: Blockchain · Reinforcement Learning (RL) · Internet of
Vehicles · Re-authentication · Markov Decision Process

1 Introduction

THIS rapid development of internet of things (IoT) technology has promoted the
transformation from traditional vehicle AD hoc networking (VANET) to Vehicle
Networking (IoV) [1]. As technology continues to evolve, vehicles can be seen as
powerful sensory platforms, able to take information from the environment [2] (or
nearby vehicles [3]) and provide information to the road infrastructure, assisting

W. Liang et al. (Eds.): SecureComm 2025, LNICST 690, pp. 56–76, 2026.
https://doi.org/10.1007/978-3-032-23456-8_4

the entire network with some management services. And the next step in this evolution is just around the corner: the Internet of self-driving cars [4]. In a sense, the future self-driving car can be seen as an intelligent robot. To address the growing challenges in traffic classification and synthesis brought by increasingly diverse network services, the FS-GAN framework was proposed in [5]. This federated self-supervised learning system, based on multiple distributed Generative Adversarial Networks, enables automatic traffic analysis and synthetic data generation across heterogeneous datasets, thereby enhancing data protection and adaptive management in autonomous networked environments.

In traditional VANET [6], the implementation of these services and functions is based on the certification of vehicles and roadside units (RSU [7]). However, because IoV is a complex topological network, it has many uncertainties. Including time-varying traffic status, diversity of information services, heterogeneity of terminal equipment and access networks, etc., these uncertainties will complicate the certification process of vehicles and RSUs. In the current vehicle and RSU certification scenario, due to the high speed of the vehicle and the limited communication range of the RSU, when a vehicle that has been successfully certified in RSU_1 moves from the jurisdiction of RSU1 to the jurisdiction of another RSU_1, RSU_1 needs to The vehicle user re-authenticates, which increases the computational complexity and communication overhead [8], and during the authentication process, authentication may be interrupted due to the high speed of the vehicle or the confirmation delay of RSU across blocks, which will make the service efficiency of the IoV network and communication efficiency is greatly reduced. At the same time, due to the open communication nature of VANET, the messages broadcast by vehicles are vulnerable to security attacks [9], so the authentication information between vehicles and RSUs is easily intercepted, modified or deleted by malicious attackers, which will affect the security of the entire system. Therefore, how to be safe and Correctly transmitting vehicle and RSU authentication information is a critical issue [10].

One potential way to make distributed systems more secure is blockchain technology [11]. Blockchain mainly has the characteristics of decentralization, anonymity, consensus mechanism, etc., and is regarded as an untamperable, unforgeable and secure distributed ledger. It can be suitable for the environment in IoV where vehicles do not trust each other, and can ensure that vehicles and The privacy of RSU certification information simultaneously completes the certification of the vehicle and RSU [12].

In recent years, significant advances have been made in techniques related to deep learning (DL) [13–15] and reinforcement learning (RL) [16–18]. A markov decision process (MDP) [19–21] is described as a fully observable environment in RL, meaning that the observed state content completely determines the characteristics required for decision-making. Almost all RL problems can be formulated as MDPs. Therefore, in order to improve the authentication efficiency of IoV and the utilization of network resources, protect the privacy of vehicles and improve the security of IoV, taking into account the complexity of its topology and high security requirements, this paper proposes a block-based Chain technology combines with the MDP framework for a disconnected security solution during vehicle certification.

The main contributions of this paper are as follows:

1. This scheme uses the advantages of blockchain's immutable and forgerable distributed ledger, including asymmetric encryption authorization technology, proof of work (PoW) and proof of stake (PoS), etc., to resist some malicious attacks in IoV, such as Sybil Attack, in order to protect vehicle privacy and improve the security of IoV.
2. A relay mining vehicle selection scheme based on blockchain and Markov decision-making is proposed to establish a feasible system model to solve the authentication disconnection problem.
3. The simulation results show that this scheme can enable the disconnected vehicle to continue to complete the authentication process after the disconnection occurs, and can effectively reduce the time and communication overhead of RSU.

2   Related Work

Considering the deployment of roadside units (RSU) along urban expressways and the structure of blockchain, the system divides them into several blocks according to the location of moving vehicles. RSU and vehicles serve as block nodes and jointly complete the creation and maintenance of block ledgers. The mutual supervision obligations between nodes and ledgers are completed through dedicated channels between mobile vehicles (MV) and RSUs. As highlighted in [22], vehicles in the Internet of Vehicles (IoV) ecosystem rely on both intra- and inter-vehicle communications to support functionalities such as autonomous driving and real-time information exchange. However, these communication protocols often expose the system to various security vulnerabilities, including unauthorized access and data tampering. Especially during vehicle-to-infrastructure interactions—such as RSU-based service authentication—malicious intrusions or protocol weaknesses can disrupt normal communication and compromise authentication reliability. Therefore, intrusion detection mechanisms and secure communication frameworks are essential to ensuring the authenticity, integrity, and availability of services within dynamic vehicular networks. In the research of Sandip Roy et al. [23], a two-wing game theory model of V2I and V2V communication was proposed, and a new routing algorithm was proposed based on this model. This article uses a reinforcement learning algorithm based on game theory to enable RSU units and vehicles to make rapid decision-making responses to the dynamic Internet of Vehicles environment. This approach works well to maximize the contribution of each telematics component. Similarly, in the view of Zhou et al. [24], the security of some security authentication schemes can be verified using a hybrid game theory model. However, in IoV application scenarios, high-speed vehicles may encounter authentication disconnections, which is a serious challenge to the security of the re-authentication process. In Zhou et al.'s scheme, there seems to be no discussion and certification of this authentication disconnection method. Huma Ghafoor et al. [25] well considered the discrete characteristics of routing links, proposed an auxiliary hybrid routing scheme based on Bayesian model, and discussed the selection of relay nodes after authentication disconnection. In their scheme, the node with the shortest message delivery time will be selected as the relay node from all neighboring nodes. However, sometimes the relay node fails to complete the task. In addition, when spectrum sensing technology is used to solve the network disconnection problem, more overhead may increase the burden on the network, while using open transmission media to transmit vehicle and RSU authentication information will bring some security issues [26].

In order to solve these security problems, some scholars, such as S. Huang et al. [27], proposed a CTIS framework among unmanned aerial vehicles (UAVs), MV and Internet of Things devices to evaluate trust and select low-cost and high-trust participants to improve data quality. The simulation results of this framework show that its performance is good. However, its implementation requires the use of drones to collect baseline data, and then validate the data reported by the MV to build global trust. Therefore, this scheme is difficult to achieve in the actual scenario, because in the real environment, it is unrealistic to use drones to collect data on so many moving vehicles. In addition, other scholars have turned to the concept of blockchain, arguing that blockchain should be a good way to solve various problems in IoV. Parmar et al. proposed a VANET privacy protection authentication scheme based on blockchain technology, which enables vehicles and trusted authorities (TA) to authenticate vehicles while protecting privacy [28]. However, introducing TA in authentication will increase communication overhead during the authentication process. Therefore, Xu, Zisang et al. [29] developed a blockchain-based authentication and key agreement protocol for the multi-TA network model, transferring the computing load of TA to RSU to improve authentication efficiency. In addition, various TAs use blockchain technology to manage the ledger that stores vehicle information, making it easy for vehicles to achieve cross-TA authentication. Taher M. Ghazal et al. [30] believe that blockchain-based encryption and hashing methods can enhance security during the authentication process. Building on this idea, recent studies have proposed a blockchain-based encryption framework tailored for electronic health monitoring systems, which addresses existing vulnerabilities—such as malicious insiders tampering with or leaking sensitive records—by leveraging computational intelligence techniques to reinforce data confidentiality and integrity. Although this solution reduces some duplication of calculations in the blockchain, it uses two blockchain [31] networks and uses the law enforcement agency (LEA) and the regional certificate authority (RCA) as peer nodes in the blockchain network. And in the existing scenario, when an authenticated vehicle user moves from one roadside unit (RSU) to another RSU area, the other RSU needs to re-authenticate the vehicle user. This solution will undoubtedly increase the computational complexity and communication overhead during the authentication process. To overcome the above challenges, Maria, Azees et al. [32] developed an efficient anonymous authentication and integrity maintenance scheme based on blockchain. This method combines blockchain and VANET, allowing certification to be completed without the involvement of a reliable third party in the verification process of vehicles and RSUs. In addition, the blockchain network also protects the confidentiality of car users' personal information and the integrity of the information. Erukala Suresh Babu et al. [33] proposed a fully distributed authentication framework for IoT devices that leverages blockchain to overcome the limitations of traditional public key infrastructures (PKI), such as the single point of failure and key escrow problems. By employing identity-based cryptography (IBC) over a blockchain network—particularly through the use of Hyperledger Fabric as a distributed private key generator—the scheme achieves secure, lightweight, and scalable authentication suitable for resource-constrained IoT environments. To enhance the authentication and security of routing information exchange in the Internet infrastructure, a blockchain-based decentralized route registration framework has been proposed [34]. This approach, named DRRS-BC, leverages a global transaction ledger formed by address prefixes and autonomous system numbers among different domains. By eliminating the dependence on centralized authentication mechanisms, the framework effectively addresses identity and behavior authentication, and offers strong resistance to prefix and subprefix hijacking attacks—providing a promising solution compared to traditional PKI-based methods. Sandip Roy et al. [23] proposed a lightweight blockchain-based access control protocol (BACHP-IoV) with handover authentication to enhance secure and efficient communication in IoV under high-mobility conditions. Similarly, Yumei Li al. [35] proposed an efficient identity-based linearly homomorphic signature scheme for wireless sensor networks, which ensures data integrity and authenticity while reducing computation overhead. Pranav Gangwani et al. [36] emphasized that trust evaluation frameworks are critical in securing wireless sensor networks (WSNs) against malicious or faulty nodes. They conducted a comparative analysis of multiple trust management models, including LTMBE, BTRES, and LDTS, and found that different models offer trade-offs between energy efficiency and security strength. Their study provides a benchmark for future research in trust evaluation mechanisms within WSNs. Yuan Liu et al. [37] proposed a blockchain-enabled reputation system for social Internet of Vehicles (SIoV), which ensures rating privacy and enhances the robustness and effectiveness of vehicle trust evaluation. P. zhang et al. [38] proposed a new model named FHIRChain, which combines public and private key pairs to complete the authentication process. The scheme inspires us to integrate blockchain with other technologies.

Hamit Mızraket al. [39] proposed a secure data sharing method by integrating JWT and blockchain technology within a layered cloud-based EHR syste. Building on this, Y. Zhang et al. [40] introduced a blockchain-based fair payment framework called BCPay to track each vehicle and verify whether its certificate is legitimate or illegal. Shalli Rani et al. [41] proposed a distributed and secure network framework for smart cities by integrating SDN and blockchain, where SDN detects potential attacks and blockchain ensures secure data transmission.

Similarly, Anichur Rahman et al. [42] proposed an architecture named DistB-SDCloud that integrates blockchain and SDN into a cloud computing platform for smart IIoT applications, aiming to enhance security, scalability, and resilience in industrial environments. while Kumar R, Kumar P [43] et al. proposed a privacy-protected vehicle-connected security framework (P2SF-IoV), although their scheme also integrates blockchain and reinforcement learning technologies, and their experimental results show that their proposed P2SF-IoV framework meets the expected requirements in both blockchain-based and non-blockchain-based solutions. However, the scheme of Kumar R, Kumar P and others, like other blockchain-based schemes, only applies the blockchain framework in the IoV environment, and lacks consideration for the environmental state and the role of nodes, and some functions may not be truly implemented. That is, as the main body of IoV, each vehicle unit has relatively independent decision-making performance. If the speed status of the vehicle is not taken into account, the success rate of certification will be greatly reduced. Similarly, Khabbaz et al. [44] proposed a greedy beam relay scheme (GBRS) without considering the vehicle speed state. The most notable feature of this approach is that a ledger is sent to every vehicle passing through the RSU. Subsequently, Khabbaz et al. proposed a probabilistic beam relay scheme that takes into account vehicle speed differences [45]. In their proposal, the RSU considered sending the ledger to faster vehicles, thereby reducing the likelihood that slower vehicles would be able to access the ledger. This scheme makes full use of the advantages of relay nodes to complete packet scheduling of the ledger. In addition, they also proposed a probabilistic packet relay strategy scheme in a double-hop vehicle fault-tolerant network [44], which corrected the account book allocation probability problem in [44,45] and further ensured the success rate. Judging from the simulation results, it can achieve the expected results, but security negligence in ledger distribution will cause certain threats.

Therefore, on the basis of analyzing the feasibility of another vehicle node as a classification carrier, issues such as the security of the authentication process, communication overhead, and high-speed vehicle authentication disconnection are considered. This paper proposes a solution based on blockchain technology, markov decision process (MDP) framework and ledger grouping scheduling model to authenticate disconnected vehicles, ensure the authenticity of data and messages and reduce the communication overhead of IoV. Figure 1 shows the flow of a distributed ledger.

3   Our Scheme

3.1   System Framework

The system framework of this paper consists of two main entities: vehicles and roadside units (RSU). Vehicles can be further subdivided into non-connected vehicles and connected vehicles. Non-connected vehicles are vehicles whose identity has not yet been authenticated by the network. A connected vehicle refers to a vehicle whose identity has been authenticated to enter the block network and a vehicle M that has been selected as a relay mining node.

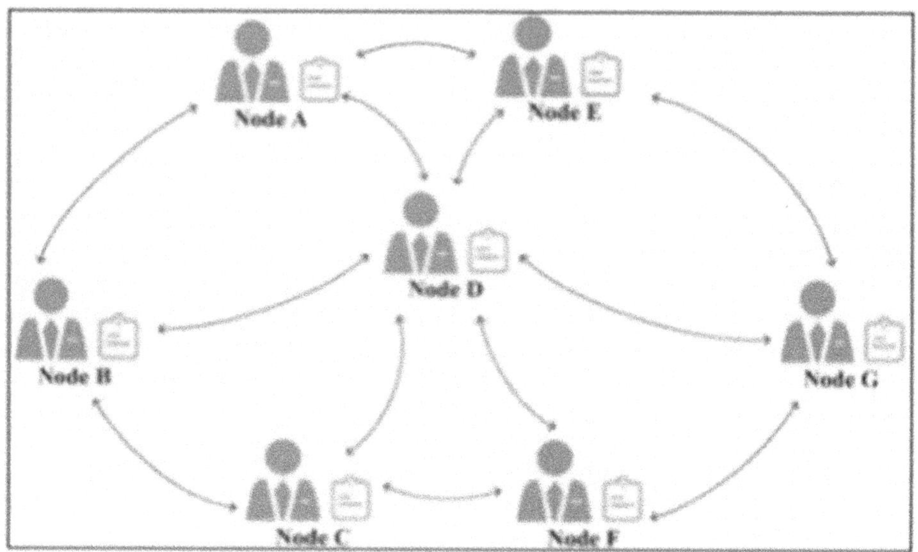

Fig. 1. The flow of distributed ledgers.

This article discusses certification of non-connected vehicles. Apply the blockchain structure to IoV and use other connected vehicles as relay mining nodes to complete the authentication of disconnected vehicles.

In order to facilitate the introduction of the idea and analysis process of this solution, we use vehicle A to represent unconnected vehicles, and vehicle B to represent vehicles that have been connected to the network. When vehicle A enters the jurisdiction of RSU_2, RSU_2 will receive vehicle A's certification application. However, because vehicle A is at the boundary governed by RSU_2 during the certification process, it may quickly pass through the jurisdiction of RSU_2 before the certification is successful, causing the vehicle certification process to be disconnected. At the same time, the manager RSU_2 of the next jurisdiction where vehicle A arrives often locates another block, and A's authentication log file cannot be transferred to the next block through negotiation voting. Our solution is to conduct a consensus election for all vehicles within the jurisdiction of RSU_2 using Proof of Work (PoW) or Proof of Stake (PoS). After the election, the vehicle M that obtains the accounting rights serves as the relay mining node of RSU_2. Because in the process of consensus election based on PoW or PoS mechanism, the higher the performance index of the vehicle's computing power and trust, the greater the probability of it obtaining the accounting right. Based on the consideration that the disconnected vehicle can be successfully reconnected, consensus election needs to select the vehicle with the best index as miner node M. In addition, RSU_2 packages the ledger information such as the authentication log file of vehicle A and sends it to vehicle M. When vehicle M approaches vehicle A, vehicle M sends a connection request to vehicle A through its on-board unit, assists vehicle A in completing the remaining authentication process, and ultimately helps vehicle A complete the entire authentication process.

When RSU_2 confirms that the authentication information of vehicle A is correct, RSU_2 will obtain the relevant information of vehicle M from the account information fed back by vehicle A, and give vehicle M a certain number of block rewards. The record of this reward will be written to the block ledger, and broadcast to other blocks for confirmation. If the record is unanimously approved, at the end of the certification, vehicle M will receive the latest ledger update and complete the upgrade of its reputation system. At the same time, in order to prevent malicious vehicles from forging their own certificates, other vehicles that provide false information or conflict with ledger data in the consensus election will be punished, and the vehicle that obtains accounting rights will write the public key of the malicious vehicle into the blockchain and broadcast to other nodes for confirmation, which effectively ensures the safety and legality of relay mining vehicles. If the RSU itself is malicious and the data it broadcasts is found to be false by other nodes, then the vehicle that has obtained the accounting rights will write the public key of the RSU into the block and broadcast it to other nodes for confirmation. Then the malicious RSU will lose its authentication rights, so that the security of the entire system can be effectively guaranteed. The entire process is shown in Fig. 2.

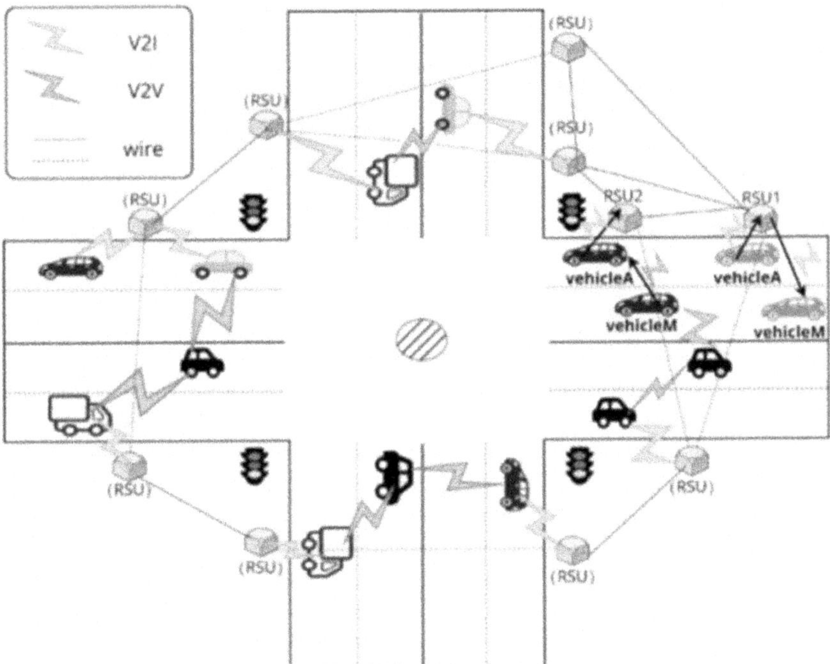

Fig. 2. System architecture and re-authentication process.

3.2 Detailed Re-authentication Process Based on Blockchain Technology

Based on the above system framework, a relay node selection method based on blockchain technology is introduced, and the Markov decision process is used to solve the disconnection problem in the vehicle certification process in detail.

1) SELECT RELAY VEHICLES BASED ON CONSENSUS MECHANISM: Aiming at the selection of relaying mining vehicles, we propose a new intelligent contract based on consensus mechanism as shown in Fig. 3.

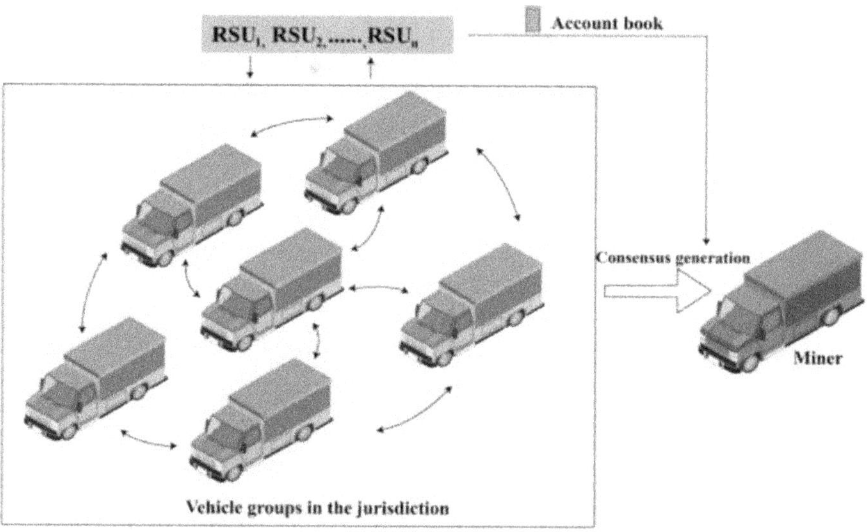

Fig. 3. An Internet of Vehicles infrastructure based on blockchain technology.

When there is a vehicle named A and it is interrupted for some reason, the RSU responsible for the A certification process will notify all vehicles within its jurisdiction to conduct a consensus election. This consensus election process utilizes PoW or PoS. After the election, the RSU selects the vehicle M that has obtained the accounting rights as the relay mining node, and then packages the corresponding account information including the vehicle A's certification log file and sends it to the vehicle M. Vehicle M will write its own information and the corresponding ledger information containing the certification log file of vehicle A into the block. At the same time, the block will be broadcast to all vehicles under the jurisdiction of the RSU. Only after it is unanimously approved by all vehicles, The block written by vehicle M can only take effect, otherwise the block is invalid and the vehicle will lose the qualification to compete as a relay mining node. Finally, if the block written by vehicle M is valid, it will carry the authentication log file of vehicle A, approach vehicle A, and help it complete the remaining re-authentication work.

2) IMPROVED FRAMEWORK AFTER COMBINING MARKOV DECISION: In the IoV scenario via fast tools, we need to assume minimal transaction latency. Based on the problem that public blockchain usually has the high transaction delay, we introduce Markov decision to improve the original scheme by combining it with blockchain technology. Markov decision-making process is a kind of decision-making method that simulates the stochastic strategies and rewards of agents in the environment. Its precondition is that its environmental state should have Markov property. That is, it conforms to the time homogeneity [46], and meets the following conditions:

$$\begin{aligned} P_r[X(t+h) = \gamma | X(t) = x(t)] \\ = P_\gamma[X(h) = \gamma | X(0) = x(0)], \forall t, h > 0 \end{aligned} \tag{1}$$

In the highway traffic scenario studied in this paper, the process of each vehicle entering the jurisdiction of a RSU obeys the Poisson process with parameter, and also meets the requirement of Markov homogeneity in terms of time.

Assume that each RSU and vehicle is an independent agent. The corresponding framework elements are as follows:

1. State: Including a number of states, such as initial state, authentication disconnection state of vehicle A, consensus election state of vehicle group B, generation stat of vehicle M, authentication success state of vehicle A.
2. Action: Including a number of actions, such as vehicle A submitting authentication information to RSU, authentication disconnection of vehicle A for some reason, RSU launching the election of vehicle M, vehicle M assisting vehicle A to complete authentication.
3. TStrategies: Including some strategies, such as RSU selecting vehicle M as a relay mining node based on the consensus results of all vehicles within its jurisdiction.
4. Reward: When vehicle M assists vehicle A in completing the certification, it can obtain the corresponding block reward.

After the system classifies the above framework elements, the set of states, actions, and rewards of the environment from the initial state S_0 to the current state S_t under the given strategy $\pi(x|a)$ is defined as a trajectory of MDP. Because the state transform and strategy selection of MDP are random, the simulated trajectory of MDP is random and unpredictable. From the trajectory of MDP.

$A_\tau = \{s_0, a_0, s_1, a_1, \gamma_1, \ldots, s_{\tau-1}, a_{\tau-1}, \gamma_{\tau-1}, s_\tau, \gamma_\tau\}$ is the trajectory of MDP, and the occurrence probability of the trajectory can be deduced as follows:

$$p(A_\tau) = p(s_0) \prod_{i=0}^{\tau-1} p(a_i|s_i) \, p(s_{i+1}|s_i, a_i) \tag{2}$$

In addition, in the MDP framework of IoV, its lifetime is limited. That is, there is a terminal state. When the terminal state is triggered, MDP framework completes an epoch and receives a reward. The finite set used to represent the reward is called discounted reward:

$$G = R_1 + \gamma R_2 + \gamma^2 R_3 + \cdots = \sum_{k=0}^{\infty} \gamma^k R_{k+1} \tag{3}$$

In this equation, $\gamma \in [0, 1]$ is a constant number, which is called the discount coefficient. As the corresponding reward of the trajectory $A = \{s_i, a_i, \gamma_i, s_{i+1}, a_{i+1}, \gamma_{i+1}, \dots\}$, G_i can be used to indicate the steps after the trajectory begins:

$$G_i = R_t + \gamma R_{i+1} + \gamma^2 R_{i+2} + \cdots = R_i + \gamma G_{i+1} \tag{4}$$

3) LEDGER PACKET SCHEDULING STRATEGY: Assuming RSU_1 can perceive the speed states of vehicles passing through its jurisdiction [47,48], RSU_1 will decide whether to send ledger information to the selected relaying mining vehicle M in its jurisdiction according to the packet queue length in its internal buffer and the speed states of all vehicles in its jurisdiction. At the same time, considering the vehicle speed state model, the RSU_1 will send the ledger containing the authentication log file of vehicle A to the optimal mining vehicle. The ledger packet scheduling strategy is as follows.

Here, we define a decision variable $x[t]$ ($x[t] \in \{0,1\}$) to indicate whether RSU_1 chooses to send a ledger to the vehicle at time t. If it decides to send a ledger, $x[t] = 1$; otherwise, $x[t] = 0$. Then, two sets of probabilities are defined: $\{b_{i,j}\}$, $\{d_{i,j}\}$, where $b_{i,j}, d_{i,j} \in \{0,1\}$. The meaning of these two sets of probabilities is as follows. When the conditions $q[t-1] = i$, $s[t] = j$ match, if a new ledger arrives at that time, $(a[t] = 1)$, the probability that RSU_1 will send the ledger to the vehicle is $b_{i,j}$, and the probability that no ledger will be sent is $1 - b_{i,j}$. And if no new ledger arrives at that time, $(a[t] = 0)$, the probability that RSU_1 will send the ledger to the vehicle at that time is $d_{i,j}$, and the probability that no ledger will be sent is $1 - d_{i,j}$.

Therefore, when the conditions $q[t-1] = i$, $s[t] = j$ match, for any $i \in [0, Q]$, $m \in [1, M+1]$, the conditional probability of scheduling decision variables $x[t]$ is expressed as follows:

$$\begin{cases} P\{x[t] = 1 | a[t] = 1, q[t-1] = i, s[t] = j\} = b_{i,j} \\ P\{x[t] = 0 | a[t] = 1, q[t-1] = i, s[t] = j\} = 1 - b_{i,j} \\ P\{x[t] = 1 | a[t] = 0, q[t-1] = i, s[t] = j\} = d_{i,j} \\ P\{x[t] = 0 | a[t] = 0, q[t-1] = i, s[t] = j\} = 1 - d_{i,j} \end{cases} \tag{5}$$

Obviously, $d_{0,j} = 0$, because when $i = 0$, there is no ledger in RSU_1's packet buffer. In addition, when the vehicle speed state is $s[t] = M + 1$ that indicates that no vehicle arrives at RSU_1 at this time, RSU_1 cannot send any ledger information to vehicles, thus $b_{i,M+1} = 0$, $f_{i,M+1} = 0$.

4) RELAYING MINING VEHICLE ELECTION PROCESS: In the environment of mutual distrust IoV, based on blockchain consensus mechanism, combined with Markov decision framework and speed state grouping decision-making scheduling, this section introduces how to select cooperative vehicle when relaying mining vehicle to complete the re-authentication.

The election process of relaying mining vehicle is mainly divided into four steps:

To simplify the process, we denote B as one vehicle of all valid vehicles in RSU jurisdiction, and M to represent relaying mining vehicle.

a) $B \rightarrow RSU$**:** S_(PoW $\|$ PoS $\|$ PK$_B$), in which S is the sending operation.

That is, B sends information about the consensus election in which it participated, along with its public key information, to the RSU.

b) $RSU \rightarrow B$**:** S_$\left(\mathrm{E_PK}_B(\mathrm{Time} \| \mathrm{Ab}_1)\right)$, in which E is an encryption operation.

That is, after receiving the information sent by B, RSU calculates the weight factor, encrypts the current timestamp and ledger of all vehicles in its jurisdiction with B's public key, and sends the weighted consensus election results to B.

c) $B \rightarrow RSU$**:** $D\_SK_B(Time \| Ab_1) \rightarrow S\_(E\_PK_{RSU}(Time_1 \| DS_{B,1} \| DS_{B,2} \| \cdots \| DS_{B,n-1} \| DS_{B,n}))$, in which D is a decryption operation.

In this process, all the vehicles participating in the consensus election decrypt the public ledger Ab1 using their private key SKb, and then evaluate the trustworthiness of all the vehicles involved in the ledger. After that, they select the best vehicle and sign the vehicle with their own digital signature (DS) as well as mark the new timestamp Time1. When all vehicles complete the consensus election, the results will be encrypted with the public key of RSU, and then respectively returned to RSU in accordance with the principle of consensus mechanism.

d) $RSU \rightarrow M$**:** $(D\_SK_{RSU}(Time_1\|DS_{B,1}\|DS_{B,2}\| \cdots \|DS_{B,n-1}\|DS_{B,n})) \rightarrow S\_ (E\_PK_M (Time_2\|Ab_1\|LF_A\|SK_f))$

The RSU received the consensus results of all vehicles and identified one vehicle named M, which received billing rights, as the relay mining vehicle. After that, the RSU will send information encrypted by the public key of M, including the latest timestamp $Time_2$, the original block ledger information, the authentication log file LFA of the disconnected vehicle A, and the license key SK_f, to vehicle M. It is important to note that the license key SK_f issued by the RSU to vehicle M has timeliness and specificity properties. That is, it can only authenticate a specific vehicle in a limited time, which effectively guarantees the privacy and security of this scheme. So far, the whole election process of relaying mining vehicles has been completed.

5) COLLABORATIVE AUTHENTICATION OF DISCONNECTED VEHICLES: After mining the selected vehicle, the selected vehicle M is motivated by the block reward to voluntarily fulfill its obligation to assist in the recertification of the disconnected vehicle A. The process is divided into two steps:

a) $M \rightarrow A$**:** in which the meaning of S and E is the same as the previous section.

$$D\_SK_M (Time_2\|Ab_1\|LF_A\|SK_f) \rightarrow S\_ (E\_PK_A (Time_3\|Ab_1\|SK_f)) \quad (6)$$

Vehicle M uses its own private key to decrypt the information from the RSU and confirms the re-authentication content. When vehicle M passes near vehicle

A, it sends vehicle A re-authentication packages encrypted by the public key of A, including the timestamp $Time_3$ and ledger information Ab_1.

b) $A \rightarrow M$:

$$D\_SK_A\,(Time_3\|Ab_1\|SK_f) \rightarrow S\_\,(E\_PK_M(Time_4\|DS_A)) \qquad (7)$$

When vehicle A receives the packets from vehicle M, it decrypts them with its private key. After confirming the legality of the ledger information and SK_f, it encrypts its personal signature and the current timestamp $Time_4$ with the public key of M, and then sends them to vehicle M. At this time, the authentication process of vehicle A has been preliminarily completed.

When vehicle M and vehicle A enter the next RSU jurisdiction, vehicle M sends the subsequent authentication data of vehicle A and the signature of vehicle A to the next RSU. The next RSU synchronizes the following block ledgers and issues corresponding block rewards to vehicle M to enhance its credibility as a relaying mining node, so as to stimulate its contribution to the disconnection authentication of other vehicles.

6) MINING VEHICLE FEEDBACK AUTHENTICATION RESULT PROCESS: To complete the re-authentication process of vehicle A, it is necessary to relay the feedback of the authentication result from relaying mining vehicle to RSU. The process is divided into three steps:

a) $M \rightarrow RSU$:

$$D\_SK_M\,(Time_4\|DS_A) \rightarrow S\_\,(E\_PK_{RSU}\,(Time_5\|CB\|DS_A)) \qquad (8)$$

Vehicle M first decrypts the packets returned by Vehicle A with its private key. When entering the next RSU jurisdiction area, M encrypts the authentication material CB of vehicle A and the digital signature of Vehicle A with the public key of the new RSU, and then sends them to the new RSU.

b) $RSU \rightarrow M$:

$$D\_SK_{RSU}\,(Time_5\|CB\|DS_A) \rightarrow S\_\,(E\_PK_M\,(Time_6\|PoS\|PoW)) \qquad (9)$$

RSU decrypts the information submitted by vehicle M with its private key and verifies its authenticity. After passing the authentication, RSU will synchronize the information of the following block ledgers, encrypt the current timestamp Time6 and the corresponding block rewards with the public key of M, and send them to M.

c) $M : D\_SK_M\,(Time_6 \parallel PoS \parallel PoW)$:

Vehicle M decrypts this task reward by using its private key. So far, the disconnected vehicle A has been successfully authenticated, the mining vehicle M has also been rewarded, and the re-authentication process has been completed.

4   Simulation

This simulation is based on Veins platform as well as the MATLAB simulation software. Veins is an open source framework for vehicle network simulation, which is based on two mature simulators: event-based network simulator called OMNET++, and road traffic simulator called SUMO. It extends these two simulators and provides a comprehensive model for the simulation of IoV. It supports network layer model of IEEE 802.11p and IEEE 1609.4 DSRC/WAVE, including multi-channel operation, access to QoS channels, noise and interference modules and so on. In Veins, the simulation of urban traffic can be real-time simulated on a single workstation or deployed on a computing cluster by MRIP distributed parallel manner. Table 1 shows our configuration information for the simulation.

Table 1. Configuration information in the simulation

Device	Parameters
CPU	Intel(R) Core(TM) i5-1240P at 1.7 GHz
RAM	4 GB
Operating system	Ubuntu (R) 16.04 (virtual machine)

4.1 Simulation Framework

As shown in Fig. 4, we use tic[11] as the RSU node and tic[0–10] as the vehicle nodes within its jurisdiction. In a certain simulation experiment, the tic[9] node was the relay mining vehicle M selected through the consensus mechanism of the vehicle group. Furthermore, in this work, we use $TicTocMsg_{15}$ to store the ledger information package.

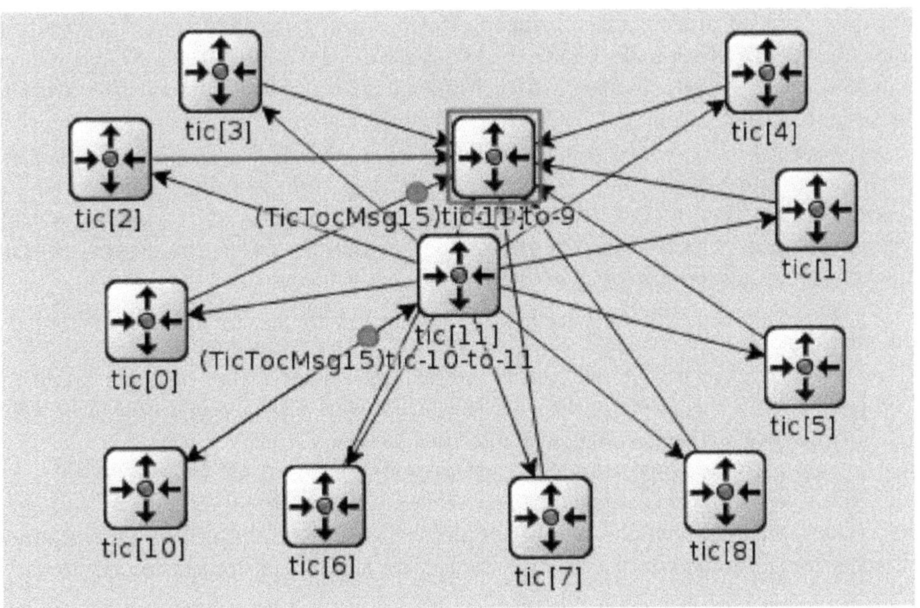

Fig. 4. Simulation framework.

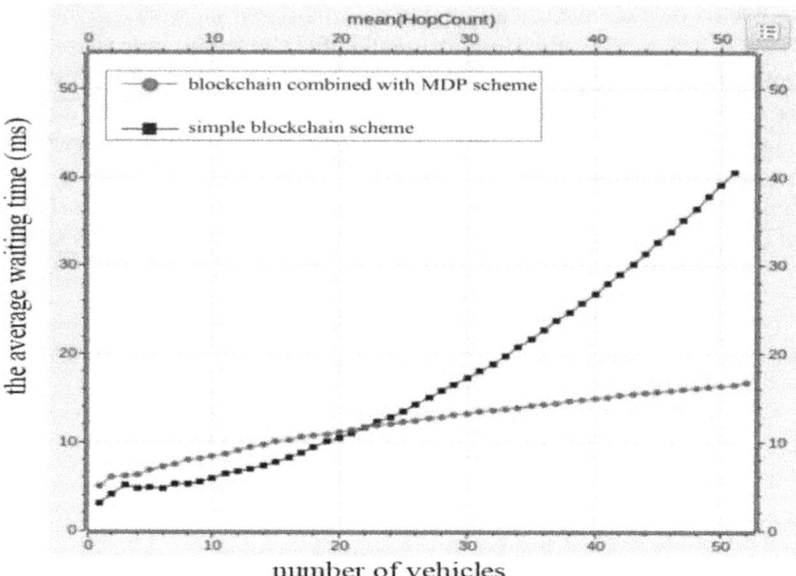

Fig. 5. Average waiting time for transaction processing.

4.2 Average Waiting Time

During the processing of every operational request and ledger, RSU follows the principle of "first come, first processed" [49], which will cause a certain end-to-end delay in the process of consensus election, and then lead to a long waiting time for each operation. In order to demonstrate the superiority of this scheme over the other simple blockchain technology scheme, we will use the average waiting time as the metric.

As shown in Fig. 5, the x-axis is the number of vehicles in the current RSU jurisdiction and the y-axis is the average waiting time in milliseconds (ms) for dealing with each vehicle in the consensus election process. The blue curve represents a simple blockchain scheme on IoV, while the red curve represents the blockchain combined with the MDP framework scheme.

It can be seen from Fig. 5 that with the increasing number of vehicles in the jurisdiction, the average waiting time of simple blockchain scheme shows a relatively rapid growth, with a trend of approaching the exponential level. Compared with the above curve, in the scheme of blockchain integrated with MDP framework, the average waiting time keeps a relatively low growth rate all the time. In addition, after the critical point of about 22 vehicles, compared with the simple blockchain scheme, our scheme has more significant advantages when the number of vehicles is large, which reflects the outstanding performance of our scheme in the control of time delay and the ledger scheduling decision.

4.3   Communication Overhead

Based on the above simulation framework, we simulated a scenario where a disconnected vehicle requires further re-certification. We assume that when a certification disconnect occurs, the 10 existing vehicles in the jurisdiction that are close to the disconnected vehicle will conduct a consensus election. In this consensus election process, the Markov decision framework and speed state group decision scheduling are combined. When the consensus election of vehicle group B is completed, RSU will select the vehicle that has obtained the accounting right as the relay mining vehicle M.

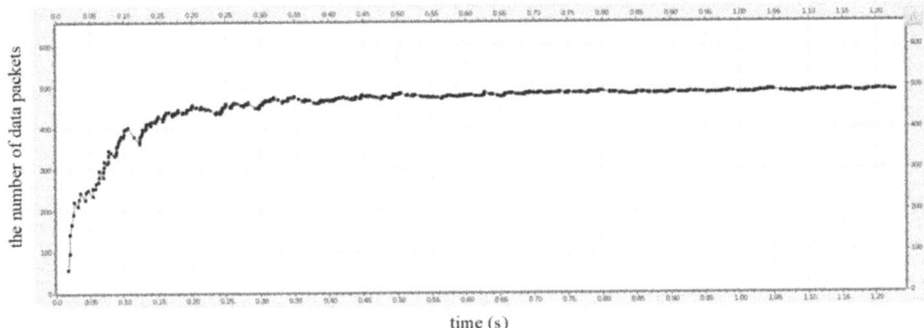

Fig. 6. Communication overhead of consensus election processing.

In Fig. 6, the X-axis represents the time required for the consensus election processing in seconds (s). The Y-axis represents the number of data packets in the consensus processing in units. It should be noted that in order to make the simulation results more clearer, here, we divide the ledgers into basic packet units and define a single packet size of 1 KB.

It can be clearly seen from the Fig. 6 that during the 1.24 s that is spent in the whole consensus election processing, except for a small amount of time spent in the system initialization, the growth rate of packets sharply increases at the beginning of the simulation, but gradually tends to be stable. The final number of packets keeps nearly 500. In terms of communication cost, it only needs about 500 KB of memory space to complete the election of relaying mining vehicle M. This trend shows that the scheme has obvious advantage in terms of communication overhead when the target block is large.

4.4   Comparative Experimental Analysis

To better highlight the advantages of this scheme in disconnection vehicle recerceration processing, we compared it with Greedy Packet Relay (GBRS) [35] and probabilistic Packet Relay (PBRS) [36] proposed by Kabazi et al., and the scheme proposed by Zhou's team [24].

Only when the mining vehicle M, also acting as the relaying node, is elected by consensus election and sends the ledger obtained from the source RSU to the disconnected vehicle A so as to assist A in completing the re-authentication, it can be rewarded by the system. We use the ledger arrival rate from RSU to vehicle A as the metric of completing the task.

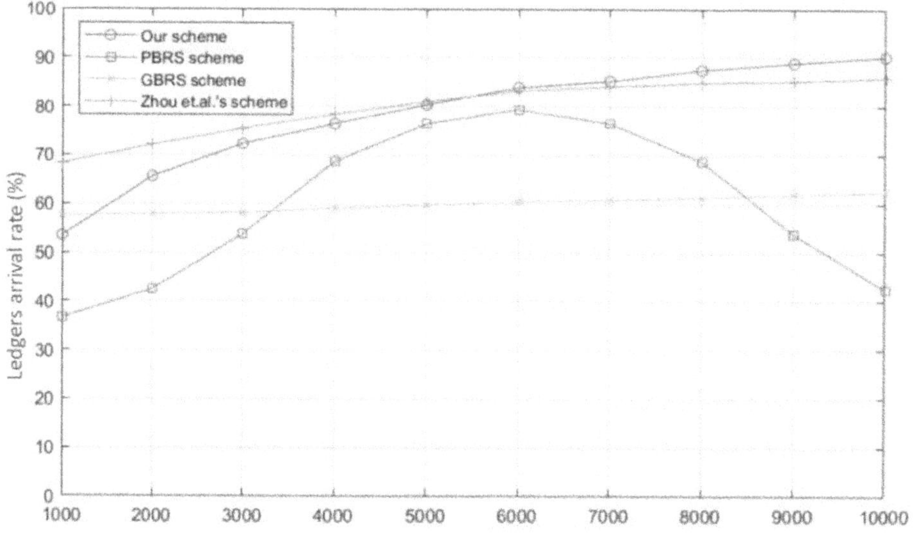

Fig. 7. The comparison of ledger arrival rate of three schemes.

As shown in Fig. 7, the X-axis represents the length of the current blockchain. According to the large scale and high density features of IoV, we set the magnitude of the blockchain length at 104. The Y-axis represents the probability of the arrival of the authentication ledger when the relaying mining vehicle M assists the disconnected vehicle A to complete reauthentication.

As seen from the Fig. 7, the arrival rate of ledgers under GBRS scheme is about 60%, and it increases slowly with the increase of blockchain length. The reason is that after an authentication disconnection, the GBRS scheme does not conduct vehicle qualification examination or select the suitable vehicle in its jurisdiction by consensus algorithm, but simply broadcasts an authentication ledger to each vehicle using a "greedy" algorithm. This scheme will not only lead to the rapid growth of communication costs, but also lack of traffic pressure considerations: When the length of blockchain is increasing, traffic congestion will inevitably occur, and this "greedy" approach obviously cannot improve the arrival rate of authentication ledgers. The more dangerous consequence is that illegal vehicles are likely to launch malicious attacks such as Sybil attacks on vehicles by illegally acquiring information from authentication ledgers without qualification examination.

In PBRS scheme, the arrival rate of authentication ledgers shows a peak trend, and reaches a peak of about 80% when the blockchain length is 6×10^4. The most fatal weakness of PBRS scheme is that RSUs tend to send authentication ledgers to faster vehicles. That is, fast vehicles are easier to be elected as relaying mining nodes because of the higher speed weighting factor, which reduces the selection probability of many vehicles with lower speed but higher trust. In fact, the faster the vehicle is, the more likely it is to be disconnected in the authentication process. In addition, this also directly leads to the RSU's difficulty in choosing high-speed vehicles when the length of blockchain is increasing and traffic congestion occurs, resulting in a significant decline in the arrival rate of authentication ledgers.

The scheme proposed by Zhou's team can well follow the change of the current blockchain's length, and with the increasing of the blockchain's length, the scheme can also maintain a high ledgers arrival rate. This is very beneficial to the PBRS and GBRS schemes mentioned above, which depends on the hybrid game can effectively screen out more successful vehicles, so as to maintain a high degree of completion. The final ledgers arrival rate of this scheme can exceed 80%.

In our scheme, we adopt Markov decision framework and ledger packet grouping scheduling strategy. Considering the current state factors of IoV, we give real-time policy based actions to the state transform, safeguard the rights and interests of relaying mining vehicle, ensure that their rewards are linked to the completion of re-authentication task, and also maintain the privacy and security of authentication information. Seen from these simulations, even encountering complex traffic status, our scheme can maintain a very high arrival rate of authentication ledger about 90%. These simulation results highlight the superiority of this scheme over other authentication schemes.

5   Conclusion

In the mutual distrust environment of IoV, the process of vehicle authentication between RSUs and vehicles may be interrupted because of the speed of vehicles or the feedback delay of cross-block RSU. In order to complete the authentication process and maintain the stability and privacy of IoV authentication functionality, this paper proposes a scheme based on blockchain and RL techniques particularly for the disconnection of vehicle authentication process. The scheme elects a trusted vehicle running in the same direction of disconnected vehicles as the relaying mining node via the consensus algorithm, designs the ledger packet group scheduling strategy based on MDP framework, and finally establishes a novel scheme to the re-authentication of disconnected vehicle. The simulation results show that this proposed scheme has high feasibility and superiority in comparison with other disconnected vehicles authentication schemes. In the future works, we will try to do further investigation of the scalability and security of the proposed scheme in large-scale IoV scenarios and make potential integration of emerging technologies such as edge computing and AI to improve the performance of the system.

References

1. Khezri, E., Hassanzadeh, H., Yahya, R.O., Mir, M.: Security challenges in internet of vehicles (IoV) for its: a survey. Tsinghua Sci. Technol. **30**(4), 1700–1723 (2025)
2. Jacques-Dumas, V., van Westen, R.M., Bouchet, F., Dijkstra, H.A.: Data-driven methods to estimate the committor function in conceptual ocean models. Nonlinear Process. Geophys. **30**(2), 195–216 (2023)
3. Zhuang, W., Ye, Q., Lyu, F., Cheng, N., Ren, J.: SDN/NFV-empowered future IoV with enhanced communication, computing, and caching. Proc. IEEE **108**(2), 274–291 (2019)
4. Badue, C., et al.: Self-driving cars: a survey. Expert Syst. Appl. **165**, 113816 (2021)
5. Xiao, Y., et al.: Distributed traffic synthesis and classification in edge networks: a federated self-supervised learning approach. IEEE Trans. Mob. Comput. **23**(2), 1815–1829 (2023)
6. Shrestha, R., Bajracharya, R., Shrestha, A.P., Nam, S.Y.: A new type of blockchain for secure message exchange in VANET. Digit. Commun. Netw. **6**(2), 177–186 (2020)
7. Yin, L., Luo, J., Qiu, C., Wang, C., Qiao, Y.: Joint task offloading and resources allocation for hybrid vehicle edge computing systems. IEEE Trans. Intell. Transp. Syst. **25**(8), 10355–10368 (2024)
8. Krekovic, D., Krivic, P., Žarko, I.P., Kušek, M., Le-Phuoc, D.: Reducing communication overhead in the IoT-edge-cloud continuum: a survey on protocols and data reduction strategies. Internet Things, 101553 (2025)
9. Aslan, Ö., Aktuğ, S.S., Ozkan-Okay, M., Yilmaz, A.A., Akin, E.: A comprehensive review of cyber security vulnerabilities, threats, attacks, and solutions. Electronics **12**(6), 1333 (2023)
10. Waqas, M., et al.: Authentication of vehicles and road side units in intelligent transportation system. Comput. Mater. Continua (1) (2020)
11. Habib, G., Sharma, S., Ibrahim, S., Ahmad, I., Qureshi, S., Ishfaq, M.: Blockchain technology: benefits, challenges, applications, and integration of blockchain technology with cloud computing. Future Internet **14**(11), 341 (2022)
12. Chen, W.W., Cao, L., Shao, C.H.: Blockchain based efficient anonymous authentication scheme for IoV. J. Comput. Appl. **40**(10), 2992–2999 (2020)
13. Dippel, O., Lisitsa, A., Peng, B.: Deep reinforcement learning for continuous control of material thickness. In: International Conference on Innovative Techniques and Applications of Artificial Intelligence, pp. 321–334. Springer (2023)
14. Janiesch, C., Zschech, P., Heinrich, K.: Machine learning and deep learning. Electron. Mark. **31**(3), 685–695 (2021)
15. Bengio, Y., Lecun, Y., Hinton, G.: Deep learning for AI. Commun. ACM **64**(7), 58–65 (2021)
16. Moerland, T.M., Broekens, J., Plaat, A., Jonker, C.M., et al.: Model-based reinforcement learning: a survey. Found. Trends® Mach. Learn. **16**(1), 1–118 (2023)
17. Matsuo, Y., et al.: Deep learning, reinforcement learning, and world models. Neural Netw. **152**, 267–275 (2022)
18. Wang, X.: Deep reinforcement learning: a survey. IEEE Trans. Neural Netw. Learn. Syst. **35**(4), 5064–5078 (2022)
19. Steimle, L.N., Kaufman, D.L., Denton, B.T.: Multi-model Markov decision processes. IISE Trans. **53**(10), 1124–1139 (2021)
20. Singh, R., Gupta, A., Shroff, N.B.: Learning in constrained Markov decision processes. IEEE Trans. Control Netw. Syst. **10**(1), 441–453 (2022)

21. Wagenmaker, A.J., Chen, Y., Simchowitz, M., Du, S., Jamieson, K.: Reward-free RL is no harder than reward-aware RL in linear Markov decision processes. In: International Conference on Machine Learning, pp. 22430–22456. PMLR (2022)
22. Taslimasa, H., Dadkhah, S., Neto, E.C.P., Xiong, P., Ray, S., Ghorbani, A.A.: Security issues in internet of vehicles (IoV): a comprehensive survey. Internet Things **22**, 100809 (2023)
23. Roy, S., Nandi, S., Maheshwari, R., Shetty, S., Das, A.K., Lorenz, P.: Blockchain-based efficient access control with handover policy in IoV-enabled intelligent transportation system. IEEE Trans. Veh. Technol. **73**(3), 3009–3024 (2023)
24. Zhou, Y., Long, X., Chen, L., Yang, Z.: Conditional privacy-preserving authentication and key agreement scheme for roaming services in VANETs. J. Inf. Secur. Appl. **47**, 295–301 (2019)
25. Ghafoor, H., Koo, I.: Infrastructure-aided hybrid routing in CR-VANETs using a Bayesian model. Wireless Netw. **25**, 1711–1729 (2019)
26. Wenhua, Z., Qamar, F., Abdali, T.-A.N., Hassan, R., Jafri, S.T.A., Nguyen, Q.N.: Blockchain technology: security issues, healthcare applications, challenges and future trends. Electronics **12**(3), 546 (2023)
27. Huang, S., Zeng, Z., Ota, K., Dong, M., Wang, T., Xiong, N.N.: An intelligent collaboration trust interconnections system for mobile information control in ubiquitous 5G networks. IEEE Trans. Netw. Sci. Eng. **8**(1), 347–365 (2021)
28. Parmar, K., Patil, S., Patel, D., Patel, V., Parikh, B., Padaria, P.: Privacy-preserving authentication scheme for VANETs using blockchain technology. Procedia Comput. Sci. **220**, 40–47 (2023)
29. Zisang, X., Liang, W., Li, K.-C., Jianbo, X., Jin, H.: A blockchain-based roadside unit-assisted authentication and key agreement protocol for internet of vehicles. J. Parallel Distrib. Comput. **149**, 29–39 (2021)
30. Ghazal, T.M., Hasan, M.K., Abdullah, S.N.H.S., Bakar, K.A.A., AlHamadi, H.: Private blockchain-based encryption framework using computational intelligence approach. Egypt. Inform. J. **23**(4), 69–75 (2022)
31. Huynh-The, T., et al.: Blockchain for the metaverse: a review. Futur. Gener. Comput. Syst. **143**, 401–419 (2023)
32. Maria, A., Rajasekaran, A.S., Al-Turjman, F., Altrjman, C., Mostarda, L.: BAIV: an efficient blockchain-based anonymous authentication and integrity preservation scheme for secure communication in vanets. Electronics **11**(3), 488 (2022)
33. Babu, E.S., Dadi, A.K., Singh, K.K., Nayak, S.R., Bhoi, A.K., Singh, A.: A distributed identity-based authentication scheme for internet of things devices using permissioned blockchain system. Expert. Syst. **39**(10), e12941 (2022)
34. Huimin, L., Tang, Yu., Sun, Y.: DRRS-BC: aecentralized routing registration system based on blockchain. IEEE/CAA J. Automatica Sinica **8**(12), 1868–1876 (2021)
35. Li, Y., Zhang, F., Liu, X.: Secure data delivery with identity-based linearly homomorphic network coding signature scheme in IoT. IEEE Trans. Serv. Comput. **15**(4), 2202–2212 (2020)
36. Gangwani, P., Perez-Pons, A., Upadhyay, H.: Evaluating trust management frameworks for wireless sensor networks. Sensors **24**(9), 2852 (2024)
37. Liu, Y., et al.: Vrepchain: a decentralized and privacy-preserving reputation system for social internet of vehicles based on blockchain. IEEE Trans. Veh. Technol. **71**(12), 13242–13253 (2022)
38. Zhang, P., White, J., Schmidt, D.C., Lenz, G., Rosenbloom, S.T.: Fhirchain: applying blockchain to securely and scalably share clinical data. Comput. Struct. Biotechnol. J. **16**, 267–278 (2018)

39. Mızrak, H., Aslan, S., Yıldırım, M.: BJWT-EHR: a novel JWT based blockchain system for electronic health records. NATURENGS **4**(2), 23–29 (2023)
40. Zhang, Y., Deng, R.H., Liu, X., Zheng, D.: Blockchain based efficient and robust fair payment for outsourcing services in cloud computing. Inf. Sci. **462**, 262–277 (2018)
41. Rani, S., Babbar, H., Srivastava, G., Gadekallu, T.R., Dhiman, G.: Security framework for internet-of-things-based software-defined networks using blockchain. IEEE Internet Things J. **10**(7), 6074–6081 (2022)
42. Rahman, A., Islam, M.J., Band, S.S., Muhammad, G., Hasan, K., Tiwari, P.: Towards a blockchain-SDN-based secure architecture for cloud computing in smart industrial IoT. Digital Commun. Netw. **9**(2), 411–421 (2023)
43. Kumar, R., Kumar, P., Tripathi, R., Gupta, G.P., Kumar, N.: P2SF-IoV: a privacy-preservation-based secured framework for internet of vehicles. IEEE Trans. Intell. Transp. Syst. **23**(11), 22571–22582 (2021)
44. Khabbaz, M.J., Fawaz, W.F., Assi, C.M.: Probabilistic bundle relaying schemes in two-hop vehicular delay tolerant networks. IEEE Commun. Lett. **15**(3), 281–283 (2011)
45. Khabbaz, M.J., Fawaz, W.F., Assi, C.M.: Modeling and delay analysis of intermittently connected roadside communication networks. IEEE Trans. Veh. Technol. **61**(6), 2698–2706 (2012)
46. Kabbilawsh, P., Sathish Kumar, D., Chithra, N.R.: Assessment of temporal homogeneity of long-term rainfall time-series datasets by applying classical homogeneity tests. Environ. Dev. Sustain. **26**(7), 16757–16801 (2024)
47. Patra, M., Thakur, R., Murthy, C.S.R.: Improving delay and energy efficiency of vehicular networks using mobile femto access points. IEEE Trans. Veh. Technol. **66**(2), 1496–1505 (2016)
48. Atallah, R., Khabbaz, M., Assi, C.: Multihop V2I communications: a feasibility study, modeling, and performance analysis. IEEE Trans. Veh. Technol. **66**(3), 2801–2810 (2016)
49. Hesselink, W.H., Buhr, P.A., Parsons, C.A.: First-come-first-served as a separate principle. ACM Trans. Parallel Comput. **11**(4), 1–20 (2024)

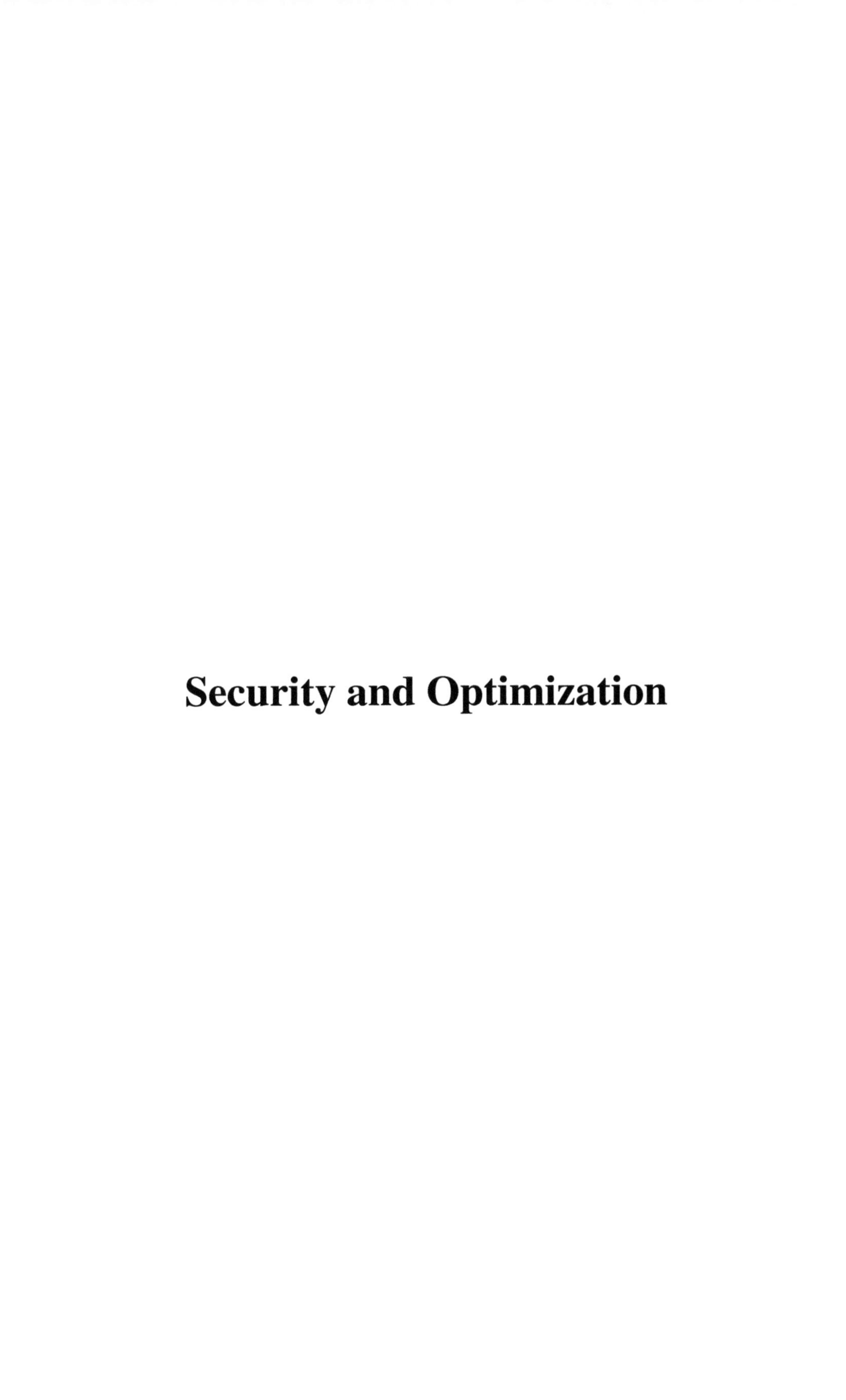

Security and Optimization

A Hybrid Adaptive Large Neighborhood Search for Secure and Efficient Single School Routing Problem

Zhangwei Cui[1], Yitao Chen[1], Qiongbing Zhang[2]([✉]), and Rui Pang[1]

[1] School of Computer Science and Engineering, Hunan University of Science and Technology, Xiangtan, China
`{zhangweicui,yitaochen,pr}@mail.hnust.edu.cn`
[2] School of Information Science and Technology, GuangDong University of Foreign Studies, Guangzhou, China
`mrtly2@whu.edu.cn`

Abstract. We address the Single School Routing Problem (SSRP) by proposing an optimized approach balancing efficiency and transportation safety. As an NP-hard variant of the Vehicle Routing Problem (VRP), SSRP aims to minimize total travel distance while satisfying vehicle capacity and time constraints. Existing approaches, such as adaptive large neighborhood search (ALNS), often generate irrational route sequences that may increase students' maximum riding time. To tackle this issue, a novel mixed integer programming (MIP) model is introduced, and a hybrid adaptive large neighborhood search (HALNS) algorithm is designed. The MIP model eliminates irrational routes passing through the school via constraint conditions. HALNS efficiently explores the solution space using five destruction operators and three repair operators, and adjusts the visiting order via shortest maximum riding time ant colony optimization (SMRTACO). Practical case calculations demonstrate that the new model improves solving speed and quality when using Gurobi. HALNS outperforms solvers like CPLEX and Gurobi, as well as ALNS, in terms of solution quality and runtime. Specifically, HALNS reduces the maximum riding time by up to 15.3%, ensuring safer and more direct routes to enhance student transportation safety. The method verifies its effectiveness in balancing efficiency and safety across small-, medium-, and large-scale datasets.

Keywords: Single school routing problem · adaptive large neighborhood search · route optimization · safe route design

1 Introduction

Assigned school buses are considered the best solution for meeting students' commuting needs and ensuring their safety in traveling between home and school [1,21]. Therefore, it is crucial to design optimal solutions and deliver high-quality

W. Liang et al. (Eds.): SecureComm 2025, LNICST 690, pp. 79–97, 2026.
https://doi.org/10.1007/978-3-032-23456-8_5

services. The school bus routing problem (SBRP) has been studied since 1969, when Newton and Thomas first proposed a method for generating school bus routes and schedules [17]. The SBRP is decomposed into five sub-problems, including bus stop selection and bus route generation. The SBRP is a variant of the VRP and includes bus route scheduling, school bell time adjustment and strategic transportation policies. The primary focus of this article is on the bus route generation aspects of the SBRP in a single-school context.

The SBRP consists of routing a fleet of school vehicles, where students must be picked up from their residences or predetermined bus stops and taken to the school. In the SBRP, as with the capacitated vehicle routing problem (CVRP), there are both vehicle capacity limits and travel time constraints [2]. There are two main types of approach to solving the SBRP, according to the number of schools served: the single-load strategy [3,15] and the mixed-load strategy [8,20]. The single-load strategy involves a school bus transporting students from only one school. The mixed-load strategy allows a school bus to transport students from multiple schools. The single-school SBRP is often considered a variant of either the CVRP or the vehicle routing problem with time windows (VRPTW) [5,10]. The multischool SBRP can be modeled via a continuous approximation approach [8] or as a pickup and delivery vehicle routing problem with time windows (PDPTW) [12,16]. The SBRP, as a variant of the VRP, is an NP-hard problem [23]. Heuristic algorithms are effective tools for finding approximate solutions of VRPs and SBRPs. Common metaheuristic algorithms adopted for the SBRP include the genetic algorithm (GA), tabu search (TS), and ant colony optimization (ACO) [9]. Recently, adaptive large neighborhood search (ALNS) has been recognized as very effective in solving the VRP and its variants, and this motivated our choice of ALNS for solving the SBRP. Wang et al. [25] (2020) implemented the ALNS algorithm to solve a variant of the VRP involving multiple compartments, trips, and staggered deliveries. Their findings revealed that ALNS could identify or approximate optimal solutions more rapidly than the exact MILP model provided by CPLEX, particularly for small- to medium-sized instances. In 2021, Özarık et al. [18] applied the ALNS algorithm to the vehicle routing and scheduling problem with time-dependent costs (VRSPTDC), demonstrating its effectiveness in generating high-quality solutions for large-scale problems. Voigt et al. [24] (2023) integrated ALNS into a population-based metaheuristic to solve the vehicle routing problem with availability profiles (VRPAPs). Their results showed that the ALNS significantly outperformed large neighborhood search (LNS) in terms of solution quality.

However, when the ALNS framework is applied to real-world road networks with the objective of minimizing the total distance traveled by school buses, it may produce routes with different visiting sequences but identical travel distances. Routes with unreasonable visiting sequences can potentially increase the maximum ride time for students. This may also lead to unrealistic scenarios in which the bus route unnecessarily passes by the school.

Therefore, this paper presents a hybrid adaptive large neighborhood search (HALNS) algorithm and a novel mixed-integer programming (MIP) model to address the challenges in the SBRP. The HALNS algorithm first employs the HALNS framework to search for solutions that minimize the total travel distance of school buses. Then, shortest maximum ride time ant colony optimization (SMRTACO) is integrated to adjust the bus visiting sequences and optimize the maximum ride time for students. The new model introduces a constraint on the integer linear programming (ILP) model described by Guo et al. (2022) [11] for solving the single school routing problem (SSRP), aiming to eliminate unreasonable routes that pass through the school. In practical applications, the HALNS algorithm delivers high-quality solutions more rapidly than do common solvers such as CPLEX and Gurobi, as well as the ALNS algorithm proposed by Chen et al. (2021) [4]. The new model, validated via the Gurobi solver, achieves better solutions more quickly than the integer linear programming (ILP) model described by Guo et al. (2022) [11] for solving the SSRP.

2   Model Formulation

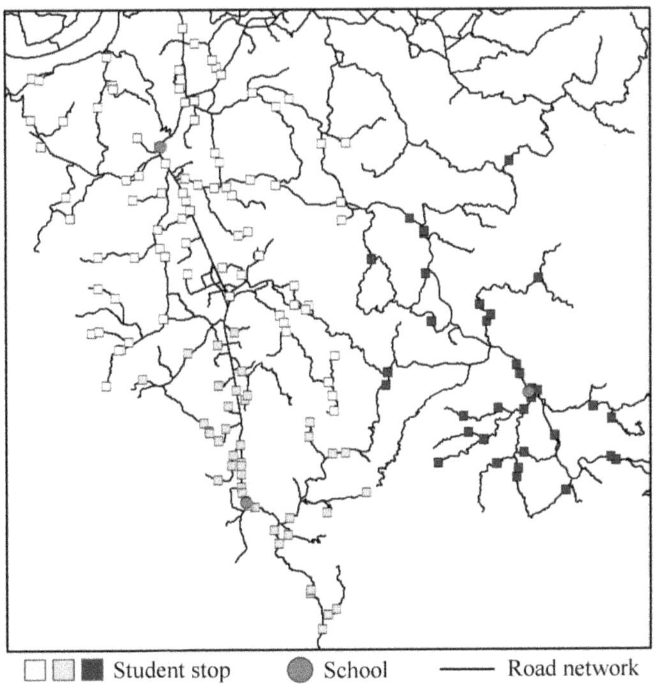

Fig. 1. Real-world scenario of township schools and student geographical distribution.

The SSRP can be described as follows: Let $G = (V, A)$ be a complete digraph. The vertex set $V = \{1, 2, 3 \ldots n\}$ represents n student stations, and 0 represents the school. The arc set $A = \{(i,j) \mid 0 \leq i, j \leq n\}$ represents potential driving paths between locations. The scenario is as follows: the school bus departs from the school location and needs to pick up students waiting at n designated stops and then return them to the school. The number of students waiting at each stop i is denoted as q_i (where $q_i > 0$ for $i = 1, 2, \ldots, n$), and the maximum capacity of each school bus is Q students (which means that $q_i < Q$). This study focuses on township schools within a real-world region. Figure 1 illustrates the actual distribution of the schools and student locations in the practical scenario. Instead of using the Euclidean distance, the road network distance is adopted to accurately define the distances between various stops. During the modeling process, the rationality of the actual vehicle travel paths is fully considered to formulate the school bus routing plans more efficiently. This plan effectively shortens the maximum riding time of students while optimizing the travel distance of the school buses.

The school bus path planning problem can be formulated as follows (Table 1):

Table 1. Notation

Symbol	Meaning
K	Number of school buses
Q	Maximum capacity of school buses
V	Set of all student stops and school stop
A	Set of all stop-to-stop paths
S	Set of all student stops
T	Maximum vehicle travel time
c_{ij}	Distance traveled by the vehicle along arc (i,j)
t_{ij}	Time for vehicles to travel along arc (i,j) and service at stop j
q_i	Number of students at stop i
x_{ijk}	Binary variable indicating whether vehicle k moves from stop i to stop j
u_{ik}	Integer variable indicating the order in which vehicle k visits stop i

$$\sum_{i=0}^{n} \sum_{j=0}^{n} c_{ij} \tag{1}$$

Formula 1 represents the sum of the path lengths consisting of all n stops in the set V.

$$\sum_{k=1}^{K} x_{ijk} \tag{2}$$

Formula 2 indicates whether vehicle k travels along the path from stop i to stop j. If it is 1, then vehicle k travels on path ij; if it is 0, then vehicle k does not travel on path ij.

$$MinZ = \sum_{i=0}^{n}\sum_{j=0}^{n}\sum_{k=1}^{K} c_{ij}x_{ijk} \tag{3}$$

Based on Formulas 1 and 2, the objective function can be expressed as follows:
s.t.

$$\sum_{k\in K}\sum_{j\in V} x_{ijk} = 1 \quad \forall i \in S \tag{4}$$

$$\sum_{i\in V} x_{ihk} - \sum_{j\in V} x_{hjk} = 0 \quad \forall h \in S, \forall k \in K \tag{5}$$

$$\sum_{j\in V} x_{0jk} = 1 \quad \forall k \in K \tag{6}$$

$$\sum_{i\in V} x_{i0k} = 1 \quad \forall k \in K \tag{7}$$

$$u_{ik} - u_{jk} + Nx_{ijk} \leq N - 1 \quad \forall i \in S, \forall j \in S, \forall k \in K \tag{8}$$

$$\sum_{i\in V}\sum_{j\in V} q_i x_{ijk} \leq Q \quad \forall k \in K \tag{9}$$

$$\sum_{i\in V}\sum_{j\in V} t_{ij} x_{ijk} \leq T \quad \forall k \in K \tag{10}$$

$$c_{ij} \neq c_{0j} + c_{i0}, \quad \forall i \in S, \forall j \in S, \forall k \in K, i \neq j, x_{ijk} = 1 \tag{11}$$

$$x_{ijk} = \begin{cases} 1, & Vehicle\ k\ travels along\ arc(i,j) \\ 0, & otherwise \end{cases} \tag{12}$$

Objective function (3) aims to minimize the total distance traveled by the vehicle. Constraint (4) requires that each student stop is served by the school bus exactly once. Constraint (5) is a flow balance constraint that ensures that if school bus k arrives at student stop i, then there is an incoming flow to i and an outgoing flow from i. Constraints (6) and (7) ensure that school bus k departs from the school and eventually returns. Constraint (8) is a subloop elimination constraint that ensures that school bus k follows a single connected route. Constraint (9) ensures that the number of students on school bus k does not exceed Q. Constraint (10) ensures that the running time of school bus k in traveling from the school and back does not exceed time T. Constraint (11) ensures that school bus k travels on one side of the school, meaning that it does not pass through the school to serve student stops. Constraint (12) ensures that the decision variables are binary.

In solving the SSRP, we explicitly account for the scenario depicted in Fig. 2. Figure 2(a) shows the distribution of five student stops and the school, where a shortest-distance travel route is generated on the basis of the Euclidean distances between student stops and from the stops to the school. This route starts at the school, visits all student stops, and finally returns to the school. In contrast, Fig. 2(b) illustrates how the same spatial distribution of these student stops and

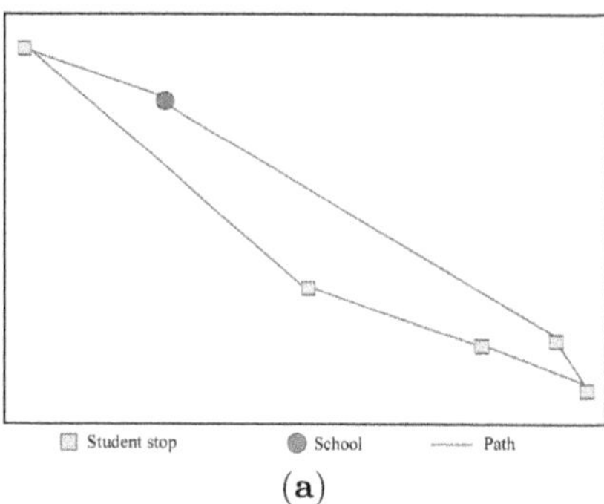

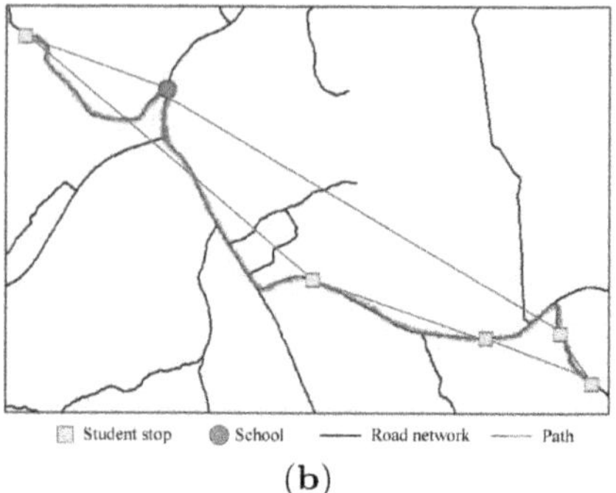

(a)   (b)

Fig. 2. The shortest Euclidean distance driving path is mapped onto the actual road network.

the school, when mapped onto an actual road network, results in an illogical scenario when seeking the shortest-distance route: the vehicle passes by the school before completing visits to all student stops. Building upon the mathematical model of the SSRP proposed by Guo et al. [11], we introduce constraint (11) to eliminate illogical routing patterns. Let c_{ij} denote the road network distance between student stops i and j, c_{0j} denote the distance from the depot (school) to student stop j, and c_{i0} denote the distance from student stop i to the depot. This constraint ensures that when a vehicle travels from student stop i to student stop j, the road network distance between these two stops cannot equal the sum of their respective distances to the school. This prevents the vehicle from passing through the school during interstop travel, thereby eliminating such illogical routing scenarios.

3   Solution Approach

In this section, we present the HALNS heuristic algorithm developed to solve the rural single school routing problem (SSRP) described in Sect. 2. The hybrid metaheuristic algorithm proposed in this paper combines five removal operators and three repair operators to consider the solution of the problem and obtain the solution set with the shortest travel distance. In addition, we propose an improved ant colony optimization (ACO) that takes the solution of the ALNS algorithm as an input to optimize the maximum ride time of the students by rearranging the order in which the student stops are visited while keeping the driving distance constant. We propose a hybrid ALNS algorithm by combining the improved ACO algorithm with ALNS to obtain the optimal solution with the shortest travel distance and the shortest maximum student ride time.

The general framework for solving our HALNS for the SSRP is shown in Algorithm 1. The removal and insertion operators used are described in Sects. 3.2 and 3.3, respectively.

Algorithm 1 is the HALNS algorithm for solving the SSRP, which relies on the set of destruction operators $\sigma_d(|\sigma_d| = 5)$ and the set of repair operators

$\sigma_r(|\sigma_r| = 3)$. In the algorithm, the variables x^b, x, and x^t denote the optimal, current, and candidate solutions, respectively. The variables σ_d and σ_r are used to store the weights of the destruction and repair operators, respectively. The developed HALNS algorithm first generates the initial solution of the SSRP through a greedy algorithm (line 1). In each major iterative step of the algorithm (lines 2 to 25), the values of σ_d, σ_r are utilized to select the destruction and repair operators d and r, respectively. A new candidate solution x^t is computed on the basis of the chosen operation (line 6). Specifically, the repair operator receives the solution generated by the destruction operator and then generates a new solution via the repair operator. Next, the new candidate solution x^t is tested by applying the acceptance criterion (see Sect. 3.5) to the new candidate solution x^t; if this solution is selected, the current solution x is updated. The best solution x^b is compared to the selected solution x^t, and x^b is updated if x^t is improved (line 11). The weights of the operators are then updated (line 13), and the algorithm is terminated when the stopping criterion is reached (see Sect. 3.6) to obtain the optimal solution x^b.

Algorithm 1. The main HALNS method for the SSRP

1: Construct initial solution x using the greedy algorithm
2: $x^b = x; \sigma_d = (0.01, ..., 0.01); \sigma_r = (0.01, ..., 0.01);$
3: **repeat**
4:     select destroy operator $d \in \Omega_d$ using σ_d;
5:     select repair operator $r \in \Omega_r$ using σ_r;
6:     $x^t = r(d(x))$;
7:     **if** accept(x^t, x) **then**
8:         $x = x^t$
9:     **end if**
10:    **if** $c(x^t) < c(x^b)$ **then**
11:       $x^b = x^t$
12:    **end if**
13:    update σ_d, σ_r
14: **until** stopping criterion is met;
15: **for** u in x^b **do**
16:    Sort the distances from node s to the school along path u in descending order to obtain u^s.
17:    **for** u in x^s **do**
18:       Obtain u^m by moving the student node s in path u to the first position.
19:       **if** ACO$(u^m) \leq$ Cost of path $c(u)$ **then**
20:          $u = u^m$
21:       **end if**
22:    **end for**
23:    $x^b(u) \leftarrow u$
24: **end for**
25: **return** solution x^b

Finally, each path in the set of optimal solutions x^b generated previously is traversed to obtain path u (line 15). The student stops on path u are sorted in descending order on the basis of their distances from the school to form the set of stops u^s (line 16). For this set u^s, each corresponding stop on path u is sequentially relocated to the first stop on path u that exits the school, while its position remains fixed (lines 17–18). The path is optimized via the classical ACO to obtain the shortest travel distance, resulting in path u^m. If $c(u^m)$ is less than or equal to $c(u)$, then path u is replaced with u^m (lines 19–21); otherwise, it remains unchanged (lines 23). After the traversal, the optimal solution x^b is returned (line 25). The components of the algorithm are described in detail below.

3.1 Generating an Initial Solution

This study focuses on township schools in a real-world region. Figure 1 shows the actual distribution of these schools and student locations in the practical scenario. During each iteration of the main algorithm, a student stop is selected and inserted into an existing (partial) route. The route is expanded by iteratively inserting additional student stops, with each insertion prioritizing the unserved stop with the lowest insertion cost. This expansion process continues until no further stops can be inserted. Upon reaching this saturation threshold, a new route is initialized, and the procedure iterates until all student stops are systematically assigned.

3.2 Destroy Operators

We employ the destroy operators commonly used in the ALNS algorithm for solving routing problems [13,14], which have proven to be highly effective. Specifically, we employ the following five operators, where the number of student stops to be removed for each operator, denoted as n_d, is randomly chosen from the interval [2, 7].

1. Random removal: This operator randomly selects n_d student stops from the solution set and then removes these student stops from the corresponding paths.
2. Related removal: This operator, known as Shaw's removal method, randomly selects a student stop i as the seed stop. In contrast to the classical Shaw operator, we design a weighting function for the SSRP problem by considering two parameters, distance and demand, obtaining the function $R(i,j) = w_1 * x + w_2 * y$. Here, $x = \frac{c_{ij}}{(c_{max} - c_{min})}, y = \frac{q_j}{(q_{max} - q_{min})}$. The weights are defined as $w_1 = 0.6$ and $w_2 = 0.4$. This function identifies n_{d-1} student stops j with attributes similar to those of the seed stop i. The function considers the distance and demand parameters. Subsequently, the n_d student stops are removed from their respective routes [19].
3. Worst removal: The student stops are initially sorted in descending order of removal cost, defined as the difference between the cost of the current route

and the cost after removing the stop. The n_d student stops with the highest removal costs on the current route are subsequently removed.

4. Random related removal: A random perturbation is incorporated into the related removal weighting function to assess the similarity between the seed stop and other student stops, which is defined by the weighting function $R(i,j) = w_1 * x + w_2 * y + w_3 * z$. Here, $x = \frac{c_{ij}}{(c_{max}-c_{min})}$, $y = \frac{q_j}{(q_{max}-q_{min})}$, and $z \in [0,1]$, with weights $w_1 = 0.4, w_2 = 0.3$, and $w_3 = 0.3$. This function considers distance and demand parameters and incorporates a stochastic component. Subsequently, n_d student stops are removed from their respective routes.

5. Random worst removal: This operator is similar to the worst removal operator, as student stops are initially sorted in descending order of removal cost. The removal cost of a specific student stop is defined as the difference between the cost of its current route and the cost after its removal. After the top three student stops with the highest removal costs are identified, one is randomly selected and removed. This process is repeated until n_d student stops have been eliminated.

3.3   Repair Operators

This paper employs three repair operators to reinsert the removed n_d student stops into the solution. The specific details of the insertion operators are provided below.

1. Best overall distance position insertion: This operator inserts the selected node into a feasible route position, minimizing the sum of the travel distances.
2. K-regret insertion: The regret insertion operator determines the insertion position of each stop on the basis of its regret value. The algorithm uses two operators: 2-regret insertion and 3-regret insertion. Specifically, 2-regret insertion is defined as the regret value representing the cost difference between a stop's best and second-best insertion positions, and 3-regret insertion represents the regret value based on the cost differences between a stop's best, second-best, and third-best insertion positions.
3. Random available position insertion: This operator inserts the selected node in a random available and feasible position within a route chosen randomly. The aim of this operator is to diversify the search.

3.4   Roulette Wheel Selection

The weights σ are initialized to 0.01 before the main algorithmic iterations of HALNS begin. This strategy assigns a weight σ to each operator and adjusts these weights as the search progresses. Let $c(x)$ represent the cost of solving x, $iter$ signify the current iteration index, and $iter_{max}$ indicate the total number of iterations. In each iteration, the weights are updated as follows: $c(x)$ represents the cost of solving x, $iter$ signifies the current iteration index, and $iter_{max}$ indicates the total number of iterations.

Let x^t be the candidate solution, x^b be the optimal solution, and x be the current solution. The process of updating the σ value of each operator in each iteration is as follows: when $c(x^t) < c(x)$, $\sigma = \sigma + \frac{c(x)-c(x^t)}{c(x)} \times \frac{iter}{iter_{max}}$; when $c(x^t) < c(x^b)$, $\sigma = \sigma + \frac{c(x^b)-c(x^t)}{c(x^b)} \times \frac{iter}{iter_{max}}$; and otherwise, $\sigma = \sigma - \sigma \times \frac{iter}{iter_{max}}$. The operator is selected on the basis of its weight and the roulette wheel mechanism.

3.5   Acceptance Criterion

The function $\text{accept}(x^t, x)$ is defined as follows: if the cost $c(x^t)$ of the candidate solution x^t is less than the cost $c(x)$ of the current solution x, then the current solution x is updated to the candidate solution, i.e., $x = x^t$. Otherwise, the acceptance rule of the simulated annealing algorithm is applied (see, e.g., Demir et al., 2012; Ropke ... Pisinger, 2006) [6,22]. We compute $u = exp((c(x) - c(x^t))/T)$, where T represents the temperature, and select a random value v uniformly from the interval $[0, 1]$. If $v < u$, then we update x to x^t and adjust the temperature T accordingly. If $T > 50$, then we set T to 0.999 * T; otherwise, we reset T to 50. The initial value of the parameter T is set to $c(x)(-0.35)/ln(0.5)$, where x represents the initial solution.

3.6   Stopping Criterion

The HALNS algorithm for obtaining the solution with the shortest total travel distance terminates when a predetermined maximum number of iterations, $iter_{max}$, is reached or the maximum number of consecutive iterations without improvement, $iter_{max}$, is reached. For small instances with fewer than 50 student stops, $iter_{max}$ is set to 30,000 iterations. For medium-sized instances with more than 50 and fewer than 100 student stops, $iter_{max}$ is set to 50,000 iterations. For large-scale instances with more than 100 student stops, $iter_{max}$ is set to 100,000 iterations. The parameter $iter_{max}$ is defined as 0.2 times the value of $iter_{max}$. When the maximum number of iterations, $iter_{max}$, or number of consecutive iterations with no improvement, $iter_{max}$, is reached, the optimal solution with the shortest total distance traveled is obtained.

3.7   Shortest Maximum Ride Time Ant Colony Optimization

The hybrid algorithm presented in this paper uses the shortest maximum ride time ant colony optimization (SMRTACO), which takes the solution generated by the ALNS algorithm as the initial solution. First, the student stops on each route of the initial solution are sorted in descending order on the basis of their distance from the school to obtain a new set of student stops. Then, the algorithm iterates through the student stops in this set and moves each corresponding student stop on the route to the first student stop that the vehicle reaches when leaving the school. The ACO [7] is used to optimize the new route with the objective of minimizing the total travel distance. Finally, if the new travel route is at least as short as the original route, the new route replaces the original route.

As demonstrated in the practical scenario in Fig. 2, modifying the service order of the student stops effectively reduces the maximum ride time for students.

4   Computational Results

The developed HALNS method is coded in Python, and the experiments are conducted on a personal computer equipped with 8 gigabytes of RAM and an Intel(R) Core(TM) i5-8250U processor clocked at 1.60 GHz as the base frequency and 1.80 GHz as the turbo max frequency for the Windows 11 operating system. The mathematical model developed in this paper is optimally solved via the exact solvers CPLEX 12.10 and Gurobi 11.0. The experimental scenario is based on a real business case in a county in Hunan Province. The dataset, which includes five school instances, is categorized into two small instances (fewer than 50 student stops), two medium instances (50 to 100 student stops), and one large instance (more than 100 student stops). Refer to Table 2 for further details.

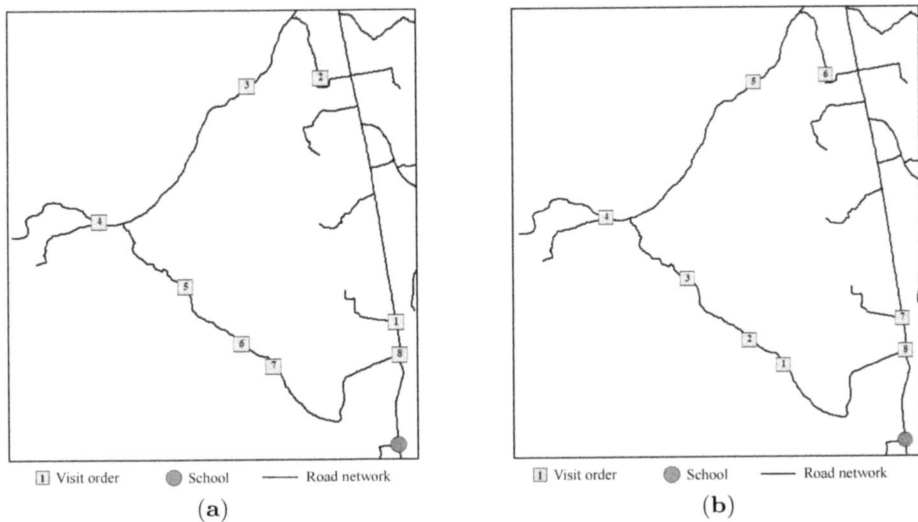

(a)   (b)

Fig. 3. Figure 3(a) shows the service order of a route generated by ALNS, and Fig. 3(b) shows the optimized result after applying the SMRTACO framework to refine the ALNS service order.

The experiment is set up so that the maximum load Q of the vehicle is 50 people, the speed v of the vehicle is 13 m/s, and the maximum service time T of the vehicle is 3600 s. The proposed new model is validated against the mathematical model proposed by Guo et al. [11] for solving the SSRP via the Gurobi solver on small- and medium-scale instances. The experiments are conducted with a time limit of 10,000 s, and the optimization objective is to minimize the total travel distance.

Table 2. Instance sets

Instances	Number of students	Number of student stops
G1	154	19
G2	249	42
G3	194	53
G4	323	77
G5	464	134

Table 3. Comparison of traditional and new model calculations

Instances	SSRP mode				New mode			
	B_S	B_{S1}	B_T	A_T	B_S	B_{S1}	B_T	A_T
G1	**30266.76**	3310.77	37.07	39.82	**30266.76**	**3249.61**	**10.11**	**12.13**
G2	**82179.11**	7643.45	2769.32	3011.1	**82179.11**	**7488.46**	**1875.33**	**1990.81**
G3	64287.77	6013.04	10000	10000	**62387.88**	**5553.55**	10000	10000
G4	178392.56	13824.70	10000	10000	**160179.45**	**13339.42**	10000	10000

Table 4. Comparison of total distance traveled results.

Instance	Algorithm	B_S	B_T	A_S	A_T
G1	Gurobi	**30266.76**	37.07	**30266.76**	39.82
	Cplex	31265.96	45.12	31265.96	56.41
	ALNS	**30266.76**	0.70	**30266.76**	26.71
	HALNS	**30266.76**	**0.32**	**30266.76**	**12.03**
G2	Gurobi	**82179.11**	2769.32	**82179.11**	3011.10
	Cplex	82664.70	3600	82664.70	3600
	ALNS	**82179.11**	8.69	82290.58	265.27
	HALNS	**82179.11**	**7.28**	**82179.11**	**183.91**
G3	Gurobi	64287.77	10000	64287.77	10000
	Cplex	71085.98	10000	71085.98	10000
	ALNS	**61358.04**	707.33	**62955.62**	449.24
	HALNS	**61358.04**	**87.22**	63810.11	**175.48**
G4	Gurobi	178392.56	10000	178392.56	10000
	Cplex	178840.76	10000	178840.76	10000
	ALNS	142300.54	209.90	148633.91	351.73
	HALNS	**140819.38**	629.80	**146461.38**	610.79
G5	Gurobi	–	–	–	–
	Cplex	–	–	–	–
	ALNS	232376.78	771.00	244532.57	780.88
	HALNS	**229540.78**	1044.21	**239702.69**	**728.39**

In Table 3, we report the results obtained by the model proposed by Guo et al. [11] for solving the SSRP and the results obtained by the new model on small- and medium-scale instances using the Gurobi solver. To evaluate the effectiveness of the current model in addressing this real-world scenario, we compare the two models on the basis of the following metrics: the B_S column represents the primary optimization objective of minimizing the total travel distance of the school buses, the B_{S1} column represents the secondary optimization objective of minimizing the maximum ride time of students, B_T indicates the shortest runtime required to obtain the optimal solution, and the A_T column shows the average runtime over 50 runs needed to achieve the optimal solution.

Table 5. Comparison of Maximum Ride Time Results.

Instance	Algorithm	B_S	B_{S1}	A_{S1}	T_{Cpu}
G1	Gurobi	**30266.76**	3310.77	3310.77	205.71
	Cplex	31265.96	3664.45	3664.45	405.60
	ALNS	**30266.76**	**3192.97**	3324.75	263.29
	HALNS	**30266.76**	**3192.97**	**3285.43**	**151.89**
G2	Gurobi	**82179.11**	7643.45	7643.45	3600
	Cplex	82664.70	8271.68	8271.68	3600
	ALNS	**82179.11**	7165.38	7925.45	592.16
	HALNS	**82179.11**	**6475.55**	**6628.90**	**321.99**
G3	Gurobi	64287.77	6013.04	6013.04	10000
	Cplex	71085.98	6823.96	6823.96	10000
	ALNS	**61358.04**	6011.02	6269.03	885.88
	HALNS	**61358.04**	**5486.52**	**5817.17**	**590.88**
G4	Gurobi	178392.56	15029.22	15029.22	10000
	Cplex	178840.76	13824.70	13824.70	10000
	ALNS	142300.54	12597.52	12820.36	1130.75
	HALNS	**140819.38**	**11895.03**	**11933.26**	1352.69
G5	Gurobi	–	–	–	–
	Cplex	–	–	–	–
	ALNS	232376.78	19654.93	20589.33	3601.43
	HALNS	**229540.78**	**17502.84**	**19331.65**	**1934.62**

The results reported in Table 3 indicate that using the Gurobi solver within a runtime limit of 1000 s, the shortest travel distances can be obtained for two small-scale instances, G1 and G2. For the maximum ride time of students, our proposed current model reduces the time by 18.5% and 2% compared to the traditional model. Additionally, the shortest runtime to obtain the optimal solution is reduced by 71.6% and 32.3%, and the average time to obtain the optimal solution is reduced by 69.7% and 33.9%. For the two medium-scale instances G3 and G4, both models failed to obtain optimal solutions within runtime limits. Compared to the traditional model, our proposed current model achieved a reduction of 3% and 10.2% in the total travel distance of school buses, while reducing the maximum student ride time by 7.6% and 3.5%.

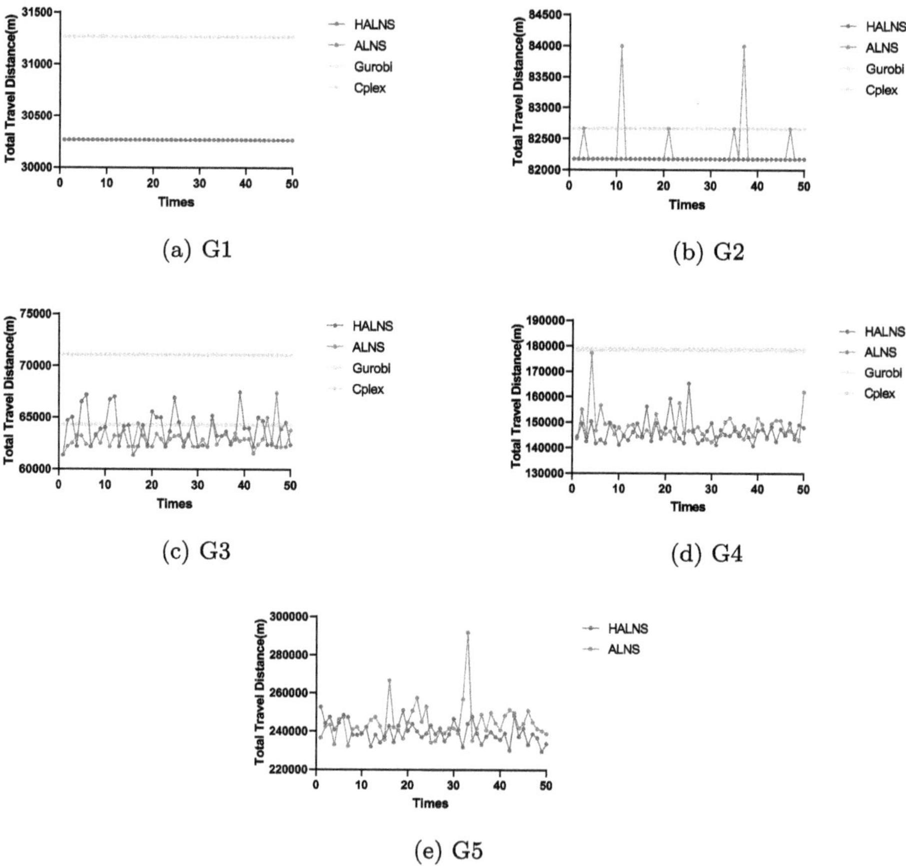

Fig. 4. Total travel distance results from 50 runs per instance (5 instances) for HALNS, ALNS, Gurobi, and CPLEX.

Table 4 reports the computational results of optimizing school bus routing distances for small-scale and medium-scale instances using the Gurobi and CPLEX solvers, the ALNS algorithm proposed by Chen et al. (2021) [4], and the HALNS algorithm. For the large-scale instance G5, Gurobi and CPLEX failed to obtain solutions within the specified time limit; thus, only results from ALNS and HALNS are shown. To evaluate the performance of HALNS in optimizing school bus route distances in this real-world scenario, we executed 50 runs for both solvers and algorithms. The B_S column denotes the shortest total travel distance obtained for school buses. The B_T column indicates the shortest computation time required to achieve the shortest total travel distance. The A_S column represents the average total travel distance. The A_T column shows the average computation time to obtain total travel distance solutions.

Table 4 demonstrates the performance of the HALNS algorithm in optimizing school bus routing distances. For small and medium-scale instances, HALNS, ALNS, and Gurobi outperformed CPLEX. In the two small-scale instances (G1 and G2), Gurobi, ALNS, and HALNS all achieved optimal solutions for the shortest travel distance. Regarding the shortest computation time required to obtain optimal solutions, HALNS was 36.75 s and 2762.04 s faster than Gurobi, and 54.3% and 16.2% faster than ALNS. In terms of average computation time, HALNS reduced runtime by 27.79 s and 2827.19 s compared to Gurobi, and by 55% and 30.7% compared to ALNS. For medium-scale instances (G3 and G4), both ALNS and HALNS performed better than Gurobi. In G3, HALNS and ALNS both achieved optimal shortest travel distances, while HALNS required 620.11 s less computation time than ALNS to reach the optimal solution. For G4, HALNS reduced the shortest travel distance by 1% compared to ALNS. For the large-scale instance G5, HALNS achieved a 12% shorter travel distance than ALNS.

Table 5 presents the computational results of small-, medium-, and large-scale benchmark instances obtained from 50 runs of the HALNS, ALNS, Gurobi, and CPLEX solvers. The B_S column indicates the shortest travel distance for school buses. The B_{S1} column represents the maximum student ride time. The A_{S1} column denotes the average maximum ride time. The T_{Cpu} column specifies the CPU computation time required to obtain the corresponding solutions. In small-scale instances, Gurobi, ALNS, and HALNS all achieve the shortest routing distance. Regarding the maximum ride time for students, HALNS reduces this metric by up to 15.3% compared to Gurobi and by up to 9.6% compared to ALNS. In terms of CPU runtime, HALNS significantly outperforms both Gurobi and Cplex solvers, with a maximum reduction of 45.6% compared to ALNS. For the medium-scale instance G3, while ALNS and HALNS obtain identical shortest total routing distances, HALNS reduces the maximum ride time and CPU time by 8.7% and 33.3%, respectively. For the large-scale instance G5, HALNS demonstrates superior performance to ALNS across all metrics. Figure 3 shows a comparison of the maximum travel time for students between HALNS and ALNS running 50 times in 5 instances.

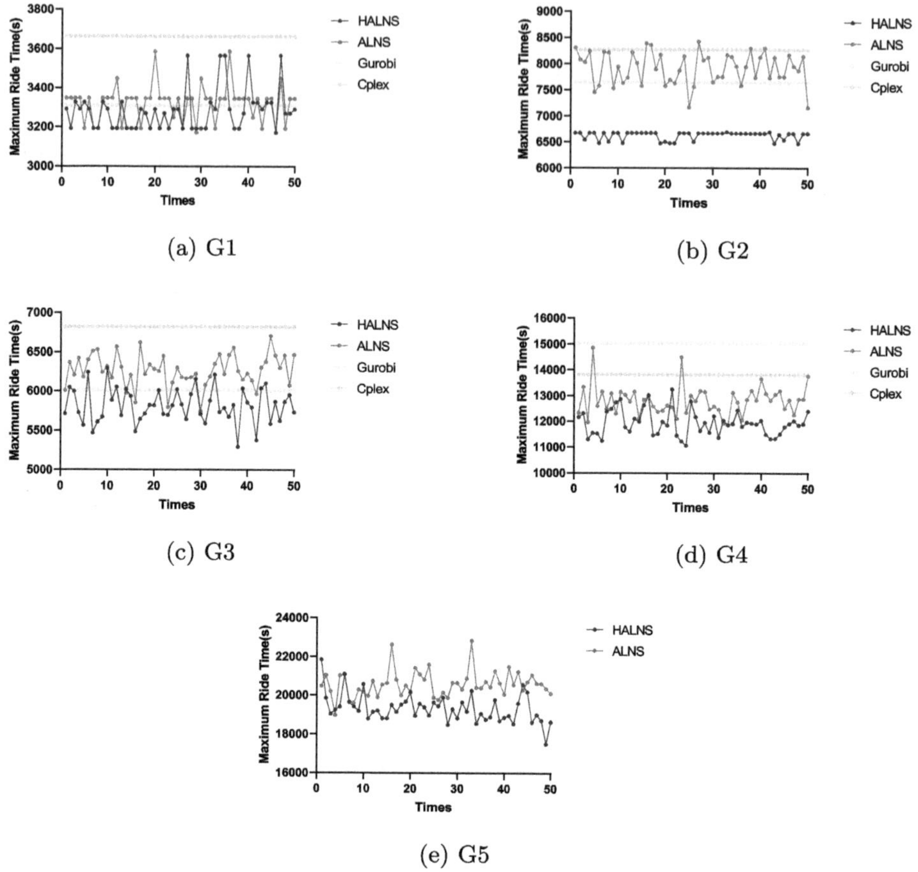

(a) G1

(b) G2

(c) G3

(d) G4

(e) G5

Fig. 5. Maximum ride time results from 50 runs per instance (5 instances) for HALNS, ALNS, Gurobi, and Cplex.

Figures 4 and 5 present the results of total travel distance and maximum student ride time obtained from 50 runs of the HALNS, ALNS, Gurobi, and CPLEX solvers. For small- and medium-scale instances, the solvers employed exact algorithms, yielding identical results across all runs. For the large-scale instance G5, the solvers failed to obtain solutions within the specified time limit; thus, only results from HALNS and ALNS are displayed.

Analysis of total travel distance (Fig. 4 and Table 4): In small-scale instances G1 and G2, HALNS and Gurobi achieved optimal total travel distances in every run, outperforming CPLEX and ALNS. For medium-scale instances G3 and G4, HALNS and ALNS demonstrated superior overall performance in total travel distance compared to Gurobi and CPLEX. In large-scale instance G5, HALNS achieved a lower average total travel distance than ALNS and consistently generated higher-quality suboptimal solutions.

Analysis of maximum student ride time (Fig. 5 and Table 5): HALNS outperformed CPLEX in all runs across all instances. For the smaller small-scale instance G1, HALNS, ALNS, and Gurobi exhibited comparable performance. In the larger small-scale instance G2, HALNS consistently achieved better results than ALNS and Gurobi. For medium-scale instances G3 and G4, HALNS produced superior results in most runs compared to ALNS and Gurobi. In large-scale instance G5, HALNS again demonstrated better performance than ALNS.

5   Conclusions

This paper addresses a highly challenging variant of the vehicle routing problem: the single school routing problem (SSRP). For real-world applications, we propose a novel mixed-integer linear programming (MILP) model that improves the solution quality and convergence speed by eliminating illogical scenarios in the solution set. Evaluations on small- and medium-scale benchmark instances demonstrate that, within a 10,000-s time limit, the Gurobi solver achieves optimal solutions more quickly than traditional models do for small-scale instances and generates higher-quality suboptimal solutions for medium-scale instances. Furthermore, the maximum ride time obtained by our model is better than those of conventional approaches.

To address the NP-hard nature of the SBRP, we develop a hybrid adaptive large neighborhood search (HALNS) heuristic. The algorithm is evaluated across small-, medium-, and large-scale real-world instances. The experimental results reveal that HALNS achieves higher-quality optimal solutions than do Gurobi, Cplex, and ALNS for small-scale instances. For medium-scale instances, it delivers higher-quality suboptimal solutions more rapidly than ALNS does for equivalent outputs. In large-scale instances, where Gurobi and Cplex fail to yield feasible solutions, HALNS consistently outperforms ALNS in generating superior suboptimal solutions. Additionally, we highlight HALNS's optimization performance regarding the maximum travel time: in small-scale instances, HALNS reduces the CPU time while obtaining shorter total routing distances and minimizing students' maximum travel time. In medium- and large-scale instances, it exhibits comprehensive superiority over ALNS across all the metrics.

References

1. Alam, M.J., Habib, M.A.: A dynamic programming optimization for traffic microsimulation modelling of a mass evacuation. Transp. Res. Part D: Transp. Environ. **97**, 102946 (2021)
2. Bektaş, T., Elmastaş, S.: Solving school bus routing problems through integer programming. J. Oper. Res. Soc. **58**(12), 1599–1604 (2007)
3. Caceres, H., Batta, R., He, Q.: School bus routing with stochastic demand and duration constraints. Transp. Sci. **51**(4), 1349–1364 (2017)
4. Chen, C., Demir, E., Huang, Y.: An adaptive large neighborhood search heuristic for the vehicle routing problem with time windows and delivery robots. Eur. J. Oper. Res. **294**(3), 1164–1180 (2021)

5. Dang, L., Hou, Y., Liu, Q., Kong, Y.: A hybrid metaheuristic algorithm for the bi-objective school bus routing problem. IAENG Int. J. Comput. Sci. **46**(3), 409–416 (2019)
6. Demir, E., Bektaş, T., Laporte, G.: An adaptive large neighborhood search heuristic for the pollution-routing problem. Eur. J. Oper. Res. **223**(2), 346–359 (2012)
7. Di Caprio, D., Ebrahimnejad, A., Alrezaamiri, H., Santos-Arteaga, F.J.: A novel ant colony algorithm for solving shortest path problems with fuzzy arc weights. Alex. Eng. J. **61**(5), 3403–3415 (2022)
8. Ellegood, W.A., Campbell, J.F., North, J.: Continuous approximation models for mixed load school bus routing. Transp. Res. Part B Methodol. **77**, 182–198 (2015)
9. Ellegood, W.A., Solomon, S., North, J., Campbell, J.F.: School bus routing problem: contemporary trends and research directions. Omega **95**, 102056 (2020)
10. Euchi, J., Mraihi, R.: The urban bus routing problem in the Tunisian case by the hybrid artificial ant colony algorithm. Swarm Evol. Comput. **2**, 15–24 (2012)
11. Guo, X., Samaranayake, S.: Shareability network based decomposition approach for solving large-scale single school routing problems. Transp. Res. Part C Emerg. Technol. **140**, 103691 (2022)
12. Hou, Y.E., Dang, L., Dong, W., Kong, Y.: A metaheuristic algorithm for routing school buses with mixed load. IEEE Access **8**, 158293–158305 (2020)
13. Konstantakopoulos, G.D., Gayialis, S.P., Kechagias, E.P., Papadopoulos, G.A., Tatsiopoulos, I.P.: A multiobjective large neighborhood search metaheuristic for the vehicle routing problem with time windows. Algorithms **13**(10), 243 (2020)
14. Liu, R., Tao, Y., Xie, X.: An adaptive large neighborhood search heuristic for the vehicle routing problem with time windows and synchronized visits. Comput. Oper. Res. **101**, 250–262 (2019)
15. López Santana, E.R., Romero Carvajal, J.d.J.: A hybrid column generation and clustering approach to the school bus routing problem with time windows. Ingeniería **20**(1), 101–117 (2015)
16. Nanry, W.P., Barnes, J.W.: Solving the pickup and delivery problem with time windows using reactive Tabu search. Transp. Res. Part B Methodol. **34**(2), 107–121 (2000)
17. Newton, R.M., Thomas, W.H.: Design of school bus routes by computer. Socioecon. Plann. Sci. **3**(1), 75–85 (1969)
18. Özarık, S.S., Veelenturf, L.P., Van Woensel, T., Laporte, G.: Optimizing e-commerce last-mile vehicle routing and scheduling under uncertain customer presence. Transp. Res. Part E Logist. Transp. Rev. **148**, 102263 (2021)
19. Pan, B., Zhang, Z., Lim, A.: A hybrid algorithm for time-dependent vehicle routing problem with time windows. Comput. Oper. Res. **128**, 105193 (2021)
20. Park, J., Tae, H., Kim, B.I.: A post-improvement procedure for the mixed load school bus routing problem. Eur. J. Oper. Res. **217**(1), 204–213 (2012)
21. Ren, J., Jin, W., Wu, W.: A two-stage algorithm for school bus stop location and routing problem with walking accessibility and mixed load. IEEE Access **7**, 119519–119540 (2019)
22. Ropke, S., Pisinger, D.: An adaptive large neighborhood search heuristic for the pickup and delivery problem with time windows. Transp. Sci. **40**(4), 455–472 (2006)
23. Toth, P., Vigo, D.: The Vehicle Routing Problem. SIAM (2002)

24. Voigt, S., Frank, M., Fontaine, P., Kuhn, H.: The vehicle routing problem with availability profiles. Transp. Sci. **57**(2), 531–551 (2023)
25. Wang, L., Kinable, J., Van Woensel, T.: The fuel replenishment problem: a split-delivery multi-compartment vehicle routing problem with multiple trips. Comput. Oper. Res. **118**, 104904 (2020)

Immediate Addressing-Based Efficient Loop Optimization for Encryption Computation

Zhihao Li[1,2]($\boxtimes$) (iD) and Yonghua Hu[1,2]

[1] School of Computer Science and Engineering, Hunan University of Science and Technology, Xiangtan 411201, Hunan, China
`zhihaoli778@163.com`, `huyh@hnust.cn`
[2] Hunan Key Laboratory for Service Computing and Novel Software Technology, Hunan University of Science and Technology, Xiangtan 411201, Hunan, China

Abstract. Encryption algorithms play a core role in data confidentiality, integrity, and authentication, with applications covering most areas of network security. Encryption algorithms involve substantial computations, which affect the algorithm's response time—an issue particularly prominent in resource-constrained terminal devices. Loop structures are common control constructs in encryption algorithms, and optimizing loop structures can facilitate the application of encryption algorithms in terminal devices. This paper proposes an efficient loop optimization method integrating immediate addressing. This method seeks to replace offset register addressing in loops with immediate addressing, expand the unrolling factor through the immediate addressing mechanism, and eliminate conditional judgment and jump instructions in loops. The method reduces computational overhead and mitigates performance degradation caused by memory access by changing the program's memory access pattern. Experimental results show that compared with traditional loop optimization methods, the proposed method achieves an average 10% performance improvement in loop programs.

Keywords: Loop Unrolling · Loop Optimization · Network Security · Encryption Algorithms

1 Introduction

With the popularization of the internet, people's awareness of privacy protection has gradually increased, and privacy protection technologies have continued to evolve. Meanwhile, encryption algorithms have increasingly become core tools in privacy protection technologies due to their excellent security, and are

Supported by Hunan Provincial Natural Science Foundation (No. 2023JJ50019), the Postgraduate Scientific Research Innovation Project of Hunan Province (No. CX20231019).

W. Liang et al. (Eds.): SecureComm 2025, LNICST 690, pp. 98–115, 2026.
https://doi.org/10.1007/978-3-032-23456-8_6

widely applied in fields such as healthcare, finance, and digital signal processing. However, the enhancement of security performance often comes with a sacrifice in program performance, a contradiction that is particularly prominent in resource-constrained embedded scenarios. This is partly due to the limited hardware resources in embedded systems, such as register resources and instruction caches. On the other hand, the volume of communication data and computational complexity have increased—for example, high-intensity encryption algorithms are difficult to run efficiently on resource-constrained terminal platforms due to their computational complexity. [1]

Digital Signal Processors have been widely applied in numerous fields such as digital communication, video surveillance, television, information security, etc. [2–4]. Inside a DSP, the Harvard architecture is adopted, and instruction scheduling employs pipelined operation, which enables the rapid completion of various digital signal processing algorithms [5]. Currently, the Very Long Instruction Word (VLIW) technology has gradually been applied in high-performance DSP architectures [6,7]. The advantage of the vector calculation unit lies in its ability to operate on multiple data simultaneously, significantly reducing the running time of the program [8]. Vector DSPs are equipped with abundant computing resources, and the architectures and instruction sets of different DSPs vary [9]. Many works on compilation optimization for vector processors are carried out manually, which is time-consuming, labor-intensive, and difficult to maintain. To save development costs and shorten the research and development cycle, it is necessary to conduct compilation optimization of programs for the architecture of vector DSPs [10].

Compilation optimization for vector DSPs requires a full consideration of the hardware resources of the chip, among which register resources are one of the most important ones [11]. In order to facilitate memory access operations, vector DSPs provide a variety of memory access registers, such as base registers and offset registers. How to make full use of various types of register resources during the program execution is one of the important parts of compilation optimization.

Encryption algorithms contain many loop structures, such as polynomial multiplication loops and polynomial addition loops in homomorphic encryption [12]. The running time of the loop structure in the algorithm accounts for a large proportion [13], so the optimization of loops is an essential part. Currently, the optimization techniques for loops mainly include loop tiling, loop unrolling [14], and software pipelining, etc. Loop unrolling is one of the most direct and effective methods among loop transformation techniques [15,16]. Its remarkable effect is to reduce the overhead of calculating the loop index and testing the loop branch conditions [14]. In addition, loop unrolling also provides opportunities for optimizations such as vectorization and data prefetching [15]. Loop unrolling is related to the characteristics of hardware resources, so the selection of the unrolling factor is an important factor [17,18]. Common methods for selecting the unrolling factor generally fall into two categories, one leverages machine learning algorithms to predict the factor [18,19], while the other constructs cost models for automatic selection [20–22].

In the instruction sequence of a loop, memory access instructions that combine a base register and an offset register are commonly used for memory access operations. However, in vector DSP processors, this is not the only type of memory access instruction. There are also memory access instructions that combine a base register with an immediate number. Compared with using an offset register for addressing, the method of using a base register in conjunction with an immediate number for addressing is more efficient. Moreover, in vector DSP processors, offset registers are a valuable resource of memory - access registers. Reducing the use of offset registers in loops helps to alleviate the pressure of subsequent register allocation.

Therefore, based on the theory in reference [19] that estimates the unrolling factor by considering register pressure, this paper proposes to use immediate addressing instead of offset register addressing during loop unrolling and increase the unrolling factor according to the immediate addressing mechanism. Meanwhile, the method proposed in this paper combines loop unrolling with loop elimination to remove loop condition judgment instructions, loop control instructions, and loop jump instructions from the instruction sequence after loop unrolling.

2   Framework and Model

2.1   Problem Analysis

Loop unrolling is generally limited to unrolling the loop while maintaining the original loop pattern. For memory access instructions, if the original loop uses register addressing mode, the addressing mode of all memory access instructions in the unrolled loop will still be register addressing. If the register addressing mode can be converted to the immediate addressing mode during the loop unrolling process, the unrolling factor of the loop unrolling can be increased without adding the allocation pressure of memory access registers. Taking the two loops in Fig. 1 as an example, if the addressing mode using immediate numbers is used to replace the register addressing mode, the loop in Fig. 1(a) can be converted into the form in Fig. 1(b). Loop unrolling creates copies of instructions in the order of the instructions. Taking loop unrolling twice as an example, as shown in Fig. 2(a), such processing does not change the addressing mode of the original loop. Figure 2(b) applies the immediate addressing mode during the loop unrolling process. By comparing the registers used in the two types of loop unrolling, it can be found that compared with the instruction sequence after loop unrolling in Fig. 2(a), the unrolled loop instruction sequence in Fig. 2(b) only increases the demand for using immediate numbers, but greatly reduces the use of offset registers.

In vector DSP processors, offset registers are a type of registers that are frequently used but in short supply. On the other hand, immediate numbers only occupy general-purpose registers. Although general-purpose registers are

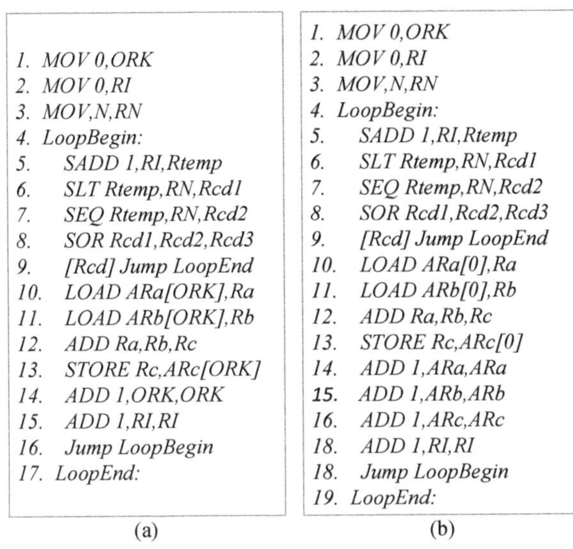

<table>
<tr><td>

1. MOV 0,ORK
2. MOV 0,RI
3. MOV,N,RN
4. LoopBegin:
5.   SADD 1,RI,Rtemp
6.   SLT Rtemp,RN,Rcd1
7.   SEQ Rtemp,RN,Rcd2
8.   SOR Rcd1,Rcd2,Rcd3
9.   [Rcd] Jump LoopEnd
10.   LOAD ARa[ORK],Ra
11.   LOAD ARb[ORK],Rb
12.   ADD Ra,Rb,Rc
13.   STORE Rc,ARc[ORK]
14.   ADD 1,ORK,ORK
15.   ADD 1,RI,RI
16.   Jump LoopBegin
17. LoopEnd:

</td><td>

1. MOV 0,ORK
2. MOV 0,RI
3. MOV,N,RN
4. LoopBegin:
5.   SADD 1,RI,Rtemp
6.   SLT Rtemp,RN,Rcd1
7.   SEQ Rtemp,RN,Rcd2
8.   SOR Rcd1,Rcd2,Rcd3
9.   [Rcd] Jump LoopEnd
10.   LOAD ARa[0],Ra
11.   LOAD ARb[0],Rb
12.   ADD Ra,Rb,Rc
13.   STORE Rc,ARc[0]
14.   ADD 1,ARa,ARa
15.   ADD 1,ARb,ARb
16.   ADD 1,ARc,ARc
18.   ADD 1,RI,RI
18.   Jump LoopBegin
19. LoopEnd:

</td></tr>
<tr><td align="center">(a)</td><td align="center">(b)</td></tr>
</table>

Fig. 1. Two different loop instruction sequences.

also used quite frequently, their quantity is usually much larger than that of offset registers. Moreover, the efficiency of immediate addressing is much higher than that of addressing using offset registers. The loop unrolling in Fig. 2(b) significantly reduces the use of offset registers, which will undoubtedly enhance the performance of the program to a great extent.

However, there is still a problem with the program after loop unrolling by using the base register in combination with immediate addressing. That is, there are a large number of loop condition judgment instructions and loop jump instructions in the instruction sequence after loop unrolling. Although the loop program using the immediate addressing mode can significantly increase the unrolling factor during loop unrolling and reduce the loop control overhead to a certain extent, it cannot completely solve this problem. If loop elimination is carried out after loop unrolling, the overhead generated by loop control can be completely eliminated, and the parallelism of the program can be improved.

2.2   Model

2.2.1   Identification of Induction Variables and Unrolling Variables

Traverse each instruction within the loop according to the definition of induction variables to identify the variables that conform to the definition. It should be noted that among the induction variables, there is one induction variable used for loop control. This variable is mainly utilized in the loop control basic block, yet its increment instruction is located in the main basic block of loop.

After identifying the induction variables in the loop, it is necessary to determine whether the recognized variables include those that use base registers and

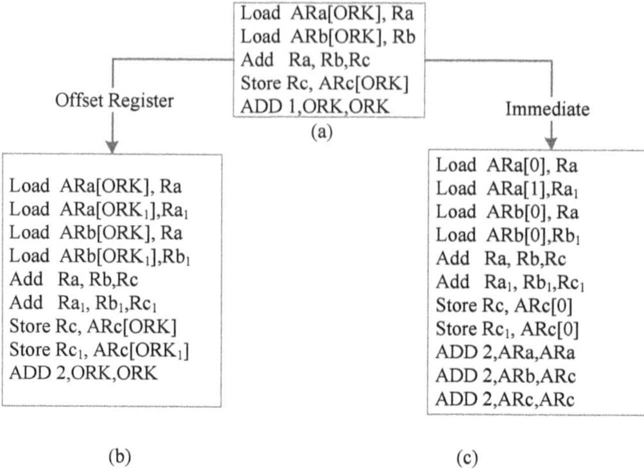

Fig. 2. Two different ways of loop unrolling.

those that use offset registers. For variables that use base registers, retain them. As for variables that use offset registers, since the method proposed in this chapter aims to replace the addressing mode of combining a base register with an offset register with the addressing mode of combining a base register with an immediate number, these variables should be removed from the set of induction variables.

2.2.2   Unrolling Factor Calculation Method Step 1: Determine the number of bits N_{Bit} occupied by the immediate number in the memory access instruction of the immediate addressing mode. Obtain the maximum value $NImm_{max}$ of the immediate number through Formula (1).

$$NImm_{max} = 2^{N_{Bit}-1} \tag{1}$$

Due to the characteristics of the vector components of vector DSPs, incrementing or decrementing the address offset by 1 will lead to redundant data calculations. Therefore, it is necessary to adjust the values of immediate addressing and subsequent register addressing according to the length of the vector processing unit of the vector DSP. This adjustment further narrows down the range of available values for the already limited immediate addressing mode. Based on the length of the data calculated by the instruction and the maximum value of immediate addressing, calculate the number N_{Imm} of values that can be provided by immediate addressing for the corresponding data length, as shown in Formula (2) below.

$$NImm = NImm_{max}/VPE \tag{2}$$

Among Formula (2), VPE represents the number of data that can be processed by the corresponding vector instruction of the vector DSP processor. In a scalar processor, its value is generally 1. In a vector processor, its value is determined according to the type of the vector component and the instruction.

Step 2: Classify the variable set S for which unrolling copies need to be created according to the register type. Find all symbolic variables in S that use base registers and put them into S_{AR}. After classification, S is composed as follows:

$$S = \{S_{AR}, S_R, S_{VR}\} \tag{3}$$

Among them, S_R and S_{VR} respectively represent the variable sets of scalar general-purpose registers and vector general-purpose registers in the vector DSP processor for which unrolling copies need to be created in the current loop.

Step 3: Obtain the number of idle register resources of all register classes before the program enters the loop, and calculate the unrolling factors of all register classes by using the unrolling factor selection method in the traditional loop unrolling approach.

Step 4: Obtain the unrolling factor BUF_{AR} of the base register according to the unrolling factor selection method in the traditional loop unrolling method, and then multiply it by N_{Imm} to obtain UF, the final unrolling factor. The specific formula is shown in Formula (4) as follows:

$$UF = BUF_{AR} \times NImm \tag{4}$$

At the same time, determine whether the register resources used after unrolling according to UF will exceed the number of idle register resources of various register types. The specific determination method is shown in Formula (5) as follows:

$$UFReg_x = UF \times UReg_x, x \in \{VR, AR\} \tag{5}$$

Among Formula (5), $UReg_x$ represents the number of registers of type x used in the original loop, and $UFReg_x$ represents the number of registers of type x used in the loop instruction sequence after unrolling with the unrolling factor UF. When unrolling is not performed using immediate numbers, the unrolling factor is derived from the pressure of various register types. Therefore, in the instruction sequence unrolled according to this unrolling factor, the situation where the used register resources exceed the number of idle registers of each type before entering the loop will not occur.

$$EReg_x = UFReg_x - FreeReg_x \tag{6}$$

$$EUFTimes = EReg_x / (UReg_x \times BUF_{AR}) \tag{7}$$

In Formula (6), $FreeReg_x$ represents the number of idle registers of type x before entering the loop, and $EReg_x$ represents the number of used registers that exceed the idle resources of registers of type x after unrolling according to the unrolling factor UF. In Formula (7), $EUFTimes$ represents the number of unrolling times when the immediate number overflows.

Step 5: After obtaining the number of unrolling times when the immediate number overflows, it is necessary to correct the unrolling factor of the immediate number. Then, based on the corrected unrolling factor of the immediate number and Formula (4), obtain the unrolling factor again. The correction method for the unrolling factor of the immediate number is shown in Formula (8) as follows:

$$NImm = NImm - EUFTimes \tag{8}$$

Step 6: Use data flow analysis to identify the constant value R_N of the loop boundary quantity. Calculate the number of loop iterations after loop unrolling according to Formula (9). Then, calculate the total instruction word length of the main basic block of loop and the maximum number of iterations allowed by the instruction cache if the loop is fully unrolled according to Formula (10).

$$UT = RN/UF \tag{9}$$

$$UT_{max} = LC / \sum_{k=1}^{n} Ins_k \tag{10}$$

Among them, Ins_k represents the instruction word length of each instruction in the loop body after loop unrolling, $SIns$ is the total instruction word length of all instructions, LC is the size of the instruction cache, and UT_{max} is the theoretical upper limit for the expansion of the unrolling factor. When $UT \leq UT_{max}$, it indicates that the unrolling factor can be expanded by making use of the instruction cache. Conversely, if $UT > UT_{max}$, the expansion cannot be carried out.

2.2.3   Code Transformation Method After determining the unrolling factor, it is necessary to transform the instruction sequence of the original loop. For the instruction sequence in the loop initialization basic block, modify the constant value in the constant assignment instruction of the offset register's unrolling factor to the number of unrolling times of the immediate number, rather than the number of unrolling times of the non - offset register. Moreover, obtain the increment of the memory - access register copy variables according to the unrolling factor of the immediate number. In the loop initialization basic block, there is no need to create initialization instructions for the copy variables of the offset register variables anymore. Instead, create initialization instructions for the copy variables of the base register variables, and the increment in these instructions is the increment obtained according to the unrolling factor of the immediate number.

If the original instruction sequence of the loop uses the addressing mode that combines a base register with an offset register, after obtaining the unrolling factor of the immediate number and the increment of the memory - access register variables, it is necessary to update the value of the offset register according to the increment. This is done to ensure that the offset stored in the offset register after the loop ends is correct. In some basic blocks after the loop, there may be instructions that access memory based on this offset register. If the value in the offset register used in the loop is not corrected, it may lead to unknown errors in the subsequent program execution.

For the main basic block of loop, since the calculation basic block of the original loop may use an offset register for memory access and update the offset register within the main basic block of loop, the identification result of the induction variable includes the offset register and an update instruction for the offset register is also generated in the unrolled instruction sequence. However, the method proposed in this chapter no longer requires the use of the offset register, so there is no need for the update instruction of the offset register either. Therefore, when unrolling the loop, the instruction that increments the offset register variable should be modified to an instruction that increments the base register variable. That is, an instruction similar to *"Add XX, ARx, ARx"* in the loop of Fig. 2(c) is used as the self-increment instruction for the memory-access induction variable, where ARx represents the variable using the base register.

3 Implementation

3.1 Unrolling Factor Calculation

The loop method incorporating immediate addressing first needs to analyze the number of bits occupied by the immediate value in memory access instructions using immediate addressing. Then, by considering the number of data items that a single vector instruction in the processor can handle, the maximum number of usable instructions for immediate-addressing memory access instructions during loop unrolling is determined. This number is then used to replace the expandable quantity of offset registers in the loop elimination method for memory access expansion.

In processors with composite addressing modes, the number of offset registers is typically limited. In contrast, the maximum addressing range supported by immediate addressing is usually far greater than the number of offset registers. Therefore, replacing offset-register addressing with immediate addressing can increase the value of the unrolling factor.

The unrolling factor selection algorithm in this paper classifies registers into three categories, namely memory-access registers, base registers, and non-memory-access registers which include vector registers and scalar registers. Firstly, according to the number of bits for immediate addressing and the vector length in the processor, the number of instructions that can perform addressing using immediate numbers is calculated, that is, to figure out how many immediate numbers can cooperate with the base register for addressing. The obtained quantity of immediate numbers that can be used for memory access together with the base register is exactly the unrolling factor of the immediate numbers. Subsequently, the calculation method of the unrolling factor in the traditional loop unrolling method is adopted to separately calculate the unrolling factor for each type of register. Multiply the unrolling factor BUF_{AR} of the base register obtained by the traditional loop unrolling method by the unrolling factor of the immediate numbers to obtain the unrolling factor expanded by the immediate numbers, and the value of the multiplication of the two unrolling factors is the maximum number of unrolling times after integrating the immediate-addressing mode.

Next, it is necessary to determine whether unrolling with the unrolling factor expanded by immediate numbers will lead to register overflow. This determination is mainly made based on the idle quantities of various types of register resources and the quantities of various types of registers used within the loop. If an overflow occurs, it is necessary to calculate the number of unrolling times that cause the overflow according to the quantity of the overflowed registers, and correct the unrolling factor of the immediate numbers based on the calculated number of unrolling times for the overflow. Finally, similar to the loop elimination method with memory access expansion, the unrolling factor needs to be further expanded through the instruction cache. The unrolling factor selection algorithm is shown in Algorithm 1.

This algorithm mainly includes the following contents: 1. Lines 2–4 of the algorithm calculate and obtain relevant information according to Formulas (1), (2), and (3).

2. Lines 5-6 of the algorithm obtain the idle quantities of various types of registers before the loop and the quantities of various types of registers used within the original loop through data flow analysis, and store the results in the sets $FreeRegS$ and $URegS$.

3. In lines 6–10 of the algorithm, R represents scalar registers and VR represents vector registers. The for - loop in this part sequentially calculates the number of scalar registers and vector registers used after unrolling. Then, it checks whether the number of used registers causes an overflow. If an overflow occurs, it calculates the number of overflowed registers and the number of unrolling times that lead to the overflow, and stores the number of overflowed registers and the number of overflowed unrolling times in the sets $ERegS$ and $EUFTimesS$ which are classified according to scalar registers and vector registers.

4. In lines 11–13 of the algorithm, the maximum number of overflowed unrolling times, $fixTimes$, is obtained from the set $EUFTimesS$ which stores the number of overflowed unrolling times classified by scalar registers and vector registers. Then, the unrolling factor UF is corrected based on this value.

5. From line 14 to the end of the algorithm, similar to the loop elimination method with memory access expansion, first, the definition instructions of the loop boundary variables are found through data - flow analysis, and the specific values defined for the loop boundary variables are analyzed. Then, the number of loop iterations is calculated according to the unrolling factor UF. Next, the instruction word length within the basic block of the loop calculation and the number of loop iterations are computed. After that, the maximum number of loop iterations allowed by the instruction cache is obtained based on the instruction cache size LC. Finally, the unrolling factor is expanded according to the number of loop iterations.

Algorithm 1 GetCstUnrollFactor

Require:

$NBit$: The number of bits for immediate addressing

VPE: The number of vector processing units

$BUFAR$: The unrolling factor of the base register

LC: The size of the instruction cache

L: The instruction sequence of the original loop

Ensure:

UF: Unrolling Factor

1: **function** GETCSTUNROLLFACTOR($NBit$, VPE, $BUFAR$, LC, L)
2:    $NImm_{max} \leftarrow 2^{NBit-1}$
3:    $NImm \leftarrow \lfloor NImm_{max}/VPE \rfloor$
4:    $UF \leftarrow BUF_{AR} \times NImm$
5:    $FreeRegS \leftarrow \text{getFreeRegNum}(L)$
6:    $URegS \leftarrow \text{getUseRegNum}(L)$
7:    **for** each $Reg \in \{R, VR\}$ **do**
8:        $UFReg \leftarrow UF \times URegS[Reg]$
9:        **if** $UFReg \geq FreeRegS[Reg]$ **then**
10:            $ERegS[Reg] \leftarrow UFReg - FreeRegS[Reg]$
11:            $EUFTimesS[Reg] \leftarrow ERegS[Reg]/(URegS[Reg] \times BUF_{AR})$
12:        **end if**
13:    **end for**
14:    $fixTimes \leftarrow \max(EUFTimesS)$
15:    $NImm \leftarrow NImm - fixTimes$
16:    $UF \leftarrow NImm \times BUF_{AR}$
17:    **for** each $Ins \in L.\text{CalcBasicBlock}$ **do**
18:        $SIns \leftarrow SIns + Ins.size$
19:    **end for**
20:    $UT \leftarrow \text{calcLoopTime}(L, UF)$
21:    $UT_{max} \leftarrow \text{calcMaxLoopTime}(LC, SIns)$
22:    **if** $UT \leq UT_{max}$ **then**
23:        $FUF \leftarrow UT \times UF$
24:        **return** FUF
25:    **else**
26:        **return** UF
27:    **end if**
28: **end function**

3.2   Code Transformation

After obtaining the unrolling factor that incorporates immediate addressing, it is necessary to start transforming the instruction sequences of each part of the loop. Before this, through control flow analysis, the program has divided the original loop into different basic blocks, namely the loop initialization basic block, the loop control basic block, and the main basic block of loop. This section describes how the code transformation is implemented on a basic block basis.

First, it comes to the transformation of the instruction sequence in the loop initialization basic block. The code transformation of the initialization basic block is shown in Fig. 3. Figure 3(a) depicts the loop initialization basic block before unrolling, while Fig. 3(b) shows it after unrolling.

The transformation of loop initialization basic block can be roughly divided into two parts. The first part involves adding definition instructions for the unrolling factor and the loop step size. The definition instructions for the unrolling factor include those for the immediate unrolling factor, the base register unrolling factor, and the final unrolling factor, as shown in Instructions 1 to 3 in Fig. 3(b). The definition instruction for the loop step size can be found in Instruction 7 in Fig. 3(b). The second part consists of the initialization instructions for the copy variables of the base register variables. As shown in Lines 8–11 in Fig. 3(b), ARa is the original base register variable, and ARa_2 to ARa_{UFAR} are the copy variables created for ARa. After the transformation of the loop initialization basic block is completed, the code in the main basic block of loop is transformed. The result of transforming this basic block is shown in Fig. 4. The main basic block of loop is mainly composed of two parts: the calculation part and the induction variable update part. Instructions 1 to 4 in Fig. 4(a) belong to the calculation part, while Instructions 5 and 6 are in the induction variable update part. The transformation of this basic block processes these two parts separately.

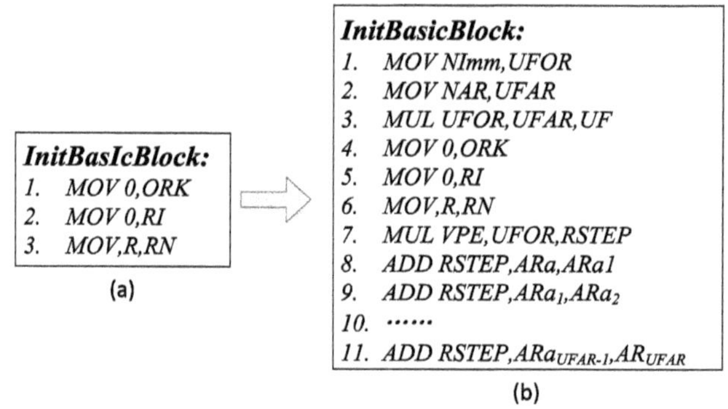

Fig. 3. The transformation of loop initialization basic block.

The first part is the transformation of the calculation section. First, an instruction sequence for immediate addressing determined by the immediate unrolling factor is added. Then, according to the unrolling factor BUF_{AR} of the base register, an instruction sequence is added. In this sequence, the generated immediate - addressing instructions are copied, and the base register variables are modified to their copy variables. Subsequently, the above operations are repeated for other base register variables until all base register variables and their copy variables have been processed. Lines 11 to 13 in Fig. 4(b) show the transformed calculation instructions, corresponding to Instruction 3. Regarding the transformation of calculation instructions, the main approach is to continuously copy the original calculation instructions according to the unrolling factor.

Meanwhile, the source and destination operands in the calculation instructions are replaced with the copy variables of the operands in the original calculation instructions.

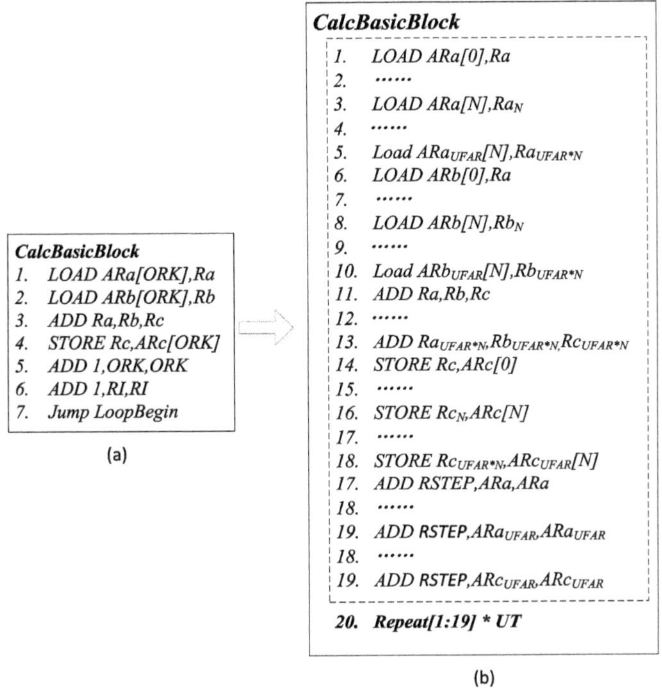

Fig. 4. The transformation of loop computation basic block.

The second part is to transform the instructions in the induction variable update section. The instructions from lines 17 to 19 at the end of Fig. 4(b) are used to update the unrolled induction variables, corresponding to instructions 5 and 6 in Fig. 4(a). In the method proposed in this paper, the transformation of the induction variable update section in the main basic block of loop mainly includes two aspects. The first is the transformation of the induction variable type. The update instructions for the induction variables are modified to update the base register variables and their copy variables. The second is to eliminate the update of induction variables related to loop control. One of the aims of the loop elimination method that integrates immediate addressing is to eliminate loops, which means eliminating the loop control overhead. Since the update of induction variables related to loop control is a form of loop control overhead, it is eliminated here.

After completing the above steps, a complete transformation of the main basic block of loop is finished. At this time, the instructions in the basic block form an instruction sequence that has been jointly unrolled using immediate numbers and base registers. To completely eliminate the loop control overhead, the instruction sequence in the basic block is copied UT times, where UT is the number of loop iterations after unrolling obtained when calculating the unrolling factor. At this point, one iteration of the instructions in the main basic block of loop is equivalent to all the iterations in the original loop, which means there is no need for loop condition judgments and loop jumps. Thus, the goal of loop elimination is achieved, and there is no redundant loop control overhead in the loop.

4   Experimental Analysis

In order to test the effectiveness of the method proposed in this paper, we have chosen the high-performance vector DSP processor YHFT-M7002 as the hardware platform for the test. YHFT-M7002 [23] adopts a three-level storage structure. Each independent computing core is equipped with a 32 KB level-1 data cache and a 512 KB vector storage space. The total capacity of the global shared cache is 2 MB. In addition, there is a large-capacity 32 GB DDR storage space available for use outside the chip.

The processor core of YHFT-M7002 is based on the VLIW architecture, which includes a scalar processing unit (SPU) and a vector processing unit (VPU). The SPU consists of a scalar execution unit (SPE), an instruction flow control unit, and a scalar memory access unit (SM). The SPE is responsible for executing the serial processing part of the application program, mainly including integer and floating-point arithmetic units. The VPU contains 16 homogeneous vector processing elements (VPEs), which are responsible for parallel computing of large-scale and data-intensive operations. The kernel architecture of YHFT-M7002 is shown in Fig. 5. The loop unrolling part of all the loop elimination methods introduced in this paper is improved based on the unrolling factor selection method of register pressure. To be more in line with the register resources of the hardware, its input is the instruction-level intermediate code of the program, and the output is the optimized instruction-level intermediate code. In order to demonstrate the advantages of the loop unrolling method in this chapter compared with the memory access expansion loop elimination method, two algorithms from the TI DSPLIB function library are selected for the experiment, namely the real array addition algorithm (ADD) and the real array multiplication algorithm (VECMUL). In addition to comparing the performance of the algorithms processed by different loop elimination methods, the experiment also makes comparisons in terms of the unrolling factor, register utilization, etc., so as to verify the efficiency of the loop elimination method integrating the immediate addressing mode on this vector DSP processor with the characteristics of composite addressing modes.

In the processing of the two algorithms selected for the experiment using two different methods, the unrolling factors of various types of registers and the final unrolling factor are shown in Table 1. Here, $TULM$ represents the experimental results obtained under the traditional loop unrolling method, and $CstLEM$

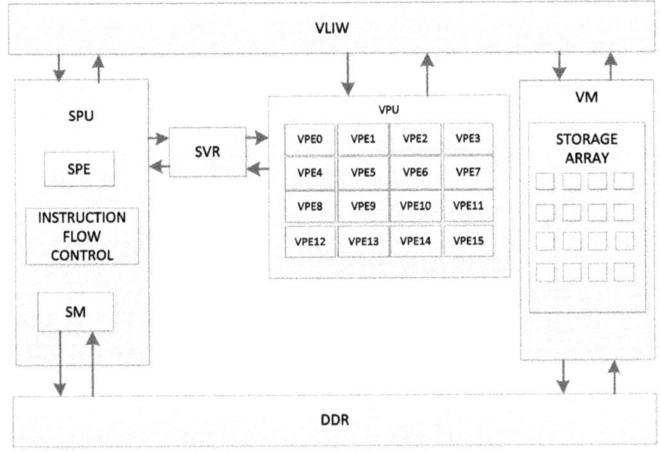

Fig. 5. Architecture of YHFT-M7002.

represents the experimental results obtained using the loop elimination method integrating immediate numbers proposed in this chapter. UF_{OR} represents the unrolling factor of the offset register, UF_{Imm} represents the unrolling factor of the immediate number, and UF_{Finall} represents the final unrolling factor.

Table 1. The unrolling factors of the ADD algorithm and the VECMUL algorithm obtained by different methods.

Method	Algorithm	UF_{AR}	UF_{OR}	UF_{Imm}	UF_{Finall}
TULM	ADD	1	8	0	8
CstLEM	ADD	2	0	15	30
TULM	VECMUL	1	8	0	8
CstLEM	VECMUL	2	0	15	30

It can be clearly seen from Table tab1 the differences in the selection of unrolling factors between the two methods. The method in this paper can obtain a larger unrolling factor when performing loop unrolling. The reason is that there are only 8 offset registers in the experimental platform, while the immediate addressing has 8 bits and the length of the VPE is 16. Through the unrolling factor selection model proposed in this paper, it can be calculated that 16 immediate numbers can be used for immediate addressing. Therefore, the maximum unrolling factor of the offset register is 8, and the maximum unrolling factor of the immediate number is 16.

The differences in the unrolling factors will lead to differences in the usage of registers in the unrolled instruction sequence. A larger unrolling factor will result in the use of more registers in the unrolled program. The usage of various types of registers in the instruction sequences of the two algorithms processed by the two processing methods is shown in Table 2.

Table 2. The number of registers used by the ADD algorithm and the VECMUL algorithm under different methods.

Method	Algorithm	AR	OR	R	VR
TULM	ADD	6	9	48	24
CstLEM	ADD	9	2	56	93
TULM	VECMUL	6	8	45	24
CstLEM	VECMUL	6	1	54	48

It can be seen from Table 2 that since the *CstLEM* method yields a larger unrolling factor, the instruction sequence processed by this method has a much higher register utilization rate than that of the *TULM* method. However, the CstLEM method abandons the unrolling of offset registers, so its usage of offset registers is lower than that of the loop elimination method with memory access expansion. The reason for abandoning the unrolling of offset registers is that offset registers are memory - access - related registers with a small quantity and high usage frequency. Reducing the use of offset registers can provide convenience for memory access of instructions outside the loop in the program.

Meanwhile, the corresponding running clock cycles are obtained through experiments. We use N to represent the data volume, $Cycle$ to represent the running clock cycles, and R to represent the speed - up ratio. The experimental results are shown in Figs. 6 and 7. For the ADD algorithm, compared with the *TULM* method, as the input data volume increases, the speed - up ratio obtained by the *CstLEM* method gradually increases, with an average speed - up ratio of approximately 1.11. As shown in Fig. 7, for the VECMUL algorithm, the method proposed in this paper can also achieve a lower number of running clock cycles for all input scales, with an average speed - up ratio of approximately 1.10. When the data volume is small, the speed - up effect of the method in this paper is not obvious. The main reason is that the instruction sequence generated by the method in this paper includes some auxiliary instructions, which limit the program's performance when calculating small - volume data. As the data volume continues to increase, the impact of the auxiliary instructions can be almost ignored, so the speed - up effect becomes more obvious.

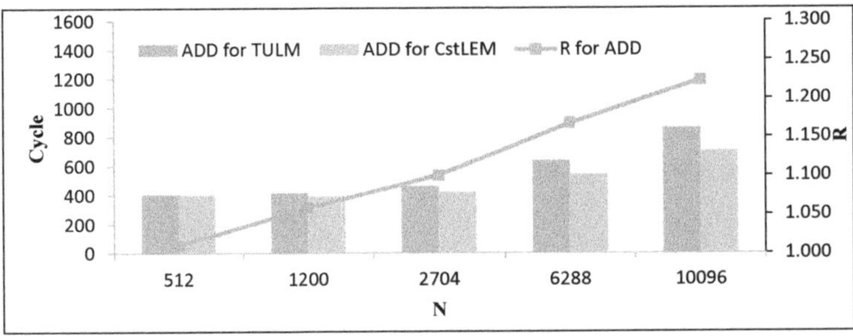

Fig. 6. The running clock cycles and speed-up ratio of the ADD algorithm.

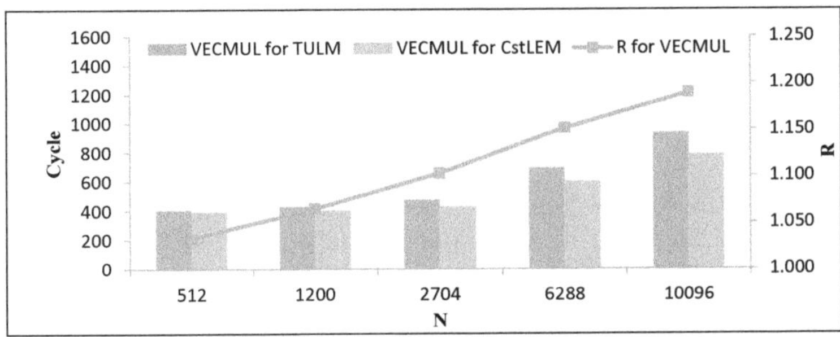

Fig. 7. The running clock cycles and speed-up ratio of the VECMUL algorithm.

5   Conclusion

Based on the architecture of the vector DSP processor, this paper analyzes the problems of the traditional loop unrolling method based on register pressure when processing programs for vector DSP processors with composite addressing modes. The main issue with the traditional loop unrolling method lies in the limitations of its unrolling factor selection. It can only perform unrolling using the type of registers under the greatest pressure, failing to fully utilize the register resources and the composite addressing mechanism of the vector DSP. Moreover, there are a large number of loop condition judgment instructions and loop jump instructions in the instruction sequence processed by the traditional loop unrolling method.

Therefore, based on the traditional loop unrolling method, this paper studies a loop elimination method that integrates immediate addressing. When unrolling the loop, this method uses immediate addressing to replace offset register addressing and expands the unrolling factor by leveraging the number of bits in immediate addressing. Subsequently, during the transformation of the instruction sequence, it eliminates the loop condition judgment instructions and loop jump instructions in the loop, while reducing the induction variable update instructions in the loop. This method can obtain a larger unrolling factor than the loop elimination method with memory access expansion, further enhancing the parallelism of the program. The experimental results on the YHFT - M7002 platform show that, compared with the loop elimination method with memory access expansion, this method can achieve a larger unrolling factor, higher register utilization, and a smaller code size. Moreover, in terms of performance, this method can bring an average improvement of 10%.

References

1. Wang, R., Lai, J., Zhang, Z., Li, X., Vijayakumar, P., Karuppiah, M.: Privacy-preserving federated learning for internet of medical things under edge computing. IEEE J. Biomed. Health Inform. **27**(2), 854–865 (2022)
2. Bariko, S., Arsalane, A., Klilou, A., Abounada, A.: Efficient parallel implementation of gaussian mixture model background subtraction algorithm on an embedded multi-core digital signal processor. Comput. Electr. Eng. **110**, 108827 (2023)
3. Khan, S., Alzaabi, A., Iqbal, Z., Ratnarajah, T., Arslan, T.: A novel digital twin (DT) model based on WiFi CSI, signal processing and machine learning for patient respiration monitoring and decision-support. IEEE Access **11**, 103554–103568 (2023)
4. Al-Dulaimi, M.A.A., Wahhab, H.A., Amer, A.A.: Design and implementation of communication digital fir filter for audio signals on the FPGA platform. J. Commun. **18**(2), 89–96 (2023)
5. Ibrahim, D., Davies, A.: The evolution of digital signal processors. In: 2019 6th IEEE History of Electrotechnology Conference (HISTELCON), pp. 25–29. IEEE (2019)
6. Van Berkel, K., Heinle, F., Meuwissen, P.P., Moerman, K., Weiss, M.: Vector processing as an enabler for software-defined radio in handheld devices. EURASIP J. Adv. Signal Process. **2005**, 1–13 (2005)
7. Damjancevic, S.A., Matus, E., Utyansky, D., van der Wolf, P., Fettweis, G.P.: Channel estimation for advanced 5G/6G use cases on a vector digital signal processor. IEEE Open J. Circ. Syst. **2**, 265–277 (2021)
8. Razilov, V., Matúš, E., Fettweis, G.: Communications signal processing using RISC-V vector extension. In: 2022 International Wireless Communications and Mobile Computing (IWCMC), pp. 690–695. IEEE (2022)
9. Mundichipparakkal, J., Bamakhrama, M.A., Jordans, R.: Fast and portable vector dsp simulation through automatic vectorization. In: Proceedings of the 21st International Workshop on Software and Compilers for Embedded Systems, pp. 47–53 (2018)
10. VanHattum, A., Nigam, R., Lee, V.T., Bornholt, J., Sampson, A.: Vectorization for digital signal processors via equality saturation. In: Proceedings of the 26th ACM International Conference on Architectural Support for Programming Languages and Operating Systems, pp. 874–886 (2021)
11. Hu, Y., Zhang, X., Wang, S., Liang, W., Li, K.C.: Research on global register allocation for code containing array-unit dual-usage register names. Concurr. Comput. Pract. Exp. **35**(19), e7519 (2023)
12. Marcolla, C., Sucasas, V., Manzano, M., Bassoli, R., Fitzek, F.H., Aaraj, N.: Survey on fully homomorphic encryption, theory, and applications. Proc. IEEE **110**(10), 1572–1609 (2022)
13. Kumar, S.A.: Enhancing the scope for automated code generation and parallelism by optimizing loops through loop unrolling. In: 2020 Fourth International Conference on Inventive Systems and Control (ICISC), pp. 790–795. IEEE (2020)

14. Cai, J., Liang, W., Li, X., Li, K., Gui, Z., Khan, M.K.: GTXchain: a secure IoT smart blockchain architecture based on graph neural network. IEEE Internet Things J. **10**(24), 21502–21514 (2023)
15. Rocha, R.C., et al.: Vectorization-aware loop unrolling with seed forwarding. In: Proceedings of the 29th International Conference on Compiler Construction, pp. 1–13 (2020)
16. Yang, C., Yang, X., Xue, J.: Improving the performance of GCC by exploiting IA-64 architectural features. In: Asia-Pacific Conference on Advances in Computer Systems Architecture, pp. 236–251. Springer (2005)
17. Stephenson, M., Amarasinghe, S.: Predicting unroll factors using supervised classification. In: International Symposium on Code Generation and Optimization, pp. 123–134. IEEE (2005)
18. Monsifrot, A., Bodin, F., Quiniou, R.: A machine learning approach to automatic production of compiler heuristics. In: Artificial Intelligence: Methodology, Systems, and Applications: 10th International Conference, AIMSA 2002 Varna, Bulgaria, 4–6 September 2002 Proceedings 10, pp. 41–50. Springer (2002)
19. Wang, D., Zhao, R., Gao, W., Li, Y.: Loop unrolling method based on random decision forest. Comput. Eng. Des. **39**(1), 199–204 (2018)
20. Wenlong, L., Li, L., Zhizhong, T.: Loop unrolling optimization for software pipelining. J. Beijing Univ. Aeronaut. Astronaut. **30**(11), 1111–1115 (2004)
21. Liu, X., Ding, L., Li, Y., Chen, G., Du, J.: Research of register pressure aware loop unrolling optimizations for compiler. In: MATEC Web of Conferences, vol. 228, p. 03008. EDP Sciences (2018)
22. Li, G., Hu, Y., Qiu, Y., Huang, W.: Investigation on the optimization for storage space in register-spilling. In: International Conference on Collaborative Computing: Networking, Applications and Worksharing, pp. 627–633. Springer (2016)
23. Hu, Y., Cheng, A., Tang, Z., et al.: LUAEMA: a loop unrolling approach extending memory accessing for vector very-long-instruction-word digital signal processor with multiple register files. Electronics **13**(8), 1425 (2024)

A Maximizing Duty-Cycle Network Lifetime Cooperative Routing Algorithm in a Smart Community Scenario

Ji Zhang[1]($\boxtimes$), Shi-ming He[2], Zhi Yan[1], and Dan Chen[1]

[1] Software School, Changsha Social Work College, Changsha 410004, Hunan Province, People's Republic of China
11942001@qq.com

[2] School of Science and Technology, Changsha University of Science and Technology, Changsha 410114, Hunan Province, People's Republic of China

Abstract. This paper proposes a Maximizing Duty-Cycle network lifetime (MDCLCR) Cooperative Routing algorithm to address the issues of short network lifetime and high maintenance costs in wireless sensor networks (WSNs) within smart communities, which are caused by high-density deployment and heterogeneous energy constraints. By integrating cooperative communication and duty-cycle techniques, the MDCLCR algorithm dynamically optimizes routing paths based on the Dijkstra framework. It combines cooperative node selection strategies and adaptive transmission mode selection strategies to jointly perceive channel states (attenuation due to building blockage), initial node energy (differences in micro-battery capacity), and dynamic residual energy, thereby achieving balanced energy consumption and alleviating hotspot problems. Experiments show that in a simulated smart community with a dense 50-node network, compared to the flow-augmenting cooperative routing algorithm (FACR), the MDCLCR algorithm extends the network lifetime by 30% to 14%. Although cooperative transmission increases average energy consumption by 16% compared to the classic cooperative algorithm (CAN), it extends the maintenance-free period of devices and reduces the frequency of community manual inspections.

Keywords: Smart community · Duty-cycle network · Cooperative Routing · Energy balance · Network lifetime

1 Introduction

Wireless Sensor Networks (WSNs) serve as the core carrier of the "perception layer" in smart communities, undertaking key functions such as environmental monitoring (temperature, humidity, air quality), intelligent security (intrusion detection, video surveillance), energy management (smart meters, lighting control), and elderly health care (wearable devices). These sensor nodes are typically powered by micro-batteries and face two major energy challenges: (1) After large-scale deployment in communities, the

W. Liang et al. (Eds.): SecureComm 2025, LNICST 690, pp. 116–133, 2026.
https://doi.org/10.1007/978-3-032-23456-8_7

cost of recovering nodes for charging or battery replacement is exorbitantly high, especially for nodes embedded in walls, underground pipelines, or high-altitude equipment; (2) In certain sensitive scenarios (e.g., emergency call systems in the homes of the elderly living alone, gas leak detection nodes), devices are required to be continuously online and cannot afford frequent maintenance interruptions. Therefore, optimizing energy utilization efficiency to extend network lifetime has become a critical issue in the construction of smart community IoT.

Current wireless communication [1, 2] in community sensor nodes predominantly employs the Single Input and Single Output (SISO) mode, which has significant drawbacks: severe channel attenuation in dense building environments leads to high data retransmission rates; high-resolution devices such as security cameras experience a surge in single-hop transmission energy consumption, accelerating node failure. To address these issues, cooperative communication technology has been introduced into community-level WSNs—by sharing the antennas and computing power of neighboring nodes (such as streetlight controllers, elevator sensors, and smart meters), a virtual multi-antenna array is constructed to utilize spatial diversity gains and reduce transmission power. For example, an alarm signal from a household gas sensor can be cooperatively transmitted to the community management center with the help of a hallway smoke detector, avoiding false negatives due to signal blockage by walls.

Cooperative routing [3–5], as a cross-layer optimization solution between the physical layer and the network layer, needs to address the unique complex requirements of smart communities [6, 7]: when planning multi-hop paths from terminal nodes (such as parking space sensors) to community cloud gateways, it is necessary to dynamically select cooperative nodes (such as nearby activated trash bin fullness monitoring devices) and optimize power allocation to balance real-time performance (e.g., emergency event reporting) and energy consumption. However, most existing studies have not fully considered the cooperative mechanism of another important energy-saving technology in smart communities—duty-cycle technology [8, 9]. Duty-cycle technology reduces idle energy consumption by scheduling periodic node sleep (e.g., turning off the wireless module of a green space humidity sensor at night), but if its sleep cycle is out of sync with the cooperative communication window, it may lead to critical data transmission failures (e.g., some cooperative nodes are in sleep mode during a sudden fire at night). Conversely, reducing sleep time to ensure cooperative availability will weaken the energy-saving effect of duty-cycle.

Duty-cycle networks can be broadly divided into two main types: random duty-cycle networks [10] and coordinated duty-cycle networks [11]. In random duty-cycle networks, sensor nodes wake up and sleep independently in a random manner. Random duty-cycle wireless sensor networks are simple in design and incur no additional overhead. In coordinated duty-cycle networks, sensor nodes communicate with each other to coordinate the switching of node working states. Although coordinated duty-cycle networks require additional communication overhead to schedule the activity/sleep of each node, this control often makes the switching of node working states more rational and the network performance more optimal. Some researchers have also proposed solutions for using cooperative communication technology in duty-cycle networks. For example, one study [12] utilized the ability of cooperative communication to expand the communication range, allowing more nodes to provide services to the gateway node, thereby effectively alleviating the "black hole" problem around the gateway node. The authors demonstrated through experiments that using cooperative communication technology in duty-cycle networks can provide higher-frequency data collection services. Another study [13] proposed a new scheduling cooperative protocol based on the characteristics of cooperative communication, enabling nodes in duty-cycle networks to wake up on demand. A third study [14] designed a reservation-based wake-up scheme to synchronize the wake-up and data transmission of cooperative nodes, thereby expanding the transmission range.

To fully leverage the energy-saving advantages of duty-cycle network technology and cooperative communication technology, we have constructed delay and energy models based on the network scenario and proposed a cooperative Routing algorithm for maximizing duty-cycle network lifetime (MDCLCR). Due to the special nature of nodes in duty-cycle networks, which are mostly in sleep mode, the MDCLCR algorithm abandons the recruitment method in cooperative node selection strategies and instead uses the preceding node as the cooperative node. Based on the unequal energy consumption of nodes in different states (standby, transmission, reception, sleep) in duty-cycle networks, an adaptive transmission mode selection strategy is formulated. When selecting routing paths, the MDCLCR algorithm jointly solves the cooperative node selection strategy and transmission costs. Experiments show that in a 50-node dense duty-cycle network, the network lifetime of the MDCLCR algorithm is extended by 30% to 14% compared to the FACR [15] algorithm; the average energy consumption is increased by 16% compared to the CAN [16] algorithm.

The remainder of this paper is organized as follows: Sect. 2 describes the research motivation; Sect. 3 constructs the system model; Sect. 4 details the cooperative node selection strategy, transmission mode selection strategy, and MDCLCR algorithm; Sect. 5 analyzes and discusses the algorithm's performance through simulation experiments; and finally, the conclusion of the paper is presented.

2 Research Motivation

We illustrate the research motivation through an example. As shown in Fig. 1, the network consists of N sensor nodes, and data information needs to be transmitted from the source node s to the destination node d. The nodes in the network are awakened at different times. The nodes s, a, c, d, and r have relatively sufficient energy, while node b has only 5% of its initial energy remaining. The network lifetime is defined as the time length from the start of the network to the depletion of the first energy-exhausted node. That is, when the residual energy R_i of any node i is 0, the network is considered dead.

Under normal circumstances, duty-cycle networks use traditional wireless routing algorithms (such as AODV, DSR, etc.) to find the best path. For example, $\{s \rightarrow a \rightarrow b \rightarrow c \rightarrow d\}$ is the traditional routing path with the minimum energy transmission power. However, node b may exhaust its energy after transmitting only a small amount of data packets, causing the network to fail. The flow-augmenting routing algorithm (FA), which incorporates residual energy indicators, would choose the path $\{s \rightarrow a \rightarrow$

r → c → d} to transmit data packets. The FA algorithm can effectively avoid energy-deficient transmission nodes, but the data packet transmission consumes more energy. We consider applying cooperative communication technology to duty-cycle networks to save energy and extend network lifetime by leveraging two advantages. First, cooperative transmission saves energy compared to traditional transmission, reducing single-hop energy consumption. Second, cooperative communication can expand the communication radius, bypassing energy-deficient nodes to complete data transmission. However, the sleep mechanism of duty-cycle networks makes the application of cooperative communication technology more challenging, and we must design strategies based on the characteristics of the network.

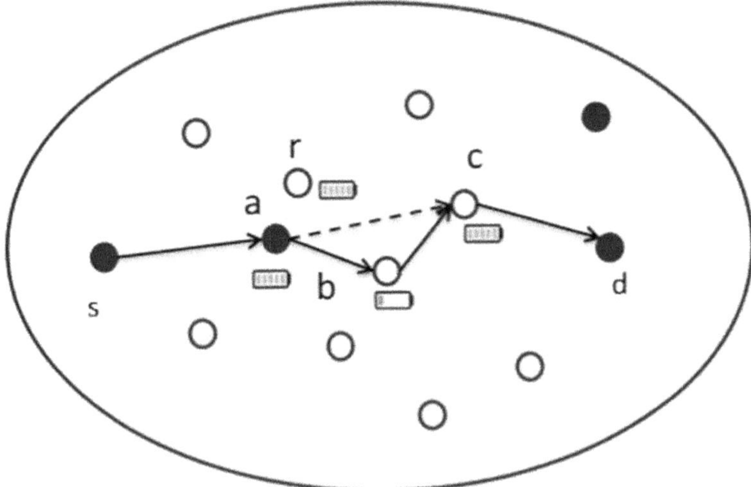

Fig. 1. Duty-Cycle Network Model

First, duty-cycle networks differ from general networks in that nodes have sleep, standby, transmission, and reception states. When designing algorithms, we need to establish energy models based on different node states, and the power allocation strategy for cooperative transmission should also consider this characteristic of duty-cycle networks.

Second, the recruitment of cooperative nodes is limited by the wake-up mechanism. As shown in Fig. 1, node a can expand its transmission radius through cooperative transmission to bypass node b and directly transmit data to node c. In a general network, node a could choose node r as a cooperative partner, with the transmission path being {s → (a,r), (a,r) → c, c → d}. However, in this network, the activity cycle of node r is not consistent with that of node a. Node a would need to transmit data to node r separately, resulting in the transmission path {s → a, a → r, (a,r) → c, c → d}. Clearly, this cooperative transmission incurs excessive additional overhead, failing to leverage the broadcast advantage of wireless communication. Moreover, the extra intermediate node would also increase network latency.

Third, in duty-cycle networks, nodes spend most of their time in sleep mode, and cooperative transmission requires waking up sleeping nodes as cooperative partners. Cooperative communication would impose additional energy costs on the cooperative partners and increase the duty cycle of the cooperative nodes. In many cases, direct transmission mode might actually require less energy. Therefore, our algorithm needs to select the transmission mode based on the energy cost.

Fourth, if the main path node's energy is insufficient during data transmission, cooperative transmission cannot fundamentally solve the problem of premature network death. For example, in Fig. 1, if the data transmission passes through the energy-deficient intermediate node b, no matter how excellent the cooperative node is chosen, it cannot fundamentally alleviate the problem of premature network death.

Therefore, this paper proposes a cooperative Routing algorithm for maximizing duty-cycle network lifetime to address the above four issues, namely: (1) How to establish an energy model for cooperative transmission in duty-cycle networks and design a power allocation scheme; (2) How to select cooperative nodes; (3) How to determine the transmission mode; (4) How to determine the optimal transmission path.

3   System Model

3.1   Network Model

The duty-cycle network model we define is shown in Fig. 1, consisting of N wireless sensor nodes. All nodes in the network are single-radio frequency, have the same transmission power, and operate in an Orthogonal Frequency Division Multiplexing (OFDM) system under Rayleigh flat slow-fading channels. Each node is equipped with an omnidirectional antenna and works in half-duplex mode. Each node has a unique ID, and during network initialization, each node can obtain information about neighboring nodes through control message exchanges. Each node has limited energy, with E_i and R_i representing the initial and residual energy of node i, respectively. If two nodes can communicate directly, their link is considered to exist, and they are mutual neighbors. Any hop in the network can communicate through cooperative transmission, and each transmitting node can adjust its transmission power P_t. When the signal-to-noise ratio received by the receiving node is greater than the threshold value SNR_{min}, the receiving node can correctly decode the data.

Each sensor node has two states: working state and sleep state. Nodes in the working state can transmit and receive data, and when there is no data communication, working nodes enter an idle listening state; nodes in the sleep state will turn off all functions except the timing function. In duty-cycle networks, nodes can wake up at any sleep moment to transmit data, but they can only receive data from neighboring nodes while in the working state.

3.2   Delay Model

In general wireless sensor networks, the transmission nodes are always in the working state and can send or receive data at any time. The data transmission delay between nodes is usually at the millisecond level and can be neglected [17]. However, in duty-cycle wireless sensor networks, the receiving nodes cannot transmit data when they are in sleep mode, and the transmitting nodes must wait for the receiving nodes to wake up before sending data. This waiting time can be several seconds or even longer. Therefore, this paper defines the time from when a transmitting node receives data intended for its neighboring node to when the neighboring node wakes up and enters the working state as the sleep delay.

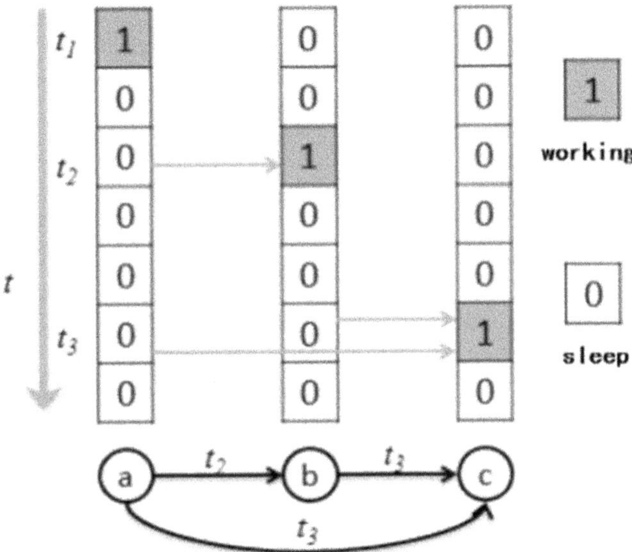

Fig. 2. Duty-Cycle Network Delay Model

In duty-cycle wireless sensor networks, sleep delay is much larger than the delay caused by normal node-to-node communication. Therefore, when considering end-to-end delay, only sleep delay is considered, and communication delay is neglected. As shown in Fig. 2, assuming T is the maximum lifetime of the entire sensor network, T is divided into several time units of equal length τ, called time slots. Suppose the characters "1" and "0" represent the working and sleep states of the nodes, respectively. At time t_1, node a has data to transmit to node b. However, node b is in sleep mode at t_1 and cannot receive data. Node a has to wait for 2 time slots until t_2 when node b wakes up to transmit the data. Similarly, at t_3, nodes a and b cooperative transmit data to node c. Therefore, the total sleep delay for a data packet sent from node a, cooperative transmitted by node b, and received by node c is 5τ.

3.3 Energy Model

In general communication transmission, there are four different transmission modes available for each hop (as shown in Fig. 3). However, in duty-cycle networks, receiving nodes cannot receive data when they are in sleep mode. This makes it very difficult to use VSIMO and VMIMO transmission modes in duty-cycle networks. Therefore, we only use SISO and VSIMO modes in duty-cycle networks.

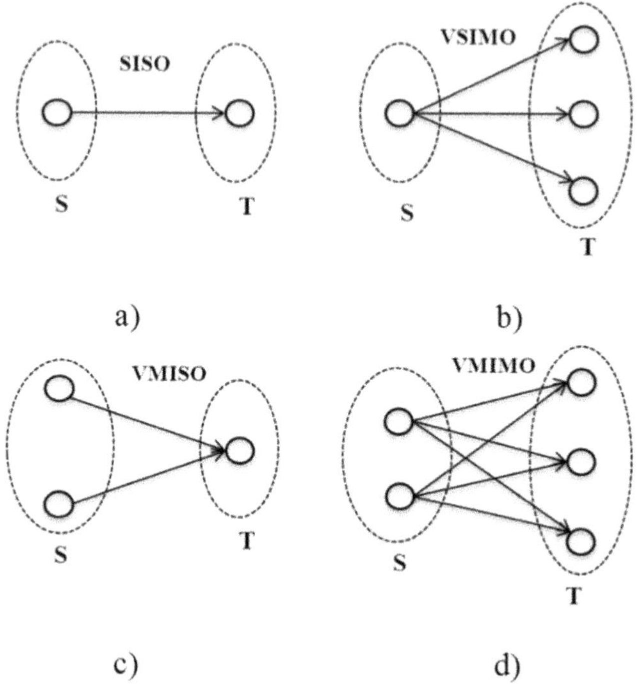

Fig. 3. Link Transmission Modes: a) VSISO b) VSIMO c) VMISO d) VMIMO

Direct Transmission

As shown in Fig. 3(a), in the direct transmission mode, the transmitting node is s, and the receiving node is t. If the signal-to-noise ratio (SNR) at the receiving end is greater than the threshold value, the receiving node can correctly decode the data. Therefore, the transmission power of the transmitting node in direct transmission mode can be expressed as:

$$\widehat{P_s} = \frac{SNR_{min}P_\eta}{E(\alpha^2)}d_{st}^\lambda \tag{1}$$

In the formula, s represents the transmitting node, t is the receiving node, $\widehat{P_s}$ is the minimum transmission power at the transmitter, P_η is the variance of the noise at the receiver, SNR_{min} is the minimum signal-to-noise ratio (SNR) threshold, a is a complex Gaussian random variable with zero mean and unit variance, d_{st} is the distance between node s and node t, and λ is the power attenuation index. The energy consumption of the transmitting node consists of two parts: circuit energy consumption and transmission energy consumption [18]. The energy expenditure of the transmitting node per unit transmission time can be expressed as:

$$E_{s\_tx} = R_d\left(a_{11} + \widehat{P_s}\right) = R_d\left(a_{11} + a_2 d_{st}^{\lambda}\right) \tag{2}$$

In the equation, R_d represents the transmission rate, a_{11} denotes the circuit energy consumption for data encoding, modulation, and demodulation, while a_2 is the energy consumption efficiency parameter of the transmit operational amplifier. In duty-cycle networks, nodes spend most of their time in sleep mode, consuming significantly less energy than when they are in the working state. Therefore, we define the energy expenditure of a transmitting node over a period t using Eq. (3):

$$Et_{s\_tx} = t\left(pE_{s\_tx} + (1 - p)E_{sleep}\right) \tag{3}$$

Here, E_{sleep} represents the energy expenditure per unit time of a sensor node in sleep mode. p denotes the average probability that the sensor node is in the working state during time t, which is also known as the duty cycle. $(1 - p)$ represents the average probability that the sensor node is in sleep mode. Similarly, we can use Eq. (4) to represent the energy expenditure of the receiving node per unit time, and Eq. (5) to represent the energy expenditure of the receiving node over a period t:

$$E_{t\_rx} = R_d a_{12} \tag{4}$$

$$Et_{t\_rx} = t\left(pE_{st\_rx} + (1 - p)E_{sleep}\right) \tag{5}$$

Here, a_{12} represents the energy consumed by the sensor node to receive 1 bit of data.

VMISO Transmission

As shown in Fig. 3(b), in the VMISO transmission mode, the transmitting node set $S = \{s_1, s_2 \ldots s_n\}$ (where n > 1), and the receiving node is t. The n transmitting nodes can synchronously send information to the destination node t. Each node in the transmitting node set S can adjust its transmission power according to demand. The power allocation scheme we use is the classic minimum power allocation method, which can be expressed as:

$$\text{Min} \sum_{i}^{n} |\omega_i|^2 \tag{6}$$

$$\text{s.t. } 0 \leq |\omega_i| \leq \sqrt{P_{\gamma i}} \tag{7}$$

$$\frac{\sum_{i=1}^{n} |\omega_i|^2 d_{it}^{-\lambda}}{P_\eta} E\left(\alpha^2\right) \geq SNR_{min} \tag{8}$$

Here, $|\omega_i|^2$ represents the transmission power of node s_i, $P_{\gamma i}$ is the rated power of node s_i, and d_{it} is the distance between node s_i and node t. The first set of constraints defines the rated power limitation, as shown in Eq. (7); the second set of constraints defines the

SNR threshold limitation, as shown in Eq. (8). Combining the objective function and the constraints, the optimal power allocation for node s_i can be obtained as:

$$\widehat{P_{si}} = |\omega_i|^2 = \frac{d_{it}^{-\lambda}\text{SNR}_{min}P_\eta}{\left(\sum_{j=1}^{n} d_{jt}^{-\lambda}\right)^2 E(\alpha^2)} \tag{9}$$

The total transmission power of the transmitting node set S can be expressed as:

$$\widehat{P_S} = \sum_{i}^{n} |\omega_i|^2 = \frac{\text{SNR}_{min}P_\eta}{\sum_{i=1}^{n} d_{it}^{-\lambda} E(\alpha^2)} \tag{10}$$

The energy expenditure of the transmitting node S_1 per unit transmission time can be expressed as:

$$E_{s_1\_tx} = R_d\left(a_{11} + |\omega_i|^2\right) = R_d\left(a_{11} + a_2\frac{d_{it}^{-\lambda}}{\left(\sum_{j=1}^{n} d_{jt}^{-\lambda}\right)^2}\right) \tag{11}$$

In the VMISO transmission mode, the energy expenditure of the receiving node is the same as that of the receiving node in the direct transmission mode. We can use Eq. (4) to represent the energy expenditure of the receiving node per unit time, and Eq. (5) to represent the energy expenditure of the receiving node over a period t. Additionally, in the duty-cycle network, some nodes do not participate in data transmission and reception during time t. These nodes are in a listening state, and their energy expenditure over time t is:

$$Et_{t\_rx} = t\left(pE_{\text{idle}} + (1-p)E_{\text{sleep}}\right) \tag{12}$$

where E_{idle} is the energy expenditure per unit time of a sensor node in idle mode.

4 Algorithm Details

4.1 Cooperative Node Selection Strategy

In general wireless sensor networks, the neighboring nodes of the transmitting node are all in the working state, and the transmitting node can select the best cooperative partner from the neighboring nodes according to routing needs. In energy-efficient cooperative routing, the transmitting node can choose the neighboring node with the best channel state as the cooperative node; in routing algorithms aimed at maximizing network lifetime, the selection of cooperative nodes needs to take into account channel state, battery capacity, and other factors.

However, in duty-cycle networks, neighboring nodes periodically switch between working and sleep states, which limits the advantage of wireless broadcasting. Therefore, the cooperative node selection strategy in general wireless sensor networks has certain limitations. As shown in Fig. 4, data is transmitted along the path a $\rightarrow$ b $\rightarrow$ c. In the transmission from b to c, the working cycles of neighboring nodes r and c are not consistent. When node c receives the data, node r is in sleep mode. If node r is recruited as the cooperative node, node b needs to transmit data to node r separately, which not only consumes additional energy from node b but also increases the sleep delay of the b → c transmission. Therefore, the cooperative node selection strategy adopted by this algorithm abandons the selection of neighboring nodes and instead uses the preceding node in the original transmission path. That is, node b can choose its preceding node a as the cooperative node for data transmission.

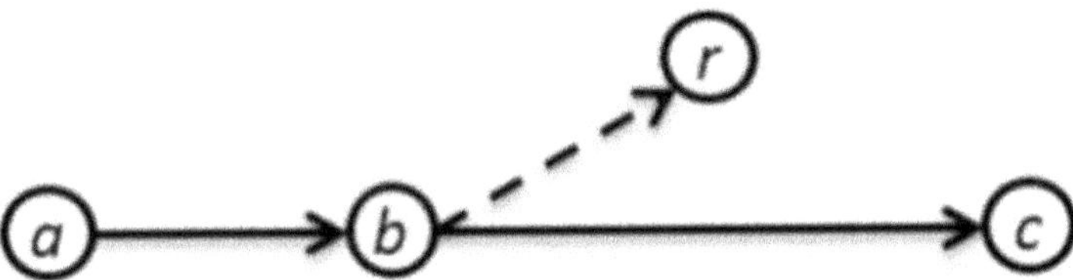

Fig. 4. Data Transmission Diagram

4.2 Transmission Mode Selection Strategy

Taking Fig. 4 as an example, according to the energy model defined in the previous section, we can determine the total energy expenditure of the direct transmission link b → c as:

$$El(b, c) = E_{b\_tx} + E_{c\_rx} \tag{13}$$

The energy expenditure of the VMISO transmission mode {a,b} → c can be expressed as:

$$El(a\&b, c) = E_{a\_tx} + E_{b\_tx} + E_{c\_rx} = R_d\left(a_{11} + |\omega_a|^2\right) + R_d\left(a_{11} + |\omega_b|^2\right) + R_d a_{12} \tag{14}$$

The algorithm in this paper aims to maximize network lifetime. Data transmission should preferentially select paths with lower energy consumption and avoid nodes with insufficient residual energy. Therefore, when designing the optimal link cost function, it is necessary to balance the energy consumption of data transmission, initial node energy, and residual energy. Referring to the FA algorithm, we have redefined the link cost function for measurement. The direct transmission link cost is defined as:

$$L(b, c) = \frac{R_b}{E_b} E_{b\_tx} + \frac{R_c}{E_c} E_{c\_rx} \tag{15}$$

where R_b represents the residual energy of node b, and E_b represents the initial energy of node b. Similarly, the VMISO transmission mode link cost is defined as:

$$L(a\&b, c) = \frac{R_a}{E_a} E_{a\_tx} + \frac{R_b}{E_b} E_{b\_tx} + \frac{R_c}{E_c} E_{c\_rx} \tag{16}$$

If the link cost of VMISO transmission L(a&b,c) is less than that of direct transmission L(b,c), VMISO transmission is selected; otherwise, direct transmission is chosen.

$$M(b, c) = \min(L(b, c), L(a\&b, c)) \tag{17}$$

4.3 MDCLCR Algorithm

STEP 1: Initialization. Create two data tables, OPEN and CLOSE, to store node information. Each table contains four fields: {NODEID, DIS_S, PARENT, ISCR}. NODEID represents the node name, DIS_S represents the distance (link cost) from the node to the source node S, PARENT represents the preceding node for data transmission to this node, and ISCR indicates whether cooperative transmission mode is used to reach this node. The source node S{S, 0, inf, inf} is added to the CLOSE table. Other nodes are added to the OPEN table. If node n is a neighboring node of the source node S, set the four fields of n to {n, L(S, n), S, 0}; if node m is not a neighboring node of the source node S, set the four fields of m to {m, ∞, inf, inf}.

Table 1. MDCLCR Algorithm

```
 1: while (OPEN!=NULL)
 2:   Find the node p in the OPEN table with the minimum DIS_S value
 3:   Move node p from the OPEN table to the CLOSE table
 4:   if (p=destination node D) break;
 5:   else{
 6:     Traverse the neighbor node set  Q of node p  Q (q∈Q){
 7:     Calculate the link costs： L(p,q) L(p.PARENT&p,q) and M(p,q)
          using equations(15， 16， 17)
 8:       if (q.DIS_S > p.DIS_S +M(p,q)){
 9:         if (M(p,q) = L(p,q))
10:           Update the entry for q in CLOSE  {q,p.DIS_S + M(p,q),p,0}.
11:         If ((p,q) = L(p.PARENT&p,q))
12:           Update the entry for q in CLOSE  {q,p.DIS_S + M(p,q),p,1}.
13:       endif
14:     endelse
15: endwhile
```

STEP 2: Node Selection. Find the node p with the smallest DIS_S value in the OPEN table, i.e., the node closest to the source node S. Move node p from the OPEN table to the CLOSE table.

STEP 3: Neighbor Node Traversal. Traverse the neighboring node set Q (where q ∈ Q) of node p in the OPEN table. Calculate the link costs ($L(p, q)$ $L(p.\text{PARENT}\&p, q)$ and $M(p, q)$) using the formulas from the previous section. If $q.\text{DIS\_S} > p.\text{DIS\_S} + M(p, q)$ update the entry q in the OPEN table. If $M(p, q) = L(p, q)$, the direct transmission mode is selected, and the entry q is set to $\{q, p.\text{DIS}\_\text{S} + M(p, q), p, 0\}$. Conversely, the VMISO transmission mode is selected, and the entry q is set to $\{q, p.\text{DIS}\_\text{S} + M(p, q), p, 1\}$.

STEP 4: Iteration. Repeat steps 2 and 3 until the OPEN table is empty or the destination node is moved from the OPEN table to the CLOSE table.

5 Simulation Experiments

5.1 Experimental Settings

We conducted simulation experiments in Matlab (R2010a) to illustrate the properties of the proposed algorithm. The experimental machine was equipped with an Intel Core i5-4590 processor and 2GB of memory. The proposed MDCLCR algorithm was compared with two types of routing algorithms.

The first type includes traditional communication-based routing algorithms, namely the Minimum Total Energy (MTE) and Flow Augmenting (FA) algorithms. The MTE algorithm aims to minimize energy expenditure, while the FA algorithm aims to maximize network lifetime.

The second type includes VMISO-based cooperative routing algorithms, namely the Classic Cooperative Algorithm (CAN) and the Flow Augmenting Cooperative Routing (FACR) algorithm. The CAN algorithm optimizes for minimum energy expenditure, while the FACR algorithm aims to maximize network lifetime.

The experimental scenario involved randomly distributing N nodes within a 200 m × 200 m area, with source node s and destination node d transmitting a fixed amount of data per unit time. If any node in the network exhausts its energy, the network is considered dead. The power loss factor α_{it}^2 between nodes i and t is inversely proportional to the square of the distance between nodes i and t. The maximum communication radius between nodes is 60 m, and each node can dynamically adjust its transmission power. The energy expenditure parameters were set according to literature [19], with detailed settings shown in Table 2. To comprehensively evaluate the MDCLCR algorithm, we compared the network lifetime, delay, and total energy consumption of the algorithms in networks with different densities and duty cycles.

Table 2. Experimental Parameter Table

Parameter Name	Parameter Value
Area	200 m*200 m
Initial Energy Eb	250j
a11	0.000000937(0.937uj/bit)
a12	0.000000787(0.787uj/bit)
a2	0.0000000172(0.0172uj/bit)
Esleep	0.00003(30uj/s)
Eidle	0.022(22mj/s)

5.2 Performance Analysis

Node Density vs. Network Lifetime

In a fixed-size area (200 × 200), we randomly distributed 30, 40, 50, 60, 70 and 80 nodes and compared the network lifetimes of the MTE, FA, CAN, FACR, and MDCLCR algorithms. To ensure fairness, the coordinates of the source and destination nodes were kept the same across different density networks. Figure 5 shows the node distribution in networks with different densities, where the red circles represent the destination and source nodes.

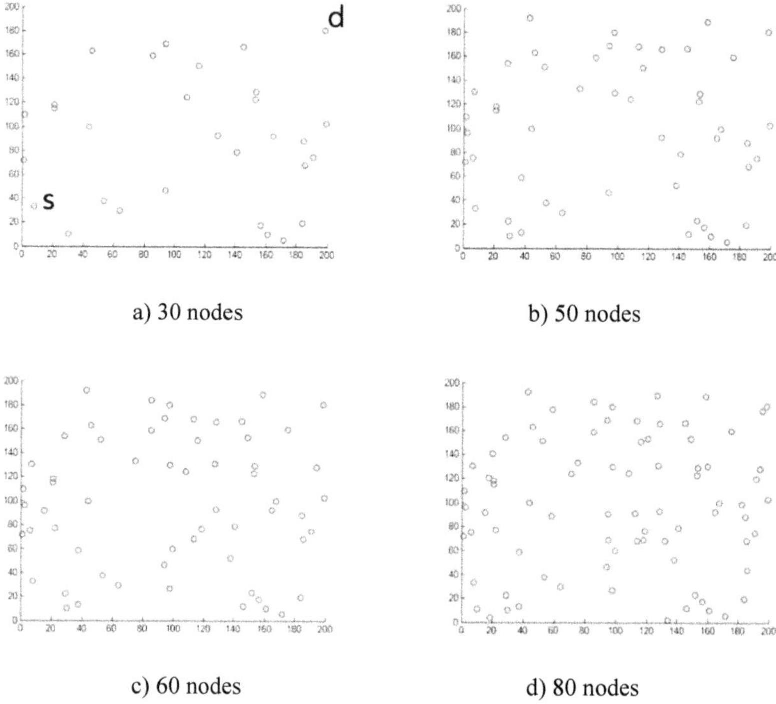

a) 30 nodes   b) 50 nodes

c) 60 nodes   d) 80 nodes

Fig. 5. Node Distribution in Networks with Different Densities

Figure 6 presents the network lifetime comparison in networks with different node densities, with the duty cycle set to 20%. The vertical axis represents the network lifetime, and the horizontal axis represents the node density, i.e., the number of nodes randomly distributed in the fixed area. As the network density increases, more nodes are available to assist in data transmission from node s to node d, resulting in an overall upward trend in network lifetime. When the number of nodes increased from 60 to 80, the change in node density did not alter the transmission paths for the MTE and CAN algorithms, so their network lifetimes remained unchanged. At low node densities (e.g., 30 nodes), the choice of transmission paths is relatively limited, and cooperative transmission can expand the transmission radius, resulting in better performance of the MDCLCR algorithm. At high node densities (e.g., 80 nodes), in our experimental scenario with relatively low data flow, more energy is consumed in the idle state, leading to a shorter network lifetime. However, regardless of the density, the MDCLCR algorithm consistently outperformed the other algorithms in terms of network lifetime. As the node density increased, the network lifetime of the MDCLCR algorithm was extended by 232%, 31%, 42%, 32%, 28%, and 23%; compared to the FA algorithm, the network lifetime was extended by 97%, 15%, 19%, 14%, 13%, and 8.5% compared to the FACR algorithm.

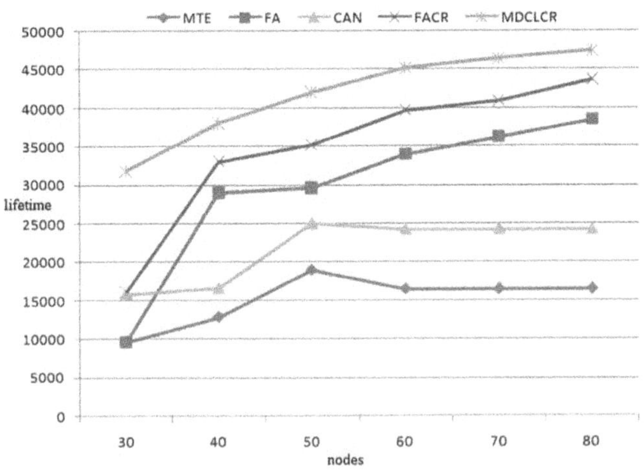

Fig. 6. Network Lifetime Comparison in Networks with Different Node Densities

Duty Cycle vs. Network Lifetime

In a fixed-size area (200 × 200), we randomly distributed 50 nodes and compared the network lifetimes of the MTE, FA, CAN, FACR, and MDCLCR algorithms under different duty cycles. Figure 7 presents the experimental results, with the vertical axis representing the network lifetime and the horizontal axis representing the duty cycle, i.e., the ratio of time spent in the working state. The experimental results show that as the duty cycle increases, the network lifetime decreases for all algorithms. This is because in low duty cycle networks, nodes spend more time in sleep mode, fully leveraging the energy-saving advantages of duty-cycle technology. Regardless of the duty cycle, the MDCLCR algorithm consistently outperformed the other algorithms in terms of network lifetime. As the duty cycle increased, the network lifetime of the MDCLCR algorithm was extended by 194% to 88% compared to the MTE algorithm; by 66% to 31% compared to the FA algorithm; by 109% to 49% compared to the CAN algorithm; and by 30% to 14% compared to the FACR algorithm.

Duty Cycle vs. Network Lifetime

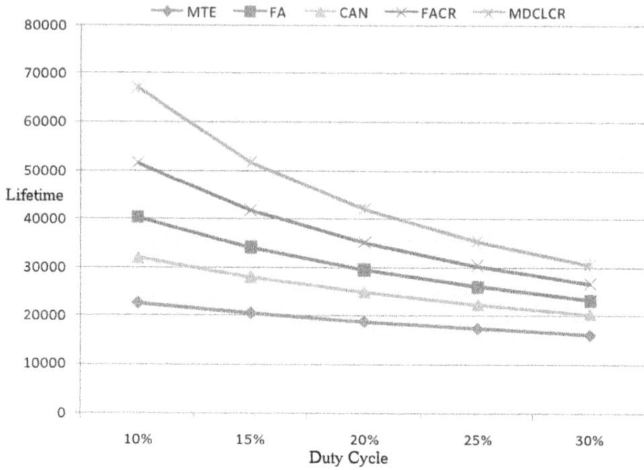

Fig. 7. Network Lifetime Comparison in Networks with Different Duty Cycles (50 Nodes)

Duty Cycle vs. Network Delay

In a fixed-size area (200 × 200), we randomly distributed 50 nodes and compared the network delays of the FA, CAN, FACR, and MDCLCR algorithms under different duty cycles. Figure 8 presents the comparison of network delays under different duty cycles, with the vertical axis representing the network delay and the horizontal axis representing the duty cycle, i.e., the ratio of time spent in the working state. The lower the duty cycle, the longer the nodes spend in sleep mode, resulting in longer network delays. The experimental results show that the delays of the FA, FACR, and MDCLCR algorithms are similar and all are better than that of the CAN algorithm.

Duty Cycle vs. Network Delay

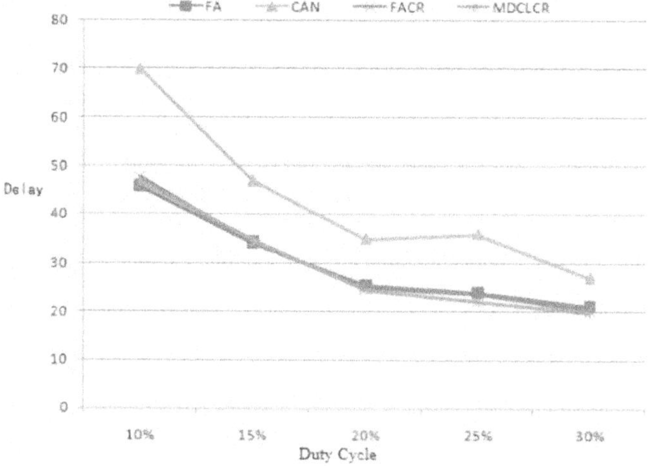

Fig. 8. Network Delay Comparison in Networks with Different Duty Cycles (50 Nodes)

Average Energy Consumption

In a fixed-size area (200 × 200), we randomly distributed 50 nodes and compared the average energy consumption of the algorithms in a network with a 10% duty cycle. Figure 9 shows the average energy consumption of data flows, with the vertical axis representing the average energy consumption, i.e., the average energy consumption of data flow transmission over 1000 time slots; the horizontal axis represents time. The lines of different algorithms have different lengths because the network lifetimes vary when using different algorithms. The average energy consumption of the MTE and CAN algorithms is a straight line because the routing paths determined by these two algorithms are fixed and do not change over time. In contrast, the FA, FACR, and MDCLCR algorithms incorporate residual node energy into the path selection criteria. As time progresses and node residual energy changes, the routing paths also change. When selecting routing paths to avoid nodes with insufficient residual energy, overall transmission energy consumption may increase. The CAN algorithm had the lowest average energy consumption (0.172J), while the MTE algorithm had the shortest network lifetime (22770 time slots). The lowest average energy consumption of the MDCLCR algorithm was 0.172J, and the highest was 0.226J, which is 116.2% of the CAN algorithm's average energy consumption.

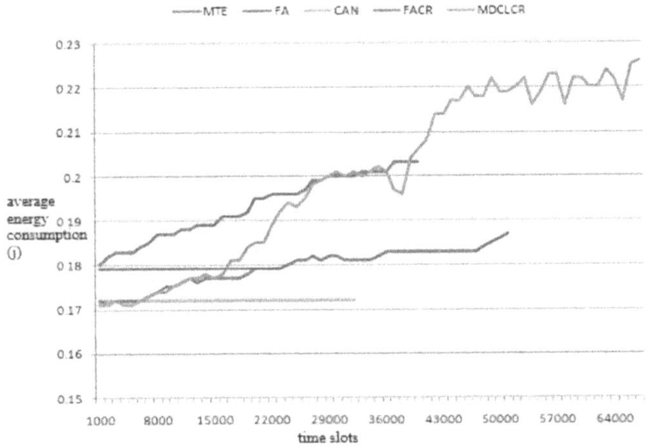

Fig. 9. Average Energy Consumption of Data Flows (50 Nodes, Duty Cycle 10%)

6 Conclusion

This paper addresses the energy constraint issues of wireless sensor networks in complex smart community perception scenarios. Based on the characteristics of cooperative duty-cycle networks that periodically switch between working and sleep states, we developed cooperative node selection and transmission mode selection strategies. By integrating the heterogeneous energy distribution characteristics of densely deployed nodes in smart communities (such as security cameras and environmental sensors) into the Dijkstra algorithm framework, we proposed a Cooperative Routing algorithm for maximizing duty-cycle network lifetime (MDCLCR). The MDCLCR algorithm jointly perceives channel states (attenuation due to building blockage), device initial energy (differences in micro-battery capacity), and dynamic residual energy to determine routing paths, balancing energy consumption among nodes and effectively alleviating "hotspot" issues. Experiments show that in a simulated smart community with a dense 50-node network, the network lifetime of the MDCLCR algorithm is extended by 30% to 14% compared to the FACR algorithm. Although cooperative transmission increases average energy consumption by 16% compared to the CAN algorithm, it extends the maintenance-free period of devices and reduces the frequency of community manual inspections. This verifies the technical advantages of our method in enabling long-term autonomous operation of embedded nodes in smart communities. Future research will further optimize the dynamic duty-cycle and cooperative mechanism by combining the spatiotemporal characteristics of community-level energy harvesting devices such as solar streetlights and elevator kinetic energy recovery.

References

1. Li, F., Yang, H., Gao, X., Han, H.: Towards IoT-based sustainable digital communities. Intell. Converged Netw. **3**(2), 190–203 (2022)
2. Eriyadi, M., Supangkat, S.H., Hidayat, F.: Sensing architecture in smart city: a review paper. In: 2023 10th International Conference on ICT for Smart Society (ICISS), Bandung, Indonesia (2023)
3. Zhang, J., Zhang, Q.: Cooperative routing in multi-source multi-destination multi-hop wireless networks. In: Proceedings of IEEE the 27th Conference on Computer Communications, INFOCOM 2008. Phoenix: IEEE Press, pp. 2369–2377 (2008)
4. Zhang, J., Zhang, D., Xie, K., et al.: A VMIMO-based cooperative routing algorithm for maximizing network lifetime. China Commun. **14**(4), 20–34 (2017)
5. Zhang, J., Zhang, D., Xie, K., et al.: A cluster cooperative routing algorithm based on evolutionary game. Acta Electron. Sin. **44**(9), 2158–2163 (2016)
6. Immanuvel Arokia James, K., Manjula, P., Mohana, M., Arthi, S.: A review on energy efficient cooperative routing algorithm for wireless sensor networks. In: 2022 International Conference on Automation, Computing and Renewable Systems (ICACRS)
7. Tripathi, N., Sharma, K.K.: Analytical review of different routing methodologies and clustering techniques in WSN/WCSN leading to Cooperative Communication. In: 2020 IEEE International Conference for Innovation in Technology (INOCON)
8. Guler, N., Hazem, Z.B.: EADS-EHWSNs: efficient energy-based adaptive duty cycle scheme for energy-harvested wireless sensor networks. In: 2023 IEEE 8th International Conference on Engineering Technologies and Applied Sciences (ICETAS)
9. Wang, X., Zhou, W., Hawbani, A., Liu, P., Zhao, L., Alsamhi, S.H.: A dynamic opportunistic routing protocol for asynchronous duty-cycled WSNs. IEEE Trans. Sustain. Comput. **8**(3), 314–327 (2023)
10. Wang, X.Y., Dokania, R.K., Apsel, A.: PCO-based synchronization for cognitive duty-cycled impulse radio sensor networks. IEEE Sens. J. **11**(3), 555–564 (2011)
11. Wang, Q., Zhang, T.: Bottleneck zone analysis in energy-constrained wireless sensor networks. IEEE Commun. Lett. **13**(6), 423–425 (2009)

12. Jung, J.W., Wang, W., Ingram, M.A.: Cooperative transmission range extension for duty cycle-limited wireless sensor networks. In: Proceedings of International Conference on Wireless Communication, Vehicular Technology, Information Theory and Aerospace & Electronic Systems Technology. Chennai: IEEE Press, pp. 1–5 (2011)
13. Lin, J., Ingram, M.A.: SCT-MAC: a scheduling duty cycle MAC protocol for cooperative wireless sensor network. In: Proceedings of IEEE International Conference on Communications. Ottawa: IEEE Press, pp. 345–349 (2012)
14. Lin, J., Ingram, M.A.: OSC-MAC: duty cycle scheduling and cooperation in multi-hop wireless sensor networks. In: Proceedings of Wireless Communications and Networking Conference. Shanghai: IEEE Press, pp. 866–871 (2013)
15. Khandani, A.E., Abounadi, J., Modiano, E.: Cooperative routing in static wireless networks. IEEE Trans. Commun. **55**(11), 2185–2192 (2007)
16. Pandana, C., Siriwongpairat, W.P., Himsoon, T., et al.: Distributed cooperative routing algorithms for maximizing network lifetime. In: Proceedings of Wireless Communications and Networking Conference 2006. Las Vegas: IEEE Press, pp. 451–456 (2006)
17. Jackson, A.w., Sterbenz, J.P.G., Condell, M.N., et al.: Active network monitoring and control: the SENCOMM architecture and implementation. In: Proceedings of Active Networks Conference and Exposition. San Francisco: IEEE Press, pp. 379–393 (2002)
18. Bhardwaj, M., Garnett, T., Chandrakasan, A.P.: Upper bounds on the lifetime of sensor networks. In: Proceedings of IEEE International Conference on Communications. Helsinki: IEEE Press, pp. 785–790 (2001)
19. Rout, R.R., Ghosh, S.K.: Enhancement of lifetime using duty cycle and network coding in wireless sensor networks. IEEE Trans. Wireless Commun. **12**(2), 656–667 (2013)

A Safety-Optimized Two-Stage Algorithm for Rural School Bus Route Planning with Heterogeneous Fleets and Mixed Loads

Cezhe Zhang[1(✉)] and Qiongbing Zhang[2]

[1] Hunan University of Science and Technology, Xiangtan, Hunan 411100, China
zczdgwd@gmail.com
[2] School of Information Science and Technology, Guangdong University of Foreign Studies, No. 2 Baiyun North Avenue, Guangzhou, China
mrtly2@whu.edu.cn

Abstract. This paper addresses the challenges of rural school bus routing, particularly in scenarios involving heterogeneous fleets and mixed student populations from different schools sharing buses. To tackle these challenges while ensuring both efficiency and safety, a specialized school bus route planning algorithm for heterogeneous fleets and mixed loads (HFML-SBRP) is proposed. First, a mixed-integer programming model is formulated to minimize total operational expenses, including fleet size, fixed costs, and distance-based costs, while adhering to safety constraints. A two-phase solution method is then introduced. The first phase employs a heuristic algorithm that integrates a greedy approach and variable neighborhood search with three neighborhood operators to generate feasible and safe bus routes. In the second phase, an adjusting clock algorithm refines these routes to further reduce the number of buses while maintaining safe and reliable transportation. Experimental results demonstrate that HFML-SBRP effectively minimizes costs, reduces fleet size, and enhances computational efficiency, all while prioritizing student safety.

Keywords: Rural school bus routing · Mixed loading · Heterogeneous fleet · Two-stage heuristic algorithm

1 Introduction

The School Bus Routing Problem (SBRP) [1] is a classic combinatorial optimization problem, with the Rural School Bus Routing Problem (RSBRP) focusing on rural areas. RSBRP aims to design optimal bus routes for safe, efficient, and cost-effective student transportation, reducing costs, resource waste, and carbon emissions. Figure 1 illustrates is a RSBRP scenario.

However, RSBRP is more challenging than SBRP due to rural-urban differences, leading to limited research in rural contexts. For example, Paul et al. [2]

W. Liang et al. (Eds.): SecureComm 2025, LNICST 690, pp. 134–151, 2026.
https://doi.org/10.1007/978-3-032-23456-8_8

addressed urban student transportation using metaheuristic and exact methods, while Aberathne et al. [3] developed a model to reduce school-related traffic congestion in Kandy, Sri Lanka. In contrast, rural research remains scarce. Existing algorithms often result in detours or buses passing schools to pick up students, as shown in Figs. 2 and 3, making SBRP methods unsuitable for RSBRP.

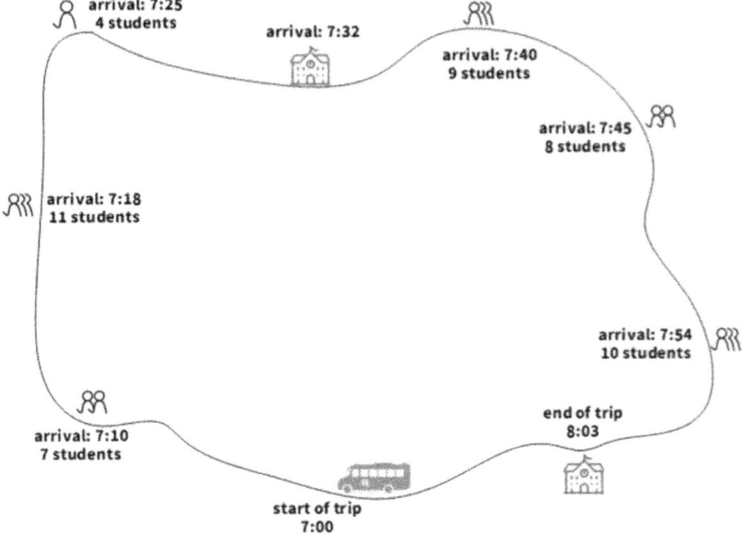

Fig. 1. A scenario of RSBRP.

In Fig. 2, the bus route passes student location 6, collects students at locations 4 and 5, and later returns to pick up student 6 before reaching school 7, creating backtracking. This inefficiency increases costs and should be avoided.

In rural areas, school buses typically start from drivers' or students' homes, often operating below capacity due to low population density. Mixed-load strategies and heterogeneous fleets are more effective in RSBRP, as single-load approaches can lead to resource waste. Bodin and Berman [4] first described mixed-load strategies in rural settings, while Chen et al. [5] highlighted the inefficiency of single-load approaches in sparse areas. Feng et al. [6] proposed a bilevel programming model for mixed-load optimization, and Sciortino et al. [7] introduced a heuristic for heterogeneous fleets. This paper integrates heterogeneous fleets and mixed loading for superior results.

We propose a heuristic algorithm, HFML-SBRP, to address RSBRP using real-world data from a rural Chinese school district with 3,194 students and 41 schools. The algorithm avoids detours and buses bypassing schools, aiming to optimize routes under mixed-fleet and mixed-load constraints. Key findings include:

- 33%–38% cost reduction compared to other mixed-load strategies, exceeding 50% against single-load strategies.

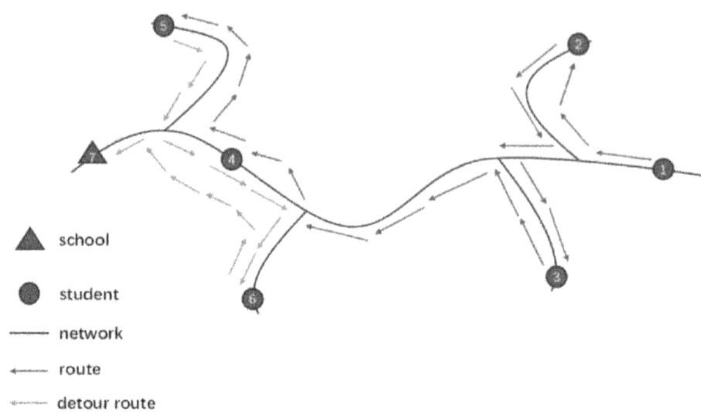

Fig. 2. A example of redundant route.

- 38%–40% fleet size reduction compared to other mixed-load strategies, surpassing 50% against single-load strategies.
- Threefold faster execution compared to single-load algorithms.

The paper is structured as follows: Sect. 2 reviews related work, Sect. 3 presents the mathematical model, Sect. 4 details the heuristic algorithm, Sect. 5 discusses experimental results, and Sect. 6 concludes.

2   Related Work

The School Bus Routing Problem (SBRP), first introduced by Newton and Thomas [1], centers on the efficient design of bus routes for student transportation. This design process must adhere to various limitations, including bus capacity, operating expenses, travel time, and other logistical factors. Park and Kim [8] suggest that the SBRP can be broken down into five sub-problems:

1. Data Preparation [9]: This sub-problem offers the data required for the other School Bus Routing Problem (SBRP) sub-problems. It includes four primary data categories: students, schools, vehicles, and the origin-destination (OD) matrix.
2. Bus Stop Selection [10]: This sub-problem seeks to determine determines bus stops and assigns students, with rural students typically picked up at home and urban students at designated stops.
3. Bus route generation: It is, in essence, a simplified version of the School Bus Routing Problem SBRP. Route generation can be categorized by load type into single load [11,12] and mixed load [6]. We can also be categorized based on fleet type into homogeneous fleets [13,14] and heterogeneous fleets [15,16].
4. School bell time adjustment [17,18]: Adjusts school timings to maximize route efficiency and reduce the number of buses needed.
5. Route scheduling [19]: By planning and coordinating the timing of each route, schools can maximize the coverage area serviced by each bus and minimize the total number of buses required to transport students.

SBRP sub-problems are often addressed independently despite their inherent interdependence. Mathematical models for SBRP, typically formulated using Mixed Integer Programming (MIP) or Nonlinear Mixed Integer Programming (NLMIP), vary by configuration. Early work by Schittekat et al. [20] and Bektas and Elmastas [21] focused on single-school scenarios, with Schittekat et al. conceptualizing schools as bus stops and Bektas and Elmastas incorporating constraints like vehicle capacity and maximum ride times. Sun et al. [22] introduced robust optimization to handle uncertainties in routing, minimizing worst-case costs while considering delays and travel time disutility.

For large-scale SBRP, heuristic methods like genetic algorithms (GAs) are widely used due to their ability to handle complex, high-dimensional solution spaces. Veeravalli et al. [23] combined reinforcement learning with GAs for dynamic scheduling, leveraging real-time data from intelligent transportation systems (ITS) to adapt to changing conditions. Ghasemi et al. [24] developed a multi-objective model addressing gender separation, mixed-loading, and accommodations for students with disabilities, using a customized GA with penalty functions to enforce constraints. Their approach was validated on a real-world case study in Tehran, demonstrating practical applicability.

Neighborhood search algorithms are also effective for complex SBRP instances. Hou et al. [25] proposed a method based on the Pickup and Delivery Problem with Time Windows (PDPTW), combining a record-to-record travel method with neighborhood operators to reduce the number of buses required. Wang and Haghani [26] integrated column generation, simulated annealing, and greedy randomized adaptive search procedures to optimize routes under time window constraints. Miranda et al. [27] extended SBRP to multi-load scenarios, using iterated local search and variable neighborhood descent to handle large-scale instances. Shafahi et al. [28] integrated scheduling information into routing for single-load SBRP, employing a two-step heuristic combining insertion heuristics, simulated annealing, and tabu search to improve solution quality.

Based on these research findings, a mixed load configuration surpasses a single load configuration in rural scenarios, and a heterogeneous fleet exhibits greater advantages compared to a homogeneous fleet. In this work, we present our approach, which employs a mixed load configuration and a heterogeneous fleet, specifically designed to address real-world scenarios.

3   Mathematical Model and Symbol Definitions

Considering the offered fleet of buses and locations of students and schools, this paper addresses the creation of bus routes for a school bus system accommodating students from multiple schools, resulting in a heterogeneous fleet and mixed student populations on each bus. This section formalizes a mixed-integer programming (MIP) model for our algorithm. Key constraints comprise student commute times, vehicle capacity, and fleet size. Our objective function minimizes the costs of the school buses.

The proposed formulation relies on these assumptions:

- A student's residence is modeled as a single stop where the school bus both picks up and drops off the student for transport to their designated school.
- Students attending different schools may share the same bus.
- A heterogeneous fleet of vehicles, each with a potentially different passenger capacity, is available for use.
- Empty and loaded buses are assumed to travel at different speeds.
- Buses maintain a constant speed while traveling between any two locations.

Table 4 demonstrates the different parameters, sets and variables for the school bus stop location and routing problem with heterogeneous fleet and mixed load (Table 1).

Table 1. Notation for the parameters, sets and variables.

Sets	
P	Set of students
S	Set of schools
A	Set of edges
B	Set of buses
K	Set of school bus types
N	Set of P and S

Parameters	
n_p	Number of the set P
n_s	Number of the set S
s_i	School of $i \in P$
b^k	Bus of type k
Q^b	Capacity for the bus $b \in B$
a_b	Cost per traveled unit distance d_{ij} for $b \in B$
f_b	Fixed cost of the bus
d_{ij}	Actual road network distance from node $i \in N$ to $j \in N$
v_{eb}	Speed of empty $b \in B$
v_{nb}	Speed of non-empty $b \in B$
t_{ijeb}	Average time for an empty bus $b \in B$ from node $i \in N$ to $j \in N$
t_{ijnb}	Average time for a non-empty bus $b \in B$ from node $i \in N$ to $j \in N$
e_s	The earliest start time of school
l_s	The latest end time of school
W_{max}	Maximum allowable variation in school working times

Decision Variables	
y_{ib}	0–1 variables determining if node $i \in N$ is assigned to vehicle $b \in B$
x_{ijb}	0–1 variables determining if bus $b \in B$ traverses arc $(i, j) \in A$
γ_b	0–1 variables determining if bus $b \in B$ is set as the startup route
ω_{ib}	Non-negative variables representing the load of bus $b \in B$ when leaving node $i \in N$
ξ_{ib}	Non-negative variables representing the time when bus $b \in B$ arrived node $i \in N$

Each school s has an associated time window $[e_s, l_s]$, where e_s represents the earliest acceptable start time and l_s the latest acceptable end time. This hard time window constraint requires buses arriving before es to wait until e_s before continuing.

To optimize scheduling and potentially reduce the number of required school buses, a maximum allowable change in school working times, denoted as W_{max}, is set. This constraint ensures that any change in the school's working times, in the range between e_s and l_s, that does not exceed W_{max}, is considered feasible. This helps to prevent scheduling times that are either undesirable or unrealistic.

The objective of the algorithm presented in this paper is to minimize operational costs, which are composed of two elements: fixed costs and variable costs. The objective function can be expressed as follows:

$$\min \sum_{b \in B} \left(f_b + \sum_{(i,j) \in A} x_{ijb} a_b d_{ij} \right) \tag{1}$$

The remaining formulas are given as follows:

$$\text{s.t.:} \quad y_{ib} \leq \gamma_b \quad \forall i \in N, b \in B, \tag{2}$$

$$\sum_{(o,j) \in A} x_{ojb} = \gamma_b \quad \forall b \in B, \tag{3}$$

$$\sum_{(i,j) \in A} x_{ijb} = \sum_{(j,i) \in A} x_{jib} \quad \forall b \in B, \tag{4}$$

$$\sum_{(i,j) \in A} x_{ijb} = y_{jb} \quad \forall b \in B, \tag{5}$$

$$\sum_{(i,j) \in A} x_{ijb} = y_{ib} \quad \forall b \in B, \tag{6}$$

$$e_i \leq \xi_{ib} \leq l_i \quad \forall i \in H, b \in B, \tag{7}$$

$$(\xi_{ib} + t_{ijb}) x_{ijb} \leq \xi_{jb} \quad \forall (i,j) \in A, b \in B, \tag{8}$$

$$\omega_{ib} x_{ijb} \leq \omega_{jb} \quad \forall (i,j) \in A, b \in B, \tag{9}$$

$$y_{ib} \leq y_{s_i b} \quad \forall i \in P, s_i \in S, b \in B, \tag{10}$$

$$x, y, \gamma \in \{0, 1\}, \tag{11}$$

$$\xi, \omega \geq 0, \tag{12}$$

where o is the starting point of each route.

Constraint (2) ensures each student is assigned to a bus, guaranteeing every student has a designated bus. Equation (3) specifies that each route is serviced by exactly one bus. Equation (4) ensures consistency in the round-trip distance for each route. Equations (5) and (6) require every road section to be assigned to a bus. Constraints (7) and (8) impose temporal restrictions on the schedule.

Constraint (9) prevents bus capacity from being exceeded at any point. Constraint (10) ensures that if a student is assigned to a bus, the bus must also visit the student's assigned school. Finally, constraints (11) and (12) define the domains for the variables.

4   HFML-SBRP

The proposed problem combines two computationally intensive components: the school bus routing subproblem, akin to the NP-hard vehicle routing problem, and the school bus scheduling subproblem. Integrating these significantly increases complexity in terms of computational time and memory. To address this, a two-stage methodology is proposed.

In the first stage, a variable neighborhood search-based heuristic generates feasible routes, ensuring constraints like arrival time windows and bus capacity are met while minimizing total travel distance. The second stage optimizes and consolidates these routes with temporal adjustments for further improvements.

4.1   Initial Solution Generation

In numerous studies, the generation of initial solutions often fails to account for scenarios where routes pass by schools to pick up students, as illustrated in Fig. 3. In this figure, triangles represent schools, and circles represent student locations. This represents an undesirable situation, as intermediate stops during a school bus route are prohibited.

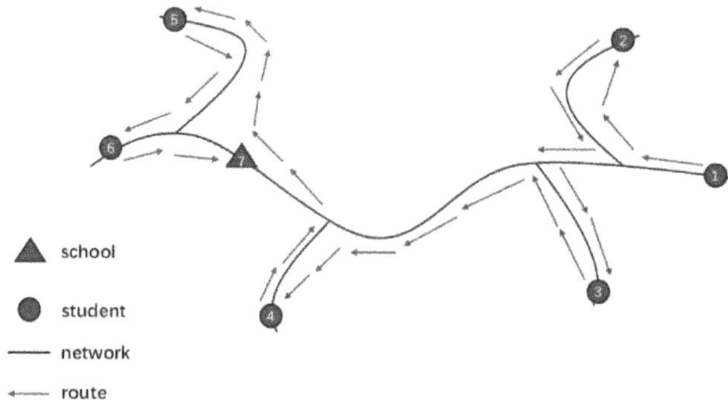

Fig. 3. An unreasonble route that by passes the school.

To address this, our algorithm uses Eq. 13 during initial solution generation to check if inserting a pickup point would cause the route to unnecessarily pass a school.

$$d_{ab} + d_{bc} = d_{ac} \tag{13}$$

where d_{ac}, d_{ab} and d_{bc} denote the distances between the points, with b represent school, a and c represent student locations. A route is considered to pass by the school if the sum of the distance from student a to the school and the distance from the school to student c is equal to the distance from student a to c.

The algorithm initializes with instance data D, including school and student locations, and distance matrices. A data structure SOL stores the solution. The set $totStopsRouted$ tracks assigned student points, excluding impractical ones: students within $2\,km$ of their school are excluded, while those beyond $16\,km$ are assumed to board directly at the school.

The algorithm iteratively inserts stops into routes while unassigned stops remain. For each school, all corresponding stops are attempted for insertion before moving to the next school. Once all schools are processed for the current route, a new route begins, enabling multi-load routes.

Algorithm 1. Constructive heuristic

1: $initialize(D, SOL)$
2: $totStopsRouted \leftarrow 0$
3: $ig\_stop(D)$
4: **while** $(totStopsRouted < |ST|)$ **do**
5:     **for** $(s = 1 \quad to \quad |S|)$ **do**
6:        $RES \leftarrow initializeRoute(v, SID_s, D)$
7:        $r, NS \leftarrow GetFromRes(RES)$
8:        **for** $(n = 1 \quad to \quad |NS|)$ **do**
9:          $ST_n \leftarrow listOfStops(NS_n)$
10:          $r \leftarrow insertSchool(r, SID_n)$
11:          $r \leftarrow insertStop(r, ST_n, SID_n)$
12:        **end for**
13:        $SOL \leftarrow UpdateInitialSolution(r)$
14:     **end for**
15:     $SOL \leftarrow ReassignVehicle(D, SOL)$
16:     $SOL \leftarrow RemoveSchool(D, SOL)$
17: **end while**

Stops farther from their schools are prioritized. For a selected stop, its school initializes a list of neighboring schools (NS), ordered by ascending distance, favoring stops near schools already on the route. The largest-capacity vehicle is assigned to the route r.

The algorithm iterates over NS, with ST_n representing stops for school NS_n. If school SID_n is not yet on the route, the algorithm attempts to insert its stops. If insertion fails, the next school is considered. Insertion uses a greedy approach, ensuring feasibility by checking for overloading, overtime, and avoiding scenarios like Fig. 3.

Once all stops are assigned, the algorithm allocates the most suitable vehicle to each route, minimizing unoccupied seats and reducing fixed costs. If a school is on a route but has no associated stops, it is removed. Algorithm 1 provides the pseudocode for this stage.

4.2   Stage 1: Variable Neighborhood Search

In the School Bus Routing Problem (SBRP), three common neighborhood operators are used in the local search set (LS) for the Variable Neighborhood Descent (VND) loop:

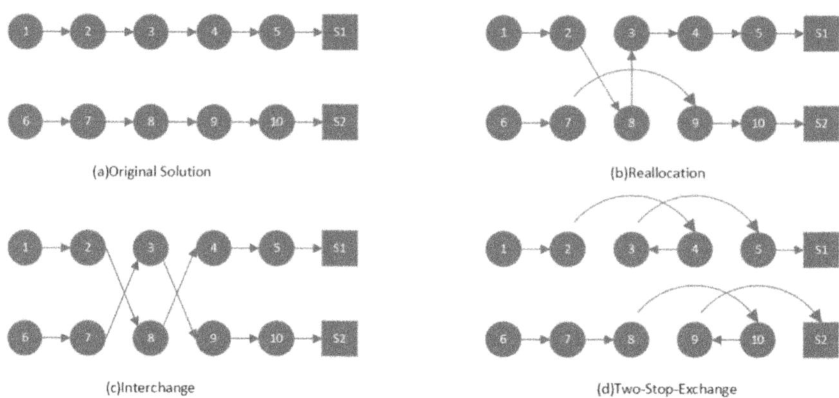

Fig. 4. The local search operators.

1. Reallocation: This operator, introduced by Osman [29], shifts stops between routes to improve the overall solution by redistributing stops.
2. Interchange: Also from Osman [29], this operator swaps stops between routes to optimize the routing plan.
3. Two-Stop-Exchange: Designed for SBRP, this operator transposes two stops within the same route to optimize stop arrangement.

Figure 4 illustrates these operators: (a) shows initial routes with stops (circles) and schools (squares); (b) depicts Reallocation, transferring a stop between routes; (c) shows Interchange, swapping stops between routes; and (d) demonstrates Two-Stop-Exchange, exchanging two stops within the same route.

Algorithm 2 serves as the main loop for local search iteration, designed to iteratively optimize the solution. Initially, ξ represents the solution from Algorithm 1, and s^* is set as the current optimal solution, starting with ξ.

In each iteration, $nPert$ counts consecutive iterations without improvement, while $maxPert$ defines the maximum allowed iterations without progress. When $nPert$ reaches $maxPert$, the loop terminates, indicating stagnation and halting further search.

The $improve$ flag checks if a new solution outperforms the current one. If so, s^* is updated, and $nPert$ is reset to 0. Otherwise, the current solution is retained. The loop continues until $nPert$ exceeds $maxPert$, signaling no further improvement. The optimal solution s^* is then returned for route merging in the second stage.

4.3   Stage 2: Route Merging and Time Optimization

Some heuristic algorithms terminate immediately after completing the neighborhood search, yet the resulting routes are often suboptimal. To address this limitation, we propose a second-stage route merging. This approach maximizes the reduction in the number of routes within an acceptable time window threshold, thereby enhancing resource utilization and lowering operational costs.

Algorithm 2. Main loop

1: $\xi \leftarrow ConstructiveHeuristics(D, SOL)$
2: $s^* \leftarrow bestsolution$
3: $s \leftarrow s^*$
4: $nPert \leftarrow 0$
5: **while** $(nPert < maxPert)$ **do**
6:      $improve \leftarrow true$
7:      **while** $(improve = true)$ **do**
8:          $s \leftarrow VND(s)$
9:          **if** $(s < s^*)$ **then**
10:              $s^* \leftarrow s$
11:              $nPert \leftarrow 0$
12:              $improve \leftarrow true$
13:          **else**
14:              $improve \leftarrow false$
15:          **end if**
16:      **end while**
17:      **if** $(nPert < maxPert)$ **then**
18:          $nPert \leftarrow nPert + 1$
19:      **end if**
20: **end while**
21: **return** s^*

This stage centers on combining the routes created in the initial stage to decrease the number of required school buses while remaining in specific temporal parameters. Each school is allocated a designated time window, $[e_s, l_s]$. The merging rule works as follows: when the initial route r_1 reaches a school, an evaluation is performed to determine whether work for the second route r_2 can be completed in the permissible time frame, W_{max}. If this proves feasible, these two routes are merged. This process then extends to include further routes, for instance r_3, to determine if they can be connected into the existing route structure without exceeding the maximum adjustment time, W_{max}. This route merging procedure is repeated iteratively until no further merges can be executed in the prescribed time constraints. A detailed description of this merging strategy is outlined in Algorithm 3.

Algorithm 3. Merge Routes

1: **Input:** s^*
2:     **for** $(r_1 = s_1^*\ \ to\ \ s^*)$ **do**
3:          $time \leftarrow RouteTime(r_1, r_2, v_{eb})$
4:         **if** $(time <= Wmax)$ **then**
5:              $r_1 \leftarrow r_1 + r_2$
6:     **end for**
7: **return:** s^*

It is essential to observe that the empty vehicle speed, v_{eb}, is utilized for this computation. This is due to the fact that, upon completion of work for route r_1, the bus is unoccupied by students prior to starting route r_2; accordingly, the travel time calculation relies on the empty vehicle speed. After the execution of all feasible merges, the loop terminates, and the final, optimized solution is returned.

5   Computational Results

In this section, we conducted experiments to compare the HFML-SBRP algorithm proposed in this paper with the single-load strategy [30] and the mixed-load strategy [27]. All heuristic algorithms were implemented in Python and tested on a Dell 3690 computer with an Intel i5 2.6 GHz six-core processor, 16 GB of RAM, and Windows 10 × 64. Spatial analysis of the results was performed using ArcGIS.

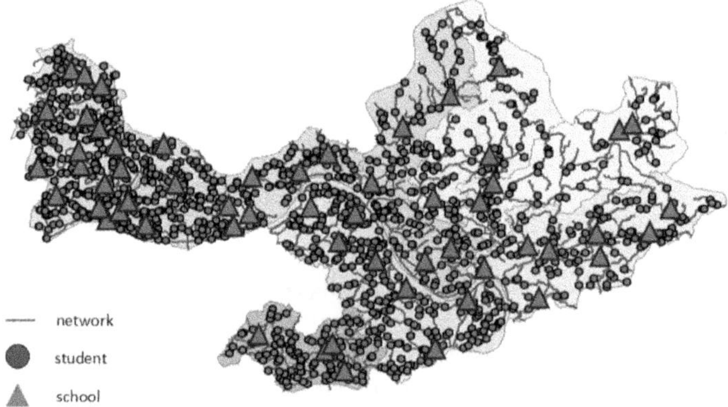

Fig. 5. Scenario data.

5.1 Experimental Setting and Data

The experimental area is located in a county in Hunan Province. Remote sensing images were obtained through open-source downloads, while road network data were commercially purchased. During preprocessing, duplicate and irrelevant road segments were removed, and missing or disconnected segments were completed. School and student location data, initially in textual address form, were converted to spatial coordinates using address matching and geocoding. All geographic data were projected into a unified coordinate system using ArcGIS. Figure 5 shows the experimental scene in ArcGIS.

Unlike most RSBRP studies that rely on pre-existing datasets and Euclidean distances, our experiment used actual road network distances calculated via the ArcGIS API. Three school bus types with capacities of 19, 36, and 56 passengers were utilized. The average speeds were set to 40 km/h for empty buses (v_{eb}) and 35 km/h for buses carrying passengers (v_{nb}). To ensure reliability, experiments were structured into four scenarios: $S1 : p = 1023, s = 11; S2 : p = 1765, s = 21; S3 : p = 2495, s = 31; S4 : p = 3194, s = 41$; where p represents the number of student pickup locations and s represents the number of schools.

5.2 Validation of the Convergence of the Algorithm

In this section, we verify the convergence rate of HFML-SBRP by comparing the objective function values generated at each iteration of HFML-SBRP with those of VRPTW [27].

For the four experimental groups, we calculated the mean objective function value per iteration, as shown in Fig. 6. The horizontal axis represents the iteration number, and the vertical axis represents the objective function value. The figure shows that HFML-SBRP converges at a rate similar to VRPTW in most scenarios. Notably, HFML-SBRP consistently achieves a lower objective function value than VRPTW, with the gap widening as the dataset size increases. This improvement stems from HFML-SBRP's additional optimization, which reduces unnecessary backtracking in routes, as illustrated in Fig. 2.

Additionally, the HFML-SBRP results in Fig. 6 reflect the state before the second stage of route combination. Since the second stage involves no iteration, no convergence check is needed. After route combination, a further reduction in the objective function value is expected, as discussed in the following subsection.

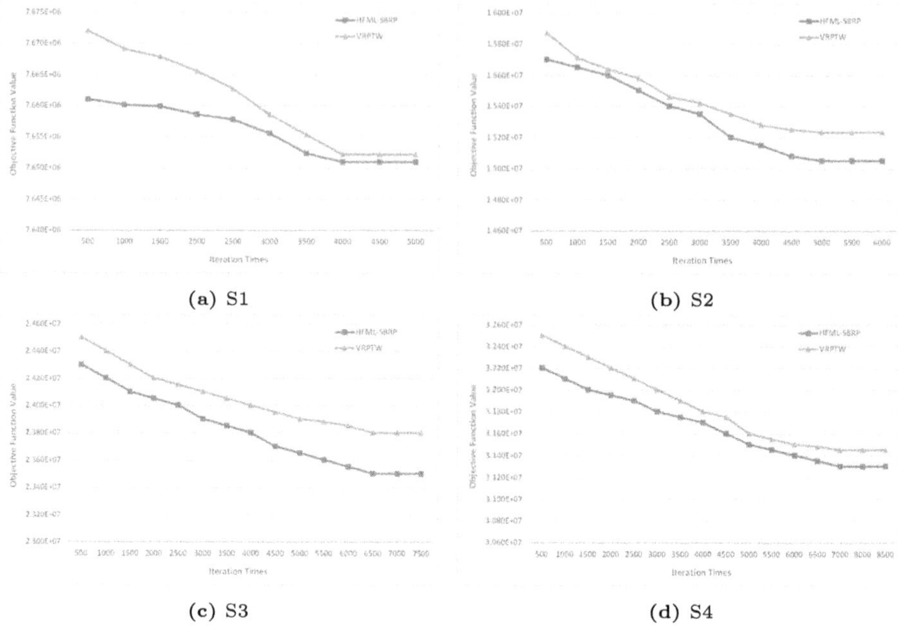

(a) S1

(b) S2

(c) S3

(d) S4

Fig. 6. Convergence Rates.

5.3   Results and Performance Analysis

This section presents a comparative analysis of the HFML-SBRP algorithm against the VRPTW algorithm and the PLRP-PS algorithm. The results displayed in Table 2 represent the average values derived from thirty trials for each algorithmic group. In the table, "Minimum distance" indicates the shortest route length in kilometers; "Total cost" corresponds to the total operational expenditure in tens of thousands of yuan; and "Execution time" signifies the algorithmic runtime in seconds.

Table 2. Analysis of performance indicators of experimental results.

Experiment	Algorithm	Min distance	Total cost	Number of routes	Execution time
S1	HFML-SBRP	9.37	510.12	26	3158
	VRPTW	3.55	765.22	40	4013
	PLRP-PS	5.30	1120.35	56	15177
S2	HFML-SBRP	10.99	995.24	54	5016
	VRPTW	3.55	1523.46	87	6367
	PLRP-PS	5.30	2280.44	114	16273
S3	HFML-SBRP	13.85	1490.37	83	7062
	VRPTW	3.55	2380.03	138	8470
	PLRP-PS	5.30	3440.67	172	18488
S4	HFML-SBRP	14.87	1940.49	108	8134
	VRPTW	3.55	3145.41	182	9196
	PLRP-PS	5.30	4460.86	223	24321

Table 2 shows that the HFML-SBRP algorithm outperforms the other two school bus routing algorithms. Compared to the VRPTW algorithm, HFML-SBRP achieved a 33% reduction in total cost and a 35% reduction in the number of school buses for scenario S1, with a 21% faster runtime. For S2, it reduced total cost by 34%, school buses by 38%, and runtime by 21%. In S3, it achieved a 37% cost reduction, a 40% reduction in school buses, and a 17% faster runtime. For S4, it demonstrated a 38% cost reduction, a 40% reduction in school buses, and a 12% faster runtime.

Compared to the PLRP-PS algorithm, HFML-SBRP achieved a 54% reduction in total cost and a 53% reduction in school buses for S1, with a 79% faster runtime. For S2, it reduced total cost by 56%, school buses by 52%, and runtime by 69%. In S3, it achieved a 56% cost reduction, a 52% reduction in school buses, and a 62% faster runtime. For S4, it resulted in a 56% cost reduction, a 52% reduction in school buses, and a 66% faster runtime. This superior performance is primarily due to the second stage of HFML-SBRP, which significantly reduces the number of school buses required.

This superior performance is primarily due to the second stage of the HFML-SBRP algorithm, which significantly reduces the number of school buses required. This effect becomes more pronounced as the dataset size increases. Additionally, the HFML-SBRP algorithm eliminates backtracking, as shown in Fig. 2. Table 4 highlights the occurrence of detours in the results of the three algorithms. Notably, our algorithm generates no detours, demonstrating its ability to avoid inefficient routing patterns and underscoring its practical effectiveness in producing logical and operationally feasible school bus routes.

Table 3. Routes and scheduled departure times.

Bus	Routes and departure times	Capacity
1	45(7:30)→78(7:41)→...→School1(7:58)→...→23(8:04)→...→School3(8:18)	19
2	21(7:30)→67(7:48)→...→School4(7:59)→...→88(8:10)→...→School7(8:25)	36
3	33(7:30)→55(7:43)→...→School6(8:00)→...→91(8:08)→...→School5(8:22)	36
4	12(7:30)→76(7:50)→...→School8(7:59)→...→89(8:09)→...→School7(8:19)	56
5	66(7:30)→28(7:38)→...→School12(7:58)→...→51(8:11)→...→School9(8:27)	19
6	43(7:30)→65(7:44)→...→School10(7:58)→...→98(8:07)→...→School11(8:16)	56
7	36(7:30)→7(7:46)→...→School14(8:00)→...→10(8:14)→...→School42(8:20)	19
8	4(7:30)→81(7:35)→...→School15(7:59)→...→15(8:06)→...→School11(8:26)	56
9	6(7:30)→9(7:40)→...→School16(8:00)→...→44(8:13)→...→School40(8:24)	19
10	56(7:30)→17(7:33)→...→School17(7:58)→...→1(8:05)→...→School50(8:28)	36

It is worth noting that the minimum driving distances for the VRPTW and PLRP-PS algorithms are 3.55 and 5.3 km, respectively. Such short distances are impractical, as they would likely lead to inefficient resource use. In contrast, the HFML-SBRP algorithm achieves a minimum driving distance exceeding 9 km, a far more realistic result. Table 3 shows the routes and scheduled departure times for 10 school buses, assuming a uniform departure time of 7:30 a.m.

Table 4. Detours in algorithm results.

Experiment	Number	VRPTW	PLRP-PS	HFML-SBRP
S1	Total routes	40	56	26
	Redundant route	9	11	0
S2	Total routes	87	114	54
	Redundant route	15	22	0
S3	Total routes	138	172	83
	Redundant route	34	46	0
S4	Total routes	182	223	108
	Redundant route	55	89	0

For example, School Bus 1 starts at the first student pickup location, proceeds through a sequence of stops, and arrives at the second pickup location. It continues to additional stops before reaching School 1, carrying students from both School 1 and School 2. Upon arrival at School 1, all School 1 students disembark, leaving only School 2 students on board. The bus then continues its route, serving only School 2 students en route to School 2, without picking up additional School 1 students. This approach avoids the problem illustrated in Fig. 3.

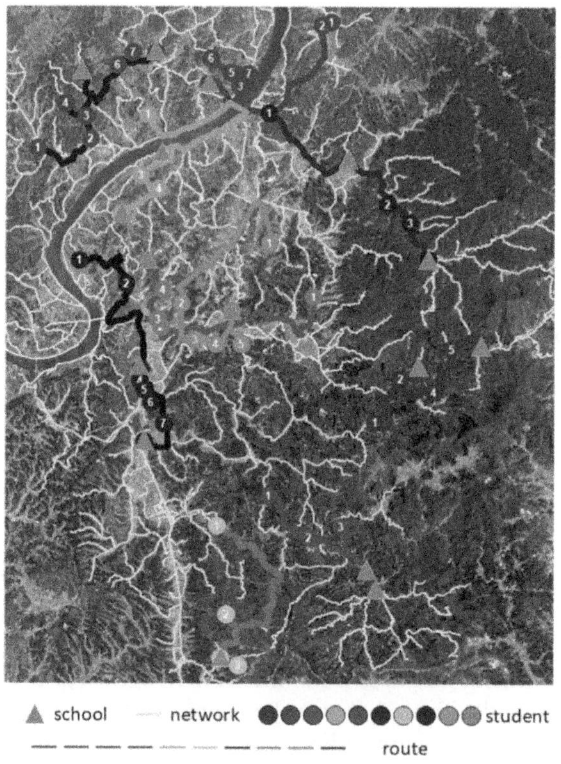

Fig. 7. Partial result of HFML-SBRP.

Analysis of school bus arrival times at the destination school shows that the HFML-SBRP algorithm adjusts school start times within the W_{max} range to enable route merging, further reducing overall costs. Figure 7 visualizes the HFML-SBRP algorithm in a real scenario, where red triangles represent schools, numbered dots indicate student pickup points and their service order, and colored curves denote different routes. The visualization confirms that HFML-SBRP avoids detours and the issue of buses passing schools to pick up students.

Compared to the VRPTW and PLRP-PS algorithms, HFML-SBRP outperforms in operating costs, the number of school buses required, and overall algorithm efficiency.

6   Conclusion

This paper proposes HFML-SBRP, a heuristic algorithm designed to solve the RSBRP with heterogeneous fleets and mixed loads. We provide detailed pseudo-code, outlining the algorithm's strategy, implementation, and results. HFML-SBRP's effectiveness was benchmarked against the VRPTW and PLRP-PS algorithms using real-world scenarios. The results demonstrate that HFML-SBRP outperforms these algorithms across multiple metrics, offering more efficient and cost-effective solutions for rural regions, particularly in developing countries.

Despite its advancements, the algorithm has limitations. Specifically, its runtime increases with larger datasets. Future research will focus on optimizing the algorithm from a software engineering perspective to address this issue. Additionally, given the dispersed nature of rural populations, we plan to explore integrating transfer points. This approach would use smaller vehicles to collect students from remote areas and transport them to central hubs, where larger vehicles would then take them to their designated schools.

References

1. Newton, R.M., Thomas, W.H.: Design of school bus routes by computer. Socioecon. Plann. Sci. **3**(1), 75–85 (1969)
2. Paul, O., Handl, J., López-Ibáñez, M.: Capacitated school bus routing problem with time windows, heterogeneous fleets and travel assistants. In: Proceedings of the Companion Conference on Genetic and Evolutionary Computation, pp. 2374–2377 (2023)
3. Aberathne, B., Nandalal, H., Satthyaprasad, I.M.S.: Application of school bus routing problem in GIS to organize school buses in Kandy city, Sri Lanka. J. Geospatial Surveying **3**, 2 (2023)
4. Bodin, L.D., Berman, L.: Routing and scheduling of school buses by computer. Transp. Sci. **13**(2), 113–129 (1979)
5. Chen, D.S., Kallsen, H.A., Snider, R.C.: School bus routing and scheduling: an expert system approach. Comput. Ind. Eng. **15**(1–4), 179–183 (1988)
6. Feng, R., Zhang, J., Wu, Y., et al.: School accessibility evaluation under mixed-load school bus routing problem strategies. Transp. Policy **131**, 75–86 (2023)

7. Sciortino, M., Lewis, R., Thompson, J.: A school bus routing heuristic algorithm allowing heterogeneous fleets and bus stop selection. SN Comput. Sci. **4**(1), 74 (2023)
8. Park, J., Kim, B.I.: The school bus routing problem: a review. Eur. J. Oper. Res. **202**(2), 311–319 (2010)
9. Kim, B.I., Jeong, S.: A comparison of algorithms for origin-destination matrix generation on real road networks and an approximation approach. Comput. Ind. Eng. **56**(1), 70–76 (2009)
10. Wang, F., Ye, M., Zhu, H., et al.: Optimization method for conventional bus stop placement and the bus line network based on the Voronoi diagram. Sustainability **14**(13), 7918 (2022)
11. Guo, X., Samaranayake, S.: Shareability network-based decomposition approach for solving large-scale single school routing problems. Transport. Res. Part C: Emerg. Technol. **140**, 103691 (2022)
12. Calvete, H.I., Galé, C.: The school bus routing problem with student choice: a bilevel approach and a simple and effective metaheuristic. Int. Trans. Oper. Res. **30**(2), 1092–1119 (2023)
13. Liu, Z., Gang, L., Yu, B., et al.: The routing problem for school buses considering accessibility and equity. Transp. Res. Part D: Transp. Environ. **107**, 103299 (2022)
14. Qian, L., Melachrinoudis, E.: An integrated neural combinatorial tabu search for optimizing school bus scheduling with bell time. Transport. Res. Part C: Emerg. Technol. **164**, 104662 (2024)
15. Shang, P., Yang, L., Zeng, Z., et al.: Solving school bus routing problem with mixed-load allowance for multiple schools. Comput. Ind. Eng. **151**, 106916 (2021)
16. Ansari, A., Farrokhvar, L., Kamali, B.: Integrated student-to-school assignment and school bus routing problem for special needs students. Transport. Res. Part E: Logist. Transport. Rev. **152**, 102416 (2021)
17. Miranda, D.M., de Camargo, R.S., Conceição, S.V., et al.: A metaheuristic for the rural school bus routing problem with bell adjustment. Expert Syst. Appl. **180**, 115086 (2021)
18. Vercraene, S., Lehuédé, F., Monteiro, T., et al.: The dial-a-ride problem with school bell time adjustment. Transp. Sci. **57**(1), 156–173 (2023)
19. Zeng, Z.L., Chopra, S., Smilowitz, K.: A bounded formulation for the school bus scheduling problem. Transp. Sci. **56**(5), 1148–1164 (2022)
20. Schittekat, P., Sevaux, M., Sorensen, K.: A mathematical formulation for a school bus routing problem. In: 2006 International Conference on Service Systems and Service Management. IEEE, vol. 2, pp. 1552–1557 (2006)
21. Bektaş, T., Elmastaş, S.: Solving school bus routing problems through integer programming. J. Oper. Res. Soc. **58**(12), 1599–1604 (2007)
22. Sun, S., Duan, Z., Xu, Q.: School bus routing problem in the stochastic and time-dependent transportation network. PLoS ONE **13**(8), e0202618 (2018)
23. Köksal Ahmed, E., Li, Z., Veeravalli, B.: Reinforcement learning-enabled genetic algorithm for school bus scheduling. J. Intell. Transport. Syst. **26**(3), 269–283 (2022)
24. Rashidi Komijan, A., Ghasemi, P., Khalili-Damghani, K., et al.: A new school bus routing problem considering gender separation, special students and mix loading: a genetic algorithm approach. J. Optim. Ind. Eng. **14**(2), 23–39 (2021)
25. Hou, Y.E., Dang, L., Dong, W., et al.: A metaheuristic algorithm for routing school buses with mixed load. IEEE Access **8**, 158293–158305 (2020)
26. Wang, Z., Haghani, A.: Column generation-based stochastic school bell time and bus scheduling optimization. Eur. J. Oper. Res. **286**(3), 1087–1102 (2020)

27. Miranda, D.M., de Camargo, R.S., Conceição, S.V., et al.: A multi-loading school bus routing problem. Expert Syst. Appl. **101**, 228–242 (2018)
28. Shafahi, A., Wang, Z., Haghani, A.: Speedroute: fast, efficient solutions for school bus routing problems. Transport. Res. Part B: Methodol. **117**, 473–493 (2018)
29. Osman, I.H.: MetaStrategy simulated annealing and tabu search algorithms for the vehicle routing problem. Ann. Oper. Res. **41**, 421–451 (1993)
30. Le Colleter, T., Dumez, D., Lehuédé, F., et al.: Small and large neighborhood search for the park-and-loop routing problem with parking selection. Eur. J. Oper. Res. **308**(3), 1233–1248 (2023)

An Energy-Efficient Scheduling Algorithm for Multiple Periodic DAGs in Safety-Critical Embedded Systems

Yuhong Chen and Jing Huang[(✉)]

School of Computer Science and Engineering, Hunan University of Science and
Technology, Taoyuan Road, Xiangtan 411201, Hunan, China
huangjing@hnust.edu.cn

Abstract. With the widespread adoption of embedded systems in industrial control, intelligent driving, and edge computing, their architectures
are increasingly evolving toward distributed and heterogeneous platforms.
In safety-critical applications, ensuring the secure and predictable execution of tasks on multiple processing units has become a key challenge.
Such tasks are typically modeled as Directed Acyclic Graphs (DAGs) to
accurately capture inter-task dependencies. To address these challenges,
this paper proposes MPDES, an energy-efficient scheduling algorithm for
multiple periodic DAGs in safety-critical embedded systems. MPDES
ensures deadline satisfaction while enhancing scheduling predictability,
resource isolation, and overall energy efficiency. The algorithm adopts a
two-phase scheduling strategy: (1) In the pre-allocation phase, tasks are
mapped to the fastest processors to guarantee timing constraints; (2) In
the energy-aware phase, idle time is exploited and processor frequency is
dynamically adjusted via DVFS technology to reduce energy consumption. This hierarchical mechanism not only lowers energy overhead but
also mitigates unpredictable behavior caused by scheduling anomalies.
Experimental results demonstrate that MPDES achieves both timing
compliance and energy efficiency in scenarios such as Fast Fourier Transform, Gaussian elimination, and randomly generated task sets. Moreover,
it provides a predictable and stable execution environment, showcasing
its practical value for safety-critical embedded systems.

Keywords: Distributed heterogeneous systems · Multiple periodic
DAGs · Safety-Critical · Embedded systems · Energy-efficient
scheduling · Dynamic Voltage and Frequency Scaling (DVFS)

1 Introduction

1.1 Motivation

With the widespread adoption of embedded systems in industrial control,
autonomous driving, and edge computing, task scheduling faces increasingly
stringent requirements for real-time performance and predictability [5,7,9]. In

© ICST Institute for Computer Sciences, Social Informatics and Telecommunications Engineering 2026
Published by Springer Nature Switzerland AG 2026. All Rights Reserved
W. Liang et al. (Eds.): SecureComm 2025, LNICST 690, pp. 152–171, 2026.
https://doi.org/10.1007/978-3-032-23456-8_9

particular, in safety-critical scenarios such as autonomous driving and medical devices, scheduling anomalies or task deadline misses can not only degrade system performance, but also trigger resource contention, task interference, and even lead to information leakage or functional failure [13,17]. Such complex tasks, characterized by temporal constraints and functional dependencies, are often modeled as Directed Acyclic Graphs (DAGs) to accurately capture the dependencies among subtasks [11]. Meanwhile, computing platforms are evolving toward heterogeneous and distributed architectures [23], and are being widely deployed from the edge to the cloud for task processing. In numerous battery-powered embedded applications (e.g., cardiac pacemakers, continuous glucose monitors), energy management is directly linked to system reliability and task sustainability, calling for more efficient multi-core task scheduling and dynamic energy control mechanisms.

To alleviate the energy pressure caused by high computational load, Dynamic Voltage and Frequency Scaling (DVFS) has been widely adopted. It reduces power consumption by dynamically adjusting the processor's voltage and frequency without violating timing constraints [15]. However, scheduling multiple periodic DAG applications on multi-core embedded systems is an NP-complete problem [20]. As task complexity grows and resources become increasingly constrained, both scheduling efficiency and feasibility face significant challenges. Although existing research has primarily focused on optimizing the scheduling of a single DAG, there remains a lack of effective mechanisms to achieve coordinated scheduling of multiple periodic DAGs in resource-competitive environments, ensuring both security and energy efficiency. Therefore, designing an efficient scheduling algorithm that simultaneously ensures security, deadline satisfaction, and energy optimization is of great theoretical significance and practical value for enhancing the reliability and energy efficiency of safety-critical embedded systems.

1.2 Our Contributions

This paper investigates the problem of collaboratively scheduling multiple independent periodic DAGs on heterogeneous distributed platforms. The objective is to minimize system energy consumption while ensuring task deadline satisfaction [6], and to enhance scheduling predictability and isolation under resource contention. The main contributions of this study are as follows:

1. We propose MPDES, an energy-efficient scheduling algorithm for safety-critical embedded systems. The algorithm ensures deadline satisfaction for multiple independent periodic DAGs, effectively optimizing overall energy consumption.
2. The MPDES algorithm adopts a two-phase strategy: (1) the pre-allocation phase ensures that each DAG meets its deadline, and (2) the energy-aware allocation phase optimizes energy efficiency through DVFS technology, significantly reducing system energy consumption.

3. Experiment results across various application scenarios demonstrate greater energy savings in MPDES compared to existing approaches under identical deadlines, indicating its practical value for safety-critical embedded systems.

The remainder of this paper is organized as follows. Section 2 discusses related work. Section 3 introduces the relevant models and formalizes the problem. Section 4 provides a detailed description of the design of the MPDES algorithm. Section 5 describes the experimental metrics and validates the effectiveness of the proposed algorithm. Finally, Sect. 6 concludes the paper.

2 Related Work

Scheduling time-constrained parallel applications on distributed platforms has become a research hotspot, attracting a large body of literature. The core objective is to efficiently assign tasks to processors (or cores) to ensure the timely completion of the entire application. As DAG scheduling is an NP-complete problem, it is difficult to obtain the optimal solution within polynomial time. Therefore, existing studies primarily focus on the design of heuristic algorithms, such as HEFT [19], CHP [4], Lookahead [3], and PEFT [2], all aiming to minimize the makespan. In recent years, with increasing attention to energy efficiency, low-power scheduling strategies have gradually gained importance. Typical examples include the NDES and NDES&GDES algorithms [24], which reduce energy consumption by evenly inserting idle time between tasks. The latter further incorporates DVFS technology to significantly optimize system energy consumption while meeting timing constraints.

For scenarios involving multiple task graphs (multi-DAGs), various strategies have been proposed. Zhao and Sakellariou [25] introduced two strategies for scheduling multiple independent DAGs on heterogeneous systems. Huang and Wang [8] developed an Online Workflow Management (OWM) method aimed at minimizing the overall makespan. Arabnejad and Barbosa [1] proposed the Fair Dynamic Workflow Scheduling (FDWS) algorithm, which further advanced the field. As system security has become an increasingly important consideration in real-time scheduling, Hu et al. [9] proposed a periodic real-time task scheduling method for safety-critical time-triggered systems, highlighting the close relationship between timing constraints and system security. Subsequently, Sunaldi et al. [7] presented the Contego framework, enabling the flexible integration of security monitoring tasks without violating real-time constraints, thereby enhancing system operational security. Further, Hu et al. [14] proposed an energy-aware scheduling approach for safety-critical time-triggered systems, which incorporates task type variations and DVFS techniques to significantly optimize system energy consumption while ensuring deadline satisfaction. In addition, Jiang et al. [12] addressed the problem of scheduling multiple workflows in heterogeneous computing systems by proposing the MWSTR algorithm, which reduces system energy consumption through idle time reclamation. Sarkar and Karfa [18] introduced DPMRS, a DVFS-enabled energy-efficient scheduling algorithm for multiple DAGs, effectively improving the energy performance of multi-task graph scheduling.

Despite significant progress in multi-DAG scheduling and energy optimization, ensuring scheduling security and timing predictability has become increasingly critical as systems evolve toward safety-critical and task-driven applications. Once a task misses its deadline, it may not only degrade system performance but also lead to severe functional failures or even safety incidents. Therefore, effectively incorporating security considerations into scheduling algorithm design has emerged as a key research direction [16]. In this context, designing a multi-periodic DAG scheduling algorithm that simultaneously ensures security, deadline satisfaction, and energy efficiency holds both theoretical significance and practical value. Based on this, this paper proposes MPDES, an energy-efficient scheduling algorithm for multiple periodic DAGs in safety-critical embedded systems. MPDES employs a hierarchical scheduling mechanism to guarantee strict deadline satisfaction and incorporates DVFS technology to reduce energy consumption, achieving a coordinated optimization among scheduling efficiency, security, and energy efficiency.

3 Models and Problem Formulation

3.1 Application Model

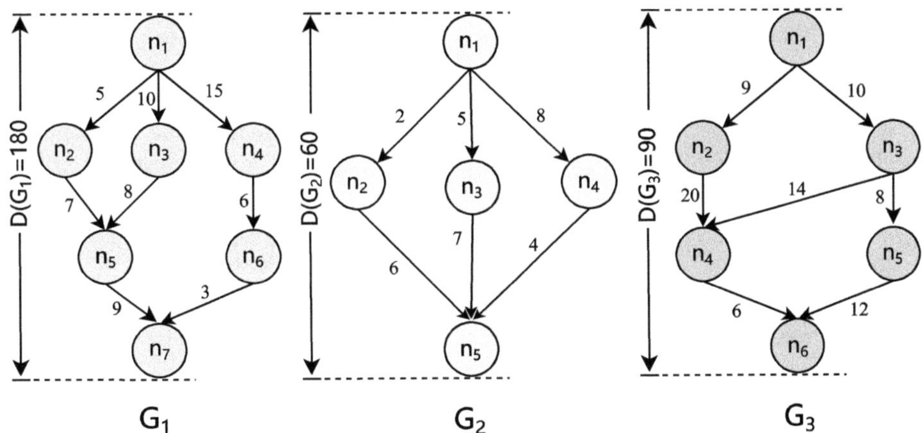

Fig. 1. An Example of three independent application DAGs.

A parallel application can be modeled as a DAG, $G = (V, E, D)$, where $V = \{n_1, n_2, \ldots, n_{|V|}\}$ is the set of nodes, and each node $n_i \in V$ represents a task. E is the set of edges, and each directed edge $e_{i,j} \in E$ represents a dependency between tasks, i.e., task n_j can only start after task n_i is completed and its output is available for n_j. The direct predecessors and successors of task n_i are denoted as pred(n_i) and succ(n_i), respectively. Tasks with no predecessors are called entry tasks (n_{entry}), and tasks with no successors are called exit tasks (n_{exit}). If there are multiple entry (or exit) tasks, they are aggregated into a single virtual entry (or exit) node through virtual edges. Each edge $e_{i,j}$ is associated with a non-negative weight $c_{i,j}$, representing the communication cost between tasks n_i and n_j. D represents the deadline, where the application's deadline is equal to its period. The system under consideration consists of a set of periodic real-time applications, represented as $\mathbf{G} = \{G_1, G_2, \ldots, G_{|G|}\}$, where each DAG has its own independent deadline (as shown in Fig. 1). It is assumed that all DAGs start execution when the system is initialized (i.e., at time zero) and continue to execute periodically until the system is turned off.

In a heterogeneous system, a set of processors is represented as $U = \{u_1, u_2, \ldots, u_{|U|}\}$. Each processor $u_k \in U$ operates at a set of discrete frequencies $F_k = \{f_{k,1}, f_{k,2}, \ldots, f_{k,|\alpha_k|}\}$, where $f_{k,1}$ and $f_{k,|\alpha_k|}$ represent the minimum and maximum available frequencies, respectively. Next, we will introduce several commonly used key attributes and formulas.

- $EST(n_i, u_k)$: The Earliest Start Time (EST) of task n_i on processor u_k, and is given by

$$EST(n_i, u_k) = \max\left\{ avail(u_k), \max_{n_j \in pred(n_i)} \left\{ AFT(n_j) + c_{j,i} \right\} \right\}. \quad (1)$$

  Where $avail(u_k)$ represents the earliest available time of processor u_k, $AFT(n_j)$ represents the actual finish time of task n_j, and $c_{j,i}$ represents the communication time between tasks n_j and n_i. If n_j and n_i are assigned to the same processor, then $c_{j,i} = 0$. For the entry task, $EST(n_{\text{entry}}, u_k) = 0$.
- $ET(n_i, u_k, f_{k,\alpha})$: The Execution Time (ET) of task n_i on processor u_k with frequency $f_{k,\alpha}$. Since the execution time of a task is linear to the frequency of the processor [10], the execution time $ET(n_i, u_k, f_{k,\alpha})$ can be estimated by

$$ET(n_i, u_k, f_{k,\alpha}) = ET(n_i, u_k, f_{k,|\alpha_k|}) \times \left(\frac{f_{k,|\alpha_k|}}{f_{k,\alpha}} \right). \quad (2)$$

  Since the execution time of tasks may vary depending on the characteristics of different processors in a heterogeneous system, as shown in Table 1, the $ET(n_i, u_k, f_{k,|\alpha_k|})$ for the example in Fig. 1 are provided.
- $EFT(n_i, u_k)$: The Earliest Finish Time (EFT) of task n_i on processor u_k. In our model, the task will not be interrupted or preemptive during its execution time. Hence, $EFT(n_i, u_k)$ can be calculated by

$$EFT(n_i, u_k) = EST(n_i, u_k) + ET(n_i, u_k, f_{k,\alpha}). \quad (3)$$

- $SL(G)$: The schedule length (or makespan) of a DAG G represents the actual finish time of the exit tasks, and is defined as follows:

$$SL(G) = AFT(n_{exit}). \quad (4)$$

Table 1. Execution times of tasks on three heterogeneous processors

	G_1							G_2					G_3					
	n_1	n_2	n_3	n_4	n_5	n_6	n_7	n_1	n_2	n_3	n_4	n_5	n_1	n_2	n_3	n_4	n_5	n_6
u_1	11	9	29	10	15	8	10	28	12	9	8	8	4	12	13	15	27	17
u_2	16	10	14	12	13	13	22	7	11	7	17	6	12	15	9	10	16	19
u_3	12	23	18	8	9	15	21	13	15	14	12	12	23	32	11	21	25	6

3.2 Power and Energy Models

The power of a processor u_k mainly consists of three components: *static power* P_k^s, *frequency-independent* and *-dependent dynamic power*, P_k^{ind} and P_k^d, where P_k^s and P_k^{ind} are often constant, while P_k^d varies with frequency and dominates the total power. For simplicity, we combine P_k^{ind} and P_k^d into $P_k^d(f_{k,\alpha})$. Therefore, the total power consumption of processor u_k when operating at frequency $f_{k,\alpha}$ is:

$$P_k(f_{k,\alpha}) = P_k^s + h \times P_k^d(f_{k,\alpha}) = P_k^s + h(P_k^{ind} + C_k^{ef} \times f_{k,\alpha}^{m_k}). \tag{5}$$

where h signifies the state of the processor, with $h = 1$ denoting the active state and $h = 0$ denoting the sleep state. The effective switching capacitance C_k^{ef} and the dynamic power exponent $m_k \in [2, 3]$ are processor-dependent constants.

For the processor u_k, the dynamic energy consumption required to complete task n_i at frequency $f_{k,\alpha}$ is the product of the processor's dynamic power and the execution time, i.e.,

$$E_d(n_i, u_k, f_{k,\alpha}) = P_k^d(f_{k,\alpha}) \times ET(n_i, u_k, f_{k,\alpha}). \tag{6}$$

The operational frequency range is bounded by $f_k^{cr} \leq f_{k,\alpha} \leq f_{k,|\alpha_k|}$, where f_k^{cr} represents the critical minimum frequency for dynamic energy efficiency. While frequency scaling down typically reduces both dynamic power dissipation and energy consumption, this benefit comes at the expense of prolonged task execution duration. Notably, although the dynamic power component P_k^d exhibits monotonic reduction with frequency scaling, this does not guarantee monotonic improvement in total energy consumption. This frequency is defined in [22] as: $f_k^{cr} = \sqrt[m_k]{P_k^{ind}/[(m_k - 1)C_k^{ef}]}$.

For a application G_r, the total dynamic energy consumption $E_d(G_r)$ for executing all tasks can be calculated as:

$$E_d(G_r) = \sum_{i=1}^{|V_r|} E_d(n_i, u_k, f_{k,\alpha}), \tag{7}$$

Let $E_s(G_r)$ represents the static energy consumption of the processors for the application G_r. It is calculated as:

$$E_s(G_r) = \sum_{k=1}^{|U|} (P_k^s \times SL(G_r)), \tag{8}$$

Table 2. Power parameters of three heterogeneous processors.

u_k	P_k^s	P_k^{ind}	C_k^{ef}	m_k	f_k^{cr}	$f_{k,|\alpha_k|}$
u_1	0.01	0.02	1.3	2.9	0.19	1.0
u_2	0.01	0.05	0.5	2.1	0.32	1.0
u_3	0.01	0.04	0.2	3.0	0.46	1.0

where $SL(G_r)$ represents the schedule length of the application G_r. If $D(G_r)$ denotes the deadline of G_r, then $SL(G_r) \leq D(G_r)$. The total energy consumption associated with the execution of the application G_r, denoted as $E(G_r)$, is given by the sum of its static and dynamic energy consumption [24], i.e.,

$$E(G_r) = E_s(G_r) + E_d(G_r). \tag{9}$$

Table 2 presents the power parameters for the three heterogeneous processors of Fig. 1 of the example system.

3.3   Problem Formulation

The problem description of this study is as follows: Given a set of periodic real-time tasks **G** and a set of fully connected DVFS-enabled processors U, design a scheduling strategy that minimizes the total energy consumption of the applications while satisfying the deadlines of each DAG in **G**. The mathematical formulation of our problem can be described as:

$$Minimize\ E(\mathbf{G}) = \sum_{r=1}^{|G|} E(G_r). \tag{10}$$

subject to:

$$\begin{cases} EFT(n_i) \leq EST(n_j), n_i \in pred(n_j), \\ SL(G_r) \leq D(G_r), 1 \leq r \leq |G|, \\ f_k^{cr} \leq f_{k,\alpha} \leq f_{k,|\alpha_k|}, 1 \leq k \leq |U|. \end{cases}$$

4   The Proposed Algorithm MPDES

4.1   Program Preprocessing

To enable synchronized scheduling and resource sharing, we assume each application $G_r \in \mathbf{G}$ initiates at time zero with period $D(G_r)$. We define a hyperperiod $D_0 = \text{LCM}(\mathbf{D})$, where $\mathbf{D} = \{D(G_1), D(G_2), \ldots, D(G_{|G|})\}$. Within each hyperperiod, all instances of the applications will arrive synchronously and generate multiple instances. Specifically, the number of invocations of application G_r within one hyperperiod D_0 is given by $I = D_0/D(G_r)$. For consecutively arriving application instances G_r^i and G_r^{i+1}, they are connected through virtual edges to maintain priority relationships. For the i-th arriving instance G_r^i of application G_r, its execution start time is at or after $D_{at}[G_r^i] = (i-1) \times D(G_r)$,

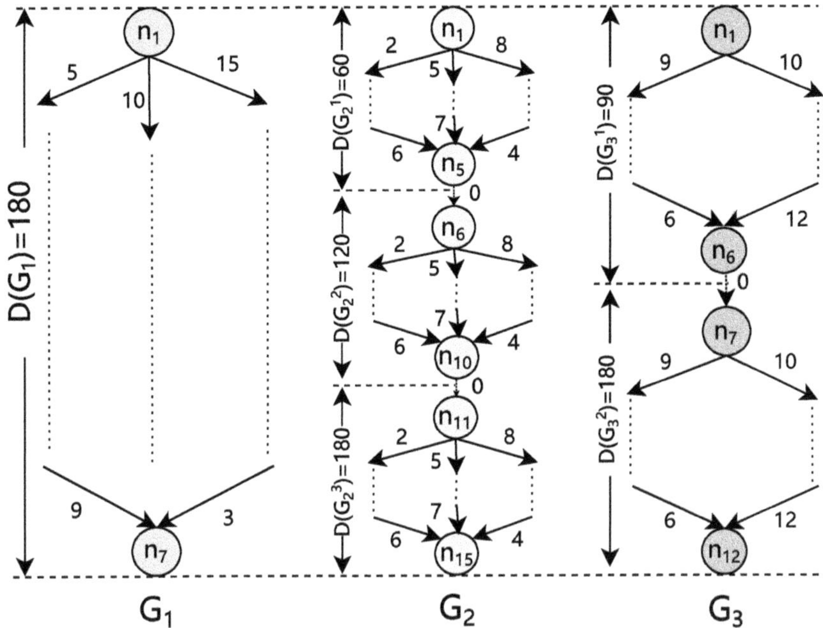

Fig. 2. DAGs after program pretreatment.

and its relative deadline is at or before $D_{\mathrm{rd}}[G_r^i] = i \times D(G_r)$. This ensures that tasks arrive and complete within their respective periods, avoiding premature or delayed execution.

In order to manage tasks effectively, the tasks will be re-indexed. The j-th task of the i-th instance of G_r is represented as $\langle G_r^i, n_j \rangle$, and is re-indexed as $\langle G_r, n_j \rangle$, where $j = i \times |V_r| + j$, and $|V_r|$ is the number of tasks in G_r. Therefore, the earliest start time $EST(n_i, u_k)$ should be determined by the following equation:

$$EST(n_i, u_k) = \begin{cases} \max\left\{ avail(u_k), D_{at}[G_r] \right\}, & \text{if}(\ n_i \in G_r(n_{entry})) \\ \max\left\{ avail(u_k), \max_{n_j \in pred(n_i)}\left\{ \right.\right. \\ \left.\left. AFT(n_j) + c_{j,i} \right\}\right\}, & \textbf{otherwise} \end{cases} \quad (11)$$

Where $G_r(n_{entry})$ denotes the entry task of application G_r. Figure 2 presents the three preprocessed DAGs from Fig. 1 with re-numbered task nodes. Let $D_0 = \mathrm{LCM}(D(G_1), D(G_2), D(G_3)) = 180$, and the vectors D_{at} and D_{rd} store the arrival times and relative deadlines, respectively. For example, $D_{at}[G_2] = 60$ and $D_{rd}[G_2] = 120$, guaranteeing timely task arrival and completion.

4.2   MPDES Pre-allocation

The *MPDES pre-allocation* (Algorithm 1) is based on a list heuristic algorithm that optimizes the task scheduling order to ensure all DAG tasks complete their

---

Algorithm 1. MPDES pre-allocation(G,U)

Input: Application set G and processor set U.
Output: $SL(G), E(G)$.
 1: Preprocess the set G. // *The total number of tasks is N.*
 2: Using Eq. (13) and (14), we obtain $OCT(n_i, u_k)$.
 3: Create the vectors $Sch\_Order[]$ and $PT[]$.
 4: Create a queue $Ready\_Pools[]$.
 5: **for** all $ct = 1$ to N **do**
 6:     Add tasks that are ready but not yet in $Ready\_Pools[]$, and record T_{ready}.
 7:     **for** each processor $u_k \in U$ **do**
 8:         Update the H values of tasks in $Ready\_Pools[]$ on processor u_k using the Eq. (12), and select the task with the maximum H value as n_{sel}.
 9:         Calculate EST and EFT using Eq. (11) and (3).
10:         Calculate $OEFT(n_{sel}, u_k)$ using Eq. (15) .
11:     **end for**
12:     Assign the task to the processor u_k with the minimum OEFT.
13:     $Sch\_Order[ct] = n_{sel}, PT[n_{sel}] = u_k$.
14: **end for**
15: **if** $\exists \langle G_r, n_{exit}\rangle | EFT(\langle G_r, n_{exit}\rangle, u_k) > D_{rd}[G_r]$ **then**
16:     **Output**: No feasible schedule can be generated.
17: **end if**
18: Calculate $SL(G)$ and $E(G)$ using Eq. (4) and (9).
19: **return** $SL(G), E(G)$;

---

execution before their respective deadlines. Static list scheduling typically consists of two steps: *task selection* and *processor allocation*. The purpose of task selection is to determine the scheduling order of tasks, while the purpose of processor allocation is to assign an appropriate processor to each task.

Task Selection: The priority metric $H(n_i, u_k)$ for task n_i on processor u_k is computed as:

$$H(n_i, u_k) = \frac{ET(n_i, u_k) + T_{wait}(n_i, u_k)}{ET(n_i, u_k)}. \tag{12}$$

where $T_{wait}(n_i, u_k) = \max\{avail(u_k) - T_{ready}(n_i)\}$ represents the waiting time, with $T_{ready}(n_i)$ representing the task's ready time. This metric balances execution time and waiting time, prioritizing tasks with prolonged waiting periods through increased H values.

When tasks share identical H values, their priorities are further distinguished by comparing the values in the Optimistic Cost Table (OCT) [2]. The OCT serves as a static urgency metric that estimates the earliest possible finish time of a task's successor chain under ideal scheduling and minimal communication overhead. The core idea is to prioritize tasks that are likely to complete earlier, thereby improving the overall scheduling efficiency. The OCT is computed as follows:

$$OCT(n_i, u_k) = \max_{n_j \in succ(n_i)} \left[\min_{u_z \in U} \left\{ OCT(n_j, u_z) + w_{j,z} + c_{i,j} \right\} \right]. \tag{13}$$

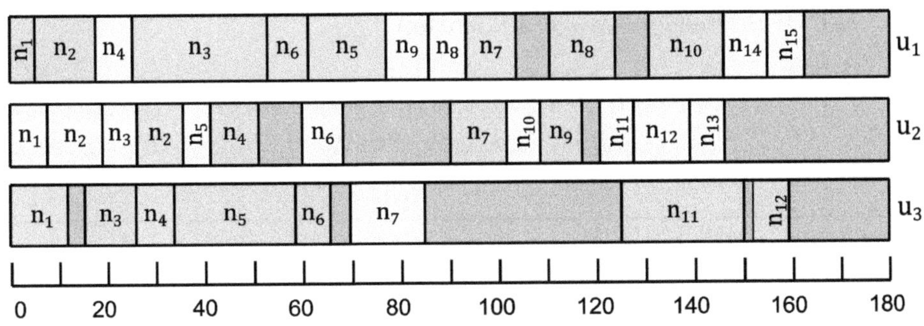

Fig. 3. Gantt chart of scheduling the sample application in Fig. 1 using MPDES pre-allocation algorithm: $SL(\mathbf{G}) = 162$ and $E(\mathbf{G}) = 279.14\ W$.

where $w_{j,z}$ represents the execution time of task n_j on processor u_z. This formula ensures the calculation of the longest successor path under optimal processor allocation, thereby reflecting the criticality of task n_i in the entire task graph. For the exit node n_i of application G_r during hyperperiod execution, the OCT is computed as:

$$OCT(n_i, u_k) = D_0 - D_{\mathrm{rd}}[n_i]. \tag{14}$$

Line 2 initializes all $OCT(n_i, u_k)$ values via Eq. (13). For exit nodes, instance-specific deadlines require OCT computation using Eq. (14). As illustrated in Fig. 2, application G_2 yields $OCT(n_5, u_k) = 120$, where $u_k \in U$.

Processor Allocation: For the selected tasks, their Optimal Earliest Finish Time (OEFT) is calculated. The task n_i with the minimum OEFT(n_i, u_k) value is allocated to processor u_k. The OEFT is defined as:

$$OEFT(n_i, u_k) = EFT(n_i, u_k) + OCT(n_i, u_k), \tag{15}$$

Line 3 initializes two vectors: $Sch\_Order[]$ which records the task scheduling sequence and $PT[]$ which stores processor allocations. Lines 5–16 describe the task allocation process: during each iteration, one task is selected from the ready pool. Specifically, in lines 7–13, for each processor, the H-value of ready tasks is calculated, and the task with the maximum H-value is selected, resulting in $|U|$ task-processor pairs $\langle n_i, u_k \rangle$. Line 14 computes the OEFT value for each $\langle n_i, u_k \rangle$ pair and selects the pair with the smallest OEFT(n_i, u_k) value, then allocates task n_i to processor u_k.

As illustrated in Fig. 3, the MPDES pre-allocation algorithm successfully schedules all tasks from Fig. 1 while meeting their deadlines. However, energy optimization is not yet addressed. In the following section, we introduce the energy-aware phase of MPDES, which leverages DVFS to exploit slack time and reduce system energy consumption.

4.3 MPDES Energy-Aware Allocation

The MPDES pre-allocation strategy prioritizes minimizing task completion time. For an application G_r, if the schedule length $SL(G_r) \leq D(G_r)$, the slack time $(D(G_r) - SL(G_r))$ can be utilized for energy-efficient scheduling. Although simul-

---

Algorithm 2. MPDES(G,U)

Input: Application set G and processor set U.
Output: SL(G), E(G).
1: $SL, E_{power} = $ MPDES pre-allocation(G, U) // (Algorithm 1)
2: Using Eq. (6), calculate the energy consumption values and sort them in ascending order to obtain $U_p(n_i)$, where $n_i \in N$.
3: A rank value is assigned to $PT[n_i]$ based on $Up(n_i)$, and stored in $R(n_i)$, $n_i \in N$.
4: $PT\_end[n_i] = PT[n_i]$, $ECL(n_i) = 1$, $n_i \in N$. $level \leftarrow |U|$.
5: **while** $level > 1$ **do**
6:     Create a queue $Sch\_opt[]$ and add tasks with $R(n_i) == level$ according to the scheduling order in $Sch\_Order[]$.
7:     **for** all tasks n_j in queue $Sch\_opt[]$ **do**
8:         **for** all tasks n_i in vector $Sch\_Order[]$ **do**
9:             **if** $n_i == n_j$ **then**
10:                 $u = Up(n_j)[ECL(n_j)]$, $ECL(n_j) = ECL(n_j) + 1$.
11:             **else**
12:                 $u = PT\_end[n_i]$.
13:             **end if**
14:             Calculate EST and EFT using Eq. (11) and (3).
15:             Assign the task n_i to processor u.
16:         **end for**
17:         **if** $\exists \langle G_r, n_{exit} \rangle | EFT(n_{exit}, u_k) > D_{rd}[G_r]$ and $ECL(n_j) < R(n_j)$ **then**
18:             Again add the task n_j to $Sch\_opt[]$.
19:         **end if**
20:         Calculate $SL(G)$ and $E(G)$ using Eq. (4) and (9).
21:         **if** $SL(G) \leq D_0$ and $E_{power} > E(G)$ **then**
22:             $SL = SL(G)$, $E_{power} = E(G)$, $PT\_end[n_j] = u$.
23:         **end if**
24:     **end for**
25:     $level = level - 1$.
26: **end while**
27: **for** all tasks n_i in vector $Sch\_Order[]$ **do**
28:     $u_k = PT\_end[n_i]$.
29:     Calculate $LFT(n_i, u_k)$ using Eq. (16) ans (17).
30:     Calculate $Slack(n_i)$ using Eq. (18).
31:     **if** $Slack(n_i) > 0$ **then**
32:         Calculate $f_{op}(n_i, u_k)$ using Eq. (19) and (20).
33:         Update $AST(n_i)$ and $AFT(n_i)$ using Eq. (21) and (22).
34:     **end if**
35: **end for**
36: Update SL and E_{power} using Eq. (4) ans (9).
37: **return** SL, E_{power}.

---

taneous optimization of both time and energy consumption represents an ideal objective, achieving this balance proves challenging due to system heterogeneity and deadline constraints. Consequently, MPDES needs to judiciously select processors to establish an optimal trade-off between time and energy consumption. The energy-aware allocation (Algorithm 2) will be elaborated in the following section.

Let $PT[n_i]$ denote the processor assigned to task n_i in Algorithm 1, which prioritizes speed over energy efficiency. To evaluate energy consumption, we sort the energy consumption of each task on all processors in ascending order, forming the set $U_p(n_i)$. Based on $U_p(n_i)$, we assign a rank value $R(n_i)$ to the processor $PT[n_i]$ (lines 2–3). For example, if $U_p(n_i) = \{u_1, u_3, u_2\}$ and $PT[n_i] = u_1$, then $R(n_i) = 1$, indicating that $PT[n_i]$ is both the fastest and most energy-efficient processor for task n_i, requiring no adjustment. On the other hand, if $PT[n_i] = u_2$, then $R(n_i) = |U|$, meaning $PT[n_i]$ is the fastest but also the most energy-consuming. In such cases, we reassign the task to a lower-energy processor while satisfying the time constraints, thereby improving the Quality of Task Assignment (QoTA).

Lines 6–29 optimize tasks with rank $R(n_i) = $ level. For each task n_j, lines 9–21 attempt to assign it to processor $U_p(n_j)[ECL(n_j)]$, where $ECL(n_j) = 1$ initially selects the most energy-efficient option. If this assignment violates the deadline (lines 19–21) and $ECL(n_j) < R(n_j)$, n_j is added to $Sch\_opt[]$ for reassignment to $U_p(n_j)[ECL(n_j) + 1]$ (line 12). This process iteratively improves processor suitability. Subsequently, we employ DVFS on residual slack time to further minimize energy consumption. The Latest Finish Time (LFT), defined as:

$$LFT(n_i, u_k) = \begin{cases} D_{rd}[G_r], & \textbf{if}(\ n_i \in G_r(n_{exit}) \ ) \\ \min_{n_j \in succ(n_i)} \{AST(n_j) - c_{i,j}\}, & \textbf{otherwise.} \end{cases} \qquad (16)$$

Here, $G_r(n_{exit})$ represents the exit task of application G_r, and $AST(n_j)$ the actual start time of task n_j. Considering task n_i is assigned to processor u_k, we define $next(n_i)$ as its direct successor on u_k. The LFT updates as:

$$LFT(n_i, u_k) = \min \{LFT(n_i, u_k), AST(next(n_i))\} . \qquad (17)$$

The slack time of task n_i is calculated as follows:

$$Slack(n_i) = LFT(n_i, u_k) - AST(n_i). \qquad (18)$$

The task n_i execution frequency on u_k then becomes:

$$f(n_i, u_k) = \frac{ET(n_i, u_k, f_{k,|\alpha_k|})}{Slack(n_i)} \times f_{k,|\alpha_k|}, \qquad (19)$$

constrained by the processor's discrete frequencies and minimum energy-efficient frequency f_k^{cr}:

$$f_{op}(n_i, u_k) = \max \{f_k^{cr}, \min \{f \mid f(n_i, u_k) \leq f, f \in F_k\}\} . \qquad (20)$$

Consequently, the actual start/finish times update to:

$$AST(n_i) = LFT(n_i) - ET(n_i, u_k, f_{k,|\alpha_k|}) \times \frac{f_{k,|\alpha_k|}}{f_{op}(n_i, u_k)}, \qquad (21)$$

$$AFT(n_i) = LFT(n_i). \qquad (22)$$

The Gantt chart in Fig. 4 demonstrates the application of the MPDES algorithm to the sample system shown in Fig. 1. As observed from the chart, the energy-aware allocation in Algorithm 2 enables MPDES to achieve 42.94% energy savings compared to Algorithm 1. The MPDES algorithm consists of two parts: pre-allocation and energy-aware allocation. The time complexity of the pre-allocation phase is $O(v^2 \cdot p)$, where v is the total number of tasks and p is the number of processors. The time complexity of the energy-aware allocation phase is $O(v^2 \cdot n)$, where n is the total number of tasks to be optimized. Therefore, the overall time complexity of the MPDES algorithm is $O(v^2 \cdot (n + p))$.

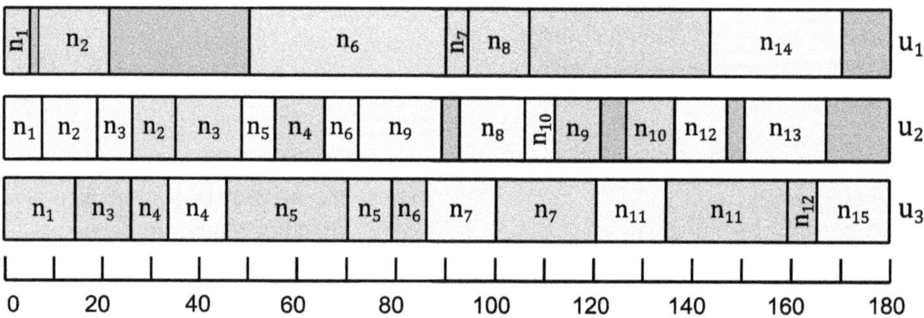

Fig. 4. Gantt chart of scheduling the sample application in Fig. 1 using MPDES pre-allocation algorithm: $SL(\mathbf{G}) = 180$ and $E(\mathbf{G}) = 159.27\ W$.

5   Experiments and Discussion

5.1   Performance Metrics

We evaluate the proposed algorithm using two key metrics:

1. **Energy Consumption** ($E(G)$): This metric evaluates the energy efficiency of applications by accounting for both static and dynamic power consumption, providing a comprehensive characterization of energy usage during execution. The proposed model calculates this metric using Eq. 9.
2. **Energy Reduction Ratio** (R): This metric is used to evaluate the energy-saving efficiency of the algorithm relative to the HEFT algorithm. It is defined as:

$$R = \frac{E_{HEFT}(G) - E_x(G)}{E_{HEFT}(G)}$$

where $E_x(G)$ and $E_{HEFT}(G)$ represent the total energy consumption produced by algorithm x and the $HEFT$ algorithm, respectively.

5.2   Comparison Algorithms

To evaluate the performance of our algorithm, we compare it with several representative scheduling algorithms, including HEFT, NDES, NDES&GDES, MWSTR, and DPMRS. HEFT is a well-known scheduling algorithm that does not consider energy costs. Comparing with HEFT effectively demonstrates the energy-saving efficiency of the other algorithms. NDES and NDES&GDES aim to minimize energy dissipation in non-DVFS and DVFS supported systems, respectively. These algorithms are designed for single-DAG scheduling, while MWSTR and DPMRS represent recent advanced research in multi-DAG scheduling, aiming to minimize system energy consumption through DVFS techniques. These algorithms are closely related to the system model presented in this paper, making them highly suitable for comparison with the MPDES algorithm we propose.

In order to adapt algorithms originally designed for scheduling a single real-time DAG to our multi-DAG system model, we modify the input during the preprocessing phase. Specifically, we introduce a virtual common entry node and exit node, connecting all applications via virtual edges without introducing any time cost, effectively transforming the problem into a single-DAG scheduling problem. This allows us to compute the total energy consumption of scheduling all applications within the super-period. Since these applications can be executed concurrently, our designed scheduling strategy can effectively approximate their scheduling energy consumption.

5.3   Experimental Setup

We conduct experiments on a simulated 32-processor platform developed in C++. The processor power parameters are as follows: $P_s = 0.01$, $P_{ind}^k \in [0.03, 0.07]$, $C_k^{ef} \in [0.2, 1.3]$, $m_k \in [2.2, 3.0]$, and $f_{k,|\alpha_k|} = 1$ GHz (discrete steps of 0.1GHz). These values emulate Intel Mobile Pentium III and ARM Cortex-A9 architectures. Task execution/communication times are uniformly distributed in [10, 100]ms. We selected three applications with distinct parallelism characteristics as workloads.

- **Fast Fourier Transform (FFT)**: High-parallelism application with task count $|N| = (2 \times \rho - 1) + \rho \log_2 \rho$, where $\rho = 2^y$ for some integer y [19],
- **Gaussian Elimination (GE)**: Low-parallelism application with $|N| = (\rho^2 + 2\rho - 2)/2$ [19], The parameter ρ enables systematic algorithm evaluation by controlling task granularity.
- **Random graphs**: Generated by the task graph generator [21] based on the following parameters:
  1. Average computation time: 50 ms.
  2. Heterogeneity factor $\beta \in \{0.1, 0.25, 0.5, 0.75, 1\}$, where a larger β value indicates greater variation in processor execution times.
  3. Communication-to-Computation Ratio (CCR) $\in \{0.1, 0.25, 0.5, 0.75, 1\}$, the smaller the CCR, the higher the communication time, and vice versa.

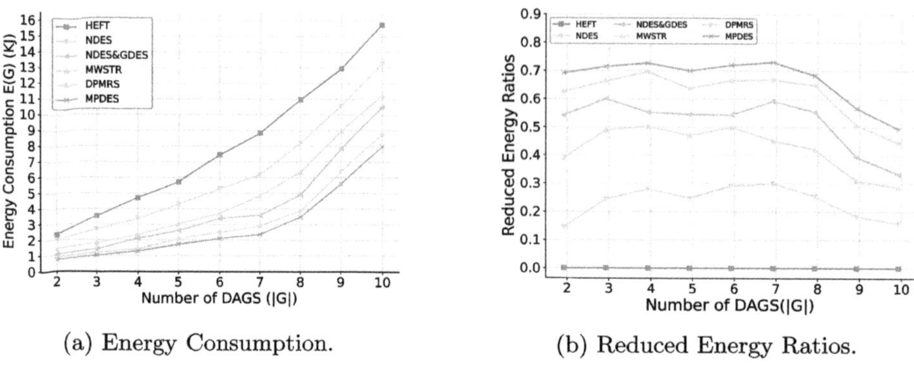

(a) Energy Consumption.

(b) Reduced Energy Ratios.

Fig. 5. Different application scales: results of applying algorithms to random applications.

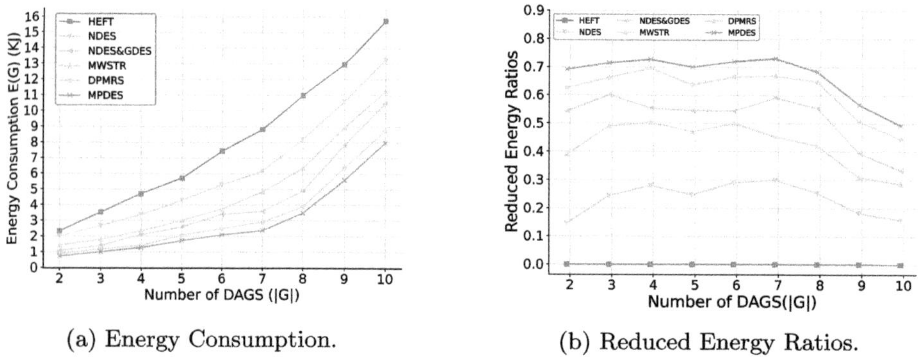

(a) Energy Consumption.

(b) Reduced Energy Ratios.

Fig. 6. Different application scales: results of applying algorithms to fast Fourier transform applications.

5.4 Experiments and Analysis

The experiment compares different algorithms from two aspects: task scale (number of tasks) and application deadline.

Experiment I: This experiment aims to evaluate the performance of different algorithms under various task scales. To conduct a comprehensive comparison, applications should cover small-scale, medium-scale, and large-scale applications. The experimental setup is as follows: the number of processors is $|U| = 8$, and the number of DAGs ranges from 2 to 10. The tasks include FFT (task numbers from 15 to 95, ρ from 2 to 4), GE (task numbers from 14 to 90, ρ from 5 to 13), and randomly generated DAGs (task numbers from 10 to 100). The range of supercycle D_0 is from 1000 to 6000. By adjusting the application cycle, the total number of tasks within the supercycle ranges from 100 (small-scale) to 2000 (large-scale). Each data point is based on the average of 200 test cases.

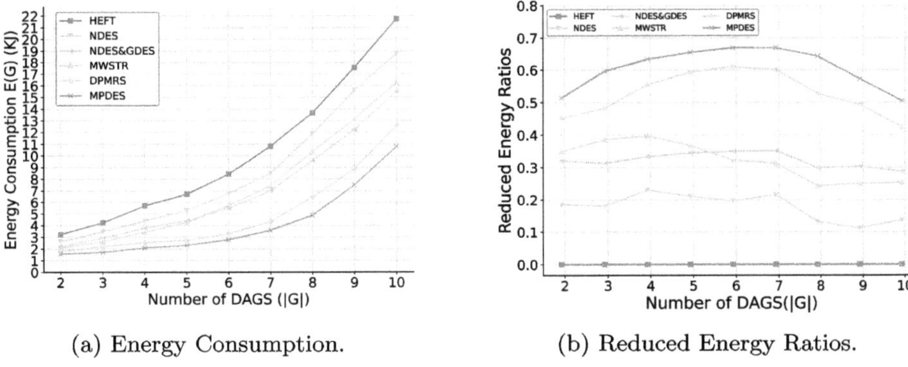

(a) Energy Consumption.   (b) Reduced Energy Ratios.

Fig. 7. Different application scales: results of applying algorithms to Gaussian elimination applications.

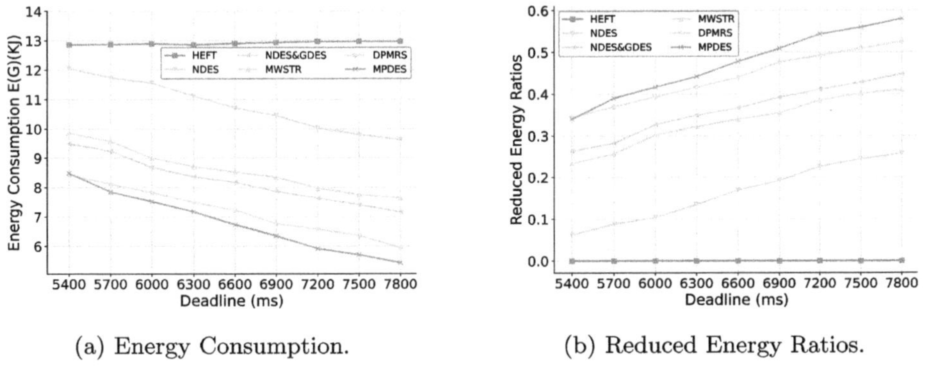

(a) Energy Consumption.   (b) Reduced Energy Ratios.

Fig. 8. Different application deadlines: results of applying algorithms to random applications.

Figures 5, 6, 7 show the results of applying the algorithm to random, Fast Fourier Transform, and Gaussian Elimination applications. From the results, we can draw the following observations.

1. The proposed MPDES algorithm demonstrates optimal energy efficiency across various application scenarios while strictly meeting task deadlines, validating the effectiveness of its energy-saving strategy.
2. Compared to other algorithms, MPDES exhibits particularly outstanding performance in medium-scale applications (N=1000). As shown in Fig. 7(b), when $|G| = 6$, MPDES achieves 66.9% higher energy savings compared to HEFT.
3. As the task scale increases, all algorithms show a declining trend in energy efficiency, though they still maintain certain energy-saving capabilities. Nevertheless, MPDES consistently outperforms other comparative algorithms in overall performance.

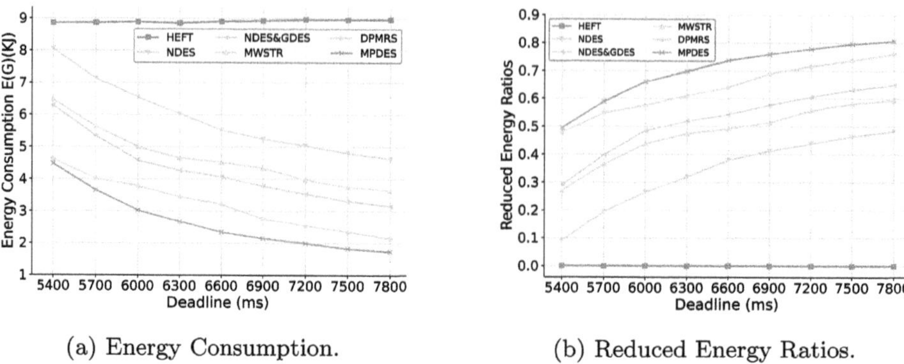

(a) Energy Consumption.

(b) Reduced Energy Ratios.

Fig. 9. Different application deadlines: results of applying algorithms to fast Fourier transform applications.

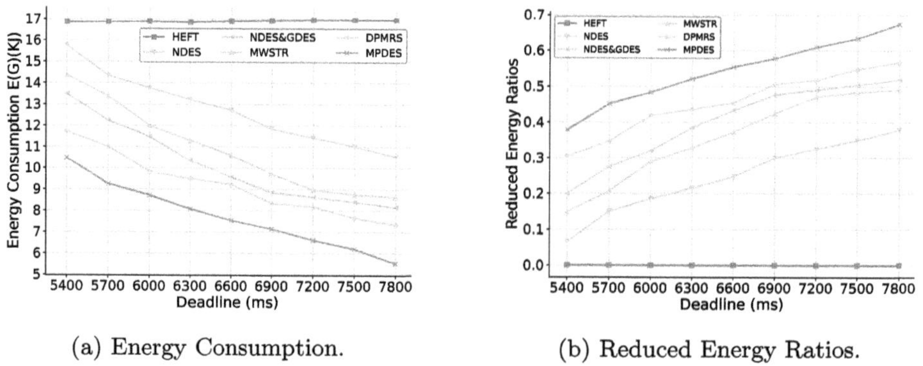

(a) Energy Consumption.

(b) Reduced Energy Ratios.

Fig. 10. Different application deadlines: results of applying algorithms to Gaussian elimination applications.

Experiment II: The purpose of this experiment is to evaluate the performance of different algorithms in utilizing slack time. In this experiment, the number of processors $|U|$ is fixed at 8. The number of DAGs $|G|$ ranges from $[1, 4]$. For the FFT application, the task count ranges from $[223, 1151]$ (with ρ in the range of $[5, 7]$), for GE, the task count ranges from $[209, 1175]$ (with ρ in the range of $[20, 48]$), for the randomly generated DAGs, the task count ranges from $[200, 2000]$. The supercycle D_0 is initially set to 5400 ms, and the application cycle T is adjusted so that the total number of tasks $|N|$ in each supercycle is kept around 1000. To study the impact of slack time, we incrementally increase the deadline D_0 by $D_0 \times 0.05$ each time, up to $D_0 \times 1.4$. Each data point is the average result of 200 test cases.

Figures 8, 9, 10 show the experimental results for the Fast Fourier Transform, Gaussian Elimination, and randomly generated DAG applications. The main observations are as follows:

1. As D_0 increases, the energy consumption of the HEFT algorithm does not remain constant. This is because changes in D_0 affect the application's D_{at} and D_{rd}, thereby influencing task scheduling and energy distribution.
2. MPDES and DPMRS demonstrate outstanding energy-saving performance. They dynamically evaluate processor energy consumption in real-time, preferentially allocating tasks to the most energy-efficient processors while fully utilizing slack time through DVFS technology.
3. In all test scenarios, the MPDES algorithm consistently exhibits the best energy-saving performance, with the effect becoming more pronounced as deadlines are extended. As shown in Figs. 8, 9, 10(b), at $D_0 \times 1.4$, MPDES saves 58.1%, 80.6%, and 67.3% more energy compared to HEFT, respectively.

The experimental results demonstrate MPDES's superior energy efficiency over existing approaches across diverse parallel applications with varying scales and deadlines.

6   Conclusion

This paper presents a static list-based real-time scheduling algorithm, MPDES, designed for multiple periodic safety-critical applications in embedded systems. MPDES aims to minimize the dynamic energy consumption of multiple periodic DAGs by leveraging DVFS technology, under the premise of ensuring task deadlines, system security, and scheduling predictability. The algorithm consists of two phases: (1) a pre-allocation phase that considers both task waiting time and processor efficiency to avoid delays and meet timing constraints, and (2) an energy-aware phase that reallocates high-energy-consumption tasks and applies DVFS to optimize slack time, thereby maximizing energy efficiency. Experimental evaluations across various parallel applications demonstrate that MPDES consistently ensures real-time performance and achieves significant energy savings. Compared with existing methods, MPDES exhibits stronger scheduling predictability and task isolation under resource contention, significantly enhancing system security and robustness. These features highlight its practical potential for deployment in safety-critical distributed heterogeneous systems.

Acknowledgments. We would like to express our sincere gratitude to the anonymous reviewers for their valuable comments and suggestions, which have significantly improved the quality of this paper. The work reported in this paper was supported by the Hunan Natural Science Foundation (Grant No. 2023JJ30263), the Hunan Provincial Educational Commitee Foundation (Grant No. 22B0510).

References

1. Arabnejad, H., Barbosa, J.: Fairness resource sharing for dynamic workflow scheduling on heterogeneous systems. In: 2012 IEEE 10th International Symposium on Parallel and Distributed Processing with Applications, pp. 633–639. IEEE (2012)

2. Arabnejad, H., Barbosa, J.G.: List scheduling algorithm for heterogeneous systems by an optimistic cost table. IEEE Trans. Parallel Distrib. Syst. **25**(3), 682–694 (2013)
3. Bittencourt, L.F., Sakellariou, R., Madeira, E.R.: Dag scheduling using a lookahead variant of the heterogeneous earliest finish time algorithm. In: 2010 18th Euromicro Conference on Parallel, Distributed and Network-Based Processing, pp. 27–34. IEEE (2010)
4. Boeres, C., Rebello, V.E., et al.: A cluster-based strategy for scheduling task on heterogeneous processors. In: 16th Symposium on Computer Architecture and High Performance Computing, pp. 214–221. IEEE (2004)
5. Buttazzo, G.C.: Hard Real-Time Computing Systems: Predictable Scheduling Algorithms and Applications. Real-Time Systems Series, 3rd edn. Springer (2011). https://doi.org/10.1007/978-1-4614-0676-1
6. Buttazzo, G.C., Buttanzo, G.: Hard Real-Time Computing Systems, vol. 356. Springer (1997)
7. Hasan, M., Mohan, S., Pellizzoni, R., Bobba, R.B.: Contego: an adaptive framework for integrating security tasks in real-time systems. arXiv preprint arXiv:1705.00138 (2017)
8. Hsu, C.C., Huang, K.C., Wang, F.J.: Online scheduling of workflow applications in grid environments. Futur. Gener. Comput. Syst. **27**(6), 860–870 (2011)
9. Hu, M., Luo, J., Wang, Y., Veeravalli, B.: Scheduling periodic task graphs for safety-critical time-triggered avionic systems. IEEE Trans. Aerosp. Electron. Syst. **51**(3), 2294–2304 (2015)
10. Huang, J., Li, R., An, J., Zeng, H., Chang, W.: A DVFs-weakly dependent energy-efficient scheduling approach for deadline-constrained parallel applications on heterogeneous systems. IEEE Trans. Comput. Aided Des. Integr. Circuits Syst. **40**(12), 2481–2494 (2021)
11. Huang, J., Li, R., Jiao, X., Jiang, Y., Chang, W.: Dynamic DAG scheduling on multiprocessor systems: reliability, energy, and makespan. IEEE Trans. Comput. Aided Des. Integr. Circuits Syst. **39**(11), 3336–3347 (2020)
12. Jiang, J., Lin, Y., Xie, G., Fu, L., Yang, J.: Time and energy optimization algorithms for the static scheduling of multiple workflows in heterogeneous computing system. J. Grid Comput. **15**, 435–456 (2017)
13. Jiang, W., Pop, P., Jiang, K.: Design optimization for security-and safety-critical distributed real-time applications. Microprocess. Microsyst. **52**, 401–415 (2017)
14. Jiang, X., et al.: Energy-efficient scheduling of periodic applications on safety-critical time-triggered multiprocessor systems. Electronics **7**(6), 98 (2018)
15. Moulik, S., Chaudhary, R., Das, Z.: Hears: a heterogeneous energy-aware real-time scheduler. Microprocess. Microsyst. **72**, 102939 (2020)
16. Pathan, R.M.: Real-time scheduling algorithm for safety-critical systems on faulty multicore environments. Real-Time Syst. **53**, 45–81 (2017)
17. Poudel, S., Ni, Z., Malla, N.: Real-time cyber physical system testbed for power system security and control. Int. J. Electr. Power Energy Syst. **90**, 124–133 (2017)
18. Senapati, D., Sarkar, A., Karfa, C.: Energy-aware real-time scheduling of multiple periodic dags on heterogeneous systems. IEEE Trans. Comput. Aided Des. Integr. Circuits Syst. **42**(8), 2447–2460 (2022)
19. Topcuoglu, H., Hariri, S., Wu, M.Y.: Performance-effective and low-complexity task scheduling for heterogeneous computing. IEEE Trans. Parallel Distrib. Syst. **13**(3), 260–274 (2002)
20. Ullman, J.D.: Np-complete scheduling problems. J. Comput. Syst. Sci. **10**(3), 384–393 (1975)

21. Unknown: Task graph generator (2015). https://sourceforge.net/projects/taskgraphgen/
22. Unsal, O.S., Koren, I.: System-level power-aware design techniques in real-time systems. Proc. IEEE **91**(7), 1055–1069 (2003)
23. Xie, G., Xiao, X., Peng, H., Li, R., Li, K.: A survey of low-energy parallel scheduling algorithms. IEEE Trans. Sustain. Comput. **7**(1), 27–46 (2021)
24. Xie, G., Zeng, G., Xiao, X., Li, R., Li, K.: Energy-efficient scheduling algorithms for real-time parallel applications on heterogeneous distributed embedded systems. IEEE Trans. Parallel Distrib. Syst. **28**(12), 3426–3442 (2017)
25. Zhao, H., Sakellariou, R.: Scheduling multiple dags onto heterogeneous systems. In: Proceedings 20th IEEE International Parallel & Distributed Processing Symposium, pp. 14–pp. IEEE (2006)

DF TransNet: Dual-Channel Fusion Transformer for Image Deraining

Zhuo He[1], Miao Liao[1], and Shuanhu Di[2(✉)]

[1] School of Computer Science and Engineering, Hunan University of Science and Technology, Xiangtan 411201, China
[2] College of Intelligence Science and Technology, National University of Defense Technology, Changsha 410073, China
dish0304@163.com

Abstract. The photos taken on rainy days suffer from degraded visual quality, posing challenges to security-critical tasks such as object detection in surveillance and autonomous systems. Existing image deraining methods often combine Transformer and CNN architectures for performance gains. However, due to the inherent discrepancy of feature extraction between CNN and Transformer, these methods struggle to model complex dependencies between rain streaks and background. To address this, we propose a dual-channel fusion-based network for image deraining, called DF TransNet. Specifically, we design a Dual-channel Fusion Transformer (DF Transformer) as the encoder, employing a dual-path structure to separately capture global semantics and local details, with cross-connections to enhance feature interaction. To deeply fuse features of different granularities, we adopt a fusion module that integrates features from channel, spatial, and frequency dimensions. Additionally, we introduce a mixed-scale gated feed-forward network to improve robustness to varying rain patterns. In the decoder of DF TransNet, a Region Transformer Cascade (RTC) is designed to distinguish the rain-affected and rain-unaffected regions by masking mechanism for targeted feature reconstruction. Extensive experiments on public datasets confirm that our method achieves state-of-the-art deraining performance, offering practical benefits for vision-based security applications in harsh weather.

Keywords: Image deraining · Dual-channel Fusion · Transformer

1 Introduction

Image deraining is a crucial preprocessing step in computer vision, particularly in safety-critical scenarios. It plays a key role in safety applications such as

This work is supported by Natural Science Foundation of Hunan Province (Grant2025J150363), Science and Technology Innovation Program of Hunan Province (2024RC3216), Scientific Research Fund of Hunan Provincial Education Department (Grant 24A0356).

W. Liang et al. (Eds.): SecureComm 2025, LNICST 690, pp. 172–189, 2026.
https://doi.org/10.1007/978-3-032-23456-8_10

intelligent video surveillance [6], autonomous driving perception [28], and remote sensing [18]. Rain streaks significantly degrade image quality, which in turn hampers the performance of downstream vision tasks such as object detection and semantic segmentation [2,41]. This degradation can lead to inaccurate recognition, missed targets, or system failure. Therefore, reliable visual perception under rainy conditions is vital for maintaining system safety and enabling accurate decision-making in complex real-world environments.

In recent years, the rapid advancement of deep learning has led to breakthroughs in image deraining. CNN-based methods [9,30,35] have significantly improved deraining performance. However, the fixed-size convolution kernels limit their receptive fields, which makes it difficult to capture global dependencies. Inspired by the success of Transformer in vision tasks [1,8], researchers have begun applying them to image deraining. Transformer achieves more comprehensive feature modeling through the self-attention mechanism [4,32,37], thereby overcoming the shortcomings of CNN in global information processing.

In real-world deraining scenarios [16,32], the diversity of rain streaks and complex backgrounds make it difficult for a single architecture to perform well. To overcome this problem, researchers combine Transformers with CNNs [3] for complementary strengths. However, most of existing models lack effective interaction and fusion mechanisms between the two architectures. CNNs focus on extracting local features, while Transformers specialize in global semantic modeling. This difference in feature extraction makes their features difficult to coordinate effectively, limiting further model performance improvements.

To solve this issue, we propose an innovative DF Transformer. This module employs a dual-channel parallel structure to extract both global and local features, followed by deep feature fusion across spatial, channel, and frequency domains. Meanwhile, a cross-connection mechanism is introduced to enable effective interaction between the two feature streams, which can enhance their complementarity. To further boost representation capability, we design a mixed-scale gated feed-forward network that enables dynamic multi-scale feature extraction. In the decoder stage, we incorporate a flexible mask mechanism [16] to distinguish rain-affected from rain-unaffected regions for targeted feature reconstruction. This design improves both feature expressiveness and adaptability to complex rain streaks.The main contributions are summarized as follows:

(1) We propose a dual-channel fusion attention mechanism that jointly captures global semantics and local details, with deep feature fusion across spatial, channel, and frequency dimensions.
(2) We introduce a mixed-scale gated feed-forward network with adaptive gating to dynamically enhance feature selection for improve the modeling of rain streaks.
(3) Our model achieves state-of-the-art performance on the Rain200L, Rain200H, DID-Data, DDN-Data, and SPA-Data datasets, offers strong potential for real-world deployment in secure perception systems under rainy weather conditions.

2   Related Work

2.1   Image Deraining in Security Applications and Perception Systems

In recent years, image deraining plays a vital role in improving the robustness of vision-based systems deployed in security-critical applications. In intelligent surveillance [19] and smart city scenarios, rain-induced image degradation can lead to false detections and missed tracking, severely affecting system reliability and decision-making accuracy. Similarly, in vehicle-to-everything communication and autonomous driving, visual sensors often serve as the primary input for object detection and navigation. However, rain streaks interfere with visual signal interpretation and reduce communication precision between perception and control layers.

To enhance the performance of these secure visual communication systems, several works have integrated image deraining into front-end perception pipelines. For instance, Sun et al. [28] proposed a CNN-based joint deraining and dehazing network to support safer autonomous driving in rain. Dey et al. [6] applied a GAN-based deraining module to improve the effectiveness of real-time surveillance systems under heavy rain. These efforts highlight the growing importance of deraining in harsh environments.

In addition, the robust deraining method helps improve the integrity of communication and network systems. At the same time, it can maintain image quality and improve the accuracy of downstream vision tasks.

2.2   Image Deraining Based on CNN

In image deraining, traditional methods [11,15,21] rely on handcrafted priors to decompose images into background and rain layers. For example, discriminative sparse coding [27] separates rain streaks by leveraging their sparsity through optimized sparse representation. However, these methods heavily depend on manually designed rules and assumptions, making them less effective in complex rain conditions. In scenarios with heavy rain, varying streak directions, or similar textures between rain and background, traditional approaches often struggle to accurately separate rain and restore the background.

In recent years, CNN-based deraining methods have achieved significant progress with the rapid development of deep learning technology. Unlike traditional approaches, deep learning models can automatically learn representations of rain and background features for better adaptation to complex rain conditions. Early CNN-based models achieved strong restoration performance, and later works further enhanced deraining by integrating rain-specific features. For instance, SPDNet [35] used wavelet-based multi-scale decomposition to capture rain's frequency characteristics and introduced a residual channel prior to improve separation accuracy. FMRNet [13] combined spatial and frequency features via a mutual refinement mechanism that bidirectionally enhances spatial representations with frequency cues for more precise restoration. Despite these methods show significant improvements over traditional manual prior strategies, the inherent limitations of convolution still hinder their ability to capture long-range dependencies in images, restricting further performance gains.

2.3   Image Deraining Based on Transformer

With their powerful sequence modeling ability, Transformers have successfully expanded from natural language processing [29] to computer vision, demonstrating superior performance over CNNs in tasks like image classification [24,26], object detection [17,39], and image segmentation [12,40]. The Vision Transformer (ViT) [8] models long-range pixel dependencies via self-attention but is computationally expensive. Therefore, Liu et al. [22] proposed Swin Transformer, which improves efficiency through local windowed attention but sacrifices some global perception capability. In image deraining, Zamir et al. [37] proposed the Restormer, which uses an innovative self-attention mechanism to effectively capture long-range pixel dependencies while maintaining large image processing capabilities. Chen et al. [4] further designed a sparse Transformer architecture with a learnable Top-K operator to optimize feature aggregation and improve detail restoration. However, these methods still face high computational complexity, limiting their application in high-resolution deraining tasks.

To reduce computational complexity while preserving global context, we propose combining self-attention with CNNs. This allows the model to learn both local and global features, improving performance in image deraining. Specifically, CNNs extract local details while attention modules capture global context, enhancing rain-background separation.

3   Proposed Method

DF TransNet adopts a U-shaped four-stage encoder-decoder architecture, consisting of a DF Transformer encoder and an RTC decoder, as shown in Fig. 1. In the encoding stage, shallow features are first extracted using a 3×3 convolution, followed by deep feature extraction via the DF Transformer. The DF Transformer includes a Dual-channel Fusion Enhanced Attention (DFEA) and a Mixed-scale Gated Feed-forward Network (MGFN). Specifically, the feature map is evenly divided into two parts along the channel dimension in DFEA. One part models long-range dependencies through the self-attention mechanism, and the other part captures short-range details through convolution. At the same time, we introduce cross-connection and fusion modules in DFEA to perform deep fusion and interaction of features from the channel, space and frequency domains. MGFN is further used for multi-scale feature extraction, enhancing robustness to complex environments. Downsampling follows each DF Transformer block, and skip connections are added to preserve intermediate features and maintain stability. In the decoder, RTC consists of three Region Transformer Blocks (RTB) and a 1×1 convolution. Each RTB includes a Region Masked Attention (RMA) and a MGFN. Before applying RTC, an auxiliary branch processes the input

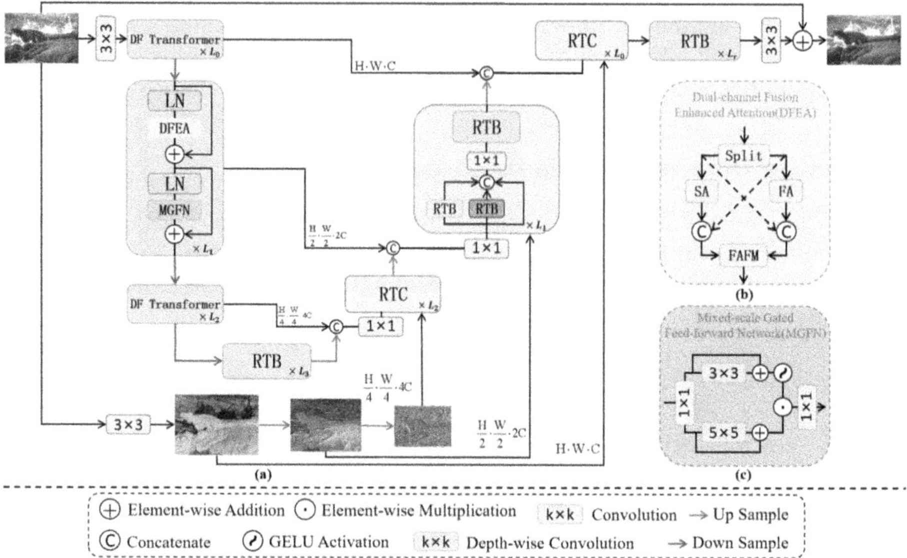

Fig. 1. The overall architecture of the proposed DF TransNet for image deraining. (a) depicts the overall framework of our model, (b) demonstrates our DFEA mechanism, and (c) illustrates our MGFN mechanism.

image with convolution and downsampling, generating a feature map fed into two RMAs. These RMAs apply attention masks to separate rain-affected and rain-unaffected regions, following [16]. Residual connections prevent loss of original features. The concatenated features are processed by a 1×1 convolution for channel reduction. An unmasked RTB then integrates three distinct feature maps into a comprehensive output with enriched feature information.

Finally, we use an RTB without masking to refine and reconstruct the image, followed by a 3×3 convolution to adjust the channel dimensions. A residual connection between the input and output is added to preserve original features and further enhance the model's representation capability.

3.1   Dual-Channel Fusion Enhanced Attention

Existing methods typically perform only shallow fusion when combining Transformers and CNNs, lacking deep interaction mechanisms. This limits effective collaboration between local details and global context, hindering further performance improvement. Therefore, we propose a DFEA, which is a dual-channel cross-connected feature extraction module designed for the deep fusion of CNN and Transformer.

The DFEA adopts a dual-path structure to extract local and global features in parallel, effectively capturing the complex contextual dependencies of rain streaks. A cross-connection mechanism is introduced to establish information

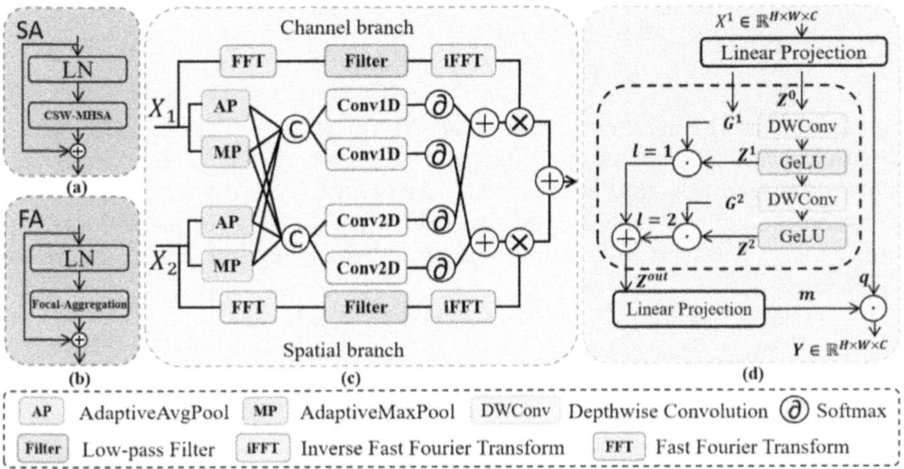

Fig. 2. The structure of each module in DFEA. (a) and (b) illustrate the structures of SA and FA, respectively. (c) presents the detailed structure of FAFM, (d) illustrates the specific details of Focal-Aggregation.

pathways, enabling deep interaction and fusion between global and local features. This mechanism also enhances the model's comprehensive understanding capability. As shown in Fig. 1(b), DFEA consists of two parallel branches. It incorporates a Self-Attention Module (SA), a Focal-Aggregation Module (FA), and a Feature Attention Fusion Module (FAFM). Specifically, the input feature $X \in \mathbb{R}^{H \times W \times 2C}$ is split equally into two sub-feature maps along the channel dimension, and fed into the two branches. SA and FA are used to capture long-range and short-range dependencies respectively. Their outputs are then concatenated along the channel dimension and passed to FAFM. This integration enhances rain streak modeling by combining local details and global semantics. The detailed structures of SA, FA, and FAFM are described in the following sections.

Self-attention Module. As shown in Fig. 2(a), SA consists of a Layer Normalization and a CSW-MHSA layer [7]. CSW-MHSA computes attention separately along horizontal and vertical directions, enabling efficient feature extraction and preserving global context. Specifically, given the input feature map $X^0 \in \mathbb{R}^{H \times W \times 2C}$, we split it equally along the channel dimension into $I_h \in \mathbb{R}^{H \times W \times 2C}$ and $I_v \in \mathbb{R}^{H \times W \times C}$, representing features for horizontal and vertical attention, respectively. For horizontal attention, I_h is evenly divided into M non-overlapping horizontal stripes with width ω. Each stripe is flattened into a sequence of length $\omega \times W$, then passed through a multi-head self-attention to obtain horizontal attention features $Y_h \in \mathbb{R}^{H \times W \times C}$. The detailed computation is as follows:

$$I_h = \left[I^1, I^2, \ldots, I^M \right], \tag{1}$$

$$Y^i = MultiHead\left(Flatten\left(I^i\right)\right), \tag{2}$$

$$Y_h = \left[Y^1, Y^2, \ldots, Y^M\right], \tag{3}$$

where M denote the number of horizontal stripes, $M = \frac{H}{\omega}$. ω is the stripe width. Adjusting ω balances computational cost and receptive field size. $Flatten(\cdot)$ denotes the operation that flattens each stripe into a sequence. $MultiHead(\cdot)$ represents the multi-head self-attention, which takes the sequence as input and learns dependencies among features via matrix multiplication. The computation is as follows:

$$Q = I \cdot W_k^Q, \quad K = I \cdot W_k^K, \quad V = I \cdot W_k^V, \tag{4}$$

$$\text{head}_k = \text{SoftMax}\left(\frac{QK^\top}{\sqrt{D}}\right) V + \text{LePE}(V), \tag{5}$$

$$\text{MultiHead}(I) = \text{Concat}\left(\text{head}_1, \text{head}_2, \ldots, \text{head}_h\right), \tag{6}$$

where h is the number of attention heads, and head_k denotes the k-th head. The projection matrices $W_k^Q \in \mathbb{R}^{C \times d_k}$, $W_k^K \in \mathbb{R}^{C \times d_k}$ and $W_k^V \in \mathbb{R}^{C \times d_k}$ correspond to query, key, and value, with d_k being the projection dimension. LePE (Local-enhanced Position Embedding) [7] is used to encode positional information.

For the vertical feature map $I_v \in \mathbb{R}^{H \times W \times C}$, attention weights are computed similarly along the vertical direction, producing attention features $Y_v \in \mathbb{R}^{H \times W \times C}$. Finally, the outputs Y_h and Y_v are concatenated to form the final attention feature map of the CSW-MHSA layer.

Focal-Aggregation Module. Image deraining requires not only modeling long-range dependencies but also effectively capturing local features to enhance detail restoration. Therefore, we propose a novel Focal-Aggregation(FA) module within the DF Transformer, as shown in Fig. 2(b). FA dynamically integrates multi-level local features through multi-scale extraction and gated fusion, allowing the model to adaptively focus on key regions and improve detail modeling for better deraining performance. FA consists of a Layer Normalization and a Focal-Aggregation. The Focal-Aggregation strengthens short-range dependencies and local features through linear projection and context aggregation operations, as shown in Fig. 2(d). Given the input feature map $X^1 \in \mathbb{R}^{H \times W \times C}$, the context aggregation process is as follows:

$$G = X^1 \cdot W^G, \quad Z^0 = X^1 \cdot W^Z, \tag{7}$$

$$Z^l = \sigma\left(\text{DWConv}\left(Z^{(l-1)}\right)\right), \tag{8}$$

$$Z^{\text{out}} = \sum_{l=1}^{L} G^l \odot Z^l, \tag{9}$$

where $G \in \mathbb{R}^{H \times W \times (L+1)}$ denote the projected features obtained by applying the projection matrix $W^G \in \mathbb{R}^{C \times (L+1)}$ to the input X. The l-th slice of G is denoted as $G^l \in \mathbb{R}^{H \times W}$. Similarly, $Z^0 \in \mathbb{R}^{H \times W \times C}$ is obtained by projecting

X with $W^Z \in \mathbb{R}^{C \times C}$. For each layer $l \in (1, 2, ..., L)$, the aggregated feature $Z^l \in \mathbb{R}^{H \times W \times C}$ is derived from $Z^{(l-1)}$ using a depth-wise convolution DWConv$(\cdot)$ followed by a GeLU activation $\sigma(\cdot)$. L is the number of aggregation layers and $\odot$ denotes element-wise multiplication. The final aggregated context feature $Z^o ut \in \mathbb{R}^{H \times W \times C}$ is obtained through hierarchical convolutional aggregation. Each G^l serves as a gating function and is broadcasted to extract context information from the corresponding layer. The aggregated features are then linearly projected and element-wise multiplied with the input to produce the final output feature $Y \in \mathbb{R}^{H \times W \times C}$. The full computation is defined as:

$$m = Z^{\text{out}} \cdot W^M, \quad q = X \cdot W^Q, \tag{10}$$

$$Y = q \odot m, \tag{11}$$

where $W^M \in \mathbb{R}^{C \times C}$, $W^Q \in \mathbb{R}^{C \times C}$ are projection matrices, and the output feature Y is obtained by element-wise multiplication of the projected features.

Feature Attention Fusion Module. Since global and local features are extracted through receptive fields of different scales, there is a significant semantic gap and feature granularity misalignment between them in terms of information representation. Simple fusion strategies struggle to effectively reconcile these intrinsic differences across multi-scale features, often leading to the loss of critical information or feature confusion, thereby degrading model performance. Rain streaks may only affect specific semantic channels. Pooling operations can be used to learn channel weights to emphasize the most relevant features in each branch, ensuring adaptive and discriminative fusion. In addition, Rain-affected regions are usually sparse in space but strong in local areas. Spatial attention mechanisms highlight such regions for focused reconstruction, enhancing the model's ability to recover clean backgrounds with fine local textures.

Therefore, we propose a Feature Attention Fusion Module for image feature fusion, which combines channel and spatial attention to weight and fuse two input features, $X_1 \in \mathbb{R}^{H \times W \times C}$ and $X_2 \in \mathbb{R}^{H \times W \times C}$, as shown in Fig. 2(c). Notably, before weighting, we apply Fourier transform to convert the features into the frequency domain, followed by preliminary processing using a low-pass filter to reduce high-frequency noise. Specifically, in the channel branch, the two feature maps are processed via cross-spatial global pooling to aggregate spatial information. The aggregation can be expressed as:

$$S_c = \text{Concat}\left(\text{AP}(X_1), \text{ MP}(X_1), \text{ AP}(X_2), \text{ MP}(X_2)\right), \tag{12}$$

where S_c denotes the aggregated spatial features, and AP$(\cdot)$ and MP$(\cdot)$ represent global average pooling and global max pooling across spatial dimensions, respectively. The aggregated spatial features are then processed through two 1D convolutional layers to obtain W_{c1} and W_{c2}, representing the channel weights of X_1 and X_2. Subsequently, Softmax is applied to W_{c1} and W_{c2} to identify important feature components. In the spatial branch, the spatial weights of X_1

and X_2 are determined similarly, highlighting key regions in the spatial dimension. Note that the spatial branch performs pooling along the channel dimension. The channel and spatial weights are then summed to obtain the overall weights, determining the most significant parts between the two features.

Finally, after denoising X_1 and X_2 in the frequency domain, the weights are used to compute a weighted sum of the features. The output can be expressed as:

$$X_1', X_2' = \mathcal{IF}\left(W^{\text{filter}} \cdot \mathcal{F}(X_1)\right), \ \mathcal{IF}\left(W^{\text{filter}} \cdot \mathcal{F}(X_2)\right), \tag{13}$$

$$Output = (W_{c1}' + W_{s1}') \cdot X_1' + (W_{c2}' + W_{s2}') \cdot X_2', \tag{14}$$

where W_{c1}', W_{c2}' represent the channel-wise attention weights, and W_{s1}', W_{s2}' denote the spatial attention weights. All weights are normalized using the Softmax function to highlight important feature components. $\mathcal{F}(\cdot)$ and $\mathcal{IF}(\cdot)$ denote the Fast Fourier Transform and its inverse, W^{filter} represents the low-pass filter mask, and Output is the fused feature. By integrating channel, spatial, and frequency-domain information through multi-level attention modeling and low-frequency filtering, this module enables dynamic weighted fusion of input features.

3.2 Mixed-Scale Gated Feed-Forward Network

Image deraining tasks require effective modeling of multi-scale rain streak features. However, existing methods often rely on single-scale processing, leading to suboptimal removal of rain streaks across varying scales in complex scenes and degrading restoration quality. Therefore, we design a Mixed-scale Gated Feed-forward Network, as shown in Fig. 1(c). Specifically, the input first undergoes a 1×1 convolution to expand channel dimensions by a ratio r, followed by two parallel branches. Multi-scale local feature extraction is performed using 3×3 and 5×5 depthwise convolutions, expressed as:

$$X_i = \text{DWConv}_{K_i \times K_i}\left(\text{Conv}_{1\times 1}(I)\right) + \text{Conv}_{1\times 1}(I), \quad i = 1, 2 \tag{15}$$

where I and X_i denote input and output features, $Conv_{1\times 1}(\cdot)$ represents 1×1 convolution, and $DWConv_{K_i \times K_i}(\cdot)$ denotes depthwise convolution. A gating mechanism then fuses the feature maps from both branches, with one branch activated by GeLU for nonlinearity. Finally, a 1×1 convolution adjusts the output channels. This process is formulated as:

$$Y = \text{Conv}_{1\times 1}\left(\phi(X_1) \odot X_2\right), \tag{16}$$

where $\phi(\cdot)$ denotes the GeLU activation. The gating mechanism adaptively weights the importance of mixed-scale local features, enhancing rain streak identification and separation while preserving background details. The introduction of MGFN significantly improves the model's adaptability in complex rain scenarios, providing robust support for image deraining tasks.

3.3 Loss Function

To explicitly suppress high-frequency noise and enhance structural fidelity in the frequency domain, we adopt a frequency-domain loss computed via the 2D Fast Fourier Transform. Given a predicted image $\breve{I}$ and ground truth image I, the frequency loss is defined as:

$$L_{freq} = \frac{1}{N} \sum_{i=1}^{N} \left| \mathcal{F}(\breve{I}_i) - \mathcal{F}(I_i) \right| \tag{17}$$

where N is the total number of pixels in the frequency domain. This formulation calculates the mean absolute difference of the complex-valued frequency components between the two images.

In addition, L_1 Loss and edge loss L_{edge} are also used as loss functions. Therefore, the total loss of the proposed method L_{total} denotes as follows:

$$L_{total} = L_1 + L_{edge} + \alpha L_{freq}, \tag{18}$$

where α is a hyperparameter and empirically set to 0.01.

We adopt frequency-domain processing by converting spatial features to the frequency domain via Fourier Transform. The Frequency Loss suppresses high-frequency noise and enhances image smoothness by evaluating spectral errors, while the Edge Loss reinforces critical contour information. Their synergistic effect significantly improves deraining performance, preserving fine details while optimizing overall image quality.

4 Experiments and Analysis

4.1 Experimental Settings

We evaluated our proposed method on several public datasets, including Rain200L [34], Rain200H [34], DID-Data [38], DDN-Data [10], and SPA-Data [31]. PSNR and SSIM were used as evaluation metrics, computed on the Y channel of the YCbCr color space, following prior works [4,5].

Our DF TransNet adopts a 4-level encoder-decoder architecture where the number of layers from L_0 to L_3 is set to 4, 4, 4, 4 with corresponding attention heads of 6, 6, 6, 6 and channel dimensions of 48, 96, 192, 384 respectively. The implementation was done using PyTorch framework and trained from scratch on a machine equipped with an NVIDIA GeForce RTX 4060Ti GPU (16GB). During training, we employed the AdamW optimizer with a patch size of 128×128 pixels, batch size of 2, and initial learning rate of 2e-4 that was gradually reduced to 2e-6 using cosine annealing schedule. The model was trained for 200 epochs on DID-Data and DDN-Data datasets, and 400 epochs on Rain200L and Rain200H datasets, with random horizontal flipping applied for data augmentation.

182   Z. He et al.

Table 1. Quantitative evaluations of the proposed approach against state-of-the-art methods on five commonly used benchmark datasets. Bold indicate the best results.

| - | Datasets | Rain200L [34] | | Rain200H [34] | | DID-Data [38] | | DDN-Data [10] | | SPA-Data [31] | |
-	Metrics	PSNR	SSIM	PSNR	SSIM	PSNR	SSIM	PSNR	SSIM	PSNR	SSIM
Prior-based methods	DSC [23]	27.16	0.8663	14.73	0.3815	24.24	0.8279	27.31	0.8373	34.95	0.9416
	GMM [21]	28.66	0.8652	14.50	0.4164	25.81	0.8344	27.55	0.8479	34.30	0.9428
CNN-based methods	DDN [10]	34.68	0.9671	26.05	0.8056	30.97	0.9116	30.00	0.9041	36.16	0.9457
	PReNet [25]	37.80	0.9814	29.04	0.8991	33.17	0.9481	32.60	0.9459	40.16	0.9816
	MSPFN [14]	38.58	0.9827	29.36	0.9034	33.72	0.9550	32.99	0.9333	43.43	0.9843
	RCDNet [30]	39.17	0.9885	30.24	0.9048	34.08	0.9532	33.04	0.9472	43.36	0.9831
	MPRNet [36]	39.47	0.9825	30.67	0.9110	33.99	0.9590	33.10	0.9347	43.64	0.9844
	DualGCN [9]	40.73	0.9886	31.15	0.9125	34.37	0.9620	33.01	0.9489	44.18	0.9902
	SPDNet [35]	40.50	0.9875	31.28	0.9207	34.57	0.9560	33.15	0.9457	43.20	0.9871
Transformer-based methods	Uformer [32]	40.20	0.9860	30.80	0.9105	35.02	0.9621	33.95	0.9545	46.13	0.9913
	Restormer [37]	40.99	0.9890	32.00	0.9329	35.29	0.9641	34.20	0.9571	47.98	0.9921
	IDT [33]	40.74	0.9884	32.10	0.9344	34.89	0.9623	33.84	0.9549	47.35	0.9930
	DRSformer [4]	41.23	0.9894	32.17	0.9326	35.35	0.9646	34.35	0.9588	48.54	0.9924
	Regformer [16]	41.51	0.9900	32.46	0.9353	35.43	0.9651	34.38	0.9591	48.60	**0.9941**
	Ours	**41.69**	**0.9901**	**32.62**	**0.9370**	**35.46**	**0.9655**	**34.45**	**0.9598**	**49.38**	0.9932

Table 2. Comparisons of model complexity against state-of-the-art methods.

Methods	#FLOPs(G)	# Params(M)
Uformer [32]	45.9	50.88
Restormer [37]	174.7	26.12
IDT [33]	61.9	16.41
DRSformer [4]	242.9	33.65
Regformer [16]	180.41	22.3
Ours	172.37	21.63

4.2 Comparisons with the State-of-the-Arts

We compared our method with prior-based approaches (DSC [23], GMM [21]), CNN-based methods (DDN [10], PReNet [25], MSPFN [14], RCDNet [30], MPR-Net [36], DualGCN [9], SPDNet [35]), and state-of-the-art Transformer-based approaches (Uformer [32], Restormer [37], IDT [33], DRSformer [4], Regformer [16]). The quantitative evaluation results on datasets [34,38], and [10] are summarized in Table 1, demonstrating our method's superior PSNR and SSIM values. Table 2 presents the performance comparison between our model and other methods.

Evaluations on Synthetic Datasets. Figure 3 displays visual results on the synthetic dataset Rain200H. The CNN-based SPDNet [35] struggles to recover fine details when handling heavy rain streaks, failing to reconstruct clear images effectively. In contrast, Transformer-based models like Restormer [37], IDT [33], DRSformer [4], and Regformer [16] excel in deraining by leveraging global contextual information for long-range modeling. However, these methods still face challenges in background reconstruction under high-intensity rain streaks, such

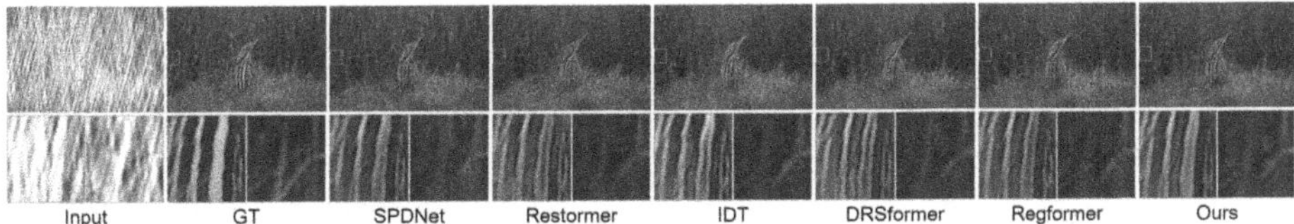

Fig. 3. Comparison of deraining results on the Rain200H dataset with heavy rain streaks.

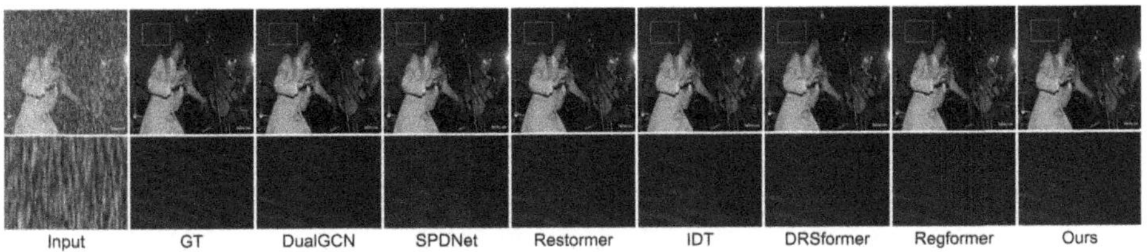

Fig. 4. Visual quality comparison on the DID-Data dataset.

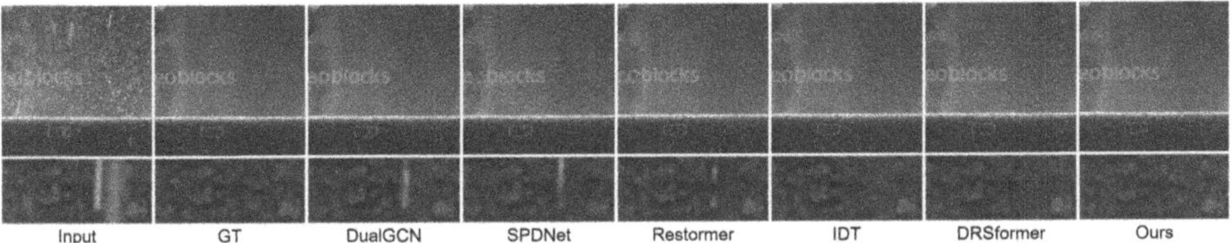

Fig. 5. Visual quality comparison on the real-world SPA-Data dataset.

as recovering details on birds obscured by rain. Compared to existing Transformer models, our proposed dual-branch fusion Transformer effectively combines local details with global context, reconstructing sharper details and more accurate image structures. Similarly, we also show the visualization results on DID-Data, as shown in Fig. 4. Our method also outperforms other methods in restoring wall textures.

Evaluations on Real-World Datasets. We further conducted comparative experiments on the real-world dataset SPA-Data. As shown in the last column of Table 1, our method improves the PSNR by 0.78dB compared with Regformer, showing a significant advantage. The visual comparison results in Fig. 5 more intuitively show the performance differences of each method. Other methods have blurred details after rain streaks (such as the rain streak area marked in the red box). However, our method can achieve better detail restoration while maintaining efficient rain removal.

4.3 Ablation Studies

Effectiveness of DFEA. To validate the effectiveness of each submodule and cross-connection in DFEA, we conducted five ablation experiments, as shown

Table 3. Ablation analysis for various different modules in DFEA. The models (a-e) are consistent with the settings in Fig. 6. Bold indicate the best results.

Models	SA	FA	FAFM	PSNR	SSIM
a	✓			41.63	0.9900
b		✓		41.57	0.9898
c	✓	✓		41.66	0.9900
d	✓	✓	✓	41.52	0.9898
e	✓	✓	✓	**41.69**	**0.9901**

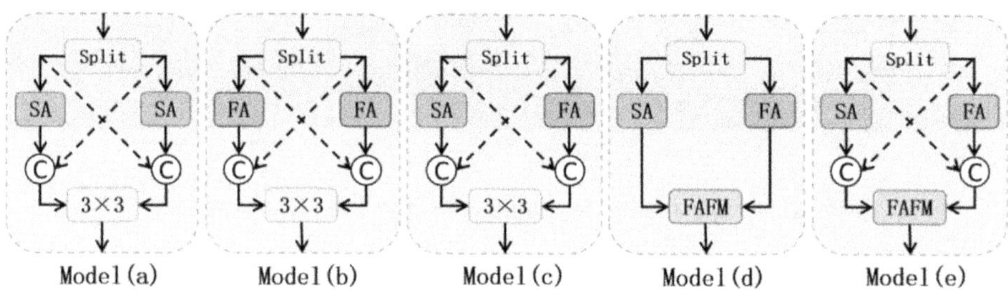

Fig. 6. Details of different versions of DFEA. Model(a) with SA, Model(b) with FA, Model(c) with SA and FA, Model(d) without cross-connection, Model (e) with all modules.

in Fig. 6. The first group used only the SA as the feature extraction unit, while the second retained only the FA, denoted as Model(a) and Model(b). The third and fifth groups progressively introduced the FA and FAFM, denoted as Model(c) and model(e) and the fourth group removed the cross-connections, denoted as Model(d). All experiments were performed on the Rain200L dataset, with results shown in Table 3. The results indicate that when DFEA contains only the SA, the model overly relies on self-attention for global context modeling, leading to insufficient local detail capture and poor rain streak recovery. Introducing the FA module significantly enhances local feature extraction and improves performance, but the lack of deep global-local feature integration limits its ability to model complex dependencies between rain streaks and backgrounds. Therefore, the FAFM is further incorporated into DFEA to enhance complex contextual modeling through spatial, channel-wise, and frequency-domain feature fusion. Comparisons between the last two groups demonstrate that cross-connections effectively promote feature interaction between parallel branches, providing richer contextual information for subsequent fusion and further boosting model performance.

Additionally, the receptive field visualization of the five models is shown in Fig. 7. It can be observed that Model(b)'s receptive field (highlighted in red) is concentrated in the central region, while Model(a) exhibits a significantly larger coverage. In Model(c), by combining the SA and FA modules, the model sig-

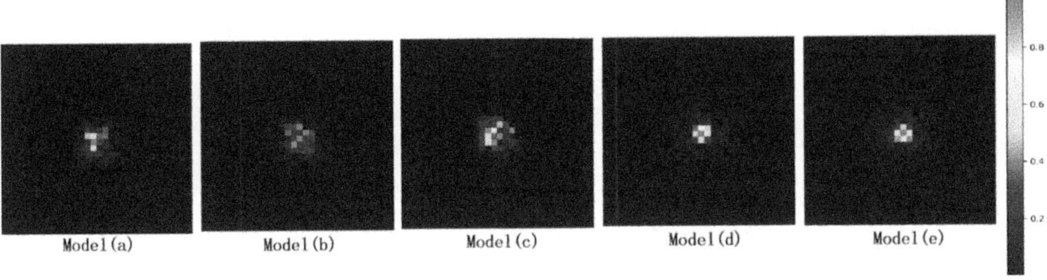

Fig. 7. Visualization comparison of different DFEA receptive field. The models (a–e) are consistent with the settings in Fig. 6. (Color figure online)

Table 4. Comparisons of four different feed-forward networks.

Methods	PSNR	SSIM
DFN [20]	41.06	0.9889
MSFN [4]	41.32	0.9893
GDFN [37]	41.47	0.9896
MGFN	41.69	0.9901

nificantly enhances the modeling ability of local details and shows a stronger local receptive field. However, Model(c) still has deficiencies in capturing information in the global scope, which limits its overall understanding of complex scenes. In contrast, Model(c) introduces the FAFM module. While maintaining strong local modeling capabilities, it effectively expands the global receptive field and achieves a deep fusion of local and global features. Especially in the image deraining task, rain streaks have local high-frequency characteristics and global distribution trends. Therefore, the model needs to have both local and global modeling capabilities. Finally, comparing Model(d) and Model(e) reveals that the latter achieves both broader receptive fields and enhanced local feature extraction, confirming that cross-connections effectively facilitate feature interaction between branches for efficient local-global fusion.

Effectiveness of MGFN. To validate the effectiveness of the proposed MGFN, we conducted comparative experiments with three representative feed-forward networks: (1) Dconv Feed-forward Network (DFN) [20]; (2) Mixed-scale Feed-forward Network (MSFN) [4]; and (3) Gated-Dconv Feed-forward network (GDFN) [37]. Table 4 gives the quantitative results of four methods on the Rain200L dataset. It can be found that although GDFN achieves some performance improvement through its dual-stream gating mechanism, it fails to fully utilize multi-scale feature information. In contrast, MGFN integrates multi-scale local feature extraction with gating mechanisms, outperforming GDFN by 0.22 dB in PSNR and demonstrating superior deraining capability. Notably, as visualized in Fig. 8, MGFN consistently leads in PSNR during training. Figure 9

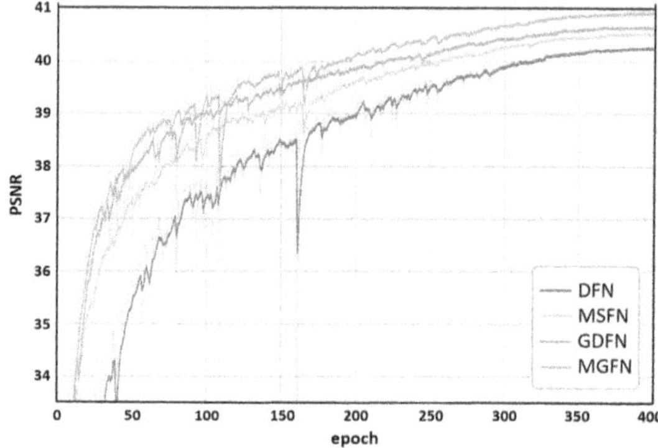

Fig. 8. Comparison of PSNR values of four feedforward networks during training.

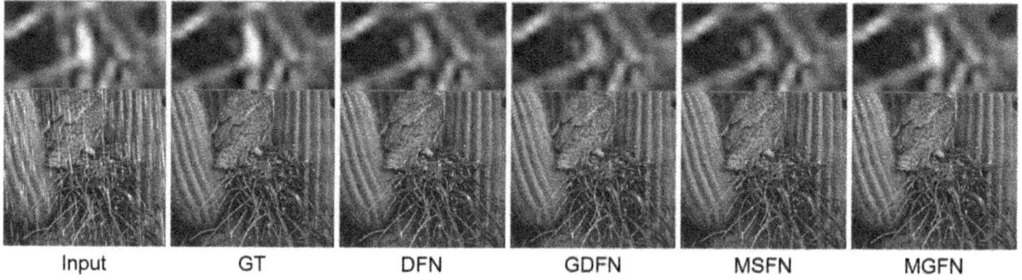

Fig. 9. Visual quality comparison on four Feed-forward networks.

shows visual comparisons of derained images. It can be seen that MGFN produces results closer to ground truth compared to other methods.

5 Conclusion

This paper presents an innovative network architecture for image deraining, denoted as DF TransNet. We design a DF Transform based on dual-channel fusion and make it serve as the encoder of DF TransNet. DF Transformer employs a dual-channel cross-connection structure to simultaneously extract local detail features and global semantic information, enhancing feature complementarity. Deep feature fusion is then performed across channel, spatial, and frequency domains by the proposed FAFM. To further fuse multi-scale features, we introduce MGFN into DF Transformer. The MGFN employs mixed-scale convolution and gating mechanism to enhance feature representation. In the decoder, we adopt the RTC module, which uses a built-in rain mask layer to precisely distinguish rain-affected areas from unaffected ones, enabling targeted feature reconstruction. Experimental results demonstrate that our DF TransNet performs favorably against state-of-the-art methods in PSNR and SSIM, proving the effectiveness of the proposed architecture.

While DF TransNet has shown strong deraining capability, particularly for security-relevant vision tasks, there are still two promising future directions that warrant our exploration. First, we aim to extend DF TransNet to real-time video deraining, enabling temporal consistency and stable performance across video frames. This is especially beneficial for intelligent surveillance and autonomous navigation, where reliability under continuous observation is critical. Second, to meet the demands of resource-constrained deployment, we plan to explore lightweight variants of DF TransNet tailored for edge devices such as drones, embedded surveillance systems, and mobile platforms. In dynamic and potentially harsh environments, these efforts will facilitate practical integration into secure visual systems operating.

References

1. Chen, H., et al.: Pre-trained image processing transformer. In: Proceedings of the IEEE/CVF Conference on Computer Vision and Pattern Recognition, pp. 12299–12310 (2021). https://doi.org/10.48550/arXiv.2012.00364
2. Chen, K., et al.: Ovarnet: towards open-vocabulary object attribute recognition. In: Proceedings of the IEEE/CVF Conference on Computer Vision and Pattern Recognition, pp. 23518–23527 (2023). https://doi.org/10.48550/arXiv.2301.09506
3. Chen, X., et al.: Hybrid CNN-transformer feature fusion for single image deraining. In: Proceedings of the AAAI Conference on Artificial Intelligence, vol. 37, no. 1, pp. 378–386 (2023). https://doi.org/10.1609/aaai.v37i1.25111
4. Chen, X., et al.: Learning a sparse transformer network for effective image deraining. In: Proceedings of the IEEE/CVF Conference on Computer Vision and Pattern Recognition, pp. 5896–5905 (2023). https://doi.org/10.48550/arXiv.2303.11950
5. Chen, X., et al.: Towards unified deep image deraining: a survey and a new benchmark. IEEE Trans. Pattern Anal. Mach. Intell. (2025). https://doi.org/10.48550/arXiv.2310.03535
6. Dey, R., Bhattacharjee, D.: Single image de-raining using GAN for accurate video surveillance. In: Intelligence Enabled Research: DoSIER 2019, pp. 7–11 (2020). https://doi.org/10.1007/978-981-15-2021-1_2
7. Dong, X., et al.: Cswin transformer: a general vision transformer backbone with cross-shaped windows. In: Proceedings of the IEEE/CVF Conference on Computer Vision and Pattern Recognition, pp. 12124–12134 (2022). https://doi.org/10.1109/CVPR52688.2022.01181
8. Dosovitskiy, A., et al.: An image is worth 16x16 words: transformers for image recognition at scale. arXiv preprint arXiv:2010.11929 (2020). https://doi.org/10.48550/arXiv.2010.11929
9. Fu, X., et al.: Rain streak removal via dual graph convolutional network. In: Proceedings of the AAAI Conference on Artificial Intelligence, vol. 35, no. 2, pp. 1352–1360 (2021). https://doi.org/10.1609/aaai.v35i2.16224
10. Fu, X., et al.: Removing rain from single images via a deep detail network. In: Proceedings of the IEEE Conference on Computer Vision and Pattern Recognition, pp. 3855–3863 (2017). https://doi.org/10.1109/CVPR.2017.186
11. Gu, S., et al.: Joint convolutional analysis and synthesis sparse representation for single image layer separation. In: Proceedings of the IEEE International Conference on Computer Vision, pp. 1708–1716 (2017). https://doi.org/10.1109/ICCV.2017.189

12. Jain, J., et al.: Oneformer: one transformer to rule universal image segmentation. In: Proceedings of the IEEE/CVF Conference on Computer Vision and Pattern Recognition, pp. 2989–2998 (2023). https://doi.org/10.48550/arXiv.2211.06220

13. Jiang, K., et al.: FMRNet: image deraining via frequency mutual revision. In: Proceedings of the AAAI Conference on Artificial Intelligence, vol. 38, no. 11, pp. 12892–12900 (2024). https://doi.org/10.1609/aaai.v38i11.29186

14. Jiang, K., et al.: Multi-scale progressive fusion network for single image deraining. In: Proceedings of the IEEE/CVF Conference on Computer Vision and Pattern Recognition, pp. 8346–8355 (2020). https://doi.org/10.48550/arXiv.2003.10985

15. Kang, L.-W., Lin, C.-W., Fu, Y.-H.: Automatic single-image-based rain streaks removal via image decomposition. IEEE Trans. Image Process. **21**(4), 1742–1755 (2011). https://doi.org/10.1109/TIP.2011.2179057

16. Li, B., et al.: Exploiting Regional Information Transformer for Single Image Deraining. arXiv preprint arXiv:2402.16033 (2024). https://doi.org/10.48550/arXiv.2402.16033

17. Li, F., et al.: Mask dino: towards a unified transformer-based framework for object detection and segmentation. In: Proceedings of the IEEE/CVF Conference on Computer Vision and Pattern Recognition, pp. 3041–3050 (2023). https://doi.org/10.48550/arXiv.2206.02777

18. Li, J., et al.: A review of remote sensing for environmental monitoring in China. Remote Sens. **12**(7), 1130 (2020). https://doi.org/10.3390/rs12071130

19. Li, M., et al.: Online rain/snow removal from surveillance videos. IEEE Trans. Image Process. **30**, 2029–2044 (2021). https://doi.org/10.1109/TIP.2021.3050313

20. Li, Y., et al.: Localvit: bringing locality to vision transformers. arXiv preprint arXiv:2104.05707 (2021). https://doi.org/10.48550/arXiv.2104.05707

21. Li, Y., et al.: Rain streak removal using layer priors. In: Proceedings of the IEEE Conference on Computer Vision and Pattern Recognition, pp. 2736–2744 (2016). https://doi.org/10.1109/CVPR.2016.299

22. Liu, Z., et al.: Swin transformer: hierarchical vision transformer using shifted windows. In: Proceedings of the IEEE/CVF International Conference on Computer Vision, pp. 10012–10022 (2021). https://doi.org/10.1109/ICCV48922.2021.00986

23. Luo, Y., Xu, Y., Ji, H.: Removing rain from a single image via discriminative sparse coding. In: Proceedings of the IEEE International Conference on Computer Vision, pp. 3397–3405 (2015). https://doi.org/10.1109/ICCV.2015.388

24. Manzari, O.N., et al.: MedViT: a robust vision transformer for generalized medical image classification. Comput. Biol. Med. **157**, 106791 (2023). https://doi.org/10.48550/arXiv.2302.09462

25. Ren, D., et al.: Progressive image deraining networks: a better and simpler baseline. In: Proceedings of the IEEE/CVF Conference on Computer Vision and Pattern Recognition, pp. 3937–3946 (2019). https://doi.org/10.48550/arXiv.1901.09221

26. Roy, S.K., et al.: Spectral-spatial morphological attention transformer for hyperspectral image classification. IEEE Trans. Geosci. Remote Sens. **61**, 1–15 (2023). https://doi.org/10.1109/TGRS.2023.3242346

27. Son, C.-H., Zhang, X.-P.: Rain removal via shrinkage-based sparse coding and learned rain dictionary. arXiv preprint arXiv:1610.00386 (2016). https://doi.org/10.48550/arXiv.1610.00386

28. Sun, H., Ang, M.H., Rus, D.: A convolutional network for joint deraining and dehazing from a single image for autonomous driving in rain. In: 2019 IEEE/RSJ International Conference on Intelligent Robots and Systems (IROS), pp. 962–969. IEEE (2019). https://doi.org/10.1109/IROS40897.2019.8967644

29. Vaswani, A, et al.: Attention is all you need. In: Advances in Neural Information Processing Systems, vol. 30 (2017). https://doi.org/10.48550/arXiv.1706.03762
30. Wang, H., et al.: A model-driven deep neural network for single image rain removal. In: Proceedings of the IEEE/CVF Conference on Computer Vision and Pattern Recognition, pp. 3103–3112 (2020). https://doi.org/10.48550/arXiv.2005.01333
31. Wang, T., et al.: Spatial attentive single-image deraining with a high quality real rain dataset. In: Proceedings of the IEEE/CVF Conference on Computer Vision and Pattern Recognition (CVPR) (2019)
32. Wang, Z., et al.: A general U-shaped transformer for image restoration. 2022 IEEE. In: CVF Conference on Computer Vision and Pattern Recognition (CVPR), pp. 17662–17672 (2022). https://doi.org/10.1109/CVPR52688.2022.01716
33. Xiao, J., et al.: Image de-raining transformer. IEEE Trans. Pattern Anal. Mach. Intell. **45**(11), 12978–12995 (2022). https://doi.org/10.1109/TPAMI.2022.3183612
34. Yang, W., et al.: Deep joint rain detection and removal from a single image. In: Proceedings of the IEEE Conference on Computer Vision and Pattern Recognition, pp. 1357–1366 (2017). https://doi.org/10.48550/arXiv.1609.07769
35. Yi, Q., et al.: Structure-preserving deraining with residue channel prior guidance. In: Proceedings of the IEEE/CVF International Conference on Computer Vision, pp. 4238–4247 (2021). https://doi.org/10.48550/arXiv.2108.09079
36. Zamir, S.W., et al.: Multi-stage progressive image restoration. In: Proceedings of the IEEE/CVF Conference on Computer Vision and Pattern Recognition, pp. 14821–14831 (2021). https://doi.org/10.48550/arXiv.2102.02808
37. Zamir, S.W., et al.: Restormer: efficient transformer for high-resolution image restoration. In: Proceedings of the IEEE/CVF Conference on Computer Vision and Pattern Recognition, pp. 5728–5739 (2022). https://doi.org/10.1109/CVPR52688.2022.00564
38. Zhang, H., Patel, V.M.: Density-aware single image de-raining using a multi-stream dense network. In: Proceedings of the IEEE Conference on Computer Vision and Pattern Recognition, pp. 695–704 (2018). https://doi.org/10.48550/arXiv.1802.07412
39. Zhou, C., et al.: OcTr: octree-based transformer for 3D object detection. In: Proceedings of the IEEE/CVF Conference on Computer Vision and Pattern Recognition, pp. 5166–5175 (2023). https://doi.org/10.48550/arXiv.2303.12621
40. Zhou, H.-Y., et al.: nnFormer: volumetric medical image segmentation via a 3D transformer. IEEE Trans. Image Process. **32**, 4036–4045 (2023). https://doi.org/10.1109/TIP.2023.3293771
41. Zhou, X., et al.: How can objects help action recognition? In: Proceedings of the IEEE/CVF Conference on Computer Vision and Pattern Recognition, pp. 2353–2362 (2023). https://doi.org/10.48550/arXiv.2306.11726

DRLPO: A Deep Reinforcement Learning Distributed Partial Offloading Scheme for Fog Computing Networks

Jiahong Xiao[1], Jiansheng Lin[1], Jigang Wen[1], Chaoyi Yang[1], Yuanqiang Tang[2], Xiaoyan Chen[3], and Tianxiong Liu[4(✉)]

[1] School of Computer Science and Engineering, Hunan University of Science and Technology, Xiangtan, China
{xiaoiaong,2305050304,yangchaoy1}@mail.hnust.edu.cn,
wenjigang@hnust.edu.cn
[2] School of Information Engineering, Xinyu University, Xinyu, China
bobtang2016@hnu.edu.cn
[3] School of Software Engineering, Xiamen University of Technology, Xiamen, China
cxy@xmut.edu.cn
[4] Research and Teaching Department, Hunan Aerospace Hospital, The Affiliated Aerospace Hospital of Hunan Normal University, Changsha, China
liutianxiong@gt.cn

Abstract. In fog computing environments, task offloading mechanisms are widely used because they can effectively alleviate the computing pressure of terminal devices. However, with the increasing demand for data privacy protection and the rise in network attack risks, achieving efficient task scheduling while ensuring data security has become a key challenge. Current research focuses on improving offloading efficiency, often ignoring the security threats that may be faced during task allocation and execution, and has certain limitations. Therefore, we propose a deep reinforcement learning task partial offloading (DRLPO) mechanism suitable for multi-user and multi-server scenarios, which divides the application device task into k subtasks, and models the offloading problem of each subtask after block as a Markov decision process (MDP) for distributed processing. By offloading subtasks instead of complete tasks, information leakage is prevented. In addition, we model the task offloading problem as a multi-objective optimization problem that takes into account energy consumption and delay, and use the Attention-DQN mechanism to keep the weighted sum of task processing delay and energy consumption at the lowest level. Experimental data show that compared with the existing baseline algorithm, the average task processing time and energy consumption of DRLPO are reduced by 2.2 s and 1.1 KJ, respectively, which can effectively reduce the response time of device tasks.

Keywords: UAV · Fog Computing Networks · Task Offloading · Deep Reinforcement Learning

W. Liang et al. (Eds.): SecureComm 2025, LNICST 690, pp. 190–209, 2026.
https://doi.org/10.1007/978-3-032-23456-8_11

1   Introduction

With the continuous advancement of mobile devices and mobile communication technologies, it has become possible to execute applications with high real-time requirements on mobile devices, such as virtual reality [25], intelligent transportation systems [11], and augmented reality [13]. However, the tasks generated by these smart devices and complex applications are not only computationally complex, but also place higher demands on data security and privacy protection. In the face of increasingly serious malicious attacks and data leakage risks, traditional cloud computing architectures upload tasks to remote cloud processing, which not only has large response delays [22], but also faces security risks in the transmission and storage of data. Therefore, fog computing, as an emerging, near-source computing paradigm, not only improves the efficiency of task processing, but also provides more secure computing support for mobile devices [16,18].

Although fog computing has the advantages of fast response and flexible deployment, it still faces many challenges in achieving efficient task offloading and resource scheduling under the premise of ensuring security. For example, how to balance the execution efficiency of offloading decisions and the security of task transmission and processing in an environment with limited resources and heterogeneous nodes [12,17]. Unreasonable task scheduling strategies may cause tasks to be executed on vulnerable nodes, thereby causing risks of privacy leakage or malicious manipulation. At the same time, due to the limited computing resources and bandwidth of fog servers, secure task scheduling strategies must also take into account the optimization of device energy consumption and delay [6]. In addition, mobile devices usually rely on battery power, and must balance performance and energy consumption when executing tasks to avoid greater computing overhead after the security protection mechanism is strengthened [1,8,19,26].

Based on the above analysis, this paper proposes a security-aware task partial offloading algorithm by studying the impact of the resource status of trusted fog nodes that changes dynamically over time on the task processing performance, security, and processing delay of mobile devices. The algorithm realizes distributed parallel processing of tasks by splitting tasks into multiple subtasks and safely offloading them to multiple trusted fog nodes for execution, and enhances the overall system's anti-attack and privacy protection capabilities. In the process of task offloading, factors such as processing delay, energy consumption, and node trust are comprehensively considered, and the weighted objective function is minimized as the optimization direction to improve task processing efficiency while ensuring system security.

- The tasks of the terminal device are divided into k subtasks, and the k subtasks are safely and reliably offloaded with distributed computing. The deep reinforcement learning (DRL) algorithm combined with the attention mechanism achieves the optimal trade-off between task delay, energy consumption and offloading safety.
- This paper adopts reinforcement learning and improved neural network methods to adaptively model the dependencies and safety levels of offloading tasks, and constructs a multi-objective offloading optimization model through state space, action strategy and reward function to improve the system's safety response capability.
- During the deep DQN training process, the parameter θ is defined to adapt to dynamically changing offloading scenarios and safety contexts. The mechanism shows good generalisation ability in optimizing resource allocation and offloading safety path selection, avoiding falling into local optimality.

2   Related Work

Most researchers define the goal of computational offloading as the optimal solution of constrained convex problems, where the constraints are mainly residual energy, task time constraints, network bandwidth capacity, etc. In [10], Jiang et al. investigated the optimization of server storage space in fog wireless access networks, optimizing and reducing the latency time of task processing by including server storage as part of the input state. In [3], they study two aspects of task placement decisions and resource allocation in task offloading computation. In [21], the authors aim to optimize offloading schemes, resource allocation, and storage caching in wireless networks. Most of the current solutions to the above problems are considered based on game theory [24,28]. However, the system simulation scenarios considered by these methods are all ideal situations, which are often not the case in reality.

Currently, many researchers focus on energy consumption in computational offloading [2,14,29]. Wang et al. [23] formulated the joint optimization problem of offloading and computing power allocation by considering factors such as dynamic channels in the natural offloading environment. [9] also considers the time delay and energy overhead and studies a resource allocation scheme. The above schemes all consider the offloading distribution between the terminal and the fog, but the cloud server is also a service device with a huge processing capacity [27].

Heuristic algorithms are proposed relative to optimization algorithms. Bitam et al. [4] suggest the Bee Life Algorithm to balance computation time and memory consumption by studying task scheduling in computing environments. Liu et al. [15] consider both together, obtaining an optimal solution through an iterative coordination process. This method is more in line with realistic user computing scenarios.

Compared with optimization methods such as heuristics that require manual rules design, DRL can achieve autonomous learning of algorithms. In [7], the author considers the system cannot predict when and where users send requests, at the same time, Q-learning can expect and count the number of user requests by training historical request data samples. However, since base stations support the traditional fog computing framework, assigning offloaded servers to users through base stations connected to users may cause problems related to information loss. With these issues in mind, Tong et al. [20] proposed a collaborative fog computing model that utilizes the historical accumulated contributions of fog computing loads to achieve distributed collaborative processing of nodes using a joint and efficient assignment of tasks and a real-time dynamic adjustment strategy of resources. At the same time, many related studies in general scenarios have not considered the service cache problem in task offloading. They all have task servers with unlimited cache space, which is unrealistic. Therefore, Dai et al. [5] By considering the influence of the joint cache of cloud service and fog service on the offloading decision, the knapsack algorithm is used to realize the dynamic load change of the service cache offloaded by the user and realize the distributed offloading of tasks.

3   System Model

We study a 2D area scene with a set of terminal devices $M = 1, 2, \ldots, M$ and N fixed fog nodes $N = 1, 2, \ldots, N$. Mobile device users will generate a series of tasks that need to be handled by themselves or in cooperation with fog computing. Each terminal device can move randomly in the area and has a certain amount of energy to maintain local computing, but its energy and computing capabilities are limited. We group user devices according to their location, and each group of mobile users can only connect to fixed fog servers within a small area. However, the fog servers can communicate directly, which means the task of the mobile user uses the linked fog server as a transfer station to offload the task to the target fog server. The framework of the model is shown in Fig. 1. Each terminal device has an application scheduler to determine where tasks are processed. But at the same time, there will be competition for communication resources and computing resources among end users, so we should also consider the real-time state of the environment during task processing.

We assume that the mobile device only generates one calculation task in each time slot, and the data size and CPU cycles required for calculation are (R_m, C_m). In particular, each task generated by the mobile device has a different data size and number of CPU cycles. When a mobile device generates a task, the task is first divided into blocks on the mobile device side. Then, the task after the block is offloaded and scheduled locally.

Let $x_i \in \{0, 1\}$ represent the execution location of the task. The delay includes calculation delay and transmission delay. However, the decision-making time is very short, so this work does not consider the delay in offloading the decision. The model considered in this article is the M/M/N model. The first M is that the task arrival rate is regarded as a Poisson process, where λ_i is the average arrival rate, the second M represents an exponential distribution of

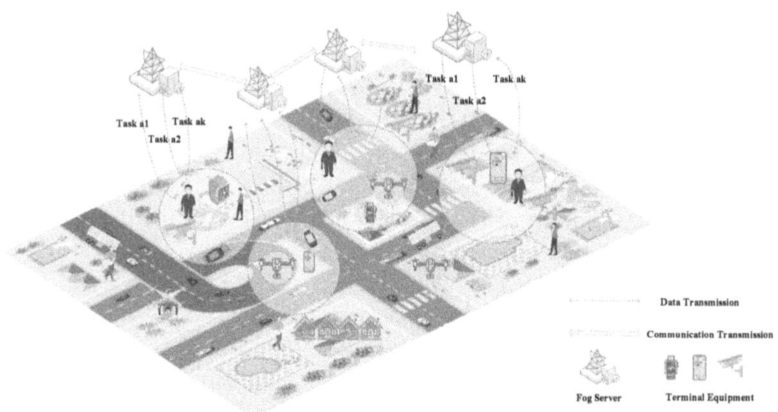

Fig. 1. Offloading models in fog environments

the task's processing rate across N fog nodes, with an average service rate of $\frac{1}{\mu}$ (seconds per packet).

3.1   Task Completion Latency Calculation Model

The fog nodes are assumed to have a sufficient buffer size to support receiving all task requests and processing data from mobile devices. The task execution delay considered in this paper includes transmission delay and computation delay. Transmission delay means the time complete transmission on the physical link, and calculation delay means the time it takes to process after arriving on the local CPU or server.

Transmission Model
The time the task spends on the physical link is described as the transmission delay, which can be divided into two parts. The first part is the time it takes to transmit the task from the mobile device to the fog server, but if the server connected to the device is not the target server of the mobile device at this time, the transmission time will include the second part, which is the time from the server the user is connected to the target server. These two parts can be expressed as:

(1) The first stage: the task of the device is transmitted to the specific server directly connected to the user through the link, and the transmission time of this stage is $D_p^o = \frac{\lambda_i^u}{f_{m,n}}$. Where, R_m is the size of the data packet, $f_{m,n}$ is the transmission rate of the data packet on the physical link.

The network considered in this article has multiple wireless channels. During the data transmission process, the data transmission between the mobile device and the fog node in one channel will be interfered with by other channels, resulting in data information loss. The communication rate can be expressed as $f_{m,n} = B\log_2(1 + \frac{P_u d_{u,n}}{N_0 + \sum_{i \in U, i \neq u} p_i d_{i,n}})$. Where, B is the channel bandwidth, P_u is the transmission power, $d_{u,n}$ is the channel gain, and $\sum P_j$ is the interference factor existing in the transmission process.

(2) The second stage: the device the user connects is not the target server for task offloading, so the task must be transmitted to the target server. The transmission time required for this part is $D_p^{o,o'} = \frac{R_m}{f_{n,n}} * h$. Where, $f_{n,n}$ is the transfer rate between servers n and n', h is the total number of hops between servers n and n'.

Similar to other studies, we ignore the transmission delay caused by returning the execution result of the task to the device. This is because the calculation result of a task is usually just text data.

Computation Model

This work considers using a single CPU to process tasks in a computational queue. If the task's offload scheduling decision is $x_i = 0$, then the task chooses to execute locally. The time required for local computation is determined by the mobile device's computing power. In consideration of many models, it is required that the computing power of the mobile device can be adjusted in real-time within a specific range of computing power according to the dynamic changes of the environment. The computing power is divided into multiple adjustable levels within its upper limit, and then select the appropriate computing power level according to the task scale and network conditions. We need to consider the time to complete the task and whether the current remaining energy of the mobile device can meet the high speed calculation. Therefore, we use f_i to represent the processing power of the mobile device, and the local processing delay using the following formula $D_t = \frac{C_m}{f_i^l}$.

The offloading schedule of the task is $x_i = 1$. In particular, the computing power of the CPU on the server is far greater than that of the local device. The server has idle core processors that can provide computing services for processing and operation, then the delay caused by the task computing on the fog can be expressed as $D_c^o = \frac{C_m}{f_i^c}$.

When a task is selected for processing on the mobile device, $x^t_i = 0$, we use $\beta^t_{i,j}$ to indicate that the task is offloaded to the j-th fog server. Therefore, we can denote the time of local execution and offload the execution of a task, jointly expressed as:

$$D_i^t = (1 - x_i^t)D_t + x_i^t \sum_{j=1}^{N} \beta_{i,j}^t (D_p^o + D_p^{o,o'} + D_c^o), \tag{1}$$

3.2 Task Completion Energy Calculation Model

The power in the mobile device can be used for the local processing of tasks or task transfer during offloading. It does not include the energy consumed to transfer to the target server. The energy collected by the mobile device can be represented by $E_i = \eta P h_i T$, where $\eta \in (0, 1)$ represents the receiving efficiency, h_i represents the channel state. The calculation formula is $h_i = Ad^{-2}$.

We model the power consumption of tasks locally processed according to the set CPU frequency of the local mobile device. The energy consumption of local processing: $E_i^l = \kappa(f_i^l)^3 D_t$. Where κ is mobile devices' energy efficiency correlation coefficient.

If offloaded, the energy consumed by task transmission can follows $E_{i,j}^o = P_{i,j} D_p$. Where $P_{i,j}$ is the transmission power. In particular, the energy consumed at this time should satisfy $E_{i,j}^o \leq E_r^t$.

Therefore, the energy consumption model can be modeled as:

$$E_i^t = (1 - x_i^t)E_i^l + x_i^t E_{i,j}^o, \tag{2}$$

At this point, we will update the remaining energy according to the energy consumed in this slot, which can be expressed as $E_r^{t+1} = E_r^t - E_i^t$.

3.3 Problem Statement

We consider the impact of time-varying fog node load on the minimum delay of fog computing system processing terminal tasks, which helps to achieve the minimum delay of terminal task requests. The low latency of terminal task requests refers to the problem of delivering task processing results within the time required by end users and ensuring the minimum delay. The goal is to keep the weighted sum between the time required for task execution and energy consumption to a minimum:

$$\min mize[ET = \sum_{t=1}^{T} w_l D_t + w_o E_t] \tag{3}$$

4 Task Offloading Method and Model Training

The problem can be formulated as a trade-off problem between mobile user computing offload decision-making scheduling and energy resource allocation, which is entirely NP-hard. After investigation, it is found that this problem is suitable for solving by reinforcement learning method, which can adaptively adjust the decision-making parameters in a dynamically changing real environment and make an offloading decision most suitable for the current environment parameters. Therefore, we formulate this offloading decision problem as an MDP decision problem.

4.1 MDP Problem Formulating

MDP is an essential concept in RL, which can be used in FC scenarios to describe the problem of mobile users' offloading and processing decisions in random environments. In MDP, the problem is usually abstracted as a five-tuple, namely $\langle S, A, P, R, \gamma \rangle$, consisting of elements such as state, action, transition probability, reward function, and strategy. Among them, the transition probability represents the probability distribution of the system transitioning from the current state to the next state under a particular current state action, through which the uncertainty and variability of the current environment can be understood. The reward function calculates the reward value or penalty value obtained by the system according to the defined reward function after executing each different offloading action in the current environment state. Using the defined reward function can help the agent find the optimal offloading strategy in the current state faster. This paper uses the MDP model to represent the decision-making of computing offload and energy resources.

State Space: The information in the state space is some decision-making information that the system observes from the current environment. The state information considered in this paper includes the data size and CPU cycles of computing tasks generated by local mobile users, the channel gain status between local mobile users and their connected servers, the load of fog servers, and the remaining energy of local mobile devices. A four-tuple can represent this state information, that is, $\langle C_n^t, H^t, \delta^t, E_r^t \rangle$.

Action Space: In each time slot, only one task of the application program is allowed to make an offloading decision, and the offloading scheduler in the mobile user can make the current offloading action decision $a^t \in A$ according to the current state S_t, where the offloading decision satisfies the condition $A \in [0, N]$.

Reward Function: In each decision slot, we need to make an offload decision for the mobile user's task. In any observed system state S_t, we can obtain the difference of the weighted sum of processing delay and energy consumption of all mobile devices in the entire system space at time slot t. After the user executes the offloading action a_t, the user will calculate the reward function R_t from the executed system state. The reward value can be considered the benefit obtained by the mobile user performing the specific action in the current state. It can be calculated as the negative increment of the weighted sum of the current processing delay and energy consumption, namely:

$$- \left[\sum_{i=1}^{M} ET_i^t - \sum_{i=1}^{M} ET_i^{t-1} \right] \tag{4}$$

According to the MDP mentioned above model, the user offloading decision and energy resource scheduling problem considered in this paper can be described as a policy decision optimization problem that maximizes the weighted sum of the discounted calculation delay reward and energy reward obtained by all mobile device users in each time slot in the FC system. Among them, the long-term discount reward can be calculated as $R_d^t = -D_t, R_e^t = -E_t$.

4.2 Action Generation and Policy Update

Using an attention mechanism is the first critical part of generating offloading actions by the DQN model. As a common operation related to deep neural networks, the attention mechanism has been widely used. The core idea of the attention mechanism is to determine the degree of attention that different input parts should receive according to their importance. In this research, an attention mechanism is used to automatically adjust the weights, which reflect the degree of attention that should be given to latency and energy consumption, and then minimize their weighted sum. The second part is the update of the parameter θ. In the tth time frame, DQN takes the load state of the fog node as input and outputs the offloading action according to its current offloading strategy $\pi_{\theta t}$, ensuring that all physical constraints listed in Eq. 4 are met. Execute the offloading action x_t obtained by the fog node, get the reward $Q(f_t, x_t)$, and finally add the newly obtained state-action pair (f_t, X_t) to experience memory.

Algorithm 1: DRLPO algorithm for solving the optimal offloading decision problem

---

Input: Fog node load situation F_t at each time frame t; terminal equipment M
Intimidation: θ =random(), Storage=ϕ, Initialize policy $\pi(x|f_{work})$, Iteration number$M$, Training intervalδ
1: **for** iteration **do**
2:     Collect initial observation state
3:     **for** $t = 1, 2, 3, \ldots, M$ **do**
4:         Divide the task into k parts on the device side
5:         Compute D_l^t, D_p^o, D_c^o
6:         Compute E_i^l, $E_{i,j}^o$
7:         Compare the processing time of these k parts separately and select the largest time as the completion time of the task
8:         Generate an offloading action X_t
9:         Compute $D_i{}^t$ and $E_i{}^t$
10:        Select $\arg\max R$ by Eq.(3)
11:        Update the replay memory
12:        Randomly select a batch of datasets from playback memory
13:        Train the DQN and update θ_t
14:        Update policy parameters
15:     **end for**
16: **end for**

The goal of us is to quickly generate the optimal offloading decision X, where $X \in \{0,1\}^N$, by monitoring the load situation f_{work} of the fog node in each time slot. Such a decision can be expressed as: $\pi(x_i|f_{work}, x_{i-1})$. That is, in state $s = (f_{work}, x_{i-1})$, the current task chooses the probability of x_i (Fig. 2).

The online training network for action generation under consideration has two fully connected neural networks. The fully connected network guarantees

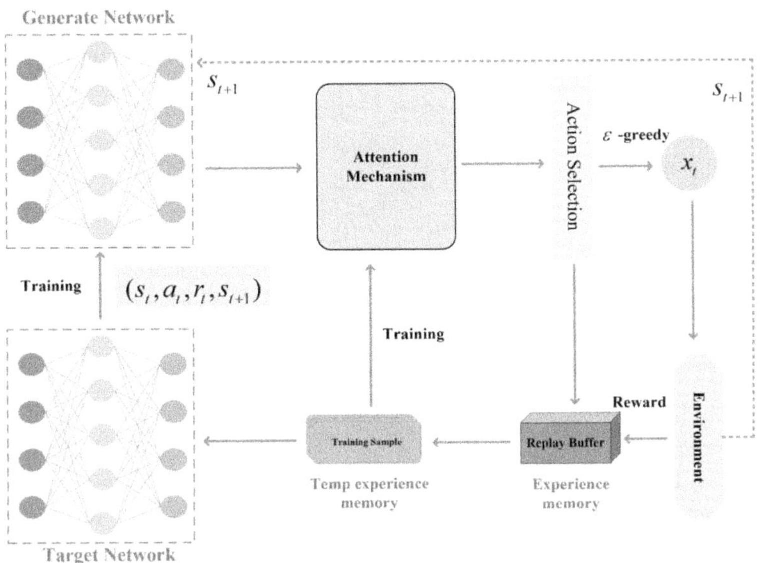

Fig. 2. DRLPO algorithm structure

that each neuron (node) can be connected to all neurons. Similarly, we can also think that each neuron in the fully connected network can receive input from all neurons in the previous layer and generate an output. Within each time slot, the input layer of the fully connected network will obtain environment vector S_t, and the dimension of this vector is N+4 dimensions. The output layer of this network outputs an action value vector Q_d^t. When we only consider the system's computationally delayed reward, the value of B reflects the action value when the system executes the current specific offloading action a_t under the current environment state. We also added an activation function Relu to each node in the two fully connected networks to help effectively solve the gradient disappearance problem and better describe the nonlinear relationship between the system environment state and the obtained offloading execution actions. Usually, the goal is not only to ensure the shortest task-processing time for all mobile device users in the entire FC system but also to minimize the time while minimizing the energy consumed in the task-processing process. Therefore, in the action selection process, we can't just consider the action that brings the maximum action value.

The model design of the attention mechanism considered in this paper is shown in Fig. 3. We use both calculations delay-based and energy consumption-based action values as part of the input of the attention mechanism, and another part of the input also includes current context information of the system, which we call the context vector v_t of the system. This context vector is some information value about the current system environment, such as calculating the time and energy consumed by the current task. The time of the current task

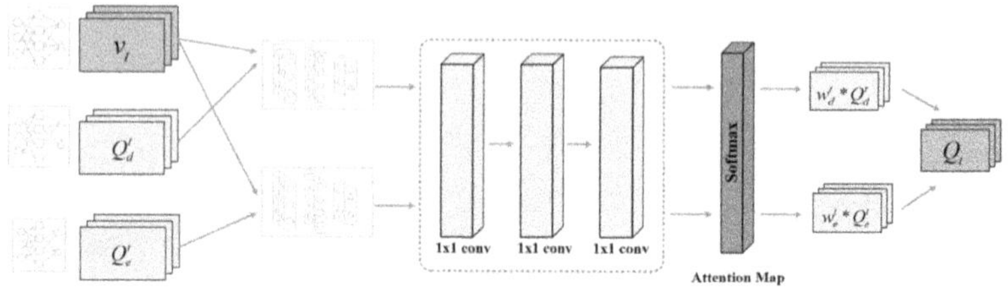

Fig. 3. Attention mechanism model design

can be expressed as $\bar{D}_t = \frac{1}{t}\sum_{i=1}^{t} D^i$ in the attention mechanism, and the energy as $\bar{E}_t = \frac{1}{t}\sum_{i=1}^{t} E^i$. Finally, the attention mechanism will assign weights to the two action values through a three-layer fully connected perception layer and softmax operation and calculate their weighted sum. It can be expressed as $Q_t = w_d^t Q_d^t + w_e^t Q_e^t$.

The training objective is to find the offloading policy with the minimum latency while satisfying the constraints. Algorithm 1 provides the DRLPO action generation and implementation process. Introducing the parameter θ in the generation process of offloading actions, combined with the memory replay function, enables the offloading decision system to adapt to the real-time changing network environment more quickly, and always maintain the optimal decision in the process of rapid dynamic changes. Additionally, all decisions made during execution are fed into an empirical memory to find optimal solutions without retraining when the environment changes suddenly. DQN takes the offloading situation f_t of the fog node at t as the training input and outputs the offloading action X_t according to the current offloading strategy $\pi_{\theta t}$. Calculate the reward function $D(F_t, X_t)$, find the best offloading action, and add the best state action pair (F_t, X_t) trained at this time to the experience memory.

5   Experimental Evaluation

This experiment compares the task processing latency of DRLPO with existing benchmark offloading algorithms under different node numbers and task arrival rates to demonstrate the performance advantages of DRLPO.

5.1   Simulation Environment and Parameters

In this experiment, 15 fog nodes ($N = 15$) are considered. These nodes represent the network structure of the fog layer in the form of an indirect graph network topology, and the propagation time between nodes is used as the weight of the links between network nodes. The fog servers are randomly and evenly distributed in this two-dimensional area, and the computing power of each fog server to reach tasks is evenly distributed within [5,10] GHz (Table 1).

Table 1. Simulation Parameters.

Parameter Type	Value	Parameter Type	Value
The number of fog servers	{3, 6, 9, 12, 15}	The number of mobile device	{1, 2, 3, 4, 5}
Task generation probability	[0.1, 0.4]	Network bandwidth	1 MHZ
Noise	$1.5 * 10^{-4}$	Task size	[20, 200] KB
CPU clock frequency	[10, 1000] MHZ	Local computing power	[300, 500] MHZ
Acceleration of the mobile device	1 m/s	Learning rate	0.01

To test whether the DRLPO algorithm can effectively balance task processing delay and energy consumption, we compared it with five benchmark algorithms in an environment with multiple fog nodes, assuming that the task is indivisible:

- Random Node Offloading method (RFN): The tasks in the loaded fog node will be offloaded to another random fog node.
- Neighborhood Node Offloading method (NFA): Transfer tasks in a loaded fog node to the fog node that is closest to it and has a larger capacity.
- Remote: All tasks are transmitted to the fog server for processing, but tasks are still divided, and the divided subtasks can be offloaded to different fog servers.
- Local: all generated tasks are processed in the local compute queue, regardless of task division.
- Single-DQN: No attention mechanism, energy, and latency are equally weighted.

5.2   Method Comparison

We compare each algorithm's average task processing delay when the number of fog nodes is different in Fig. 4. The task processing delay of the DRLPO algorithm and the Single-DQN algorithm is generally in a low trend in increasing the number of fog nodes, and they can always maintain the efficient processing of tasks. NFA and RWA are two methods of full offloading, which respectively offload tasks to the nearest fog node and randomly select offloading nodes. The average processing delay of tasks in the random offloading method is higher than that in the nearest neighbor offloading method. This may be because random offloading may select a server far away from the server that the user can connect to, resulting in excessive transmission overhead, while the transmission delay caused by the proximity method is always the smallest.

Figure 5 shows the energy consumed by the terminal device processing tasks under different task offloading scheduling methods. This experiment does not consider NFA and RWA, because these two methods offload tasks to random fog nodes and the nearest fog node respectively, and both belong to the method of complete offloading, which can be considered remote. As can be seen from the figure, local processing consumes much more energy than others. This is because the local processing of each task consumes more energy than the transfer task. The energy consumed by the DRLPO method for processing tasks is

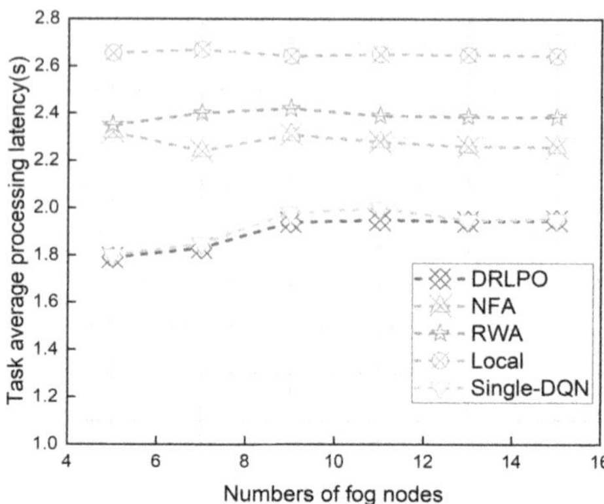

Fig. 4. Comparing the average processing delay of different algorithms when the number of fog nodes changes

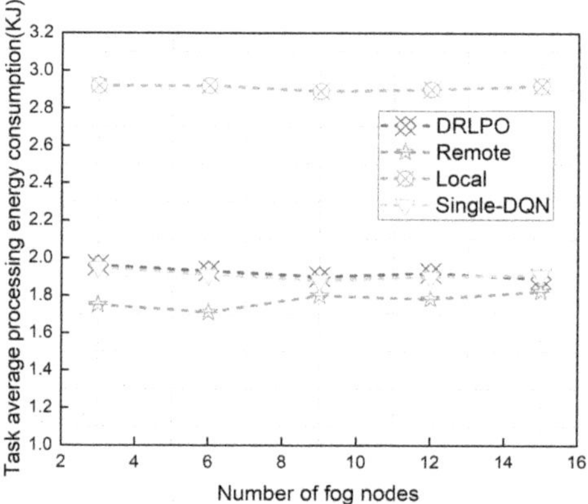

Fig. 5. Compare the average energy consumption of different algorithms when the number of fog nodes increases

between Local and Remote because some tasks in this method are processed locally because it consumes more energy than full-transmission input fog node processing. In the process of increasing the number of fog nodes, the fluctuation of the energy consumed by the full remote mode is small. Because when the number of fog nodes increases, the power consumption variation of tasks in terms of transmission fluctuates less. Of course, this is also determined by the location of the fog server and device because the location of the mobile device considered in this paper moves randomly within the two-dimensional range, so the magnitude of the energy will also change dynamically, which cannot be accurately predicted. In addition, this experiment is also compared with Single-DQN. The energy with DRLPO is slightly lower than that of Single-DQN at some moments because the attention mechanism can adaptively allocate energy and delay weights.

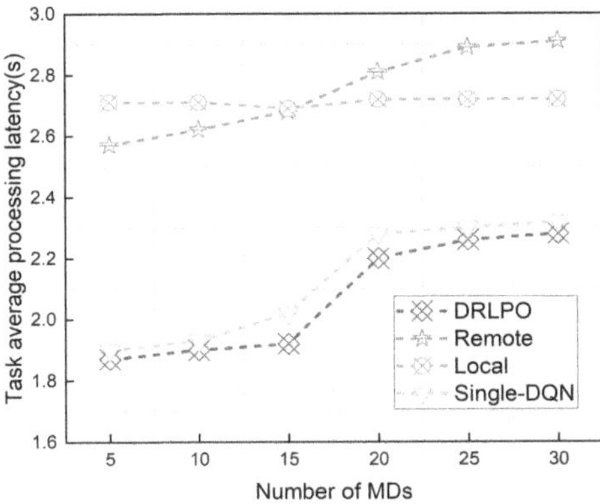

Fig. 6. Comparing the average processing delay of different algorithms when the number of mobile devices increases

Figure 6 is to observe different algorithms' average task processing delay by increasing the number of mobile users. The average task processing delay of all methods will increase with devices. When the number of mobile devices increases, it may cause tasks to queue up in the fog nodes for too long, which brings about big delay problems. However, the DRLPO method can still control the delay within a small range. One is that it can divide tasks into blocks for parallel processing, and the other is that it performs offloading and scheduling between nodes by obtaining the load information of nodes in the fog layer, which effectively avoids the long waiting times for tasks in one node.

We compare the task execution success rate of different algorithms when the number of mobile devices increases in Fig. 7. The success rate of local execution is not affected by the devices. When the number of mobile devices increases, the task execution rate of the complete offload method is most affected. Still, as the number of devices increases, the task execution success rate drops sharply. This is because when the tasks of all mobile devices need to be uploaded to the fog nodes, it will cause severe congestion in the fog layer, which will cause the charges to be processed over time and cause timeout retransmission. In particular, although the success rate of task execution under the DRLPO method will also be affected by the increase in the number of user devices, it remains high, which can significantly avoid task discarding and retransmission during execution.

In Fig. 8, we fix the packet type as heavy packets, filter the light packet data in the task, increase the number of hefty packets arriving at the fog layer, and then compare the average delay of DRLPO and several benchmark algorithms when the number of task arrivals increases. In this experiment, we sequentially increase the number of heavy packets from 8.35×10^6 to 8.95×10^6. According to the experimental data, the average task processing delay of DRLPO, Remote, Local, and Single-DQN is proportional to the fluctuation of the data packets. While the processing rate of tasks remains constant, tasks are congested in the

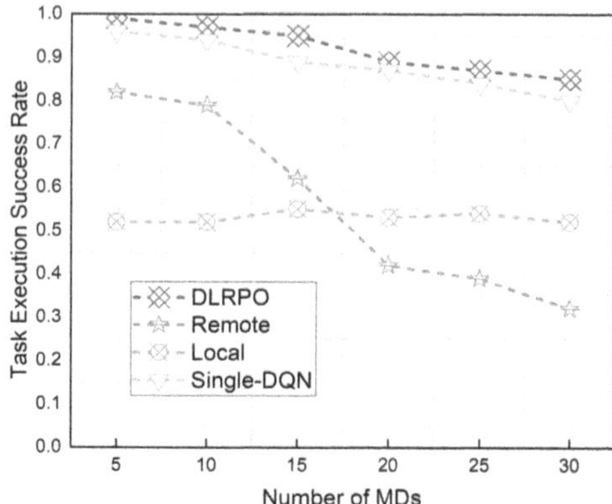

Fig. 7. Comparing the task execution success rate of different algorithms when the number of mobile devices increases

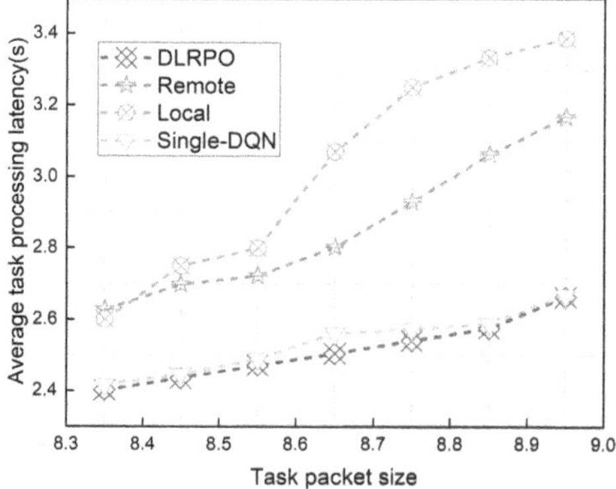

Fig. 8. Comparing the processing latency of different algorithms as the number of task arrivals increases

queue, increasing the latency of this part of the task. Experiments also show that although the task processing delay induced by DRLPO increases with the task arrival rate, it is always lower than the baseline algorithm. However, when the number of packets increases to 8.95×10^6, the growth rate of DRLPO increases significantly, which may be because the arrival rate of tasks is close to the processing rate of tasks at this time, resulting in a longer waiting time in the queue.

In Fig. 9, we compare the success rate under different methods by increasing the arrival rate of tasks reaching the fog layer. It can be seen from the fluctuation trend of the data in the figure that the successful execution rate of DRLPO, Remote, Local, and Single-DQN tasks is inversely proportional to the increase in the task arrival rate. All methods increase the packet loss rate of device tasks as the task arrival rate increases, because when the task arrival rate is close to the processing capacity of the local mobile device and the fog server, congestion will occur, resulting in the inability to process tasks in time. In particular, meth-

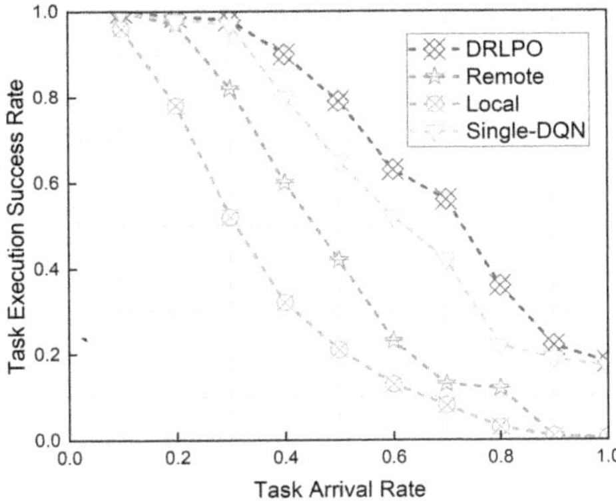

Fig. 9. Comparing the task success rate of different algorithms when the task arrival rate increases

ods other than all local mobile device processing can achieve a task processing success rate close to 100% when the rate is low. However, when the rate reaches 0.5, except for the DRLPO and Single-DQN methods that can maintain the task success rate at 60%, the task success rate of other baseline methods drops sharply, even below 50%. Finally, when the task arrival rate is close to 1, the success rate of the Local and Remote methods is close to 0. In contrast, the task execution success rate of the method proposed in this paper remains at about 20%, which is still much higher than the two baseline algorithms.

The task generated by the actual mobile device will have a task deadline, and the task will be considered successful if it is executed within the deadline required by the task. Still, if it exceeds the defined time, the task will be discarded and retransmitted for processing. In Fig. 10, we compare the performance of each offloading method in terms of task loss rate under different task deadlines. In the figure, the task loss rate of DRLPO is always lower than that of the benchmark algorithm, which can ensure that at least 80% of the tasks can be successfully executed. Especially in the case of defined tasks with short deadlines, the task drop rate of DRLPO is significantly lower than that of other baseline algorithms. When the task deadline is increased to 2.7 s, the task loss rate of all methods is close to 0, and all tasks can be successfully executed within this period. At this time, it isn't very sensible to increase the task deadline.

When arrival rate increases, the task processing latency of all offloading algorithms increases accordingly. In Fig. 11, we fix the packet type as heavy packets, and the task arrival rate is close to the task processing rate. This experiment compares the maximum/minimum average delay and maximum/minimum energy consumption caused by DRLPO with Local, Remote and Single-DQN. From the experimental results, no matter the circumstances, the average task processing delay of DRLPO is significantly lower than the three baseline algorithms, and it performs better task offloading.

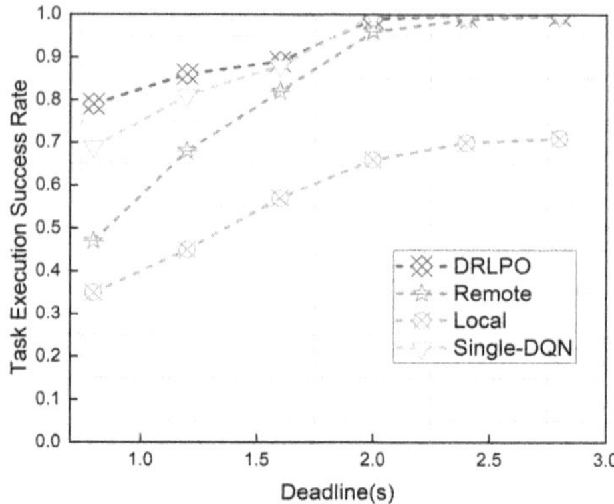

Fig. 10. Comparing the task success rate of different algorithms under different task deadlines

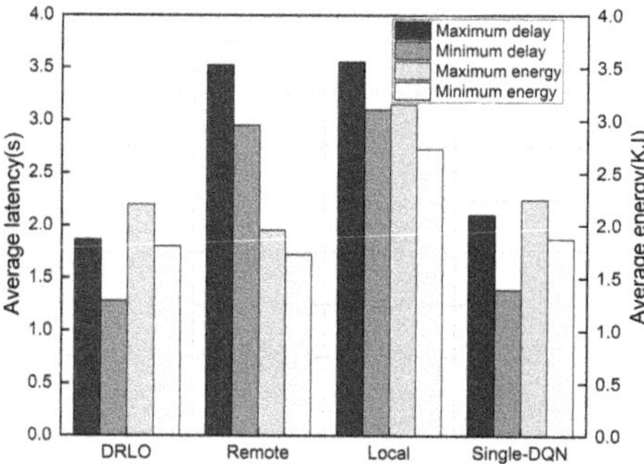

Fig. 11. Compare the maximum performance of task processing under different algorithms

In summary, the proposed DRLPO achieves lower latency and energy consumption than existing baseline methods under different conditions and the maximum delay in task processing. The DRLPO algorithm can more efficiently solve the problem of dynamic load levels among fog nodes, thus achieving a lower task processing delay and more efficient resource allocation.

6   Concluding Remarks

In this paper, we study the problem of partial offloading computation of tasks in multi-service scenarios and solve the optimal offloading decision of multiple tasks with the objective of minimizing the average processing delay and energy consumption of all mobile device tasks. Considering the limited energy of mobile terminal devices in fog computing environments, we designed DRLPO, a method supporting distributed offloading of mobile device tasks, to solve the problem of processing failure due to the long execution time of latency-sensitive tasks. DRLPO divides the tasks of a mobile device into optimal k blocks for distributed parallel scheduling. DRLPO can solve the dynamic load level problem of fog nodes, realize the optimal balance between processing time and energy consumption, and improve the environmental adaptability of fog computing task offloading. Experimental data show that compared with the existing baseline algorithms, DRLPO's average task processing time and energy consumption are reduced by 2.2 s and 1.1 KJ, respectively, which can effectively reduce the response time of device tasks.

Acknowledgement. This work was supported in part by the Hunan Provincial Natural Science Foundation of China under Grant 2026JJ90204, in part by the Postgraduate Scientific Research Innovation Project of Hunan Province under Grant CX20251515, in part by Science Foundation of Bureau of Science and Technology of Changsha Municipality under Grant kh2502057 and in part by Science Foundation of Hunan Aerospace Hospital under Grant 2025YJ03.

References

1. Abd Elaziz, M., Abualigah, L., Attiya, I.: Advanced optimization technique for scheduling IoT tasks in cloud-fog computing environments. Futur. Gener. Comput. Syst. **124**, 142–154 (2021)
2. Basu, S., et al.: An intelligent/cognitive model of task scheduling for IoT applications in cloud computing environment. Futur. Gener. Comput. Syst. **88**, 254–261 (2018)
3. Bi, S., Zhang, Y.J.: Computation rate maximization for wireless powered mobile-edge computing with binary computation offloading. IEEE Trans. Wireless Commun. **17**(6), 4177–4190 (2018)
4. Bitam, S., Zeadally, S., Mellouk, A.: Fog computing job scheduling optimization based on bees swarm. Enterp. Inf. Syst. **12**(1–5), 1–25 (2018)
5. Dai, X., et al.: Task offloading for cloud-assisted fog computing with dynamic service caching in enterprise management systems. IEEE Trans. Industr. Inf. **19**(1), 662–672 (2022)
6. Goudarzi, M., Wu, H., Palaniswami, M., Buyya, R.: An application placement technique for concurrent IoT applications in edge and fog computing environments. IEEE Trans. Mob. Comput. **20**(4), 1298–1311 (2020)
7. Guo, K., Yang, C., Liu, T.: Caching in base station with recommendation via Q-learning. In: 2017 IEEE Wireless Communications and Networking Conference (WCNC), pp. 1–6. IEEE (2017)
8. Hu, N., Zhang, D., Xie, K., Liang, W., Hsieh, M.Y.: Graph learning-based spatial-temporal graph convolutional neural networks for traffic forecasting. Connect. Sci. **34**(1), 429–448 (2022)
9. Huang, X., Cui, Y., Chen, Q., Zhang, J.: Joint task offloading and QoS-aware resource allocation in fog-enabled internet-of-things networks. IEEE Internet Things J. **7**(8), 7194–7206 (2020)
10. Jiang, Y., et al.: Analysis and optimization of cache-enabled fog radio access networks: Successful transmission probability, fractional offloaded traffic and delay. IEEE Trans. Veh. Technol. **69**(5), 5219–5231 (2020)

11. Kaffash, S., Nguyen, A.T., Zhu, J.: Big data algorithms and applications in intelligent transportation system: a review and bibliometric analysis. Int. J. Prod. Econ. **231**, 107868 (2021)

12. Liang, W., Huang, Y., Xu, J., Xie, S.: A distributed data secure transmission scheme in wireless sensor network. Int. J. Distrib. Sensor Netw. **13**(4) (2017)

13. Liang, W., et al.: TMHD: twin-bridge scheduling of multi-heterogeneous dependent tasks for edge computing. Futur. Gener. Comput. Syst. **158**, 60–72 (2024)

14. Lin, Y., Liu, T., Chen, F., Li, K.C., Xie, Y.: An energy-efficient task migration scheme based on genetic algorithms for mobile applications in clonecloud. J. Supercomput. **77**, 5220–5236 (2021)

15. Liu, Z., Dai, P., Xing, H., Yu, Z., Zhang, W.: A distributed algorithm for task offloading in vehicular networks with hybrid fog/cloud computing. IEEE Trans. Syst. Man Cybern. Syst. 1–14 (2021)

16. Mahmud, R., Ramamohanarao, K., Buyya, R.: Application management in fog computing environments: a taxonomy, review and future directions. ACM Comput. Surv. (CSUR) **53**(4), 1–43 (2020)

17. Malik, U.M., Javed, M.A., Zeadally, S., Ul Islam, S.: Energy-efficient fog computing for 6G-enabled massive IoT: recent trends and future opportunities. IEEE Internet Things J. **9**(16), 14572–14594 (2021)

18. Martinez, I., Hafid, A.S., Jarray, A.: Design, resource management, and evaluation of fog computing systems: a survey. IEEE Internet Things J. **8**(4), 2494–2516 (2020)

19. Ren, J., Zhang, D., He, S., Zhang, Y., Li, T.: A survey on end-edge-cloud orchestrated network computing paradigms: transparent computing, mobile edge computing, fog computing, and cloudlet. ACM Comput. Surv. (CSUR) **52**(6), 1–36 (2019)

20. Tong, S., Liu, Y., Chang, X., Mišić, J., Zhang, Z.: Joint task offloading and resource allocation: a historical cumulative contribution based collaborative fog computing model. IEEE Trans. Veh. Technol. (2022)

21. Wang, C., Liang, C., Yu, F.R., Chen, Q., Tang, L.: Computation offloading and resource allocation in wireless cellular networks with mobile edge computing. IEEE Trans. Wireless Commun. **16**(8), 4924–4938 (2017)

22. Wang, J., Luo, W., Liang, W., Liu, X., Dong, X.: Locally minimum storage regenerating codes in distributed cloud storage systems. China Commun. **14**(11), 82–91 (2017)

23. Wang, K., Zhou, Y., Li, J., Shi, L., Chen, W., Hanzo, L.: Energy-efficient task offloading in massive MIMO-aided multi-pair fog-computing networks. IEEE Trans. Commun. **69**(4), 2123–2137 (2020)

24. Wang, Y., et al.: A game-based computation offloading method in vehicular multi-access edge computing networks. IEEE Internet Things J. **7**(6), 4987–4996 (2020)

25. Xiong, J., Hsiang, E.L., He, Z., Zhan, T., Wu, S.T.: Augmented reality and virtual reality displays: emerging technologies and future perspectives. Light Sci. Appl. **10**(1), 216 (2021)

26. Zahmatkesh, H., Al-Turjman, F.: Fog computing for sustainable smart cities in the IoT era: caching techniques and enabling technologies-an overview. Sustain. Cities Soc. **59**, 102139 (2020)

27. Zhang, G., Shen, F., Yang, Y., Qian, H., Yao, W.: Fair task offloading among fog nodes in fog computing networks. In: 2018 IEEE International Conference on Communications (ICC), pp. 1–6. IEEE (2018)

28. Zhou, S., Jadoon, W.: The partial computation offloading strategy based on game theory for multi-user in mobile edge computing environment. Comput. Netw. **178**, 107334 (2020)
29. Zhu, X., Li, K.C., Zhang, J., Zhang, S.: Distributed reliable and efficient transmission task assignment for WSNs. Sensors **19**(22), 5028 (2019)

BMI: A Bidirectional Spatio-Temporal Selective State Space Model for Data Imputation

Jigang Wen[1], Wenqian Nie[2], Xiaocan Li[2,3(✉)], Kun Xie[2(✉)], Yong Xie[4], Yuxiang Chen[1], Zigeng Fu[2], and Quan Feng[5]

[1] Hunan University of Science and Technology, Xiangtan, China
{wenjigang,chenyuxiang}@hnust.edu.cn
[2] Hunan University, Changsha, China
{niewenqian,hnulxc,xiekun,HubertFu}@hnu.edu.cn
[3] Greater Bay Area Institute for Innovation, Hunan University, Changsha, China
[4] Nanjing University of Posts and Telecommunications, Nanjing, China
yongxie@njupt.edu.cn
[5] Hunan Vanguard Group Corporation Limited, Hunan, China

Abstract. Missing value imputation is a fundamental challenge in spatio-temporal data modeling. To address this issue, we propose a novel model named Bidirectional Mamba Imputation (BMI), which incorporates the selective state space model, Mamba, into the missing data recovery task. The proposed BMI leverages bidirectional information flow to capture both past and future dependencies in time series, and introduces a spatio-temporal block design to jointly learn temporal and spatial patterns. Moreover, a selective mechanism is embedded in the state transition process to adaptively focus on crucial variables and time steps. Extensive experiments conducted on four real-world datasets demonstrate that BMI significantly outperforms existing traditional and deep learning baselines under both point and block missing scenarios. Ablation studies confirm the effectiveness of the bidirectional design and the selective state space module. Additionally, efficiency analysis shows that BMI is well-suited for deployment in resource-constrained environments due to its high memory and I/O efficiency.

Keywords: Spatio-temporal data imputation · Bidirectional Mamba · Time series forecasting

1 Introduction

Since the integrity of input time series data directly impacts the accuracy of various tasks (e.g., anomaly detection, network security operations and maintenance), the data missing phenomena frequently occur due to a variety of reasons (e.g., network transmission errors, downsampling, or malfunctions of data collection devices). To address this issue, several studies have proposed matrix completion or tensor completion techniques [5, 9–11, 13, 14, 18–20] to interpolate missing

© ICST Institute for Computer Sciences, Social Informatics and Telecommunications Engineering 2026
Published by Springer Nature Switzerland AG 2026. All Rights Reserved
W. Liang et al. (Eds.): SecureComm 2025, LNICST 690, pp. 210–228, 2026.
https://doi.org/10.1007/978-3-032-23456-8_12

data. However, these methods typically leverage only the low-rank properties of the data while neglecting its complex nonlinear characteristics.

To more effectively utilize the internal features of data, a wide range of neural network models [1,3,4,6,17] have been applied to data imputation tasks, including RNNs, LSTM, Graph Convolutional Network, and Transformer. These models typically take historical time series data as input and estimate missing values by iteratively updating hidden states. However, they often encounter performance bottlenecks when dealing with long time series. With the advancement of deep learning techniques, many researchers have started to apply Transformer models to data imputation tasks. Although the Transformer excels at capturing long-range dependencies, its high computational complexity $(O(n^2))$ makes it less suitable for long sequences in resource-constrained environments [7]. Moreover, most of these models adopt a unidirectional information flow, i.e., information only flows from past to future, thus ignoring the potential impact of future data on current missing values.

With the emergence of state space models (SSMs) [8,15], many of the challenges faced by Transformer and RNN architectures have been effectively addressed. The Mamba architecture [7] improves upon the SSM by demonstrating significant potential in optimizing both performance and computational efficiency. It leverages convolutional computation to capture sequential information while eliminating the need for hidden states. Although pure SSM architectures have shown certain limitations in data imputation, Mamba enhances the model's ability to identify and filter information through the introduction of selective mechanisms. Extensive experimental results have shown that Mamba achieves remarkable performance in the NLP domain [21], frequently realizing a win-win in terms of model accuracy and computational cost. Therefore, this study explores the application of the Mamba architecture in data imputation tasks.

Despite the promising performance of unidirectional Mamba models on visual data, they exhibit several significant limitations. First, the unidirectional Mamba can only process information from past to future, restricting its ability to capture the potential influence of future data on current and past points. Furthermore, unidirectional Mamba models generally lack positional awareness, which can lead to suboptimal performance when handling time series data requiring global context.

To tackle these problems, we propose the Bidirectional Mamba Imputation (BMI) model based a bidirectional spatio-temporal selective state space. The BMI model can simultaneously process forward and backward information in time series, capturing dependencies from past to future, and further leveraging future information to enhance the understanding of current and past states. Moreover, In addition, we incorporate positional embeddings to enhance the model's position-awareness, thereby improving its ability to capture data dependencies. Among which, the S6 (i.e., Mamba: Linear-Time Sequence Modeling with Selective State Spaces) [7] selective state space mechanism dynamically adjusts the model's focus based on data characteristics, thereby enhancing the BMI model's ability to handle varying temporal scales and more accurately capture time series features. Moreover, the BMI model reduces GPU memory usage and training time. In this paper, we conduct extensive experiments on multiple real-world datasets to provide a detailed analysis of the BMI model's performance, demonstrating its practical effectiveness and superiority.

In summary, the main contributions of this paper are as follows:

1) **Bidirectional Information Processing Mechanism:** We propose a Bidirectional Mamba model which, in contrast to its unidirectional variant, captures dependencies not only from past to future but also from future to past. This bidirectional design enables a more comprehensive understanding of the entire sequence, leading to improved interpretation and prediction—especially in the presence of substantial missing data.

2) **Selective State Space:** Based on the S6 selection mechanism, our model can dynamically and selectively focus on important information based on the characteristics of the input data, while ignoring irrelevant parts. This not only enhances the model's performance but also reduces unnecessary computation, thereby improving its flexibility, generalizability, and adaptability across various application scenarios.

3) **Linear Time Complexity:** The BMI model exhibits linear time complexity ($O(L)$), making it more efficient for long time series data. This contributes to a significant improvement in the accuracy and efficiency of time series imputation tasks, particularly in environments with severe data loss or complex temporal dynamics.

4) **Extensive experiments:** We conducted extensive comparative experiments with seven state-of-the-art algorithms on four datasets. The experimental results demonstrate that our proposed BMI model achieves superior performance in both point missing and block missing scenarios.

2   Problem Formulation

The time series data is typically represented as a matrix $X \in \mathbb{R}^{T \times N}$, where N denotes the number of samples and T denotes the number of time slots. However, due to the network transmission errors, downsampling, or malfunctions of data collection devices, the data matrix X is always highly sparse, as shown in Fig. 1 (a).

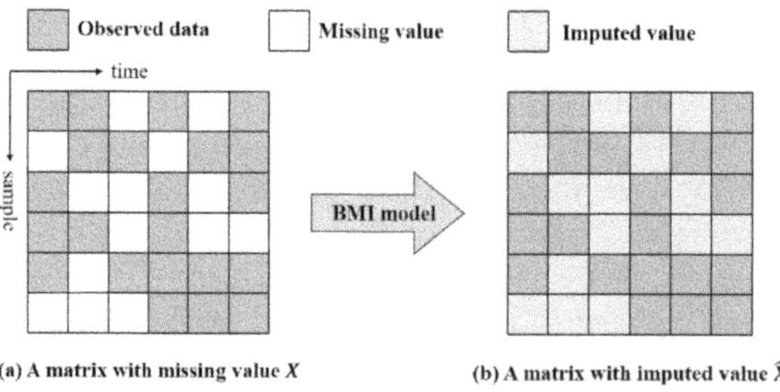

Fig. 1. Time series data matrix X and its imputed results $\hat{X}$

To model the missing values in X, we consider a binary mask $M \in \{0,1\}^{T \times N}$ at each time step, where m_{tn} indicates whether the attribute x_{tn} of node n at time step t is observed. Specifically, $m_{tn} = 1$ means that the data point x_{tn} is observed, while $m_{tn} = 0$ indicates that it is missing.

To ensure the integrity of time series data, it is vital to complete the missing data in X by solving the missing data imputation problem defined as:

$$L(\hat{X}, X, M) = \frac{\sum_{t=1}^{T} \sum_{n=1}^{N} |\hat{x}_{tn} - x_{tn}| m_{tn}}{\sum_{t=1}^{T} \sum_{n=1}^{N} m_{tn}} \tag{1}$$

where, $\hat{x}_{tn}$ denotes the imputed value at position (t, n) in $\hat{X}$, x_{tn} is the ground truth at the same position in X, and m_{tn} is the corresponding mask entry indicating whether the value is missing. T is the total number of time steps, and N is the number of features.

The loss function $L(\hat{X}, X, M)$ computes the Mean Absolute Error between the imputed values $\hat{X}$ and the ground truth values X, considering only those entries that are marked as missing by the mask M. The MAE is normalized by the total number of valid (non-missing) entries as indicated by the mask.

3   Theoretical Background

The goal of BMI is to introduce advanced State Space Models (SSMs), specifically Mamba [7], into the field of data imputation. This section first presents the necessary background on SSMs, including the Structured State Space Sequence model (S4) and the Mamba architecture.

The Mamba architecture is primarily built upon the State Space Model (SSM) framework. In this subsection, we briefly introduce the SSM architecture. An SSM can represent any recurrent process with latent states. It uses first-order differential equations to describe the evolution of internal system states and another set of differential equations to relate the latent states to the output sequence. The SSM learns to map the input $x(t)$ to the output $y(t)$ through an intermediate state $h(t)$. Here, x, y, and h are all functions of time. S4 relates them using three continuous parameter matrices A, B, and C. Specifically, the input sequence $x(t) \in \mathbb{R}^{D}$ is mapped to the output sequence $y(t) \in \mathbb{R}^{N}$ via the latent state $h(t) \in \mathbb{R}^{N}$, using the following two equations:

$$\begin{aligned} h(t) &= Ah(t-1) + Bx(t) \\ y(t) &= Ch(t) \end{aligned} \tag{2}$$

where $A \in \mathbb{R}^{N \times N}$ and $B, C \in \mathbb{R}^{N \times D}$ are learnable matrices.

SSMs are the continuous-time counterparts of discrete systems. However, in practice, data such as text or time series are inherently discrete. Therefore, the continuous parameters A, B, and C of the SSM must be discretized into $\bar{A}$, $\bar{B}$, and $\bar{C}$ using a discretization step Δ. A commonly used method for this transformation is Zero-Order Hold (ZOH), which is defined as:

$$\bar{A} = \exp(\Delta A)$$
$$\bar{B} = (\Delta A)^{-1}(\exp(\Delta A) - I) \cdot \Delta B \tag{3}$$

Once discretized, the system can be represented by the following discrete equations:

$$h_t = \bar{A}h_{t-1} + \bar{B}x_t$$
$$y_t = Ch_t \tag{4}$$

Finally, the model computes the output using a global convolution operation:

$$K = (C\bar{B}, C\bar{A}\bar{B}, \ldots, C\bar{A}^{M-1}\bar{B})$$
$$y = x * K \tag{5}$$

where M is the length of the input sequence x, and K is a structured convolution kernel.

These equations form a recurrence similar to a Recurrent Neural Network (RNN), where at each time step t, the model combines the previous hidden state h_{t-1} and the current input x_t to produce a new hidden state h_t.

4   Model Architecture

An overview of the proposed BMI model is shown in Fig. 2. The model consists of a position embedding layer and multiple spatio-temporal blocks, which can be stacked to form a deep architecture for extracting high-level spatio-temporal features.

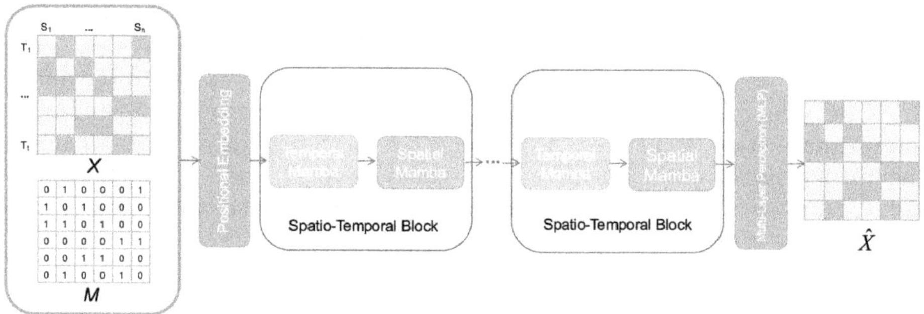

Fig. 2. Overview of the BMI model

Specifically, the input sequence is first passed to the l-th layer of the BMI model, producing an output T_l. The final output T_L is then normalized and fed into a MLP head to generate the final prediction $\hat{p}$:

$$T_l = \text{BMI}(T_{l-1}) + T_{l-1} \tag{6}$$

Here, T_{l-1} represents the input token sequence to the l-th layer, and $\text{BMI}(T_{l-1})$ denotes the output of the BMI block at that layer. Each layer adds new information to the token sequence. The residual connection helps to combine the learned features with the original input, alleviating the vanishing gradient problem and enabling deeper networks to learn more complex representations.

$$f = \text{Norm}(T_L) \tag{7}$$

Normalization stabilizes the value ranges during training and improves training efficiency.

$$\hat{p} = \text{MLP}(f) \tag{8}$$

The normalized feature vector f is fed into a MLP to generate the final prediction $\hat{p}$. The MLP typically consists of one or more dense layers to transform the feature vector into the final output.

4.1   Position Embedding

As shown in Fig. 2, the proposed BMI model integrates a position embedding mechanism since the standard Mamba is designed for 1D sequences and lacks temporal ordering information. To incorporate sequential order, positional encoding $\mathbf{PE}$ is introduced using sinusoidal functions.

For a position $pos \in [0, N-1]$ (where N is the maximum sequence length) and dimension $i \in [0, d_{\text{model}} - 1]$, the positional encoding $\mathbf{PE}$ is defined as:

For even $i = 2k$:

$$\mathbf{PE}(pos, 2k) = \sin\left(pos \cdot \frac{1}{10000^{2k/d_{\text{model}}}} \right) \tag{9}$$

For odd $i = 2k + 1$:

$$\mathbf{PE}(pos, 2k + 1) = \cos\left(pos \cdot \frac{1}{10000^{2k/d_{\text{model}}}} \right) \tag{10}$$

These encodings map each position pos into a high-dimensional space with different frequencies across dimensions, helping the model perceive sequence order.

The position encodings are added to the input data $\mathbf{x}$ to preserve temporal information:

$$\bar{\mathbf{x}} = \text{MLP}(\mathbf{x}) + \mathbf{PE} \tag{11}$$

Here, $\mathbf{x}$ is the original input matrix, transformed via MLP into a shape of (N, d_{model}), where N is the sequence length and d_{model} is the model dimension. $\mathbf{PE}$ is the position encoding matrix of the same shape.

4.2   Spatio-Temporal BMI Module

As shown in Fig. 3, each spatio-temporal block is composed of a spatial Mamba and a temporal Mamba to jointly extract latent spatio-temporal features. This section introduces a block that integrates spatial and temporal information to model dependencies across both dimensions for accurate data imputation.

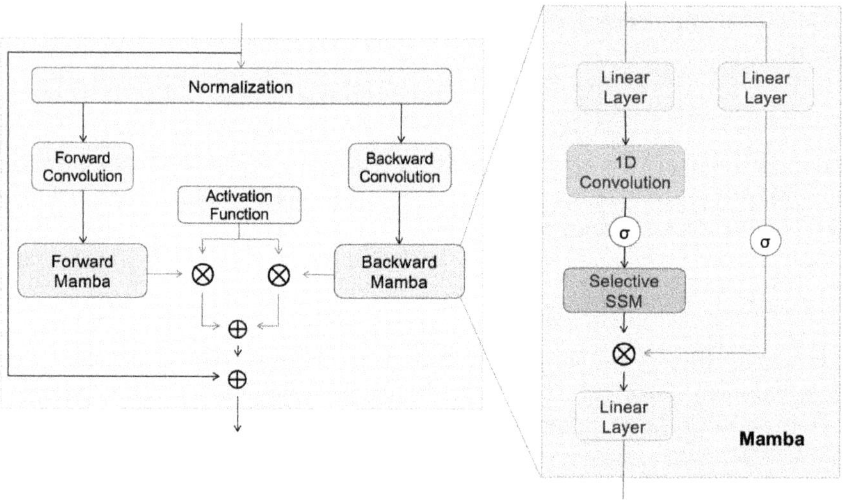

Fig. 3. Overview of the Spatio-Temporal Mamba Block

Unidirectional Mamba. Since traditional SSMs lack selectivity, they treat all input time steps equally. For instance, in traffic datasets, the correlation of traffic flow between the same road segment during morning and evening rush hours is usually stronger than that between non-peak periods. Without selectivity, the model allocates equal attention to all time points, failing to focus on the most influential ones. By introducing a selective mechanism, the model can focus on the most relevant timestamps and ignore less important ones, thus improving imputation accuracy. Therefore, this study uses the Mamba model, which incorporates a selective mechanism into the SSM.

Unlike traditional SSMs where the parameters A, B, and C are constants, Mamba dynamically adjusts these parameters based on the input data. The latent state is represented as:

$$
\begin{aligned}
h_t &= s_A(x_t)h_{t-1} + s_B(x_t)x_t \\
y_t &= s_C(x_t)h_t
\end{aligned}
\tag{12}
$$

The unidirectional Mamba model, based on the SSM architecture, takes an input $x \in \mathbb{R}^{B \times L \times D}$, where B is the batch size, L is the sequence length, and D is the model dimension. Inspired by the Mamba architecture, we employ an S6 block with a gated MLP and a convolutional layer. Since Mamba is designed for 1D data, a 1D convolution is used. The complete Mamba module is defined as:

$$
\begin{aligned}
x' &= \mathrm{SiLU}(\mathrm{Conv1d}(\bar{x})) \\
B &= \mathrm{Linear}^{B}(x') \\
C &= \mathrm{Linear}^{C}(x') \\
\Delta &= \log(1 + \exp(\mathrm{Linear}^{\Delta}(x') + \mathrm{Parameter}^{\Delta})) \\
A &= \Delta \otimes \mathrm{Parameter}^{A} \\
B &= \Delta \otimes B \\
Y &= \mathrm{SSM}(A, B, C)(x')
\end{aligned}
\tag{13}
$$

Here, Linear^{B}, Linear^{C}, and Linear^{Δ} represent distinct linear transformations (with superscripts indicating their specific purposes). Conv1d denotes 1D convolution, SiLU is the Sigmoid Linear Unit activation function, $\mathrm{Parameter}^{A}$ and $\mathrm{Parameter}^{\Delta}$ are learned parameters, SSM refers to the state space module, and $\otimes$ denotes element-wise (broadcasted) multiplication.

Bidirectional Mamba. The Transformer architecture has greatly facilitated feature learning due to its ability to comprehensively capture the influence of all variables on a specific target. However, as the number of variables increases, the quadratic complexity of Transformers leads to significantly higher computational costs. In contrast, Mamba's selective mechanism effectively identifies the importance of different variables, and its computation scales linearly with the number of variables. Nevertheless, the unidirectional nature of Mamba limits it to processing only forward information, lacking the global receptive field of Transformers, and possibly failing to capture the full dynamics of data.

To overcome this limitation, we develop a bidirectional Mamba layer that integrates two Mamba blocks to comprehensively capture correlations between variables, including both causes and effects in causal relationships. This design enables the system to consider the influence of future information on past values.

Algorithm 1. BMI Block

Require: Token sequence $T_{l-1} : (B, M, D)$
Ensure: Token sequence $T_l : (B, M, D)$

1: /* Normalize the input sequence */
2: $T'_{l-1} \leftarrow \mathrm{Norm}(T_{l-1})$
3: $x \leftarrow \mathrm{Linear}^x(T'_{l-1})$
4: $z \leftarrow \mathrm{Linear}^z(T'_{l-1})$
5: /* Process in both directions */
6: **for** o in {forward, backward} **do**
7:     $x'_o \leftarrow \mathrm{SiLU}(\mathrm{Conv1d}_o(x))$
8:     $B_o \leftarrow \mathrm{Linear}^B_o(x'_o)$
9:     $C_o \leftarrow \mathrm{Linear}^C_o(x'_o)$
10:     $\Delta_o \leftarrow \log(1 + \exp(\mathrm{Linear}^\Delta_o(x'_o) + \mathrm{Parameter}^\Delta_o))$
11:     $A_o \leftarrow \Delta_o \otimes \mathrm{Parameter}^A_o$
12:     $B_o \leftarrow \Delta_o \otimes B_o$
13:     $y_o \leftarrow \mathrm{SSM}(A_o, B_o, C_o)(x'_o)$
14: **end for**
15: /* Gate the outputs */
16: $y'_{\mathrm{forward}} \leftarrow y_{\mathrm{forward}} \otimes \mathrm{SiLU}(z)$
17: $y'_{\mathrm{backward}} \leftarrow y_{\mathrm{backward}} \otimes \mathrm{SiLU}(z)$
18: /* Residual connection */
19: $T_l \leftarrow \mathrm{Linear}_T(y'_{\mathrm{forward}} + y'_{\mathrm{backward}}) + T_{l-1}$
20: **return** T_l

The proposed Bidirectional Mamba innovates upon the traditional unidirectional Mamba by introducing a reverse state space mechanism, enabling the modeling of both forward and backward dependencies in time series. Each module maintains its own independence: the forward module aggregates information from the beginning to the end of the sequence, while the backward module processes the sequence in the reverse order. This architecture ensures that each time step captures features from both the past and the future, enabling a more comprehensive understanding of temporal dynamics and improving the model's accuracy in imputing missing values

Traditional Mamba models solely address the forward-flowing features of data, which may result in an incomplete exploitation of temporal context. To overcome this limitation, our Bidirectional Mamba model integrates both forward and backward processing modules, allowing it to capture both antecedent and consequent relationships within time series data. By combining the unidirectional Mamba model with a reverse state space mechanism, the proposed model enhances its capability to effectively model bidirectional temporal dependencies.

Let f and b denote forward and backward directions respectively. The forward module updates its hidden state h^f_t from past to future, while the backward module updates its state h^b_t from future to past. This allows each time step to receive contextual information from both directions. The mathematical formulation of the Bidirectional Mamba is as follows:

$$h_t^f = A^f h_{t-1}^f + B^f x_t$$
$$h_t^b = A^b h_{t+1}^b + B^b x_t \tag{14}$$
$$y_t = C^f h_t^f + C^b h_t^b$$

where, $h_t^f = A^f h_{t-1}^f + B^f x_t$ denotes the forward state update, with A^f as the forward transition matrix and B^f as the forward input transformation matrix. Similarly, $h_t^b = A^b h_{t+1}^b + B^b x_t$ denotes the backward state update. The final output y_t combines both forward and backward outputs through transformation matrices C^f and C^b.

By leveraging bidirectional processing, the Mamba model captures more complex dependencies in time-series data. This design provides a robust mechanism for accurate data imputation, combining forward and backward flows for a richer understanding of temporal structures. Compared to Transformers, the Bidirectional Mamba maintains high computational efficiency with significantly lower cost, making it suitable for large-scale data and resource-constrained environments.

The operation of the BMI block is shown in Algorithm 1. The input token sequence T_{l-1} is first normalized, then projected linearly into representations x and z of dimension E. For each direction, x is convolved via a 1D convolution to obtain x_o', which is then linearly projected into B_o, C_o, and Δ_o. These are used to compute A_o, B_o, and the output of the SSM. The resulting outputs from both directions are gated using z, combined, and finally passed through a residual connection to obtain T_l.

The hyperparameters of the BMI architecture are as follows:

- L: Number of blocks
- D: Hidden dimension
- E: Expanded dimension
- N: Dimension of the SSM

The BMI model first applies a projection layer with a kernel size of 16×16 to obtain 1D sequence embeddings. Then, L BMI blocks are stacked. By default, we set the number of blocks $L = 24$, SSM dimension $N = 16$, hidden dimension $D = 128$, and expanded dimension $E = 256$.

5   Model Feature Analysis

5.1   The Analysis of Bidirectional Information Processing Mechanism

Unlike missing data imputation models, which solely extract forward temporal dependency information and may lead to incomplete utilization of temporal context, the BMI model we propose employs a bidirectional Mamba structure (according to Eq.(14)). This structure simultaneously captures both forward and backward temporal dependencies, thereby enabling more robust temporal feature extraction and facilitating more accurate missing data imputation.

5.2   Efficiency Analysis of BMI Model

Traditional SSM-based methods utilize Fast Fourier Transform (FFT) to enhance convolutional operations, as in Eq.(5). In contrast, the SSM operation in Line 11 of Algorithm 1 within Mamba and BMI is no longer equivalent to convolution. To address this, Mamba and the proposed BMI adopt a hardware-friendly strategy to ensure efficiency. The key optimization is designed to overcome input/output (IO) bottlenecks and memory limitations on modern accelerators (GPUs).

IO Efficiency. High-bandwidth memory (HBM) and static random-access memory (SRAM) are two critical memory components in GPUs. While SRAM offers higher bandwidth, HBM provides larger capacity. The standard SSM implementation requires IO complexity of $O(BMEN)$. Inspired by Mamba, BMI first loads $O(BME + EN)$ bytes of memory $(\Delta_o, A_o, B_o, C_o)$ from HBM to SRAM. Discrete matrices of shape (B, M, E, N) for A_o and B_o are then computed in SRAM, and the resulting output of shape (B, M, E) is written back to HBM. This strategy reduces the IO complexity from $O(BMEN)$ to $O(BME + EN)$.

Memory Efficiency. To avoid memory overflow and enable efficient processing of long sequences, BMI employs the same strategy as Mamba—recomputing intermediate states of shape (B, M, E, N) during backpropagation instead of storing them. Intermediate activations such as outputs of activation functions and convolutions are also recomputed rather than stored, as they are fast to recompute and consume significant memory.

Computational Efficiency. Both the SSM in BMI (Line 11 of Algorithm 1) and self-attention in Transformers provide global adaptive context. In terms of computational complexity, self-attention is quadratic in the sequence length M, while SSM is linear (with fixed dimension $N = 16$ by default). Given a sequence $T \in \mathbb{R}^{1 \times M \times D}$ and default $E = 2D$, the complexities are:

$$\begin{aligned}
\Omega(\text{self-attention}) &= 4M^2D^2 + 2M^2D \\
\Omega(\text{SSM}) &= 3M(2D)N + M(2D)N
\end{aligned} \tag{15}$$

Overall, the BMI model we propose not only achieves more accurate missing data imputation but also ensures the efficiency of the model in terms of IO, Memory, and Computational resources. Next, we will verify these advantages of the BMI model through experiments.

6   Experimental Results and Analysis

6.1   Experimental Results

In this section, the effectiveness of the proposed BMI model is evaluated using four datasets from three real-world application domains. Specifically, the datasets include two traffic datasets (METR-LA and PEMS-BAY) [12], and two air quality datasets (AQI and AQI-36) [22]. Two types of missing data scenarios are simulated: point missingness (as shown in Fig. 4(a)) and block missingness (as shown in Fig. 4(b)). Point missingness typically represents random data loss, while block missingness simulates more extreme conditions, such as sensor failure leading to consecutive data loss. The performance is evaluated using three standard metrics: Mean Absolute Error (MAE), Mean Squared Error (MSE), and Mean Relative Error (MRE).

To assess the model's capability under various conditions, we compare the BMI model against several baselines, including Mean Imputation, KNN [2,16], Matrix Factorization, MICE [1], SAITS [6], Transformer [17], BRITS [4]. Experiments are conducted under varying missing rates (from 4% to 50%), and performance is evaluated separately for point missingness and block missingness.

On both METR-LA and PEMS-BAY datasets, the BMI model consistently achieves the lowest MAE across all missing rates (see Table 1 and Table 2). The superiority is particularly evident under low sampling rates (below 10%). For instance, on METR-LA with 4% point missingness, the BMI model achieves an MAE of only 4.019. Similarly, on the PEMS-BAY dataset, the MAE at a 4% sampling rate reaches as low as 2.2221, demonstrating the model's strong ability to handle missing data.

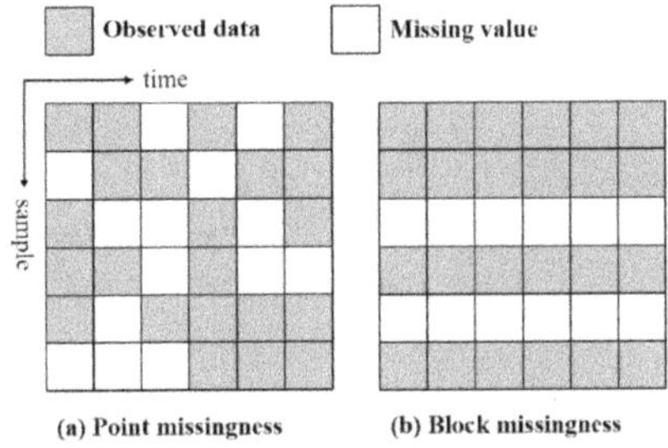

Fig. 4. Overview of the point missingness and block missingness

The MSE results (see Table 3 and Table 4) further confirm the robustness and efficiency of BMI. On METR-LA, BMI achieves significantly lower MSE than all baselines, especially under high missing rates—for example, achieving an MSE of 65.5922 at a 4% sampling rate. Similar trends are observed on the PEMS-BAY dataset.

Table 1. MAE results under point and block missingness on METR-LA dataset

Missing Type	Model / Rate	4%	6%	8%	10%	25%	50%
Point	Mean Imputation	7.5073	7.5058	7.5047	7.5038	7.5076	7.4919
	KNN	40.575	34.2888	29.1789	25.0185	10.9494	8.2103
	Matrix Factorization	7.1603	6.9366	6.7677	6.1582	5.1798	4.7159
	MICE	5.4396	4.9752	4.6643	4.4655	3.701	3.1855
	SAITS	5.1581	4.8451	3.9593	3.7953	3.5391	2.4800
	Transformer	6.6288	5.9292	5.2053	4.8038	3.7391	3.0381
	BRITS	4.1020	3.8423	3.6819	3.5393	3.0222	2.6428
	BMI	**4.0190**	**3.6027**	**3.3613**	**3.1448**	**2.5621**	**2.2648**
Block	Mean Imputation	7.5041	7.5028	7.5048	7.5031	7.5019	7.4919
	KNN	41.1625	34.9992	29.9549	25.7082	11.3521	8.2103
	Matrix Factorization	7.1365	6.9817	6.8230	6.3093	5.0778	4.6794
	MICE	5.4990	5.0287	4.7363	4.5016	3.7264	3.1855
	SAITS	5.9513	5.2451	4.9563	4.7963	3.6319	3.0831
	Transformer	7.6845	6.9119	6.2320	6.0696	4.1005	3.3654
	BRITS	4.1086	3.8757	3.7035	3.5937	3.0643	2.6951
	BMI	**4.0767**	**3.6644**	**3.4105**	**3.1911**	**2.6220**	**2.3321**

Table 2. MAE results under point and block missingness on the PEMS-BAY dataset

Missing Type	Model / Sampling Rate	4%	6%	8%	10%	25%	50%
Point Missing	Mean Imputation	5.434	5.4337	5.4341	5.433	5.4316	5.4423
	KNN	41.7462	34.1616	28.0048	23.0615	7.1597	4.4957
	Matrix Factorization	4.2481	3.4793	3.2493	3.1557	2.9007	2.8637
	MICE	5.2667	5.1832	5.1035	5.0212	4.4499	3.6720
	SAITS	4.3151	4.2085	3.9572	2.9141	1.4915	1.2796
	Transformer	3.9454	3.5219	3.1657	2.9360	1.5195	1.3789
	BRITS	2.6344	2.4910	2.4129	2.3529	2.1024	1.9501
	BMI	**2.2221**	**1.8649**	**1.6293**	**1.5007**	**1.0645**	**0.8271**
Block Missing	Mean Imputation	5.4341	5.4338	5.4344	5.4336	5.4380	5.4423
	KNN	42.4368	35.0328	8.8765	23.9030	7.5685	4.4957
	Matrix Factorization	4.2629	3.6232	3.2885	3.1664	2.9281	2.8941
	MICE	5.2735	5.1940	5.1160	5.0378	4.4939	3.6720
	SAITS	4.2796	4.1397	3.9833	3.0941	1.5215	1.2496
	Transformer	4.0051	3.5582	3.2856	2.9696	1.6403	1.3567
	BRITS	2.6398	2.5291	2.4453	2.3684	2.1390	1.9836
	BMI	**2.2262**	**1.8949**	**1.6931**	**1.5428**	**1.1222**	**0.8966**

Notably, the BMI model also demonstrates superior performance in terms of Mean Relative Error (MRE) (see Table 5 and Table 6), achieving the lowest relative error among all compared models. These results indicate that BMI not only excels quantitatively but also ensures high accuracy in data recovery.

Table 3. MSE results under point and block missingness on the METR-LA dataset

Missing Type	Model / Sampling Rate	4%	6%	8%	10%	25%	50%
Point Missing	Mean Imputation	142.5133	142.4343	142.3802	142.3409	142.5285	141.8274
	KNN	2284.9488	1841.9605	1488.1925	1204.4182	298.7052	145.0057
	Matrix Factorization	148.9847	144.7381	141.0804	119.3803	93.3133	78.0482
	MICE	80.6066	68.6597	61.1633	56.4545	39.8744	29.5690
	SAITS	76.9593	68.9593	52.7698	48.8732	44.0583	18.2261
	Transformer	135.5170	110.9247	88.4255	76.5043	44.0583	25.2474
	BRITS	58.9600	50.5516	47.2208	42.7020	29.5063	21.8634
	BMI	**65.5922**	**51.6620**	**45.6381**	**37.9597**	**22.8586**	**16.0496**
Block Missing	Mean Imputation	142.3754	142.3333	142.3951	142.3516	142.2788	141.8274
	KNN	2325.6349	1890.6649	1540.7575	1251.0557	321.7091	145.0057
	Matrix Factorization	146.6025	145.0509	142.2099	124.8078	87.8519	78.0482
	MICE	81.6064	69.7375	62.7956	57.3972	40.5242	29.5690
	SAITS	96.9593	82.9593	78.7698	68.8732	40.0583	27.2261
	Transformer	171.0240	144.6158	121.6525	113.8869	54.7035	36.1111
	BRITS	58.5121	53.3852	47.4551	43.8503	30.4272	22.7110
	BMI	**68.4555**	**52.6277**	**46.0529**	**38.9564**	**24.3072**	**17.5550**

Table 4. MSE results under point and block missingness on the PEMS-BAY dataset

Missing Type	Model/Sampling Rate	4%	6%	8%	10%	25%	50%
Point Missing	Mean Imputation	87.1069	87.1009	87.1141	87.0740	86.9594	87.2722
	KNN	2489.6869	1954.9769	1529.7198	1195.1041	192.6311	56.5265
	Matrix Factorization	77.8922	53.8846	49.1320	47.0803	40.5561	40.4832
	MICE	82.2904	79.9368	77.7403	75.4389	60.2879	41.9525
	SAITS	67.7862	63.5565	49.3142	38.3126	9.9164	4.8094
	Transformer	65.5622	54.2969	45.2432	39.4831	11.0916	4.9194
	BRITS	28.2008	25.7503	24.1964	23.0710	18.0257	15.1815
	BMI	**25.0582**	**18.1882**	**13.8123**	**11.7095**	**5.1824**	**2.5734**
Block Missing	Mean Imputation	87.1258	87.1046	87.1129	87.0766	87.2228	87.2722
	KNN	2538.4850	2014.9568	1588.7291	1251.0415	215.4243	56.5265
	Matrix Factorization	79.6518	59.1762	49.7152	46.9315	42.8314	41.4699
	MICE	82.5035	80.2374	78.0428	75.8269	61.5772	41.9525
	SAITS	75.7862	62.6236	52.3142	41.3126	12.9164	8.8094
	Transformer	69.2640	55.2070	48.5828	41.3330	14.0329	10.2922
	BRITS	28.2518	26.4654	24.7685	23.3950	18.4862	15.4290
	BMI	**26.5058**	**19.4226**	**15.2060**	**12.7675**	**6.2039**	**3.8231**

In summary, the BMI model shows significant advantages in handling both point and block missingness on the METR-LA and PEMS-BAY datasets. Through comprehensive evaluation metrics including MAE, MSE, and MRE, the BMI model proves its robustness and superior performance under high missing rate scenarios. These findings highlight the model's capability in dealing with complex and incomplete data and underline its potential in real-world applications.

Table 5. MRE results under point and block missingness on the METR-LA dataset

Missing Type	Model/Sampling Rate	4%	6%	8%	10%	25%	50%
Point Missing	Mean Imputation	0.1300	0.1299	0.1299	0.1299	0.1300	0.1297
	KNN	0.7024	0.5936	0.5051	0.4331	0.1896	0.1421
	Matrix Factorization	0.1240	0.1201	0.1172	0.1066	0.0897	0.0810
	MICE	0.0942	0.0861	0.0807	0.0773	0.0641	0.0551
	SAITS	0.0845	0.0765	0.0863	0.0641	0.0507	0.0398
	Transformer	0.1147	0.1026	0.0900	0.0831	0.0647	0.0526
	BRITS	0.0710	0.0665	0.0637	0.0613	0.0523	0.0457
	BMI	**0.0682**	**0.0623**	**0.0581**	**0.0544**	**0.0443**	**0.0395**
Block Missing	Mean Imputation	0.1299	0.1299	0.1299	0.1299	0.1299	0.1297
	KNN	0.7125	0.6059	0.5186	0.4450	0.1965	0.1421
	Matrix Factorization	0.1235	0.1209	0.1181	0.1092	0.0879	0.0810
	MICE	0.0952	0.0870	0.0820	0.0779	0.0645	0.0551
	SAITS	0.1145	0.1065	0.0963	0.0891	0.0627	0.0498
	Transformer	0.1329	0.1196	0.1078	0.1051	0.0709	0.0583
	BRITS	0.0711	0.0671	0.0641	0.0622	0.0530	0.0467
	BMI	**0.0695**	**0.0634**	**0.0590**	**0.0552**	**0.0453**	**0.0403**

Table 6. MRE results under point and block missingness on the PEMS-BAY dataset

Missing Type	Model/Sampling Rate	4%	6%	8%	10%	25%	50%
Point Missing	Mean Imputation	0.0870	0.0870	0.0870	0.0870	0.0869	0.0871
	KNN	0.6683	0.5469	0.4483	0.3692	0.1146	0.0720
	Matrix Factorization	0.0674	0.0557	0.0520	0.0505	0.0464	0.0459
	MICE	0.0843	0.0830	0.0817	0.0804	0.0712	0.0588
	SAITS	0.0689	0.0622	0.0617	0.0451	0.0247	0.0207
	Transformer	0.0632	0.0564	0.0507	0.0468	0.0253	0.0217
	BRITS	0.0422	0.0399	0.0386	0.0376	0.0337	0.0312
	BMI	**0.0355**	**0.02987**	**0.02609**	**0.02403**	**0.0170**	**0.01324**
Block Missing	Mean Imputation	0.0870	0.0870	0.0870	0.0870	0.0871	0.0871
	KNN	0.6794	0.5608	0.4623	0.3827	0.1212	0.0720
	Matrix Factorization	0.0682	0.0580	0.0526	0.0507	0.0471	0.0463
	MICE	0.0844	0.0831	0.0819	0.0806	0.0719	0.0588
	SAITS	0.0732	0.0638	0.0597	0.0488	0.0253	0.0220
	Transformer	0.0641	0.0570	0.0526	0.0475	0.0262	0.0227
	BRITS	0.0422	0.0405	0.03917	0.0379	0.0342	0.0317
	BMI	**0.0356**	**0.0303**	**0.0271**	**0.0247**	**0.01798**	**0.01437**

We further conducted evaluations on the AQI and AQI36 datasets (see Table 7 and Table 8). The BMI model achieves outstanding performance, significantly outperforming all baseline models in terms of MAE, MSE, and MRE. Specifically, on the AQI dataset, BMI yields MAE, MSE, and MRE of 14.2211, 880.3414, and 0.2287, respectively. Similarly, on the AQI36 dataset, it continues

Table 7. Results on the AQI dataset

Model	MAE	MSE	MRE
Mean Imputation	40.2627	3276.696	0.6025
KNN	34.1740	3614.958	0.5114
Matrix Factorization	26.2433	1957.239	0.3927
MICE	31.0673	2350.401	0.4649
SAITS	27.2390	2026.834	0.4042
Transformer	28.3935	2194.366	0.4113
BRITS	20.2305	1156.908	0.3027
BMI	**14.2211**	**880.3414**	**0.2287**

Table 8. Results on the AQI36 dataset

Model	MAE	MSE	MRE
Mean Imputation	55.0812	4715.698	0.7907
KNN	29.5539	3059.955	0.4242
Matrix Factorization	30.1841	2774.002	0.4333
MICE	29.4408	2549.720	0.4226
SAITS	21.2391	659.406	0.3068
Transformer	27.3025	2711.788	0.3723
BRITS	13.7439	531.8731	0.1973
BMI	**11.8172**	**456.7164**	**0.1617**

to outperform, achieving MAE of 11.8172, MSE of 456.7164, and MRE of 0.1617. These results validate BMI's powerful capability in handling missing data and highlight its high accuracy and reliability for air quality prediction. Particularly under high missing ratios, BMI provides more accurate imputation than other models.

Among the compared methods, traditional approaches such as Mean Imputation, KNN, Matrix Factorization, and MICE—though widely used—experience severe performance degradation under high missing ratios. Deep learning methods like SAITS, Transformer, and BRITS perform well under low missing conditions but are limited as missing ratios increase.

As the missing rate increases, the performance advantage of BMI becomes more evident. This is attributed to BMI's ability to effectively adapt to characteristics of high-missing data. Its significant advantage stems from the capability to model high dynamics, high dimensionality, and severe missingness in time series. The BMI model's effectiveness on both datasets can be attributed to the synergy of RMSNorm normalization and the bidirectional Mamba layer. RMSNorm enhances the model's adaptation to input fluctuations by effectively scaling the features, while the bidirectional Mamba layer captures both forward and backward dependencies in time series data, enabling richer contextual understanding and improved prediction accuracy. **This architecture enables BMI to robustly model complex temporal dependencies in air quality data and optimize predictive results.**

6.2   Ablation Study

To further validate the proposed model, we conduct a series of ablation studies on the METR-LA, AQI, and AQI36 datasets to compare the performance of unidirectional and bidirectional Mamba models.

As shown in Table 9, the bidirectional Mamba consistently outperforms its unidirectional counterpart across all metrics. The performance gains are particularly notable at lower missing rates. For instance, at a 50% missing rate, the bidirectional Mamba achieves an 8.2% reduction in MAE and a 25.6% reduction in MSE compared to the unidirectional version.

Table 9 presents the ablation results on the METR-LA dataset. As shown, the bidirectional Mamba model consistently outperforms the unidirectional variant in terms of MAE, MSE, and MRE, particularly under low missing rates. For instance, at a 50% missing rate, the bidirectional Mamba achieves 8.2% and 25.6% reductions in MAE and MSE, respectively.

As shown in Table 10, the bidirectional Mamba model consistently outperforms other methods on both the AQI and AQI-36 datasets with respect to MAE and MSE. Notably, on AQI36, the bidirectional model reduces MAE and MSE by 28.2% and 55.7%, respectively, indicating its ability to more effectively leverage both past and future information for imputation.

The ablation study demonstrates that **the bidirectional Mamba is highly effective at exploiting the bidirectional dependencies in time series data**, resulting in improved imputation accuracy. This bidirectional mechanism is especially suitable for environments with high temporal dynamics and correlations, such as traffic and air quality monitoring. Moreover, the model exhibits strong robustness and adaptability across various missing rates, making it a promising tool for real-world applications.

Table 9. Ablation results on the METR-LA dataset

Metric	Direction	4%	6%	8%	10%	25%	50%
MAE	Uni	4.0767	3.6720	3.4708	3.3455	2.8467	2.5393
	Bi	**4.0190**	**3.6644**	**3.4105**	**3.1911**	**2.6220**	**2.3321**
MSE	Uni	68.3642	57.1390	51.6920	47.3511	31.9821	23.5954
	Bi	**68.4555**	**52.6277**	**46.0529**	**38.9564**	**24.3072**	**17.5550**
MRE	Uni	0.0695	0.0635	0.0600	0.0579	0.0492	0.0439
	Bi	**0.0695**	**0.0634**	**0.0590**	**0.0552**	**0.0453**	**0.0403**

Table 10. Ablation study on the AQI and AQI-36 datasets

Metric	Direction	AQI	AQI36
MAE	Uni	17.4049	16.4435
	Bi	**14.2211**	**11.8172**
MSE	Uni	990.0747	1031.705
	Bi	**880.3414**	**456.7164**
MRE	Uni	0.2541	0.2226
	Bi	**0.2287**	**0.16174**

7 Conclusion

In this paper, we propose the Bidirectional Mamba Imputation (BMI) model, which builds upon the advanced state space architecture, Mamba, to substantially improve both the performance and efficiency of data imputation tasks. By incorporating a bidirectional information flow mechanism alongside selective state space techniques, the BMI model captures both forward and backward dependencies within time series data, facilitating the inference of global context and enhancing the model's understanding of dynamic data patterns. Furthermore, the integration of the S6 selective mechanism enables BMI to dynamically adjust its information processing strategy based on the characteristics of the input data, thereby further optimizing computational efficiency and prediction accuracy. Extensive experiments conducted on four real-world datasets underscore the effectiveness and robustness of the BMI model, particularly in scenarios involving complex data with high missing rates, demonstrating its significant potential for future data imputation applications.

Acknowledgment. The work was supported in part by the National Natural Science Foundation of China under Grants 62025201, 62472159, 62202156 and 62472167, in part by the Hunan Provincial Natural Science Foundation of China under Grants 2024JJ3014 and 2024JJ5165, and in part by the Key Research and Development Program of Hunan Province under Grant 2023GK2001, and in part by the Guangdong Basic and Applied Basic Research Foundation 2025A1515010305. Xiaocan Li and Kun Xie are co-corresponding authors, and their contributions are equal.

References

1. Azur, M.J., Stuart, E.A., Frangakis, C., Leaf, P.J.: Multiple imputation by chained equations: what is it and how does it work? Int. J. Methods Psychiatr. Res. **20**(1), 40–49 (2011)
2. Beretta, L., Santaniello, A.: Nearest neighbor imputation algorithms: a critical evaluation. BMC Med. Inform. Decis. Mak. **16**(3), 197–208 (2016)
3. van den Berg, R., Kipf, T.N., Welling, M.: Graph convolutional matrix completion (2017)

4. Cao, W., Wang, D., Li, J., Zhou, H., Li, L., Li, Y.: Brits: bidirectional recurrent imputation for time series. In: Advances in Neural Information Processing Systems, vol. 31 (2018)

5. Du, R., Chen, C., Yang, B., Guan, X.: Vanet based traffic estimation: a matrix completion approach. In: 2013 IEEE Global Communications Conference (GLOBE-COM), pp. 30–35 (2013). https://doi.org/10.1109/GLOCOM.2013.6831043

6. Du, W., Côté, D., Liu, Y.: SAITS: self-attention-based imputation for time series. Expert Syst. Appl. **219**, 119619 (2023)

7. Gu, A., Dao, T.: Mamba: Linear-time sequence modeling with selective state spaces. arXiv preprint arXiv:2312.00752 (2023)

8. Gu, A., Goel, K., Ré, C.: Efficiently modeling long sequences with structured state spaces. arXiv preprint arXiv:2111.00396 (2021)

9. Gürsun, G., Crovella, M.: On traffic matrix completion in the internet. In: Proceedings of the 2012 Internet Measurement Conference, pp. 399–412. IMC '12, Association for Computing Machinery, New York, NY, USA (2012). https://doi.org/10.1145/2398776.2398818

10. Li, X., et al.: Tripartite graph aided tensor completion for sparse network measurement. IEEE Trans. Parallel Distrib. Syst. **34**(1), 48–62 (2022)

11. Li, X., et al.: Multi-view matrix factorization for sparse mobile crowdsensing. IEEE Internet Things J. **9**(24), 25767–25779 (2022)

12. Li, Y., Yu, R., Shahabi, C., Liu, Y.: Diffusion convolutional recurrent neural network: data-driven traffic forecasting. arXiv preprint arXiv:1707.01926 (2017)

13. Mardani, M., Giannakis, G.B.: Robust network traffic estimation via sparsity and low rank. In: 2013 IEEE International Conference on Acoustics, Speech and Signal Processing, pp. 4529–4533 (2013). https://doi.org/10.1109/ICASSP.2013.6638517

14. Roughan, M., Zhang, Y., Willinger, W., Qiu, L.: Spatio-temporal compressive sensing and internet traffic matrices (extended version). IEEE/ACM Trans. Network. **20**(3), 662–676 (2012). https://doi.org/10.1109/TNET.2011.2169424

15. Smith, J.T., Warrington, A., Linderman, S.W.: Simplified state space layers for sequence modeling. arXiv preprint arXiv:2208.04933 (2022)

16. Troyanskaya, O., et al.: Missing value estimation methods for DNA microarrays. Bioinformatics **17**(6), 520–525 (2001)

17. Vaswani, A., et al.: Attention is all you need. In: Advances in Neural Information Processing Systems, vol. 30 (2017)

18. Xie, K., et al.: Accurate recovery of internet traffic data under variable rate measurements. IEEE/ACM Trans. Network. **26**(3), 1137–1150 (2018). https://doi.org/10.1109/TNET.2018.2819504

19. Xie, K., et al.: Sequential and adaptive sampling for matrix completion in network monitoring systems. In: 2015 IEEE Conference on Computer Communications (INFOCOM), pp. 2443–2451 (2015). https://doi.org/10.1109/INFOCOM.2015.7218633

20. Xie, K., et al.: Accurate recovery of missing network measurement data with localized tensor completion. IEEE/ACM Trans. Network. **27**(6), 2222–2235 (2019). https://doi.org/10.1109/TNET.2019.2940147

21. Yang, Z., Mitra, A., Kwon, S., Yu, H.: ClinicAlmamba: a generative clinical language model on longitudinal clinical notes. arXiv preprint arXiv:2403.05795 (2024)

22. Zheng, Y., Yi, X., Li, M., Li, R., Shan, Z., Chang, E., Li, T.: Forecasting fine-grained air quality based on big data. In: Proceedings of the 21th ACM SIGKDD International Conference on Knowledge Discovery and Data Mining, pp. 2267–2276 (2015)

Multi-dimensional Cost-Driven LDSP Instruction Scheduling Optimization

Ting Peng[1], Min Shi[2(✉)], and Xinlian Zhou[1]

[1] Hunan University of Science and Technology, Xiangtan 411100, Hunan, China
[2] Hunan University, Changsha 410000, Hunan, China
shimin22@hnu.edu.cn

Abstract. As one of the core basic software tools in modern processor architecture, the compiler plays a key role in hardware resource utilization and program performance optimization. Addressing the dual challenges of limited register resources and low instruction-level parallelism efficiency faced by LDSP accelerator in the embedded real-time control domain, this paper conducts research on instruction scheduling optimization based on the LLVM compilation framework. Traditional heuristic scheduling methods, lacking dynamic register pressure sensing mechanism, frequently cause register spilling during the processing of large-scale data computations, resulting in a large number of redundant memory access instructions, which seriously restricts the release of hardware performance. To this end, this paper proposes an instruction scheduling algorithm based on quantification register pressure (QRP) and an improved Max-Min Ant System (MMAS). This algorithm estimates program performance by sensing the number of memory access instructions required for register spilling and guides instruction scheduling to achieve synergistic optimization of instruction-level parallelism and register pressure. Testing with eight classic DSP algorithms, the experimental results show that the algorithm can achieve an average performance speedup ratio of 1.1, effectively enhancing the performance of LDSP in computation-intensive programs.

Keywords: Instruction Scheduling · LLVM · Compiler Optimization

1 Introduction

With the continuous evolution of computer architecture and the increasing complexity of processor designs, modern processors demand enhanced capabilities for exploiting Instruction-Level Parallelism (ILP) [1]. As a critical bridge between hardware and software, the optimization efficacy of compilers directly impacts the performance of generated code. In the context of deep integration between heterogeneous computing and embedded systems, the trend towards diversification of processor architectures imposes even more severe challenges on compilation technology. Particularly for LDSP accelerators targeting real-time control

W. Liang et al. (Eds.): SecureComm 2025, LNICST 690, pp. 229–242, 2026.
https://doi.org/10.1007/978-3-032-23456-8_13

and signal processing domains, the unique hardware characteristics of LDSP accelerators, which employ Very Long Instruction Word (VLIW) architectures, significantly differ from those of general processors: 1) The limited capacity of the register file struggles to support the storage demands of data-intensive algorithms; 2) The VLIW architecture relies significantly more on the compiler's instruction scheduling capabilities compared to traditional out-of-order execution processors [2,3]. Under the constraints of limited register capacity and memory bandwidth in LDSP, leveraging compiler instruction scheduling to enhance ILP has become a critical technological challenge.

Instruction scheduling, as one of the core optimization techniques in compilers, aims to rearrange the instruction sequence to minimize performance losses caused by resource conflicts or delays, while satisfying data dependencies and hardware constraints. The ultimate goal is to maximize ILP and hardware utilization [4]. In recent years, with the rapid development of high-performance computing, artificial intelligence, large language models and other fields, processor architectures have become increasingly complex, while the scale and complexity of programs continue to grow. And the performance of instruction scheduling optimization algorithms has become increasingly critical. However, traditional scheduling algorithms based on heuristic approaches have gradually revealed limitations: 1) Heuristic algorithms often adopt greedy strategies, which are prone to falling into local optima; 2) Traditional scheduling algorithms, such as list scheduling, fail to establish a quantifiable relationship between ILP and register pressure [5]. Therefore, exploring more efficient instruction scheduling algorithms has become an urgent and important issue to address, with significant practical implications.

In view of the aforementioned issues, this paper focuses on the compilation optimization requirements of LDSP accelerators, and proposes an instruction scheduling framework based on an improved MMAS [6]. Building on this, the dynamic QRP method is introduced, and a quantitative evaluation model of ILP that balances ILP gains and register spill costs is established, thereby enabling the search for a globally optimal scheduling solution under register resource constraints. Experimental results demonstrate that the proposed QRP-MMAS scheduling algorithm effectively retains the ILP exploration capability of traditional scheduling algorithms while significantly reducing performance degradation caused by register spilling, thereby enhancing program execution performance.

2   Related Work

The evolution of instruction scheduling algorithms is closely tied to advancements in processor architecture [7,8]. During the era dominated by single-issue scalar processors, the primary goal of instruction scheduling was to mitigate pipeline conflicts, with technical efforts focused on optimizing instruction ordering within basic blocks. For instance, methods such as eliminating empty operations (NOP) instructions or filling delay slots(Delay Slot Filling) [9,10] effectively reduced pipeline stalls and improved instruction throughput. These approaches rely on static analysis and characterized by low overhead, which makes it consistently used in modern compilers. With the popularity of Superscalar and VLIW architectures [11], the multi-issue mechanism imposed higher demands on the exploitation of ILP. Traditional local scheduling could no longer meet these requirements because it is limited to the basic block, leading to the emergence of global scheduling techniques. The Trace Scheduling [12], significantly enhanced the parallelism of the long instruction sequences by rearranging instructions across basic blocks along high-frequency execution paths. However, such methods rely on accurate program behavior predictions and often idealize hardware resource allocation, making them susceptible to branch predictions failure and complex program control flows in practical applications.

In recent years, the scheduling techniques for complex architectures such as VLIW and Single Instruction Multiple Data (SIMD) have become increasingly refined. The stringent constraints on memory bandwidth and register resources in heterogeneous computing scenarios have prompted researchers to reexamine the assumptions limitations of traditional scheduling algorithms. For instance, much of the existing research is based on idealized assumptions about register resources, often overlooking the implicit constraints that register pressure on ILP in embedded scenarios. Specifically, when compilers overly schedule instructions to enhance ILP, the memory access overhead caused by register spills may offset or even exceed the benefits of parallelization [13]. Consequently, researchers began to focus on multi-objective collaborative optimization [5,14,15]. Some have attempted to incorporate register pressure awareness into instruction scheduling optimization, as seen in approaches like SLIL [16]. However, since the overhead of memory access instructions and the performance penalty caused by register spilling vary across different architectures, such methods relying solely on the number of register uses struggle to practically quantify it.

3   Algorithm Introduction and Implementation

This section, with the core goal of balancing ILP and QRP, provides a detailed exposition of the implementation framework of the QRP-MMAS algorithm. Firstly, based on an improved MMAS algorithm, an instruction scheduler and decision model are designed. By extensively searching the solution space for feasible solutions that satisfy dependency constraints, the optimal scheduling scheme is selected. Secondly, to address the challenge of quantifying the cost of register spilling in traditional scheduling algorithms, a static analysis of the instruction dependency graph is used to construct a quantitative model for the register spilling load induced by different scheduling sequences. This model, combined with the scheduling length, designs a cost function to provide critical information for the MMAS scheduler's decision-making, aiming to minimize both the scheduling length and register pressure.

The overall architecture of the algorithm is illustrated in Fig. 1. The input Directed Acyclic Graph(DAG) is fed into both the heuristic scheduler and the

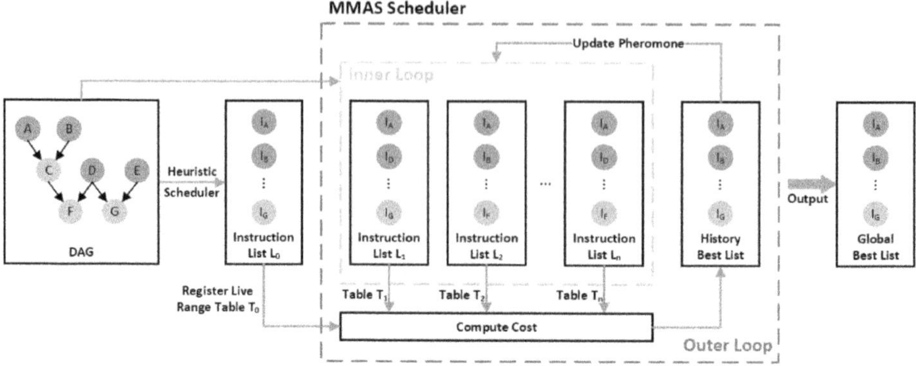

Fig. 1. Flowchart of the QRP-MMAS Instruction Scheduling Algorithm.

MMAS scheduler. The heuristic scheduler generates a scheduling scheme L_0, while the MMAS scheduler produces multiple scheduling schemes $L_1...L_n$. Meanwhile, during the scheduling process, the register live range tables $T_0...T_n$ are obtained by analyzing the program. Based on the register live range tables and the scheduling schemes, the register pressure is quantified, and the Cost of each scheme is calculated. The optimal scheduling scheme is selected and saved as the current best solution. When updating the pheromone, an elite solution strategy is employed to expand the search space. Upon meeting the termination condition, the optimal scheduling scheme is output.

3.1 Implementation of an Improved MMAS for Instruction Scheduling

This algorithm, based on the MMAS framework, achieves efficient optimization for complex instruction sequences. By introducing a dynamic pheromone concentration boundary constraint mechanism, adaptive adjustment of pheromone concentration is realized, enhancing the search space in the early stages of the algorithm. This prevents premature convergence and avoids being trapped in local optima. To improve the convergence speed in the later stages of the algorithm, a stagnation detection strategy based on the convergence rate of the cost value is designed, as shown in Eqs. (1), (2), and (3). The setup and calculation method of the cost function are introduced in Sect. 3.2.

Let Cost_t, Cost_{best} respectively represent the cost value of the local optimal scheduling solution generated in the current iteration and that of the historical optimal scheduling solution. Let Cost_i be the set of locally optimal cost values produced in each of five successive iterations. ΔCost_{best} is defined as the difference rate between the locally optimal cost value of the current iteration and the historically optimal cost value, while ΔCost_{max} is defined as the difference rate between the maximum and minimum locally optimal cost values over five consecutive iterations.

$$\Delta\text{Cost}_{\text{best}} = \frac{\text{Cost}_t - \text{Cost}_{\text{best}}}{\text{Cost}_{\text{best}}} \tag{1}$$

$$\Delta\text{Cost}_{\max} = \frac{\max \text{Cost}_i - \min \text{Cost}_i}{\max \text{Cost}_i} \tag{2}$$

$$\text{Cost}_i = \{\text{Cost}_{t-4},\ \text{Cost}_{t-3},\ \text{Cost}_{t-2},\ \text{Cost}_{t-1},\ \text{Cost}_i\} \tag{3}$$

By comparing $\Delta\text{Cost}_{\text{best}}$ and $\Delta\text{Cost}_{\max}$, the convergence rate of the algorithm is assessed. If $\Delta\text{Cost}_{\text{best}} < 0.005$ and $\Delta\text{Cost}_{\max} < 0.02$, it is considered that the scheduling process has reached a stable state, and the algorithm is terminated early. Furthermore, in order to enhance the quality of the generated scheduling solutions, an elite solution strategy is introduced. In each iteration, three high-quality solutions are retained along with the historically optimal solution to participate in the pheromone update process. This mechanism prevents the algorithm from being trapped in local optimal solution.

The overall flow of the MMAS instruction scheduling algorithm is show in **Algorithm** 1. By quantifying the register pressure and scheduling length, the proposed algorithm selects the scheme with the smallest cost function for scheduling in a large number of scheduling schemes. The input to the algorithm is a DAG based on a basic block, where each DAG consists of a certain number of instructions with dependency relationships.

Line 1 represents the upper and lower bound of the initialized pheromone concentration and the historical optimal scheduling scheme. Line 2 indicates that the algorithm exits when the algorithm reaches the maximum number of iterations or reaches a steady state, and outputs the historical optimal scheduling scheme, otherwise continue the algorithm. Lines 3-19 are an independent scheduling process, and each scheduling process generates a scheduling scheme path$_{\text{ant}}$ and its corresponding cost value C$_{\text{ant}}$. Line 4 initializes the path of the current schedule, register live range LR spill information SPI, quantified register pressure QRP$_{\text{ant}}$, cost value C$_{\text{ant}}$, and ready queue rea$_q$. Lines 6-12 are the instruction scheduling scheme generation process, ins is the instruction of the current cycle scheduling, and θ represents two scheduling strategies. When $\theta = 1$, the heuristic strategy is used to select the instruction with the highest priority for scheduling, and when $\theta = 2$ the roulette wheel method is employed to select an instruction from the ready queue based on pheromone concentration. The choice of scheduling strategy is determined by the random number rand between 0 and 1, If rand < 0.3, the heuristic strategy is chosen; if rand ≥ 0.3, the roulette wheel method is selected. Lines 13-14 update the register live range, ready queue, and scheduling scheme based on the selected instruction. Lines 16-18 are the program information analysis stage. When the scheduling is completed, the spill information SPI is calculated according to the register live range, and the quantified register pressure and generation value of the current scheduling scheme are obtained through the cost function. The calculation method is described in Sect. 3.2. Lines 20-21 are the scheme selection stage. After the current iteration

---

Algorithm 1. The MMAS Instruction Scheduling Algorithm

Require: DAG
Ensure: $\text{path}_{\text{best}}$
 1: $\text{path}_{\text{best}} \leftarrow \emptyset$ $\varepsilon(\text{phe}_c \mid \text{boundary}_1) \leftarrow \text{dval}$ $\varepsilon(\text{phe}_c \mid \text{boundary}_2) \leftarrow \text{uval}$;
 2: **while** $(c < 50 \mid ((\Delta\text{Cost}_{best} < 0.005)\&(\Delta\text{Cost}_{max} < 0.02)))$ **do**
 3:   **for** $\text{ant} \in \text{num}$ **do**
 4:     $\text{path}_{\text{ant}} \leftarrow \emptyset$ $\text{LR} \leftarrow \emptyset$ $\text{SPI} \leftarrow \emptyset$ $\text{QRP}_{\text{ant}} \leftarrow \emptyset$ $\text{C}_{\text{ant}} \leftarrow \emptyset$ $\text{rea}_q \leftarrow \text{list}_{\text{ins}}$;
 5:     **while** $\text{rea}_q \neq \emptyset$ **do**
 6:       $\text{rea}_q = \partial[0 \cdots 1]$;
 7:       **if** $(\text{rand} < 0.3)$ **then**
 8:         $\text{ins} \leftarrow \Delta(\text{rea}_q, \mid \theta, 1)$;
 9:       **end if**
10:       **if** $(\text{rand} \geq 0.3)$ **then**
11:         $\text{ins} \leftarrow \tau(\Delta(\text{rea}_q, \mid \theta, 2), \text{phe}_c)$;
12:       **end if**
13:       $\text{LR} \leftarrow \lambda(\text{ins}, \text{cycle})$ $\text{rea}_q \leftarrow \vartheta(\text{ins}, \text{DAG})$;
14:       $\text{path}_{\text{ant}} \ni \text{ins}$;
15:     **end while**
16:     $\text{SPI} \leftarrow \xi(\text{LR})$;
17:     $\text{QRP}_{\text{ant}} \leftarrow \varphi(\text{LR}, \text{SPI})$;
18:     $\text{C}_{\text{ant}} \leftarrow \phi(\text{QRP}_{\text{ant}}, \text{L})$;
19:   **end for**
20:   $\text{path}_{\text{best}} \leftarrow \sigma(\text{path}_{\text{best}}, \text{path}_{\text{ant}} \mid \min)$;
21:   $\text{phe}_c \leftarrow \delta(\text{QRP}_{\text{ant}}, \text{path}_{\text{ant}} \mid \text{ant} \in \text{num})$;
22: **end while**

---

completes, among the num generated scheduling schemes and the historically optimal scheduling scheme, the scheme with the minimum cost value is selected and saved as the historically optimal scheduling scheme, and the pheromone concentration of all edges is updated according to the elite solution.

3.2   QRP Algorithm and Cost Function

In some previous studies, the Peak Register Pressure (PERP) was adopted as the cost function to evaluate the register pressure of programs, with the aim of finding a scheduling scheme that minimizes PERP within a scheduling region. However, in most scheduling regions, there may exist multiple cycles exhibiting high register pressure, and a cost function based on PERP is inadequate to accurately assess such scenarios. Additionally, due to variations in the latency of memory access instructions across different architectures, the performance degradation caused by register spills also varies. Therefore, direct through register usage quantities cannot accurately evaluate program performance.

The register pressure quantification method proposed in this paper evaluates register pressure by calculating the number of Load/Store instructions required in the scheduling region, thereby predicting the performance loss caused by register pressure. In a given basic block, each virtual register has one definition and multiple uses. The live range of a register refers to the number of cycles from its definition to its last use. When register pressure exists, the common register allocation strategy tends to spill the register with the longest live range. By this approach, the number of additional Load/Store instructions required for the scheduling region can be calculated, thereby estimating the performance loss caused by register spilling. We quantify register pressure using the total execution latency of additional memory access instructions incurred by register spilling, defined as QRP, as shown in Eq. (4). The value is derived by calculating the cumulative summation of execution latencies associated with store and load instructions required during register spilling operations across all register types. Here, n represents the number of register types in the current processor, α_s^i denotes the latency of the store instruction used when spilling the corresponding type of register, and β_l^i denotes the latency of the load instruction for loading data from memory or cache for a register of type load. The number of additional store and load instructions required for each register type in the current scheduling scheme are represented by N_s^i and N_l^i, respectively.

$$Q_{\mathrm{rp}} = \sum_{i=1}^{n} (N_s^i \cdot \alpha_s^i + N_l^i \cdot \alpha_l^i) \qquad (4)$$

Figure 2 illustrates the calculation process of QRP for three different scheduling schemes. Figure 2a depicts a DAG composed of seven instructions, assuming each instruction has an execution latency of 1 and the current processor is equipped with 2 physical registers. The tables of Fig. 2(b), Fig. 2(d), and Fig. 2(f) represent three distinct scheduling schemes, where the third column lists the registers active in the current cycle, and the fourth column indicates in the current cycle, the required Load/Store instructions as well as the registers to be spilled. Figure 2(c), Fig. 2(e) and Fig. 2(g) respectively illustrate the register live range for the three scheduling schemes, where the shaded regions indicate the cycles in which register spilling is required. For example, in Fig. 2(e), the shaded region indicates that register spilling is required at cycle 6 for scheduling scheme 2. At this point, the active registers are Rd, Rf, and Re, with remaining live ranges of 1, 2, and 1 cycles, respectively. In this case, register Rf is spilled, necessitating an additional Store instruction and a Load instruction. Consequently, the QRP value for the scheduling scheme depicted in Fig. 2(e) is calculated as follows:$\alpha_s + \beta_l$.

As illustrated in Fig. 2, it is impossible to differentiate the execution performance of the three scheduling schemes based solely on the number of registers used. All three scheduling schemes encounter situations where the number of registers used exceeds the number of physical registers, leading to register spilling. Minimizing the QRP can effectively reduce the performance loss caused by register spilling. In complex basic blocks, there may also exist multiple distinct types of register spilling. In most processor architectures, different Load/Store instructions are typically employed to handle different types of register spilling, which makes evaluating scheduling schemes based on the number of registers used both complex and inaccurate. By employing QRP, the performance losses

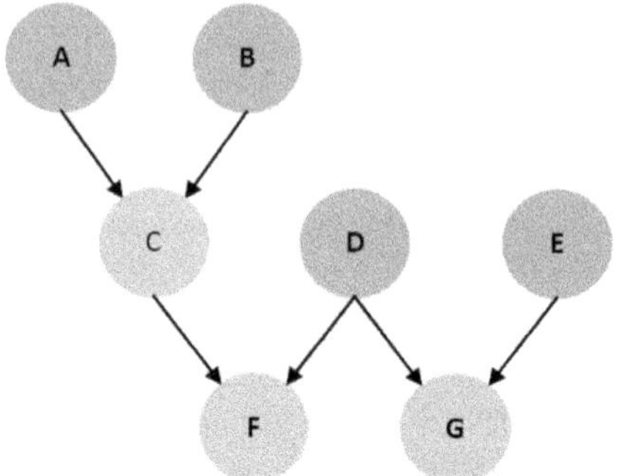

(a) A Simple DAG.

Cycles	Instr	Alive Regs	Reg Spill
1	A	R_A	None
2	B	R_A, R_B	None
3	C	R_C	None
4	D	R_C, R_D	None
5	E	R_C, R_D, R_E	S R_E
6	F	R_D, R_E, R_F	S R_F, L R_E
7	G	R_F, R_G	L R_F

(b) Schedule List 1.

(c) Register Live Range Table 1.

Cycles	Instr	Alive Regs	Reg Spill
1	A	R_A	None
2	B	R_A, R_B	None
3	C	R_C	None
4	D	R_C, R_D	None
5	F	R_D, R_F	None
6	E	R_D, R_E, R_F	S R_F
7	G	R_F, R_G	L R_F

(d) Schedule List 2.

(e) Register Live Range Table 2.

Cycles	Instr	Alive Regs	Reg Spill
1	A	R_A	None
2	B	R_A, R_B	None
3	D	R_A, R_B, R_D	S R_D
4	C	R_C, R_D	None
5	F	R_D, R_F	L R_D
6	E	R_D, R_E, R_F	S R_F
7	G	R_F, R_G	L R_F

(f) Schedule List 3.

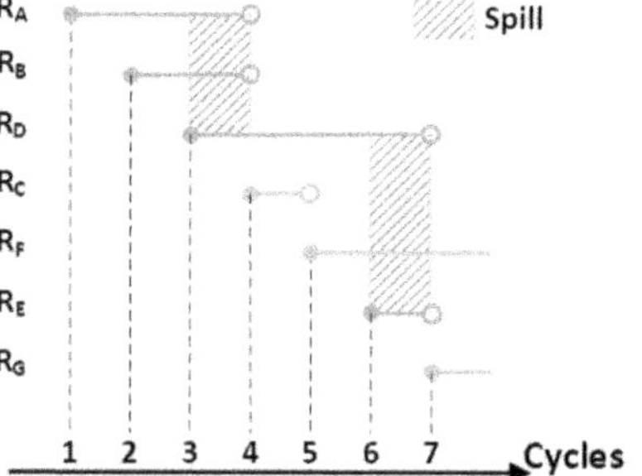

(g) Register Live Range Table 3.

Fig. 2. QRP Calculation.

resulting from any type of register spilling can be accurately captured, enabling a more precise quantification of the performance penalties associated with register overflow.

To accurately evaluate the overall execution performance of a scheduling scheme, this paper constructs a cost evaluation function based on QRP and critical path feature extraction. The value is formulated as a weighted summation of execution latencies under both the QRP and the incumbent scheduling scheme as shown in Eq. (5). In this equation, Latency represents the total delay of the current scheduling scheme, Q_{rp} represents the QRP, and ω_1, ω_2 are the weighting coefficients. Although Q_{rp} is regarded as a performance loss caused by register spilling, it cannot directly be used to calculate the actual program performance. Therefore, weighting coefficients are introduced to balance the scheduling length and the register pressure. Concurrently, the instruction scheduling strategy can be dynamically biased towards either register pressure-optimized solutions or latency-minimized configurations through coordinated modulation of weighting coefficients ω_1, ω_2.

$$\text{Cost(S)} = \omega_1 \cdot \text{Latency} + \omega_2 \cdot Q_{rp} \tag{5}$$

3.3 QRP Algorithm Implementation

During the scheduling process, the def-use information of each virtual register is analyzed to save the cycle value at its first def and the cycle value at each use, such as $Reg_1 : (Start, End)$. Each cycle also checks whether the current active register of each type corresponds to the number of physical registers. If the number exceeds the available physical registers, the cycle information and the register type exceeding the number of physical registers are saved to the spill information. After the scheduling is completed, go through all the overflow information, analyze the register type that needs to spill of each cycle, calculate the remaining survival cycle of the active register as $End - Cycle$, and mark the register with the longest remaining survival cycle as spilling. All subsequent use of this register is considered as necessary to add a Load instruction. Assuming that 2 instructions use the register after a register spills, the corresponding quantified register pressure is $\alpha_s + 2\beta_l$. The quantized register pressure of the base block is the sum of the execution cycles resulting from all register spills. The specific algorithm description is provided in **Algorithm 2.**, which omits the detailed scheduling process and only shows the analysis process of quantified register pressure.

Line 1 represents the initialization of the register life cycle LR, spill information SPI, register type RegType, quantified register pressure QRP, and the maximum number of physical registers $PhyReg_{RT}$ per type. Lines 2-19 are the information collection stage. In the scheduling process of each instruction, the required information is saved, where DefReg represents the register defined by the current instruction and UseReg represents the set of registers used by the current instruction. Lines 4-5 are after complete the scheduling of instruction ins according to the scheduling strategy, Store cycle information in the variable

---

Algorithm 2. The Quantification Register Pressure Algorithm

Require: DAG
Ensure: QRP
 1: $LR \leftarrow \emptyset$ $SPI \leftarrow \emptyset$ $RT \leftarrow n$ $PhyReg_{RT} \leftarrow m$ $QRP \leftarrow \emptyset$;
 2: **while** $rea_q \neq \emptyset$ **do**
 3:    $DefReg \leftarrow \emptyset$ $UseReg \leftarrow \emptyset$;
 4:    $ins \leftarrow \Delta(rea_q \mid \Theta)$;
 5:    $ins \leftarrow currcycle$ $DefReg, UseReg \leftarrow \xi(ins)$;
 6:    **if** $!(DefReg \in LR)$ **then**
 7:       $LR \leftarrow \tau(DefReg, cycle)$;
 8:    **end if**
 9:    **for** $Reg \in UseReg$ **do**
10:       **if** $\delta(Reg)$ **then**
11:          $LR \leftarrow \tau(Reg, cycle)$;
12:       **end if**
13:    **end for**
14:    **for** $Type \in RT$ **do**
15:       **if** $\sigma(LR, Type > PhyReg_{RT})$ **then**
16:          $SPI \leftarrow \xi(Type, cycle)$;
17:       **end if**
18:    **end for**
19: **end while**
20: **for** $Type \in \lambda(RT)$ **do**
21:    $SL_{Type} \leftarrow \alpha_{Type}$ $LL_{Type} \leftarrow \beta_{Type}$ $SpReg \leftarrow \emptyset$ $S_{SpReg} \leftarrow 1$ $L_{SpReg} \leftarrow \emptyset$;
22:    **for** $Type \in \lambda(RT)$ **do**
23:       $SpReg, L_{SpReg} \leftarrow \Phi(LR, Type)$;
24:       $QRP+ \leftarrow S_{SpReg} \cdot SL_{Type} + L_{SpReg} \cdot LL_{Type}$;
25:    **end for**
26: **end for**

---

cycle, and extract the instruction's def-use information, placing it into DefReg and UseReg, respectively. Lines 6-8 update the LR according to DefReg. Lines 9-13 analyze the UseReg information and if there is a register that is being used for the last time, the LR is updated accordingly. Lines 14-18 analyze whether the number of registers of each type used in the current cycle by the LR exceeds the hardware limit $PhyReg_{RT}$, and if so the record corresponds to cycle and register type. Lines 20-26 are the quantified register pressure QRP calculation stage. This phase iterates through the overflow conditions of each register type in each cycle and spills the register SpReg with the longest remaining live range. SL_{type} represents the number of cycles required for Type type register to overflow into memory, LL_{type} represents the number of cycles required for Type type register to load data from memory, and S_{SpReg} and L_{SpReg} represent the number of Store instructions and Load instructions required for overflow register SpReg, respectively.

Table 1. The Compilation Test Results.

	Number of execute passes	Execute pass rate
Before optimization	156	100%
After optimization	156	100%

Table 2. The Execution Test Results.

	Number of compile passes	Compile pass rate
Before optimization	153	98.08%
After optimization	153	98.08%

4   Test and Analysis

4.1   Test Platform and Test Set

In order to verify the correctness and effectiveness of the instruction scheduling optimization algorithm proposed in this paper on the LDSP accelerator, this section conducts testing and analysis from both functional and performance perspectives. The QRP-MMAS scheduling algorithm is implemented based on LLVM 14.0 and tested using the LDSP accelerator as the hardware platform. For functional testing, 156 intermediate description file composition of the .ll suffices written based on LLVM IR are selected. For performance testing, a selection of classic DSP algorithms is used to evaluate the execution performance of the generated code before and after optimization.

4.2   Functional Testing and Analysis

To verify the functional correctness of the instruction scheduling optimization, 156 .ll files from the llvm/test/CodeGen/LDSP directory were selected for testing, and the results are shown in Tables 1 and 2. Both before and after optimization, the compilation success rate remained at 100%, and the execution success rate was 98.08% in both cases. The failure of three test cases was attributed to features unsupported by the hardware platform. The instruction scheduling optimization algorithm proposed in this paper did not introduce additional errors and ensured the correctness of the generated executable code.

4.3   Performance Testing and Analysis

Eight classical DSP algorithms, including FIR, IIR, LMS, and FFT, were selected for performance testing to compare the optimization performance of the QRP-MMAS scheduling algorithm with the traditional list scheduling algorithm. All tests were conducted using the same input data, and the average values from multiple test runs were selected for comparative analysis to avoid result randomness. The test results are shown in Fig. 3 and Fig. 4.

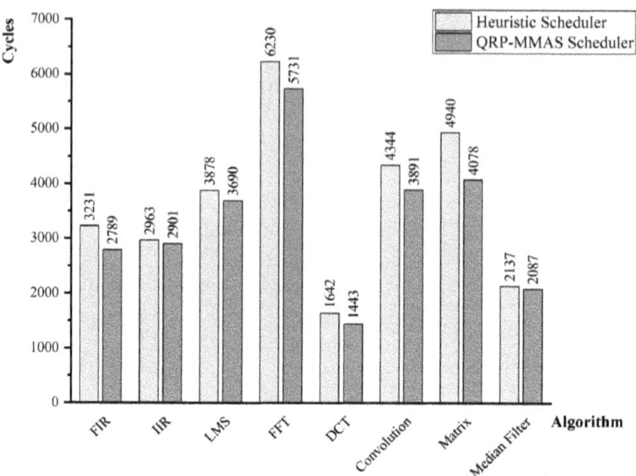

Fig. 3. Execution Cycle of Heuristic-Scheduler and QRP-MMAS Scheduler.

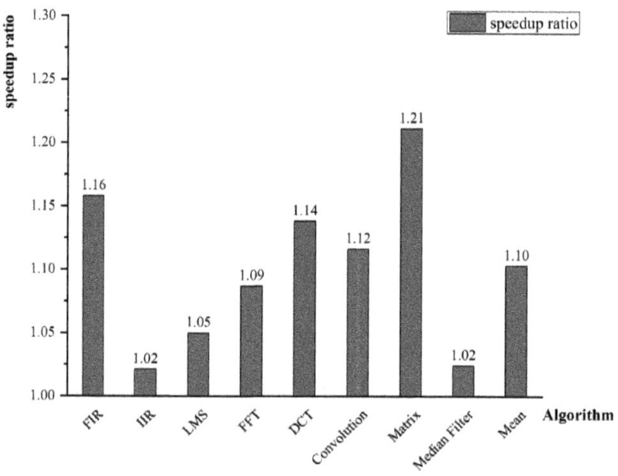

Fig. 4. Speed Ratio of QRP-MMAS.

Figure 3 compares the number of execution cycles of programs compiled using the QRP-MMAS scheduling algorithm and the traditional list scheduling algorithm. The QRP-MMAS scheduling algorithm consistently and significantly reduces program execution time, thereby improving program performance.

Figure 4 illustrates the performance speedup ratio of the QRP-MMAS scheduling algorithm compared to traditional heuristic scheduling. Across the eight test programs, the QRP-MMAS scheduling algorithm achieves an average performance speedup ratio of 1.1, with the highest speedup ratio reaching 1.21.

5   Conclusion

This paper proposes a multi-dimensional cost-driven instruction scheduling optimization method tailored for LDSP accelerators. By integrating an improved MMAS system with a dynamic register pressure quantification model, it effectively addresses the performance bottleneck of traditional scheduling algorithms in scenarios with limited register resources. Experimental results demonstrate that this method not only enhances ILP but also significantly reduces the performance loss caused by register spilling, providing new insights and practical references for compiler optimization of LDSP accelerators in embedded real-time control applications. In the future, we plan to continue focusing on improving ILP as the core objective, refine multi-objective collaborative optimization mechanisms, establish a more precise register pressure quantification model, and deliver higher-performance compilers for users.

References

1. Giesemann, F., Gerlach, L., Paya-Vaya, G.: Evolutionary algorithms for instruction scheduling, operation merging, and register allocation in vliw compilers. J. Sig. Process. Syst. **92**(7), 655–678 (2020)
2. Six, C., Boulmé, S., Monniaux, D.: Certified and efficient instruction scheduling: application to interlocked vliw processors. Proceedings of the ACM on Programming Languages 4(OOPSLA), 1–29 (2020)
3. Six, C., Gourdin, L., Boulmé, S., Monniaux, D., Fasse, J., Nardino, N.: Formally verified superblock scheduling. In: Proceedings of the 11th ACM SIGPLAN International Conference on Certified Programs and Proofs, pp. 40–54 (2022)
4. Carvalho, J.F.N., Sousa, B.L., Araújo, M.R., Bigonha, M.A.S.: The register allocation and instruction scheduling challenge. In: Proceedings of the 21st Brazilian Symposium on Programming Languages, pp. 1–9 (2017)
5. Roberto Castañeda Lozano, Mats Carlsson, Gabriel Hjort Blindell, and Christian Schulte. Combinatorial register allocation and instruction scheduling. *ACM Transactions on Programming Languages and Systems (TOPLAS)*, 41(3):1–53, 2019
6. Stützle, T., Hoos, H.H.: Max-min ant system. Futur. Gener. Comput. Syst. **16**(8), 889–914 (2000)
7. Kessler, C.W.: Compiling for vliw dsps. In: Handbook of Signal Processing Systems, pp. 979–1020. Springer (2018)
8. Wong, H., Betz, V., Rose, J.: High-performance instruction scheduling circuits for superscalar out-of-order soft processors. ACM Trans. Reconfigurable Technol. Syst. (TRETS) **11**(1), 1–22 (2018)
9. Ying, H., Zhu, H., Xue, Z., Wang, D., Hou, C.: A delay slot scheduling framework for vliw architectures in assembly-level. In: 2013 IEEE 11th International Conference on Dependable, Autonomic and Secure Computing, pp. 231–234. IEEE (2013)
10. Aa, T.V., Mei, B.-F., De Sutter, B.: A backtracking instruction scheduler using predicate-based code hoisting to fill delay slots. In: Proceedings of the 2007 International Conference on Compilers, Architecture, and Synthesis for Embedded Systems, pp. 229–237 (2007)

11. Hwu, W.-M.W., et al.: The superblock: An effective technique for vliw and super-scalar compilation. In: Instruction-Level Parallelism: A Special Issue of The Journal of Supercomputing, pp. 229–248. Springer (2011)
12. Jablin, J.A., Jablin, T.B., Mutlu, O., Herlihy, M.: Warp-aware trace scheduling for gpus. In: Proceedings of the 23rd International Conference on Parallel Architectures and Compilation, pp. 163–174 (2014)
13. Rawat, P.S., Sukumaran-Rajam, A., Rountev, A., Rastello, F., Pouchet, L.-N., Sadayappan, P.: Associative instruction reordering to alleviate register pressure. In: SC18: International Conference for High Performance Computing, Networking, Storage and Analysis, pp. 590–602. IEEE (2018)
14. Deng, C., Chen, Z., Shi, Y., Ma, Y., Wen, M., Luo, L.: Optimizing vliw instruction scheduling via a two-dimensional constrained dynamic programming. ACM Trans. Des. Automation Electron. Syst. **29**(5), 1–20 (2024)
15. Xuesong, S., Hui, W., Xue, J.: An efficient wcet-aware instruction scheduling and register allocation approach for clustered vliw processors. ACM Trans. Embedded Comput. Syst. (TECS) **16**(5s), 1–21 (2017)
16. Shobaki, G., Kerbow, A., Pulido, C., Dobson, W.: Exploring an alternative cost function for combinatorial register-pressure-aware instruction scheduling. ACM Trans. Architecture Code Optim. (TACO) **16**(1), 1–30 (2019)

More Bang for Your Buck: Gaining Collateral Benefit from Partial ROV Deployment

Yuxuan Chen[1,2(✉)], Hui Zou[1,2], Yanbiao Li[1,3], Xin Wang[4], and Gaogang Xie[1,2]

[1] Computer Network Information Center, Chinese Academy of Sciences, Beijing, China
`{chenyuxuan,zouhui,lybmath,xie}@cnic.cn`
[2] School of Computer Science and Technology, University of Chinese Academy of Sciences, Beijing, China
[3] Hangzhou Institute for Advanced Study, University of Chinese Academy of Sciences, Hangzhou, China
[4] Department of Electrical and Computer Engineering, Stony Brook University, Stony Brook, NY, USA
`x.wang@stonybrook.edu`

Abstract. The Resource Public Key Infrastructure (RPKI) is a system designed to improve Internet routing security. However, the protection scope of RPKI remains limited due to ineffective deployment of Route Origin Validation (ROV), the process that verifies the legitimacy of BGP announcements using RPKI data. Several deployment strategies have been proposed to increase the security benefits of partial ROV deployment. However, these strategies fail to detect the hidden propagation paths that can be exploited by illegitimate routes, resulting in their protection being vulnerable to hijacking attacks. In this paper, we introduce `ihege`, a novel metric that effectively captures the hidden propagation paths of RPKI-invalid routes. The `ihege` employs the routing model to discover possible propagation paths that are not observed in BGP data and prioritize ASes by their ability to eliminate the possible propagation paths of RPKI-invalid routes. We then propose `ihege`-based deployment strategy and evaluate its security impact under various hijacking scenarios. Experimental results show that, when deploying ROV on the same number of ASes, the `ihege`-based strategy reduces the number of infected ASes by 25.9%–74.7% in comparison with other strategies.

Keywords: Routing Security · BGP · RPKI · ROV

1 Introduction

The Border Gateway Protocol (BGP) [1] is the de-facto inter-domain routing protocol that facilitates the exchange of routing information among different

W. Liang et al. (Eds.): SecureComm 2025, LNICST 690, pp. 243–266, 2026.
https://doi.org/10.1007/978-3-032-23456-8_14

Autonomous Systems (ASes) in the Internet. However, BGP is inherently vulnerable to routing attacks for its default-trust model where routers accept all route information from peers without verifying its correctness. *Prefix hijacks* are the most common and effective routing attacks against BGP. In a prefix hijack, an attacker AS originates routes for prefixes that it does not legitimately own, thereby attracting traffic destined for the victim AS, which engages in malicious activities such as traffic disruption [2], sending spam [3,4], DoS attacks [5], or stealing crypto currencies [6,7]. Prefix hijacks are frequently observed in today's Internet. According to Qrator Labs [8], there are 13,438 hijacking incidents observed in Q3 2024, including one global incident that hijacked 479 IPv4 prefixes with maximum propagation of 89%.

To defend against prefix hijacks, many BGP security mechanisms have been proposed [9–15]. Among them, Resource Public Key Infrastructure (RPKI) [16] has been standardized by IETF and gets increasingly deployed in practice. RPKI is designed to authenticate the ownership and legitimate use of Internet number resources. Through RPKI, the owner of IP prefix p can create *Route Origin Authorizations (ROAs)* [17] to specify which ASes are authorized to originate routes for this prefix. When a router receives BGP announcements of prefix p or any sub-prefix of p, it can apply *Route Origin Validation (ROV)* [18–20] to verify the legitimacy of the origin AS using ROAs and then discard the announcements with invalid origins, thereby preventing prefix hijacks. RPKI has demonstrated its effectiveness in real-world scenarios. For example, the prefix hijack targeting Twitter in 2022 [21] did not propagate far because Twitter created an ROA for hijacked prefix and other network operators implemented ROV to drop RPKI-invalid routes. Currently, RPKI-ROV has been recommended by global initiatives [22,23], regional Internet registries [24,25] and governments [26,27] as a critical mechanism to enhance the security and resilience of the inter-domain routing.

Currently, over 55% of IPv4 address space has been protected by ROAs [28, 29]. However, according to recent ROV measurements [30–35], the majority of ASes ($¿70\%$) still accept RPKI-invalid routes, revealing the ineffective deployment of ROV. To enhance the effectiveness of ROV, various approaches have been proposed. These approaches can be divided into two categories: ROV extensions and deployment strategies. ROV extensions [36–39] usually modify the process of route validation and route selection with techniques such as blackholing (e.g. ROV++ [36]) or notifications (e.g. RPKIN [37]) to more effectively prevent the propagation of invalid routes. However, these extensions require highly customized modifications on ROV and BGP, which is hard to implement on commodity routers.

Deployment strategies [33,40–42] prioritize ASes by their importance in ROV deployment and suggest the most important ones to deploy ROV first. These strategies utilize publicly accessible metrics (e.g. ASRank [43]) or metrics derived from public BGP data (e.g. routing betweenness [42]) to offer recommendations, so they are more likely to be accepted by network operators. However, the effectiveness of these strategies is constrained by their dependence on BGP data visibility. Since most of the observed RPKI-invalid routes are likely to be benign [39] and the hijacking routes are usually short-lived [4], existing strategies remain vulnerable to hijacking attacks that exploit alternative paths to reach corners of Internet [41]. As ROV is increasingly deployed, more RPKI-invalid routes would become invisible from route collectors [30], thereby compromising the effectiveness of existing strategies.

In this paper, we propose `ihege`, a novel metric to quantify the security benefits of deploying ROV on an AS. To discover the *hidden* propagation paths that are not observed by BGP data collection platforms, we employ the routing model to analyze the derived possible paths instead of observed paths [41] or synthesized paths [42]. The `ihege` seeks to capture the *collateral benefit* of ROV deployment, where an ROV AS can protect other non-ROV ASes by filtering out illegitimate routes to prevent the propagation of these routes. Therefore, we compute the `ihege` score through the following steps: (a) generating *all possible* propagation paths of BGP routes with the inter-domain routing model [44]; (b) identifying the propagation paths that can be exploited by the attacker to launch a prefix hijack, namely *insecure paths*; and (c) prioritizing ASes by their *occurrences* in insecure paths, where the AS that occurs most frequently should deploy ROV first. Additionally, we develop an algorithm to achieve fast approximation of `ihege`, saving significant time compared to analyzing the massive propagation paths.

In summary, this paper makes the following contributions:

1. We propose `ihege`, a novel metric to quantify the security benefits of deploying ROV on an AS. Through the analysis of all possible propagation paths, the `ihege` more precisely captures the collateral benefit of deploying ROV on an AS.
2. We design an adaptive deployment strategy based on `ihege`. Our proposed strategy dynamically updates its recommendation as ROV deployment status changes, providing substantial security benefits in different phases of ROV deployment.
3. We implement an algorithm to accelerate the computation of `ihege`. This algorithm allows `ihege`-based strategy to efficiently offer recommendations for the Internet's large-scale topology.
4. We evaluate the effectiveness of our proposed strategy over an empirical Internet topology. Experimental results show that, when deploying ROV on the same number of ASes, the `ihege`-based strategy reduces the number of infected ASes by 25.9%–74.7% in comparison with other strategies.

The paper is organized as follows. The background and motivation are introduced in Sect. 2. We introduce the details of `ihege` in Sect. 3. In Sect. 4, we present the evaluation of `ihege`. The related work is investigated in Sect. 5. Discussion and conclusion are provided in Sect. 6 and Sect. 7.

2   Background and Motivation

2.1   Background

BGP. Routers exchange reachability information across the Internet through Border Gateway Protocol (BGP). A BGP route consists of an IP prefix and a sequence of Autonomous Systems (ASes), indicating data packets should traverse along these ASes to reach the origin AS of this prefix. An example of BGP route is as follows:

Prefix: 223.193.0.0/16
AS_PATH: AS12389 AS174 AS7497

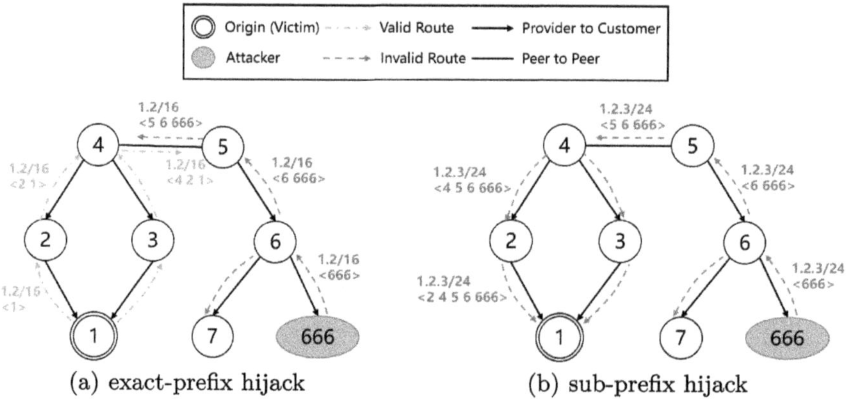

(a) exact-prefix hijack   (b) sub-prefix hijack

Fig. 1. Example of Prefix Hijacks.

In this example, AS7497 is the origin AS of the route and claims to be the owner of prefix 223.193.0.0/16. When neighboring routers receive this route, they install it into their routing information tables (RIBs) and propagate it to their own neighbors. If there exist multiple routes for the same IP prefix, the router would process route selection to determine the best route based on commercial relationships, path lengths, or other factors.

Prefix Hijacks. Prefix hijacks occur when an AS announces routes for a prefix it does not legitimately own. Due to the lack of security features in original BGP standards, illegitimate routes would propagate across the Internet and redirect traffic to the hijacking network, resulting in serious security issues such as service outages and financial losses.

We take Fig. 1 to demonstrate two examples of prefix hijacks. Assume that AS1 is the legitimate owner of prefix 1.2.0.0/16 and AS666 is a malicious attacker that intends to steal traffic destined for AS1. In Fig. 1(a), AS666 illegitimately announces a route of prefix 1.2.0.0/16. The routers learn routes for prefix 1.2.0.0/16 but with two different origins: the legitimate origin AS1 and the illegitimate origin AS666. Since the route with a shorter AS path is preferred in BGP, the ASes close to the hijacker are more likely to select illegitimate routes, causing parts of the Internet polluted. This type of prefix hijacks is called exact-prefix hijack.

The other type of prefix hijacks is sub-prefix hijack, where the hijacker announces a more specific prefix. As shown in Fig. 1(b), AS666 announces a route for prefix 1.2.3.0/24, which is a sub-prefix of 1.2.0.0/16. Since AS1 has not announced any route for prefix 1.2.3.0/24, routers would straightforwardly install and propagate the illegitimate routes, causing the entire Internet polluted. Therefore, sub-prefix hijacks propagate further than exact-prefix hijacks and cause more serious damage.

Route Origin Validation. When receiving a BGP route, the router can process Route Origin Validation (ROV) [19] to examine it through a set of rules and assign a validation state to it. The router employs the authorization tuples *(prefix, maxLength, ASN)* called Validated ROA Payloads (VRPs), which are extracted from Route Origin Authorizations (ROAs) [17].

The router first checks if the received route is covered by any VRP, where the covering means the route prefix is either identical to the VRP prefix or more specific than the VRP prefix. If the route is covered by a VRP, the validation proceeds by checking if (1) the length of the route prefix is equal to or less than VRP maxLength, and (2) the route origin ASN is the same as VRP ASN. If both criteria are satisfied, the route is considered to be matched by the VRP.

A BGP route is assigned to be *valid* if at least one VRP matches the route, *invalid* if at least one VRP covers the route but no VRP matches it, and *unknown* if no VRP covers the route. By rejecting RPKI-invalid routes, ROV routers can prevent the potential damage of hijacking attacks and improve the reliability of inter-domain routing system.

Partial ROV Deployment. The full-scale deployment of ROV is theoretically capable of preventing all prefix hijacking attacks recognized by RPKI. Many efforts have been made [24–27,45] towards full ROV deployment. Despite these efforts, merely 12.3% of ASes have fully implemented ROV in 2023 [33]. Therefore, it can be anticipated that ROV will be deployed partially over a long period.

In the stage of partial deployment, the effectiveness of ROV varies for different ASes. We take Fig. 2 to illustrate the effectiveness of ROV under partial deployment. In this example, the attacker AS666 launches a sub-prefix hijack by announcing prefix 1.2.3.0/24. We omit the victim that announces prefix 1.2.0.0/16 because it does not affect the propagation of sub-prefix routes. As shown in Fig. 2(a), AS2's deploying ROV only prevents itself from accepting illegitimate routes. Even though AS2 would not send any illegitimate route to AS1, AS1 still receives an illegitimate route from the other neighboring AS. In Fig. 2(b), we demonstrate the case when AS4 deploys ROV. By dropping the

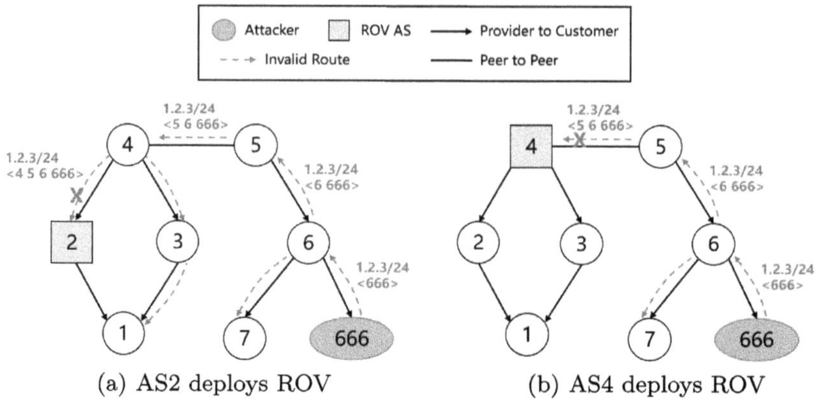

(a) AS2 deploys ROV   (b) AS4 deploys ROV

Fig. 2. Example of Partial ROV Deployment.

illegitimate route and prevent its propagation to customers, AS4 can protect not only itself but also its direct customers (AS2 and AS3) and even the indirect customer (AS1) against the sub-prefix hijack. In this case, deploying ROV on an AS can shield other ASes that do not perform ROV from illegitimate routes. Such protective influence is referred to as *collateral benefit* [40]. Through the exploitation of collateral benefit, a deployment strategy would help the Internet to gain significant security benefits from partial ROV deployment.

2.2   Motivation

To improve the effectiveness of ROV, many deployment strategies leverage the paths observed by BGP data collection platforms [46,47] to offer recommendations. Du et al. [41] took the mean AS hegemony score considering paths of RPKI-valid routes and then the score considering paths of RPKI-invalid routes, where the ASes that have larger AS hegemony score for RPKI-invalid routes are suggested to serve as a starting point for future ROV deployment. Since the RPKI-invalid routes account for less than 1% of collected routes [39], their approach can only be applied to a small set of ASes (with size of 163). The recently proposed ROVReco [42] chooses to construct hijacking scenarios by synthesizing paths of RPKI-invalid routes from those of RPKI-valid routes. However, as ROV is increasingly deployed, the propagation of these two types of routes has been much different [30]. Since only a small fraction of ASes announce RPKI-invalid routes and the propagation of these routes has been much different, it is difficult to derive the propagation paths of RPKI-invalid routes from collected BGP data.

In this paper, we try to capture the *hidden* propagation paths that have not been observed by BGP data collection platforms, to locate the important ASes in preventing the propagation of illegitimate routes. To this end, we employ the inter-domain routing model to generate *all possible* propagation paths of BGP routes and then analyze the set of paths that can be exploited by illegitimate routes, which we call the *insecure paths*. Furthermore, we propose `ihege`, a new metric to prioritize ASes according to their ability to eliminate insecure paths. Compared to other metrics, the `ihege` pays more attention to hidden propagation paths instead of observed propagation paths. Through analyzing a wider range of propagation paths, the `ihege`-based deployment strategy achieves better protection against hijacking attacks.

3   Our Method

3.1   Inter-domain Routing Model

We employ the routing model [44,48] which has been widely used in many BGP research works [35,40,49,50] to discover the hidden propagation paths.

AS-Level Graph. We model the Internet as an *AS-level graph* $G = (V, E)$ where each node $v \in V$ represents an AS and each edge $e \in E$ represents a BGP connection between two ASes. Since each AS is managed by a single administrative entity, the relationships between these entities are crucial for ASes to make routing decisions. We consider two types of common relationships: (1) *provider-to-customer* (or *customer-to-provider*) where the customer AS pays the provider AS for the use of transit service, and (2) *peer-to-peer* where two ASes agree to exchange traffic directly without the payment of transit fees. Similar to prior works [36,51], the other types of relationship (e.g., sibling) are not considered. For ASv, we denote the set of its providers as $Prov(v)$, the set of its peers as $Peer(v)$, and the set of its customers as $Cust(v)$.

Valley-Free Routing. The *valley-free routing* is a set of assumptions for the exchange of routing information: when exchanging routes with a customer, an AS can export its routes, the routes learned from other customers, as well as the routes learned from providers and peers; when exchanging routes with a provider or a peer, an AS can export its routes and the routes of its customer, but can not export the routes learned from other providers or peers. Following the assumptions, an AS never relays routes received from a non-customer neighbor to another non-customer neighbor, and no valley would be formed in the routing path. Although the valley-free routing assumptions sometimes deviate from real-world BGP behaviors [52–55], we adapt it for this work because of the lack of better models.

3.2   Insecure-Path Hegemony

Definition. We introduce a new metric, *insecure-path hegemony* (`ihege` for short), to quantify the collateral benefit of deploying ROV on an AS. Among the *all possible* propagation paths derived from the routing model, we focus on the set of propagation paths that contain only non-ROV ASes, denoted by *insecure paths*. Due to the lack of RPKI-invalid filtering, the insecure paths are likely to be exploited to facilitate the propagation of RPKI-invalid routes in a prefix hijack.

Through deploying ROV on an AS, the insecure paths that traverse this AS would be eliminated, thereby mitigating the spread of hijacking attacks and protecting other ASes. Therefore, we propose to quantify the collateral benefit of deploying ROV with the number of eliminated insecure paths. More specifically, given the set of all possible propagation paths S and the set of ASes that have deployed ROV R, we define the `ihege` score of ASv as:

$$\mathbf{ihege}(v) = \frac{1}{|S|} \sum_{p \in S} I\big[\sigma(p) \cap R = \emptyset \wedge v \in \sigma(p)\big] \tag{1}$$

where $I[\cdot]$ is an indicator function that outputs 1 if the proposition is satisfied and 0 otherwise, and $\sigma(p)$ is the set of ASes that are located on path p. The `ihege` of ASv indicates the proportion of eliminated insecure paths by deploying ROV on ASv to the entire set of all possible propagation paths within the network.

Computation. The computation of `ihege` is straightforward according to its definition once we get the two input sets S and R. Since the set R can be obtained from public ROV measurement platforms [56–58], we focus on the construction of set S. For the computation of S, we reserve the propagation paths that follow the valley-free principle but take a detour to reach its destination, because these paths can also be exploited as an alternative to launch hijacking attacks.

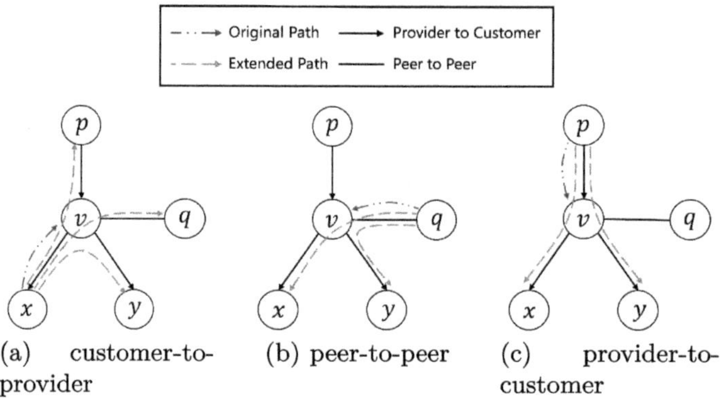

Fig. 3. Categories of Valley-Free Propagation Paths.

We develop an algorithm to construct all possible valley-free propagation paths within the AS-level graph, as described in Algorithm 1. Our algorithm is based on the observation that we can obtain a valley-free propagation path by removing the last AS from another path with length of more than one. Conversely, by appending an appropriate AS, we can extend a valley-free propagation

---

Algorithm 1: Path Expansion Algorithm

Data: Graph $G = (V, E)$ with AS relationships
Result: Set of all possible propagation paths S

1 Initialize $S_2 \leftarrow \emptyset$;
2 **for** $v \in V$ **do**
3   **for** $w \in Prov(v) \cup Peer(v) \cup Cust(v)$ **do**
4        $S_2 \leftarrow S_2 \cup \{[v, w]\}$;
5   **end**
6 **end**
7 $S \leftarrow S_2$;
8 $d \leftarrow 2$;
9 **while** $S_d \neq \emptyset$ **do**
10   Initialize $S_{d+1} \leftarrow \emptyset$;
11   **foreach** $p \in S_d$ **do**
12       $v \leftarrow$ the last AS of p;
13       $u \leftarrow$ the second to last AS of p;
14   **if** $u \in Cust(v)$ **then**
15   **for** $w \in \big(Prov(v) \cup Peer(v) \cup Cust(v)\big)/\sigma(p)$ **do**
16           $S_{d+1} \leftarrow S_{d+1} \cup \{p +\!\!+ [w]\}$;
17   **end**
18   **else**
19   **for** $w \in Cust(v)/\sigma(p)$ **do**
20           $S_{d+1} \leftarrow S_{d+1} \cup \{p +\!\!+ [w]\}$;
21   **end**
22   **end**
23   **end**
24    $S \leftarrow S \cup S_{d+1}$;
25    $d \leftarrow d + 1$;
26 **end**

---

path. To identify the appropriate ASes to append, we categorize the valley-free propagation paths by the relationship of the last two ASes: (1) customer-to-provider, (2) peer-to-peer, and (3) provider-to-customer. As shown in Fig. 3(a), when the original path ends with ASx (customer of ASv) and ASv, we can extend the path by appending a neighbor of ASv without violation of valley-free principle. If the second to last AS is a peer of a provider of the last AS, only customers of the last AS can be appended to the original path, as illustrated in Fig. 3(b) and Fig. 3(c). By iteratively appending new ASes to discovered propagation paths, we would finally obtain the set of all possible propagation paths, namely S.

Deployment Strategy. Our `ihege`-based strategy prioritizes ASes with the `ihege` score and recommends the AS with the highest `ihege` score to deploy ROV first. However, the collateral benefit would be affected by the ROV deployment status of other ASes. For example, an ROV AS can prevent the propaga-

---

Algorithm 2: Insecure-Path Counting Algorithm

Data: Graph $G = (V, E)$ with AS relationships and the set R of ROV ASes
Result: Array h where $h[v]$ indicates the approximate number of insecure
paths that contains ASv

1 **for** v *in* V/R *by ascending order of customer cone sizes* **do**
2 $\quad$ $g_c[v] \leftarrow 0$;
3 $\quad$ **for** $u \in Cust(v)/R$ **do**
4 $\quad\quad$ $\mid$ $g_c[v] \leftarrow g_c[v] + g_c[u] + 1$;
5 $\quad$ **end**
6 **end**
7 **for** $v \in V/R$ **do**
8 $\quad$ $g_r[v] \leftarrow 0$;
9 $\quad$ **for** $u \in Peer(v)/R$ **do**
10 $\quad\quad$ $\mid$ $g_r[v] \leftarrow g_r[v] + g_c[u] + 1$;
11 $\quad$ **end**
12 **end**
13 **for** v *in* V/R *by descending order of customer cone sizes* **do**
14 $\quad$ $g_p[v] \leftarrow 0$;
15 $\quad$ **for** $u \in Prov(v)/R$ **do**
16 $\quad\quad$ $\mid$ $g_p[v] \leftarrow g_p[v] + g_p[u] + g_r[u] + g_c[u] + 1$;
17 $\quad$ **end**
18 **end**
19 **for** $v \in V/R$ **do**
20 $\quad$ $\mid$ $h[v] \leftarrow (g_c[v] + 2)(g_c[v] + g_r[v] + g_p[v]) + g_c[v] \cdot (g_r[v] + g_p[v])$;
21 **end**

---

tion of RPKI-invalid routes to its neighbors, thereby providing collateral benefit. But when all the neighbors start to deploy ROV, the AS would not receive any RPKI-invalid route, then the collateral benefit becomes negligible. To adapt to the dynamic changes of ROV deployment status, our proposed strategy would update the `ihege` score when a new AS deploys ROV, which captures the collateral benefit in different phases of ROV deployment.

3.3 Approximation Algorithm

Due to the extremely fast expansion of possible propagation paths, the running time of Algorithm 1 grows exponentially as the topology scales up (which we evaluate in Sect. 4.5). Therefore, we develop an approximation algorithm to accelerate the computation of `ihege`, as described in Algorithm 2. The key to computing `ihege` lies on counting the insecure paths that contain the given AS. Our algorithm consists of two phases: (1) counting all insecure paths where the paths are categorized by their last AS and the relationship between the last two ASes, and (2) counting the insecure paths that pass through an AS by concatenating insecure paths under the constraints of valley-free principle.

Counting All Insecure Paths. We define $g_c(v)$, $g_r(v)$, $g_p(v)$ as the approximate number of insecure paths where ASv is the last AS and the relationship of the last two ASes is customer-to-provider, peer-to-peer, or provider-to-customer, respectively.

Recall that R is the set of ASes that have deployed ROV. If $v \in R$, the propagation paths that end with ASv contain at least one ROV AS, thereby $g_c(v) = g_r(v) = g_p(v) = 0$. Otherwise, we construct insecure paths that end with ASv by appending ASv to other insecure paths. Assume ASu is a non-ROV customer of ASv, namely $u \in Cust(v)/R$. Since ASu only exports routes learned from its customers to ASv, we can only append ASv to the insecure paths whose last relationship is customer-to-provider. Therefore, we can construct $g_c(u)$ insecure that ends with ASv by appending ASv to the insecure paths that end with ASu. Besides, we can obtain an extra insecure path with length of 2 by appending ASv to ASu. So there are $g_c(u) + 1$ insecure paths that pass through the customer ASu and end with ASv, which derives the approximation formula of $g_c(v)$:

$$g_c(v) = \sum_{u \in Cust(v)/R} (g_c(u) + 1) \tag{2}$$

Similarly, the peer of ASv only exports routes learned from its customer to ASv, so we have:

$$g_r(v) = \sum_{u \in Peer(v)/R} (g_c(u) + 1) \tag{3}$$

As for the provider of ASv, all routes learned from its neighbors are exported to ASv, so we can append ASv to any propagation paths that end with the provider. Hence,

$$g_p(v) = \sum_{u \in Prov(v)/R} \big(g_c(u) + g_r(u) + g_p(u) + 1\big) \tag{4}$$

By summing up the number of insecure paths that end with each AS, we approximate the total number of *all* insecure paths, denoted as w:

$$w = \sum_{v \in V} \big(g_c(v) + g_r(v) + g_p(v)\big) \tag{5}$$

Counting Passing-Through Paths. We define $h(v)$ as the approximate number of paths passing through ASv and categorize these paths by the position of ASv: (1) ASv is at the start of the path, (2) ASv is at the end of the path, (3) ASv is in the middle of the path. For the first two categories, we observe that the reversal of an insecure path is also an insecure path, so we approximate the number of insecure paths that start with ASv or end with ASv as:

$$h_1(v) = h_2(v) = g_c(v) + g_r(v) + g_p(v) \tag{6}$$

For the case that ASv is in the middle of the path, we choose to construct insecure paths by concatenating two paths that start with ASv or end with ASv. As shown in Fig. 3, under the constraints of the valley-free principle, a path that ends with customer-to-provider relationship can be concatenated with the path that starts with any relationship, while a path that ends with peer-to-peer or provider-to-customer relationship can only be concatenated with the path that starts with provider-to-customer relationship. Therefore, we can approximate the insecure path that contains ASv in the middle as :

$$h_3(v) = g_c(v) \cdot \big(g_c(v) + 2g_r(v) + 2g_p(v)\big) \tag{7}$$

By summing up the number of insecure paths of each category, we approximate the number of insecure paths passing through ASv as:

$$h(v) = \big(g_c(v) + 2\big)\big(g_c(v) + g_r(v) + g_p(v)\big) + g_c(v) \cdot \big(g_r(v) + g_p(v)\big) \tag{8}$$

Time Complexity. As dictated by Eqs. (2), (3), and (4), the computation of $g_c(v)$, $g_r(v)$, and $g_p(v)$ only involves the neighboring nodes of ASv. Therefore, the process of approximating the number of all insecure paths operates within a time complexity of $O(|V| + |E|)$, where $|V|$ and $|E|$ denote the number of nodes and edges in the AS-level topology, respectively. Furthermore, for each AS (i.e. ASv), the approximate number of categorized paths passing through ASv is calculated in constant time using Eqs. (6), (7) and (8). As a result, our proposed algorithm exhibits efficient time complexity, scaling linearly with the size of the topology, specifically at $O(|V| + |E|)$.

4   Evaluation

In this section, we conduct Internet-scale simulations to evaluate the effectiveness of `ihege`-based strategy and verify its superiority in comparison with other strategies. Besides, we evaluate the performance of the approximation algorithm for `ihege` in terms of running time and accuracy.

4.1   Simulation Setup

To simulate the propagation of routes, we employ the routing tree algorithm [59] used in recent works [35,60]. Our simulation uses CAIDA's Internet-scale AS topology (January 2025) with relationships of provider-to-customer or peer-to-peer [61]. The topology contains more than 77,000 ASes and 483,000 relationships. Following prior works [36,51], we distinguish three types of ASes according to the relationships: (1) tier-1 ASes, the top-tier ASes that have no providers, (2) transit ASes, the ASes that have multiple neighbors including at least one customer, (3) edge ASes, the ASes that only have BGP connections to their providers.

Hijacking Scenarios. We extracted 2,818 exact-prefix hijacks and 1,039 sub-prefix hijacks from the BGP anomalies reported by BGPMon [62], which we call the scenarios of *reported hijacks*. We adapt the scenario settings of recent works [35, 51] to generate hijacking scenarios for the *exact-prefix hijacks* and the *sub-prefix hijacks*.

For the exact-prefix hijack, the victim's legitimate route competes against the attacker's illegitimate route, and the one which has the higher local preference and the shorter AS path takes precedence. We design two types of exact-prefix hijacking scenarios: (1) single attacker, and (2) multiple attackers. For each type of scenarios, we generate 100,000 exact-prefix hijacking incidents where the attacker and the victim are both randomly selected from edge ASes (for multiple attackers, 10 ASes are selected from edge ASes).

For the sub-prefix hijack, the victim's legitimate route does not mitigate the spread of attacker's illegitimate route since they have different route prefixes. We generate 100,000 sub-prefix hijacking incidents where the attacker and the victim are both randomly selected from edge ASes.

Deployment Strategies. We evaluate the effectiveness of four ROV deployment strategies: ASRank-based strategy [33, 40], transit-based strategy [30], the ROVReco [42] and the `ihege`-based strategy we proposed.

The ASRank-based strategy sorts ASes by the *customer cone size*, the number of direct and indirect customers, and recommends the AS with the largest customer cone size to deploy ROV. The transit-based strategy sorts ASes by the *transit degree*, the number of neighbors that use its services for transit, and recommends the AS with the largest transit degree to deploy ROV. The ROVReco calculates the *routing betweenness* for ASes that propagate invalid routes and recommends the AS with the highest routing betweenness to deploy ROV. Our proposed `ihege`-based strategy computes the number of *insecure paths*, the possible propagation paths that can be exploited by hijacking attacks, and suggests the AS that occurs most frequently on insecure paths to deploy ROV.

The ASRank and transit degree are provided by CAIDA [43], while the recommendation list of ROVReco is presented by Li et al. [42]. For `ihege`-based strategy, we obtain the recommendation through Algorithm 2 and update the recommendation as new AS deploys ROV.

RPKI Deployment Status. We assume that all illegitimate routes are recognized by RPKI and all RPKI-invalid routes are rejected by ROV ASes. We explore two types of ROV deployment scenarios: *from-scratch deployment* and *incremental deployment*. For from-scratch deployment, we assume that no AS deploys ROV at the beginning. For incremental deployment, we take the measurement results of Hlavack et al. [34] and assume the ASes with strong evidence on ROV enforcement have fully deployed ROV. For the evaluation of deployment strategy, we iteratively deploy ROV on the most recommended AS of the strategy until the number of additional ROV ASes reaches 100. As for incremental deployment, ROVReco can only recommend 70 additional ROV ASes because its recommendation list overlaps with the list of ROV ASes.

Routing Policy. We employ the routing policies developed by Gao et al. [44] and used in recent BGP research works [35,63]. When receiving multiple routes for the same prefix, the AS process *route selection* on the routes destined to this prefix to determine the best route, which would be installed into Route Information Base (RIB) and sent to neighbors for further propagation. The AS that deploys ROV would perform validation on all received routes and exclude the invalid ones from route selection. When selecting among multiple routes to a destination prefix, the AS follows three principles to make decisions:

1. **Local Preference:** Prefer routes received from a customer over routes received from a peer over routes received from a provider.
2. **Shortest Path:** Among the routes with highest local preference, prefer routes with shortest AS paths.
3. **Tie Break:** Use a tiebreaker to select a route from remaining routes which have the same local preference and AS path length. We use a random tiebreaker for this work.

The *export policy* determines which routes (if any) are sent to neighbors. Since the customer pays for transit traffic, an AS should be willing to export routes learned from its customer to all its neighbors. However, if a route is learned from a provider or peer, it is restricted to be exported only to the customers.

Effectiveness Metric. We focus on the *infection rate*, i.e., the percent of ASes that install illegitimate routes originated by the attacker (or attackers in the multi-attacker case) into their RIBs. For the comparison of different strategies, we compute the *average infection rate* for each type of hijacking scenarios.

4.2   Exact Prefix Hijacks

Single Attacker. Figure 4 presents the average infection rates under the exact-prefix hijacks from a single attacker. Due to the lack of guidance, the current deployment of ROV only reduces the average infection rate to 19.0% with 589 ROV ASes (see the leftmost point in Fig. 4(b)). In contrast, by adopting the `ihege`-based strategy, deploying ROV on 30 ASes is enough to achieve a lower average infection rate (18.7%).

As shown in Fig. 4(a), with our proposed strategy, starting from scratch to deploy ROV on 60 ASes can reduce the average infection rate to lower than 10% in the exact-prefix hijacking attacks, while the other strategies would require at least 80 ROV ASes to achieve the same level of protection. In the cases of incremental deployment, as illustrated in Fig. 4(b), our proposed strategy reduces the average infection rate to 5% by additionally deploying ROV on 40 ASes, while the other strategies need at least 1.5x the number of ASes to achieve the same level of protection. We can see that adopting the deployment strategy with `ihege` is more effective in preventing exact-prefix hijacks compared to other metrics in different phases of ROV deployment.

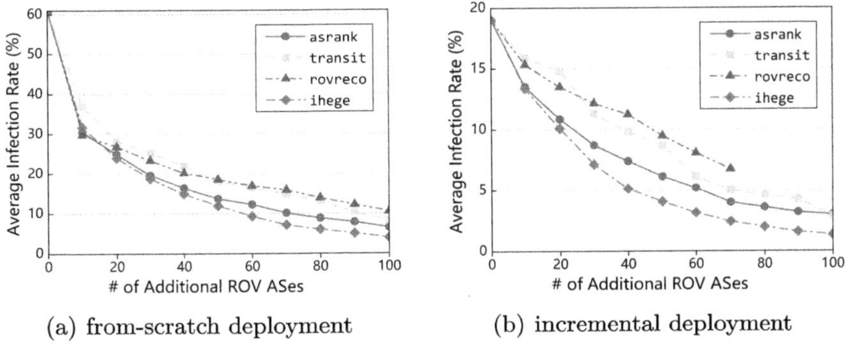

(a) from-scratch deployment   (b) incremental deployment

Fig. 4. Defenses against Exact-Prefix Hijacks from Single Attacker.

Multiple Attackers. Figure 5 plots the results of defenses against exact-prefix hijacking from 10 attackers. Compared to the results with a single attacker in Fig. 4, it is clear that multiple attackers lead to a significantly higher infection rate. If no AS deploys ROV (see the leftmost point in Fig. 4(a) and that in Fig. 5(a)), the multiple-attacker hijacks would infect more than 95% ASes while the single-attacker hijacks infect about 60% ASes on average.

When there are only several additional ROV ASes, the `ihege`-based strategy performs similarly to the ASRank-based strategy. As the number of ROV ASes grows, the average infection rate of `ihege`-based strategy becomes much lower than other strategies. When the number of additional ROV ASes reaches 100 (see the rightmost point in Fig. 5(a) and that in Fig. 5(b)), the `ihege`-based strategy reduces the number of infected AS by 25.9% in comparison with other strategies in the from-scratch deployment, and demonstrates a reduction of 45.6% on the number of infected ASes compared to other strategies in the incremental deployment.

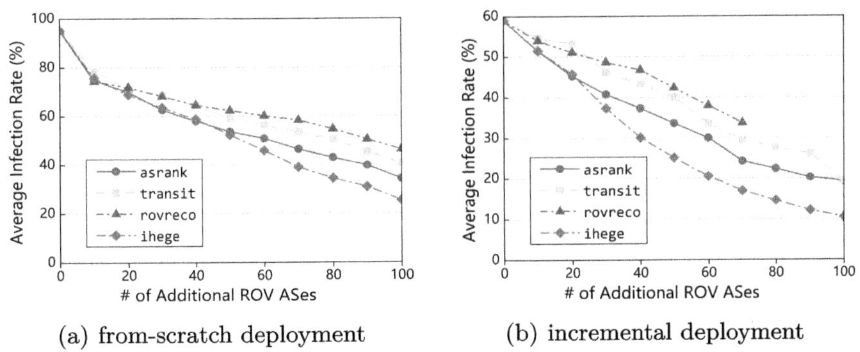

(a) from-scratch deployment   (b) incremental deployment

Fig. 5. Defenses against Exact-Prefix Hijacks from Multiple Attackers.

4.3 Sub-prefix Hijacks

Figure 6 demonstrates the results of average infection rates under sub-prefix hijacks. As shown in Fig. 6(a), due to the lack of competing routes, nearly all ASes are infected by the illegitimate sub-prefix routes when no AS deploys ROV. In the current deployment of ROV, as shown in Fig. 6(b), the sub-prefix hijacks have been less effective, but still infect about 50% of the ASes.

In the from-scratch deployment, as shown in Fig. 6(a), our strategy reduces the average infection rate to less than 20% by deploying ROV on 70 ASes, while the other strategies need at least 90 ASes for additional deployment to provide the same level of protection. In the incremental deployment, as shown in Fig. 6(b), the **ihege**-based strategy achieves an infection rate of 11.0% with 50 additional ROV ASes, while the other strategies need to additionally deploy on 1.4x the number of ASes to get a lower infection rate. Hence, our **ihege**-based strategy requires the fewest ASes to achieve the desired protection against sub-prefix hijacks across various phases of ROV deployment.

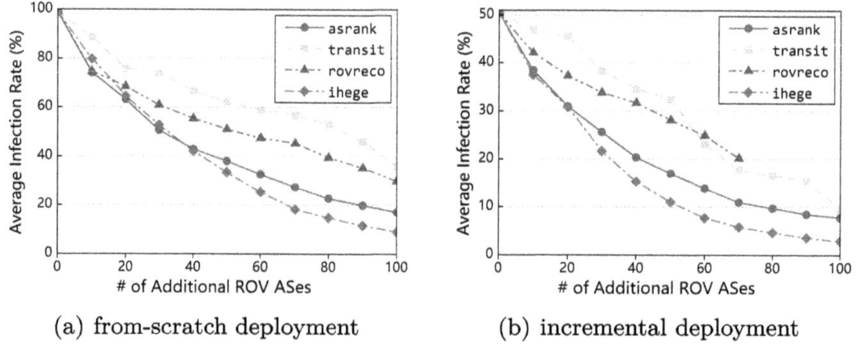

(a) from-scratch deployment   (b) incremental deployment

Fig. 6. Defenses against Sub-Prefix Hijacks.

4.4 Reported Hijacks

Figure 7 shows the effectiveness of ROV deployment strategies against the reported hijacking incidents, including 2,818 exact-prefix hijacks and 1,039 sub-prefix hijacks.

As shown in Fig. 7(a), the **ihege**-based strategy reduces the average infection rate from 75.6% to 7.3% by deploying ROV on 100 ASes. As demonstrated in Fig. 7(b), under the incremental deployment with a constraint of 100 additional ROV ASes, the **ihege**-based strategy achieves a reduction of 3.9% on average infection rate compared to ASRank-based strategy, which extends route protection to approximately 3,000 additional ASes. Therefore, the **ihege**-based strategy exhibits significant security benefits against report hijacks.

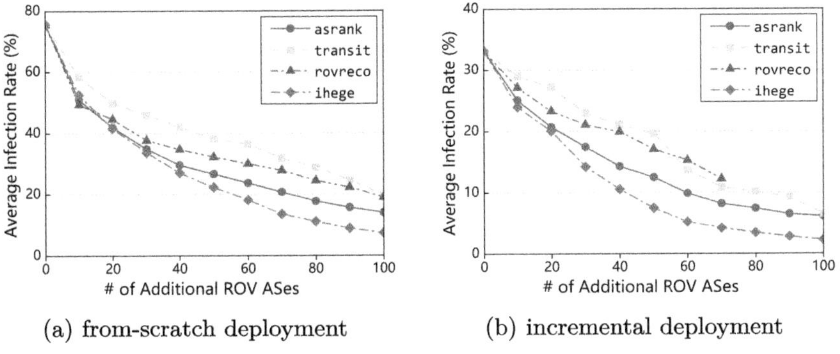

(a) from-scratch deployment   (b) incremental deployment

Fig. 7. Defenses against Reported Hijacks.

4.5   Algorithm Performance

To evaluate the performance of our approximate algorithm, we construct 10 AS topologies ranging from 1,000 to 10,000 nodes. The topologies are derived from the CAIDA's Internet-scale topology [61] by iteratively removing the leaf nodes until reaching the target node count. For each topology, we compute the number of all possible propagation paths with Algorithm 1 and Algorithm 2. Both algorithms are implemented in Python3 and executed on AMD EPYC 7742 @ 2.25GHz. For Algorithm 2, the number of all possible propagation paths is approximated with Eq. (5) by setting $R = \emptyset$.

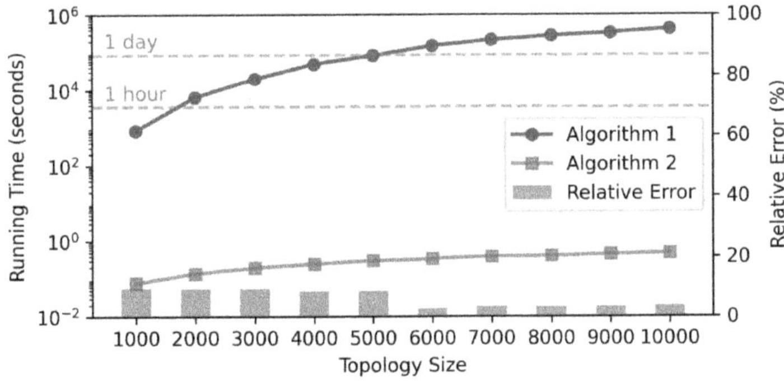

Fig. 8. The Running Time and Relative Error of Approximation Algorithm.

Figure 8 demonstrates the running time of each algorithm and the relative error of the approximation algorithm. As the size of the topology scales up, the running time of Algorithm 1 grows exponentially, requiring nearly 5 days to process the topology with 10,000 nodes. In contrast, the approximation algorithm (Algorithm 2) can achieve fast computation of `ihege` (less than 1 s) with an acceptable loss of accuracy (a relative error lower than 10%).

5   Related Work

We review the literature and summarize related works in following three categories.

5.1   Measurement of RPKI Deployment Status

Several studies measured the deployment status of RPKI, mainly focusing on ROA and ROV. The measurements on ROAs concentrate on the coverage and quantity of ROAs [64–66] and related solutions [67], as well as the RPKI protection state of DNS resolvers [68] and web servers [69]. The measurements of ROV aim to identify which ASes have deployed ROV to filter invalid BGP announcements. Gilad et al. [40] measured the ROV adoption rate using passive control-plane measurements. Reuter et al. [70] proposed the use of controlled and verifiable methodology for measuring ROV. Rodday et al. [32] tried to identify the ROV-enforcing ASes based on vantage points using controlled experiments. Testart et al. [30] extended prior works and introduced a passive method to detect ROV filters on full-feeder ASes which shared most of their preferred routes with BGP collectors. Li et al. [33] presented an ROV measurement framework that leveraged the IP-ID side channel and in-the-wild RPKI-invalid prefixes for scalable ROV measurement.

5.2   Evaluation of Security Benefits Provided by RPKI

The security benefits of RPKI and its applications (e.g., ROV, BGPsec) have been extensively studied. Chan et al. [71] proposed a model to evaluate the adoptability of secure BGP protocols, such as S-BGP, the predecessor of RPKI. Goldberg et al. [50] evaluated the ability of S-BGP to defend against prefix hijacks. Lychev et al. [72] found that the path security mechanism (e.g. BGPsec) can provide only meager benefits over origin authentication (e.g. ROV). Gilad et al. [40] demonstrated that the security benefits provided by RPKI were limited unless top ISPs deployed ROV. Testart et al. [30] demonstrated that the deployment of ROV indeed brought direct benefits to networks, limiting the propagation of illicit announcements. Rodday et al. [63] compared random and selective deployment strategies for two path plausibility algorithms, finding that both algorithms perform better in a top-down deployment strategy.

5.3   Recommendations for RPKI-ROV Deployment

Motivated by the revenue generation goals of ISPs, Gill et al. [49] proposed the global deployment strategy for S*BGP (e.g., S-BGP), and evaluated the effectiveness of this strategy through theoretical analysis and large-scale simulations. Gilad et al. [40] showed that enforcing ROV only at top ISPs can gain substantial benefits from RPKI, and advocated boosting ROV adoption amongst the top ISPs. Hlavacek et al. [34] found that large ASes, ISPs, and IXPs have more incentives to deploy ROV compared to stub ASes. They concluded that deploying ROV on large ASes and Tier-1 providers can bring global security benefits, while IXPs provide only localized protection against hijacks. Testart et al. [30] held the view that the benefit of RPKI depends on whether transit providers validate and filter invalid BGP announcements. Li et al. [33] emphasized the importance of higher-ranked ASes adopting ROV to have a larger collateral benefit. Du et al. [41] suggested using AS hegemony as a metric to guide ROV deployment efforts. Goldberg [50] recommended to use secure routing protocols (e.g., soBGP and S-BGP) along with mechanisms like defensive filtering to manage export policies and improve network security. Qin et al. [35] proposed deploying ROV at the provider interface instead of the customer interface via simulation experiments, which is contrary to the recommendation of MANRS. Li et al. [42] proposed ROVReco to offer detailed ROV deployment recommendations based on routing betweenness, and they employed graph neural networks to address scalability issues in routing analysis.

6   Discussion

Obstacles to ROV Adoption. Although the importance of deploying ROV has been demonstrated in practice, the operators still hesitate to adopt ROV for economical and technical reasons. On the one hand, adopting ROV would incur costs for equipment upgrades, as well as extensive human efforts for operation and maintenance [35]. On the other hand, adopting ROV may result in losing connection with the legitimate networks due to erroneous ROAs or inter-organization dependencies [40]. Therefore, we advocate prioritizing ROV deployment on large ISPs for their superiority in capital and technology. Also, we suggest that ISPs should use ROAs to carefully check the validity state of their address space and that of their customers' address space before deploying ROV.

Limitations. The `ihege` employs a routing model with many levels of abstraction. Such abstraction deviates from real-world routing system in the following aspects: (1) the valley-free assumption does not always hold, as a significant fraction of valley paths have been observed in both BGP updates and BGP tables [52], (2) the AS-level model is insufficient to capture the advanced routing behaviors, such as hot-potato routing [73] and partial transit [74], and (3) the other security mechanisms in place are not considered, e.g., MANRS Action 1 [75]. Nevertheless, the `ihege` should be treated as an indication of security benefits rather than an accurate prediction.

Future Work. As for future work, we are exploring the following three directions: (1) evaluating the performance of our proposed deployment strategy under more realistic simulation settings, e.g., by taking account of real-world routing decisions, instead of only using valley-free routing, (2) proposing a new deployment strategy that takes into account not only the security benefits, but also the cost of deploying ROV, such as hardware requirements, software licensing, staff training, and so on, and (3) exploring the compatibility with other ROV deployment recommendations, such as deploying ROV at provider interfaces [35].

7   Conclusions

In this paper, we propose `ihege`, a new metric to quantify the security benefits of deploying ROV on an AS. The `ihege` employs the routing model to discover hidden propagation paths that can be exploited by attackers to launch prefix hijacks. We then propose the `ihege`-based deployment strategy which dynamically updates its recommendation as ROV deployment status changes. Compared to other strategies, `ihege`-based strategy can protect more ASes with fewer deployment efforts under various hijacking scenarios. Hence, we suggest deploying ROV on the set of ASes with the highest `ihege` for improved future ROV deployment.

Acknowledgements. We sincerely thank the anonymous reviewers for their insightful and constructive suggestions. This work was supported by the National Key R&D Program of China under Grant No.2022YFB3104800 and the National Natural Science Foundation of China under Grant No.62302476. The corresponding authors of this paper are Yanbiao Li and Gaogang Xie.

References

1. Rekhter, Y., Hares, S., Li, T.: A Border Gateway Protocol 4 (BGP-4). RFC 4271 (2006)
2. RIPE NCC. YouTube Hijacking: A RIPE NCC RIS case study. https://www.ripe.net/publications/news/youtube-hijacking-a-ripe-ncc-ris-case-study/ (2008)
3. Ramachandran, A., Feamster, N.: Understanding the network-level behavior of spammers. SIGCOMM Comput. Commun. Rev. **36**(4), 291–302 (2006)
4. Vervier, P.-A., Thonnard, O., Dacier, M.: On the stealthiness of malicious BGP Hijacks. In: NDSS, Mind your blocks (2015)
5. Ferlin, S., Alvarez, M.: BGP internet routing: What are the threats? https://www.ibm.com/think/x-force/bgp-internet-routing-what-are-the-threats (2017)
6. Apostolaki, M., Zohar, A., Vanbever, L.: Hijacking Bitcoin: routing attacks on cryptocurrencies. In: 2017 IEEE Symposium on Security and Privacy (SP), pp. 375–392 (2017)
7. Loshin, P.: BGP routing security flaw caused amazon route 53 incident. https://www.techtarget.com/searchsecurity/news/252439945/BGP-routing-security-flaw-caused-Amazon-Route-53-incident (2018)
8. Qrator Labs. Q3 2024 DDoS, bots and BGP incidents statistics and overview reports. https://blog.qrator.net/en/q3-2024-ddos-bots-and-bgp-incidents-statistics-and_209/ (2024)
9. Holterbach, T., Alfroy, T., Phokeer, A., Dainotti, A., Pelsser, C.: A system to detect forged-origin BGP hijacks. In: 21st USENIX Symposium on Networked Systems Design and Implementation (NSDI 24), pp. 1751–1770 (2024)

10. Qin, L., Li, D., Li, R., Wang, K.: Themis: accelerating the detection of route origin hijacking by distinguishing legitimate and illegitimate moas. In: 31st USENIX Security Symposium (USENIX Security 22), pp. 4509–4524 (2022)
11. Sermpezis, P., et al.: ARTEMIS: neutralizing BGP hijacking within a minute. IEEE/ACM Trans. Networking **26**(6), 2471–2486 (2018)
12. Schlamp, J., Holz, R., Jacquemart, Q., Carle, G., Biersack, E.W.: HEAP: reliable assessment of BGP hijacking attacks. IEEE J. Sel. Areas Commun. **34**(6), 1849–1861 (2016)
13. Kent, S., Lynn, C., Seo, K.: Secure border gateway protocol (S-BGP). IEEE J. Sel. Areas Commun. **18**(4), 582–592 (2000)
14. Karlin, J., Forrest, S., Rexford, J.: Pretty good BGP: improving BGP by cautiously adopting routes. In: Proceedings of the 2006 IEEE International Conference on Network Protocols, pp. 290–299. IEEE (2006)
15. White, R.: Securing BGP through secure origin BGP (soBGP). Bus. Commun. Rev. **33**(5), 47–53 (2003)
16. Lepinski, M., Kent, S.: An infrastructure to support secure internet routing (2012)
17. Snijders, J., Maddison, B., Lepinski, M., Kong, D., Kent, S.: A Profile for Route Origin Authorizations (ROAs). RFC 9582 (2024)
18. Huston, G., Michaelson, G.G.: Validation of Route Origination Using the Resource Certificate Public Key Infrastructure (PKI) and Route Origin Authorizations (ROAs). RFC 6483 (2012)
19. Mohapatra, P., Scudder, J., Ward, D., Bush, R., Austein, R.: BGP Prefix Origin Validation. RFC 6811 (2013)
20. Bush, R.: Origin Validation Operation Based on the Resource Public Key Infrastructure (RPKI). RFC 7115 (2014)
21. Siddiqui, A.: Lesson learned: Twitter shored up its routing security. https://manrs.org/2022/03/lesson-learned-twitter-shored-up-its-routing-security/ (2022)
22. MANRS. RPKI ROV deployment reaches major milestone. https://manrs.org/2024/05/rpki-rov-deployment-reaches-major-milestone/ (2024)
23. IAB. IAB statement on the RPKI. https://datatracker.ietf.org/doc/statement-iab-2010-statement-on-the-rpki/ (2010)
24. RIPE NCC. What is RPKI? https://www.ripe.net/manage-ips-and-asns/resource-management/rpki/what-is-rpki (2025)
25. Michael Waidner. RPKI: Deployed is better than perfect. https://blog.apnic.net/2024/10/01/rpki-deployed-is-better-than-perfect/ (2024)
26. MANRS. The white house's roadmap to enhancing routing security. https://manrs.org/2024/09/roadmap-to-routing-security/ (2024)
27. Forum Standaardisatie. Secured internet routing of Dutch government by end of 2024. https://www.forumstandaardisatie.nl/nieuws/secured-internet-routing-dutch-government-end-2024/ (2023)
28. NIST. NIST RPKI monitor. https://rpki-monitor.antd.nist.gov (2025)
29. MANRS. MANRS observatory. https://observatory.manrs.org/ (2025)
30. Testart, C., Richter, P., King, A., Dainotti, A., Clark, D.: To filter or not to filter: measuring the benefits of registering in the RPKI today. In: Passive and Active Measurement: 21st International Conference, PAM 2020, Eugene, Oregon, USA, March 30–31, 2020, Proceedings 21, pp. 71–87. Springer (2020)
31. Geoff Huston. Measuring ROAs and ROV. https://blog.apnic.net/2021/03/24/measuring-roas-and-rov/ (2021)
32. Rodday, N., et al.: Revisiting RPKI route origin validation on the data plane. In: Proceedings of Network Traffic Measurement and Analysis Conference (TMA), IFIP (2021)

33. Li, W., et al.: RoVista: measuring and analyzing the route origin validation (ROV) in RPKI. In: Proceedings of the 2023 ACM on Internet Measurement Conference, pp. 73–88 (2023)
34. Hlavacek, T., Shulman, H., Vogel, N., Waidner, M.: Keep your friends close, but your routeservers closer: insights into {RPKI} validation in the internet. In: 32nd USENIX Security Symposium (USENIX Security 23), pp. 4841–4858 (2023)
35. Qin, L., Chen, L., Li, D., Ye, H., Wang, Y.: Understanding route origin validation (ROV) deployment in the real world and why MANRS action 1 is not followed. In: NDSS (2024)
36. Morillo, R., Furuness, J., Morris, C., Breslin, J., Herzberg, A., Wang, B.: ROV++: improved deployable defense against BGP hijacking. In: NDSS (2021)
37. Zeng, M., Huang, X., Zhang, P., Li, D., Xie, K.: Improving prefix hijacking defense of RPKI from an evolutionary game perspective. IEEE Transactions on Dependable and Secure Computing (2024)
38. Hlavacek, T., Shulman, H., Waidner, M.: Smart RPKI validation: avoiding errors and preventing hijacks. In: European Symposium on Research in Computer Security, pp. 509–530. Springer (2022)
39. Schulmann, H., Zhao, S.: Learning to identify conflicts in RPKI. In: Proceedings of the 19th ACM Asia Conference on Computer and Communications Security (2025)
40. Gilad, Y., Cohen, A., Herzberg, A., Schapira, M., Schulmann, H.: Are we there yet? On RPKI's deployment and security. In: 24th Annual Network and Distributed System Security Symposium, NDSS 2017. The Internet Society (2017)
41. Du, B., Testart, C., Fontugne, R., Snoeren, A.C., Claffy, K.: Poster: taking the low road: how RPKI invalids propagate. In: Proceedings of the ACM SIGCOMM 2023 Conference, pp. 1144–1146 (2023)
42. Li, P., Liu, Y., Su, J., Yu, B.: ROVReco: An ROV deployment recommendation approach with GNN based on routing betweenness. Available at SSRN 5170823
43. CAIDA. As rank. https://asrank.caida.org/asns (2025)
44. Gao, L., Rexford, J.: Stable internet routing without global coordination. IEEE/ACM Trans. Networking 9(6), 681–692 (2001)
45. Anirban Datta. What is route origin validation? https://manrs.org/2020/10/what-is-rov/ (2020)
46. RIPE NCC. Ripe routing information service (RIS). https://www.ripe.net/analyse/internetmeasurements/routing-information-service-ris/ (2024)
47. University of Oregon. RouteViews. https://www.routeviews.org/routeviews/ (2025)
48. Griffin, T.G., Shepherd, F.B., Wilfong, G.: The stable paths problem and interdomain routing. IEEE/ACM Trans. Netw. 10(2), 232–243 (2002)
49. Gill, P., Schapira, M., Goldberg, S.: Let the market drive deployment: a strategy for transitioning to BGP security. ACM SIGCOMM Comput. Commun. Rev. 41(4), 14–25 (2011)
50. Goldberg, S., Schapira, M., Hummon, P., Rexford, J.: How secure are secure interdomain routing protocols. ACM SIGCOMM Comput. Commun. Rev. 40(4), 87–98 (2010)
51. Morris, C., Herzberg, A., Wang, B., Secondo, S.: BGP-iSec: improved security of internet routing against Post-ROV attacks. In: 31st Annual Network and Distributed System Security Symposium, NDSS 2024, San Diego, California, USA, February 26 - March 1, 2024. The Internet Society (2024)
52. Mazloum, R., Buob, M.-O., Auge, J., Baynat, B., Rossi, D., Friedman, T.: Violation of interdomain routing assumptions. In: International Conference on Passive and Active Network Measurement, pp. 173–182. Springer (2014)

53. Anwar, R., Niaz, H., Choffnes, D., Cunha, Í., Gill, P., Katz-Bassett, E.: Investigating interdomain routing policies in the wild. In: Proceedings of the 2015 Internet Measurement Conference, pp. 71–77 (2015)
54. Madhyastha, H.V., Katz-Bassett, E., Anderson, T.E., Krishnamurthy, A., Venkataramani, A.: iPlane nano: path prediction for peer-to-peer applications. In: NSDI, vol. 9, pp. 137–152 (2009)
55. Mühlbauer, W., Feldmann, A., Maennel, O., Roughan, M., Uhlig, S.: Building an as-topology model that captures route diversity. ACM SIGCOMM Comput. Commun. Rev. **36**(4), 195–206 (2006)
56. Netsecurelab VT. Rovista. https://rovista.netsecurelab.org/ (2025)
57. APNIC. RPKI ROV drop-invalid. https://stats.labs.apnic.net/rpki (2025)
58. Cloudflare. Is BGP safe yet? https://isbgpsafeyet.com/ (2025)
59. Gill, P., Schapira, M., Goldberg, S.: Modeling on quicksand: dealing with the scarcity of ground truth in interdomain routing data. ACM SIGCOMM Comput. Commun. Rev. **42**(1), 40–46 (2012)
60. Ivanović, M., Wirz, F., Subirà Nieto, J., Perrig, A.: Charting censorship resilience and global internet reachability: a quantitative approach. In: 2024 IFIP Networking Conference (IFIP Networking), pp. 529–535 (2024)
61. CAIDA. As relationships. https://www.caida.org/catalog/datasets/as-relationships/ (2025)
62. CISCO. BGPmon. https://www.bgpmon.net (2025)
63. Rodday, N.M., Rodosek, G.D., Pras, A., van Rijswijk-Deij, R.M.: Exploring the benefit of path plausibility algorithms in BGP. In: IEEE/IFIP Network Operations and Management Symposium, NOMS 2024. IFIP (2024)
64. Chung, T., et al.: RPKI is coming of age: a longitudinal study of RPKI deployment and invalid route origins. In: Proceedings of the Internet Measurement Conference, pp. 406–419 (2019)
65. Iamartino, D.: Study and measurements of the RPKI deployment (2015)
66. Xu, W., Chang, D., Li, X.: On the classification and false alarm of invalid prefixes in RPKI based BGP route origin validation. In: 2019 IFIP/IEEE Symposium on Integrated Network and Service Management (IM), pp. 654–658. IEEE (2019)
67. Li, Y., et al.: The hanging ROA: a secure and scalable encoding scheme for route origin authorization. In: IEEE INFOCOM 2022-IEEE Conference on Computer Communications, pp. 21–30. IEEE (2022)
68. Brouwer, M., Dekker, E.: The current state of DNS resolvers and RPKI protection (2020)
69. Wählisch, M., Schmidt, R., Schmidt, T.C., Maennel, O., Uhlig, S., Tyson, G.: RIPKI: the tragic story of RPKI deployment in the web ecosystem. In: Proceedings of the 14th ACM Workshop on Hot Topics in Networks, pp. 1–7 (2015)
70. Reuter, A., Bush, R., Cunha, I., Katz-Bassett, E., Schmidt, T.C., Wählisch, M.: Towards a rigorous methodology for measuring adoption of RPKI route validation and filtering. ACM SIGCOMM Comput. Commun. Rev. **48**(1), 19–27 (2018)
71. Chan, H., Dash, D., Perrig, A., Zhang, H.: Modeling adoptability of secure BGP protocol. ACM SIGCOMM Comput. Commun. Rev. **36**(4), 279–290 (2006)
72. Lychev, R., Goldberg, S., Schapira, M.: BGP security in partial deployment: is the juice worth the squeeze? In: Proceedings of the ACM SIGCOMM 2013 Conference on SIGCOMM, pp. 171–182 (2013)
73. Teixeira, R., Shaikh, A., Griffin, T., Rexford, J.: Dynamics of hot-potato routing in IP networks. In: Proceedings of the Joint International Conference on Measurement and Modeling of Computer Systems, SIGMETRICS '04/Performance '04, pp. 307–319, New York, NY, USA (2004). Association for Computing Machinery

74. Giotsas, V., Luckie, M., Huffaker, B., Claffy, K.: Inferring complex as relationships. In: Proceedings of the 2014 Conference on Internet Measurement Conference, IMC '14, pp. 23–30, New York, NY, USA (2014). Association for Computing Machinery
75. MANRS. Network operator actions. https://manrs.org/netops/network-operator-actions/ (2021)

On Analyzing SSO Permissions Across Web and Android Platforms

Fahimeh Rezaei[1]([✉])(iD), Matteo Lupinacci[2](iD), Mohammad Mannan[1](iD), and Amr Youssef[1](iD)

[1] Concordia University, Montreal, Canada
{fahimeh.rezaei,m.mannan,amr.youssef}@concordia.ca
[2] University of Calabria, Rende, Calabria, Italy
matteo.lupinacci@unical.it

Abstract. Federated Single Sign-On (SSO) is a widely used authentication method that delegates user login to Identity Providers (IdPs) such as Google and Facebook. While convenient, SSO raises privacy and security concerns, particularly, as we observed, when permissions vary across different platforms (web vs. mobile, even different versions of an app). Existing work on SSO logins completely lacks the exploration of such variances, and their privacy consequences, even though many users may use a service both via web and mobile platforms. This study examines such discrepancies at scale, alongside an analysis of dangerous permissions specifically requested on websites and Android apps. We developed a framework to automate SSO logins on both platforms, systematically measuring permission discrepancies. Our analysis, based on 661 and 318 successful logins using Google and Facebook SSO, respectively, across both the Android app and its corresponding website for the same service, reveals a 12.58% discrepancy in Facebook SSO permissions and a 3.48% discrepancy in Google SSO permissions between web and Android platforms. These findings, along with our analysis of top-5K Tranco websites, indicate that Android apps tend to request more intrusive permissions, underscoring the need for incremental authorization mechanisms to minimize unnecessary data exposure.

Keywords: Single Sign-on · Privacy · Web vs. Mobile SSO Permissions · Google SSO · Facebook SSO

1 Introduction

Federated Single Sign-On (SSO) has emerged as a widely adopted authentication strategy, permitting websites to delegate the login process to established Identity Providers (IdPs) such as Google, Facebook, and Apple. By employing SSO protocols such as OAuth and OpenID Connect, websites allow users to access applications using their existing IdP accounts. This approach effectively integrates the user's account on the new platform with their pre-existing online identity, thus removing the need for users to manage distinct credentials for

W. Liang et al. (Eds.): SecureComm 2025, LNICST 690, pp. 267–295, 2026.
https://doi.org/10.1007/978-3-032-23456-8_15

each site, leading users to prefer social logins over website-specific registration mechanisms. For example, a survey conducted by LoginRadius [44] indicates that 73.69% of individuals aged 18–25 prefer using social logins over other login and registration methods. On the flip side, through SSO, websites, referred to as Relying Parties (RPs), can access more comprehensive user profiles by requesting additional data from users, such as their birthday, location, and interests.

Privacy and security concerns of social logins have long been significant issues for users [15]. Consequently, considerable research has been focused on analyzing such issues in public SSO-supported services, and SSO protocols [47], with several frameworks [17,22,23,37,38,49] developed to measure these issues. Specifically, Dimova et al. [14] assessed the privacy implications of OAuth authentication by examining the SSO permissions requested by various IdPs, finding that 18.53% of websites using OAuth request at least one non-minimal permission (largely unnecessary, not requested by other IdPs). Moreover, Morkonda et al. [34] discovered that popular RPs request varying amounts of user data from different IdPs, with some being significantly more privacy-intrusive, a phenomenon comparable to dark patterns in website design. In subsequent work, they introduced SPEye [35], a browser extension prototype that extracts and displays permission request information from SSO login options in RPs, focusing on three major IdPs. Several past user studies (e.g., [8,9]) also revealed that users frequently grant permissions without fully understanding the scope of data being shared with the RPs.

A significant gap in previous research is the lack of privacy analysis on SSO permissions for mobile apps, and more critically, the discrepancies (if any) in permissions between web and mobile platforms. This is important as many users rely on mobile apps for accessing online services, and users also switch between mobile and web services at least for specific applications (e.g., checking notifications on the app and more involved usage on the website). Users may assume that logging into a mobile app with a specific IdP results in consistent data access as logging into the corresponding website; however, existing work in SSO privacy does not shed light into such specific issue. As SSO implementations on mobile apps also differ from those on websites [12,26] (although transparent to users), privacy issues need a closer look on both platforms.

To address this gap, we develop *SSO-Scoper*, a framework designed to automate Google and Facebook social logins on websites and Android mobile apps. We choose Android due to its popularity compared to other mobile platforms (e.g., iOS), and Google and Facebook IdPs, as they are most commonly supported by websites (see e.g., [7,14,23]. We use *SSO-Scoper* to automatically identify, login, and collect requested permissions by RPs for a given set of website domains (top sites from the Tranco [39] list) and downloaded apps (top apps from Google Play). After collecting the list of permissions for top apps and websites, we perform various privacy analyses, including: generate statistics about the permissions, especially the more sensitive ones (beyond the minimum scopes allowed by the IdPs); and systematically compare the permissions requested on web and Android platforms for the same services, and identify the discrepancies (if any) between web vs. app.

Our seemingly straightforward approach encountered several challenges, including: the complexities of UI automation (e.g., finding the correct login buttons) in websites (see the example in appendix A.4), and specifically in Android apps, due to the numerous ways that developers implement UI in websites and apps; the lack of an obvious mapping between an app and its corresponding website (if exists); Captcha challenges and other UI banners on some sites; and the variations in SSO login implementations across IdPs. We adequately addressed these challenges to enable our large-scale analysis. For instance, while our tool relies on text-based searches to locate SSO-related buttons, it currently cannot identify IdP logos/images on websites or apps. To mitigate Google reCAPTCHA triggers during domain login searches, we used proxy servers to rotate *SSO-Scoper*'s IP addresses. For preventative UI banners on websites (e.g., cookie consent pop-ups and ads), we installed two browser extensions to handle these interruptions.

Our main contributions and notable findings include:

1. We design and implement *SSO-Scoper*, an SSO permission measurement tool capable of automating SSO logins on both websites and Android apps using Facebook and Google IdPs. Using *SSO-Scoper*, we conduct a large-scale measurement study by logging into 1,716 Android apps and 1,286 websites via Google SSO, and 678 Android apps and 523 websites via Facebook SSO, systematically collecting and analyzing the permissions requested during the login process.

2. Our measurements show that Android apps generally request more permissions than websites: 1.06 permissions per app versus 1.01 permissions per website for Google SSO, and 2.25 permissions per app versus 2.09 permissions per website for Facebook SSO. Similarly, the number of permissions requested from Facebook is generally higher than those requested from Google.[1] Such trend underlines the importance of evaluating SSO permissions for apps.

3. We identify the frequent use of non-minimal permissions (i.e., permissions beyond basic profile information), particularly in mobile apps. These permissions are more privacy-intrusive and, in many cases, not essential for users, as confirmed by our manual analysis (see Sect. 6)

4. Surprisingly, for the same service offered via a website and Android app, the app generally requests more intrusive permissions than the website (the opposite is also true in a few cases). Considering all the apps and websites

---

[1] We conducted a statistical analysis with a 95% confidence level. For the comparison between the average number of permissions requested from Google (apps vs. websites), a p-value of 0.0048 was calculated. For the average number of permissions requested from Facebook (apps vs. websites), the p-value was 0.0357. Both p-values indicate statistically significant results. Additionally, when comparing the average number of permissions requested from Facebook and Google using the same platform, the p-values were less than 0.0001, further confirming significant differences in both cases.

offering the same service, for Facebook, we identified these permission discrepancies in 12.58% of the RPs (40/318), and for Google, 3.48% (23/661) of the RPs. When a service requests different sets of permissions on its web and mobile versions, users who access both platforms may unintentionally grant the more intrusive permissions, even if a single login on the more demanding platform (web or mobile) is performed. Such potential oversharing has not been reported on past work due to their focus on websites alone.

5. We discover a novel client-side attack that enables unauthorized permission injection during Facebook SSO logins, prompting Facebook to fix the vulnerability and award us a bounty; see Sect. 7.

Ethics and Disclosure. Our experiments primarily involved logging into websites and Android apps. We used test accounts with email addresses containing the keyword "test" to clearly indicate their purpose as non-personal, experimental accounts. Throughout our automatic and manual analyses, we strictly avoided actions that could interfere with the normal operation of the websites or mobile apps. No malicious or heavy data requests were sent, and we limited our interactions to essential login and permission analysis tasks, minimizing any potential impact on the services being tested. For the 14 case study apps mentioned in Sect. 6, we contacted each app's developer, using the contact information available on their Google Play Store page, to report our findings, and inquire about the observed discrepancies. We received responses only from Smule, Badoo, and Cupid Media. Smule's response indicated that the mandatory permissions remain the same across both platforms, while the optional permissions differ. Badoo team stated that both the app and web versions only require members to share their Facebook name and profile picture—although they ask for additional non-minimal permissions. Cupid Media explained that the Android app requests additional information, like gender and birthday, to streamline the user experience by auto-populating profiles, while the web platform only requires basic authentication. Additionally, to responsibly address the risks associated with permission adjustments in Sect. 7, we disclosed our findings to both Facebook and Google. Facebook acknowledged the vulnerability, awarded us a bounty, and has since implemented a patch at the time of writing this paper.

2 Background

OAuth [21] is an open standard for access delegation that enables websites or apps to obtain limited access to user information without exposing user credentials. This standard was developed to provide a method for third-party applications to request access to protected resources hosted by service providers like Google, Facebook, and Apple. The access is granted by users through a consent-based mechanism, where they authorize the third-party service to access their data without sharing their login credentials. Over time, OAuth has become a fundamental protocol for modern web and mobile apps, enabling secure third-party access to user resources hosted at popular services like Facebook/Google.

Table 1. Summary comparison for logins and platform coverage in related measurement studies

Ref	Year	Focus	IdPs	Platform	Target Size	# FB Logins	# Google Logins
[49]	2014	security	FB	web	17,913	1,660	-
[43]	2019	security	FB +2	mobile	550	128	-
[32]	2021	privacy	FB G +2	web	2,500	676	688
[16]	2022	security	FB	web	100K	1,900	-
[7]	2023	SSO prevalence	FB G +7	web	10K	293	339
[14]	2023	privacy	FB G +33	web	100K	4,743	3,400
[23]	2024	security	FB G +10	web	1M	18,560	21,473
Our work	2025	privacy	FB G	**mobile**	**21,163**	**678**	**1,716**
				web	6,322	523	1,286

During SSO login, users are typically prompted to grant specific permissions to the requesting application, such as access to their profile information, email address, and other personal data. These SSO permissions are often presented in a dialog box, where users can review and modify the scope of access before proceeding. The granularity of permissions allows users to control which aspects of their data are shared. If a user wishes to revoke or edit these permissions after the initial login, they can do so through the IdP website, which provides a centralized interface to manage the granted permissions, including revoking access entirely or adjusting the permissions to limit the data shared with the application.

In the context of implementing SSO using OAuth 2.0, developers are required to register their applications with an IdP such as Google or Facebook. This registration process results in the issuance of a unique application identifier, known as an *app ID*, which is used to identify the application during the OAuth authorization flow. Typically, developers provide information such as the application's name, website domain, and redirect URL during registration. Often, the application's requirements remain consistent across web and mobile platforms, necessitating the same set of SSO permissions for both web and mobile users. In such cases, developers usually opt for a single app ID with uniform permissions across platforms.

However, when different SSO permissions are required for web and mobile platforms, developers have two possible strategies. The first strategy is to use a single app ID for both platforms, adjusting the permissions in the client-side code to meet the specific needs of each platform. Alternatively, developers may register two separate app IDs–one for the web and one for the mobile platform–allowing for platform-specific control over settings, SSO permissions, and security configurations, thus addressing the distinct requirements of each platform more effectively. Regardless of the chosen strategy, IdPs recommend developers to adopt incremental authorization when requesting SSO permissions [19,28]. This method enhances user trust and privacy by requesting permissions only when they are required for a specific functionality, rather than requesting all permissions upfront; however, such incremental permission request is yet to be adopted by RPs (c.f. [14]).

3   Related Work

The research on SSO systems, especially regarding automated login and social login usage, has been extensive due to rising concerns about security and privacy issues [5,10,18,22,25,37,38,41,42,48]. Most work primarily however examined SSO implementations on websites, not mobile apps. Below we discuss example studies more relevant to our work.

One of the first tools developed in this domain was SSOScan [49], which aimed to uncover SSO-related vulnerabilities (e.g., access token misuse, user credential leakage) in websites that used Facebook as the IdP. Out of the 1660 sites with Facebook SSO (taken from top 20k websites), over 20% were found to be vulnerable. More recently, in the similar vein, Ghasemisharif et al. [16] introduced SAAT, a tool designed to assess account and session management practices on websites using Facebook SSO, and reveal security issues such as the lack of implementing re-authentication by most RPs to prevent compromise from hijacked IdP cookies. Jannett et al. [23] proposed SSO-MONITOR, a framework aimed at continuously monitoring/archiving the security and implementation of SSO systems on websites. From 89k SSO authentication flows on the top 1M websites, the authors found 33k violations of OAuth security best practices and 339 severe security vulnerabilities (e.g., 30 username and password leaks).

In terms of SSO security analysis, Shi et al. [43] assessed SSO implementation in Android apps with support for Facebook, WeChat, and Sina Weibo IdPs. Their study primarily identified vulnerabilities stemming from incorrect SSO implementations by testing and analyzing network traffic. Out of 23,936 apps, they successfully examined 550 apps, and found that 397 of them had flawed SSO implementations.

On the privacy analysis of SSO permissions, Dimova et al. [14] examined unnecessary data collection practices in 6211 SSO-supported websites (chosen from the CrUX top 100K websites, over 30 different IdP services). Their findings revealed that when websites request a non-minimal scope of user data, much of the information collected is often excessive (as apparent from the support of alternative SSO options like Apple that allow access to very little user data).

To understand variations in the permissions requested by websites for different IdPs (Google, Facebook, Apple, and LinkedIn), Morkonda et al. [32] developed OAuthScope, a tool for semi-automated scanning and analysis of OAuth 2.0 parameters and permissions. By checking the SSO login options on popular websites (Alexa top 500 from five countries), they revealed that websites request different categories and amounts of personal data from different IdP providers. Their work is focused on identifying privacy concerns, including dark patterns in the placement and ordering of SSO login buttons, often nudging users toward selecting IdPs that requested more permissions than others.

Apart from security or privacy issues, Ardi and Calder [7] examined the prevalence of SSO logins on top 10K CrUX websites using nine different IdPs, including Google and Facebook. They found that 51% of these websites offer a login option, and about 30% of the top 10K sites allow login via 3rd-party IdPs.

In terms of user studies focusing SSO login usage, recent work by Balash et al. [8] found that 89% of their 432 survey participants have used Google SSO at least once to log into 3rd-party apps/services. In their second survey with 214 participants, they used a browser extension to collect information about apps that have access to users' Google accounts, and surveyed users about their awareness and understanding of such access. Their findings include: most participants were not concerned about third-party apps' access to their Google account, although a significant number of participants could not fully understand what an app can do with a specific permission (e.g., "view personal info"). Majority of the participants also reported not to review what services have access to their Google account.

In a 2013 study by Bauer et al. [9], reported that participants' understanding of the information IdPs shared with RPs was not influenced by the content of consent dialogs displayed by the IdPs, or how much information was being shared with RPs. Participants were also generally unaware of RPs' access rights (e.g., durations, frequencies) to user data.

Recently, Morkonda et al. [33]conducted a 200-participant study and found that 55% of participants preferred an SSO login option as their initial login choice, and 28% of participants decided to change their login choice after viewing the comparative IdP permissions.

Research Gaps. As apparent from the above discussion, there is significant research in SSO security, privacy, and usability—mostly around the use of SSO logins for websites. Surprisingly, no privacy measurement study has been done on mobile SSO privacy issues. Consequently, our study explores privacy-sensitive permissions requested by Android apps, as well as, covers the use of non-minimal permissions in both websites and apps, and reveals the discrepancies between permission requests for the same services offered via websites and apps.

Table 1 provides a summary of relevant studies closely related to our research. For each study, the table indicates the successfully analyzed IdPs, the successfully tested dataset size, and the final number of successful logins. Our work contributes to this domain by offering a side-by-side analysis of websites and Android apps using the two most common IdPs, Facebook and Google.

4   Methodology

This section outlines the methodology we adopted for automating logins on apps and websites, as well as for analyzing the requested permissions on each platform. We detail the detection and login techniques utilized by *SSO-Scoper* along with its approach to permission analysis; see Fig. 1 for an overview. The framework comprises two primary components for automating social logins on apps and websites, along with a third component dedicated to extracting and analyzing requested permissions.

Both Facebook and Google SSO login processes allow users to edit the permissions shown during login, enabling them to proceed with the minimal default permissions, which typically include only the public information of the SSO account and the user's email address. However, in our experiment, we assumed that users do not alter the presented permissions in the login pop-up and proceed with them (c.f. [8,9]).

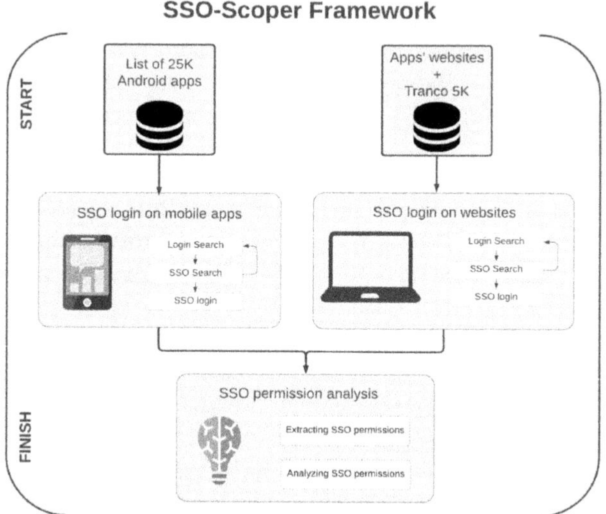

Fig. 1. *SSO-Scoper* overview

4.1   SSO Logins on Android Apps

The *SSO-Scoper* component for Android app automation is designed to analyze screen elements, specifically targeting login buttons to identify available SSO options, and then execute the login process using our SSO test accounts. The orchestration and management module processes a list of predefined IdPs, specifically Facebook and Google, and conducts separate analyses for each IdP. We utilize text-based keyword searches to locate relevant buttons within the authentication process. We first identify login or registration buttons on the screen and then interact with these buttons to find Google/Facebook SSO options. If an SSO button is detected, the tool initiates the login procedure. The authentication process is divided into three distinct phases: login search, SSO search, and SSO login. Depending on the execution of each phase, a specific set of keywords is searched within the screen elements. In the login search method, a set of hard-coded strings (e.g., register, login; for the full list, see Table 6 in the appendix), derived from a manual inspection of 50 random apps, is used to identify login or signup buttons. If these buttons are found, we then search for the IdP names (Facebook, Google) within the text of the screen elements. We also perform this search on the app's start page, as the manual analysis of 50 apps revealed that some apps present SSO login options directly on their start page. During the SSO search phase, if any screen element's text attribute contains the IdP name, the corresponding button is clicked, and the SSO login process begins, searching for our test IdP account name or email on the screen. To ensure a successful login into an application, the IdP accounts are logged into on the device. For Facebook, the Facebook app is installed and logged in, allowing it to open and request permissions when logging in to other apps using Facebook SSO. For Google, a Google account is signed in on the device, so that when logging in with Google SSO, a dialog box displaying the Google email appears. In both cases, the tool identifies the account name or email, and selects it to complete the login process.

After a successful login, the app data is erased from the device, and it is re-launched in a fresh state for the analysis of the next IdP. When both IdPs are tested, the tool uninstalls the installed app and removes its associated data from the device. The process then continues with the installation and analysis of the next app. After the tool has finished running, a list of successfully logged-in apps, along with the permissions granted to them, is automatically extracted from the IdP accounts and saved. This information is subsequently used for our analysis.

We developed this module on top of the ThirdEye framework [40] to leverage its capabilities in app execution, orchestration, and UI interaction. In addition to making modifications to the existing code-base to suit our requirements, we added approximately 600 lines of code to the UI interactor module to implement the SSO search and login processes.

4.2 Mapping of Android Apps and Websites

For our comparison between apps and websites SSO permissions for the same services, it is essential to map Android apps to their corresponding websites. Each app's Google Play Store listing includes two URL fields: the website URL, which refers to the official domain, and the privacy policy URL. Since some apps do not have the website field populated by the developer, we also collect the privacy policy URLs (assuming that may lead to the corresponding service's website). By leveraging the Python library "tldextract" [24], we extract the domain from the privacy policy URL and use it as the corresponding website for the mobile app. This process of retrieving website and privacy policy URLs is automated via the Google Play API [36]. The final output consists of websites associated with Android apps, with the privacy policy domain used for apps without a website URL.

We manually compared the website and privacy policy domains of 100 randomly selected apps. In 79 cases, both the website and privacy policy fields matched. For 12 cases, however, the website domain differed from the privacy policy URL domain: the website field referred to the app's official site, while the privacy policy field either pointed to a static landing page—common for entertainment apps—an unrelated website used solely for hosting legal documents, or a shortened URL such as bit.ly. For 9 apps, the website field was left blank on the app's Google Play Store page, with the privacy policy field containing the app's website.

4.3   SSO Logins on Websites

To automate social logins on websites, we utilized the Python library "undetected_chromedriver" [46], an optimized Selenium WebDriver designed to bypass detection by potential antibot systems. This approach, previously adopted by Pham et al. [37], was complemented by using the latest version of the Chrome browser for user interface automation.

SSO-Scoper begins by processing a list of website domains (collected from apps as described in Sect. 4.2, augmented with Tranco top-5K sites). For each domain, a Google search is performed using the "login" keyword to locate the login page. The first result that matches the input domain is selected, and the tool attempts to locate the SSO login button on this page. If the button is not found, the tool sequentially examines the second search result and the root domain webpage. However, it does not consider any other links from the search results, as our manual analysis of 100 websites indicated that the login page typically appears within the first two search results.

Once a webpage is selected and opened, *SSO-Scoper* initiates a heuristic, text-based search, scanning for SSO-related regex-based keywords (see Table 7 in the appendix), within all attributes of page elements. The list of keywords is curated based on a manual analysis of 100 websites, as mentioned. The search prioritizes buttons first, followed by all other elements, while disregarding those with zero height or width to limit the search space and optimize performance. The list of keywords, priorities, and filters was developed from a manual analysis of 100 websites. If the tool locates these clickable keywords, it proceeds to the login phase, where it searches for the SSO account name or email address on the screen. If no SSO-related elements are found, a third phase (login search) begins, targeting keywords related to login or registration (see Table 8 in the appendix). Once a login button is identified, *SSO-Scoper* resumes its search for SSO login buttons and proceeds with the login process if the related buttons are detected.

After each click on SSO buttons, *SSO-Scoper* calls a method to analyze the current page, and determines if SSO login can be performed. The main functionality of this method is to check if the IdP URLs used for SSO login initiation are contained in the actual URL login page that has been opened in the browser. For Facebook SSO, this pattern includes the presence of "facebook.com/login" or "facebook.com/privacy/consent" in the URL. For Google, it includes "/v3/signin/identifier?", "/o/oauth", "/gsi/select?", or "/oauth/-google". The presence of these strings within the URL guides the tool to proceed with the login method.

One key aspect of our approach is the use of a fixed, pre-configured Chrome profile to facilitate the login process and address issues such as non-English websites and preventative pop-ups. In this profile, both Facebook and Google accounts are logged in, along with the installation of two Chrome extensions to further simplify the interaction with websites. The first extension, "Accept All Cookies" [1], is a Google Chrome extension that automatically accepts cookie consent on various forms of notifications or pop-ups, minimizing user interaction with the website. The second extension, "AdGuard Adblocker" [2], is employed to block advertisement pop-ups on web pages.

To address the issue of non-English languages on some websites, the Chrome profile is configured to automatically translate all content into English. This ensures that, immediately after a page loads, it is translated, allowing the tool to accurately identify login and SSO-related buttons. Based on a manual analysis of 20 non-English websites, we observed that the translation process typically completes in under 2 s. As a result, *SSO-Scoper* is programmed to pause for 3 s before processing the webpage. Additionally, the tool detects and avoids social media pages and links that might be mistakenly identified as SSO login links during analysis.

A primary challenge we encountered during this stage was frequently triggering Google's reCAPTCHA when searching for website login pages. To enhance the human-like behavior of our automation and reduce Captcha triggers, we implemented pauses between actions and used Selenium's Python module, "Action Chains" [4], to simulate mouse movements. Additionally, we set up four dedicated proxy servers for our experiment and configured Selenium WebDriver to rotate the proxy IP after analyzing every 20 domains.

Finally, a list of successfully logged-in websites' SSO names and their granted SSO permissions is automatically extracted from the IdP accounts and saved. This information is subsequently used to compare the SSO permissions requested on the corresponding websites.

4.4   Collection and Analysis of SSO Permissions

Facebook imposes a rate limit on viewing app permissions, locking the account temporarily if a certain threshold is reached. To avoid such issues, we extract all app permissions from our test Facebook and Google accounts after completing the login process for all apps and websites (i.e., not after each app/site testing). Each app appears in the Facebook and Google dashboards under its configured app SSO name (configured SSO name by the app's developer).

To map SSO names across the web and Android platforms and compare SSO permissions for each app and its corresponding website, we employed two approaches; app ID comparison, and fuzzy string matching using Levenshtein distance.

For Facebook, each app is assigned a unique app ID—a numeric string included in the query string of the URL displaying permissions. Because this app ID is unique and consistent for each service, we used it to compare app SSO

Table 2. Summary of app installation and login success

# Total Android apps	25,000
# Successfully installed and analyzed	21,163/25,000 (84.65%)
# Successful login with Facebook	678/21,163 (3.20%)
# Successful login with Google	1,716/21,163 (8.11%)

permissions across two different profiles, one associated with the web experiment and the other with the mobile experiment.

For Google, since the app IDs are not accessible through the Google dashboard, we employed the "fuzzywuzzy" [13] Python library, which uses Levenshtein distance to measure the differences between sequences of app SSO names. To ensure the accuracy of the final mapping, we manually verified the mapped SSO names across both platforms.

5   Results

In this section, we present our findings on the prevalence of SSO logins in Android apps and websites, followed by an analysis of SSO permissions and their discrepancies across the two platforms. Note that our experiments were conducted from December 2023 to September 2024. For testing apps, we utilized Pixel 4 and Pixel 6 Android devices running rooted Android 12 images, alongside a desktop running Ubuntu 22.04 to orchestrate the execution of the target apps.

5.1   Prevalence of SSO Logins on Android Apps

We began by collecting a dataset of 25K popular Android package names from various sources, including Androidrank [3], AndroZoo [27], and the Google Play Store. During analysis, 3,837 apps failed to install on our devices due to app incompatibility or geographic restrictions. Of the remaining apps, *SSO-Scoper* successfully logged into 678 apps (3.20%) using Facebook as the IdP and 1716 apps (8.11%) using the Google IdP; see Table 2.

For the remaining apps where *SSO-Scoper* was unable to log in, either Facebook or Google SSO was not supported, or the login process was too complex to navigate. This complexity often stemmed from lengthy login flows with nonstandard keywords for login-related buttons, or the presence of advertisements during app startup or before the login process; see Fig. 8. We manually installed and evaluated 50 apps to assess the efficiency of *SSO-Scoper*. Out of these apps, 8 supported login with Facebook SSO, and 11 supported Google SSO. *SSO-Scoper* successfully logged into 5 apps using Facebook SSO and 7 using Google SSO. For the remaining apps, *SSO-Scoper* failed to log in due to the challenges mentioned.

In terms of permissions distribution, as expected, most apps (except a few games) request the default minimal permissions. For Facebook SSO, 99.71% of the apps requested "Name and profile picture" and 91.89% requested "Email address", and for Google SSO, 98.86% of the apps requested "See your profile info". Other commonly requested permissions include: "Birthday", "Gender", and "Photos" (for Facebook); and "Create, edit, and delete your Google Play Games activity", "See and download your exact date of birth", and "See, create, and delete its own configuration data in your Google Drive" for Google. See Figs. 6 and 7.

To compare Facebook vs. Google SSO permissions requested by the same apps, we identified 424 apps with successful SSO logins using both IdPs. In 55 apps (12.97%), Facebook permissions were more privacy-intrusive than Google permissions; and in 8 apps (1.89%), Google permissions were more privacy-intrusive than Facebook. In one app ("Fotka"), both Facebook and Google requested different non-minimal permissions (Facebook SSO requested for "Name and profile picture", "Gender", "Email address", "Birthday", "Current city", and "Hometown", while Google SSO requested "See your profile info" and "View Google Photo Library"). Note that for Google SSO results, in some cases, we used the exact permission names as appear in a user's Google account dashboard.

5.2 Prevalence of SSO Logins on Websites

We perform our tests on two sets of websites: domains that are collected from our Android apps (to compare between apps with websites), and Tranco top-5K websites (for general websites).

We extracted 1724 unique websites corresponding to the tested apps with successful IdP logins. In total, *SSO-Scoper* successfully logged into 318 websites using Facebook SSO and 661 websites using Google SSO, which corresponds to 46.90% and 38.52% successful login rates for Facebook and Google, respectively.

To validate our results, we manually checked 100 randomly-selected URLs for Facebook SSO and 100 URLs for Google SSO. Surprisingly, for Facebook, only 58 of these URLs offered Facebook SSO as a login method, while 22 were static websites with no login capability, often serving as simple landing pages for mobile apps, especially common in the entertainment and gaming categories. Therefore, the true success rate of our tool is estimated at 75.86% (44/58) for Facebook SSO. In contrast, for Google SSO, 30 websites were static pages with no login option. Of the remaining URLs, 56 websites supported Google SSO, and *SSO-Scoper* successfully logged into 48 of them, achieving a success rate of 85.71%.

From the Tranco top 5K websites, 1,170 domains (23.4%) did not have login pages (as from our search results). Among the remaining websites, it successfully logged into 733 using Google SSO and 265 websites using Facebook. To assess the success rate, we randomly selected 100 websites from the top 3K Tranco domains where *SSO-Scoper* did not complete the login process. Of these 100 domains, the tool failed on 10 sites: 4 required Captcha or a confirmation button before login, and 6 used extensive customization with non-standard button names.

Overall, we assessed a total of 6,322 websites, including the top 5K Tranco sites and the websites corresponding to the Android apps. See Figs. 4 and 5 for the distribution of permissions. Top 3 common permissions for Facebook are "Birthday", "Gender", and "Current City"; note that the "Current City" permission takes precedence over the "Photos" permission, which ranks higher for Android apps. For Google, the top three most common website permissions differ significantly from those on Android: "See and download your exact date of birth", "See and download your contacts", and "See your age group".

To compare Facebook vs. Google SSO permissions requested by the same websites, we identified 254 websites with successful SSO logins using both IdPs. In 23 sites (9.05%), Facebook permissions were more privacy-intrusive than Google permissions. In one case (0.39%), Google permissions were more privacy-intrusive than Facebook. On two websites, both Facebook and Google requested different non-minimal permissions.

5.3   Discrepancy of SSO Permissions Across Web and Android Apps

For Facebook SSO, we identified 40 services with different permissions between the web and Android platforms. Among these, TikTok was the only service where the Android app's *app ID* differed from that of the website. 20 additional permissions were requested exclusively by the websites, while 38 extra permissions were requested solely by the apps. For Google SSO, we found permissions discrepancies in 23 cases. Among these, 22 additional permissions were requested exclusively by the Android apps, while 14 extra permissions were requested only by the websites. The statistics of apps with permission discrepancies are shown in Table 3. Based on these findings, the Android platform typically requests more permissions than the web platform (see Fig. 2 and Fig. 3), underscoring the varying privacy practices across different SSO implementations.

Table 3. Breakdown of successful SSO logins and permissions discrepancies across Android apps and corresponding websites

	Facebook	Google
# Successful login on apps	678	1716
# Successful login on the apps' websites	318/678 (46.90%)	661/1716 (38.52%)
# Different permissions	40/318 (12.58%)	23/661 (3.48%)

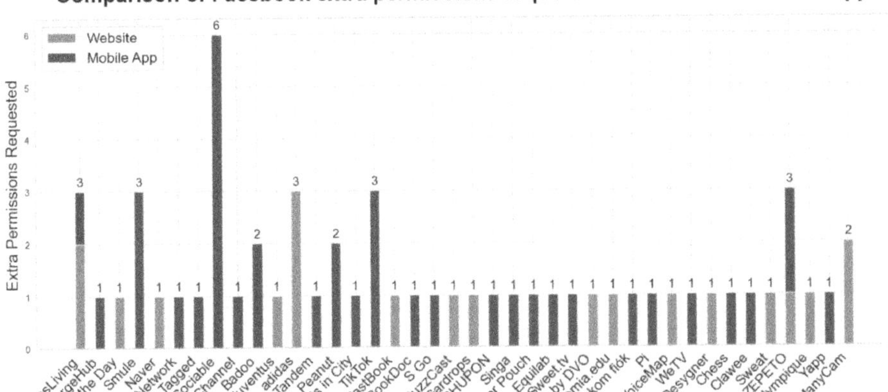

Fig. 2. SSO permissions discrepancies: extra permissions requested for Facebook SSO

Table 4. Privacy-intrusive permissions requested by Facebook and Google on web and Android platforms

		Android App	Website	Example App/Website (#DL)
Facebook	Photos	32	14	Tinder (100M+)
	Friends list	30	11	StarMaker (100M+)
	Page likes	3	1	Sociable (1M+)
	Publish videos to timeline	0	1	Manycam.com
Google	Gmail Emails (full access)	5	0	Yahoo Mail (100M+)
	Google Calendar (full access)	5	2	TypeApp mail (1M+)
	Google Calendar (read access)	2	2	Lich Van Nien 2024 (5M+)
	Contacts (full access)	2	0	Microsoft Outlook Lite (10M+)
	Contacts (read access)	2	4	Truecaller (1B+)
	Youtube Account (full access)	1	0	AutoGuard Dash Cam (1M+)
	Youtube Account (read access)	2	0	AmpMe (10M+)
	Google Fit Physical Activity (write access)	1	0	Yoga Club (100K+)
	Google Drive (read access)	1	0	Microsoft Outlook Lite (10M+)
	Google Photos (read access)	1	1	Fotka (1M+)
	Google Classroom Information (read access)	1	1	ThingLink (100K+)
	Personal Phone numbers (read access)	1	2	Class101.net
	Street Addresses (read access)	0	1	Dbl.id

5.4   Privacy-Intrusive Permissions

Throughout this study, we encountered several revealing and potentially dangerous permissions requested during login by websites and mobile apps using Facebook and Google social login options. These permissions extend beyond basic profile access, posing significant privacy risks by requesting access to more sensitive data. While some services may require these permissions for specific functionalities, IdPs like Google and Facebook recommend developers adopt incremental authorization [19, 28]. This approach ensures that permissions are requested only when the user activates the related feature (e.g., importing Facebook photos into the app), reducing unnecessary access to sensitive information for features users may choose not to use; see Table 4.

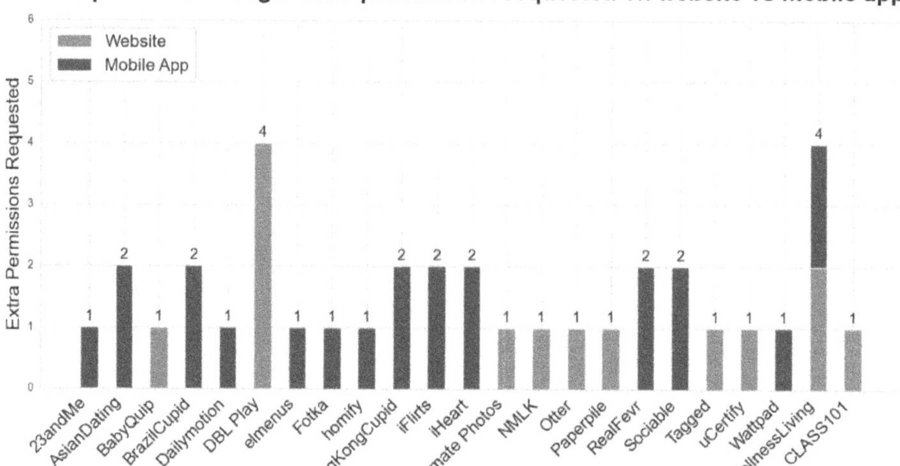

Fig. 3. SSO permissions discrepancies: extra permissions requested for Google SSO

In the case of Facebook, the following less common but highly intrusive permissions were observed in our experiments: Photos, Friends list, Page likes (Allows the RP to view a list of all Facebook Pages a user has liked, potentially disclosing personal interests, affiliations, and political views), Publish videos to timeline (Grants the RP the ability to publish live videos to a user's timeline, group, event, or Page).

For Google, we identified the following permissions that grant extensive access to personal information: Gmail Emails (full access), Google Calendar (full access), Google Calendar (read access), Contacts (full access), Contacts (read access), Youtube Account (full access), Youtube Account (read access), Google Fit Physical Activity (write access) which access individual activities like walking, running, number of calories burned, step count or any workout activity that other apps have added to Google Fit. It also access information about physical habits that may be sensitive and could be used to make assumptions about users' fitness. Google Drive (read access), Google Photos (read access), Google Classroom Information (read access) which include access to users' Google classes and the list of students (rosters) , Personal Phone numbers (read access), Street Addresses (read access).

6   Discussions

Here we discuss the results of our manual analysis of 14 RPs (out of 60 unique cases with discrepancies, see Sect. 5.3), where there are significant permission differences between an app and its corresponding website. We provide a summary of the discrepancies in Table 5; for details of these services, see appendix A.3.

We found only minor differences in functionality (not in core features) between web and Android versions of these services. This raises questions about the necessity of the extra permissions requested, as these differences do not seem to justify the additional data access.

Furthermore, our review of the privacy policies for these fourteen services revealed only in six cases, the extra permissions are mentioned in the privacy policy page, while eight of them provided only broad descriptions of data collection, such as basic permissions for email and name, without disclosing the additional permissions requested on the more intrusive platform. For example, the ZEPETO app requests access to the "Friends list" only on its mobile version, yet this is not mentioned in its privacy policy. Additionally, while all the services investigated had a single privacy policy covering all versions of their service, none specified platform-specific permissions for web and app versions. This lack of transparency leaves users unaware of the permissions requested on different versions of the app, raising concerns about the justification for such requests.

With the exception of two cases (Cupid Media, and ManyCam), the other apps provide an Apple SSO option for login on their websites or iOS versions. As Apple's documentation states [6], Apple only shares the user's name and/or email with RPs. Therefore, offering Apple SSO indicates that the service can operate with minimal SSO permissions.

We further compared SSO login options with manual registration by creating user accounts on both the web and Android versions of each service. With the exception of the Sociable app, which only offers SSO options for login and registration, for 9/14 services, the SSO login option was found to be more intrusive than manual registration. In 2 cases, both options had comparable privacy levels. Only for Cupid Media, manual registration required more information (country and city on the app) than Google SSO login (no Facebook SSO support).

Table 5 provides a summary for all services. The permissions listed in the "Extra Permissions" column are those that were requested exclusively on either the website or Android app, with the corresponding platform not requiring the same permissions. Note that we disclosed our observations to all the developers of these apps as mentioned in the Introduction.

7   Privacy Risks from Permission Adjustments

In both Google and Facebook IdPs, users have the right to deny any permissions beyond the default (which includes only basic profile information) during login, or afterward through the IdP's dashboard. Dimova et al. [14] also explored the removal of non-minimal permissions as a way to reduce privacy exposure (most websites were found to function properly without the extra permissions). While this option is available to users, we examine a potential abuse of it—to forcibly increase SSO permissions by modifying the OAuth flow from the client side by a malicious RP. For testing purposes, we selected certain websites that use Google and Facebook SSO and attempted to inject extra permissions into the OAuth

Table 5. Extra permissions requested on either the mobile platform or website for notable services

Application	#DL	SSO Type	Platform	Extra Permissions
TikTok	1B+	f	mobile	Email, Age range, Friends list
Smule	100M+	f	mobile	Email, Age range, Friends list
Badoo	100M+	f	web	Birthday, Gender
Zepeto	100M+	f	mobile	Email, Friends list
iHeart	50M+	G	mobile	Birthday, Gender
adidas	50M+	f	web	Birthday, Gender, Age range
Chess	50M+	f	web	Friends list
Tagged	50M+	f	mobile	Photos
		G	web	Contacts (read access)
Desygner	5M+	f	web	Photos
Sociable	1M+	f	mobile	Email, Birthday, Gender, Friends list, Page likes, Photos
		G	mobile	Birthday, Gender
ManyCam	1M+	f	web	Email, Publish video to timeline
AsianDating BrazilCupid HongKongCupid	1M+	G	mobile	Birthday, Gender
WellnessLiving Achieve	100K+	f	web	Gender, Timeline link
		G	mobile	Birthday, Google Calendar (full access)
		G	web	Secondary Google Calendars (full access), Google Calendar (read access)
InmatePhotos	100K+	G	web	Google Photos

scopes transferred in the requests. Importantly, these tests were conducted on existing websites rather than personal test applications, and all findings were responsibly disclosed to the respective IdPs. As documented [20,29], both Google and Facebook require developers to undergo a review process when requesting non-minimal permissions to ensure the necessity and non-malicious intent of the developers. However, we found that this review process can be bypassed in Facebook's case, allowing a malicious developer to request more permissions than those allowed in the review process.

We noticed that by injecting extra permissions in the "params[steps]" parameter within Facebook SSO requests, a developer can forcibly request additional permissions beyond those initially approved during the Facebook review process. This means a developer could release an app with minimal permissions or less intrusive permissions to avoid or facilitate Facebook's review process, but later request additional permissions from users to gain access to their resources. Importantly, the consent screen still displays *all* requested permissions to the user, regardless of the initial approval. We responsibly reported this finding to Facebook as a lack of permission validation on Facebook's side—i.e., not checking the requested permissions against the reviewed permissions. Facebook confirmed the vulnerability and addressed it accordingly, awarding us a bounty in recognition of our responsible disclosure.

In contrast, Google categorizes its SSO scopes into three broad levels: non-sensitive, sensitive, and restricted. The review process is conducted based on these categories. If an application is granted access to non-sensitive scopes (e.g., gender), it can access all scopes within this category (e.g., birthday, street address, and classroom rosters). Similarly, applications validated for sensitive scopes (e.g., contacts) can access any other scopes in the sensitive or non-sensitive categories. For restricted scopes, such as those related to Gmail or Google Drive, access implicitly includes all lower-tier categories. However, Google's documentation does not explain this categorization, nor did they provide clarification when directly queried. Therefore, we observed that developers can verify their application for a specific non-sensitive scope, such as a user's birthday, and later request additional permissions within the same category, such as the user's street address.

Additionally, attempts to inject a sensitive scope into the OAuth flow on a service configured for non-sensitive scopes result in a non-preventative error message. This error message reveals the developer's Gmail address, submitted as contact information during the SSO setup. In contrast, attempts to inject a restricted scope result in a stricter response, with Google blocking the OAuth flow entirely and preventing the user from proceeding.

These variations in behavior suggest that Google has implemented some safeguards to handle unforeseen permission requests, potentially mitigating associated risks to a certain extent. We responsibly disclosed our findings to Google, and their response confirmed that these behaviors are intentional.

8   Conclusion

This study analyzes discrepancies in permissions requested by Google and Facebook SSO across Android and web platforms. As part of this work, we developed *SSO-Scoper*, an automated framework for SSO logins, enabling a systematic comparison of permissions between platforms and identifying more privacy-intrusive requests. Our findings show that SSO permissions differ significantly: Facebook SSO generally requests more intrusive permissions than Google SSO, and Android apps demand more permissions than web apps. Specifically, we observed a 12.58% discrepancy in Facebook SSO and a 3.48% discrepancy in Google SSO permissions between web and Android platforms. We also uncovered potential risks, including permission validation gaps in Facebook and inconsistent behaviors in Google's review process that could allow permissions to bypass checks. These findings highlight the need for incremental authorization, where permissions are requested only when necessary, to enhance user privacy.

Acknowlegement. This research is supported by the Office of the Privacy Commissioner of Canada (OPC). The views expressed herein are those of the authors and do not necessarily reflect those of the OPC.

A Appendix

A.1 Detection Keywords for SSO Buttons

This appendix presents the keywords used by *SSO-Scoper* to detect SSO-related buttons in both apps and websites for login automation.

Table 6. Keywords for login detection in apps

Keywords

"register", "login", "sign up", "signup", "don't have an account? sign up", "create an account", "join", "join now", "log in", "sign in", "log in to your account", "login/signup", "profile", "login/register", "login or signup", "login or register", "register/login", "profile", "user", "continue", "options"

Table 7. Keywords for SSO button detection

SSO Provider	Keywords
Google SSO	"google", "gmail", "google+"
Facebook SSO	"facebook", "fb[*]?login", "fb[*]?sign"

Table 8. Regular expressions used for login detection in websites

Keywords

```
''^(Log|Sign)[\s]?in$'',
''^Log in to your account$'',
''^Login(/|or)(SignUp|Register)$'',
''^Register/Log[\s]?in$'',
''^sign[\s]?up$'',
''^Profile$'',
''^Don't have an account? sign up$'',
''^Create an Account$'',
''^(Join|Register)[\s]?Now[\s]?$''
```

A.2 Distribution of SSO Permissions Across Websites and Android Apps

Figure 4 and Fig. 5 show the distribution of Facebook and Google permissions across websites, while Fig. 6 and Fig. 7 show the distribution of Facebook and Google permissions across websites .

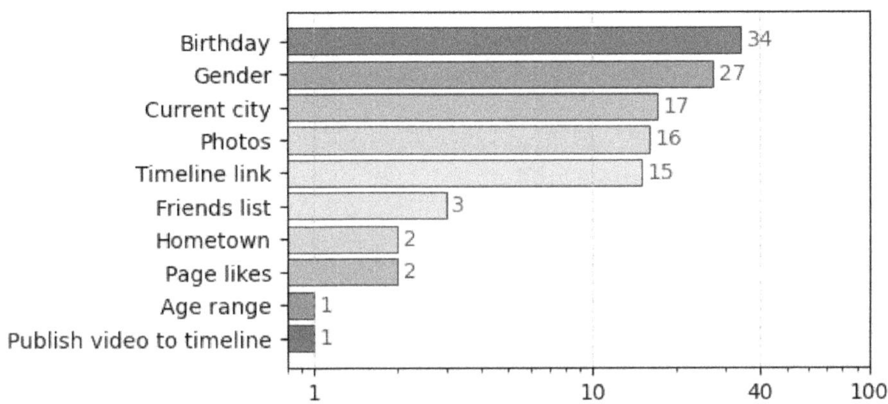

Fig. 4. Distribution of Facebook permissions in websites without the two minimal permissions of "Name and profile picture" and "Email".

A.3 Example Cases

Below, we detail a subset of RPs showing SSO permission discrepancies between their apps and websites, beyond basic permissions.

TikTok. This app is the third most popular social media app worldwide [45] with over 1 billion downloads from the Google Play Store, employs different Facebook app IDs for handling its mobile and web applications separately. During our experiments, we observed that while TikTok only requests the "Name and profile picture" permission on its website, it requests three additional permissions— "Email address", "Age range", and "Friends list"—on its Android app. The "Friends list" permission pertains to the user's list of friends who also use Tik-Tok. When logging in with Google SSO, the app requests only the minimal permission "See your profile info" on both the web and Android platforms.

Smule: Karaoke Songs and Videos. Smule is a popular entertainment app with over 100 million downloads, supporting both Facebook and Google SSO on its mobile and web platforms. Our analysis revealed discrepancies in the permissions requested between the web and Android platforms when using Facebook SSO. On Android, Smule requests access to three additional data fields: "Email address", "Age range", and "Friends list", whereas on the web platform, it only

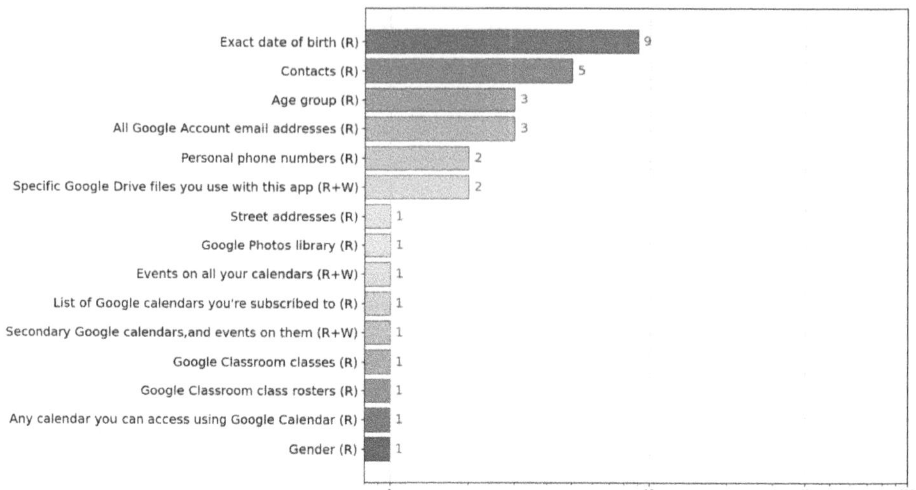

Fig. 5. Distribution of Google permissions in websites without the minimal permission "See your profile info". The labels in parentheses indicate whether the permission involves *read* (R) and/or *write* (W) access.

requests the "Name and profile picture" permission. Additionally, when using Google SSO, the app requests only the minimal permission, "See your profile info". We reached out to the Smule support team regarding the discrepancies in permissions. Their response indicated that the mandatory permissions remain the same across both platforms, while the optional permissions differ. They clarified that it is up to the user's discretion to grant additional permissions, as they are not mandatory. According to Facebook's specifications [31], the only mandatory permission is the "Name and profile picture" field, allowing users to deny any additional permissions by modifying them during the login process. However, since these extra permissions are still presented as default requirements during login, our experiment did not account for users deliberately modifying permissions.

Badoo Dating App: Meet and Date. Badoo is recognized as the fourth most popular dating app worldwide, according to Statista's 2024 report [11]. Unlike most apps, Badoo requests more permissions when users log in using Facebook SSO on a web browser. The additional permissions include the user's "Birthday" and "Gender" from their Facebook profile, while this information is not required on the Android app or during the Google SSO login process. When using Google SSO, the app only requests the minimal permission, "See your profile info". In response to our inquiry about the differing permissions across the two platforms, they replied, stating that "both the app and web versions only require members to share their Facebook name and profile picture. Members can then optionally choose to share their email address, gender, and birthday from Facebook if they

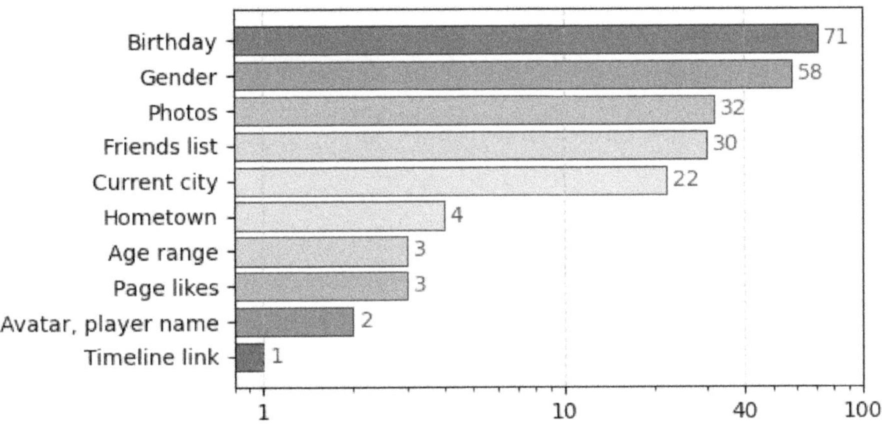

Fig. 6. Distribution of Facebook permissions in Android apps without the two minimal permissions of "Name and profile picture" and "Email"

wish." However, their response did not justify the current permissions, and they did not address our follow-up question regarding the reason behind the existing difference.

ZEPETO: Avatar, Connect and Live. ZEPETO is a virtual role-playing game that allows users to create digital avatars, boasting over 100 million downloads on the Google Play Store. While the app requests only the "Name and profile picture" permission when logging into the web version via Facebook SSO, the Android version requires two additional permissions: "Email address" and "Friends list". The functionality review revealed that user registration can only be completed through the mobile app, forcing users to grant the extra permissions regardless of their necessity, as the additional permissions appear unnecessary for the app's functionality.

iHeart: Music, Radio, Podcasts. iHeart is a well-known music, radio, and podcast app with over 50 million downloads from the Google Play Store. This app requests minimal permissions from users on its web platform during Google SSO login. However, when using the Android app or logging in with a Facebook account, the app consistently requests access to the user's "Birthday" and "Gender", regardless of the platform.

adidas: Shop Shoes and Clothing. Adidas is a renowned shopping brand that offers web and mobile apps for online shopping, with over 50 million downloads. When using Google SSO to log in to this app, both the web and Android app platforms require only minimal mandatory permissions, while the permissions for "Age Group" and "Exact Date of Birth" are presented as optional, allowing the user to choose whether to grant them. In contrast, when

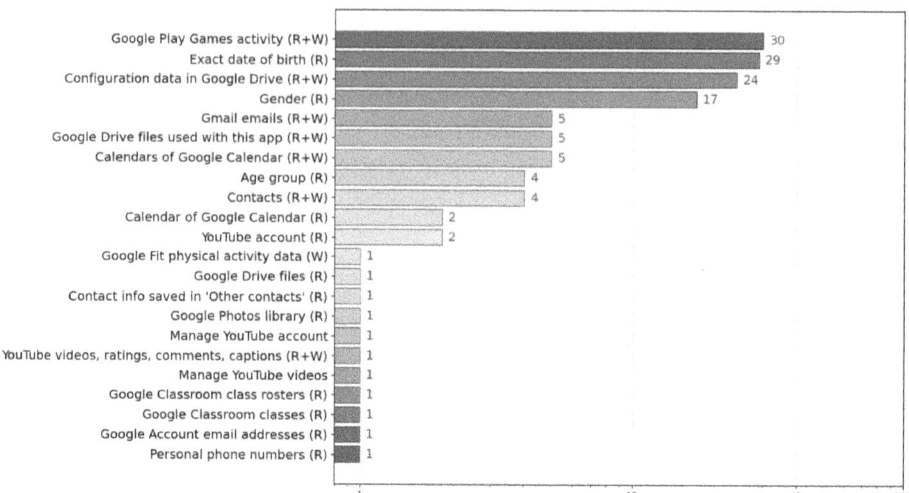

Fig. 7. Distribution of Google permissions in Android apps without minimal permission "See your profile info". The labels in parentheses indicate whether the permission involves *read* (R) and/or *write* (W) access.

using Facebook SSO on the web platform, the same permissions—"Age Group" and "Birthday"—along with the user's "Gender", are requested as mandatory, whereas these permissions are not requested on the Android app.

Chess - Play and Learn. Chess is a free, unlimited chess game with over 50 million downloads. This gaming app requests access to its users' list of friends who also use the app, only when a user logs in with their Facebook account on a web browser. In contrast, when using the mobile app or logging in with Google SSO, the app requests only the minimal permissions.

Tagged - Meet, Chat and Dating. Tagged is a dating app with over 50 million users. On the Android app of this service, the "Photos" permission is requested, granting read access to the photos a user has uploaded to Facebook [30], which may include personal and sensitive images. In contrast, logging in with Google SSO on the web results in an additional permission, "See and download your contacts", which provides read access to all of the user's Google contacts. Google specifies that this permission allows the app to view and make a copy of the user's Google Contacts, which may include names, phone numbers, addresses, and other information about the user's acquaintances.

Desygner: Graphic Design Maker. Desygner is a business marketing app with over 5 million downloads from the Google Play Store. While the app requests minimal permissions when logging in with Google SSO, it requests access to the user's Facebook photos when the user chooses to log in with Facebook on a web browser. This permission ("Photos") is not required when the user uses the same SSO option to log in on an Android device. Regarding functionality, both the app and website offer similar functionality, allowing users to upload or import photos from Facebook. However, the web version requests the "Photos" permission during login but requires re-authentication later to access photos, while the Android app requests the permission only when the user navigates to the Gallery to upload images.

Sociable - Social Games and Chat. Sociable is a social gaming app with over 1 million downloads. This app exhibits several discrepancies in its requested permissions across web and mobile platforms, as well as between Facebook and Google SSOs. Overall, the app requests more permissions on its Android app compared to its website version. When using Facebook SSO, the app requests sensitive additional permissions, such as access to the user's photos posted on Facebook ("Photos") and a list of all Facebook Pages the user has liked ("Page likes"), among other permissions; see Table 5. In contrast, when using Google SSO, the app requests access to the user's birth date and gender exclusively on the Android platform.

After reviewing the functionality of Sociable, we found that full registration and core features like gaming are only available on the mobile app, with the website encouraging users to install the app for the complete experience. Despite extensive permission requests via Facebook and Google SSO, these permissions were not visibly utilized in either version.

ManyCam - Easy Live Streaming. ManyCam is a virtual camera and live streaming software with over 1 million downloads on the Google Play Store. This app requests minimal permissions when logging in with Google SSO on both Android and web platforms, as well as during Facebook login on the Android app. However, when using Facebook SSO on the web, it requests permission to publish live videos to the user's timeline, group, event, or page ("Email address", "Publish video to your timeline on your behalf"). The ManyCam mobile app enables video streaming to Facebook, requesting permissions "Publish video to your timeline on your behalf", "Create and manage content on your Page", "Read content posted on the Page", and "Show a list of the Pages you manage". only when the user decides to initiate a stream. In contrast, the website serves as an administrative panel with no recording capabilities, making the permission to publish videos to the Facebook timeline excessive and unnecessary on the web platform.

AsianDating: Asian Dating, BrazilCupid: Brazilian Dating, and HongKongCupid Hong Kong Dating. These three popular region-based dating apps are owned by "Cupid Media" and share the same theme and configurations. When logging in with Google SSO on the Android app, these apps require permissions for the user's birthday and gender, whereas these permissions are not requested on the web platform. In response to our inquiry, the vendor explained that the Android app requests additional information, like gender and birthday, to streamline the user experience by auto-populating profiles, while the web platform only requires basic authentication. However, despite this explanation, both the website and the Android app ask users for this information directly, rendering the granted permissions unnecessary.

WellnessLiving Achieve. WellnessLiving is a software solution designed for art and sports studios, supporting both Google and Facebook SSO login on its web and mobile platforms. This app requests different permissions depending on the platform. When logging in with Facebook SSO, the Android app requests only "Name and profile picture" and "Email address". However, on the web browser, it additionally requests the "gender" and a "Timeline link" to access the user's profile link. When a user chooses to log in using Google SSO, the app requests more extensive permissions on the Android platform, including access to the user's birthday ("Exact Date of Birth") and full access to all of their Google calendars ("Google Calendar, see, edit, share, and permanently delete all the calendars you can access using Google Calendar"). This permission allows the app to make changes to the user's calendars, as well as any calendar they can access via Google Calendar, including creating, changing, or deleting calendars, updating individual calendar events, modifying settings such as who can view the events, and altering who the calendar is shared with. This is a sensitive permission, as a user's calendar may contain personal contacts and private appointments. In contrast, when logging in with Google SSO on the WellnessLiving website, the service requests the following permissions: "Make secondary Google calendars, and see, create, change, and delete events on them" and "See the list of Google calendars you're subscribed to". Although Google OAuth scopes do not provide a detailed explanation for this permission, the general description suggests that the app requests full access to all of the user's calendars. Functionality testing revealed that logging into the app was not possible due to restricted access for specific accounts, though we successfully logged in on the website. However, the requirement to complete medical information forms prevented a full review of the features, leaving our functionality assessment incomplete and inconclusive.

Inmate Photos: Photos to Jail. Inmate Photos is an app designed for delivering photos and pictures to inmates. While this app requests access to users' photos during both Google and Facebook SSO login, it notably does not request this permission when logging in with Facebook SSO on the Android app.

A.4   Example of Complex Login Path in Android App

Figure 8 shows an example of an Android app where the navigation path to the login is too complex for *SSO-Scoper* to detect effectively.

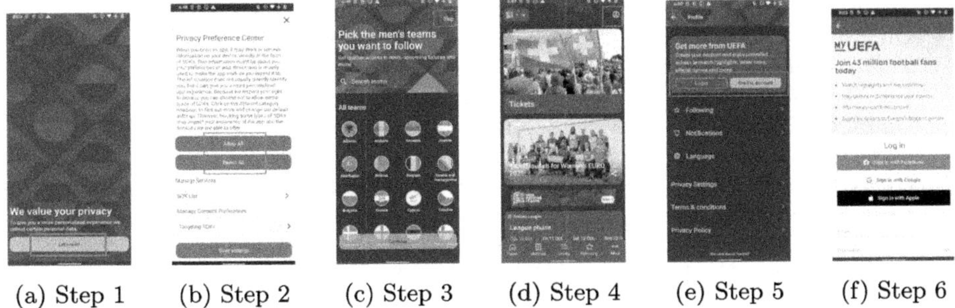

(a) Step 1   (b) Step 2   (c) Step 3   (d) Step 4   (e) Step 5   (f) Step 6

Fig. 8. Login process of the "Nations League & Women's EURO" app, requiring five clicks on buttons with uncommon keywords to reach the login screen.

References

1. Accept all cookies (2024). https://chromewebstore.google.com/detail/accept-all-cookies/ofpnikijgfhlmmjlpkfaifhhdonchhoi, version 1.0.3
2. Adguard adblocker (2024). https://chromewebstore.google.com/detail/adguard-adblocker/bgnkhhnnamicmpeenaelnjfhikgbkllg, version 4.4.22
3. Adnroidrank (2024). https://www.androidrank.org/
4. Selenium 4.25.0 documentation (2024). https://www.selenium.dev/selenium/docs/api/py/webdriver/selenium.webdriver.common.action_chains.html
5. Al Rahat, T., Feng, Y., Tian, Y.: OAUTHLINT: an empirical study on OAuth bugs in android applications. In: 2019 34th IEEE/ACM International Conference on Automated Software Engineering (ASE), pp. 293–304. IEEE (2019)
6. Apple: Request an authorization to the sign in with apple server (2024). https://developer.apple.com/documentation/sign_in_with_apple/request_an_authorization_to_the_sign_in_with_apple_server
7. Ardi, C., Calder, M.: The prevalence of single sign-on on the web: towards the next generation of web content measurement. In: Proceedings of the 2023 ACM on Internet Measurement Conference, pp. 124–130 (2023)
8. Balash, D.G., Wu, X., Grant, M., Reyes, I., Aviv, A.J.: Security and privacy perceptions of third-party application access for google accounts. In: 31st USENIX Security Symposium (USENIX Security 22), pp. 3397–3414 (2022)
9. Bauer, L., Bravo-Lillo, C., Fragkaki, E., Melicher, W.: A comparison of users' perceptions of and willingness to use Google, Facebook, and Google+ single-sign-on functionality. In: Proceedings of the 2013 ACM Workshop on Digital Identity Management, pp. 25–36 (2013)
10. Benolli, M., Mirheidari, S.A., Arshad, E., Crispo, B.: The full gamut of an attack: an empirical analysis of OAuth CSRF in the wild. In: Detection of Intrusions and Malware, and Vulnerability Assessment: 18th International Conference, DIMVA 2021, Virtual Event, July 14–16, 2021, Proceedings 18, pp. 21–41. Springer (2021)
11. Ceci, L.: Most popular dating apps worldwide in June 2024, by number of monthly downloads (2024). https://www.statista.com/statistics/1200234/most-popular-dating-apps-worldwide-by-number-of-downloads/
12. Chen, E.Y., Pei, Y., Chen, S., Tian, Y., Kotcher, R., Tague, P.: OAuth demystified for mobile application developers. In: Proceedings of the 2014 ACM SIGSAC Conference on Computer and Communications Security, pp. 892–903 (2014)

13. Cohen, A.: FuzzyWuzzy (2020). https://pypi.org/project/fuzzywuzzy/
14. Dimova, Y., Van Goethem, T., Joosen, W.: Everybody's looking for ssomething: a large-scale evaluation on the privacy of OAuth authentication on the web. In: Proceedings on Privacy Enhancing Technologies (2023)
15. Gafni, R., Nissim, D.: To social login or not login? Exploring factors affecting the decision. Issues Inf. Sci. Inf. Technol. **11**(1), 57–72 (2014)
16. Ghasemisharif, M., Kanich, C., Polakis, J.: Towards automated auditing for account and session management flaws in single sign-on deployments. In: 2022 IEEE Symposium on Security and Privacy (SP). pp. 1774–1790. IEEE (2022)
17. Ghasemisharif, M., Ramesh, A., Checkoway, S., Kanich, C., Polakis, J.: O single sign-off, where art thou? An empirical analysis of single sign-on account hijacking and session management on the web. In: 27th USENIX Security Symposium (USENIX Security 18), pp. 1475–1492 (2018)
18. Göçer, B.D., Bahtiyar, Ş.: An authorization framework with OAuth for fintech servers. In: 2019 4th International Conference on Computer Science and Engineering (UBMK), pp. 536–541. IEEE (2019)
19. Google: Incremental authorization (2024). https://developers.google.com/identity/protocols/oauth2/web-server#incrementalAuth
20. Google: OAuth app verification (2024). https://support.google.com/cloud/answer/13463073
21. Hardt, D.: The OAuth 2.0 authorization framework (2012). https://datatracker.ietf.org/doc/html/rfc6749
22. Jannett, L., Mladenov, V., Mainka, C., Schwenk, J.: DISTINCT: identity theft using in-browser communications in dual-window single sign-on. In: Proceedings of the 2022 ACM SIGSAC Conference on Computer and Communications Security, pp. 1553–1567 (2022)
23. Jannett, L., Westers, M., Wich, T., Mainka, C., Mayer, A., Mladenov, V.: SoK: SSO-monitor - the current state and future research directions in single sign-on security measurements. In: 2024 IEEE 9th European Symposium on Security and Privacy (EuroS&P) (2024). https://doi.org/TBD
24. John.Kurkowski: Tldextract (2024). https://pypi.org/project/tldextract/
25. Li, W., Mitchell, C.J., Chen, T.: OAuthGuard: protecting user security and privacy with OAuth 2.0 and OpenID connect. In: Proceedings of the 5th ACM Workshop on Security Standardisation Research Workshop, pp. 35–44 (2019)
26. Liu, X., Liu, J., Wang, W., Zhu, S.: Android single sign-on security: issues, taxonomy and directions. Futur. Gener. Comput. Syst. **89**, 402–420 (2018)
27. du Luxembourg, U.: Androzoo (2016). https://androzoo.uni.lu/
28. Meta: Facebook login best practices (2024). https://developers.facebook.com/docs/facebook-login/best-practices
29. Meta: Permissions/login review (2024). https://developers.facebook.com/docs/facebook-login/guides/permissions/review/
30. Meta: Permissions reference for meta technologies APIs (2024). https://developers.facebook.com/docs/permissions
31. Meta: Permissions with Facebook login (2024). https://developers.facebook.com/docs/facebook-login/guides/permissions/
32. Morkonda, S.G., Chiasson, S., van Oorschot, P.C.: Empirical analysis and privacy implications in OAuth-based single sign-on systems. In: Proceedings of the 20th Workshop on Workshop on Privacy in the Electronic Society, pp. 195–208 (2021)
33. Morkonda, S.G., Chiasson, S., van Oorschot, P.C.: Influences of displaying permission-related information on web single sign-on login decisions. Comput. Secur. **139**, 103666 (2024)

34. Morkonda, S.G., van Oorschot, P.C., Chiasson, S.: Exploring privacy implications in OAuth deployments. arXiv preprint arXiv:2103.02579 (2021)
35. Morkonda Gnanasekaran, S., Chiasson, S., Van Oorschot, P.: "sign in with... privacy": Timely disclosure of privacy differences among web SSO login options. ACM Transactions on Privacy and Security (2025)
36. Olano, F.: google-play-API (2024). https://github.com/facundoolano/google-play-api
37. Pham, T.H., Vo, Q.H., Dao, H., Fukuda, K.: SSOLogin: a framework for automated web privacy measurement with SSO logins. In: Proceedings of the 18th Asian Internet Engineering Conference, pp. 69–77 (2023)
38. Philippaerts, P., Preuveneers, D., Joosen, W.: OAuch: exploring security compliance in the OAuth 2.0 ecosystem. In: Proceedings of the 25th International Symposium on Research in Attacks, Intrusions and Defenses, pp. 460–481 (2022)
39. Pochat, V.L., Van Goethem, T., Tajalizadehkhoob, S., Korczyński, M., Joosen, W.: Tranco: A research-oriented top sites ranking hardened against manipulation. arXiv preprint arXiv:1806.01156 (2018)
40. Pourali, S., Samarasinghe, N., Mannan, M.: Hidden in plain sight: exploring encrypted channels in android apps. In: Proceedings of the 2022 ACM SIGSAC Conference on Computer and Communications Security, pp. 2445–2458 (2022)
41. Rahat, T.A., Feng, Y., Tian, Y.: Cerberus: query-driven scalable vulnerability detection in OAuth service provider implementations. In: Proceedings of the 2022 ACM SIGSAC Conference on Computer and Communications Security, pp. 2459–2473 (2022)
42. Sadqi, Y., Belfaik, Y., Safi, S.: Web OAuth-based SSO systems security. In: Proceedings of the 3rd International Conference on Networking, Information Systems & Security, pp. 1–7 (2020)
43. Shi, S., Wang, X., Lau, W.C.: MoSSOT: an automated blackbox tester for single sign-on vulnerabilities in mobile applications. In: Proceedings of the 2019 ACM Asia Conference on Computer and Communications Security, pp. 269–282 (2019)
44. Soni, R.: LoginRadius releases consumer identity trend report 2022, key login methods highlighted (2022). https://www.loginradius.com/blog/identity/loginradius-consumer-identity-trend-report-2022/
45. Team, B.: Most popular apps (2024). https://backlinko.com/most-popular-apps
46. UltrafunkAmsterdam: undetected_chromedriver (2024). https://pypi.org/project/undetected-chromedriver/
47. Wang, K., Bai, G., Dong, N., Dong, J.S.: A framework for formal analysis of privacy on SSO protocols. In: Security and Privacy in Communication Networks: 13th International Conference, SecureComm 2017, Niagara Falls, ON, Canada, October 22–25, 2017, Proceedings 13, pp. 763–777. Springer (2018)
48. Wei, H., Hassanshahi, B., Bai, G., Krishnan, P., Vorobyov, K.: MoScan: a model-based vulnerability scanner for web single sign-on services. In: Proceedings of the 30th ACM SIGSOFT International Symposium on Software Testing and Analysis, pp. 678–681 (2021)
49. Zhou, Y., Evans, D.: SSOScan: automated testing of web applications for single sign-on vulnerabilities. In: 23rd USENIX Security Symposium (USENIX Security 14), pp. 495–510 (2014)

Replication-Based Fault-Tolerant Scheduling Algorithm for Heterogeneous Real-Time Systems

Yanghao Yu[1,2], Jiayin Zhou[1,2], and Jing Wu[1,2(✉)]

[1] School of Computer Science and Technology, Wuhan University of Science and Technology, Wuhan 430065, Hubei, China
{yuyanghao,wujingecs}@wust.edu.cn
[2] Hubei Province Key Laboratory of Intelligent Information Processing and Real-Time Industrial System, Wuhan 430065, China

Abstract. In real-time systems, low response time and high reliability are critical yet conflicting performance metrics. The scheduling of parallel applications with data dependencies in heterogeneous systems has been proven to be an NP-complete problem. Traditional active replication methods, while improving reliability, often introduce resource contention, increasing task response times and jeopardizing real-time requirements. To address this challenge, this paper proposes a Maximum Reliability Fault-Tolerance Algorithm based on Limited Replication (LDFTS). Our algorithm first generates an initial scheduling solution using a limited replication strategy, then iteratively replicates tasks starting from the least reliable ones while verifying temporal constraints, ultimately yielding an optimal replication scheme that maximizes system reliability. Experiments on heterogeneous multi-core platforms demonstrate that, compared to DB-FAST and BLMR, our algorithm significantly enhances system reliability while reducing the overall scheduling length.

Keywords: heterogeneous multi-core · real-time systems · task replication · reliability · scheduling algorithm

1 Introduction

With the increasing demand for computation and the rapid development of computer science and technology, parallel and distributed computing [13–15] has gradually become a hot spot for research, and hard real-time systems have been widely used in industrial control, UAV navigation, autonomous driving, and other fields. Such systems are usually composed of multiple heterogeneous processors, which can efficiently execute parallel tasks while consuming low power [16–18]. We usually represent our set of tasks as a *directed acyclic graph* (DAG), and in modern applications, these tasks not only have obvious data dependencies, but also some strict priority constraints, and it has been proven that the task scheduling problem in such systems is NP-complete, and the difficulty of its solution rises dramatically as the system size becomes larger.

W. Liang et al. (Eds.): SecureComm 2025, LNICST 690, pp. 296–312, 2026.
https://doi.org/10.1007/978-3-032-23456-8_16

In real-world operating environments, systems usually face severe reliability challenges [20, 26], whether they are personal hosts, servers, or embedded devices that are subject to disturbances such as those in the external environment during use, which may lead to failures. There are two types of failure: transient failures and permanent failures. Permanent failures are usually caused by defects in the hardware itself, causing the processor to malfunction and requiring hardware replacement; transient failures are usually caused by electromagnetic interference, cosmic ray radiation, and other factors, affecting only the execution of tasks at the current point in time and occurring at a relatively high frequency. Both transient faults and permanent faults will affect the normal execution of the system. Reliability is an important indicator in real-time systems. This paper focuses on the study of transient faults under the improvement of reliability.

In order to improve the reliability of the system, two fault-tolerant techniques are proposed, namely, active replication and passive replication techniques. Active replication is to consider the replication of tasks before the scheduling starts, assigning the execution scheme of all tasks and their replica tasks in advance, and the main and replica task sets are executed concurrently during the scheduling process. Passive replication uses checkpointing techniques, which usually set up checkpoints at certain nodes of the task execution, and when the checking error occurs, the passive replicated task is re-executed to ensure the normal execution of the program, which requires additional hardware devices for checking. Both techniques increase the number of executions of tasks in the program due to replication thus increasing the overhead of the system, and since passive replication also requires additional hardware costs, in this paper we consider the active replication approach to improve the reliability of the system.

Excessive replication will lead to a large amount of redundancy in the system, significantly increasing the response time of the system and affecting the real-time requirements, so our algorithm will limit the number of replications per task. We improve the reliability of the system by replicating low reliability task nodes when the real-time requirement can be met.

The contributions of this paper are mainly as follows:

1) A new fault-tolerant scheduling algorithm is proposed, which can shorten the scheduling length while improving the reliability of the system, thus solving the problem of reduced system reliability due to transient failures in the system.
2) The effectiveness of our algorithm is proved experimentally, compared with DB-FTSA and BLMR algorithms, our algorithm LDFTS algorithm shortens the scheduling length by an average of 4.57% to 6.01%, and improves the reliability by an average of 14.62% to 15.26%.

2 Related Work

2.1 Scheduling Based on Replication

The purpose of replication-based scheduling is to increase the number of redundant copies of a task through replication, allowing subsequent tasks to execute faster and reducing the impact of inter-task communication costs. This type of scheduling usually has three phases: a prioritization phase, a replication phase, and a processor selection phase. Earlier Ahmad et al. proposed the *Critical Path Fast Duplication* (CPFD) algorithm [1], which duplicates the parent of a task that has a parent node on the critical path and the parent node is not executing on the same processor to execute on the same processor as the task without delaying the execution of the current task; Kruatrachue et al. proposed the *Heuristic Duplication* (DSH) algorithm [2], which duplicates the predecessor task of a task that is waiting to be the predecessor task of a scheduled task into the free time slot of the current processor to reduce the running time of the whole system. When the HEFT algorithm was proposed, Tang et al. proposed the *Heterogeneous Earliest Fulfillment Duplication* (HEFD) algorithm [3], which uses an iterative task allocation strategy that traverses all the processors when scheduling node n_i, calculates the *Data Arrival Time* (DAT) of the predecessor task n_j in a non-increasing order, and then duplicates n_j if n_i can start earlier.

2.2 Fault-Tolerant Scheduling

Fault-tolerant scheduling is a key guarantee for real-time systems, which is mainly used to increase the reliability value of the system by increasing redundant copies of tasks through task replication to ensure the smooth execution of tasks. Wei et al. proposed the DB-FTSA algorithm [4], which uses deadlines as constraints and replicates the tasks in the order of their priority to increase the reliability of the system. Liu et al. proposed the DBSA algorithm [5], which aims to increase the reliability of the system by replicating the permanent failures that occur in the system. The purpose is to increase the reliability of the system by replicating the permanent failures of the system. Mao et al. proposed the BLMR algorithm [8], which argues that when the number of backup tasks is more than two, it does not help much to increase the reliability of the application, so it needs to go back and forth to each task twice in order to fully utilize the processor resources, thus increasing the reliability of the system. Wei et al. [19] studied reliable data collection techniques in underwater wireless sensor networks, which is very useful in various applications [20–22]. Song et al. [23] proposed a retraining strategy-based domain adaptation network for intelligent fault diagnosis, which inspired many new followers in optimization approach in that direction [24–26]. Chen et al. [27] proposed multicenter hierarchical federated learning with fault-tolerance mechanisms, which leads the machine learning approach for fault-tolerance research [28–30].

Unlike the above algorithms, our algorithm studies real-time heterogeneous systems with data-dependent applications, and the use of restricted replication not only meets the demand for real-time but also solves the problem of transient failures in the system that lead to a reduction in the reliability of the system.

3 Model and Problem Definition

3.1 System Model

We assume that a heterogeneous system consists of multiple heterogeneous processors that form a processor set $P = \{p_1, p_2, ..., p_m\}$, , where m is the number of processes. It is assumed that these processors are fully connected, communicate over a bus (interconnect), and that there is no contention during processing [10–12].

3.2 Application Model

In task scheduling, we usually represent our application model with prioritization constraints by a weighted directed acyclic graph (DAG) G = {T, P, C, W}. As shown in Fig. 1, $T = \{t_1, t_2, ..., t_n\}$ denotes the set sum of tasks and n is the number of tasks. P is the set of processors. C is the set sum of communication costs, representing the transmission delay between each task, denoted on each edge, and $c_{i,j} \in C$ denotes the task t_i to task t_j communication cost. W is an m*n adjacency matrix, shown in Table 1, $w_{i,j}$ denoting the execution time of a task t_i on a processor p_j. Where pred(t_i) denotes the predecessor task of the task t_i, the ingress task has no predecessor task; succ(t_i) denotes the successor task of the task t_i, the egress task has no successor task, and if there are more than one ingress or egress task in the DAG graph, a virtual ingress or egress task with no weight and with dependency relationship is added.

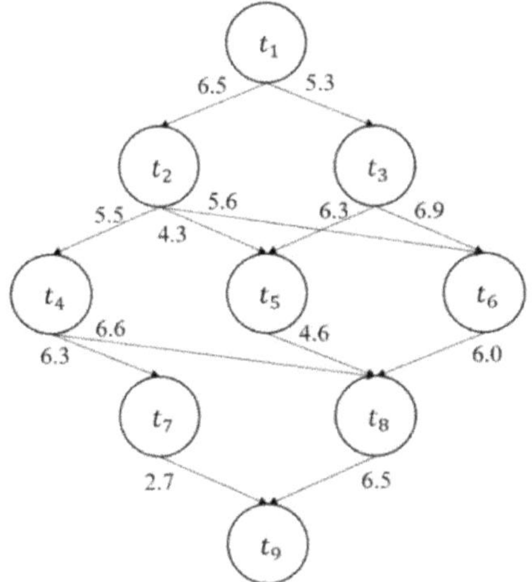

Fig. 1. Apply DAG graph

Table. 1. Task execution schedule on different processing levels

	p1	p2	p3	p4
t1	4.1	2.1	2.2	
t2	9.8	6.8	11.8	13.3
t3	14.1	4.9	12.3	7.8
t4	4.0	6.9	4.2	3.8
t5	7.1	16.2	18.0	14.5
t6	16.4	6.3	6.4	11.9
t7	16.7	20.4	21.1	18.3
t8	7.7	12.2	8.9	11.7

(continued)

Table. 1. (*continued*)

	p1	p2	p3	p4
t9	7.1	6.9	4.9	3.0

3.3 Reliability Model

The incidence of transient failures of tasks in general DAG graph-based applications follows a pineapple distribution [6]. We denote the reliability of a task t_i on a processor p_k by $R(t_i, p_k)$:

$$1 - R(t_i, p_k) = 1 - e^{-\lambda_k W_{i,k}} \tag{1}$$

where λ_k denotes the failure rate per unit time for different processors and $w_{i,k}$ denotes the execution time of the task t_i on the processor p_k. So when the probability of a task execution failing once is:

$$1 - R(t_i, p_k) = 1 - e^{-\lambda_k w_{i,k}} \tag{2}$$

Methods to improve reliability mainly use task replication, executing multiple identical tasks can improve the reliability of that task and reduce the probability that the application will fail to run due to an error in that task. Denote the set of task V_i and its backup task by $V = \{V_i, V_i\}$. The application will only fail when both of them are wrong at the same time, so the more backup tasks the higher the reliability, but in order to balance the execution time, the algorithm in this paper supports backing up at most one task. According to the reliability formula [1] and [2] the probability of task execution failure after replication can be calculated as:

$$1 - R_i = \prod_{t_i \in V} (1 - R(t_i, \mathrm{proc}(t_i))) \tag{3}$$

where V contains the master copy task after replication and proc(v) denotes the processor core on which task t_i runs. So the probability of successful execution of the replicated task is:

$$R_i = 1 - \prod_{t_i \in v} (1 - R(t_i, \mathrm{proc}(t_i))) \tag{4}$$

Successful execution of the application requires that each task can be executed successfully, so the reliability of the whole application is calculated as:

$$R(G) = \prod_{i=1}^{n} R_i \tag{5}$$

In this paper, we use active replication, i.e., a running scheme that schedules all tasks before actually running the application, without considering passive replication for error checking. The algorithm in this paper does not schedule the backup $t_i\prime$ of task t_i on the same processor core since the backup task also needs to be computed and putting multiple identical tasks together in sequence cannot reduce the completion time.

3.4 Problem Description

In fault-tolerant algorithms, we try to give a maximum scheduling length, or deadline denoted as D. Our goal is to optimize reliability by replicating under this condition, otherwise unlimited replication may result in a very high reliability, but the scheduling length will grow extremely fast and will not be able to meet the real-time requirements of the application.

We study task scheduling and fault tolerance. So, our problem is input n node DAG G = {T, P, C, W} and there is a time cutoff D in a heterogeneous system $P = \{p_1, p_2, ..., p_m\}$ with m processors. We need to optimize our reliability as much as possible while satisfying the time cutoff D. We need to optimize our reliability as much as possible.

$$R(G) = \max \prod_{i=1}^{n} R_i \tag{6}$$

Subject to:

$$makespan \leq D \tag{7}$$

4 Fault Tolerant Scheduling Algorithm Based on Replication

4.1 Scheduling Strategy

We use $\overline{w}_i$ to denote the average computational cost of the task t_i over all processors, with the formula:

$$\overline{w_i} = \sum_{j=1}^{p} w_{i,j}/p \tag{8}$$

We use level(t_i) to denote the level at which the task is located, which is the maximum value of the number of edges in the path from the entry task to the current task node, computed by the following formula, assuming that the level of the entry task level(entry) = 0:

$$level(t_i) = \max_{q \in pred(t_i)} \{level(q)\} + 1 \tag{9}$$

DP(level) denotes the maximum number of replications of a task at a particular level, calculated by the following formula:

$$DP(level) = num(p) - \sum_{t_i \in V_{level}} t_i \tag{10}$$

where num(P) is the number of processsor cores and V_{level} is the current tier level.

TDP(t_i) denotes the maximum number of replications for a particular task and is calculated by the following formula:

$$TDP(t_i) = \sum_{j=1}^{x} t_j - 1, t_j \in succ(t_i) \tag{11}$$

$EST(t_i, p_j)$ denotes the earliest time at which a task t_i starts executing on a processor p_k, which is calculated by the following formula:

$$EST(n_i, p_j) = \max\{T_{avl}(p_j), \max_{t_m \in pred(t_i)}\{AFT(t_m) + c_{m,i}\}\} \tag{12}$$

where $T_{avl}(p_j)$ denotes the processor p_j ready time, $AFT(t_m)$ is the actual completion time of the task t_m, and the communication cost is 0 if the predecessor task t_m is also executing on the processor p_j.

$EFT(t_i, p_j)$ denotes the earliest completion time of the task t_i on the processor p_k, which is obtained by adding the earliest start time to the execution time:

$$EFT(t_i, p_j) = EST(t_i, p_j) = w_{i,j} \tag{13}$$

$DAT(t_i, t_j)$ denotes the time when the task t_i data arrives at the task t_j, which is the earliest possible start time of the successor task t_j, and is obtained from the following equation:

$$DAT(t_i, t_j) = AFT(t_i) + c_{i,j} \tag{14}$$

Not considered in the case of evaluation replication, task t_i and t_j executed on the same processor.

Our algorithm first uses the replication strategy of Guo et al. [7] for the initial scheduling of the application to optimize the scheduling length, then the initial reliability of each task is incrementally sorted and then traversed from low to high reliability, replication and scheduling is performed according to our algorithm, if the deadline is met then replication is performed otherwise no fault tolerant replication is performed, the specific pseudo-code of the execution process is shown in Algorithm 1.

Algorithm 1:LDFTS Algorithm Scheduling Function_allotProcessor

---

Input:application's task set G, execution time matrix W, heterogeneous multicore processor P,OCT table with rank, parameter flist (empty array by default)

1. Re-calculate DP,TDP table for all tasks,reset status of tasks and processors.

2. Create an empty list ready-list and put t_{entry} as initial task.

3. while ready-list is not empty do

4. $t_i \leftarrow$ Task popped from ready-list which has the highest $rank_{oct}$.

5.   for processor p_j in processor-set P do

6.   Calculate EFT(t_i, p_j) and o_{EFT} (t_i, p_j),record EFT(t_i, p_j) to eftList.

7.   end for

8.   Assign task t_i to the processor p_{best} which minimize o_{EFT} value.

9.   if DP[level(t_i)] > 0 and TDP(t_i) > 0 then

10.   Create empty list skipped to record tasks that has less DAT.

11.   for processor p_d in processor-set P- p_{best} do

12.   Calculate EFT(t_i, p_d) and minDAT(t_i).

13.   if EFT(t_i, p_d) $\geqslant$ minDAT(t_i) then

14.   ADD t_{min} that minimize minDAT(t_i) to skipped.

15.   Reduce TDP(t_i) by 1,then continue rhe loop.

16.   else

17.   Duplicate task t_i on processor p_d .

18.   Reduce DP[level(t_i)] and TDP(t_i) by 1.

19.   end if

20.   Once TDP(t_i) < 1,break task duplication loop.

21.   end for

22.   end if

23.   if t_i task id in flist and t_i not duplicated then

24. $p_f \leftarrow$ Find processor that has minimim EFT in eftList except p_{best} .

25.   Duplicate task t_i on processor p_f .

26.   end if

27.   Update ready-list with $t_j \in$ succ(t_i) if t_j not in ready-list.

28. end while

Output:scheduling scheme for this iteration based on the flist parameter

---

The LDFTS algorithm first calculates the initial finite replication limit table DP, TDP based on Eqs. 10 and 11, then calculates the OCT table required for scheduling as well as rank_{oct}, puts the entry task into the ready-list ready-list. Line five enters the scheduling phase calculates the EFT and O_{EFT} and records the core P_{best} that makes the O_{EFT} smallest, scheduling the task on it. The ninth line starts replication only if the replication policy is satisfied. Line ten enters the replication phase and line thirteen starts replication judgment to determine which replicas can lower the deadline. After line twenty-three, the fault-tolerant replication phase is entered, with the parameter flist controlling the tasks that can be fault-tolerant replicated, and active replication is performed if the task t_i in the schedule is not replicated and its task id exists in flist; in line twenty-four, the cores that minimize the EFT of the task are identified based on the previously saved eftList, and are excluded P_{best} to ensure that the task can be scheduled in parallel to the other cores.

Algorithm 2 :LDFTS algorithm

Inputs: application task set G, execution time matrix W,heterogeneous multicore processorP

1.   Calculate OCT table and rank_{oct}
2.   initialScheme ← Scheduling upon _allotProcessor([]).
3.   rlist ← Task id and corresponding reliability of tasks in initialScheme.
4.   Sort rlist in ascending order of tasks reliability,create empty array flist.
5.   for task id r in rlist do
6.   Append task id r to flist.
7.   tmpSchene ← Scheduling upon _allotProcessor(flist).
8.   if makespan of tmpScheme exceeds M then
9.   Remove task id r from flist.
10.   end if
11.   end for
12.   Scheduling to system using _allotProcessor(flist).

Output:Fault-tolerant scheduling solution for applications

The overall algorithm requires several iterations to determine the final solution, and Algorithm 2 shows the pseudo-code of the external complete flow of the LDFTS algorithm. First the OCT table and rank_{oct} is computed and used to model the scheduling. After that, an empty array is used instead of flist for the initial scheduling; the reliability of each task can be determined after the scheduling. As shown in the third line of Algorithm 2, the ids of the applications and the reliability of the corresponding tasks are stored in rlist, and then sorted in ascending order, with the one with the smallest reliability at the top; after that, in the fifth line, a loop is performed on the set of tasks to iterate over the tasks, take out the ids of the tasks from the rlist in order, add them to flist, which represents the list of task ids that are taken into account in the fault-tolerant replication policy, and simulate scheduling based on the list; if this list is empty, the scheduling is done in the first line. If the result of this scheduling exceeds the deadline M, the fault-tolerant replication of the task corresponding to r is discarded, otherwise it will be kept in flist; after the simulation of all task ids, the flist is the final list of ids that can be fault-tolerant replicated, and the twelfth line will be dispatched to the real system to complete the scheduling.

LDFTS algorithm due to the use of multiple iterations for scheduling simulation, it will be in the simulation of scheduling to increase the time complexity of v, its increase in fault-tolerant replication strategy (as shown in Algorithm 1 of the twenty-three to twenty-six rows) does not increase the algorithm's time complexity, so the LDFTS algorithm overall time complexity is o(v^3*p).

4.2 Experiment

This section briefly compares the scheduling results of the application modeled in Chapter 3 using the LDFTS algorithm for fault-tolerant scheduling and with the DB-FTSA algorithm and BLMR algorithm, which are consistent with the research. The comparison metrics include not only the scheduling length makespan, but also the reliability of the application, R(G), since our algorithm takes into account both real-time and reliability.

Figures 2, 3 and 4 show the results of scheduling applications using DB-FTSA, BLMR and our own LDFTS algorithm respectively, where the white color indicates the main task and the gray color indicates the replica task, and it is proved that our algorithm not only improves the reliability of the system effectively, but also shortens the running time of the application.

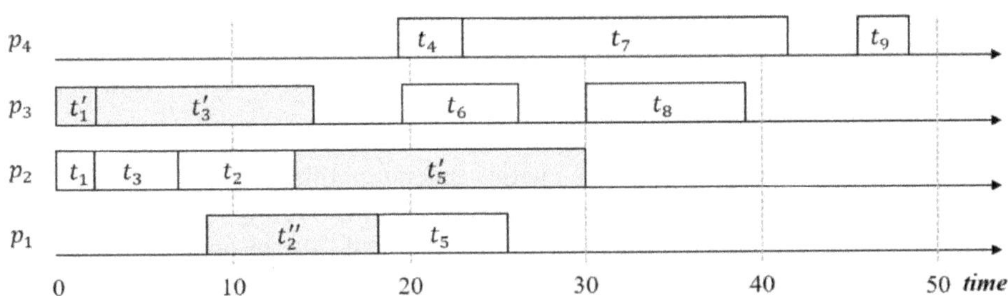

Fig. 2. Example diagram of DB-FTSA algorithm scheduling, makespan = 48.5, R(G) = 65.28%

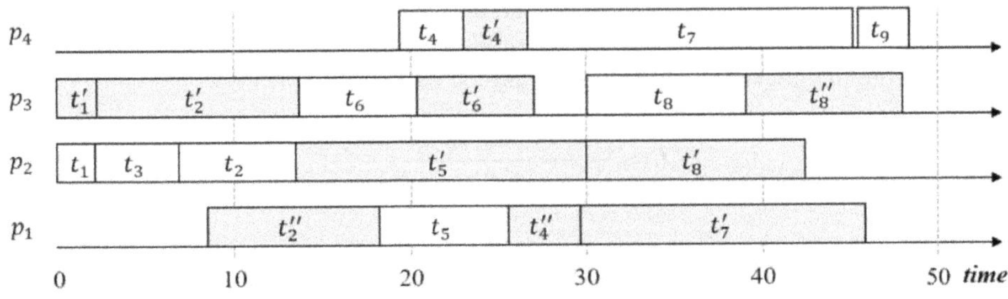

Fig. 3. Example diagram of BLMR algorithm scheduling, makespan = 48.5, R(G) = 82.54

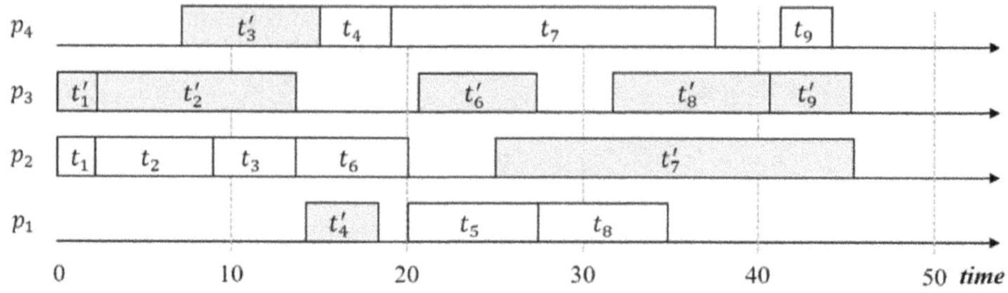

Fig. 4. Example diagram of LDFTS algorithm scheduling, makespan = 45.7, R(G) = 88.09%

Our algorithm LDFTS reduces the scheduling time by 5.77% compared to DB-FTSA and BLMR, and improves the reliability by 25.89% vs. 6.3%, which is a more significant improvement.

5   Experimental Results and Discussion

In this section, we evaluate the effectiveness of our proposed algorithm by comparing our algorithm with two excellent fault-tolerant scheduling algorithms, DB-FTSA and BLMR. We will also perform random generation of task graphs using various parameters as well as simulation of real applications and finally present the comparison results for each parameter. The simulation of the application model and processor model, the analysis of the results and the visualization of the data have been implemented using Python language on a computer with a CPU of 3.50 GHz and 32 GB of RAM.

5.1   Algorithm Comparison Metrics

Comparison of scheduling algorithms metrics generation time is one of the most basic measures of algorithmic strengths and weaknesses [5]. In fault-tolerant scheduling, it is equally important, although in order to meet the real-time or application has special requirements on time, fault-tolerant scheduling algorithms need to complete the scheduling within the deadline D, the results produced are also different [9]. In addition to fault-tolerant scheduling algorithms also need to ensure that the application can be executed normally to ensure the reliability of the system, so the reliability of the algorithm scheduling results is also one of the indicators of the strength of the algorithm.

Since the scheduling time of large applications is too long, this paper uses Scheduling Length Ratio (SLR) to normalize the scheduling length to a smaller range to evaluate the scheduling length of the algorithm is defined by Eq. 15.

$$SLR = \frac{makespan}{\sum t_i \in CP_{\text{MIN}} \min_{p_j \in P}\{w_{i,j}\}} \tag{15}$$

where the denominator is the sum of the minimum execution times of the tasks on the path.

The comparison experiments in this chapter will be scheduled under the constraint that the deadline D is set to 1.1 times the completion time of the PEFT, while the failure rate λ of each processor core in the simulation will be set uniformly to simplify the problem. The comparison of algorithms will be analyzed and compared based on makespan, SLR,R(G), SLR is calculated as shown in Eq. 15, and the application reliability is calculated based on Eq. 5 and the related contents of the subsection on reliability model. Among them, the lower the value of completion time and SLR the better the algorithm is, the higher the reliability R(G) the more fault tolerant the algorithm is, the strength of the algorithm is based on this comprehensive assessment of the conclusion.

5.2 Experiments and Results Analysis Based on Randomly Generated Task Sets

In order to evaluate the skills we define some parameters are 1) the number of tasks n; 2) CCR, the ratio of the sum of the weights of the edges in the DAG to the sum of the node weights; 3) β, the processor heterogeneity factor; and 4) the number of processor cores, processor.

The generated parameters in this section are shown in Table 2.

Table. 2. Randomly generate a list of parameter values

parameters	experimental value
n	[10,20,30,40,50]
CCR	[0.5,1,4,8,10,20]
β	[0.5,1,1.5]
processor	[8, 15]

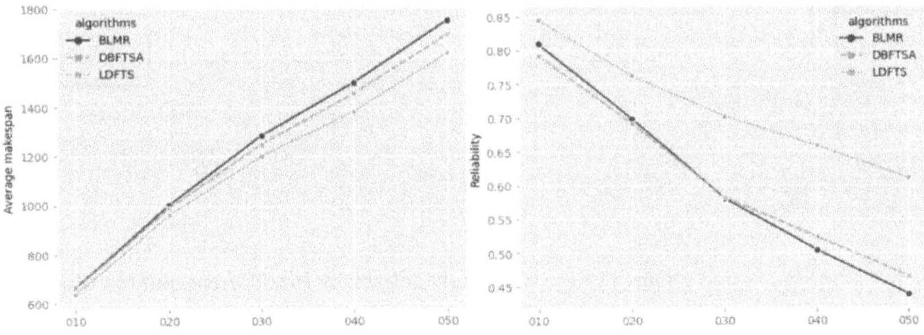

Fig. 5. Comparative line graphs of (a) scheduling length and (b) reliability for different number of tasks

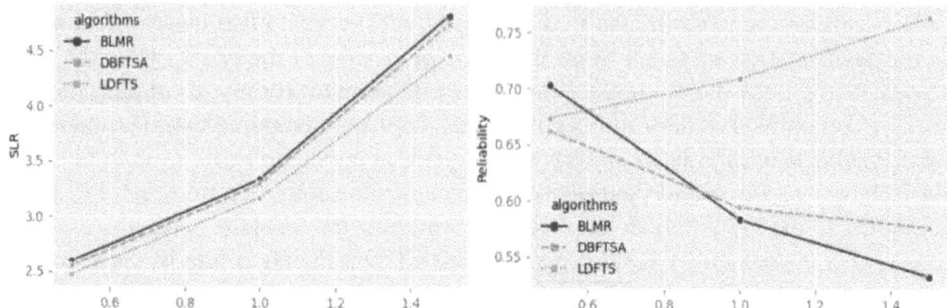

Fig. 6. Comparative line plots of (a) SLR and (b) reliability under different processor heterogeneity β

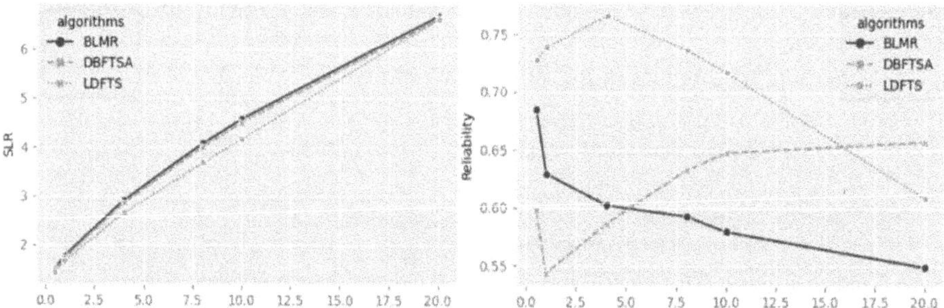

Fig. 7. Comparative line graphs of (a) SLR and (b) reliability under different CCRs

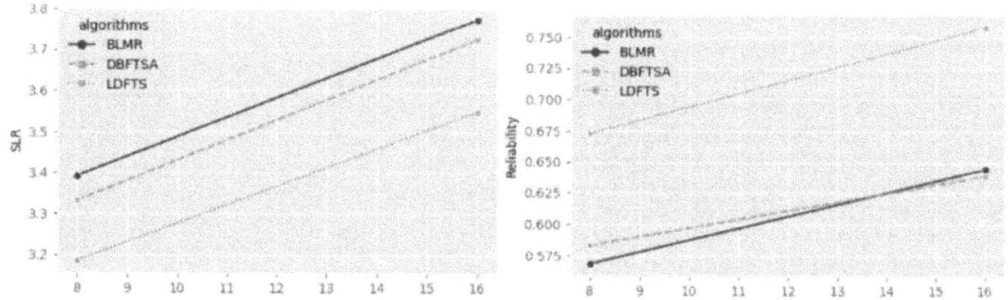

Fig. 8. Comparative line graphs of (a) SLR and (b) reliability for different number of processor cores

From the above comparison graph, it can be seen that the overall experimental results of the BLMR algorithm, compared to DB-FTSA, do not have a large gap in terms of reliability, and will outperform the DB-FTSA algorithm in specific cases, but the scheduling length is consistently higher than that of the DB-FTSA algorithm. However, the LDFTS algorithm proposed in this chapter not only outperforms the other two algorithms in terms of average scheduling length but also has a great improvement in reliability (Figs. 5, 6, 7 and 8).

5.3 Experiments and Results Analysis Based on Real Applications

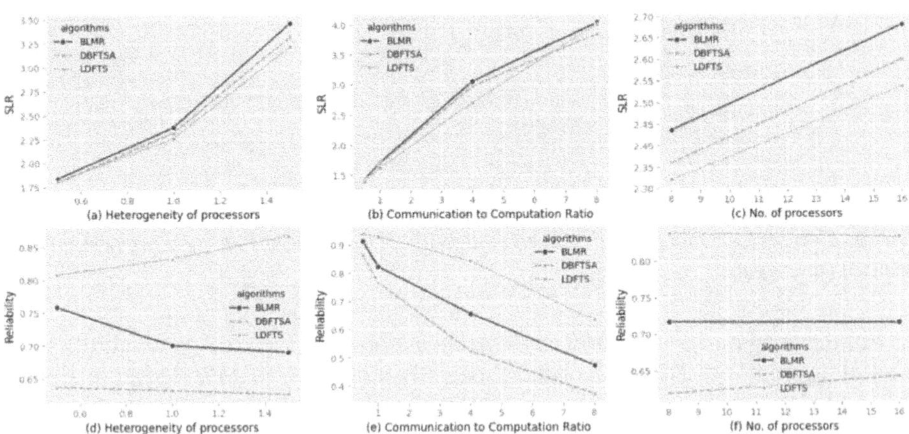

Fig. 9. Comparative line graphs of SLR and reliability of Gaussian elimination elements applied to different parameters.

Figure 9 shows the comparison between LDFTS algorithm and the comparison algorithm in simulated scheduling with Gaussian elimination application. The upper part of Fig. 9(a), (b), (c) shows the SLR comparison results, and the lower part of Fig. 9(d), (e), (f) shows the reliability comparison results. According to Fig. 9(a), (d) it can be seen that under the simulation of the heterogeneity parameter β the LDFTS algorithm shortens the scheduling length on average (1.57%,4.77%,7.06%) and improves the reliability on average (6.04%,15.87%,20.45%) for the BLMR algorithm, respectively; and compares the DB-FTSA algorithm with the average shortening of the scheduling length (-0.51%, 2.53%, and 3.09%) and average reliability improvement (21.16%,24.13%,27.89%). Figure 9(b), (e) shows that the scheduling length of LDFTS algorithm is inferior to DB-FTSA algorithm at higher CCR, but the improvement in reliability is larger. As for the number of processor cores, Figs. 9(c) and (f) show that the LDFTS algorithm outperforms the other two compared algorithms in terms of scheduling length and reliability.

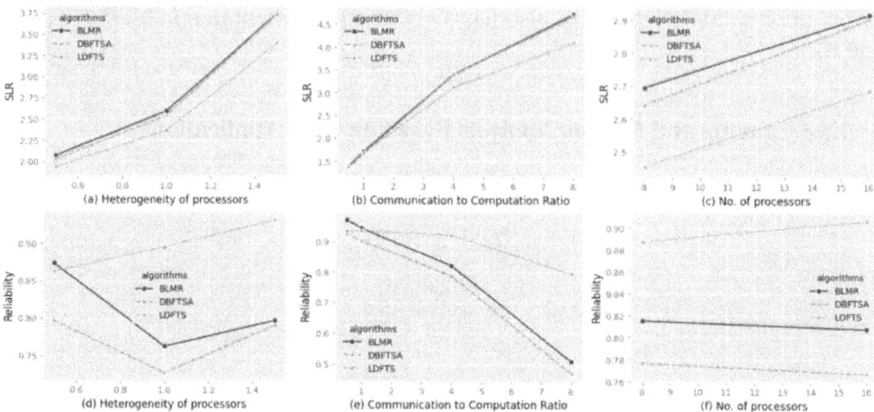

Fig. 10. Comparative line plots of SLR and reliability of fast Fourier transform applications with different parameters.

For the fast Fourier transform application, as shown in Fig. 10, the reliability of the scheduling result of LDFTS algorithm is slightly inferior to BLMR algorithm at lower CCR and processor heterogeneity, and LDFTS algorithm is better in the rest of the cases, no matter in the completion time or reliability. Comprehensive fast Fourier transform application experimental results, LDFTS algorithm than BLMR algorithm to shorten the scheduling length of an average of 8.39%, an average increase in reliability of 9.51%; than the DB-FTSA algorithm to shorten the scheduling length of an average of 7.30%, an average increase in reliability of 13.93%.

The experimental results based on real applications show that the scheduling length and reliability of LDFTS algorithm are better than BLMR algorithm and DB-FTSA algorithm in the average case.

6 Conclusions and Future Work

In this paper, we studied the fault-tolerant scheduling algorithm in real-time systems and proposed a new fault-tolerant scheduling algorithm for real-time systems based on limited duplication, the LDFTS (*Limited Duplication based Fault Tolerant Scheduling*) algorithm. The algorithm first makes the limited duplication to generate the initial scheduling results, which can shorten the scheduling length while improving the reliability of some tasks; after that, it is iterated according to the fault-tolerant strategy to maximize the application reliability while meeting the real-time requirements, and finally arrives at the fault-tolerant scheduling results. The experimental results showed that we not only shorten the scheduling length but also improve the reliability of the system. In the future, we will consider improving the reliability of the system with the addition of energy consumption limitations.

References

1. Ahmad, I., Kwok, Y.: A new approach to scheduling parallel programs using task duplication. IEEE. Int. Conf. Parallel Process. **2**, 47–51 (1994)

2. Kruatrachue, B., Lewis, T.G.: Grain size determination for parallel processing. IEEE Softw. **5**, 23–32 (1998)

3. Tang, X., Li, K., Liao, G., Li, R.: List scheduling with duplication for heterogeneous computing systems. J. Parallel Distrib. Comput. **70**, 323–329 (2010)

4. Wei, M., Liu, J., Li, T., Xu, X., Hu, W., Zhao, D.: Fault-tolerant scheduling of real-time tasks on heterogeneous systems. In: 2017 12thIEEE Conference on Industrial Electronics and Applications (ICIEA), pp. 1006–1011. IEEE (2017)

5. Liu, J., Wei, M., Hu, W., Xu, X., Ouyang, A.: Task scheduling with fault-tolerance in real-time heterogeneous systems. J. Syst. Architect. **90**, 23–33 (2018)

6. Xie, G., et al.: Minimizing redundancy to satisfy reliability requirement for a parallel application on heterogeneous service-oriented systems. IEEE Trans. Serv. Comput. (2017)

7. Guo, H., Zhou, J., Gu, H.: Limited duplication-based list scheduling algorithm for heterogeneous computing system. Micromachines **13**, 1067 (2022)

8. Mao, D., Hu, W., Gan, Y., Liu, J., Gu, H.: Fault-tolerant scheduling algorithm based on local maximum reliability replication policy in real-time heterogeneous systems. SMC, 3192–3197 (2022)

9. Abdulhamid, S.M., Abd Latiff, M.S., Madni, S.H.H., Abdullahi, M.: Fault tolerance aware scheduling technique for cloud computing environment using dynamic clustering algorithm. Neural Comput. Appl. **29**(1), 279–293 (2016). https://doi.org/10.1007/s00521-016-2448-8

10. Roy, A., Aydin, H., Zhu, D.: Energy-aware standby-sparing on heterogeneous multicore systems. In: 2017 54th ACM/EDAC/IEEE Design Automation Conference (DAC), pp. 1–6, IEEE (2017)

11. Li, J., Qiu, M., Niu, J., Yang, L., Zhu, Y., Ming, Z.: Thermal-aware task scheduling in 3D chip multiprocessor with real-time constrained workloads. ACM Trans. Embed. Comput. Syst. (TECS) **12**(2), 1–22 (2013)

12. Shao, Z., Wang, M., et al.: Real-time dynamic voltage loop scheduling for multi-core embedded systems. IEEE Trans. Circ. Syst. II Express Briefs **54**(5), 445–449 (2007)

13. Qiu, M., Dai, W., Vasilakos, A.: Loop parallelism maximization for multimedia data processing in mobile vehicular clouds. IEEE Trans. Cloud Comput. **7**(1), 250–258 (2016)

14. Qiu, M., Li, J.: Real-Time Embedded Systems: Optimization, Synthesis, and Networking. CRC Press (2011)

15. Gai, K., Qiu, M., Liu, M., Xiong, Z.: In-memory big data analytics under space constraints using dynamic programming. Future Gener. Comput. Syst. **83**, 219–227

16. Gao, Y., Iqbal, S., et al.: Performance and power analysis of high-density multi-GPGPU architectures: a preliminary case study. In: IEEE 17th HPCC (2015)

17. Huang, H., Chaturvedi, V., et al.: Throughput maximization for periodic real-time systems under the maximal temperature constraint. ACM Trans. Embed. Comput. Syst. (TECS) **13**(2s), 1–22 (2014)

18. Qiu, M., Guo, M., et al.: Loop scheduling and bank type assignment for heterogeneous multi-bank memory. J. Parallel Distrib. Comput. **69**(6), 546–558 (2009)

19. Wei, X., Guo, H., et al.: Reliable data collection techniques in underwater wireless sensor networks: a survey. IEEE Comm. Surveys **24**(1), 404–431 (2021)

20. Qiu, M., Qiu, H.: Review on image processing based adversarial example defenses in computer vision. In: IEEE 6th Big Data Security (2020)

21. Qiu, M., Zhang, K., Huang, M.: Usability in mobile interface browsing. Web Intell. Agent Syst. **4**(1), 43–59 (2006)

22. Zhang, Y., Qiu, M., Gao, H.: Communication-efficient stochastic gradient descent ascent with momentum algorithms. IJCAI, 4602–4610 (2023)

23. Song, Y., Li, Y., et al.: Retraining strategy-based domain adaption network for intelligent fault diagnosis. IEEE Trans. Ind. Inf. **16**(9), 6163–6171 (2019)

24. Cui, Y., Cao, K., et al.: Client scheduling and resource management for efficient training in heterogeneous IoT-edge federated learning. IEEE TCAD (2021)
25. Lu, H., Wang, X., et al.: The effects of using chaotic map on improving the performance of multi-objective evolutionary algorithms. Math. Probl. Eng. 1, 2014 (2014)
26. Zhang, Y., Qiu, M., et al.: Health-CPS: healthcare cyber-physical system assisted by cloud and big data. IEEE Syst. J. 11(1), 88–95 (2015)
27. Chen, X., Xu, G., et al.: Multicenter hierarchical federated learning with fault-tolerance mechanisms for resilient edge computing networks. In: IEEE Trans. Neural Networks and Learning Systems, vol. 36, no. 1, pp. 47–61 (2025)
28. Wang, Z., Qiu, M., et al.: Toward fair graph neural networks via real counterfactual samples. Knowl. Inf. Syst. 66(11), 6617–6641 (2024)
29. Qiu, Y., Fang, H., et al.: A closer look at GAN priors: exploiting intermediate features for enhanced model inversion attacks. In: ECCV, vol. 32, pp. 109–126 (2024)
30. Xiong, F., Sun, H., et al.: Graph attention network with high-order neighbor information propagation for social recommendation. IJCAI, 2478–2486 (2024)

Research on Mixed-Precision Optimization Compilation Techniques for Loop Programs in Privacy-Preserving Computing

Fan Luo[1,2]([envelope]) [ORCID], Yonghua Hu[1,2], Huifu Zhang[1,2], Yüxiang Gao[1,2], and Anxing Xie[1,2]

[1] School of Computer Science and Engineering, Hunan University of Science and Technology, Xiangtan 411201, Hunan, China
{22010501023,axie}@mail.hnust.edu.cn, huyh@hnust.cn, hfzhang@hnust.edu.cn
[2] Hunan Key Laboratory for Service Computing and Novel Software Technology, Hunan University of Science and Technology, Xiangtan 411201, Hunan, China

Abstract. The continuous development of privacy-preserving technologies has increasingly enhanced data security, but it also poses challenges to program performance. This contradiction is particularly prominent in resource-constrained scenarios. Related algorithms often contain computational loops. Mapping the precision-tolerant parts of these loops to a low-precision form to obtain performance improvement is a way to alleviate this contradiction. Therefore, under the LLVM (Low-Level Virtual Machine) framework, this paper proposes an automatic mixed-precision code generation method for loop programs. First, the method preprocesses input data to eliminate type conversion operations in data flows. Subsequently, corresponding to the modified data formats, a type conversion optimization strategy is proposed for low-precision computations to accelerate execution speed. Finally, mixed-precision code sequences are generated through sampled analysis of input data combined with error thresholds. Experimental results demonstrate that, under acceptable error tolerance thresholds, the proposed method effectively improves computational speed and minimizes error accumulation. Using the computational speed of high-precision programs as the baseline, the mixed-precision implementation achieves an average 17% improvement in computing performance.

Keywords: Privacy-preserving · LLVM · Mixed-precision Optimization · Code Generation

Supported by Hunan Provincial Natural Science Foundation (No. 2023JJ50019), the Postgraduate Scientific Research Innovation Project of Hunan Province (No. CX20231019).

W. Liang et al. (Eds.): SecureComm 2025, LNICST 690, pp. 313–331, 2026.
https://doi.org/10.1007/978-3-032-23456-8_17

1 Introduction

With increasing emphasis on cybersecurity, privacy-preserving technologies have achieved significant advancements. Current solutions have evolved into a multi-layered architecture encompassing encryption, data anonymization, access control, and other mechanisms, widely applied in healthcare, finance, and other sectors. However, enhanced security often comes at the cost of degraded computational performance. This trade-off becomes particularly acute in resource-constrained embedded scenarios, attributable to two factors: hardware limitations and growing communication overhead/computational complexity. For instance, high-intensity encryption algorithms with extreme computational demands struggle to operate on resource-constrained platforms. Federated learning [20], due to its distributed architecture, requires frequent model parameter transmission and aggregation. Additionally, defense mechanisms against model inversion attacks in federated learning further escalate computational burdens.

In recent years, many new hardware architectures have continuously achieved breakthroughs in performance while continuously enhancing their support for different accuracies. For example, multiple GPU architectures of NVIDIA [15], such as Volta, Turing, Ampere, etc., all provide dedicated hardware support for FP16. Moreover, due to the fact that the FP16 data format occupies less memory, NVIDIA has also optimized memory management. Intel's support for different precisions is also continuously evolving. Some versions of the ARM architecture, such as ARMv7 [2], all support FP16. In addition, Intel uses FP16 in the Sapphire Rapids [14] architecture, and since the Ivy Bridge [18] architecture, FP16 has existed as a storage format.

Common privacy-preserving technologies include cryptographic algorithms, differential privacy [23], federated learning, and reinforcement learning-driven privacy mechanisms [12]. Many of these techniques involve precision-tolerant computations. For instance, intermediate layer computations in federated learning and dynamic training phases often contain precision-insensitive operations. Supported by multi-precision architectures, adopting mixed-precision computations for programs with tolerable accuracy loss can maintain error bounds while enhancing computational efficiency. In 2018, Baidu and NVIDIA [13] jointly published "Mixed Precision Training," proposing the use of FP16 floating-point formats for neural network training to improve overall performance. While most parameters and intermediate results in artificial neural networks are traditionally stored and computed using FP32 formats, increasingly complex model architectures have made FP32 computations a critical performance bottleneck. Strategic mapping of precision-tolerant operations to lower-precision formats effectively reduces memory overhead and accelerates execution. To address challenges in federated learning—including limited device-side computational resources, high communication costs, and insufficient quantization precision—Bokun Wang et al. [19] developed an 8-bit floating-point (FP8) framework. This approach implements device-side FP8 model training through quantization-aware training (QAT), employs stochastic quantization for unbiased communication compression, and optimizes server-side aggregation. Experimental results demonstrate at least 2.9× communication reduction while maintaining model accuracy comparable to FP32 baselines, with accuracy improvements observed in certain scenarios due to regularization effects. This methodology effectively balances efficiency and performance in federated learning, enabling privacy-preserved large-scale collaborative training on edge devices.

The programming process adheres to a principle: a program spends about 90% of its execution time on less than 10% of the code [8]. These codes generally have loop structures. Many loop structures exist in privacy-preserving technology-related algorithms, such as the round function in AES [9] encryption programs, the polynomial multiplication loop in homomorphic encryption [1], and model training in federated learning.

Compared with other programs, loop programs consume more computational resources and have a greater impact on the precision of calculation results. If loop programs that can tolerate a certain amount of error are directly mapped to low - precision computational programs, it often leads to relatively large errors in the results. Such errors are not allowed in many cases. Optimizing loop programs with mixed precision has become an important way to strike a balance between performance and error. However, there are few existing automatic mixed - precision optimization methods for loop programs. How to control the mixed - precision ratio of loop programs to improve performance and reduce errors has become a difficult problem.

To solve this problem, this paper implements an automatic generation framework for mixed-precision optimized code based on error analysis. This framework takes the C language source program as input, further converts the program into LLVM IR (Intermediate Representation) within the LLVM framework, and then uses the subsequent conversion processes and optimization methods to further generate the code optimized with mixed precision.

The rest of this paper is organized as follows: Sect. 2 introduces the relevant concepts of the LLVM compiler and the research status of automatic mixed-precision optimization methods. Section 3 presents the overall framework and implementation, which includes data preprocessing, code mapping methods, low-precision code optimization methods, as well as the analysis and implementation of automatic mixed-precision optimization. Section 4 conducts experimental comparisons and analyses. Finally, a summary and outlook of the entire paper are provided.

2 Related Work

2.1 LLVM Compiler

LLVM is a collection of modular and reusable compiler and toolchain technologies [3]. LLVM IR is the intermediate representation of the LLVM framework. It has the style of RISC assembly and is characterized by not being related to any architecture. Through different front-end compilers, various source languages can be converted into LLVM IR, enabling subsequent compilation to be analyzed and optimized in a general way. There are mainly three forms of expression for IR: textual form, data structure in memory, and bytecode form, and these three forms are equivalent to each other. The memory model of IR is roughly divided into four basic concepts: Module, Function, Basic Block, and Instruction. A source code is regarded as a module, which contains the global information of the source code such as functions, global variables, etc. A function is composed of several basic blocks and arranged in order. Each basic block is composed of several instruction sequences.

LLVM Pass is a plug-in component for the LLVM compiler infrastructure. It is one of the core mechanisms of the LLVM compilation framework. By using this mechanism, researchers can implement the functions of code analysis and transformation according to their own needs. Cherubin et al. [6] proposed a tool named TAFFO for floating-point to fixed-point tuning based on LLVM. It achieves a full trade-off between precision and solution time during precision tuning. In addition, it is provided to users in the form of an LLVM Pass. Rubio-González et al. developed a dynamic program analysis tool called Precimonious [16]. This tool can tentatively reduce the precision of program variables on the premise of meeting precision constraints and performance goals, so as to achieve the goal of improving performance.

In our research, we have successfully implemented a code mapping framework for a new architecture by utilizing the extension mechanism of LLVM Pass. Taking LLVM IR as the input, this framework can generate correct assembly sequences through a series of processes. Additionally, within the code mapping framework, we have implemented an optimization method for low-precision code generation. This method accomplishes the transformation of a high-precision computational program into a low-precision computational program, which serves as a prerequisite for the automatic generation method of mixed-precision optimized code.

2.2   Mixed Precision Optimization

Mixed precision optimization is an optimization method for floating-point calculations. It improves program performance by using floating-point variables and basic functions of different precisions in a mixed manner. Compared with the approach of reducing the overall floating-point precision of the program to improve computational performance, mixed precision optimization can, to a certain extent, mitigate excessive precision loss. Xu J et al. [22] proposed an overall method named PrecTuner. It can automatically generate and optimize the mixed - precision code of affine programs. Eventually, through testing, compared with Luls [5] and Pluto [4], the programs optimized by this method have achieved favorable performance improvements. Lev Denisov et al. proposed a method for rapidly selecting a mixed-precision software-hardware combination based on FPGA [7]. This method supports both floating-point and fixed-point calculations. In benchmark tests, compared with traditional methods, the hardware energy consumption has been significantly reduced, and the computational performance has been improved remarkably.

In addition, mixed-precision optimization can be divided into variable level and operator level in terms of hierarchy. Variable-level mixed-precision optimization is mainly used in various precision tuning and analysis tools, such as AMPT-GA [10], FPTuner [17], Autoscaler For C [11], and so on. Operator-level mixed-precision optimization improves the overall efficiency of the code by using operators with different precisions. A typical application is mixed-precision training in the field of artificial intelligence.

At present, the main research directions of mixed-precision optimization mainly focus on the levels of variable declaration and operators, and there is very little research on the optimization methods for the loop structure of programs. Compared with a complete low-precision computational program, a program using mixed precision has fewer errors. In addition, the mixing ratio of different precisions affects the magnitude of the errors. Therefore, the mixed-precision optimization method in this paper is guided by the relative error introduced in the process of input data precision conversion, further predicts the error of the result and calculates the mixing ratio, and dynamically controls the mixing ratio of computational programs with different precisions, so as to improve the comprehensive performance of the program.

3 Introduction and Implementation of the Overall Framework

This paper proposes an automated hybrid-precision optimized code generation method for loop programs, building upon the foundation of mapping high-precision code to low-precision code, with the objectives of further enhancing acceleration effects and reducing errors introduced by program transformation. Taking IR programs as input, the method automatically generates hybrid-precision code blocks through iteration space partitioning and code generation. Additionally, based on user-specified data computation methods, the method can automatically append data preprocessing routines and error calculation routines. The data preprocessing routines implement precision conversion while calculating the error between original and converted data. The error calculation routines compute the output's average error based on the discrepancy between high/low-precision data and user-defined error thresholds. The iteration space partitioning process utilizes both the average error and predicted output mean to determine the iteration partitioning factor, subsequently deriving the outermost loop partitioning coefficient to guide the hybrid-precision code generation.

The execution order of the framework's components is shown in Fig. 1.

3.1 Data Preprocessing

The data preprocessing module consists of three components: data rearrangement, precision conversion, and error calculation, as illustrated in Fig. 2.

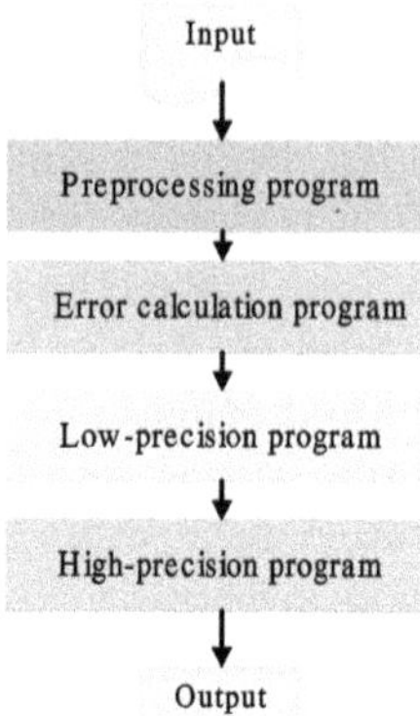

Fig. 1. Execution Order of Framework Components.

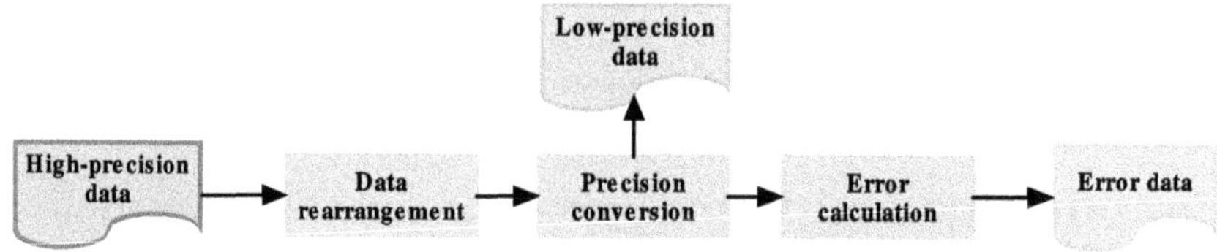

Fig. 2. Data Preprocessing Workflow for High-Precision Data.

Among them, data rearrangement reorganizes input data according to computational characteristics (such as one-dimensional computation, matrix computation, etc.) to ensure continuous address space during data retrieval, overcoming the inability to generate efficient load instructions due to memory alignment requirements. Additionally, the data rearrangement duplicates tail data to adapt to the characteristics of low-precision computation. For example, Fig. 3 illustrates the data preprocessing process for array data. In the diagram, the input data type is FP32, which is converted into FP16 output data. During data rearrangement, considering that general-purpose registers typically have 32-bit length (where a single register can simultaneously accommodate two FP16 data elements), and conversion instructions need to read two FP32 data elements. However, when encountering an odd number of data elements, as the aforementioned feature cannot be utilized, the tail data requires separate processing. The solution for this scenario is to duplicate the tail data once. This approach eliminates the need to add tail processing logic during data preprocessing while better supporting reciprocal and division operations in subsequent computational phases.

From a format perspective, data of different precisions exhibit structural differences. For example, FP32 data consists of 1 sign bit,8 exponent bits, and 23 mantissa bits, while FP16 data is 16 bits in total, comprising 1 sign bit, 5 exponent bits, and 10 mantissa bits. These differences lead to significant vari-

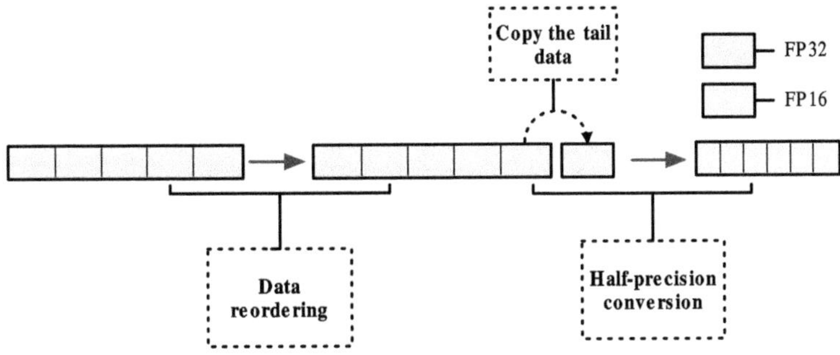

Fig. 3. Process of Data Reordering and FP32-to-FP16 Precision Conversion.

ations in their numerical representation ranges. Typically, due to the reduced mantissa length, FP16 data can accurately represent approximately 3 decimal digits, which is 4 fewer digits than FP32. Consequently, during precision conversion (FP32 to FP16), truncation or rounding of excess bits is required, introducing quantization errors between the original and converted data. This trade-off between precision and computational efficiency is a critical consideration in low-precision computing workflows.

The error calculation process aims to quantify the deviation between data values before and after precision conversion. Let the high-precision value be denoted as v_h the low-precision value as v_l and the error as Δ_v. The calculation follows Eq. (1):

$$\Delta_v = v_h / v_l \tag{1}$$

This formula directly measures the numerical discrepancy introduced by precision reduction. The error magnitude reflects the cumulative impact of truncation, rounding, and range limitations inherent to low-precision formats. Such quantification is essential for analyzing algorithmic stability, error propagation, and performance-accuracy trade-offs in mixed-precision computing systems.

3.2   Introduction to Code Mapping Frameworks

This paper presents a code mapping framework developed as an LLVM pass. The framework replaces the traditional DAG-based LLVM backend process. It takes standard C language as input and outputs assembly code. The framework consists of five main phases: Preprocessing, Type Renaming, Legitimization, Instruction Selection, and Virtual Register Allocation. The overall workflow of the framework is illustrated in Fig. 4.

Each operand in LLVM IR has a data type, but the target architecture may have incompatibilities with the original data types. Therefore, defining a data type set adapted to the target architecture is necessary. The role of type renaming is to rename the operand types of instructions based on their semantic meaning.

Fig. 4. Framework Processing Workflow.

The legalization process addresses type incompatibility issues caused by the former, incorporating an optimized type renaming method. Instruction selection is divided into two parts:

1. Special instruction handling: Deals with instructions that cannot be directly mapped.
2. Instruction mapping: Handles ordinary instructions.

Virtual register allocation is responsible for reassigning virtual register names to operands based on their data types. After applying the above transformation processes, we ultimately obtain an assembly code sequence for the target architecture, as illustrated in Fig. 5.

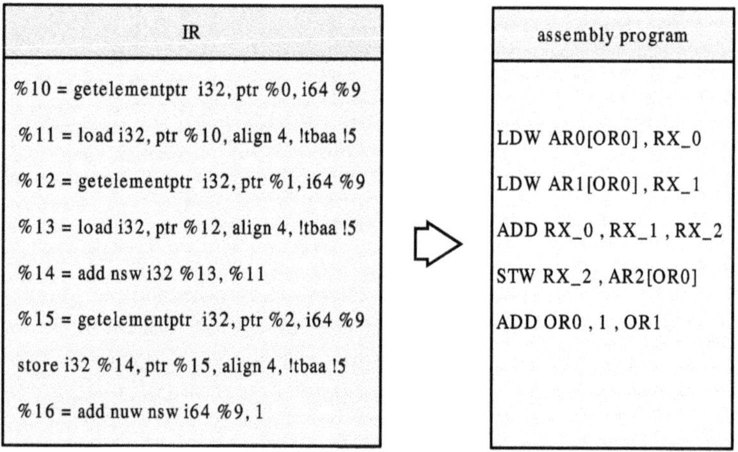

Fig. 5. Comparison diagram before and after converting IR to assembly code.

3.3 Optimization Methods for Type Conversion in Low-Precision Computation Programs

The aforementioned code mapping framework incorporates an optimization method for low-precision code generation. This method revolves around instruction fusion, with its core idea being to analyze data dependencies between instructions, select appropriate instruction combinations, and map them to corresponding low-precision instructions. While preserving the original data processing flow, the method inserts data precision conversion steps and adds code for handling trailing data. For code with complex control structures, the method generates a significant number of control instructions to enforce low-precision mapping constraints. This introduces substantial overhead, leading to rapid degradation of acceleration benefits. As shown in Fig. 6, we consider a floating-point array multiplication operation.

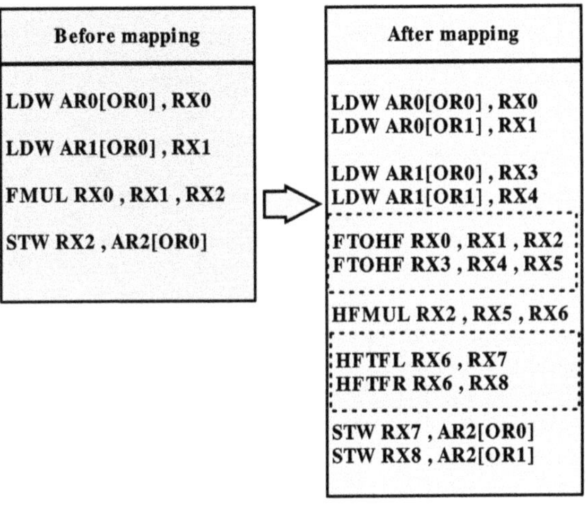

Fig. 6. Comparison diagram of high-precision and low-precision calculation codes before and after conversion.

The left side of Fig. 6 illustrates the program state before code mapping. After applying the low-precision code generation optimization method, the code shown in the figure is generated. Leveraging the capability of low-precision compute units to perform two operations per cycle, the optimization method duplicates the entire data processing pipeline. This involves two type conversion steps, corresponding to the content within the green dashed boxes in the figure. By switching the data format from FP32 to FP16:

1. The number of LDW instructions is halved.
2. The precision conversion instruction FTOHT (FP32-to-FP16 conversion) is eliminated entirely.

These changes collectively achieve significant acceleration. The mixed-precision optimization code auto-generation method proposed in this paper incorporates data reorganization and precision conversion during the data preprocessing phase. Correspondingly, this approach eliminates the precision conversion steps and modifies the data fetching process generated by the original code generation method. Building upon the original framework, we propose a Type Conversion Optimization (TCO) method for low-precision computation programs to adapt to the holistic optimization framework. The TCO method consists of the following steps:

1. Analyze and group load instructions with adjacent memory addresses.
2. Analyze data dependencies of load instructions to identify precision conversion operations.
3. Replace load instructions and eliminate precision conversion instructions.
4. Adjust address offsets.
5. Remove redundant instructions based on the number of dependent instructions relying on a specific instruction's output.

The TCO method is detailed in Algorithm (1).

Algorithm 1 TCO

Input: $Ifunc$: custom function class;
1: $Loads \Leftarrow \{\}$ //Loads refers to a container that stores the objects corresponding to load instructions.
2: **for** each $ins \in Ifunc$ **do**
3:     **if** GetOpcode(ins) $\neq$ $load$ **then**
4:         $Loads \rightarrow$ append(ins)
5:         $SecondLoad \Leftarrow$ FindNeighborLoad($Ifunc$, ins)
6:         **if** $SecondLoad \neq$ NULL **then**
7:             $Loads \rightarrow$ append($SecondLoad$)
8:         **end if**
9:         $PrecisionTransIns \Leftarrow$ FindNeighborIns($Loads$)
10:         **if** $PrecisionTransIns \neq$ NULL **then**
11:             $newload \Leftarrow$ InsertNewLoad($Loads$, $PrecisionTransIns$)
12:             ModOffset($newload$)
13:             Delete($Loads$)
14:             Delete($PrecisionTransIns$)
15:         **end if**
16:     **end if**
17: **end for**
18: $DependNum \Leftarrow 0, Oprands \Leftarrow \{\}$
19: **for** each $ins \in Ifunc$ **do**
20:     $DependNum \Leftarrow$ AcountInsDependNum(ins)
21:     **if** $DependNum == 0$ **then**
22:         $Oprands \rightarrow$ Copy($ins \rightarrow$ GetOprand())
23:         Delete(ins)
24:         **for** each $op \in Oprands$ **do**
25:             DeleteRedundantIns(op)
26:         **end for**
27:     **end if**
28: **end for**
29: **return** $Ifunc$

3.4   Mixed-Precision Optimization Method

3.4.1   Single-Cycle Error Estimation Method

After preprocessing, high-precision data is converted into low-precision data and data errors. The optimized low-precision code processes the low-precision data, yielding results with propagated errors, which may exceed the original data errors. To proactively estimate the result errors, this paper implements error propagation methods tailored to specific computational operations, such as addition, subtraction, and complex function operations. These error calculation methods are integrated into the project as a program library and provided to users through a lookup table approach for invocation.

The first step of this method is to determine the computational operations and functional relationships. Let the original data be $v_{h1}, v_{h2}, ..., v_{hn}$, and the computational operation be $y = f(v_1, v_2, ..., v_n)$, After precision reduction, the data becomes $v_{l1}, v_{l2}, ..., v_{ln}$ and the precision conversion error can be calculated using Eq. (1), The second step involves deriving error propagation formulas for each computational operation using the total differential formula, as shown in Eq. (2).

$$dy = \frac{\partial f}{\partial v_1}dv_1 + \frac{\partial f}{\partial v_2}dv_2 + ... + \frac{\partial f}{\partial v_n}dv_n \tag{2}$$

Here, dv_i corresponds to Δ_{vi}, and dy represents the result error Δ_y, This enables the calculation of the error for each computational result in the program. For example, in Fig. 7, the program's computation is defined as $y = m * x_1 + x_2$. Using the total differential formula, the error estimation formula for this program is derived as $\Delta_y = m * \Delta_{x1} + \Delta_{x2}$.

```
void Linear_function(const float *x1, const float *x2, const
float m, float *y, const int nx){
    int i;
    for (i = 0; i < nx; i++){
        y[i] = m * x1[i] + x2[i];
    }
}
```

Fig. 7. Example of Standard C Language Program.

3.4.2   Average Error Calculation Method

Building upon the error estimation methods, this paper proposes the Cumulative Error Calculation (CECAL) method for average error analysis across all data. This method aims to provide a basis for iterative space partitioning in mixed-precision optimization. We define the input data range as [0.1, 100]. Through numerical analysis, the relative error of most single-cycle computations for final results falls within 0.1%–1%. Therefore, we set the user-defined error threshold (E_{th}) within $[0.01, 0.0001]$ and perform data sampling on each dataset to estimate the cumulative relative error of the overall results.

The CECAL method treats the innermost loop body of a computational program as the fundamental computational unit, defining the input data and its data size N. Subsequently, the method performs random sampling on each input dataset to obtain sample data. Let the sampling ratio be P and the sample data size be n, which are calculated using Eq. (3) and Eq. (4), respectively.

$$P = 1 - \frac{E_{th}}{0.01} \tag{3}$$

$$n = N * P \tag{4}$$

Finally, the method averages the sampled data and their errors, and calculates the estimated result error using the corresponding error estimation method. For example, in Fig. 5, the high-precision data for the program are $x_1[N_1]$ and $x_2[N_2]$, the sampled data are $\widehat{x}_1[n_1]$ and $\widehat{x}_2[n_2]$, and the estimated result error $\Delta_{\widehat{y}}$ is computed as shown in Eq. (5).

$$\Delta_{\widehat{y}} = \frac{m}{n_1} * \sum_{i=0}^{n_1} \Delta_{\widehat{x_1}[i]} + \frac{1}{n_2} * \sum_{i=0}^{n_2} \Delta_{\widehat{x_2}[i]} \tag{5}$$

3.4.3   Iterative Space Partitioning Method

Iterative space partitioning refers to the process of dividing a loop-nested computational space into two disjoint iterative spaces by calculating a partitioning factor K_{isp}, enabling precision-specific computations within each partitioned space. While programs may contain multi-layer loop nests, this work focuses solely on partitioning outer-loop iterations.

Prior to iterative space partitioning, this work requires pre-partitioning result estimation. The estimation method involves substituting sampled input data into the computational formula. Let the computed results be y[n]; then, the partitioning factor K_{isp} can be derived using Eq. (6) and rounded down via floor rounding.

$$K_{isp} = \frac{E_{th}}{n * \Delta_{\widehat{y}}} * \sum_{i=0}^{n} y[i] \tag{6}$$

In nested loops, the iteration counts for each loop level are denoted as $T_1, T_2, ..., T_n$. The partitioning coefficient Q for the outermost loop can be calculated using Eq. (7).

$$Q = \frac{K_{isp}}{\prod_{i=2}^{n} T_i} \tag{7}$$

3.4.4   Code Generation

The code generation framework maps the original program into a mixed-precision program using the outermost loop partitioning coefficient Q. The execution sequence arranges the low-precision computational block to run first, followed by the high-precision computational block. Through data dependency analysis, the upper bound of the outermost loop in the low-precision block and the lower bound of the outermost loop in the high-precision block are adjusted to Q. This work focuses on loop programs with known iteration counts, where inputs, outputs, and parameters are explicitly declared in the parameter list. The code generation process employs a mixed-precision code stitching method, comprising four steps:

1. Stitching low- and high-precision code blocks.
2. Parameter passing identification and handling.
3. Return value processing.
4. Redundant instruction elimination.

4   Experimental Analysis

To validate the effectiveness of the automatic mixed-precision optimization method, this paper employs a code mapping framework to generate original programs, low-precision programs, and mixed-precision programs tailored for the FT-M7004 processor development platform. These programs are then benchmarked to analyze their differences in performance and accuracy.

4.1   Introduction to Experimental Platform

The FT-M7004 is a high-performance DSP chip that uses a three-level storage structure, with a single computing core having 32KB of first-level data cache and 512KB of vector memory (AM), a total global shared Cache of 2 MB, and 32 GB of large-capacity DDR storage outside the core [21].

The processor kernel FT-MT is based on the very long instruction word (VLIW) structure and contains a scalar processing unit (SPU) and a vector processing unit (VPU), which exchange data through a set of scalar-vector shared registers (SVRs). The SPU consists of a scalar execution unit (SPE), an instruction flow control unit, and a scalar data memory unit (SM), which is the computational engine of the scalar processing unit and is responsible for the serial processing part of the application. The SPE is the computation engine of the processing unit and is responsible for the serial processing part of the application, which mainly includes the integer unit and the floating-point unit. The FT-MT core structure is shown in Fig. 8.

4.2   Performance Test Results

This paper selects common floating-point array multiplication, binary linear computation, and sum-of-squares functions in privacy protection as the experimental targets. These three groups of computations often appear in scenarios

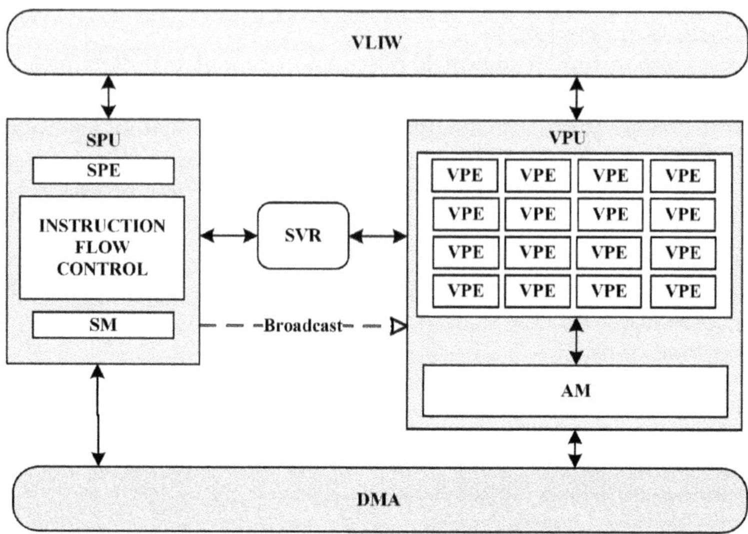

Fig. 8. FT-MT2 Kernel Architecture.

such as federated learning, differential privacy, and secure aggregation. To evaluate the computational speed of programs generated by different methods, the data scale (input size) is chosen as the independent variable, while the cycle count (clock cycles) and speedup ratio are measured as dependent variables. The experimental results are presented in Fig. 9, Fig. 10 and Fig. 11. In the figures:

1. Single-Float: Denotes the single-precision floating-point program (baseline).
2. Half-Float1: Represents the baseline half-precision floating-point program.
3. Half-Float2: Indicates the optimized half-precision floating-point program.
4. Mix-Float: Refers to the mixed-precision floating-point program.

Additionally, the speedup ratio ($R_{Speedup}$) is calculated using Eq. (8), where:

- N_{cycle1}: Cycle count before optimization.
- N_{cycle2}: Cycle count after optimization.

$$R_{speedup} = N_{cycle1}/N_{cycle2} \tag{8}$$

In all the experimental test diagrams, H1/S denotes the ratio of Half-Float1 to Single-Float, H2/S represents the ratio of Half-Float2 to Single-Float, and M/S indicates the ratio of Mix-Float to Single-Float.

In the experiment, the E_{th} is set to 0.0060, and the iteration count is fixed at 60 cycles. According to the iterative space partitioning method in the automatic mixed-precision optimization framework, the outermost loop partitioning coefficient for the floating-point array multiplication function is determined as

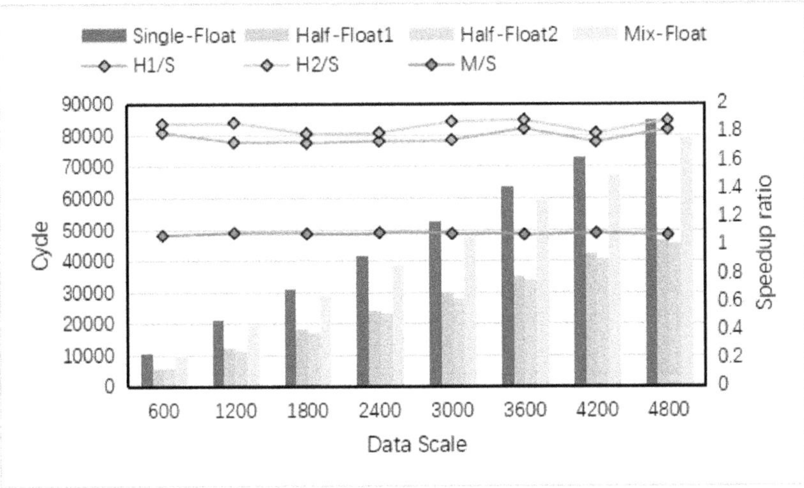

Fig. 9. Floating-point Array Multiplication Experimental Test Diagram.

23. This signifies that the first 23 iterations execute half-precision floating-point computations, while the remaining iterations perform single-precision floating-point computations.

As shown in Fig. 9, the Half-Float2 achieves an average speed improvement of 10% compared to the baseline Half-Float1. However, the Mix-Float exhibits a less pronounced acceleration relative to the full half-precision program, with an average speed gain of 7%.

In the experiment on the binary linear function, the experimental setup remained consistent with the former. After testing, the outermost loop segmentation coefficient of the binary linear function experiment was determined to be 34. As shown in Fig. 9, the H2/S configuration achieved a 4% improvement in computational speed compared to H1/S. The mixed-precision program demonstrated an average computational speed enhancement of 37%.

In the experiment on the sum of squares function, the experimental conditions remained consistent with the previous two groups. As shown in Fig. 10, the H2/S configuration achieved an average computational speed improvement of 14% compared to H1/S. The mixed-precision computation demonstrated an average execution speed enhancement of 8%.

4.3   Error Test Results

To assess the impact of different mixing ratios on precision, this study selects Mix Ratio as the horizontal axis and Maximum Error (Error) as the vertical axis. Here, Error is calculated by taking the high-precision computation results as the reference and determining the difference between the results obtained from the two computation methods. The Mix Ratio represents the proportion of the outermost loop executed in half-precision computation, with a horizontal

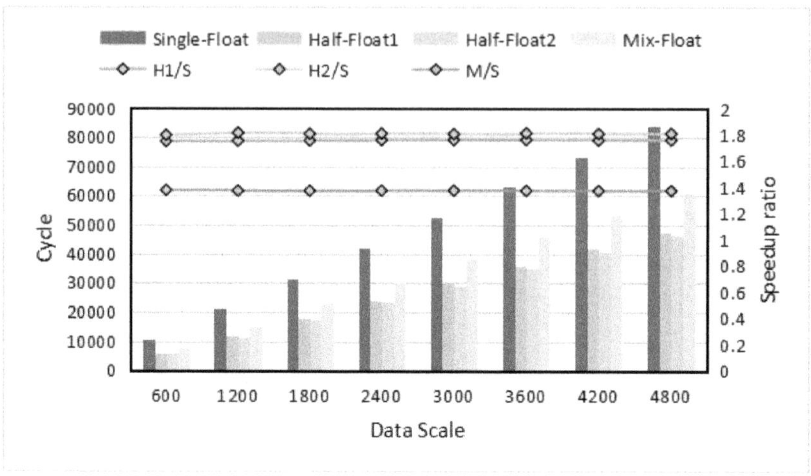

Fig. 10. Binary Linear Computation Experimental Test Diagram.

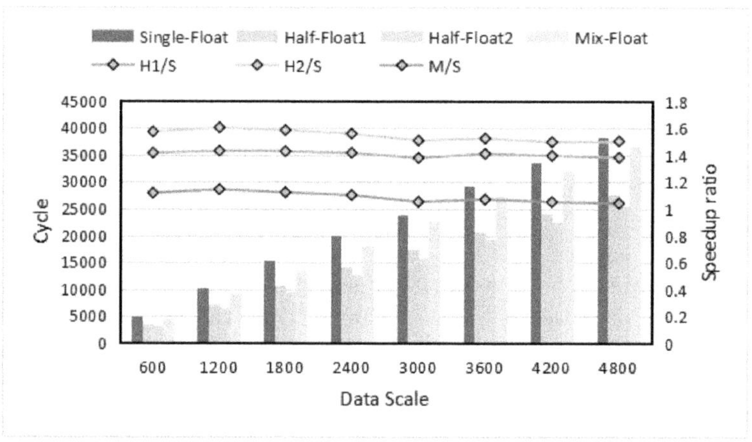

Fig. 11. Sum of Squares Experimental Test Diagram.

coordinate value of 1 indicating fully half-precision execution. Error denotes the total error in the output results when executing the half-precision program. The experimental results are illustrated in Fig. 12, Fig. 13, and Fig. 14.

Figure 12 and Fig. 13 correspond to the functions of floating-point array multiplication and binary linear computation, respectively. Since the output contains multiple values, Error represents the cumulative error. The floating-point array multiplication is defined as, with a maximum error of 3.9. The binary linear computation function is defined as, with a maximum error of 2.5.

Figure 14 illustrates the error testing results for the sum-of-squares function with varying partitioning ratios of the outermost loop. This function differs in

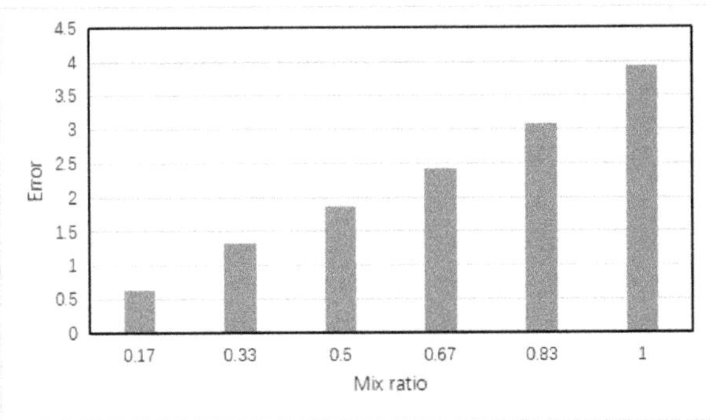

Fig. 12. Floating-point Array Multiplication Experimental error test chart.

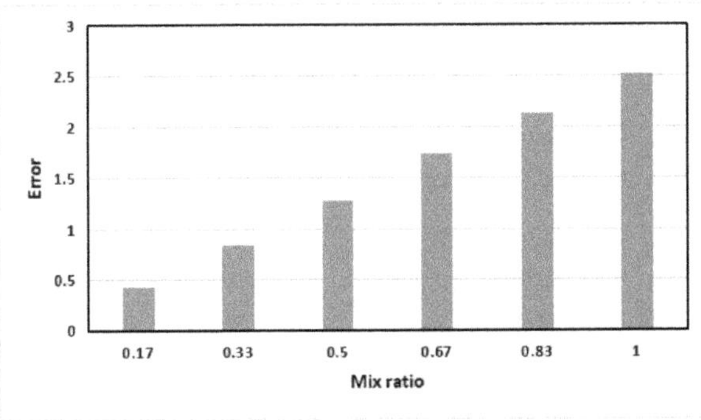

Fig. 13. Binary Linear Computation Experimental Error Test Chart.

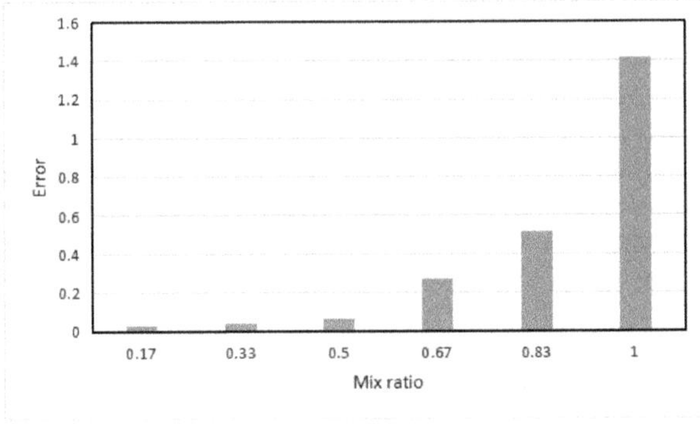

Fig. 14. Sum of Squares Experimental error Test Diagram.

computation methodology from the previous two cases. While the former operations are element-wise, the sum-of-squares function is an aggregation-based computation. Since the function outputs only a single value, the Error calculation

focuses solely on this single output. The mixed-precision computation for the sum-of-squares function achieves a maximum error of 1.4, as shown in Fig. 14.

5   Conclusion and Future Work

This paper proposes an automated code generation method for mixed-precision optimization targeting loop-based programs, leveraging error analysis to guide the process. By incorporating data preprocessing and adaptive adjustments to low-precision computations, the method aims to compensate for errors introduced by reduced precision while ensuring a measurable acceleration performance. Experimental results demonstrate that the proposed method has largely achieved its intended objectives. However, there remain limitations in its current implementation. For instance, the approach shows limited applicability to specialized computations such as multi-dimensional convolution and matrix transposition. Future work will focus on extending this approach to more complex code structures and broadening its applicability to diverse computational patterns, thereby enhancing the method's generalizability.

References

1. Acar, A., Aksu, H., Uluagac, A.S., Conti, M.: A survey on homomorphic encryption schemes: theory and implementation. ACM Comput. Surv. (CSUR) **51**(4), 1–35 (2018)
2. Ashfaq, S., AskariHemmat, M., Sah, S., Saboori, E., Mastropietro, O., Hoffman, A.: Accelerating deep learning model inference on ARM CPUS with ultra-low bit quantization and runtime. arXiv preprint arXiv:2207.08820 (2022)
3. Balasubramanian, K.K., Di Salvo, M., Rocchia, W., Decherchi, S., Crepaldi, M.: Designing RISC-V instruction set extensions for artificial neural networks: an LLVM compiler-driven perspective. IEEE Access (2024)
4. Bondhugula, U., Ramanujam, J., Sadayappan, P.: A practical and fully automatic polyhedral program optimization system. ACM SIGPLAN PLDI (2008) (2007)
5. Cattaneo, D., Chiari, M., Fossati, N., Cherubin, S., Agosta, G.: Architecture-aware precision tuning with multiple number representation systems. In: 2021 58th ACM/IEEE Design Automation Conference (DAC), pp. 673–678. IEEE (2021)
6. Cherubin, S., Cattaneo, D., Chiari, M., Di Bello, A., Agosta, G.: TAFFO: tuning assistant for floating to fixed point optimization. IEEE Embed. Syst. Lett. **12**(1), 5–8 (2019)
7. Denisov, L., Galimberti, A., Cattaneo, D., Agosta, G., Zoni, D.: Design-time methodology for optimizing mixed-precision CPU architectures on FPGA. J. Syst. Architect. **155**, 103257 (2024)
8. Hennessy, J.L., Patterson, D.A.: Computer Architecture: A Quantitative Approach. Elsevier (2011)
9. Jang, K., Baksi, A., Kim, H., Song, G., Seo, H., Chattopadhyay, A.: Quantum analysis of AES. Cryptology ePrint Archive (2022)
10. Kotipalli, P.V., Singh, R., Wood, P., Laguna, I., Bagchi, S.: AMPT-GA: automatic mixed precision floating point tuning for GPU applications. In: Proceedings of the ACM International Conference on Supercomputing, pp. 160–170 (2019)

11. Kum, K.I., Kang, J., Sung, W.: AutoScaler for C: an optimizing floating-point to integer c program converter for fixed-point digital signal processors. IEEE Trans. Circ. Syst. II: Analog Digit. Sig. Process. **47**(9), 840–848 (2000)
12. Lei, Y., Ye, D., Shen, S., Sui, Y., Zhu, T., Zhou, W.: New challenges in reinforcement learning: a survey of security and privacy. Artif. Intell. Rev. **56**(7), 7195–7236 (2023)
13. Micikevicius, P., et al.: Mixed precision training. arXiv preprint arXiv:1710.03740 (2017)
14. Nassif, N., et al.: Sapphire rapids: The next-generation intel XEON scalable processor. In: 2022 IEEE International Solid-State Circuits Conference (ISSCC), vol. 65, pp. 44–46. IEEE (2022)
15. Peng, H., et al.: FP8-LM: training FP8 large language models. arXiv preprint arXiv:2310.18313 (2023)
16. Rubio-González, C., et al.: Precimonious: tuning assistant for floating-point precision. In: Proceedings of the International Conference on High Performance Computing, Networking, Storage and Analysis, pp. 1–12 (2013)
17. Solovyev, A., Baranowski, M.S., Briggs, I., Jacobsen, C., Rakamarić, Z., Gopalakrishnan, G.: Rigorous estimation of floating-point round-off errors with symbolic Taylor expansions. ACM Trans. Programm. Lang. Syst. (TOPLAS) **41**(1), 1–39 (2018)
18. Vieublé, B.: Mixed precision iterative refinement for the solution of large sparse linear systems. Ph.D. thesis, Institut National Polytechnique de Toulouse-INPT (2022)
19. Wang, B., Berg, A., Acar, D.A.E., Zhou, C.: Towards federated learning with on-device training and communication in 8-bit floating point. In: FedKDD: International Joint Workshop on Federated Learning for Data Mining and Graph Analytics (2024)
20. Wang, R., Lai, J., Zhang, Z., Li, X., Vijayakumar, P., Karuppiah, M.: Privacy-preserving federated learning for internet of medical things under edge computing. IEEE J. Biomed. Health Inform. **27**(2), 854–865 (2022)
21. Xie, A., Hu, Y., Cheng, A., Tang, Z., Liu, P., Zhang, X.: Advancing matrix decomposition efficiency: a study on ft-matrix DSP based SVD optimization. In: 2023 IEEE 10th International Conference on Cyber Security and Cloud Computing (CSCloud)/2023 IEEE 9th International Conference on Edge Computing and Scalable Cloud (EdgeCom), pp. 464–469. IEEE (2023)
22. Xu, J., Song, G., Zhou, B., Li, F., Hao, J., Zhao, J.: A holistic approach to automatic mixed-precision code generation and tuning for affine programs. In: Proceedings of the 29th ACM SIGPLAN Annual Symposium on Principles and Practice of Parallel Programming, pp. 55–67 (2024)
23. Zhao, Y., Chen, J.: A survey on differential privacy for unstructured data content. ACM Comput. Surv. (CSUR) **54**(10s), 1–28 (2022)

ReForGe: A Secure Fusion Model with Recursive Feature Engineering for Aircraft Engine Predictive Maintenance

Yingzi Huo[1,2(✉)], Yufeng Xiao[1,2], Jiahong Cai[1,2], Yanbing Wu[1,2], and Chengjun Yang[3]

[1] School of Computer Science and Engineering, Hunan University of Science and Technology, Xiangtan 411201, China
[2] Sanya Institute of Hunan University of Science and Technology, Sanya 572024, China
`yingzihuo02@mail.hnust.edu.cn`
[3] College of Artificial Intelligence and Manufacturing, Hechi University, Hechi 546300, China

Abstract. With the rapid growth of global air transport, traditional time-based maintenance models relying on flight hours have struggled to adapt to complex operational environments and the nonlinear degradation characteristics of equipment. Meanwhile, frequent cyberattacks during data transmission pose severe challenges to aviation maintenance safety. To address these issues, this paper proposes ReForGe, a secure predictive maintenance model based on an ensemble learning framework. The model integrates recursive feature elimination with decision path analysis to accurately identify core features from multi-source heterogeneous sensor data. Additionally, it embeds a lightweight security verification mechanism to effectively mitigate risks of malicious tampering and data theft during transmission. Furthermore, by introducing an expected-cost-driven dynamic weight adjustment mechanism, ReForGe adaptively balances operational risks between over-maintenance and fault omission, significantly improving the accuracy of remaining useful life prediction and the reliability of maintenance decisions. Experimental results demonstrate that ReForGe achieves a fault prediction accuracy of 93%, with its F1-score surpassing conventional models by 4.49%. It also exhibits exceptional robustness and cost-effectiveness under complex operational conditions.

Keywords: predictive maintenance · aircraft engines · data security · feature downgrading · machine learning

1 Introduction

As the core power infrastructure of modern aviation transportation systems, the operational safety of aircraft engines directly determines the mission sustainability and survivability of the aircraft [1]. With global annual passenger

W. Liang et al. (Eds.): SecureComm 2025, LNICST 690, pp. 332–351, 2026.
https://doi.org/10.1007/978-3-032-23456-8_18

turnover exceeding 10 trillion passenger-kilometers, the aviation transportation system faces dual challenges of exponential growth in operational intensity and the increasing complexity of extreme working conditions [2]. According to the International Air Transport Association, in 2023 alone, flight delays caused by planned engine maintenance accounted for 320,000 flights, resulting in direct economic losses exceeding $12 billion. This passive, reactive maintenance strategy not only struggles to cope with unexpected failures but also leads to a lack of adaptive regulation for critical infrastructure when faced with extreme loads, material aging, and environmental changes [3]. Additionally, digital transformation has integrated key components, such as engine control systems and maintenance data management platforms, deeply into networks, making them vulnerable to malicious attacks [4]. These attackers can manipulate maintenance decisions by tampering with sensor data, forging maintenance instructions, and even triggering cascading system failures, severely threatening flight safety [5].

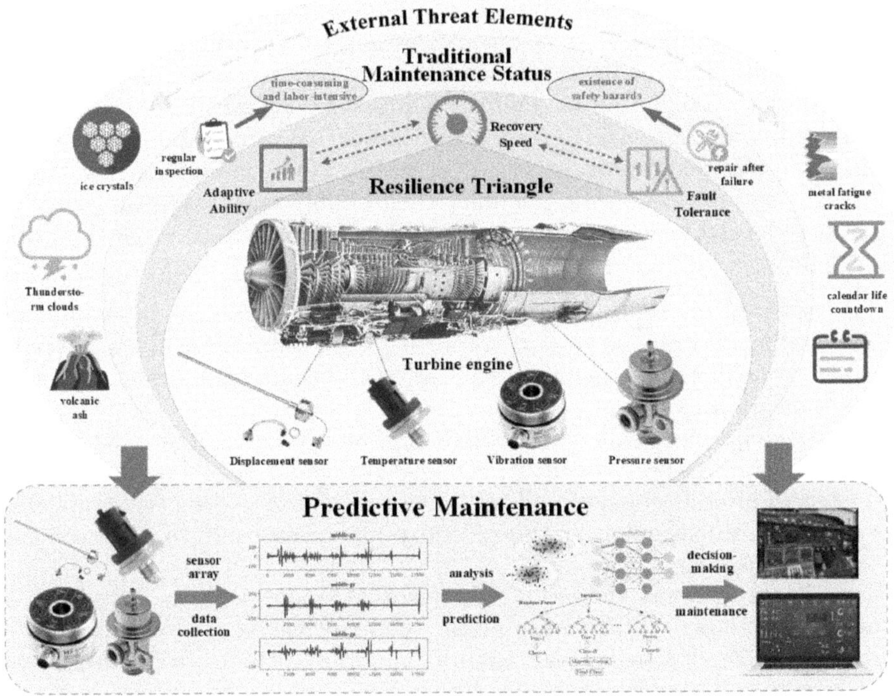

Fig. 1. Predictive maintenance architecture for aircraft engines.

Predictive maintenance, through the integration of sensor data, machine learning algorithms, and real-time analytics, can identify engine performance degradation trends in advance [6], shifting the maintenance cycle from "periodic" to "on-demand," significantly reducing the risk of unplanned downtime, as shown in Fig. 1. However, under complex conditions, existing predictive maintenance models exhibit structural defects that do not align with the resilience needs of critical infrastructure [7]. Early physics-based methods (such as thermodynamic equilibrium equations) could describe steady-state engine characteristics, but their linear assumptions are inadequate for capturing the nonlinear degradation characteristics of multi-component coupling in aircraft engines, resulting in delayed maintenance decisions [8]. On the other hand, data-driven single machine learning models face the problem of high-dimensional sparsity [9]. When dealing with multiple sensor parameters, the utilization of feature crossovers is insufficient, making it difficult to capture the nonlinear relationships between parameters such as temperature, vibration, and pressure [10]. Moreover, data-driven approaches often focus on fault feature extraction when handling high-dimensional sensor data, neglecting the verification of data integrity and source authenticity [11]. Attackers can inject small disturbances to cause misjudgments in vibration signals or manipulate sensor readings via man-in-the-middle attacks, leading to erroneous predictions and influencing normal engine maintenance [12].

To address this, this paper proposes a Random Forest-driven hybrid Model for predictive maintenance with Recursive-Gaussian fusion, referred to as the ReForGe model. This model constructs a nonlinear degradation analysis framework with deep integration of multiple features to achieve high-accuracy predictions of key aircraft engine component degradation trends and dynamic optimization of maintenance decisions. At the same time, the model integrates a lightweight security validation module to effectively ensure the integrity and authenticity of data during transmission. The main contributions of this paper are as follows:

1. The proposal of the ReForGe model for aircraft engine predictive maintenance, which is oriented toward optimizing expected cost, using an ensemble model to predict the remaining life cycle of the engine and optimize maintenance decisions.
2. The development of a secure data mining and feature interaction method, which improves the cross-utilization of features by selecting core features related to aircraft engines, and introduces an end-to-end security validation mechanism to ensure the integrity and tamper-proof nature of sensor data during transmission.
3. Experimental results show that the ReForGe model performs excellently in multi-dimensional performance evaluations and can accurately predict the remaining life cycle of aircraft engines, confirming the model's effectiveness and practicality in aircraft engine health management.

The remaining articles in this paper are organized as follows: Sect. 2 analyzes the secure maintenance methods of aircraft engines and the application of machine learning in predictive maintenance. Section 3 describes A Random Forest-Driven Hybrid Model for Predictive Maintenance with Recursive-Gaussian Fusion proposed in this paper. Section 4 presents an experimental comparison of the ReForGe model with other models. Section 5 summarizes the work of this paper.

2   Related Work

2.1   Secure Maintenance Methods of Aircraft Engine

The aircraft engine is a highly complex and sophisticated thermomechanical system. Its built-in intelligent sensors and control systems monitor operational status in real-time through a data transmission network [13]. However, engines operating under extreme conditions such as high temperatures, high pressures, high rotational speeds, and strong vibrations not only endure significant mechanical and thermal stresses but also face potential cyberattacks targeting the data transmission links, such as the injection of erroneous instructions or tampering with performance parameters [14]. In such harsh internal and external environments, any failure of a component or anomaly in data transmission could lead to serious flight accidents, resulting in significant loss of life and property damage [15].

Traditional aircraft engine maintenance methods both domestically and internationally are primarily based on time-based maintenance and condition-based maintenance. Time-based maintenance involves periodic inspections at preset time intervals or flight hours [16]. For example, Fedele et al. developed an evaluation system for the CFM56 engine [17], which is convenient for management and execution but can lead to over- or under-maintenance due to neglecting individual differences [18]. Condition-based maintenance, on the other hand, assesses health status by real-time monitoring of operational parameters such as vibration and temperature. For instance, Zheng et al. dynamically optimized maintenance and spare parts replenishment strategies by real-time monitoring of the degradation state of K-out-of-N systems and integrating spare parts order information using a Markov decision process [19]. De et al. proposed a method for discretizing a static continuous-time continuous state non-decreasing degradation process, transforming it into a discrete-time Markov chain and representing it with a transition probability matrix [20]. However, condition-based maintenance methods require advanced monitoring technology and data analysis capabilities [21].

With the development of the aviation industry and advancements in technology, predictive maintenance has been widely applied in the field of aircraft engine maintenance [22]. This method leverages sensors, big data, and machine learning technologies to monitor engine operational status in real-time, predict fault risks through data analysis, and develop maintenance plans. For example, De et al. constructed a fleet maintenance scheduling framework based on dynamic prediction of remaining useful life (RUL), using convolutional neural networks and integer linear programming to optimize task scheduling, with a safety factor mechanism controlling fault costs to 7.4% of total maintenance costs. Xiong et al. proposed a digital twin-driven maintenance framework, mining implicit digital twin models for engine maintenance [23]. Compared to traditional maintenance, predictive maintenance can provide early warnings of faults, enabling maintenance personnel to repair issues in time, improving flight safety. The analysis results can also provide a basis for engine design optimization, driving technological development.

However, predictive maintenance highly depends on the massive operational data collected by sensors for analysis and modeling [24]. If the data is tampered with or stolen during transmission, it could lead to incorrect maintenance decisions, potentially resulting in serious safety incidents [25]. To address this issue, Mahlake et al. proposed integrating security IoT algorithms with sensor network security protocols to develop lightweight security algorithms [26]. These algorithms ensure data security while effectively maintaining system performance. In the field of anomaly detection, threshold-based anomaly detection methods, due to their intuitiveness and ease of use, are widely applied in various scenarios. Adrian et al. summarized various supervised and unsupervised threshold selection strategies in their study of network anomaly detection literature [27]. These algorithms set normal threshold ranges for key parameters such as data transmission rates and IP access frequencies. Once the actual monitoring data in the sensor network exceeds these ranges, the system immediately triggers an alert [28].

2.2 Application of Machine Learning in Predictive Maintenance

Predictive maintenance technology based on machine learning is widely used in the modern aviation field to ensure the operational safety of aircraft engines. By deploying multiple types of high-precision sensors (including vibration, temperature, oil pressure and other sensors) in the key parts of the engine, the system is able to collect real-time data on the engine's operating status [29]. After preprocessing and feature extraction, these data are used to construct an engine health state assessment model. Among them, machine learning algorithms (e.g., random forests, LSTM and other time-series models) are able to effectively learn the normal operating mode of the engine and identify potential abnormal features by analysing massive historical operating data [30]. Predictive maintenance based on machine learning can identify potential risks at the early stage of failure and avoid worsening of the problem, thus significantly improving the reliability and safety of the engine, while reducing the operational losses caused by sudden failures [31].

Machine learning offers unique advantages in predictive maintenance over traditional physical model-based approaches [32]. Firstly, data-driven approaches are able to adaptively learn degradation characteristics of complex systems that are difficult to describe with physical equations. Cheng et al. proposed a predictive maintenance framework that combines building information modelling and IoT technologies to overcome the limitations of traditional reactive and preventive maintenance through real-time data integration and machine learning algorithms to predict the future state of mechanical, electrical, and plumbing components [33]. Xiong et al. proposed an adaptive deep learning-based residual service life prediction framework, which integrates a physical information failure mode classifier with a deep convolutional neural network, and improves the interpretability and robustness of the model prediction through an operating condition smoothing technique [34]. Secondly, with the development of edge computing technology, lightweight models can be deployed on airborne devices for real-time monitoring. Yu et al. proposed an industrial IoT big data ecosystem based on a three-tier architecture that improves the efficiency of fault detection in manufacturing predictive maintenance through the integration of edge computing and autoencoder technology [35]. Mourtzis et al. proposed the design and initial development in order to distribute computational loads to nodes and extended it to be able to utilise machine learning techniques to calculate the RUL of critical machine components [36]. In addition, hybrid learning methods are able to further improve the accuracy of fault diagnosis by fusing multi-source sensor data. Hajiha et al. proposed a physically regularised data-driven approach for health prediction of complex engineered systems with multiple hidden and dependent health states [37]. Xue et al. proposed a new fault diagnosis of electric motor bearings in terms of multi-transform domain and multi-source data fusion framework that enables feature extraction and fusion from various source data in the time, frequency and time-frequency domains [38].

However, data-driven models require high quality and quantity of data, which may affect the accuracy and reliability of the model if the data are noisy, missing or biased [39]. Traditional machine learning models often show strong limitations when facing complex and changing operating conditions, and it is difficult to accurately capture the subtle changes in the operating state of equipment and potential fault characteristics [40]. When dealing with high-dimensional and non-linear data, these models are prone to overfitting or underfitting problems, resulting in less accurate and reliable prediction results.

3   ReForGe Model

To achieve accurate prediction of the RUL of aircraft engines and ensure the security of data transmission, this paper proposes the ReForGe model, whose architecture is shown in Fig. 2. Section 3.1 introduces a security-enhanced data mining and feature interaction method. This method utilizes recursive feature elimination and decision path analysis to identify key degradation features from multi-source sensor data such as vibration, temperature, and pressure. It enhances nonlinear interactions between features by constructing product and ratio terms, and embeds a lightweight security verification mechanism during data transmission to ensure data integrity and authenticity. Section 3.2 presents an expected cost-oriented dynamic weight adjustment strategy, which focuses on the ensemble of machine learning models. By integrating multiple models, the strategy accurately captures complex patterns in the data and quantifies the operational risks of over-maintenance and missed fault detection, thereby enabling joint optimization of RUL prediction and maintenance decision-making.

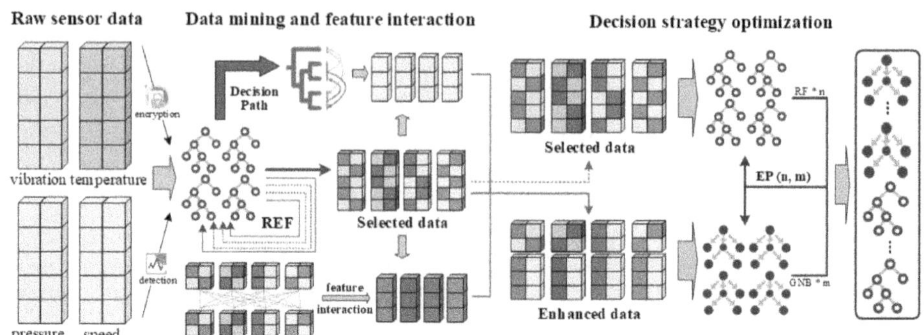

Fig. 2. ReForGe model architecture.

3.1 Security-Enhanced Data Mining and Feature Interaction Method

During the operation of aircraft engines, sensors continuously collect vast amounts of real-time data encompassing key parameters such as vibration, temperature, pressure, and rotational speed. However, this raw data is not only high-dimensional—with some features exhibiting low correlation to the engine's RUL—but is also highly susceptible to cyberattacks such as data poisoning and traffic hijacking. These threats can introduce abnormal data into the training set, severely degrading the accuracy and reliability of predictive models.

To address this issue, this paper proposes a security-enhanced data processing method. The method employs a lightweight hash verification mechanism combined with traffic behavior analysis to validate the integrity of the collected data and detect anomalous network traffic, thereby ensuring the reliability of the dataset. Subsequently, the Recursive Feature Elimination (RFE) algorithm is used to iteratively train the Random Forest (RF) model. Based on the feature importance scores from the RF model, redundant features are gradually removed, ultimately yielding an optimal feature subset that enhances the model's generalization capability, pseudo code can be found in Algorithm 1.

Assume a pre-collected sensor dataset D. The SHA-256 hashing algorithm is applied to each data record D_i, generating a unique fixed-length digest $H(D_i)$. A hierarchical hash aggregation mechanism is then used to iteratively combine individual hash values. Suppose there are n data records. At the j-th aggregation level, the hash is computed as:

$$H_j = H_{\text{merge}}\left(H_{(j-1)_{\text{left}}},\ H_{(j-1)_{\text{right}}}\right), \tag{1}$$

where H_{merge} is the hash merge function. The final root hash value H_{root} is stored in a secure and trusted environment.

During data transmission, real-time monitoring nodes are deployed. When data arrive at the input layer of the model, the hash value of the received data $H'(D_i)$ is recalculated and compared bit by bit with the encrypted hash value

Algorithm 1. Security-Enhanced Data Mining and Feature Interaction Method

Input: Collected dataset D, minimum feature threshold f_{TH}, number of important features K_{top}, anomaly dataset E

Output: F_{opt}, X_{opt}, F_{en}, X_{en}, R

1: Initialize $L \leftarrow \lceil \log_2 n \rceil$, $F_N \leftarrow \{1, 2, \ldots, n\}$, $I_{\min} \leftarrow \infty$, $F_{opt} \leftarrow F_N$, $P_{all} = []$;
2: **for** i in D **do**
3: $\quad$ $H(D_i) = $ SHA-256(D_i);
4: **end for**
5: $H_{\text{root}} \leftarrow$ Eq.(1);
6: **for** i in D **do**
7: $\quad$ **if** $H'(D_i) \neq H(D_i)$ or $D_i \notin [\mu - k\sigma, \mu + k\sigma]$ **then**
8: $\quad\quad$ $E \leftarrow D_i$;
9: $\quad$ **else**
10: $\quad\quad$ $D_{\text{safe}} \leftarrow D_i$;
11: $\quad$ **end if**
12: **end for**
13: $N \leftarrow D_{\text{safe}}$;
14: **while** $|F_N| \geq f_{TH}$ **do**
15: $\quad$ $I_j \leftarrow$ train RF model $R(X[:, F_N], Y)$ $\qquad\qquad$ ▷ Calculate feature importance
16: $\quad$ **if** $I_j < I_{min}$ **then**
17: $\quad\quad$ $I_{min} \leftarrow I_j$, $F_{opt} \leftarrow F_N$
18: $\quad$ **end if**
19: $\quad$ **if** $|F_N| = f_{TH}$ **then**
20: $\quad\quad$ **break**
21: $\quad$ **end if**
22: $\quad$ $f_{drop} \leftarrow \text{argmin}_{j \in F_N} I_j$
23: $\quad$ $F_N \leftarrow F_N \setminus f_{drop}$
24: **end while**
25: $F_{en} \leftarrow F_{opt}$
26: **for each** tree $t \in R$ **do**
27: $\quad$ Path $\leftarrow t.$decision_path(F_{en})
28: $\quad$ $P_{all}.$append(Path)
29: **end for**
30: $I_{top} \leftarrow$ sort$(I_{[-K_{top}:]})$ $\qquad\qquad\qquad$ ▷ Get top K_{top} important features
31: $X_{top} \leftarrow X_{opt}[:, I_{top}]$
32: $M_{mul} \leftarrow X_{top} \otimes X_{top}$ $\qquad\qquad\qquad\qquad$ ▷ Element-wise product
33: $M_{div} \leftarrow X_{top} \oslash X_{top}$ $\qquad\qquad\qquad\qquad$ ▷ Element-wise division
34: $F_{en}.$append(OneHotEncode(P_{all}), M_{mul}, M_{div})

stored $H(D_i)$. If $\exists i$, $H'(D_i) \neq H(D_i)$, the system immediately triggers a alert mechanism. Finally, the intelligent decision module automatically discards the abnormal data and generates a security event report containing information such as the tampering time, original hash value, and transmission path, ensuring that all data entering the model maintains complete authenticity and reliability.

In addition, based on historical data distribution, reasonable ranges for sensor parameters are defined. Assuming the normal distribution of sensor parameters follows a Gaussian distribution with mean μ and standard deviation σ, thresholds are set statistically in the interval $[\mu - k\sigma, \mu + k\sigma]$ (where k is a coefficient set according to risk tolerance). If real-time collected sensor data falls outside this range, it is determined to be abnormal flow, which may be caused by DoS attacks or signal interference. Abnormal flow data is temporarily stored and reported for manual verification to prevent adverse effects on the model.

After completing the security verification, the RF model is trained using all its feature sets F_N and the model performance is evaluated by calculating the Root Mean Square Error (RMSE) of the model through cross-validation:

$$\text{RMSE}(F_N) = \sqrt{\frac{1}{n} \sum_{i=1}^{n} (y_i - \hat{y}(F_N))^2}, \tag{2}$$

Where y_i is the true value and $\hat{y}(F_N)$ is the predicted value. Next, the contribution of each feature to the model's prediction accuracy is evaluated by the RF model's feature importance metrics I, to remove the least contributing feature. The importance of each feature is obtained by calculating the decrease in the mean square error (MSE) due to each feature in T decision tree over multiple splits:

$$I_j = \sum_{t=1}^{T} \sum_{s \in S(j,t)} \Delta I(s,t), \tag{3}$$

where I_j represents the importance of feature f_j, $S(j,t)$ denotes the splits related to feature f_j in tree t, and $\Delta I(s,t)$ represents the reduction in MSE caused by the split of feature f_j. After calculating the importance of all features in each round, the feature with the lowest importance $f_{\min}$ is removed, and the feature set is updated. This process is repeated until the number of features is reduced to the specified feature threshold f_{TH}. Finally, the feature subset that yields the smallest Root Mean Squared Error (RMSE) is selected as the optimal feature selection result F_{opt} and the sample matrix X_{opt}.

After performing feature selection on the initial dataset N to obtain F_{opt}, in order to further explore potential information in the data and enhance the descriptive capability of features for aircraft engine operating states using the Gaussian Naive Bayes (GNB) model, this paper subsequently performs data augmentation on F_{opt} from two aspects: decision paths and feature interactions. Assuming the RF model consists of T decision trees $T_1, T_2, \cdots, T_L$, for a sample x, to compute its decision path in decision tree T_i, we start from the root node and traverse downward step by step according to the decision conditions at each node based on the sample's feature values, until reaching a leaf node. This decision path can be represented as an ordered sequence of nodes $P_{t,x} = \{n_{t,x}^1, n_{t,x}^2, \cdots, n_{t,x}^{l_x}\}$, where $l_{t,x}$ denotes the path length of sample x in decision tree T_i, and $n_{t,x}^j$ represents the j-th node along the path. Based on this, we can construct the path feature matrix $X_{path} = [X_{path1}, X_{path2}, \cdots, X_{pathT}]$ for F_{opt}, where $X_{patht} \in \mathbb{R}^{n \times l_t}$ and l_t is the number of leaf nodes in tree T_i.

In terms of feature interaction, it is first necessary to sort the feature importance of F_{opt} to obtain the top K_{top} important feature set, and then construct the product term X_{mul} and ratio term X_{div} using Eq.(3) and Eq.(4):

$$X_{mul} = \{x_p \cdot x_q \mid p, q \in [1, top_k], p < q\}, \tag{4}$$

$$X_{mul} = \{x_p \cdot x_q \mid p, q \in [1, top_k], p < q\}, \tag{5}$$

where x_p represents the p-th most important feature. The product term exhibits symmetry: $x_p \cdot x_q = x_q \cdot x_p$, which can capture synergistic effects between features, demonstrate nonlinearity, and is sensitive to feature scales. On the other hand, the ratio term exhibits asymmetry $\frac{x_p}{x_q} \neq \frac{x_q}{x_p}$ and is insensitive to feature scales, capable of capturing proportional relationships between features.

Finally, we convert X_{path} into one-hot encoded format for sorting and organization, then merge it with the feature interaction terms into F_{opt} to form a new feature set F_{en} and sample matrix $X_{en} \in \mathbb{R}^{n \times m}$, where $m = k + \sum_{t=1}^{T} l_t + |X_{mul}| + |X_{div}|$, F_{en} not only contains the original features highly correlated with engine RUL, but also incorporates latent feature information extracted from decision paths and feature interaction information. This enables a more comprehensive representation of the engine's operational state.

3.2   Expectation Cost Oriented Dynamic Weight Adjustment Strategy

Single machine learning models often have limitations when dealing with complex operational data of aircraft engines, and it is difficult to comprehensively capture

---

Algorithm 2. Expected Cost Oriented Dynamic Weight Adjustment Strategy

---

Input: Dataset to be validated X, X_{opt}, X_{en}, Y_{tune}, RF model $\mathbb{R}$
Output: The ReForGe model M, dataset prediction results Y

1: Initialize $w_R, w_G \leftarrow 0.5$, $EP_{pred} \leftarrow +\infty$
2: $P_R \leftarrow \mathbb{R}.\text{predict}(X_{opt})$
3: $P_N \leftarrow G.\text{predict}(X_{en})$ ▷ GNB model prediction
4: **while** convergence $=$ **true do**
5:       $P_M \leftarrow w_R P_R + w_G P_N$
6:       $EP \leftarrow EP(P_M, Y_{tune})$
7:       $EP_R \leftarrow EP(P_R, Y_{tune})$
8:       **if** $|EP_{cur} - EP_{pred}| <$ tol **then**   ▷ Check convergence threshold
9:           **break**
10:      **else**
11:          $EP_{pred} \leftarrow EP_{cur}$
12:          $w_R \leftarrow w_R + \alpha \frac{EP - EP_R}{EP}$
13:          $w_G \leftarrow 1 - w_R$
14:          $Y \leftarrow P_M(X)$
15:      **end if**
16: **end while**

---

the key information in the data. For this reason, this model adopts the Stacking integrated learning framework, selects GNB and RF as the base learner, and uses the weighted summed linear regression model as the meta-model to construct the aircraft engine RUL prediction model, pseudo code can be found in Algorithm 2.

The RF model constructs multiple decision trees by self-sampling and feature random selection mechanism, which predicts the probability of engine failure for the samples X_{opt} after feature selection:

$$P_R(y|x_{opt}) = \frac{1}{T} \sum_{t=1}^{T} \frac{1}{l_t} \sum_{l \in l_t} \mathbb{I}(y_l = y), \tag{6}$$

where $\frac{1}{l_t} \sum_{l \in l_t} \mathbb{I}(y_l = y)$ denotes the prediction probability of the t-th decision tree, and $\mathbb{I}(\cdot)$ is the indicator function. The GNB model is based on Bayes' theorem for classification prediction of X_{en} after feature enhancement:

$$P_\alpha(y|x_{en}) \propto P(y) \prod_{i=1}^{m} P(x_i|y),$$

$$\text{where } m = |F_{en}|, \quad P(x_i|y) = \frac{1}{\sqrt{2\pi\sigma_{y,i}^2}} \exp\left(-\frac{(x_i - \mu_{y,i})^2}{2\sigma_{y,i}^2}\right), \tag{7}$$

where $\mu_{y,i}$ and $\sigma_{y,i}^2$ denote the mean and variance of the feature i under the category y, respectively.

The RF model is able to capture the nonlinear mapping relationship between sensor parameters and is robust to data noise and outliers. The GNB model assumes that the features are independent of each other and is able to utilise all possible combinations of features, and performs well in dealing with conditional independence between features. To integrate the advantages of both, weighted integration is used to obtain the final prediction probability:

$$P(y|x) = w_R P_R(y|x_{opt}) + w_G P_G(y|x_{en}),$$
$$\text{where } w_R + w_G = 1, w_R, w_G \geq 0. \tag{8}$$

Meanwhile, in order that this model can automatically specify a reasonable model selection strategy in different scenarios, this paper proposes an expected cost oriented dynamic weight adjustment strategy to optimise the weights of the ReForGe model with the objective of minimising the expected cost (EP) with the objective function:

$$\min_{w_R, w_G} EP(w_R, w_G)$$
$$\text{s.t. } w_R + w_G = 1, \tag{9}$$
$$w_R, w_G \in [0, 1].$$

The EP function is evaluated by calculating the cost of the risk of occurrence in the predictive maintenance process, which consists of two main risks: over-repair and missed failures, defined by the formula:

$$EP = R_L \times P_L \times C_L + P_B \times C_B,$$

$$\text{where } P_L = \frac{FP}{TP + TN + FP + FN}, P_B = \frac{FN}{TP + TN + FP + FN}. \tag{10}$$

Here R_L denotes the predicted remaining life cycle of the engine, P_L denotes the proportion of safe samples that the model incorrectly predicts as faulty samples (false positive rate), P_B denotes the proportion of faulty samples that the model incorrectly predicts as safe samples (false negative rate), and C_L and C_B denote the corresponding costs. TP (True Positive) indicates a sample that the model correctly predicts as a positive sample, TN (True Negative) indicates a sample that the model correctly predicts as a negative sample, FP (False Positive) indicates a sample that the model incorrectly predicts as a positive sample, and FN (False Negative) indicates a sample that the model incorrectly predicts as a negative sample.

After calculating the expected cost of the model through the EP function, the weights can be iteratively updated with the formula:

$$w'_R = w_R + \alpha \frac{EP - EP_R}{EP},$$
$$w'_G = 1 - w'_R, \tag{11}$$

where α is the learning rate, EP_R is the expected cost of the RF model, and EP is the expected cost of ReForGe model. By dynamically adjusting the weighting strategy, the ReForGe model is able to directly optimise the cost objective related to the actual application, fully consider the actual impact of different types of errors on the cost, and is able to adaptively adjust the weight allocation to improve the accuracy of the prediction.

4 Experiments and Discussions

4.1 Experimental Environment and Data Set

This experiment is carried out on a computer with a high-performance configuration, which is equipped with a processor of Intel Core i5 - 13400K, 32 GB of RAM, a graphics card of NVIDIA GeForce RTX 4060, an operating system of Windows 11 Professional, a programming environment based on Python 3.8, and the use of NumPy, Pandas, The programming environment is based on Python 3.8, using NumPy, Pandas, Matplotlib, Scikit - learn and other commonly used Python libraries for data processing, analysis and model construction.

In this paper, we study the turbofan engine degradation simulation dataset provided by the NASA platform [41], which simulates the operating conditions of various aircraft engines under different operating conditions, and the dataset contains a wealth of sensor data, such as the data collected by vibration sensors, temperature sensors, and pressure sensors. The samples in the dataset are arranged in chronological order, and each sample corresponds to the operating state of the engine at a specific moment. The purpose of the experiment in this paper is to determine whether the engine will fail in the next cycle.

4.2 Indicators for Assessing Model Performance

In order to comprehensively and accurately evaluate the model performance, this paper selects the commonly used evaluation indexes, including Accuracy, Precision, Recall, F1 Score and ROC AUC.

Accuracy is a measure of the number of samples correctly predicted by the model as a proportion of the total number of samples, and is calculated by the formula:

$$Accuracy = \frac{TP + TN}{TP + TN + FP + FN},\tag{12}$$

Accuracy reflects the overall accuracy of the model's predictions; a higher accuracy means that the model is able to make the right judgement in most cases, but it can be affected by factors such as sample imbalance.

The precision rate measures the proportion of samples predicted by the model to be positive and actually also positive to the proportion of samples predicted by the model to be positive, and is calculated as follows:

$$Precision = \frac{TP}{TP + FP},\tag{13}$$

The accuracy rate reflects the accuracy of the positive samples predicted by the model. In the engine failure prediction scenario, a higher accuracy rate indicates that the samples in which the model predicts that the engine is about to fail account for a higher proportion of the samples in which the failure will actually occur, i.e., the model's prediction results are more reliable, and it can effectively avoid the occurrence of false alarms and reduce unnecessary maintenance costs and resource wastage.

The recall rate represents the proportion of the number of samples that are actually positive and correctly predicted to be positive to the total number of actual positive samples, and is calculated by the formula:

$$Recall = \frac{TP}{TP + FN},\tag{14}$$

The accuracy rate reflects the accuracy of the positive samples predicted by the model. In the engine failure prediction scenario, a higher accuracy rate indicates that the samples in which the model predicts that the engine is about to fail account for a higher proportion of the samples in which the failure will actually occur, i.e., the model's prediction results are more reliable, and it can effectively avoid the occurrence of false alarms and reduce unnecessary maintenance costs and resource wastage.

The F1 score is a reconciled average that combines precision and recall to provide a more comprehensive assessment of model performance, and is calculated as:

$$F1 - Score = 2 \times \frac{Precision \times Recall}{Precision + Recall}.\tag{15}$$

ROC-AUC is used to evaluate the classification performance of the model under different classification thresholds. In a binary classification problem, a series of different true positive rates (i.e., recall rates) and false positive rates are obtained by continuously adjusting the classification threshold $FPR = \frac{FP}{FP+TN}$, and these points are connected to form a ROC curve, and ROC - AUC is the area under the curve. The closer the value of ROC - AUC is to 1, the better the classification performance of the model, and the value ranges from 0 to 1. When ROC - AUC is 0.5, it means that the prediction effect of the model is no different from random guessing; and when ROC - AUC is greater than 0.5, the model has a certain classification ability, and the larger the value, the stronger the model's ability to distinguish between positive samples and negative samples under different thresholds, and for the prediction model that distinguishes whether the engine is about to break down or not, the higher ROC - AUC means that the model can have better performance under different decision criteria. criteria can perform better.

4.3 Experimental Results and Discussion

According to the results of the bar chart comparison in Fig. 3a, the ReForGe model performs more balanced in all the indexes without obvious shortcomings. On the basis of ensuring high accuracy and precision of the model, the Recall rate is increased by 1% to 93%. The increase of the Recall rate enables the model to detect potential faulty engines more comprehensively, reducing the risk of missed detection and ensuring flight safety. This is because even if only one engine fault is missed, it may cause a serious accident during the flight. The F1 score combines the precision and Recall rates, and the ReForGe model improves the F1 score by 4.49% to 92.9%, which further shows that the model's ability in identifying samples of the positive class (i.e., samples predicted to be of the positive class are actually also of the positive class) performs well, while the false alarm rate is also effectively controlled. A good balance is achieved between the Precision and Recall rates.

From the radar plot comparison in Fig. 3b, it can be seen that the ReForGe model has the largest area in the radar plot. The radargram is able to visually display the model's comprehensive performance on multiple performance indicators, and a larger area means that the model performs relatively well on all indicators and the overall performance is more balanced. This further proves that the overall performance of the ReForGe model has been optimised compared with other comparative models, which makes its fault prediction under complex working conditions more reliable, and enables it to accurately judge and predict both normal fluctuations during engine operation and complex potential fault characteristics.

In this paper, experimental comparisons of model performance before and after feature engineering were conducted and the results are shown in Fig. 4a. The experiments were conducted to compare the model performance of a single RF model, a single GNB model, a simple integrated model of RF and GNB, and a ReForGe model, respectively. From the comparison of F1 scores in Fig. 4(a), it

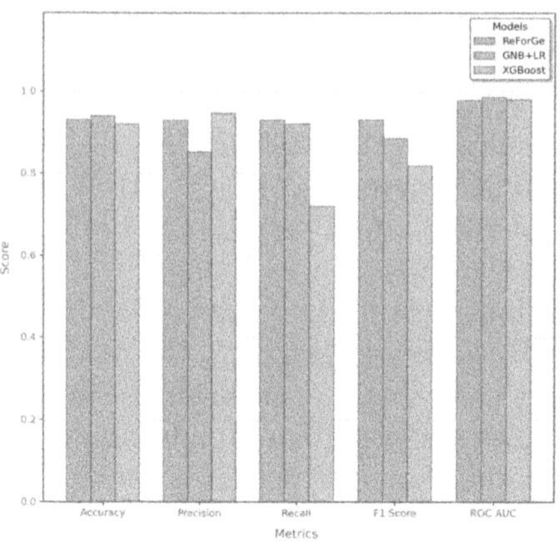

(a) Bar chart comparison of model performance metrics

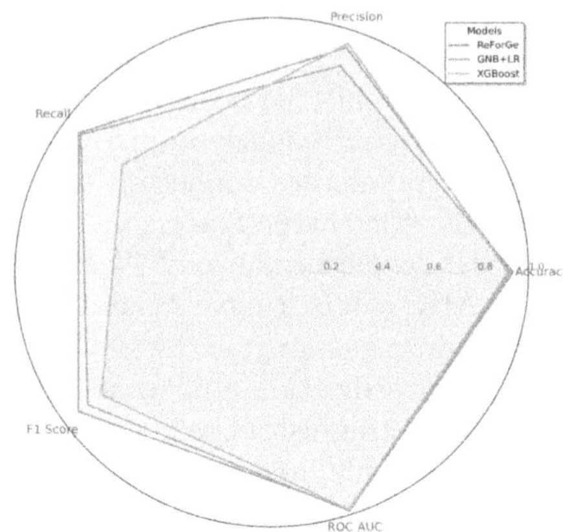

(b) Radar map comparison of comprehensive performance

Fig. 3. Performance comparison of ReForGe model with other models

can be clearly seen that ReForGe improves the model performance by 4.4% compared to the single machine learning model and the simple integration model. This is due to the fact that the subset of features screened by the RFE algorithm in combination with the RF model can more effectively reflect the relationship between the engine operating state and the remaining service life. By removing redundant and interfering features in the original data through feature selection, the model is able to focus on key features related to engine failures, which reduces the model complexity, reduces the risk of overfitting, and improves the generalisation ability of the model, which is able to better adapt to different engine operation data and accurately predict the remaining service life and the likelihood of engine failures.

The prediction probability distributions in Fig. 4b clearly show the prediction characteristics of the different models. the Naive Bayes model provides the most dispersed prediction distributions, which means that the model is more broad in predicting the probability of engine failures, with a larger uncertainty, and it is difficult to accurately give a clear conclusion on the failure prediction. the Random Forest model, with its obvious bimodal distribution, c tends to make more extreme predictions, and may not be accurate enough to judge some engine operating states in critical or complex conditions. The Random Forest model has obvious bimodal distribution characteristics and tends to make more extreme predictions, c may simply divide the engine operating state into two extreme cases of normal or failure, and is not accurate enough to judge the operating state of the engine in some critical or complex working conditions. The Simple Ensemble model shows a certain prediction tendency while maintaining the stability, but in the face of the complex data, its prediction However, when facing complex data, there is still room for improvement in the compre-

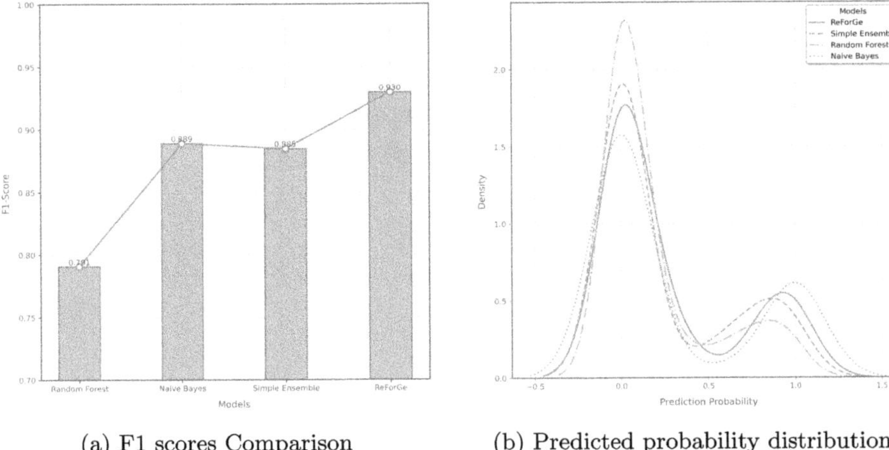

(a) F1 scores Comparison   (b) Predicted probability distribution

Fig. 4. Comparison of model performance before and after feature selection

hensiveness and accuracy of its prediction. The ReForGe model, on the other hand, has the smoothest distribution and achieves the most stable prediction distribution through its integration strategy and feature engineering. This shows that the ReForGe model is able to fully integrate the advantages of different models to provide a more comprehensive and in-depth analysis of the engine operation data, and thus can give more reasonable, stable and accurate results when predicting the probability of engine failure.

The experimental results show that the difference in the strength of the correlation between the different features can be visualised from the thermogram in Fig. 5 (a). The positive correlation between the engine vibration and temperature parameters under some operating conditions may be due to the increase in vibration and friction caused by the wear or failure of internal engine components, which leads to an increase in temperature; the negative correlation between the pressure and speed parameters under certain circumstances is due to the change in the engine intake pressure, which affects the combustion efficiency and hence the engine speed. These correlations help to understand the engine operation mechanism and potential causes of failure, and also provide a key basis for model optimisation.

Figure 5 (b) illustrates the corresponding number of predicted samples for TP, TN, FP, and FN. From the figure, it can be visualised that the number of correctly predicted samples of the model (TP + TN) is significantly higher than the cases of missed (FN) and false (FP) alarms. The large number of correctly predicted samples indicates that the model is able to accurately identify the normal operating state and faulty state of the engine, which provides a reliable support for the actual aircraft engine maintenance decision-making, and the small number of missed alarms and false alarms are also within the acceptable range.

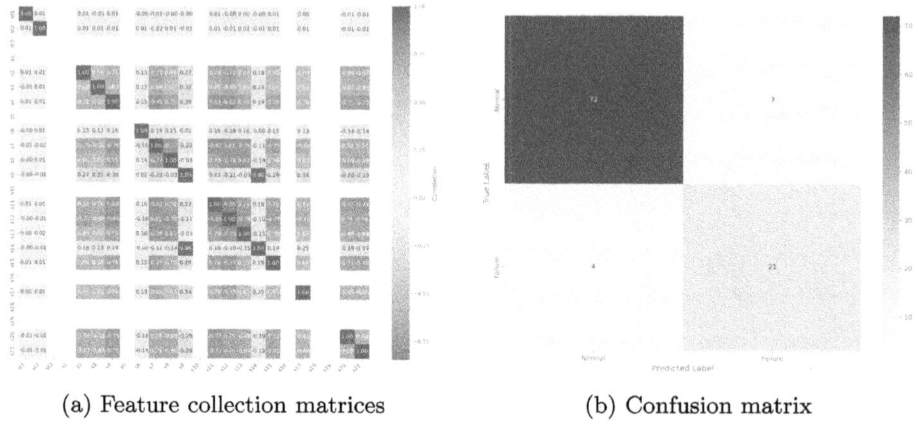

(a) Feature collection matrices   (b) Confusion matrix

Fig. 5. Analysis of feature correlation and prediction results of ReForGe

5   Conclusion and Future Work

In the field of predictive maintenance for aircraft engines, traditional methods suffer from low fault prediction accuracy and data leakage risks due to limitations of linear assumptions and insufficient data security protection. To address these issues, this paper proposes the ReForGe secure integration model. The model selects core features using the RFE algorithm and constructs feature interaction terms to uncover hidden relationships in the data. It ensures data security through lightweight hash verification and traffic analysis techniques. Based on a Stacking framework, the model integrates GNB and RF, optimizing prediction accuracy through dynamic weight adjustment. Experimental results show that the model achieves 93% fault prediction accuracy on the NASA dataset, with a 4.49% improvement in F1 score over traditional models, and demonstrates better performance under extreme conditions. Future work could explore integrating physical degradation mechanisms and expert experience, strengthening cybersecurity protections, and improving the model's interpretability and reliability for maintenance decisions.

References

1. Sai, Y.: Developing key sustainability indicators for aviation (2024)
2. Wild, G.: Urban aviation: the future aerospace transportation system for intercity and intracity mobility. Urban Sci. **8**(4), 218 (2024)
3. Li, Y., Liang, W., Xie, K., Zhang, D., Li, K., Xiong, N.N.: EventMon: real-time event-based streaming network monitoring data recovery. IEEE Trans. Dependable Secure Comput. (2024)
4. Möller, D.P.F.: Cybersecurity in digital transformation. In: Guide to Cybersecurity in Digital Transformation: Trends, Methods, Technologies, Applications and Best Practices, pp. 1–70, Springer, (2023). https://doi.org/10.1007/978-3-031-26845-8_1

5. Babu, C.S., Pal, A.: Enhancing security for unmanned aircraft systems in IoT environments: defense mechanisms and mitigation strategies. Unmanned Aircraft Syst., 429–476 (2024) Wiley Online Library

6. Xiao, Y., Huo, Y., Cai, J., Gong, Y., Liang, W., Kołodziej, J.: ERF-XGB: an edge-IoT-based explainable model for predictive maintenance. IEEE Trans. Consum. Electron. **70**(1), 4016–4025 (2024)

7. Shaik, M.A., Sneha, P.: Revolutionizing infrastructure resilience: AI-driven predictive maintenance and structural health monitoring (2025)

8. De Giorgi, M.G., Menga, N., Ficarella, A.: Exploring prognostic and diagnostic techniques for jet engine health monitoring: a review of degradation mechanisms and advanced prediction strategies. Energies **16**(6), 2711 (2023)

9. Liang, W., Liu, Y., Yang, C., Xie, S., Li, K., Susilo, W.: On identity, transaction, and smart contract privacy on permissioned and permissionless blockchain: a comprehensive survey. ACM Comput. Surv. **56**(12), 1–35 (2024)

10. Zhang, Y., et al.: Review of the field environmental sensing methods based on multi-sensor information fusion technology. Int. J. Agri. Biol. Eng. **17**(2), 1–13 (2024)

11. Chintaiah, N., Vignesh, M., Charan, K., Sanjana, M., Gowthami, P.: Advancing sensor data integrity with deep learning-based fault detection. Int. Res. J. Multidiscip. Scope **5**(2)

12. Mohammed, A.: Detection and mitigation strategies for cyber-attacks in offshore oil and gas industrial networks. PhD thesis, Cardiff University (2024)

13. Cai, J., Liang, W., Li, X., Li, K., Gui, Z., Khan, M.K.: GTXChain: a secure IoT smart blockchain architecture based on graph neural network. IEEE Internet Things J. **10**(24), 21502–21514 (2023)

14. Liang, W., Xie, S., Li, K.C., Li, X., Kui, X., Zomaya, A.Y.: MC-DSC: a dynamic secure resource configuration scheme based on medical consortium blockchain. IEEE Trans. Inf. Forensics Secur. **19**, 3525–3538 (2024)

15. Hou, N., et al.: Failure modes, mechanisms and causes of shafts in mechanical equipment. Eng. Fail. Anal. **136**, 106216 (2022)

16. Zhang, Q., Chung, S.H., Ma, H.L., Sun, X.: Robust aircraft maintenance routing with heterogenous aircraft maintenance tasks. Transport. Res. Part C: Emerg. Technol. **160**, 104518 (2024)

17. Fedele, L., Di Vito, L., Ramundo, F.E.: Increasing efficiency in an aeronautical engine through maintenance evaluation and upgrades: analysis of the reliability and performance improvements under financial issues. Energies **13**(12), 3059 (2020)

18. Zhao, N., et al.: Identifying bad software changes via multimodal anomaly detection for online service systems. In: Proceedings of the 29th ACM Joint Meeting on European Software Engineering Conference and Symposium on the Foundations of Software Engineering, pp. 527–539 (2021)

19. Zheng, M., Lin, J., Xia, T., Liu, Y., Pan, E.: Joint condition-based maintenance and spare provisioning policy for a k-out-of-n system with failures during inspection intervals. Eur. J. Oper. Res. **308**(3), 1220–1232 (2023)

20. De Pater, I., Reijns, A., Mitici, M.: Alarm-based predictive maintenance scheduling for aircraft engines with imperfect remaining useful life prognostics. Reliab. Eng. Syst. Saf. **221**, 108341 (2022)

21. Randall, R.B.: Vibration-Based Condition Monitoring: Industrial, Automotive and Aerospace Applications. Wiley (2021)

22. Stanton, I., Munir, K., Ikram, A., El-Bakry, M.: Predictive maintenance analytics and implementation for aircraft: challenges and opportunities. Syst. Eng. **26**(2), 216–237 (2023)

23. Xiong, M., Wang, H., Fu, Q., Xu, Y.: Digital twin-driven aero-engine intelligent predictive maintenance. Int. J. Adv. Manuf. Technol. **114**(11), 3751–3761 (2021)
24. Achouch, M., et al.: On predictive maintenance in industry 4.0: overview, models, and challenges. Appl. Sci. **12**(16), 8081 (2022). MDPI
25. Shafik, W.: Data loss software reason and hardware reason. In: Data Recovery Techniques for Computer Forensics, pp. 27–61, Bentham Science Publishers (2025)
26. Mahlake, N., Mathonsi, T.E., Du Plessis, D., Muchenje, T.: A lightweight encryption algorithm to enhance wireless sensor network security on the internet of things. J. Commun. **18**(1), 47–57 (2023)
27. Komadina, A., Martinić, M., Groš, S., Mihajlović, Ž.: Comparing threshold selection methods for network anomaly detection. IEEE Access (2024)
28. Dargie, W., Wen, J., Panes-Ruiz, L.A., Riemenschneider, L., Ibarlucea, B., Cuniberti, G.: Monitoring toxic gases using nanotechnology and wireless sensor networks. IEEE Sensors J. **23**(11), 12274–12283 (2023) IEEE
29. Xie, S., Xiao, L., Han, D., Xie, K., Li, X., Liang, W.: HCVC: a high-capacity off-chain virtual channel scheme based on bidirectional locking mechanism. IEEE Trans. Netw. Sci. Eng. **11**(5), 3995–4006 (2023)
30. Shahid, S.M., Ko, S., Kwon, S.: Real-time abnormality detection and classification in diesel engine operations with convolutional neural network. Expert Syst. Appl. **192**, 116233 (2022)
31. Zhang, D., et al.: Failure analysis and reliability optimization approaches for particulate filter of diesel engine after-treatment system. Int. J. Autom. Manuf. Mater. (2025)
32. Wang, H., Zhang, W., Yang, D., Xiang, Y.: Deep-learning-enabled predictive maintenance in industrial internet of things: methods, applications, and challenges. IEEE Syst. J. **17**(2), 2602–2615 (2022)
33. Cheng, J.C., Chen, W., Chen, K., Wang, Q.: Data-driven predictive maintenance planning framework for MEP components based on BIM and IoT using machine learning algorithms. Autom. Constr. **112**, 103087 (2020)
34. Xiong, J., Zhou, J., Ma, Y., Zhang, F., Lin, C.: Adaptive deep learning-based remaining useful life prediction framework for systems with multiple failure patterns. Reliab. Eng. Syst. Safety **235**, 109244 (2023)
35. Yu, W., Liu, Y., Dillon, T., Rahayu, W.: Edge computing-assisted IoT framework with an autoencoder for fault detection in manufacturing predictive maintenance. IEEE Trans. Industr. Inf. **19**(4), 5701–5710 (2022)
36. Mourtzis, D., Angelopoulos, J., Panopoulos, N.: Design and development of an edge-computing platform towards 5g technology adoption for improving equipment predictive maintenance. Procedia Comput. Sci. **200**, 611–619 (2022)
37. Hajiha, M., Liu, X., Lee, Y.M., Ramin, M.: A physics-regularized data-driven approach for health prognostics of complex engineered systems with dependent health states. Reliab. Eng. Syst. Safety **226**, 108677 (2022)
38. Xue, Y., Wen, C., Wang, Z., Liu, W., Chen, G.: A novel framework for motor bearing fault diagnosis based on multi-transformation domain and multi-source data. Knowl. Based Syst. **283**, 111205 (2024)
39. Liu, P., Wang, L., Ranjan, R., He, G., Zhao, L.: A survey on active deep learning: from model driven to data driven. ACM Comput. Surv. (CSUR) **54**(10s), 1–34 (2022)

40. Moşteanu, N.R.: Adapting to the unpredictable: building resilience for business continuity in an ever-changing landscape. Eur. J. Theor. Appl. Sci. **2**(1), 444–457 (2024)
41. Saxena, A., Goebel, K., Simon, D., Eklund, N.: Damage propagation modeling for aircraft engine run-to-failure simulation. In: 2008 International Conference on Prognostics and Health Management, pp. 1–9. IEEE (2008)

Real-World Image Dehazing via Degradation Modeling, Spectral-Spatial Fusion, and Prior Guidance

Jiali Rong[1], Miao Liao[1], and Shuanhu Di[2(✉)]

[1] School of Computer Science and Engineering, Hunan University of Science and Technology, Xiangtan 411201, China
[2] College of Intelligence Science and Technology, National University of Defense Technology, Changsha 410073, China
dish0304@163.com

Abstract. Image dehazing serves as a fundamental low-level computer vision task that aims to recover high-quality images from haze-corrupted observations. This technology plays a critical role in safety-critical applications such as autonomous driving, intelligent transportation systems, and urban security monitoring. The performance of image dehazing directly impacts the perception accuracy and overall safety of vision-based systems. However, owing to the complexity of degradation factors in real-world hazy images and the difficulty in capturing paired hazy-clear data, existing methods face significant challenges in real-world image dehazing. In this paper, we focus on three key aspects to improve adaptability in real-world scenarios. Specifically, (1) to simulate the complex haze degradation process, we design a haze degradation model incorporating multiple scattering effects and diverse degradation factors. (2) To improve frequency-domain distortions, we introduce a Spectral-Spatial Fusion Module into the network, which adaptively processes both spatial and frequency information. (3) To effectively incorporate prior knowledge, we incorporate a Prior-Guided Feedforward Network into the network architecture. Comprehensive experiments show that the proposed method achieves better dehazing performance than other state-of-the-art real-world image dehazing methods. This method can improve the perception accuracy of vision-based systems and enhance their reliability in safety-critical tasks.

Keywords: Real-world image dehazing · Haze degradation model · Spectral-spatial fusion · Prior guidance

Supported by the Natural Science Foundation of Hunan Province (Grant No. 2025J150363); the Science and Technology Innovation Program of Hunan Province (Grant No. 2024RC3216); and the Scientific Research Fund of Hunan Provincial Education Department (Grant No. 24A0356).

W. Liang et al. (Eds.): SecureComm 2025, LNICST 690, pp. 352–370, 2026.
https://doi.org/10.1007/978-3-032-23456-8_19

1   Introduction

Owing to the absorption and scattering of visible light by suspended particles in the atmosphere, images captured in haze conditions often suffer from color distortion, detail loss, and low contrast. This degradation may cause recognition errors and decision biases in safety-critical applications, such as autonomous driving, intelligent transportation systems, and urban security monitoring [1,7, 12,18], posing serious safety risks. Consequently, image dehazing has become a research hotspot in the field of computer vision, with significant research value and practical significance.

Nowadays, existing image dehazing methods can be divided into two categories: those based on image priors and those based on deep learning. Dehazing methods based on image priors typically rely on the atmospheric scattering model (ASM), utilizing image statistical priors to estimate its parameters. For example, He et al. [11] proposed the Dark Channel Prior (DCP) by observing that minimum channel values in non-sky regions of clear images tend to be near zero. Utilizing this prior, their method estimates both the transmission and global atmospheric light to recover clear images. Zhu et al. [31] discovered a linear relationship between scene depth and the difference between brightness and saturation, proposing a dehazing method based on the Color Attenuation Prior. Berman et al. [2] estimated the transmission using the haze-line prior, and further refined it through a regularization term. Ling et al. [16] proposed a novel prior called the Saturation Line Prior, which effectively estimates transmission by leveraging the linear relationship between pixel saturation and the reciprocal of brightness. While these methods perform well in specific hazy conditions without the need for training, their handcrafted priors often struggle to adapt to the complexity and variability of real haze.

With the rapid development of deep learning, dehazing methods based on deep learning have made significant progress. Early research, such as DehazeNet [3], obtained clear images by constructing a convolutional neural network to learn the mapping between hazy images and transmission maps. Ren et al. [22] designed two sub-networks that progressively estimate transmission maps from coarse to fine. However, estimation errors of these parameters may be progressively amplified in subsequent computations, ultimately affecting dehazing performance. Therefore, researchers have proposed some end-to-end methods [13] that directly restore clear images to avoid cumulative errors. For example, Qin et al. [20] proposed the Feature Fusion Attention Network, which integrates both channel and pixel attention mechanisms, achieving remarkable performance across multiple benchmark datasets. Lu et al. [17] enhanced dehazing performance by incorporating multi-scale convolution and parallel attention to better capture local textures and handle uneven haze distribution. Cui et al. [6] introduced a dual-domain channel attention mechanism that combines channel interactions in both spatial and frequency domains, significantly enhancing image restoration performance across various tasks. Although these methods achieve promising results on synthetic datasets, their performance degrades considerably in real-world hazy conditions, primarily due to their limited generalization capability in complex and diverse scenarios.

Given the substantial domain discrepancy between synthetic and real hazy images, a series of dehazing methods specifically designed for real-world hazy images have been progressively proposed in recent years. For example, Chen et al. [4] proposed a two-stage dehazing method (PSD), which involves pretraining on synthetic datasets followed by unsupervised fine-tuning on real-world hazy images using physical prior constraints. This approach effectively enhances generalization in complex environments. Yang et al. [28] introduced a self-enhanced dehazing framework (D4) that uses unpaired data to learn scattering coefficients and scene depth within the ASM, enabling effective haze generation and removal in real-world scenarios. UCL-Dehaze [26] proposed an unsupervised contrastive learning-based image dehazing method, which constructs positive and negative sample pairs from unpaired data and incorporates adversarial training to achieve domain adaptation. HazeCLIP [25] innovatively leverages CLIP's [21] zero-shot recognition capability to bridge the domain gap in real-world dehazing without requiring labeled hazy-clean pairs. However, constrained by the complexity of real-world scenarios and the diversity of degradation factors, these methods still exhibit limited robustness in real-world image dehazing tasks.

To address the challenges in real-world image dehazing, this work systematically enhances the adaptability of the dehazing model through three key aspects. (1) To generate realistic hazy images that conform to natural degradation patterns, we propose an enhanced haze degradation model that incorporates multiple scattering effects and various degradation factors, thereby providing high-fidelity training samples for image dehazing network. (2) Existing dehazing methods primarily remove haze interference by modeling local structures in the spatial domain, but real-world hazy images often suffer from severe noise interference. Haze and noise exhibit distinct characteristics in the frequency domain: haze typically causes attenuation of high-frequency components, while noise introduces excessive high-frequency artifacts, resulting in inconsistent spectral properties in hazy images. Therefore, we introduce a Spectral-Spatial Fusion Module (SSFM) into the network, which adaptively processes spatial texture information and frequency-domain structural features. (3) Considering that traditional prior knowledge with potential guiding value, which is often underutilized in existing methods. We introduce a Prior-Guided Feedforward Network (PGFN) into the network.

In summary, the main contributions of this work are as follows:

1. We propose a haze degradation model that incorporates multiple scattering effects and diverse degradation factors to more realistically simulate haze formation in complex natural environments, thereby mitigating the distributional discrepancy between synthetic and real domains and enhancing the model's generalization capability on real-world images.
2. We propose a SSFM that integrates spatial and frequency domain features, addressing the local detail blurring caused by haze in the spatial domain and

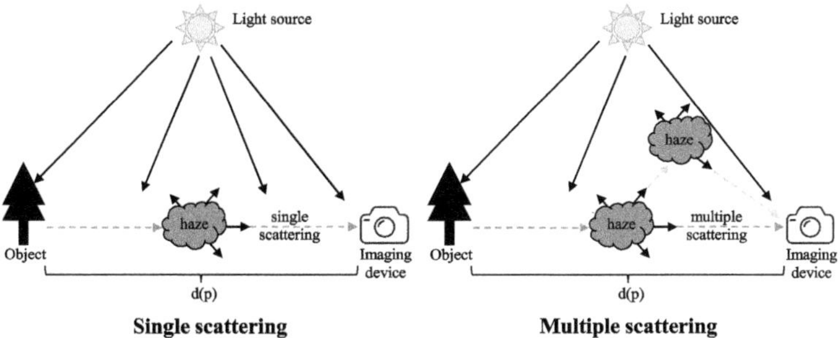

Fig. 1. Effect of single scattering and multiple scattering in the atmosphere on imaging. The tree is the target object, the camera is the imaging device that captures hazy images, and the cloud represents the haze particles in the atmosphere. $d(p)$ represents the distance from the target object to the imaging device and the sun represents the light source.

the differing characteristics of haze and noise interference in the frequency domain.
3. We construct a PGFN to explore task-relevant physical priors, which significantly enhance the network's capability to extract haze-related features.

2   Method

2.1   Haze Degradation Model Construction

Designing data generation strategies is an effective approach to improving single-image dehazing performance in real-world scenarios. Classic strategies typically rely on the ASM, The haze degradation process based on the ASM assumes that light is scattered by haze particles at most once after being reflected from the target object. The left part of Fig. 1 demonstrates the single scattering process. However, in real atmospheric environments, light often undergoes multiple scattering during propagation [30] (the right part of Fig. 1), resulting in more complex image degradation phenomena such as halo effects and image blurring. In addition, real-world hazy scenes are often affected by various degradation factors, such as color shift, noise, and artifacts, making the actual degradation process more complex than the ASM. Therefore, we extend the ASM based on multiple scattering effects and various degradation factors, establishing an enhanced haze degradation model. The specific formula is as follows:

$$I(p) = JPEG\{((1-\alpha)I(p) + \alpha \sum_{i \in \Omega} w(i)I(i)e^{-\beta d(i)} + N)T(p) +$$

$$(1 - T(p))(A + \Delta A)\} \tag{1}$$

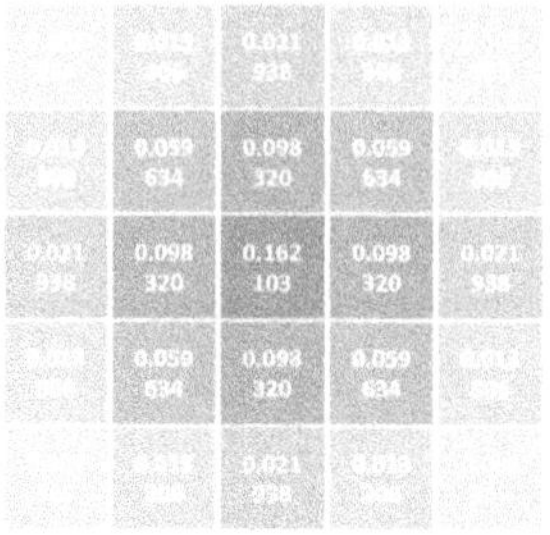

Fig. 2. Gaussian weight function $w(i)$, where $i \in \Omega$, the window size of ω is set to 5.

where, p denotes the position of a pixel. $I(p)$ and $J(p)$ represent the intensity of the observed image and the ground truth intensity of the target image, respectively. $T(p)$ denotes the transmission, which reflects the attenuation of light during propagation, while A represents the global atmospheric light. $\sum_{i \in \Omega} w(i) I(i) e^{-\beta d(i)}$ represents the multiple scattering term, where Ω refers to the multiple scattering domain, $w(i)$ is the scattering weight of neighboring pixel i, $J(i)$ is the target intensity, and $e^{-\beta d(i)}$ represents the transmission. β and $d(i)$ denote the scattering coefficient and scene depth, respectively. The parameter $\alpha \in (0, 1)$ controls the contribution of the multiple scattering term, adjusting its influence on the overall image intensity. N represents Gaussian noise, and ΔA denotes a color deviation perturbation. The $JPEG\{\cdot\}$ denotes compression artifacts. The haze degradation model extends the ASM by incorporating multiple scattering effects, color shifts, as well as noise and artifacts. A detailed explanation of each component is provided below.

Multiple Scattering: To accurately simulate the physical properties of light propagation in real hazy environments, we use a Gaussian weight function $w(i)$ to represent the scattering contribution from neighboring pixels i to the central pixel p. As shown in Fig. 2, under the influence of the Gaussian weight function, the scattering contribution of neighboring pixels to the central pixel decreases with distance. As the key parameters in the haze degradation model, we employ a depth estimation network [15] to obtain depth images $d(i)$, and use $\beta \in [0.3, 1.5]$ to control the scattering intensity. The scattering coefficient, scene depth, and multiple scattering weight jointly determine the distribution and density variations of hazy images. By adjusting these three parameters, the haze degradation model can effectively simulate hazy images with varying degrees of degradation, providing diverse and realistic training data for the dehazing network.

Color Bias: To generate more diverse hazy images, we introduce color bias into the global atmospheric light A. The global atmospheric light A is a three-channel vector, which is constrained in the range of $[0.75, 0.95]$ to ensure reasonable brightness distribution. Additionally, to enhance color randomness, a perturbation term ΔA is added to each channel, which is randomly sampled from the

Fig. 3. Visual comparison of hazy images. (a) clear image, (b) hazy images generated by the proposed haze degradation model, (c) hazy images from the RESIDE dataset.

range of $[-0.025, 0.025]$. This design effectively simulates the color variations of haze under different lighting conditions in real-world environments.

Noise and Artifacts: Noise is also one of the degradation factors of real hazy images. In this paper, Gaussian noise is introduced into the haze degradation model. Furthermore, to better align with the characteristics of actual imaging systems, *JPEG* compression is applied in the final stage of the haze degradation model, reproducing the typical *JPEG* artifacts caused by the compression algorithm in the simulated hazy images.

We randomly select 500 clear images from the SOTS-outdoor to construct paired training data, with hazy images dynamically generated by the haze degradation model during the training process. Figure 3 presents a comparison between hazy images generated by the proposed haze degradation model and those hazy images from the RESIDE dataset. It can be observed that the haze produced by our model is denser and more complex, with spatial distribution and visual appearance that more closely resembles real-world haze conditions, thereby enhancing the realism and diversity of the training data.

2.2 Dehazing Network Construction

Overall Pipeline. Based on the proposed haze degradation model, we design an end-to-end dehazing network architecture. As illustrated in Fig. 4, the overall architecture adopts a three-stage symmetric encoder-decoder framework. It takes a hazy image as input and initially extracts low-level features through a 3×3 convolutional layer. At the same time, an initial dehazed image is estimated from the input using the DCP, providing a prior foundation for subsequent feature enhancement. In the backbone network, each stage consists of a varying number of stacked Mixed-domain Feature Blocks (MFBlock), which operate at different resolutions and channel numbers across stages to extract multi-scale features. The MFBlock is designed based on the basic framework of the Transformer Block [23]. Each MFBlock incorporates a SSFM, which extracts local spatial textures and global frequency domain structures, preserving image details while enhancing the perception of frequency characteristic differences. At the same time, the PGFN enhances texture edges and detail information, fully leveraging the guiding role of prior knowledge. Specifically, the prior branch (PB) extracts features from the initial dehazed image and integrates the extracted prior information into the PGFN. The feature downsampling and upsampling processes respectively employ pixel-unshuffle and pixel-shuffle operations, which effectively preserve the image's structural information while improving the accuracy of context alignment. Additionally, to prevent information loss during downsampling. The skip connections are established at each stage, allowing the features extracted by the encoder to be directly passed to the corresponding decoder stage, enabling cross-layer feature fusion. Finally, a 3×3 convolution layer is used to transform the high-dimensional features into image space, producing a residual image. This residual image is subsequently added to the input image to produce the dehazed image J, represented as:

$$J = I + R \tag{2}$$

where, R is the residual image, I is the input hazy image.

Spectral-Spatial Fusion Module. Most existing dehazing approaches primarily focus on restoring local structures and texture details in the spatial domain. However, in complex real-world environments, images are not only affected by haze but may also suffer from other degradation factors such as noise. Various degradation types manifest differently in the frequency domain. Specifically, haze suppresses high-frequency components, resulting in blurred visual content, while noise introduces excessive high-frequency perturbations that compromise the integrity of the spectral distribution. The inconsistency in frequency-domain properties makes it difficult to fully compensate for degradation information through spatial-domain modeling alone. To address this issue, we introduce a SSFM, which enhances the representation capacity of the network by adaptively modeling spatial and frequency domain features.

As illustrated in Fig. 4, the SSFM consists of three main components: a spatial branch, a frequency branch, and an adaptive fusion mechanism. Within the spatial branch, we employ a lightweight residual architecture, which utilizes 3×3 convolution and 3×3 depthwise convolution layers for feature extraction. Residual connections are incorporated to retain the original feature representations. The corresponding process can be formulated as:

$$X_{\text{spatial}} = \text{Conv}\left(\text{Dconv}\left(\text{Conv}(X_f)\right)\right) + X_f \tag{3}$$

where, X_f denotes the input feature, Conv represents the 3×3 convolution, Dconv denotes the 3×3 depthwise convolution, and X_{spatial} indicates the feature produced by the spatial branch.

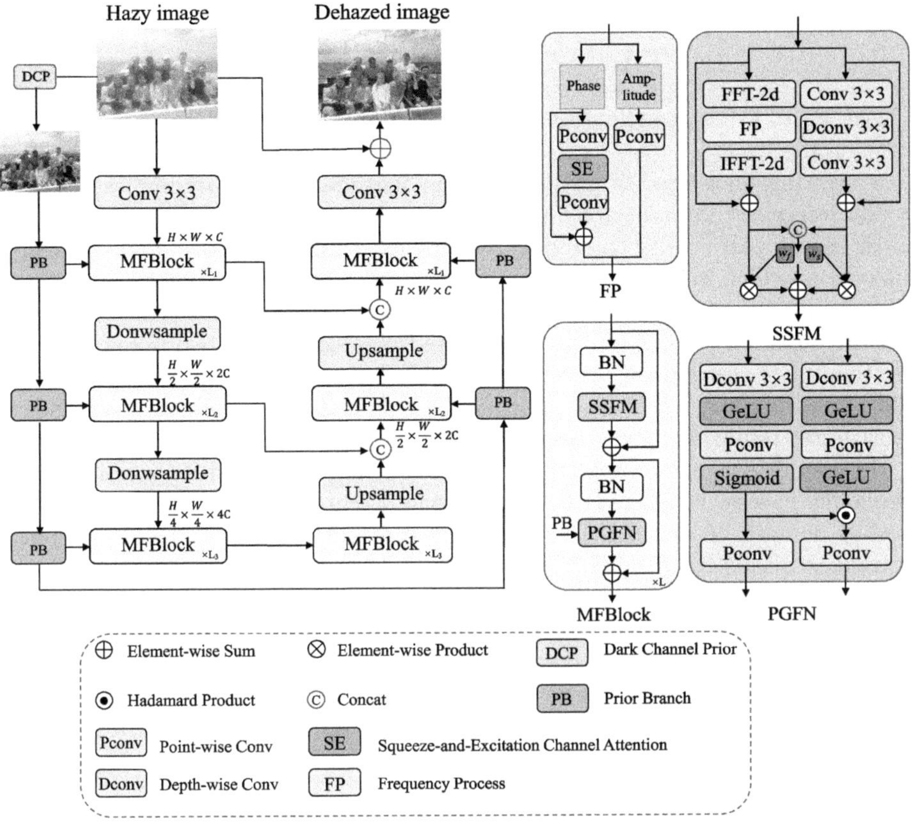

Fig. 4. The Structure of the proposed Network. This network is a three-stage symmetric encoder-decoder framework embedded in MFBlock. The MFBlock integrates a SSFM and a PGFN.

In the frequency branch, the input features X_f are first transformed using the Fourier Transform $F(X_f)$, which can be formalized as:

$$F(X_f)(u,v) = \sum_{h=0}^{H-1} \sum_{w=0}^{W-1} X_f(h,w) e^{-j2\pi\left(\frac{h}{H}u + \frac{w}{W}v\right)} \tag{4}$$

where, (h,w) and (u,v) respectively refer to the spatial and frequency coordinates, and H and W indicate the height and width of the input feature. The frequency-domain feature $F(X_f)$ is represented as: $F(X_f) = R(X_f) + jI(X_f)$, where $R(X_f)$ and $I(X_f)$ correspond to its real and imaginary components. These components are then converted into amplitude and phase spectra, which are computed as follows:

$$A(X_f)(u,v) = \sqrt{R^2(X_f)(u,v) + I^2(X_f)(u,v)} \tag{5}$$

$$P(X_f)(u, v) = \arctan\left(\frac{I(X_f)(u, v)}{R(X_f)(u, v)}\right) \tag{6}$$

where, $A(X_f)$ denotes the amplitude spectrum, and $P(X_f)$ denotes the phase spectrum.

According to related literature [29], the degradation characteristics of images in the frequency domain are predominantly manifested in the amplitude spectrum. Specifically, haze commonly results in reduced contrast and brightness distortion, which manifests as attenuation in the amplitude information. On the other hand, the phase spectrum, which focuses on structural and contour details, remains relatively stable and is less affected by degradation. Consequently, during the image restoration process, effectively enhancing the magnitude features while utilizing the structural information retained in the phase spectrum can contribute to improving the restoration quality.

In response to the aforementioned phenomena, we introduce a collaborative frequency process strategy (FP) for the magnitude and phase spectra in the frequency domain branch. In the magnitude spectrum branch, a 1×1 convolution is used to recover the magnitude spectrum and dynamically adjust its intensity distribution, thereby mitigating brightness distortion caused by haze. In the phase spectrum branch, a 1×1 convolution and SE channel attention mechanism are introduced to compensate for subtle phase change degradation factors, while residual connections are employed to preserve the original feature information. This design improves representational capacity without compromising computational efficiency. The computation formula is as follows:

$$A^1\left(X_f\right)(u, v) = \mathrm{Pconv}\left(A\left(X_f\right)(u, v)\right) \tag{7}$$

$$P^1\left(X_f\right)(u, v) = \mathrm{Pconv}\left(\mathrm{SE}\left(\mathrm{Pconv}\left(P\left(X_f\right)(u, v)\right)\right)\right) + P\left(X_f\right)(u, v) \tag{8}$$

where, Pconv represents the 1×1 convolution, SE represents the channel attention mechanism, and $A^1\left(X_f\right)(u, v)$ and $P^1\left(X_f\right)(u, v)$ respectively denote the processed magnitude spectrum and phase spectrum. Subsequently, the real and imaginary components are computed as follows:

$$R^1\left(X_f^{(t-1)}\right)(u, v) = A^1\left(X_f\right)(u, v) \cdot \cos\left(P^1\left(X_f\right)(u, v)\right) \tag{9}$$

$$I^1\left(X_f^{(t-1)}\right)(u, v) = A^1\left(X_f\right)(u, v) \cdot \sin\left(P^1\left(X_f\right)(u, v)\right) \tag{10}$$

Finally, the feature maps are transformed back into the spatial domain, as formulated below:

$$X_{\mathrm{frequency}} = F^{-1}\left(R^1\left(X_f^{(t-1)}\right)(u, v), I^1\left(X_f^{(t-1)}\right)(u, v)\right) \tag{11}$$

where, $X_{\mathrm{frequency}}$ denotes the feature obtained from the frequency-domain branch, and F^{-1} represents the inverse Fourier transform.

Ultimately, the features obtained from the spatial and frequency-domain branches are concatenated along the channel axis and subsequently integrated through a 1×1 convolution. The corresponding formulation is as follows:

$$X_{\text{cat}} = \text{Pconv}\left(\text{Concat}\left(X_{\text{spatial}}, X_{\text{frequency}}\right)\right) \tag{12}$$

where, Concat denotes channel-wise concatenation. Subsequently, the Softmax function is applied along the channel dimension to generate adaptive fusion weights w_s and w_f, corresponding to the spatial and frequency branches, respectively:

$$[w_f, w_s] = \text{Softmax}\left(X_{\text{cat}}\right) \tag{13}$$

The output X'_f is obtained by computing the weighted fusion of the two types of features.

$$X'_f = w_s \cdot X_{\text{spatial}} + w_f \cdot X_{\text{frequency}} \tag{14}$$

This adaptive fusion mechanism can automatically adjust the contributions of spatial and frequency information according to different inputs, enabling the network to more effectively integrate local details and global structural information, improving the quality of dehazed results.

Prior-Guided Feed-Forward Network. In this paper, we propose a PGFN, which incorporates DCP to guide the network's attention to hazy regions and fine structures. DCP is a classic prior-based image dehazing method, which can generate dehazed images quickly and without training, while preserving detail. Though DCP is effective in many scenarios, it often introduce artifacts in the sky regions of dehazed images. Therefore, we employs a gating mechanism to adaptively regulate the integration of prior information, retaining the advantages of DCP while minimizing its limitations.

As illustrated in Fig. 4, the PGFN consists of two parallel branches. The prior branch first takes the DCP-based dehazed image as input, which is employed to adaptively modulate the feature representations in the main branch. Firstly, detail features are captured through a 3×3 depthwise convolution, a GELU activation function, and followed by a 1×1 convolution. Then, a Sigmoid activation function normalizes the feature values to the $[0, 1]$, producing the gating mask X^1_{DCP}. Finally, to restore the original channel dimension, another 1×1 convolution is employed, yielding X'_{DCP}, which is fed into the next PGFN. The corresponding formulation is given as follows:

$$X^1_{\text{DCP}} = \text{Sigmoid}\left(\text{Pconv}\left(\sigma\text{Dconv}\left(X_{\text{DCP}}\right)\right)\right) \tag{15}$$

$$X'_{\text{DCP}} = \text{Pconv}\left(X^1_{\text{DCP}}\right) \tag{16}$$

where, σ denotes the GELU activation function.

In the main branch, firstly, detail features are extracted using a 3×3 depthwise convolution, a GELU activation function, and followed by a 1×1 convolution, which is similar to the prior branch. Then, the extracted features X^1_f are element-wise multiplied by the gating mask X_{DCP}^1 to achieve adaptive feature modulation. Finally, the features X_f' of the main branch are obtained through a 1×1 convolution and fed into the next PGFN. The corresponding formulation is as follows:

$$X_f^1 = X_{\mathrm{DCP}}' \cdot \sigma\left(\mathrm{Pconv}\left(\sigma \mathrm{Dconv}\left(X_f\right)\right)\right) \tag{17}$$

$$X_f' = \mathrm{Pconv}\left(X_f^1\right) \tag{18}$$

Loss Function. To improve the quality of dehazed images, a jointly optimized loss function is proposed. It consists of two components: L1 loss and contrastive learning loss.

L1 Loss: To enhance the similarity between the dehazed result J' and the clear image J in the pixel space, an L1 loss is adopted to constrain the reconstruction accuracy. The calculation is as follows:

$$L_1 = \|J - J'\|_1 \tag{19}$$

where, $\|\cdot\|_1$ denotes the L1 norm.

Contrastive Learning Loss: To enhance the network's ability to distinguish image structures and semantics, a contrastive loss based on feature similarity is introduced. It encourages the network to produce the dehaze result J' that closely resembles the clear image J while diverging from hazy image I. The definition is as follows:

$$L_{\mathrm{con}} = \sum_{i=0}^{n} w_i \frac{\|R_i(J) - R_i(I')\|_1}{\|R_i(I) - R_i(I')\|_1} \tag{20}$$

where, R_i denotes the feature extracted from the i-th layer of the VGG, and w_i represents the corresponding weighting coefficient.

The total loss function L_{total} is formulated as follows:

$$L_{\mathrm{total}} = L_1 + \lambda L_{\mathrm{con}} \tag{21}$$

where, λ represents the hyperparameter that balances the two components.

3   Experimentals

3.1   Dataset

RESIDE [14] has been widely recognized as a benchmark dataset in the image dehazing community. It consists of multiple subsets of synthetic and real hazy images for training and testing, including ITS/OTS, SOTS-indoor/outdoor, HSTS, RTTS, and URHI. Specifically, ITS and OTS serve as training sets, SOTS-indoor and SOTS-outdoor are primarily used for testing, HSTS facilitates small-scale comparative analysis, and RTTS and URHI offer real hazy scenes for validating the network's generalization ability under real-world conditions. In this work, we randomly select 500 clear images from the SOTS-outdoor subset.

Their depth images are estimated using algorithm [15], and the corresponding hazy images are dynamically generated via the proposed haze degradation model, forming paired data for training. In addition, another set of 500 clear images is selected from the SOTS-outdoor subset, and hazy images are generated using the same approach to construct a test set for evaluating the effectiveness of the proposed modules. During the evaluation phase, both qualitative and quantitative analyses are performed on the RTTS subset. Meanwhile, to comprehensively validate the dehazing capability of the proposed method, the Fattal [9] dataset is also used in this paper, which consists of 34 natural hazy images, including 31 outdoor scenes and 3 indoor scenes.

3.2 Metrics

To comprehensively evaluate the performance of the proposed method, different types of evaluation metrics are used for synthetic and real-world datasets. For synthetic data, we use the Peak Signal-to-Noise Ratio (PSNR) and Structural Similarity Index (SSIM) to quantitatively evaluate the restoration quality of dehazed results. In real-world scenarios where reference images are unavailable, we use several no-reference metrics, including the FADE [5] for measuring residual haze, BRISQUE [19] for assessing image distortion, and NIMA [24] for evaluating perceptual aesthetics. Specifically, lower values of FADE and BRISQUE correspond to higher image quality, while a higher NIMA score reflects better visual appeal.

3.3 Implementation Details

All experiments in this paper are conducted on a hardware platform equipped with an NVIDIA GeForce RTX 4060 TI GPU, 32 GB of memory, and an Intel (R) Core (TM) i5-13600KF processor. Python 3.9 and Pytorch 2.1.0 are used for training. The optimizer used is AdamW, with momentum parameters β_1 and β_2 set to 0.9 and 0.999. The batch size is 2, and the model is trained for 300 epochs. The initial learning rate lr is set to 1e-3 and is decayed to 1e-5 using a cosine annealing schedule. During training, samples are randomly cropped to 256×256 and augmented by random rotation and horizontal flipping. The depth configuration of the model is set to $\{2, 3, 4, 3, 2\}$, and the embedding dimensions are set to $\{24, 48, 96, 48, 24\}$.

3.4 Comparison with State-of-the-Art Methods

To validate the effectiveness of the proposed method, we conduct both quantitative and qualitative comparisons on real hazy images using several state-of-the-art dehazing algorithms, including MSBDN [8], PSD [4], D4 [28], RIDCP [27], KA_Net [10], and HazeCLIP [25]. Among them, MSBDN achieves superior performance on synthetic datasets, while the other methods are specifically designed for real-world image dehazing, representing the mainstream research direction in this field.

Table 1. Quantitative PSNR and SSIM values on the SOTS-outdoor and HSTS datasets. Bold and underline indicate the best results and the second-best, respectively.

Method	Publication	RTTS			Fattal		
		FADE↓	BRISQUE↓	NIMA↑	FADE↓	BRISQUE↓	NIMA↑
Hazy image	–	2.484	37.011	4.3250	1.025	14.360	5.1992
MSBDN [8]	CVPR'2020	1.3630	28.743	4.1401	0.542	13.997	5.3520
PSD [4]	CVPR'2021	0.920	25.239	4.3459	0.413	18.572	4.9448
D4 [28]	CVPR'2022	1.358	33.206	3.7239	0.291	14.869	<u>5.4785</u>
RIDCP [27]	CVPR'2023	0.944	18.782	4.4267	0.378	17.244	5.3560
KA_Net [10]	TPAMI'2024	0.869	20.882	<u>4.9281</u>	0.366	13.635	5.4376
HazeCLIP [25]	ICASSP'2025	**0.638**	<u>18.567</u>	4.5510	**0.237**	<u>13.154</u>	5.3113
Ours	-	<u>0.687</u>	**13.318**	**5.0955**	<u>0.276</u>	**12.457**	**5.4962**

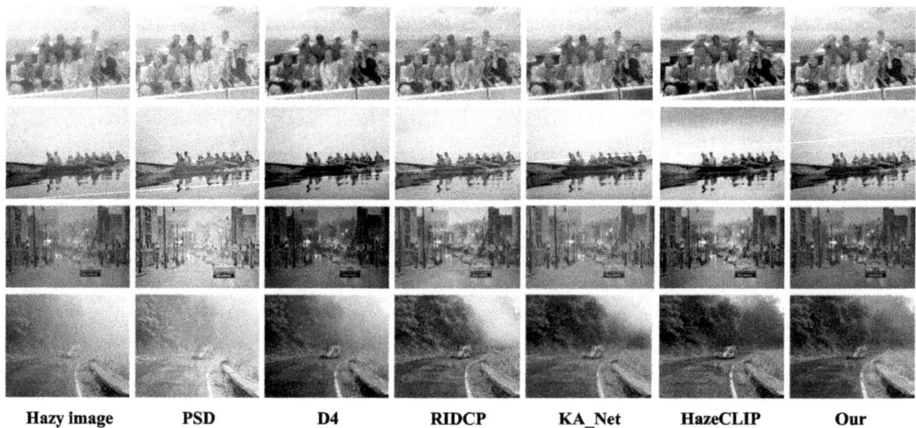

Fig. 5. Qualitative Comparison on the RTTS Dataset.

Quantitative Comparison. Table 1 shows the quantitative comparison of different dehazing methods on the RTTS and Fattal datasets, where bold and underline respectively indicate the best and second-best performance. As shown in Table 1, our method achieves the best performance on two key metrics, BRISQUE and NIMA. Specifically, on the RTTS dataset, our method reduces the BRISQUE score by 28.3% and increases the NIMA score by 3.4% compared to the second-best method. On the Fattal dataset, the improvements are 5.3% and 0.32%. In the FADE metric evaluation, our method ranks second with a slight margin behind the HazeCLIP [25]. This is mainly due to the latter use of the cross-modal understanding ability of the CLIP, which enhances adaptability in complex scenes. In general, the quantitative experimental results comprehensively confirm the superior dehazing performance of our method.

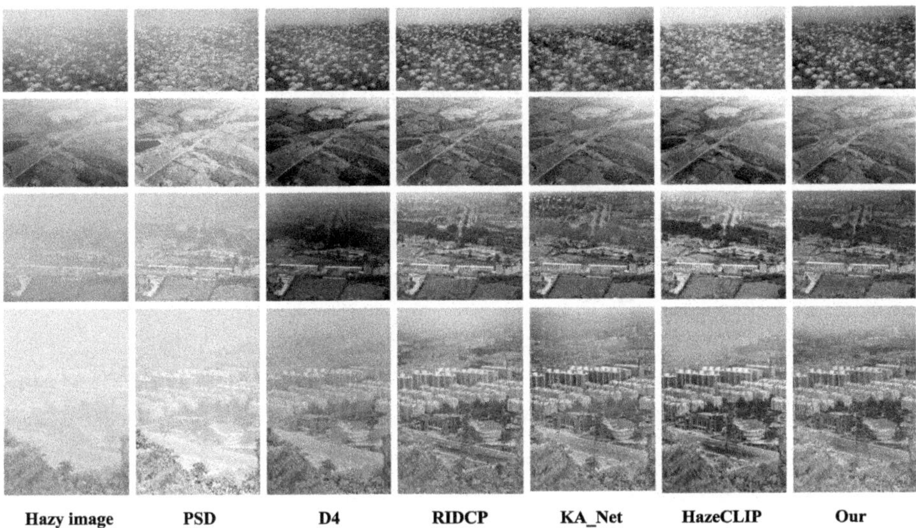

Fig. 6. Qualitative Comparison on the Fattal Dataset.

Qualitative Comparison. Figure 5 and Fig. 6 illustrate the dehazed results of different methods on the RTTS and Fattal datasets. As shown in the figures, although PSD [4] leverages the bright channel priors to produce brighter images, it fails to achieve a substantial dehazing effect. D4 [28] demonstrates noticeable dehazing effects in certain areas, but the overall image appears darker. This is attributed to the inaccurate depth estimation, which leads to inadequate transmission recovery and consequently reduces the image brightness. Since the high-quality prior matching relied on by RIDCP [27] is not suitable for all hazy scenes, it leads to noticeable color shifts in the results. KA_Net [10] shows better dehazing performance in the near areas of the image, but the dehazing effect weakens in the distant regions. HazeCLIP [25] can significantly remove haze in some images but also introduces artifacts and distortion. Compared to these methods, the proposed method in this paper delivers superior visual results in handling brightness, color, and haze residue.

3.5 Computational Complexity

To evaluate the lightweight and efficient nature of the proposed method in practical deployment, we calculated the number of parameters and floating-point operations (FLOPs) of different methods on image patches of 256×256. As shown in Table 2, due to the compact embedding dimensions and relatively shallow model depth, our method not only exhibits the lowest number of parameters but also demonstrates competitive Flops, indicating that the proposed method has the advantage in practical deployment scenarios.

Table 2. Comparison of model complexity on parameters and FLOPs. Bold and underline indicate the best results and the second-best, respectively.

Method	Publication	Params (M)	FLOPs (G)
MSBDN	CVPR'2020	31.35	83.16
PSD	CVPR'2021	33.11	91.27
D4	CVPR'2022	<u>10.73</u>	**4.43**
RIDCP	CVPR'2023	29.48	386.88
KA_Net	TPAMI'2024	55.66	<u>11.43</u>
HazeCLIP	ICASSP'2025	28.36	47.11
Ours	-	**1.66**	31.81

Fig. 7. Ablation Comparison on the Fattal Dataset. Our-RESIDE is trained on the RESIDE dataset, and Our-MD is trained on data produced by the proposed haze degradation model.

4 Ablation Study

In order to assess the contribution of each key component, we conduct a series of ablation experiments. This section discusses the effectiveness of the proposed haze degradation model, the SSFM, and the PGFN.

4.1 Effectiveness of the Haze Degradation Model

To validate the effectiveness of the proposed haze degradation model, we train our network on the RESIDE dataset synthesized using the ASM (serves as Our-RESIDE) and on the dataset generated by the proposed haze degradation model (serves as Our-MD), and then evaluate it on real-world datasets RTTS and Fattal. Table 3 shows that the network trained with the newly proposed haze degradation model outperforms the one trained on the RESIDE in real-world scenarios. Figure 7 presents the visual dehazed results on real images using two training data. The model trained with our haze degradation model produces more realistic results in brightness, color, and haze removal, and outperforms the one trained on RESIDE. This highlights the importance of using more realistic degradation data to improve performance in real-world dehazing tasks.

Table 3. Ablation comparison of the haze degradation model on the RTTS and Fattal datasets. Our-RESIDE is trained on the RESIDE dataset, and Our-MD is trained on data produced by the proposed haze degradation model.

Dataset	Method	FADE↓	BRISQUE↓	NIMA↑
RTTS	Our-RESIDE	1.484	29.259	4.8705
	Our-MD	0.687	13.318	5.0955
Fattal	Our-RESIDE	0.436	14.682	5.4098
	Our-MD	0.276	12.457	5.4962

Table 4. Ablation study of key components in the SSFM and PGFN.

Module	Component	Baseline-a	Baseline-b	Baseline-c	Baseline-d	Ours
SSFM	spatial branch		✓	✓	✓	✓
	frequency branch	✓		✓	✓	✓
	adaptive fusion				✓	✓
PGFN	prior branch	✓	✓	✓		✓
	main branch	✓	✓	✓	✓	✓
Metric	PSNR ↑	22.1529	23.8482	24.4428	24.4472	25.0309
	SSIM ↑	0.8200	0.8727	0.8762	0.8757	0.8822

4.2 Effectiveness of the Spectral-Spatial Fusion Module

The proposed SSFM consists of three components: a spatial branch, a frequency branch, and an adaptive fusion mechanism. To evaluate the contribution of each component, we conduct ablation experiments by removing key modules, allowing for a thorough analysis of the complementary benefits of spatial and frequency domain features in dehazing. As presented in Table 4, baseline-a, baseline-b, and baseline-c correspond to the ablation settings remove the spatial branch, frequency domain branch, and adaptive fusion mechanism, respectively. Specifically, when the spatial or frequency branch is removed, the corresponding adaptive fusion mechanism becomes inapplicable due to the lack of multi-source information, and is removed. The results indicate that each component contributes significantly to the final performance, confirming the complementarity between spatial and frequency domain features and the crucial role of the adaptive fusion strategy in information integration.

4.3 Effectiveness of Prior-Guided Feedforward Network

The PGFN proposed in this paper uses the initial dehazed image generated by the DCP as a guidance mask and employs a gating mechanism to effectively regulate and fuse the backbone features. To validate the role of the prior branch in the overall network, an ablation experiment was designed, removing the prior branch to evaluate its impact on dehazing performance. As shown in Table 4, Baseline-d represents the network structure without the prior branch. Specifically, while the main branch of the PGFN is kept, the gating mechanism is removed due to the absence of prior information. Experimental results show that this setting yields lower PSNR and SSIM values compared to the full model. This demonstrates that integrating prior knowledge can provide effective guidance for the network, positively facilitating the dehazing task and highlighting the potential of traditional prior knowledge in data-driven methods.

5   Conclusion

With the development of safety-critical applications such as autonomous driving, intelligent traffic systems, and urban security monitoring, improving the performance of image dehazing technologies is crucial for ensuring the perceptual accuracy and overall safety of vision-based systems. This paper proposes a multi-faceted collaborative enhancement dehazing method to address key issues in real-world image dehazing, such as domain gaps, complex degradation modeling, and limited prior knowledge usage. Specifically, a haze degradation model based on multiple scattering mechanisms and multiple degradation factors is constructed to effectively mitigate the domain gap between synthetic and real domains; a Spectral-Spatial Fusion Module is designed to enhance the model's ability to adapt to complex degradation features; and the Prior-Guided Feedforward Network fully exploits and integrates dark channel prior information, effectively enhancing the model's perception and modeling capability for hazy regions. Experimental results on several real image datasets demonstrate that the proposed method outperforms existing mainstream dehazing methods in both visual quality and quantitative metrics, validating its effectiveness and advancement for real-world image dehazing. Future work will focus on improving the model's robustness and real-time performance under extreme weather conditions, further enhancing the safety assurance and intelligence level of dehazing techniques in real-world applications such as autonomous driving, intelligent transportation, and urban security monitoring.

References

1. Azfar, T., Li, J., Yu, H., Cheu, R.L., Lv, Y., Ke, R.: Deep learning-based computer vision methods for complex traffic environments perception: a review. Data Sci. Transport. **6**(1), 1 (2024)
2. Berman, D., treibitz, T., Avidan, S.: Non-local image dehazing. In: Proceedings of the IEEE Conference on Computer Vision and Pattern Recognition (CVPR) (June 2016)
3. Cai, B., Xu, X., Jia, K., Qing, C., Tao, D.: Dehazenet: an end-to-end system for single image haze removal. IEEE Trans. Image Process. **25**(11), 5187–5198 (2016)

4. Chen, Z., Wang, Y., Yang, Y., Liu, D.: Psd: principled synthetic-to-real dehazing guided by physical priors. In: Proceedings of the IEEE/CVF Conference on Computer Vision and Pattern Recognition (CVPR), pp. 7180–7189 (June 2021)
5. Choi, L.K., You, J., Bovik, A.C.: Referenceless prediction of perceptual fog density and perceptual image defogging. IEEE Trans. Image Process. **24**(11), 3888–3901 (2015)
6. Cui, Y., Knoll, A.: Exploring the potential of channel interactions for image restoration. Knowl.-Based Syst. **282**, 111156 (2023)
7. Dilek, E., Dener, M.: Computer vision applications in intelligent transportation systems: a survey. Sensors **23**(6) (2023)
8. Dong, H., Pan, J., Xiang, L., Hu, Z., Zhang, X., Wang, F., Yang, M.H.: Multi-scale boosted dehazing network with dense feature fusion. In: Proceedings of the IEEE/CVF Conference on Computer Vision and Pattern Recognition (CVPR) (June 2020)
9. Fattal, R.: Dehazing using color-lines. ACM Trans. Graph. **34**(1) (Dec 2015)
10. Feng, Y., Ma, L., Meng, X., Zhou, F., Liu, R., Su, Z.: Advancing real-world image dehazing: perspective, modules, and training. IEEE Trans. Pattern Anal. Mach. Intell. **46**(12), 9303–9320 (2024)
11. He, K., Sun, J., Tang, X.: Single image haze removal using dark channel prior. IEEE Trans. Pattern Anal. Mach. Intell. **33**(12), 2341–2353 (2011)
12. Hu, S., Chen, L., Wu, P., Li, H., Yan, J., Tao, D.: St-p3: end-to-end vision-based autonomous driving via spatial-temporal feature learning. In: Avidan, S., Brostow, G., Cissé, M., Farinella, G.M., Hassner, T. (eds.) Computer Vision - ECCV 2022, pp. 533–549. Springer Nature Switzerland, Cham (2022)
13. Li, B., Peng, X., Wang, Z., Xu, J., Feng, D.: Aod-net: all-in-one dehazing network. In: Proceedings of the IEEE International Conference on Computer Vision (ICCV) (Oct 2017)
14. Li, B., et al.: Benchmarking single-image dehazing and beyond. IEEE Trans. Image Process. **28**(1), 492–505 (2019)
15. Li, Z., Snavely, N.: Megadepth: learning single-view depth prediction from internet photos. In: Proceedings of the IEEE Conference on Computer Vision and Pattern Recognition (CVPR) (June 2018)
16. Ling, P., Chen, H., Tan, X., Jin, Y., Chen, E.: Single image dehazing using saturation line prior. IEEE Trans. Image Process. **32**, 3238–3253 (2023)
17. Lu, L., Xiong, Q., Xu, B., Chu, D.: Mixdehazenet: mix structure block for image dehazing network. In: 2024 International Joint Conference on Neural Networks (IJCNN), pp. 1–10 (2024)
18. Lysova, T.: Intersecting perspectives: video surveillance in urban spaces through surveillance society and security state frameworks. Cities **156**, 105544 (2025)
19. Mittal, A., Moorthy, A.K., Bovik, A.C.: No-reference image quality assessment in the spatial domain. IEEE Trans. Image Process. **21**(12), 4695–4708 (2012)
20. Qin, X., Wang, Z., Bai, Y., Xie, X., Jia, H.: Ffa-net: feature fusion attention network for single image dehazing. In: Proceedings of the AAAI Conference on Artificial Intelligence, vol. 34(07), pp. 11908–11915 (2020)
21. Radford, A., et al.: Learning transferable visual models from natural language supervision. In: Meila, M., Zhang, T. (eds.) Proceedings of the 38th International Conference on Machine Learning. In: Proceedings of Machine Learning Research, 18–24 Jul, vol. 139, pp. 8748–8763. PMLR (2021)

22. Ren, W., Liu, S., Zhang, H., Pan, J., Cao, X., Yang, M.H.: Single image dehazing via multi-scale convolutional neural networks. In: Leibe, B., Matas, J., Sebe, N., Welling, M. (eds.) Computer Vision - ECCV 2016, pp. 154–169. Springer International Publishing, Cham (2016). https://doi.org/10.1007/978-3-319-46475-6_10

23. Song, Y., He, Z., Qian, H., Du, X.: Vision transformers for single image dehazing. IEEE Trans. Image Process. **32**, 1927–1941 (2023)

24. Talebi, H., Milanfar, P.: Nima: neural image assessment. IEEE Trans. Image Process. **27**(8), 3998–4011 (2018)

25. Wang, R., et al.: Hazeclip: towards language guided real-world image dehazing. In: ICASSP 2025 - 2025 IEEE International Conference on Acoustics, Speech and Signal Processing (ICASSP), pp. 1–5 (2025)

26. Wang, Y., et al.: Ucl-dehaze: toward real-world image dehazing via unsupervised contrastive learning. IEEE Trans. Image Process. **33**, 1361–1374 (2024)

27. Wu, R.Q., Duan, Z.P., Guo, C.L., Chai, Z., Li, C.: Ridcp: revitalizing real image dehazing via high-quality codebook priors. In: Proceedings of the IEEE/CVF Conference on Computer Vision and Pattern Recognition (CVPR), pp. 22282–22291 (June 2023)

28. Yang, Y., Wang, C., Liu, R., Zhang, L., Guo, X., Tao, D.: Self-augmented unpaired image dehazing via density and depth decomposition. In: Proceedings of the IEEE/CVF Conference on Computer Vision and Pattern Recognition (CVPR), pp. 2037–2046 (June 2022)

29. Yu, H., Zheng, N., Zhou, M., Huang, J., Xiao, Z., Zhao, F.: Frequency and spatial dual guidance for image dehazing. In: Avidan, S., Brostow, G., Cissé, M., Farinella, G.M., Hassner, T. (eds.) Computer Vision - ECCV 2022, pp. 181–198. Springer Nature Switzerland, Cham (2022)

30. Yuan, Z., Wu, L., Wang, Y., Sun, M., Xia, M.: Image dehazing based on multiple scattering model. In: Proceedings of the 2020 4th International Conference on Electronic Information Technology and Computer Engineering, EITCE 2020, pp. 454–458. Association for Computing Machinery, New York (2021)

31. Zhu, Q., Mai, J., Shao, L.: A fast single image haze removal algorithm using color attenuation prior. IEEE Trans. Image Process. **24**(11), 3522–3533 (2015)

On the Decision Problem of a Class of Automata Used for Security Verification of Network Protocols

Qingxia Long[1,2], Yong He[1,2], and Zhenhe Cui[1,2(✉)]

[1] School of Computer Science and Engineering, Hunan University of Science and Technology, Hunan 411201, Xiangtan, China
`yonghe@hnust.edu.cn`
[2] Sanya Institute of Hunan University of Science and Technology, Hunan 572024, Sanya, China
`zhhcui@hnust.edu.cn`

Abstract. As the core model of discrete control systems and security verification, the order structure of automata on their state sets plays a key role in network security protocols, quantum secure communication, privacy protection, cryptography, dynamic obstacle avoidance control and other scenarios. Based on this, we study a class of automata with special order structures —monotonic automata (automata whose state set admits a compatible total order) are the extreme case of partially ordered automata. If an automaton A is a monotonic automaton, then its state set forms a forest under the action of any input symbol. We define the structural total order of such forests and prove that A is monotonic if and only if all forests of A corresponding to the input symbols have a common structural total order. Accordingly, a decision algorithm of monotonic automata with time complexity $O(mn^3)$ is designed.

Keywords: network security protocols · compatible total order · structural total order · aperiodic symbol

1 Introduction

An automaton is a mathematical computational model of transition and action between a finite number of states. It serves as an abstraction for many discrete control systems and is widely applied in fields such as information security, security control, security verification, privacy protection [1–4]. In the field of network security protocols, researchers often use automata to verify the security of network protocols, for example, Kurkowski *et al.*. [5] constructs a network model of 18 automata modeling executions of the participants and 20 knowledge automata to perform distributed semantic modeling of the NSPK protocol, and uses BMC technology to convert the protocol session path reachability problem into verification of SAT coding. Fathinavid *et al.*. [6] design an algorithm that implements intrusion detection in a zone using the learning automata approach

W. Liang et al. (Eds.): SecureComm 2025, LNICST 690, pp. 371–391, 2026.
https://doi.org/10.1007/978-3-032-23456-8_20

to detect attacks. It can adjust based on node behavior feedback to achieve real-time identification and isolation of malicious nodes. The above fully demonstrates that automaton theory plays an irreplaceable role in the study of some related properties of network protocols.

An automaton whose state set has an ordered structure is called a partially ordered automaton [7–11]. Existing research results show that most network security protocols can be modeled as partially ordered automata, for example, Xiao Mingming *et al..* [12] proposed a new general protocol modeling method, the process of this implementation is essentially the state transition process of the protocol, and the key elements of the protocol trigger the state transformation between messages in each protocol session (the protocol state machine is composed of a series of ordered states, which represents the basic structure of the application protocol). They introduce a grammatical inference algorithm to derive finite state machine models of protocols such as HTTP and SMTP from network traffic, and automatically generate specifications that can be used to parse messages of certain types. Inspired by this, we consider the research of further exploring the properties of network protocols through automaton modeling from the perspective of partially ordered structure.

In this paper, we study a special class of partially ordered automata for network protocol security verification, called monotonic automata. Specifically, we study the decision problem of monotonic automata. Monotonic automata are the automata that the state set admits a compatible total order. It is the extreme case of partially ordered automata, which are not only dendriform but also bounded. In formal language, monotonic automata have been used to classify regular languages according to their sortability. Nicola Cotumaccio's establishes a unified parameterization that simultaneously captures various automata-related measures [13]. For the synchronizing automaton, Ananichev and Volkov demonstrated that the shortest synchronizing word length for an n-state synchronizing monotonic automaton does not exceed $n - 1$ [14]. They further extended the monotonic automata to two broader classes of partially ordered automata —generalized monotonic automata and weakly monotonic automata —proving that the shortest synchronizing word length for n-state generalized monotonic automata is also bounded by $n - 1$ [7], while weakly monotonic automata with additional constraints satisfy Černý's conjecture [8]. In the above studies on monotonic automata and formal languages, it is not considered what conditions any automaton satisfy to have a compatible total order. This paper will study the decision methods of monotonic automata. Thus began the study of decision methods of various automata with special partially ordered structures.

This paper consists of six sections: Sect. 2 introduces preliminary work that will be extensively utilized. Section 3 presents a decision method for monotonic automata. Building on this, Sect. 4 provides an algorithm for deciding the base-connected monotonic automata. Section 5 illustrates the decision algorithm with a concrete example. Finally, Sect. 6 concludes the contributions of this paper.

2 Preliminaries

2.1 Basic Concepts and Notations

All sets under discuss are non-empty. Unless explicitly stated otherwise, undefined terms and notations are in accordance with the conventions of Howie [15], Grätzer [16], and Kolman [17].

A collection of ordered pairs on a set X is called a relation on X. The adjacency digraph of a relation R is the digraph (X, R) that has the vertexs of X and edge R. In general, we do not distinguish between a relation and its adjacency digraph. A relation R is said to be reflexive if every vertex in R has a self-loop. A relation R is said to be antisymmetric if for arbitrary distinct vertices x and y, the existence of both edges (x, y) and (y, x) is impossible. A relation R is said to be transitive if for arbitrary vertices x, y, z the presence of edges (x, y) and (y, x) necessarily implies the existence of (x, z). The smallest reflexive relation, the smallest symmetric relation, and the smallest transitive relation in X that contain R are termed the reflexive closure, symmetric closure, and transitive closure of R, denoted as R^r, R^s and R^t.

Lemma 1. *[17] The reflexive closure R^r of a relation R on set X is defined by $R \cup \{(x, x) | x \in X\}$, while the symmetric closure R^s is given by $R \cup R^{-1}$. For an n-element set, the transitive closure R^t of a relation can be computed in $O(n^3)$ time using the Warshall algorithm.*

Lemma 2. *Detecting whether a relation is symmetric or antisymmetric can be accomplished in $O(n^2)$ time, where n is the number of vertices in the relation.*

Proof. To decide the symmetry of a relation R, it needs to traverse all vertices of R and check for each vertex, whether every outgoing edge (excluding self-loops) has a corresponding reverse edge. If a non-self-loop edge (x, y) in R is found to have its reverse edge (y, x) also present, then R is symmetric; If no such reverse edges exist for an arbitrary edge (x, y), then R is antisymmetric. Since there are at most n^2 edges in the relation, the time complexity of this procedure is evidently (n^2). This completes the proof.

A relation R on a set X is called an equivalence relation if it is reflexive, symmetric, and transitive. A relation R in X is termed a partial order (denoted by the symbol $\leq$) if it is reflexive, antisymmetric, and transitive. In this case, the pair $(X, \leq)$ is said to form a partially ordered set. Elements a and b in X are said to be comparable if $a \leq b$ or $b \leq a$ holds; otherwise, they are incomparable. An element $a \in X$ is called the minimum element if $a \leq x$ for all $x \in X$, while an element $b \in X$ is the maximum element if $x \leq b$ for every $x \in X$. Any partially ordered set can have at most one minimum element and at most one maximum element [17].

A partially ordered set in which arbitrary elements are comparable is called a chain. A partially ordered set with a minimum element is termed a dendriform partially ordered set, while a set possessing both a maximum and a minimum element is called a bounded partially ordered set. The partial orders defined on chains, dendriform partially ordered sets, and bounded partially ordered sets are respectively called total order, dendriform partial order, and bounded partial order. Clearly, every finite chain is a partially ordered bounded set, and every bounded partially ordered set is a dendriform partially ordered set [9].

An automaton $A = (Q, \Sigma, \delta)$ consists of a state set Q, the input symbols Σ, and a transition function $\delta : Q \times \Sigma \to Q$. Where: Q is a finite set whose elements are called states of the automaton, Σ represents the input commands through its symbols, and δ defines the state transition induced by all input symbols, expressed as $\delta(q, a)$, where ϵ denotes the empty word. The size of A is defined as the ordered pair (n, m), where n is the number of states and m the number of input symbols. The transition diagram of automaton is an edge-labeled digraph with Q as its vertex set and Σ as the set of edge labels: an edge labeled a from vertex q to vertex p exists if and only if $\delta(q, a) = p$. We generally do not distinguish between an automaton and its state transition diagram.

Let $A = (Q, \Sigma, \delta)$ be an automaton. For a relation R on the state set Q of A, define

$$R\Sigma = \{(qa, pa)|(q, p) \in R, a \in \Sigma\} \text{ and } R\Sigma^* = \{(qw, pw)|(q, p) \in R, w \in \Sigma^*\}.$$

If $R\Sigma \in R$, then R is said to be compatible with A or R is termed a compatible relation A.

Lemma 3. *Checking the compatibility of a relation with an automaton on its state set can be done in $O(mn^2)$ time.*

Proof. Let A be an automaton of size (n, m), and let R be a relation on A. Since R can contain at most n^2 ordered pairs, computing $R\Sigma$ requires $O(mn^2)$ time. Subsequently, verifying whether $R\Sigma \in R$ holds can be completed in $O(n^2)$ time. Therefore, the total time complexity for deciding the compatibility of R with A is $O(mn^2)$.

Lemma 4. *A relation R on the state set Q of an automaton $A = (Q, \Sigma, \delta)$ is compatible with A if and only if $R = R\Sigma^*$.*

Proof. Suppose R is compatible with A. We first show $R = R\Sigma^*$. Since $R = R\epsilon \subseteq R\Sigma^*$ (where ϵ denotes the empty word) and the compatibility condition $R\Sigma \subseteq R$ implies $R\Sigma^* \subseteq R$, it follows that $R = R\Sigma^*$.

Conversely, suppose $R = R\Sigma^*$. To prove R is compatible with A, observe that

$$R\Sigma = R\Sigma^*\Sigma \subseteq R\Sigma^* = R.$$

This directly implies $R\Sigma \subseteq R$, satisfying the definition of compatibility.

For a relation R on the state set Q of an automaton $A = (Q, \Sigma, \delta)$, if R' is the smallest A-compatible relation on Q that contains R, then R' is called the A-compatible closure of R. Similarly, if R' is the smallest A-compatible and transitive relation on Q that contains R, it is termed the A-compatible transitive closure of R.

2.2   Structural Total Order of Trees and Forests

Now we define the structural total order on the vertex sets of trees and forests. Each monotonic automaton corresponds to a forest. There is a tree (T, v_0), where v_0 is the root of T, V and E are the sets of vertex and the sets of edge of T. For each vertex $v \in V$, two functions are defined as follows:

  1. Layer polarity function $y : V \to Z$. Satisfies the following:

(1) $y(v_0) = 0$;
(2) $|y(v)|$ represents the level of v in the tree;
(3) If v and u are parent-child relationships in T, then $y(v)y(u) > 0$.

2. Sibling order function $z : V \to Z^+$, satisfies that when v and u are sibling relationships in T, then $z(v) \neq z(u)$.

Any node v in T can be assigned to a pair constructed by the layer polarity function and the sibling order function: $v \to (y(v), z(v))$. Arbitrary nodes v_1 and v_2 in T compare the size of $(y(v), z(v))$ in lexicographic order $\leq_i$. The rules are as follows:

$$v_1 \leq_i v_2 \Leftrightarrow \begin{cases} y(v_1) < y(v_2) \\ y(v_1) < y(v_2) \ and \ z(v_1) < z(v_2) \end{cases},$$

when $y(v_1) \neq y(v_2)$ or $y(v_1) = y(v_2)$ and $z(v_1) \neq z(v_2)$, then

$$(y(v_1), z(v_1)) \neq (y(v_2), z(v_2)).$$

Obviously, each v has a unique corresponding $(y(v), z(v))$, so the structural total order of the tree holds.

There is a forest $F = (V, E)$ that contains k trees. For the maximal subtree T in F, a function $x : V \to Z^+$ is defined, which satisfies that arbitrary nodes v and u are vertices of the same maximal subtree if and only if $x(v) = x(u)$. This function indicates that all trees in the forest are assigned a unique positive integer number $x(v)$ to decide the order. Define a triple $(x(v), y(v), z(v))$ for each node $v \in V$ in the forest. According to lexicographic order $\leq_i$, the following rules apply:

$$v_1 \leq_i v_2 \Leftrightarrow \begin{cases} x(v_1) < x(v_2) \\ x(v_1) = x(v_2) \ and \ y(v_1) < y(v_2) \\ x(v_1) = x(v_2) \ and \ y(v_1) = y(v_2) \ and \ z(v_1) < z(v_2) \end{cases},$$

Obviously, the function $v \to (x(v), y(v), z(v))$ is injective, so arbitrary node v in the forest has a unique corresponding $(x(v), y(v), z(v))$. Therefore, the structural total order of the forest can be produced on the basis of this triple.

3   An Decision Method of Monotonic Automata

If the automaton $A = (Q, \Sigma, \delta)$ has no loop other than a self-loop under the action of an input symbol, the symbol is called the aperiodic symbol.

Lemma 5. *If an automaton A is monotonic, then all symbols of A are aperiodic.*

Proof. Suppose that there exists a symbol in A that is not aperiodic, then the automaton A is not monotonic.

For an existing automaton $A = (Q, \Sigma, \delta)$, when the input symbol $a \in \Sigma$ acts on different states $s_1, s_2, s_3, \cdots, s_k$, there exists a loop:

$$s_1 a = s_2, s_2 a = s_3, \cdots, s_{k-1} a = s_k, s_k a = s_1.$$

Assuming $s_1 \leq s_2 \leq s_3 \leq \cdots \leq s_k$, we have

$$s_2 = s_1 a \leq s_2 a = s_3, s_3 = s_2 a \leq s_3 a = s_4, \cdots, s_k = s_{k-1} a \leq s_k a = s_1.$$

Therefore $s_1 = s_2 = s_3 = \cdots = s_k$, which contradicts the assumption. In summary, A is not monotonic. Proof completed.

If the directed edges in the state transition graph of the automaton A are considered to be connected after being regarded as undirected edges, then the automaton is called a base-connected automaton. An arbitrary automaton can be regarded as composed of one or more base-connected automata. The existing automaton $A = (Q, \Sigma, \delta)$ is composed of k base-connected automata $A = (Q_1, \Sigma_1, \delta_1)$, $A = (Q_2, \Sigma_2, \delta_2)$, $\cdots$, $A = (Q_k, \Sigma_k, \delta_k)$.

Given an automaton A whose symbols are all aperiodic, for an arbitrary input symbol $a \in \Sigma$ induces a forest composed with its corresponding edges, called an a-forest, where:

1. Each base-connected component can be regarded as an a-tree T_i of the forest;
2. The state with self-loops is the root v_0 of T_i;

There is a unique path from the other vertices to the root v_0 without passing through self-loops.

Lemma 6. *If the base-connected automaton A has only one input symbol, then there is only one tree in the corresponding forest.*

Proof. According to the definition of base-connected automaton, if the automaton A corresponds to two or more trees, the automaton is not connected after the directed edges of the state transition graph are regarded as undirected edges, which contradicts the definition of base-connected automaton, so the proposition holds.

Lemma 7. *If every base-connected automaton contained in automaton A is monotonic, then A is monotonic.*

Proof. We now define the total order on $\leq$, for arbitrary states $p \in Q_i$ and $q \in Q_j$(where $i, j \leq k$), the total order on the base-connected automaton A_i is $\leq_i$, and the following holds:

$$p \leq q \Leftrightarrow \begin{cases} i = j, \ p \leq_i q \\ i < j \end{cases},$$

When $i = j$, the monotonicity of A_i directly implies $pa \leq qa$. For $i < j$, arbitrary states $p \in Q_i$ and $q \in Q_j$ satisfy $p \leq q$, and since $pa \in Q_i$ and $qa \in Q_j$, we have $pa \leq qa$. In summary, A is compatible, and its state set admits a compatible total order structure $\leq$, thus establishing the monotonicity of A.

Corollary 1. *The total order relationship between different trees of the monotonic automaton $A = (Q, \Sigma, \delta)$ under the same symbol can be arbitrarily defined and still satisfy the compatibility.*

Proof. The monotonic automaton $A = (Q, \Sigma, \delta)$ is a new automaton $B = (Q, a, \delta)$ under the same symbol a. Obviously, each tree of B is a base-connected automaton. The Corollary 1 can be proved by Lemma 7.

Lemma 8. *Every tree in the automaton is monotonic.*

Proof. According to Sect. 2 of this paper, we define a total order $\leq_i$ for the state set on an arbitrary tree T_i, v_0. For arbitrary states $p, q \in T_i$, the following pair $(y(p), z(p))$ holds:

$$p \leq_i q \Leftrightarrow \begin{cases} y(p) < y(q) \\ y(p) = y(q) \ and \ z(p) < z(q) \end{cases},$$

For example: $y(p) = -2 \leq y(q) = +1$, because the negative layer is always smaller than the positive layer.

Due to the uniqueness of each pair $(y(p), z(p))$ in the tree, the total order holds.

We now prove that if $p \leq q$, then $pa \leq qa$ holds for an arbitrary input symbol a. Discuss the following cases:

1. When $p = q$, $pa \leq qa$ obviously holds, so we will not discuss it any further.
2. When $p = v_0$(with $y(p) = 0$), then $pa \leq qa$ means that q is a positive layer state. Under the action of the symbol a, we have $pa = v_0 \Rightarrow y(pa) = 0$. Since q is a positive layer state, we know that $y(qa) = y(q) - 1 \geq 0$, so $pa = v_0 \leq pa$.
3. When $q = v_0$(with $y(q) = 0$), then $pa \leq qa$ means that p is a negative layer state. Under the action of the symbol a, we have $y(pa) = y(p) + 1 \leq 0$, then $pa = v_0 \Rightarrow y(qa) = 0$, so $pa = v_0 \leq pa$.
4. When p and q are both in positive layer states, we can get $y(p) = +k$, $y(q) = +m$ (where k and m are positive integers, which will not be explained later). If $p \leq q$ and $+k < +m$, then under the action of symbol a, we know that
$$y(pa) = +k - 1 < +m - 1 = y(qa),$$
so $pa \leq qa$. If $p \leq q$ and $k = m$, then under the action of symbol a, we have $pa = qa$, so $pa \leq qa$.
5. When p and q are both in negative layer states, then $y(p) = -k$, $y(q) = -m$, if $p \leq q$ and $-k < -m$, then under the action of the symbol a, we know that
$$y(pa) = -k + 1 < -m + 1 = y(qa),$$
so $pa \leq qa$. if $p \leq q$ and $k = m$, then under the action of symbol a, we have $pa = qa$, so $pa \leq qa$.

6. When p is a negative layer state and q is a positive layer state, we can get $y(p) = -k$, $y(q) = +m$, if $p \leq q$, then $-k \leq +m$, under the action of symbol a, we know that

$$y(pa) = -k + 1 \leq +m - 1 = y(qa),$$

so $pa \leq qa$.

Due to the aperiodic of the symbols in Lemma 5, the state cannot move away from the root through the symbols(otherwise a cycle will be formed). In summary, for arbitrary states $p, q \in T_i$, if $p \leq q$, then for the input symbol a, we have $pa \leq qa$. Therefore, the states on the same tree are in compatible total order.

Lemma 9. *In a monotonic automaton, for arbitrary state p, q and input symbol a, when $pa \neq qa$, the inequality $p \leq q$ holds if and only if $pa \leq qa$.*

Proof. Discuss two situations:

1. When p and q belong to the same tree T_i.

(1) When $p = q$, we have $pa = qa$, which conflicts with the proposition condition and will not be discussed further.
(2) When p is the root node: From $y(p) = y(pa) = 0$, we know that $p \leq q \Leftrightarrow pa \leq qa$ always holds. When q is the root node, the same logic holds.
(3) When p and q are both negative layer states: The proof of $p \leq q \Rightarrow pa \leq qa$ is consistent with Case 5 in Lemma 8. In contrast, consider $y(pa) = -k+1$ and $y(qa) = -m + 1$. if $pa \leq qa$ and $-k + 1 < -m + 1$, then $y(p) = -k < -m = y(q)$, which directly implies $p \leq q$; if $pa \leq qa$ and $-k + 1 = -m + 1$, then $y(p) = -k = -m = y(q)$ is true, in this case, $z(pa) < z(qa) \Rightarrow z(p) < z(q)$, thus enforcing $p \leq q$. The same applies when p and q are both positive layer states.
(4) When p is a negative layer state and q is a positive layer state: we can get $p \leq q \Rightarrow pa \leq qa$ with case 6 in Lemma 8. In contrast, $pa \leq qa$ implies $-k \leq +m$, hence $p \leq q$.

2. When p, q belong to different trees T_i and T_j.
   According to Corollary 1, the trees can be arbitrarily sorted. If $T_i \leq T_j$, then for arbitrary $p \in T_i$ and $q \in T_j$, there is $p \leq q$. Under the action of the symbol a, we have $pa \in T_i$, $qa \in T_j$, so $pa \leq qa$. Vice versa. We know that

$$p \leq q \Leftrightarrow T_i \leq T_j \Leftrightarrow pa \leq qa.$$

The partially ordered set of the monotonic automaton $A = (Q, \Sigma, \delta)$ is a compatible total order (i.e. chain) and its total order structure is $\leq$. For arbitrary states $p, q \in Q$, the following interval I is defined:

$$[p, q] = \{r \in Q | p \leq r \leq q\}.$$

When an interval I_i is contained in another interval I_j, it is written as $I_i \prec I_j$.

Lemma 10. *Each tree of a monotonic automaton $A = (Q, \Sigma, \delta)$ is an interval.*

Proof. Suppose that there is a tree whose state is non-continuous in the total order of A, then there are states $p, q \in T_i$ and $r \in T_j$, where $T_i \neq T_j$, v_i is the root of T_i, and v_j is the root of T_j, satisfying $p \leq r \leq q$.

Because all states converge to the root through the input sequence of a, there exists a positive integer k under the action of the symbol a such that $pa^k = qa^k = v_i$, $ra^k = v_j$. According to the compatibility, $pa^k \leq ra^k \leq qa^k$. If $T_i \leq T_j$, then $T_i \leq T_j \leq T_i$. The trees are intertwined in the total order, resulting in a contradiction. Therefore, each tree of a monotonic automaton A is an interval.

In order to more efficiently describe the total order of the automaton $A = (Q, \Sigma, \delta)$, we define the triple:

$$\tau_a(p) = (x_a(p), y_a(p), z_a(p)),$$

that is for each state $p \in Q$ and input symbol $a \in \Sigma$ of A according to the structural total order of the forest in Sect. 2 . The structural total order of the input symbol a is denoted by $\leq_a$.

Theorem 1. *An automaton $A = (Q, \Sigma, \delta)$ is monotonic if and only if all forests of A corresponding to the input symbols have a common structural total order.*

Proof. First, prove that if A is monotonic, then the forest corresponding to all input symbols have a common structural total order.

If the automaton A is monotonic, then there exists a compatible total order $\leq$. Now construct a triple τ_a based on the total order $\leq$. For an arbitrary input symbol a, given the total order $\leq$ can know the ordering relationship between arbitrary nodes, the order $z_a(p)$ between an arbitrary node p and other nodes at the same layer polarity in the tree to which it belongs can be determined. Then, we can determine $x_a(p)$ by defining the order of the tree through Corollary 1 and $y_a(p)$ by Lemma 8. In summary, for each input symbol a, the chain obtained τ_a with $\leq_a$ is compatible and consistent with the monotonic chain of A. Therefore, $\leq_a = \leq$, and the forests corresponding to all symbols have a common structural total order.

Prove further that if the forests corresponding to all input symbols of automaton A have a common structural total order, then the automaton is monotonic.

For arbitrary states p and q that satisfy

$$p \leq q \Rightarrow (x_a(p), y_a(p), z_a(p)) \leq (x_a(q), y_a(q), z_a(q))$$

on an arbitrary input symbol a, we can get $pa \leq qa$. Therefore, each state sorted by $\leq_a$ is compatible, so the automaton A is monotonic.

Lemma 11. *When there are states p and q in the monotonic automaton $A = (Q, \Sigma, \delta)$ that cannot be sorted in all forests, the order of these states can be arbitrarily defined on the monotonic chain.*

Proof. Because all forests cannot sort the order of p and q, for an arbitrary input symbol $a \in \Sigma$, if $pa \neq qa$, it is necessary to satisfy $p \leq q \Rightarrow pa \leq qa$, then the order relationship between pa and qa is also undetermined, and then their order can continue to be arbitrarily defined without contradiction. If $pa = qa$, the order relationship is naturally maintained.

For example: define $p \leq q$, then for arbitrary input symbol a, if $pa \neq qa$, it is necessary to satisfy $pa \leq qa$. Since the order of pa and qa in all forests is still indistinguishable. In order to form a recursive order consistency, we can continue to define $pa \leq qa$. Similarly, the definition of $q \leq p$ also holds.

Based on Theorem 1, we propose a decision method for monotonic automata. Recalling the Lemma 7, we can decide whether any automaton is monotonic by deciding whether any base-connected automaton is monotonic. We now give a deciding method for the base-connected monotonic automaton. Suppose that there is an arbitrary base-connected automaton $A = (Q, \Sigma, \delta)$, whose forest consists of several trees $\{T_1, T_2, \cdots, T_u\}$. The decision method is generally divided into two steps:

1. Determine the order of all trees in the automaton.

(1) Choose arbitrary trees T_i and T_j, satisfying $T_j \subsetneq T_i$ and $T_j \subsetneq T_i$, and divide the state sets of these trees into three non-intersecting intervals

$$I_1 \cup I_2 \cup I_3 = (T_i - T_j) \cup (T_j - T_i) \cup (T_i \cap T_j).$$

Lemma 10 shows that if the automaton A is monotonic, then I_1, I_2, I_3 are continuous intervals, and the order is $I_1 \leq I_3 \leq I_2$ or $I_2 \leq I_3 \leq I_1$;

(2) Select arbitrary unprocessed tree T_k. If there are sorted intervals $I_1 \leq I_2 \leq \cdots \leq I_v$, check the intersection between T_k and these intervals. If T_k and interval I_k are not subsets of each other and the intersection is not empty, then further divide the intersection between T_k and each interval I_k. If the states of T_k are distributed in multiple non-adjacent intervals, then T_k is impossible to form a continuous interval in the total order, which contradicts Lemma 10. Therefore, the automaton A is not monotonic;

(3) If no contradiction is detected, merge the division result of step (2) into the sorted interval to form a more refined interval sequence. Repeat step (2) until all trees are processed, and finally obtain the sorted interval chain L covering all states.

2. Determine the position of nodes within each tree in the automaton, including the node layer polarity and the order of nodes with the same father.

Interval chain $L = [I_1, I_2, \cdots, I_m]$, where each interval $I_i \subseteq Q$ is a set of ordered continuous states. Define $f(I_i) = i$, which represents the position of interval I_i in the total order chain. The larger the f value, the larger the state order.

(1) The layer polarity $y(p)$ of the states on each tree T_i can be determined based on the unequal values of $f(I_i)$, and the original interval can be divided into

finer sub-intervals based on $y(p)$. The ordering of states at the same layer polarity is processed as follows: if $p \in I_i$, $q \in I_j$, and $f(I_i) < f(I_j)$, then $p \leq q$.

(2) Merge the refinement results of all trees to obtain a more refined interval chain L, and update $f(I_i)$.

(3) If there is an interval in chain L that contains non-continuous states from different trees, then Lemma 10 is contradicted and the automaton A is not monotonic.

(4) Iterate and repeat steps (1)–(3) until chain L no longer changes or a contradiction is detected.

(5) When there is still an interval I_i in the chain L that contains multiple states and the positive and negative layers are unknown, it is classified one of the states as a negative layer according to Lemma 11, and go to step (1).

(6) When there is still an interval I_i in the chain L that contains multiple states and is at the same layer polarity, its order relationship is arbitrarily defined according to Lemma 11.

Step 1 determines $x_a(p)$ in the triple of Theorem 1, and step 2 determines $y_a(p)$ and $z_a(p)$ in the triple of Theorem 1. Therefore, if the base-connected automaton A is monotonic, this decision method can obtain a unique monotonic chain L. When every base-connected automaton contained in an arbitrary automaton B is monotonic, then Lemma 7 shows the compatible total order of B.

4   An Algorithm for Deciding the Base-Connected Monotonic Automata

The corresponding decision algorithm is designed based on the decision method the base- connected monotonic automata in Sect. 3. The main algorithm contains two sub-algorithms. Sub-algorithm 1 corresponds to step 1 of the decision method, and sub-algorithm 2 corresponds to step 2 of the decision method. The input is an arbitrary base-connected automaton $A = (Q, \Sigma, \delta)$, and the output is a monotonic chain L. If L is not an empty set, then the automaton is monotonic, and vice versa. During the execution of the algorithm, the set L' is used to represent the ordered interval chains in the monotonic chain L. When each interval of L' contains only one state, the set L' is the final monotonic chain L. The forest where A corresponds to all symbols is represented by F. When calling the sub-algorithm, in order to keep F unchanged, an invariant copy $F' = F$ is initialized.

Algorithm 1. Main(A): Deciding the base-connected monotonic automata

---

Input: The base-connected automata $A = (Q, \Sigma, \delta)$.
Output: The chain L.
 1: Let $L = \emptyset$, $L' = \emptyset$, $F' = \emptyset$.
 2: **if** there exists a symbol in A that is not aperiodic **then**
 3:     **return** L.
 4: **end if**
 5: **if** $|\Sigma| = 1$ **then**
 6:     Sort A in the tree and get chain L'.
 7:     **return** $L = L'$.
 8: **else**
 9:     Let $F' = F$, $L' = $ Sub-algorithm1(F').
10: **end if**
11: **if** $L' = \emptyset$ **then**
12:     **return** $L = L'$.
13: **end if**
14: Let $F' = F$, $L' = $ Sub-algorithm2(F', L').
15: **return** $L = L'$.

In Sub-algorithm 1, T_i and T_j represent arbitrary trees in the forest F'. Their intersecting intervals are stored in a chain $L' = \{X_1, X_2, \cdots, X_{max}\}$, where each X_i is an interval, X_1 is the head of the chain L', and X_{max} is the tail of the chain L'. Next, select an arbitrary tree T_k from F', compute a new interval for the intersection between T_k and X_i, and add these new intervals to L'. To track the order of intervals in L', define a function f such that $f(X_i) = i$, where the domain of f is L' and its range is $[1, max]$. Here, s denotes an arbitrary state in F'.

In Sub-algorithm 2, (T_i, v_0) represents arbitrary tree in the forest F', the states in T_i are represented by s_i, s_j, the state of the leaf node is represented by s_e and s'_e, the branch where s_i in T_i is located is represented by B_{s_i}, the interval obtained by sorting the states in the T_i is represented by the chain L''. When A is a monotonic automaton, L'' is the sub-chain of the interval chain L'. Define the function y to record the layer polarity of each state. When $y(s_i) < 0$, s_i is a negative layer; when $y(s_i) = 0$, $s_i = v_0$; and when $y(s_i) > 0$, s_i is a positive layer. Therefore, the range of value y is an integer. In Line 17–22 of Subalgorithm 2 uses Lemma 12 and in Line 24–31 uses Lemma 13.

Lemma 12. *In a monotonic automaton $A = (Q, \Sigma, \delta)$, for arbitrary leaf node s_e and node s_h in a tree T_i. When $|y(s_e)| > |y(s_h)|$ and $|y(s_h)| \neq 0$, if $s_e \leq s_h$ in the interval chain L, then $y(B_{s_e}) < 0$; if $s_h \leq s_e$ in the interval chain, then $y(B_{s_e}) > 0$.*

Proof. Each tree corresponds to a continuous interval $I(T_i)$ in the total order chain L. From the state sorting rule in the tree in Lemma 8, we can see that the following holds: For the negative layer branch B, if $y(p) = -k$, then $k_1 > k_2 \Rightarrow p_1 \leq p_2$ (the farther the negative layer is from the root, the smaller the

---

Algorithm 2. Sub-algorithm1(F'): Tree sorting algorithm

Input: The forest F'.
Output: The chain L'.
1: Choose arbitrary trees $T_i \in F'$ and $T_j \in F'$ satisfying $T_i \cap T_j \neq \emptyset$, $T_j \subsetneq T_i$ and $T_j \subsetneq T_i$.
2: Let $X_1 = T_i - T_j$, $X_2 = T_i \cap T_j$, $X_3 = T_j - T_i$.
3: Define the function $f(X_1) = 1$, $f(X_2) = 2$, $f(X_3) = 3$, let $F' = F' - T_i - T_j$, $L' = \{X_1, X_2, X_3\}$, $X_{max} = f^{-1}(max f(X_i))$, $X_i \in L'$.
4: **if** $F' = \emptyset$ **then**
5:     **return** L'.
6: **end if**
7: Let L^* be a chain.
8: **repeat**
9:     Update $L^* = L'$.
10:     **repeat**
11:       Choose an arbitrary tree $T_k \in F'$.
12:       **if** $T_k \cap L' \neq \emptyset$ **then**
13:         **if** all states of $T_k \cap L'$ cannot form an interval in L' **then**
14:           **return** $\emptyset$.
15:         **end if**
16:         **if** $T_k - L' \neq \emptyset$ and $T_k - L'$ is at the beginning of the chain of L' **then**
17:           Let $X_{max+1} \leftarrow X_{max}, \ldots, X_{k+1} \leftarrow X_k, \ldots, X_2 \leftarrow X_1, X_1 \leftarrow T_k - L'$,
    $X_{max} \leftarrow X_{max+1}$.
18:         **else if** $T_k - L' \neq \emptyset$ and $T_k - L'$ is at the end of the chain of L' **then**
19:           Let $X_{max} \leftarrow T_k - L'$.
20:         **end if**
21:         Update the function f such that $f(X_i) = i$.
22:       **end if**
23:       **while** $T_k \cap X_k \neq \emptyset$ and $T_j \subsetneq T_i$ and $T_j \subsetneq T_i$ **do**
24:         **if** $X_k \neq X_{max}$ **then**
25:           Let $X_{max+1} \leftarrow X_{max}, \ldots, X_{k+2} \leftarrow X_{k+1}, X_{max} \leftarrow X_{max+1}$.
26:         **end if**
27:         **if** exists a state $s \in T_k - X_k$ such that $f(s) < f(X_k)$ **then**
28:           Update $X_{k+1} \leftarrow X_k - T_k$, $X_k \leftarrow X_k \cap T_k$.
29:         **else**
30:           Update $X_{k+1} \leftarrow X_k \cap T_k$, $X_k \leftarrow X_k - T_k$.
31:         **end if**
32:         Update the function f such that $f(X_i) = i$.
33:       **end while**
34:       Let $F' = F' - T_k$.
35:     **until** $F' = \emptyset$
36:     Let $F' = F$.
37: **until** $L^* = L'$
38: **return** L'.

---

order); for the positive layer branch B, if $y(p) = +k$, then $k_1 > k_2 \Rightarrow p_2 \leq p_1$ (the farther the positive layer is from the root, the larger the order).

From $|y(s_e)| > |y(s_h)|$, we can see that the farther s_e is from the root, since $|y(s_h)| \neq 0$, s_h is not a root node. When $s_e \leq s_h$, assuming that B_{s_e} is a negative layer, the larger $|y(s_e)|$ is, the smaller the order is, so $s_e \leq s_h$, and the assumption holds; assuming that B_{s_e} is a positive layer, since the larger $|y(s_e)|$ corresponds to a larger order, this would enforce $s_h \leq s_e$, contradicting $s_e \leq s_h$.

Algorithm 3. Sub-algorithm2(F', L'): Detailed division of interval chain L'

Input: The forest F', the chain L'.
Output: The chain L'.
1: **repeat**
2:   **repeat**
3:     **repeat**
4:       Choose an arbitrary tree $T_i \in F'$, let $F' \leftarrow F' - T_i$.
5:       **if** choose every pairs in T_i all satisfying $f(s_i) < f(s_j)$ and $|y(s_i)| \neq |y(s_j)|$. **then**
6:         **if** $s_i = v_0$ **then**
7:           Let $y(B_{s_j}) > 0$.
8:         **else if** $s_j = v_0$ **then**
9:           Let $y(B_{s_i}) < 0$.
10:         **else if** $|y(s_i)| > |y(s_j)|$ and $B_{s_i} = B_{s_j}$ **then**
11:           Let $y(B_{s_i}) < 0$.
12:         **else if** $|y(s_i)| < |y(s_j)|$ and $B_{s_i} = B_{s_j}$ **then**
13:           Let $y(B_{s_i}) > 0$.
14:         **end if**
15:       **end if**
16:       **if** exists state s_e such that cannot distinguish layer polarity **then**
17:         **if** $|y(s_e)| > |y(s_h)|$ and $y(s_h) \neq 0$. **then**
18:           **if** $f(s_e) < f(s_h)$ **then**
19:             Let $y(B_{s_e}) < 0$.
20:           **else if** $f(s_e) > f(s_h)$ **then**
21:             Let $y(B_{s_e}) > 0$.
22:           **end if**
23:         **end if**
24:         **while** there is no branch in T_i that satisfies $y(B_{s'_e}) < 0$ and $y(B_{s'_e}) > 0$ **do**
25:           **if** there is no branch in T_i that satisfies $y(B_{s'_e}) < 0$ and $|y(s'_e)| < |y(s_e)|$ **then**
26:             Let $y(B_{s_e}) < 0$.
27:           **end if**
28:           **if** there is no branch in T_i that satisfies $y(B_{s'_e}) > 0$ and $|y(s'_e)| < |y(s_e)|$ **then**
29:             Let $y(B_{s_e}) > 0$.
30:           **end if**
31:         **end while**
32:         **if** $|y(s_e)| > |y(f^{-1}(f(v_0) - 1))|$ or $|y(s_e)| > |y(f^{-1}(f(v_0) + 1))|$ **then**
33:           **return** $\emptyset$.
34:         **end if**
35:         **if** exists state s_k that cannot distinguish layer polarity **then**
36:           Record the possible range of s_k.
37:         **end if**
38:       **end if**
39:       **if** If T_i cannot form a continuous state in L' according to the order in the tree **then**
40:         **return** $\emptyset$.
41:       **else**
42:         Sort T_i to form sub-chain L'', and then refer to L'' to refine L' to form a smaller interval.
43:       **end if**
44:       Update the function f such that $f(X_i) = i$.
45:     **until** $F' = \emptyset$
46:     Let $F' = F$.
47:   **until** the function f and the layer polarity of T_i remain stable
48:   Choose an arbitrary T_i with branch B_i that cannot determine the layer polarity $y(B_i)$, let $y(B_i) < 0$.
49:   Sort T_i to form sub-chain L'', and then refer to L'' to refine L' to form a smaller interval.
50:   Update the function f such that $f(X_i) = i$, let $F' = F$.
51: **until** the layer polarity of all branches B_i in the forest is determined
52: **if** $|f^{-1}(f(X_i))| > 1$ **then**
53:   Arbitrarily order these states to obtain a chain L' with only one state in each interval.
54: **end if**
55: **return** L'.

Thus, B_{s_e} can only be a negative layer, that is, $y(B_{s_e}) < 0$. When $s_h \leq s_e$, by the same logic, B_{s_e} can only be a positive layer, that is, $y(B_{s_e}) > 0$. The proof is complete.

Lemma 13. *In the decision process of the monotonic automaton $A = (Q, \Sigma, \delta)$, for an arbitrary tree T_i, the branches whose layer polarity can be determined by the interval chain L are represented by $B_{s'_e}$, its leaf node is s'_e, and the remaining branches with undetermined layer polarity are represented by B_{s_e}, its leaf node is s_e. If A is monotonic, the following hold:*

1. *If $B_{s'_e}$ has both positive and negative layers, then $|y(s_e)| < |y(s'_e)|$;*
2. *If $B_{s'_e}$ has only positive layers and $|y(s'_e)| < |y(s_e)|$, then $y(B_2) < 0$;*
3. *If $B_{s'_e}$ has only negative layers and $|y(s'_e)| < |y(s_e)|$, then $y(B_2) > 0$.*

Proof. In a monotonic automaton, each tree T_i corresponds to a continuous interval in the total order chain, and all states are strictly ordered according to the layer polarity function.

In 1, since $B_{s'_e}$ has both positive and negative levels, the maximum and minimum elements in the continuous interval $I(T_i)$ where T_i is located are in branch $B_{s'_e}$. Assuming $|y(s'_e)| < |y(s_e)|$, the leaf node s_e farthest from the root node is the maximum or minimum element in $I(T_i)$, so the layer polarity of B_{s_e} can be determined, and the assumption does not hold. Therefore, $|y(s_e)| < |y(s'_e)|$, the proposition is proved.

In 2, since $B_{s'_e}$ has only positive layers, the maximum element of the continuous interval $I(T_i)$ is located in the branch $B_{s'_e}$. Assuming B_{s_e} is a positive layer, because $|y(s'_e)| < |y(s_e)|$, then the leaf node s_e farthest from the root node is the maximum element of $I(T_i)$, so the layer polarity of B_{s_e} can be determined, and the assumption does not hold. Assuming B_{s_e} is a negative layer, because $|y(s'_e)| < |y(s_e)|$, then the leaf node s'_e farthest from the root node is the maximum element of $I(T_i)$, and because B_{s_e} is a negative layer, it can be known that $y(s_e) < 0$, which reveals that s_e cannot be the maximum element of $I(T_i)$, so the assumption holds. Thus, B_{s_e} is a negative layer, that is, $y(B_2) < 0$. 3 can be obtained by the same logic and will not be discussed again. The proposition is proved.

Algorithm time complexity analysis: Suppose that the size of the automata is (n, m). The main algorithm contains two sub-algorithms. Sub-algorithm 1 constructs the initial interval chain L. The time complexity of processing the interval divided by two trees each time is $O(n)$. The time complexity of calculating each tree intersection with the existing chain to divide the finer intervals is $O(n)$. Therefore, the overall time complexity of sub-algorithm 1 is $O(n^2)$. In sub-algorithm 2, the time complexity of traversing the chain L to determine the layer polarity of each tree T_i and traversing the layer polarity of each tree T_i to refine the chain L is $O(n^2)$, In the worst case, it needs to be iterated n times until the chain L no longer changes. There are m input symbols in total, so the time complexity of sub-algorithm 2 is $O(mn^3)$. Therefore, the time complexity of the main algorithm is $O(mn^3)$.

5   An Example of the Decision Algorithm

Now we give an example of a base-connected automaton $A = (Q, \Sigma, \delta)$, and decide its monotonicity according to the algorithm. where $Q = \{1, 2, 3, \cdots, 33\}$, $\Sigma = \{a, b, c\}$. The corresponding

$$a\text{-forest} = \{(T_1, 24), (T_2, 1), (T_3, 21), (T_4, 12)\},$$
$$b\text{-forest} = \{(T_5, 23), (T_6, 16), (T_7, 12), (T_8, 2), (T_9, 24)\},$$
$$c\text{-forest} = \{(T_{10}, 31), (T_{11}, 22), (T_{12}, 11)\},$$

we can see in Figs. 1, 2 and 3(The green state is v_0).

Because $|\Sigma| \neq 1$, we execute sub-algorithm 1 for A. Suppose that the arbitrary trees selected at this time are T_1 and T_5, satisfying $T_1 \cap T_5 \neq \emptyset$ and neither is a subset of the other. By executing in Line 1–6 of sub-algorithm 1 to obtain the interval chain L', as shown in Table 1.

Table 1. The chain L' got by executing 1–6 on the T_1 and T_5 in Sub-algorithm 1.

Interval	State
$f(X_1) = 1$	$17, 18, 19, 20, 21$
$f(X_2) = 2$	$22, 23$
$f(X_3) = 3$	$24, 25, 26, 27, 28, 29, 30, 31$

Choose T_4 to satisfy $T_4 \cap L' \neq \emptyset$, and execute in Line 11–33 of sub-algorithm 1 to obtain L' as shown in Table 2.

Table 2. Select T_4 to execute in Line 11–33 of sub-algorithm 1 to obtain chain L'

Interval	State
$f(X_1) = 1$	$6, 7, 8, 9, 10, 11, 12, 13, 14, 15, 16$
$f(X_2) = 2$	$17, 18, 19$
$f(X_3) = 3$	$20, 21$
$f(X_4) = 4$	$22, 23$
$f(X_5) = 5$	$24, 25, 26, 27, 28, 29, 30, 31, 32, 33$

By executing in Line 34–38 of sub-algorithm 1, all trees are iterated until L' no longer changes. Sub-algorithm 1 ends and returns L' as shown in Table 3.

Because $L' \neq \emptyset$, calling sub-algorithm 2. Assuming that the tree selected at this time is T_1, and in Line 4–44 are executed to label each state of T_1 with positive or negative layers, we can see from T_1 in Fig. 4. Sort the tree T_1 according to the positive and negative layers to obtain the interval chain L'' as shown in the green part of Table 4. L' is shown in Table 4.

Table 3. The chain L' returned by sub-algorithm 1

Interval	State
$f(X_1) = 1$	$1, 2, 3, 4, 5$
$f(X_2) = 2$	$6, 7$
$f(X_3) = 3$	$8, 9, 10, 11, 12$
$f(X_4) = 4$	$13, 14$
$f(X_5) = 5$	$15, 16$
$f(X_6) = 6$	$17, 18, 19$
$f(X_7) = 7$	$20, 21$
$f(X_8) = 8$	$22, 23$
$f(X_9) = 9$	$24, 25, 26, 27$
$f(X_{10}) = 10$	$28, 29, 30, 31, 32, 33$

Table 4. The chain L' got by sorting the tree T_1 in sub-algorithm 2

Interval	State
$f(X_1) = 1$	$1, 2, 3, 4, 5$
$f(X_2) = 2$	$6, 7$
$f(X_3) = 3$	$8, 9, 10, 11, 12$
$f(X_4) = 4$	$13, 14$
$f(X_5) = 5$	$15, 16$
$f(X_6) = 6$	$17, 18, 19$
$f(X_7) = 7$	$20, 21$
$f(X_8) = 8$	$22, 23$
$f(X_9) = 9$	24
$f(X_{10}) = 10$	$25, 26, 27$
$f(X_{11}) = 11$	$28, 29, 30$
$f(X_{12}) = 12$	$31, 32$
$f(X_{13}) = 13$	33

Each tree is iterated for one round until the positive and negative layers of T_i and the function f no longer change. When a state of the tree cannot determine the positive and negative layers, for example, state 11 in T_4, the size between 11 and 10, 12 cannot be determined in L'', it is recorded. After one round of iteration, the positive and negative layers of all trees are as shown in Fig. 4.

Currently, state 11 in T_4 and T_7, states 10 and 12 in T_{12} cannot be classified into positive and negative layers. However, L' shows $10 < 12$, which allows state 11 to be placed either before or after states 10 and 12. By executing in Line (48)-(50) of Algorithm 2, we obtain the updated interval chain L', as shown in Table 5.

Table 5. Execute in Line (48)–(50) in sub-algorithm 2 to obtain the chain L'

Interval	State	Interval	State
$f(X_1) = 1$	1	$f(X_{17}) = 17$	18
$f(X_2) = 2$	2	$f(X_{18}) = 18$	19
$f(X_3) = 3$	3, 4	$f(X_{19}) = 19$	20
$f(X_4) = 4$	5	$f(X_{20}) = 20$	21
$f(X_5) = 5$	6	$f(X_{21}) = 21$	22
$f(X_6) = 6$	7	$f(X_{22}) = 22$	23
$f(X_7) = 7$	8	$f(X_{23}) = 23$	24
$f(X_8) = 8$	9	$f(X_{24}) = 24$	25
$f(X_9) = 9$	10	$f(X_{25}) = 25$	26
$f(X_{10}) = 10$	11	$f(X_{26}) = 26$	27
$f(X_{11}) = 11$	12	$f(X_{27}) = 27$	28
$f(X_{12}) = 12$	13	$f(X_{28}) = 28$	29
$f(X_{13}) = 13$	14	$f(X_{29}) = 29$	30
$f(X_{14}) = 14$	15	$f(X_{30}) = 30$	31
$f(X_{15}) = 15$	16	$f(X_{31}) = 31$	32
$f(X_{16}) = 16$	17	$f(X_{32}) = 32$	33

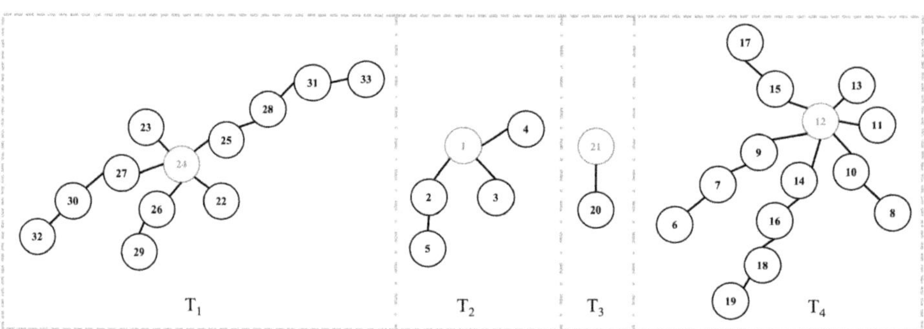

Fig. 1. The a-forest corresponding to the input symbol a.

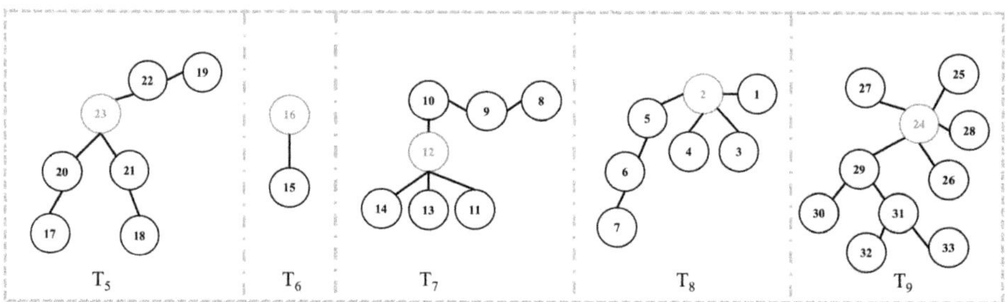

Fig. 2. The b-forest corresponding to the input symbol b.

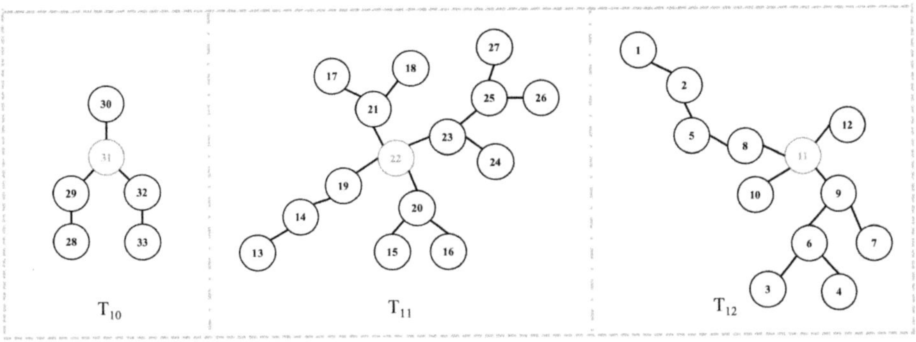

Fig. 3. The c-forest corresponding to the input symbol c.

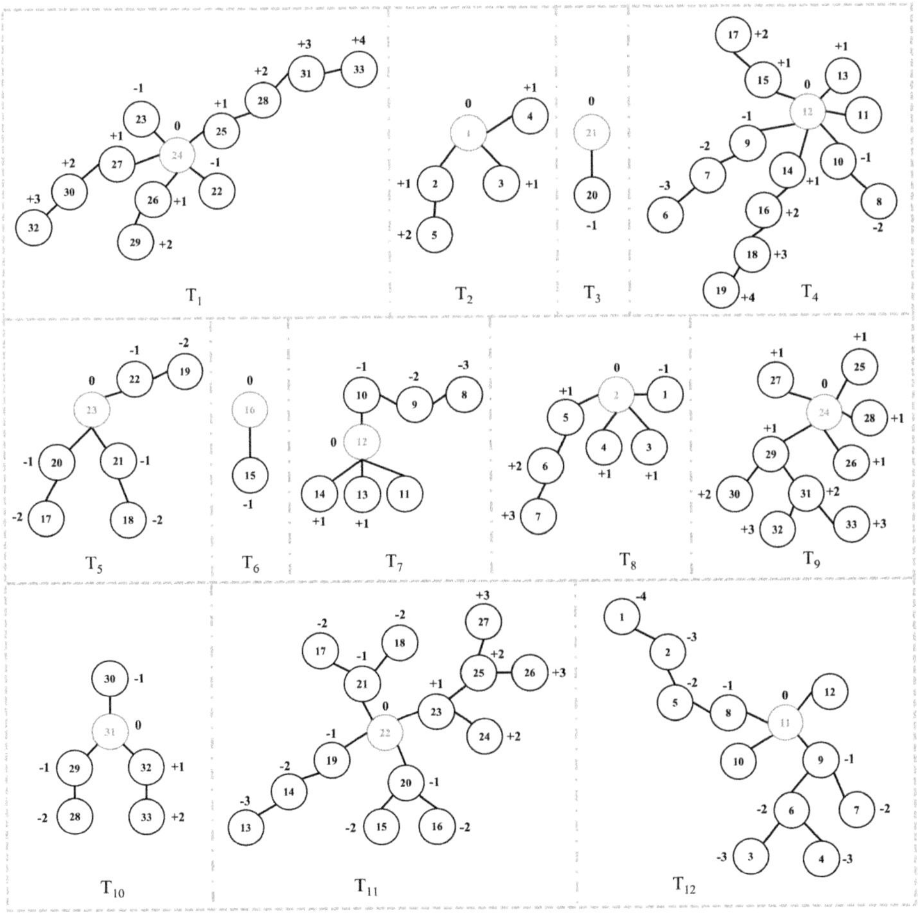

Fig. 4. Positive and negative layer corresponding to F.

In the interval chain L', we observe that $|f^{-1}(f(X_3))| > 1$, indicating that the order between states 3 and 4 cannot be resolved. We arbitrarily assign their order as $3 < 4$, we can obtain a complete monotonic chain L'. This chain is returned to the main algorithm and the output is $L = L'$.

6   Conclusion

This paper gives the structural total order of trees and forests. Each input symbol of a monotonic automaton is aperiodic, and the structural total order of the corresponding forest is compatible. Based on this, we prove that the necessary and sufficient condition for an automaton to be monotonic is that the forest corresponding to all input symbols have a common structural total order. Each monotonic automaton is composed of k base-connected automata. Since Sect. 6 of this paper proves that each base-connected automaton contained in an arbitrary automaton A is monotonic, it follows that automaton A is monotonic. Thus, we propose a method and algorithm for deciding the of base-connected monotonic automata. Subsequent research on the application of automata with order structures to the network protocol security field provides a new model.

Acknowledgements. This paper was supported by National Natural Science Foundation of China (No. 62406108), Hainan Provincial Natural Science Foundation of China (No. 625QN362), Research Foundation of Education Bureau of Hunan Province of China (No. 23B0471).

References

1. Xu, Q., Zhang, Z., Yan, Y., Xia, C.: Security and privacy with K-step opacity for finite automata via a novel algebraic approach. Trans. Inst. Meas. Control. **43**(16), 3606–3614 (2021)
2. Colombo C., Pace G.J., Schneider G.: LARVA—safer monitoring of real-time java programs (Tool Paper). In: 2009 Seventh IEEE International Conference on Software Engineering and Formal Methods, pp. 33–37 (2009)
3. Soliman, D., Thramboulidis, K., Frey, G.: Transformation of function block diagrams to UPPAAL timed automata for the verification of safety applications. Annu. Rev. Control. **36**(2), 338–345 (2012)
4. Ouedraogo, L., Kumar, R., Malik, R., Akesson, K.: Nonblocking and safe control of discrete-event systems modeled as extended finite automata. IEEE Trans. Autom. Sci. Eng. **8**(3), 560–569 (2011)
5. Kurkowski, M., Penczek, W.: Verifying security protocols modelled by networks of automata. Fund. Inform. **79**(3–4), 453–471 (2007)
6. Fathinavid A.H., Aghababa A.B.: A protocol for intrusion detection based on learning automata in forwarding packets for distributed wireless sensor networks. In: 2012 International Conference on Cyber-Enabled Distributed Computing and Knowledge Discovery, pp. 373–380 (2012)
7. Ananichev, D.S., Volkov, M.V.: Synchronizing generalized monotonic automata. Theoret. Comput. Sci. **330**(1), 3–13 (2005)

8. Volkov, M.: Synchronizing automata preserving a chain of partial orders. Theoret. Comput. Sci. **410**(37), 3513–3519 (2009)
9. Cui, Z.H., He, Y., Sun, S.Y.: Synchronizing bounded partially ordered automata. Chinese J. Comput. **42**(3), 610–623 (2019)
10. Cui Z.H., Wang Z.X., He.Y.: On the synchronizing problem of tree-Like partially ordered automata. Chinese J. Comput. **46**(9), 1960–1976 (2023)
11. Wang, Z.X., Jiang, G.D.: Synchronizing algorithms for bounded partially ordered automata. Comput. Sci. **50**(S1), 841–845 (2023)
12. Xiao M.M., Yu S.Z., Wang Y.: Automatic network protocol automaton extraction. In: 2009 Third International Conference on Network and System Security, pp. 336–343 (2009)
13. Cotumaccio, N., D'Agostino, G., Policriti, A.: Co-lexicographically ordering automata and regular languages-part. J. ACM **70**(4), 1–73 (2023)
14. Ananichev, D.S., Volkov, M.V.: Synchronizing monotonic automata. Theoret. Comput. Sci. **327**(3), 225–239 (2004)
15. Howie, J.: Automata and languages. Clarendon Press, Oxford (1991)
16. Grätzer, G.: Lattice theory: foundation. Switzerland. Birkhäuser, Basel (2011)
17. Kolman B., Busky R.C., Ross S.C.: Discrete mathematical structures. 6th Edn. Pearson Education Inc. (2012)

A Self-adaptive Moving Target Defense Decision-Making Method Based on Bounded-Rationality Supermodular Games

Rongbo Sun[✉], Jinlong Fei, and Yuefei Zhu

Key Laboratory of Cyberspace Security, Ministry of Education, Zhengzhou, China
satoshi626@163.com

Abstract. Existing research on moving target defense (MTD) decision-making methods predominantly relies on game models under the assumption of complete rationality, failing to adequately account for the bounded rationality of attackers and defenders. Additionally, traditional MTD strategies face issues of rigidity and resource inefficiency in dynamic environments, rendering them ineffective against continuously evolving adversarial scenarios. To address these limitations, this paper proposes a dynamically self-adaptive decision-making method based on supermodular games under bounded rationality. First, the adversarial process is modeled using a supermodular game framework that incorporates prospect theory to capture bounded rational behavior. Furthermore, a constrained payoff function that balances MTD security, performance, and affordability is designed. Second, an innovative Prospect-Theoretic Multi-Agent Advantage Actor-Critic (PT-MAA2C) algorithm is proposed to solve the game, leveraging its adaptive and efficient strategy exploration and exploitation capabilities to derive optimal equilibrium solutions. Finally, through experiments simulating MTD methods against DDoS attacks in a network topology deception scenario, the proposed method is demonstrated with significantly enhanced defense efficiency, system robustness, and resource optimization, offering both theoretical and practical value.

Keywords: Cyber Security · Moving Target Defense · Multi-agent Reinforcement Learning · Security Metrics · Game Theory

1 Introduction

While current network architectures exhibit significant advancements in intelligence, automation, and integration, security architectures suffer from a pronounced asymmetry in offensive and defensive capabilities: attackers can launch effective attacks using simple methods, small tools, and security vulnerabilities, whereas defense systems rely on complex algorithms to construct coordinated and systemic protection mechanisms. This operational dynamic results in a marked asymmetry in cyber attack and defense interactions.

© ICST Institute for Computer Sciences, Social Informatics and Telecommunications Engineering 2026
Published by Springer Nature Switzerland AG 2026. All Rights Reserved
W. Liang et al. (Eds.): SecureComm 2025, LNICST 690, pp. 392–409, 2026.
https://doi.org/10.1007/978-3-032-23456-8_21

To transcend the limitations of traditional static defense paradigms, researchers have proposed the Moving Target Defense (MTD) theory based on principles of shuffling, diversity, and redundancy [1]. The core of MTD lies in constructing a time-varying dynamic defense mechanism that dynamically contracts the attack surface within a controllable threshold through multi-dimensional coordination. This proactive defense architecture continuously resets the system's attack surface, forcing attackers into a perpetual state of environmental awareness and vulnerability matching, thereby disrupting the temporal and continuous construction of attack chains and enhancing the system's defensive efficacy against hybrid security threats.

MTD research offers a rich array of defense mechanisms for various security threats, primarily focusing on three main research directions: (1) specific MTD technical designs, (2) MTD timing decision methods, and (3) MTD spatial decision methods. The first category pertains to strategy formulation, while the latter two concern decision mechanisms. Existing MTD decision-making methods predominantly employ game theory for strategy development [2,3], assuming complete rationality on the part of both attackers and defenders, with limited consideration of bounded rationality.

In reality, complete rationality in game theory requires three conditions: (1) both attackers and defenders must fully understand every factor influencing decision outcomes, (2) they must fully consider all possible outcomes and their probabilities, and (3) they must be capable of ranking their preferences for each outcome. However, in cyber attack and defense scenarios, the differing understandings and reactions of attackers and defenders to the cybersecurity landscape result in varied prediction and decision-making mechanisms. For instance, defenders have limited knowledge of attack experiences, capabilities, and objectives, while attackers have limited understanding of the target system's MTD strategies. This makes it challenging for both parties to make nearly perfect judgments and decisions during the adversarial process. Therefore, researching MTD decision-making methods under bounded rationality, which refers to the strategies defenders should adopt under constrained rational conditions to counter attackers' behaviors, is of significant practical importance. This paper proposes a Prospect-theoretic Multi-agent Advantage Actor-critic (PT-MAA2C) algorithm to solve MTD decision-making problems based on bounded-rationality supermodular games (BRSMG). Compared to existing research, our main contributions are as follows:

1. Abstracting the cyber attack and defense process as a BRSMG game, incorporating bounded rationality based on prospect theory: By introducing a supermodular game framework and incorporating prospect theory to model bounded rational behavior, we construct a BRSMG model that closely aligns with real-world cyber attack and defense scenarios, providing a precise abstraction of the actual environment to aid in the dynamic learning and updating of MTD decision-making methods.

2. Proposing an improved multi-agent A2C algorithm to solve the game: We introduce prospect theory's behavioral decision model into a multi-agent

reinforcement learning framework for the first time, leveraging reinforcement learning's adaptive exploration and exploitation mechanisms in high-dimensional strategy spaces. This addresses the disconnect between the complete rationality assumption in classical game theory and the bounded rational behavior in real-world scenarios, offering a high-yield decision-making method that converges rapidly.

3. Validating the robustness and practicality of PT-MAA2C in BRSMG-based topology deception experiments: We conduct comparative experiments with existing topology deception research based on three-dimensional metrics of security, performance, and affordability. Through detailed data analysis, we demonstrate that our PT-MAA2C algorithm effectively balances the costs, defense efficacy, and security of different MTD strategies under bounded rationality conditions.

The remainder of this paper is organized as follows: Sect. 2 reviews related work on MTD decision-making methods and the progress of approaches related to our method; Sect. 3 details the BRSMG model and the PT-MAA2C algorithm; Sect. 4 presents a case study using topology deception MTD methods against DDoS attacks to validate the feasibility and effectiveness of our proposed method. Section 5 concludes the entire article.

2   Related Work

MTD decision-making mechanism research primarily focuses on how and when to move the attack surface to achieve optimal defense effects against different security risks. Most existing research employs game theory as a mathematical tool to describe and analyze multi-agent interactions [4]. Game theory is particularly suited for MTD decision-making research due to two key points:

1. Resource Antagonism: Attackers exploit system vulnerabilities to expand breach surfaces, while defenders constrain exposures via dynamic configuration shifts (e.g., randomization, diversification) [5].
2. Interdependent Decision-Making: The efficacy of adversarial strategies hinges on mutual behavioral adaptations [3].

These MTD adversarial characteristics align with game theory features, making game theory a popular tool for modeling MTD solutions, proving equilibrium convergence, and deriving equilibrium strategies [6].

Traditional MTD research designs equilibrium strategies under the assumption of complete rationality, overlooking the cognitive limitations of defenders in real-time responses [7]. To enhance the realism of decision models, some scholars have attempted to integrate bounded rationality theory with MTD mechanisms. For example, Schlenker et al. [8] used the Level-k model to simulate the limited reasoning depth of attackers and defenders, demonstrating the robustness of defense strategies under asymmetric information. Xu et al. [9] optimized defense action selection through loss aversion parameters. However, existing work is often limited to single-agent decision-making or simplified game structures, lacking explicit modeling of multi-party strategy complementarity and cooperative equilibrium, making it challenging to address large-scale complex attack scenarios.

Bounded rationality game theory aims to model decision-makers' strategic behaviors under real-world constraints such as incomplete information, limited computational resources, and cognitive biases. Simon [10] first introduced the concept of "bounded rationality," emphasizing that decision-makers tend to seek satisfactory solutions rather than global optima. Camerer et al. [11] validated the effectiveness of Quantal Response Equilibrium (QRE) in predicting human game behavior through behavioral experiments, where players choose strategies with Logit probabilities, enhancing the modeling of non-completely rational decision-making. McKelvey et al. [12] extended QRE to dynamic games, laying the foundation for bounded rationality analysis in complex scenarios. Recently, deep reinforcement learning (DRL) has been introduced to bounded rationality modeling, such as Kulkarni et al. [13] proposed a hierarchical belief update mechanism based on DRL, effectively capturing cognitive constraints in multi-stage games. However, existing research often focuses on static payoff matrices or complete information assumptions, with limited attention to behavioral heterogeneity in dynamic environments, such as reference point dependence and loss aversion.

Supermodular games, known for their strategy complementarity, have become essential tools for analyzing adversarial decision systems. Topkis [14] proved the existence of pure strategy Nash equilibria and convergence conditions using lattice theory, while Vives [15] extended these findings to stochastic dynamic game scenarios. Classic solution methods like best response dynamics rely on monotonic strategy updates for global convergence but face computational efficiency bottlenecks in high-dimensional action spaces [16]. Recently, reinforcement learning techniques have been applied to supermodular game solving, such as Narang et al. [17] proposed a Q-learning-based strategy search framework, which reduces dimensionality through state abstraction. However, existing RL methods do not fully consider decision-makers' bounded rational behaviors, such as reference point anchoring effects, potentially leading to equilibrium shifts or convergence oscillations.

The Actor-Critic (AC) framework balances exploration and exploitation efficiency by combining policy gradients with value function estimation. To enhance training stability, A2C (Advantage Actor-Critic) synchronously updates policy and value networks, demonstrating superior sample efficiency through parameter sharing and experience replay mechanisms. For multi-agent game scenarios, Lowe et al. [18] proposed an MADDPG algorithm, which mitigates environmental non-stationarity challenges through a centralized training and decentralized execution hybrid architecture. However, existing AC algorithms face two limitations when handling decision-making under bounded rationality: (1) advantage function estimation does not incorporate behavioral economic models, making it difficult to capture real decision-makers' risk preferences; and (2) cross-agent strategy coordination mechanisms rely on shared networks or global signals, lacking formal constraints on local interaction structures, which can lead to equilibrium instability.

3   Model and Methodology

Under the BRSMG, both attackers and defenders are intelligent agents utilizing reinforcement learning algorithms, capable of making decisions by observing the environment. The multi-agent game relies on reinforcement learning algorithms to solve for the game's equilibrium points [17]. Section 3.1 models the game, defining and explaining each component of the model. Section 3.2 introduces the MTD scenario based on this game. Section 3.3 introduces the multi-agent reinforcement learning framework of MTD decision-making method to solve this MTD game.

3.1   Bounded-Rationality Supermodular Game Model

Theorem 1. *(Supermodularity Conditions): A supermodular game satisfies the following conditions:*

a) *Partial order of action sets: Each participant's action set is a partially ordered set, typically a real interval or discrete set.*

b) *Supermodularity of Payoff Functions: Each participant's payoff function is supermodular, meaning that for any actions $a^P \leq a^{P\prime}$ and $a^{\overline{P}} \leq a^{\overline{P}\prime}$, the following condition holds for satisfying strategy complementarity:*

$$R^P\left(a^{P\prime}, a^{\overline{P}\prime}\right) + R^P\left(a^P, a^{\overline{P}}\right) \geq R^P\left(a^{P\prime}, a^{\overline{P}}\right) + R^P\left(a^P, a^{\overline{P}\prime}\right) \tag{1}$$

This formula indicates that when one participant chooses a higher action, the marginal benefit of other participants choosing higher action increases. The core feature of supermodular games is the adversarial interaction between participants' strategies. This property ensures the existence of Nash equilibrium and algorithmic convergence. Under these conditions, supermodular games can be applied to the cyber attack and defense process: an increase in the attacker's attack intensity will drive the defender to increase MTD intensity, and vice versa. The properties of supermodular games remain valid even when both attackers and defenders are boundedly rational. Therefore, the supermodular game is adapted to a bounded-rationality supermodular game (BRSMG) based on real-world cyber attack and defense processes, defined as a quadruple $< P, S, A, R >$. The elements are explained as follows:

Participants P. $P = \{P^D, P^A\}$, where P^D represents the defender and P^A represents the attacker. For convenience, $\overline{P}$ denotes the opponent.

State Space S. The game state is described through three dimensions of the defense system's attack surface, which is the set of exposed exploitable resources. At time t, the state s_t can be expressed as:

$$s_t = (s_t{}^S, s_t{}^C, s_t{}^P) \in \mathbb{R}^3 \tag{2}$$

Structural Exposure $s_t{}^S$. The number of exposed network interfaces and service ports (discrete value, normalized to [0,1]).

Configuration Vulnerability $s_t{}^C$. The weighted sum of unpatched vulnerabilities' CVSS scores (continuous value, weighted average to [0,1]).

Protocol Detectability $s_t{}^P$. The entropy of fingerprintable features in communication protocols (low entropy $\Rightarrow$ easy to detect, normalized to [0,1]).

State changes are primarily based on these three components. For example,a_t^D = "port randomization," leading to $s_t^S \rightarrow s_{t+1}^S$, and $s_t = (s_t^S, s_t^C, s_t^P) \rightarrow s_{t+1} = (s_{t+1}^S, s_t^C, s_t^P)$. The defender's goal is to minimize $\|s_t\|$, while the attacker aims to maximize it. This quantitative framework is compatible with various MTD techniques, such as IP hopping, topology deception, and service migration.

Local Observation Space O. Based on the state space, the local observations o_t^P for both attackers and defenders are defined. Due to visibility constraints, neither party can directly observe $\|s_t\|$. The defender can only infer it by sensing partial attack traffic, while the attacker's initial estimate of $\|s_t\|$ is based on historical results, which may be outdated and updated only through exploratory attacks. Thus, local observations are noisy mappings:

$$o_t^P = g^P(s_t) \tag{3}$$

where $g^P()$ is a noisy mapping function simulating bounded rationality under incomplete information.

Action Space A. $A = \{A^D, A^A\}$, where at time t, the action is a_t^P. Participants' action choices are derived from the strategy function $\pi^P(a_t^P|o_t^P)$. To ensure BRSMG adheres to supermodular game properties, the discrete actions of both parties are defined with a partial order, and actions are sorted based on the output values of the strategy function. Under bounded rationality, the defender's conservative tendency toward "false security" states manifest as delayed strategy switching, meaning defense actions must satisfy a minimum activation interval and cannot be adjusted continuously. The attacker exhibits an anchoring effect on historical attack success rates, over-relying on initial scan results and underestimating the defender's dynamic adjustment capabilities.

Payoff Function R. $R = \{R^D, R^A\}$. The payoff function incorporates prospect theory's loss aversion and subjective probability weighting mechanisms:

$$R^P(o_t^P, a_t^P) = v(r) \cdot w(\pi(o_t^P, a_t^P)) \tag{4}$$

A probability weighting mechanism is introduced in calculating payoff, because game participants adjust their strategies based on immediate rewards, indicating that action selection probabilities influence payoffs. To reflect bounded rationality, a rationality factor γ is incorporate into the probability weighting mechanism to describe the tendency to overvalue short-term rewards.

Perceived Value Function(Loss Aversion and Gain Sensitivity)

$$v(r) = \begin{cases} r^\alpha & r \geq 0 \\ -\lambda(-r)^\beta & r < 0 \end{cases} \tag{5}$$

where γ is the participant's loss aversion factor, typically greater than 1. α and β are factors that capture the diminishing marginal effects of gains and losses. We assume $\alpha = 0.88$ and $\beta = 0.92$ (Kahneman-Tversky parameters) [19]. To address the security-performance-affordability trilemma in attack and defense games, we reconstruct r as a composite optimization objective:

$$r = \Delta\|s\|_2 - \overline{\Delta\|s\|_2} - C \tag{6}$$

where $\Delta\|s\|_2$ represents the norm change in the attack surface, $\overline{\Delta\|s\|_2}$ represents the rate of norm change in the attack surface, and C is the normalized strategy cost. $\Delta\|s\|_2$ intuitively indicates the impact of the strategy on security:

$$\Delta\|s\|_2 = \frac{\|s_t\|_2 - \|s_{t-1}\|_2}{\|s_{t-1}\|_2 + \dot{0}} \tag{7}$$

The value is normalized to [0,1], where $\dot{0} = 1$ when $\|s_{t-1}\|_2 = 0$, and 0 otherwise. $\overline{\Delta\|s\|_2}$ is included as a penalty term because rapid adjustments to the attack surface can cause service jitter. This value is positive for attackers and negative for defenders:

$$\overline{\Delta\|s\|_2} = \pm\frac{\Delta\|s_t\|_2}{\Delta\|s_t\|_{2max} + \dot{0}} \tag{8}$$

where $\Delta\|s_t\|_{2max}$ is the maximum attack surface norm change up to time t. This value does not require normalization because if the attack surface norm change at time t exceeds the maximum norm change up to $t - 1$, $\overline{\Delta\|s\|_2} = 1$, ensuring the value remains within $[0, 1]$.

Subjective Strategy Weighting Function (Bounded Rationality in Action Selection)

$$w(\pi) = \frac{\pi^\gamma}{(\pi^\gamma + (1 - \pi)^\gamma)^{1/\gamma}}, \gamma < 1 \tag{9}$$

where γ is the rationality factor. In reality, the attacker's γ^A is lower, reflecting a non-rational preference for low-probability, high-risk attack paths, such as exploiting high-risk vulnerabilities with a 0.1% success rate. The defender's γ^D is relatively higher, indicating a more rational assessment of risk probabilities. Parameter settings are based on traditional game theory assumptions of complete rationality and utility maximization, while in real-world attack and defense scenarios, attackers are often driven by "gambler's fallacy", and defenders are overly sensitive to critical node failures. By incorporating prospect theory, the model better aligns with real-world behavior patterns [20]. Table 1 compares our model with traditional complete rationality models. According to **Theorem 1**, supermodular games are convergent to Nash equilibrium, and the BRSMG

Table 1. Comparison with traditional models

Model Characteristics	Complete Rationality Model ($\gamma = 1$)	BRSMG Model ($\gamma \neq 1$)
Behavioral Assumption	Strict adherence to expected utility maximization	Irrationality quantified and cognitive biases considered
Strategy Diversity	Single optimal strategy	Strategy spectra generated based on γ
Practical Adaptability	Difficult to simulate non-rational behaviors like social engineering	Attackers' exploratory and gambler's fallacy behaviors captured
Learning Convergence Difficulty	Precise probability models required	Exploration noise and rationality factors balanced for convergence

with PT-modified payoff functions retains the convergence property of equation in (1).

If the original payoff function R is supermodular, and the PT-modified perceived value function $v(\cdot)$ satisfies the following conditions:

1. The marginal value function $v\prime(\cdot) \geq 0$;
2. The second derivative $v\prime\prime(\cdot) \geq 0$(convex for loss regions, can be relaxed for gain regions).

Then the BRSMG remains supermodular and will gradually converge to a Nash equilibrium.

3.2   A Multi-stage BRSMG-MTD Scenario

The combination of BRSMG and MTD is detailed below.

Stage 1: System Initialization of Attack Surface State. The initial attack surface state $s_0 = (s_0{}^S, s_0{}^C, s_0{}^P) \in \mathbb{R}^3$, which is determined by the system's default configuration. For example, at time $t = 0$, the SSH port is open, and the initial state value is presumably set as $s_0 = (0.3, 0, 0)$.

Stage 2: Alternating Strategy Execution Based on Local Observations. a) Defender's Turn: The defender observes $o_0^D = g^D(s_0) = (0.23, 0, 0)$, and selects an action a_0^D (e.g., "closing non-essential ports") based on the strategy function $\pi^D(a_0^D|s_0) = 0.5$. The action updates the state $s_0 \rightarrow s_1 = (0.15, 0, 0)$, and the defender receives a reward $R^D(s_0, a_0^D) = -1.99$ from the environment, which is used to update the strategy function $\pi^D(a_0^D|s_0) = 0.2$. The negative reward in the initial stage is due to service jitter caused by rapid adjustments to the attack surface. b) Attacker's Turn: The attacker observes $o_1^A = g^A(s_1) = (0.06, 0, 0)$ and selects an action a_1^A (e.g., "scanning new ports") based on the strategy function $\pi^A(a_1^A|s_1) = 0.5$. The action triggers a state transition $s_1 \rightarrow s_2 = (0.23, 0, 0)$, and the attacker receives a reward $R^A(s_1, a_1^A) = 0.52$ from the environment, which is used to update the strategy function $\pi^A(a_1^A|s_1) = 0.75$.

...

Stage n: Equilibrium Convergence. The payoff of participants converges under Theorem 1 and the following conditions:

$$\forall a^P, \mathbb{E}[R^P(a^{P*}, a^{\overline{P}*})] \geq \mathbb{E}[R^P(a^P, a^{\overline{P}*})] \tag{10}$$

The game reaches a Nash equilibrium, where $\|s_t\|_2$ stabilizes.

3.3 PT-MAA2C for BRSMG-MTD

Based on the above BRSMG-MTD scenario, the PT-MAA2C algorithm framework under the guidance of prospect theory is proposed to model the strategy function and efficiently solve the game. The overall algorithm architecture is based on the A2C framework, where the policy network and value network are RNNs with T layers. Both the defender and attacker maintain their own policy networks, which take the state as input and output action probability distributions. They share a centralized value network (Critic), which takes the global state and actions as input and outputs the value. Figure 1 illustrates the architecture. In the standard A2C algorithm, the value network provides an advantage function by comparing the current action's reward to previous actions, and the policy network updates itself based on the advantage function. To solve the BRSMG, the advantage function must be modified to a PT-advantage function, and the action selection probability must incorporate the subjective strategy weighting function.

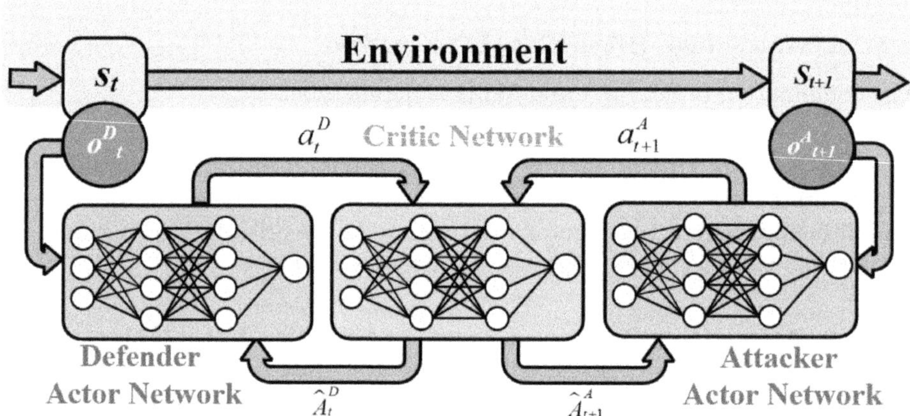

Fig. 1. The architecture of PT-MAA2C

Modification of the Advantage Function. In terms of value perception, a reference point must be introduced. The preference of attackers and defenders for actions is no longer based on the immediate reward's sign but on the difference between the immediate reward and the expected value of historical actions:

$$\phi(s) = \mathbb{E}_{a \sim \pi_{old}}[Q(s, \alpha)] \tag{11}$$

$$v(\Delta Q) = \begin{cases} (Q(s,a) - \phi(s))^\alpha & Q \geq \phi \\ -\lambda(\phi(s) - Q(s,a))^\beta & Q < \phi \end{cases} \tag{12}$$

The PT-advantage function is used to evaluate the current strategy:

$$\widehat{A}(s, a) = v(\Delta Q) - V(s) \tag{13}$$

Policy Gradient and Value Function Updates. In terms of policy updates, in supermodular games, when participant P tends to choose a higher-order action a^P, the corresponding probability increases, and the opponent $\overline{P}$'s policy network will also increase the probability of higher-order actions $a^{\overline{P}}$ to maintain mutual benefits. The original policy gradient $\nabla_{\theta^P} \log \pi^P \cdot \hat{A}^P$ ensures individual bounded rationality but may not satisfy strategy complementarity. Therefore, the policy gradient is adjusted by adding a complementary coupling term to ensure cooperative changes in action probabilities:

$$\nabla_{\theta^P} J^P = \mathbb{E}\left[\nabla_{q^n} \log w(\pi^P) \cdot \hat{A}^P\right] + \mathbb{E}_{a^P}\left[\nabla_{\theta^P} \frac{\partial \log(\pi^P)}{\partial \theta^P} \cdot \frac{\partial \log(\pi^{\overline{P}})}{\partial \theta^{\overline{P}}}\right] + H(\pi^P) \tag{14}$$

where $H(\pi^P)$ is the entropy regularization term, and ϕ is the entropy coefficient, initially set to 0.01 and decayed to 95% of its value every 200 steps to balance exploration and exploitation (high exploration in early training, strong exploitation in later stages):

$$H(\pi^P) = -\phi \sum_{a^P} w\left(\pi^P(a^P \mid o^P)\right) \log w\left(\pi^P(a^P \mid o^P)\right) \tag{15}$$

The value network is updated using TD error, and the loss function is computed using the mean squared error (MSE) method:

$$L_{critic} = \sum \left(R + \sigma V(s_{t+1}; \varphi) - V(s_t; \varphi)\right)^2 \tag{16}$$

Maintaining Supermodularity in Discrete Action Spaces. Through the complementary coupling term, the action probabilities of both attackers and defenders maintain supermodularity, mathematically equivalent to explicitly reinforcing the positivity of cross-partial derivatives $\frac{\partial^2 R^P}{\partial a^P \partial a^{\overline{P}}}$. Additionally, the PT-modified value function $v(\Delta Q)$ remains non-decreasing with respect to ΔQ, ensuring that the gradient update direction of PT-MAA2C converges to the Nash equilibrium. The overall algorithm is as follows:

4   Experiment

This section aims to validate the effectiveness of our proposed method through experiments simulating topology deception against DDoS attacks. The experimental design focuses on evaluating algorithm performance, strategy optimization capabilities, and practical application value to ensure that the proposed model and algorithm are not only theoretically innovative but also feasible in real-world applications.

In this section, we conduct simulation experiments to demonstrate the superior performance of our algorithm in outputting optimal strategies. Subsection 4.1 describes the experimental setup, including the design of the simulation environment and strategies for both attackers and defenders. In Subsect. 4.2 the convergence of the proposed method is compared with other classic reinforcement

---

Algorithm 1. PT-MAA2C for BRSMG-MTD

Input: $< P, S, A, R >$, episode_num, and batch_size;
Output: π^{D*} and π^{D*};
1: initialize θ^D, θ^A for policy π^D, π^A and φ for critic V
2: **while** episode_num>0 **do**
3:    **for** $i = 1$ to batch_size **do**
4:       τ^D, $\tau^A=[]$ two empty lists
5:       initialize $h^D_{(0,\pi^D)},h^A_{(0,\pi^A)}$ for actor RNN states and $h^D_{(0,v^D)}$, $h^A_{(0,v^A)}$ for critic RNN states
6:       **for** $t = 1$ to T **do**
7:          defender updates by observing $o^D_t = g^D(s_t)$
8:          $p^D_t, h^D_{(t,\pi^D)} = \pi^D(o^D_t, h^D_{(t-1,\pi^D)}); \theta^D$
9:          defender executes action $a^D_t \sim p^D_t$
10:         $v^D_t, h^D_{(t,v^D)} = V(s_t, h^D_{(t-1,v^D)}); \varphi$
11:         defender observes R^D_t, o^D_{t+1}
12:         $t+ = 1$
13:         attacker updates by observing $o^A_t = g^A(s_t)$
14:         $p^A_t, h^A_{(t,\pi^A)} = \pi^A(o^A_t, h^A_{(t-1,\pi^A)}); \theta^A$
15:         attacker executes action $a^A_t \sim p^A_t$
16:         $v^A_t, h^A_{(t,v^A)} = V(s_t, h^A_{(t-1,v^A)}); \varphi$
17:         attacker observes R^A_t, o^A_{t+1}
18:      **end for**
19:    **end for**
20:    update RNN hidden states h from the first hidden state
21:    update θ^D, θ^A from $J(\theta^D), J(\theta^A)$ with b
22:    update φ from $L(\varphi)$ with b
23: **end while**

---

learning algorithms. In Subsect. 4.3 our method is compared with other classical algorithms and experimental analysis is provided.

4.1 Experiment Setup

Topology deception [21] is a key MTD technology that dynamically reconstructs virtual network logical architectures based on the principle of dynamic heterogeneity. By generating false network topology information, it hides the real network topology, delaying or evading DDoS attacks. Topology deception primarily deploys honeypot hosts and deception servers in the virtual topology to mislead attackers. Its architecture is based on three components:

a) Virtualization Control Layer

Topology deception requires an SDN controller (e.g., POX) to maintain a dynamically heterogeneous virtual logical topology. The virtualization control layer uses VXLAN tunnels to decouple the logical topology from the physical network. Additionally, the logical topology must appear valid to attackers through dynamic OpenFlow flow table configurations.

b) Honeypot Hosts

   In addition to real hosts, the virtual topology includes numerous honeypot hosts to deceive attackers. Defenders deploy fake services (e.g., SSH/HTTP) on these honeypot hosts and record attack fingerprints, guiding attackers to use them as bait servers for attack deployment. Defenders can collect attack traffic through these honeypot hosts for further analysis and monitoring. To maintain the changing virtual topology, defenders periodically unbind honeypot hosts' IP addresses from the physical topology.

c) Deception Servers

   Defenders deploy deception servers in the network, ensuring each switch is directly connected to a deception server. The deception server modifies the TTL value of data packets and generates response packets, making the virtual topology appear real to attackers. Furthermore, the design of topology deception requires presenting different virtual topologies to different external IPs when facing distributed traffic from attackers, preventing attackers from discovering exploitable bait servers and critical links.

The experiment is implemented using the Mininet network. We create an Open-Flow switch network in Mininet, with the real topology based on Abilene [22], with 210 hosts surrounded, which can be infected as Zombies. The virtual topology is implemented using the Ryu SDN simulator as the control plane, as shown in Fig. 2. Specifically, the Ryu application invokes various topology deception methods to generate the virtual network topology. The actions for attackers and defenders are listed in Tables 2 and 3, respectively. The normalized costs are derived from normalized historical experience [23]. The table lists each action's bounded rationality features, indicating that both attackers and defenders have subjective preferences for these actions, suitable for subjective action probabilities.

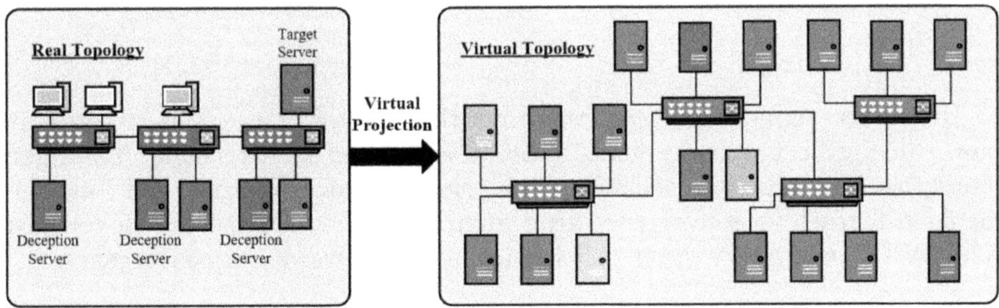

Fig. 2. Virtual projection of network topology

Table 2. Defender's action set

Action ID	Action Name	Action Type	Bounded Rationality Feature	Cost	Description
a^{D1}	Dynamic Virtual Node Generation	Topology Obfuscation	Overexposure of Deception Features	0.8	Maintaining virtual topology consistency
a^{D2}	Deception Server TTL Randomization	Path Obfuscation	Response to current attack features only	0.4	Real-time modification of packet headers
a^{D3}	Traffic to Honeypot Redirection	Attack Induction	No active adaptation to attacker's behavior	0.6	Honeypots handling high-concurrency traffic
a^{D4}	Honeypot Service Type Adjustment	Deception Enhancement	Relying on historical honeypot configurations	0.5	Dynamic deployment of different service containers, compatibility risks
a^{D5}	Static Traffic Filtering Rules Configuration	Traffic Cleaning	Relying on initial rule sets	0.3	Missed detections by rule update delay
a^{D6}	Intermittently Disconnection to Real Nodes	Dynamic Protection	Overly susceptive to node failures	0.7	Susceptible normal business availability
a^{D7}	Route Hop Count Feedback Forge	Path Deception	Exaggerating false path lengths	0.5	Decoupling from physical topology

Table 3. Attacker's action set

Action ID	Action Name	Action Type	Bounded Rationality Feature	Cost	Description
a^{A1}	ICMP Subnet Scanning	Topology Mapping	Preference to historical successful scans	0.3	Consuming bandwidth, easily detected
a^{A2}	TCP SYN Port Scanning	Service Discovery	Ignoring unexpected port responses	0.4	Triggering defense mechanisms, attack intent exposable
a^{A3}	ARP Spoofing	Node Location	Assuming local ARP cache not poisoned	0.6	High energy consumption, sensitive to network topology stability
a^{A4}	SYN Flood Attack	Network-layer DDoS	Underestimating defender's cleaning capability	0.7	Continuous packet sending, traffic patterns easily identified
a^{A5}	UDP Reflection Amplification Attack	Application-layer DDoS	Overly trusting third-party reflection servers	0.8	Relying on external distributed servers, high anonymity cost
a^{A6}	HTTP Slow Attack	Application-layer DDoS	Fixed use of Slowloris mode	0.5	Maintaining half-open connections, consuming computational resources

4.2 Experiment Configuration and Convergence Comparison

Through a series of preliminary experiments, we ensure that the algorithm converges within 1,000 episodes. Therefore, we set the number of episodes to 1,000, with each episode consisting of 100 steps, and repeat the experiment 100 times. We set different rationality levels based on Table 4. We assume the experiment is conducted under resource-constrained edge node defense. To demonstrate the superiority of our algorithm in convergence and optimal strategy output, we compare our method with commonly used reinforcement learning algorithms, including DQN [24], PPO [25], and Actor-Critic [26], under the BRSMG framework.

Table 4. Rationality factor configuration

Scenario Description	γ^D	γ^A
Regular Defense(Baseline Model)	0.85	0.45
Advanced Persistent Threat	0.92 → Increasing rationality to defend against hidden attacks	0.25 → Enticing attacker to expose intention
Resource-Constrained Edge Node Defense	0.75 → Allowing moderate exploration of new strategies	0.6 → Suppressing blind attacks to conserve resources

Under the same conditions, the algorithm's convergence and rewards are shown in Fig. 3. The convergence episode is pointed as a triangle. The figure shows that our algorithm achieves the highest reward, close to 2, and converges the fastest, reaching convergence after approximately 400 episodes. In contrast, A2C, PPO, and DQN exhibit deficiencies in both reward and convergence.

4.3 Experiment Analysis

In the following experiments, we compare our method with static defense, MVNAH [27], and IBM [28] under the same BRSMG framework. The bounded rationality features include:

1. Incomplete Information: Both attackers and defenders have partial observations of the network state in different algorithms.

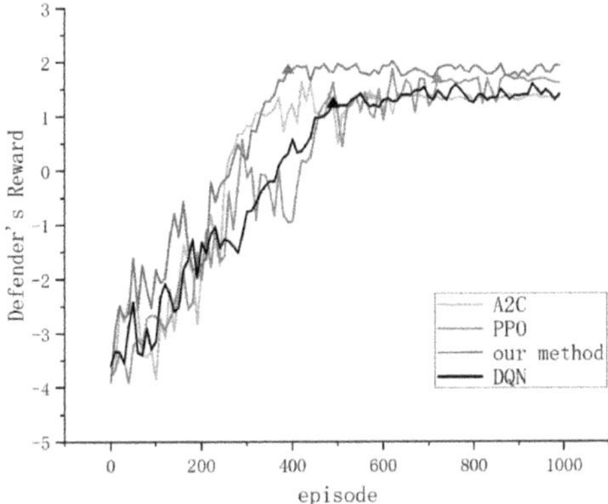

Fig. 3. Defender's reward after 1000 episodes of different RL algorithms

2. Strategy Update Delay: Both attackers and defenders can adjust their strategies only every 3 s.
3. Behavioral Preferences: Both attackers and defenders base their actions on prospect theory's loss aversion and subjective probability functions, reflecting bounded rationality in network attack and defense.

Based on these conditions, the experimental results are analyzed from three perspectives: security, system performance, and defense affordability.

Security Analysis. For security analysis, Honeypot Redirection Rate (HRR) is used to measure the proportion of attack traffic successfully redirected to honeypots:

$$HRR = \frac{NT^H}{NT} \tag{17}$$

where NT^H represents the number of attack flows successfully redirected to honeypots (e.g., through ARP spoofing or BGP hijacking), and NT represents the total number of attack flows (including all traffic before and after cleaning).

The results are shown in Fig. 4. In the static network, the number of honeypot hosts is fixed. As the attack and defense process continues, attackers gradually identify and mark honeypot hosts, reducing the attack traffic sent to them. By 20 s, all honeypot hosts are identified, and HRR drops to 0%. The other three methods are all able to maintain $HRR > 0$, indicating that they can, to some extent, limit the attacker's further analysis and attacks. However, our method outperforms the other two approaches, which we attribute primarily to the advantages brought by our self-adaptive algorithm.

Performance Analysis. For performance analysis, server response latency is measured to evaluate the impact of the algorithm on system performance [29]. Lower server response latency and higher file transfer rates indicate better network service responsiveness and system performance. Server response latency is

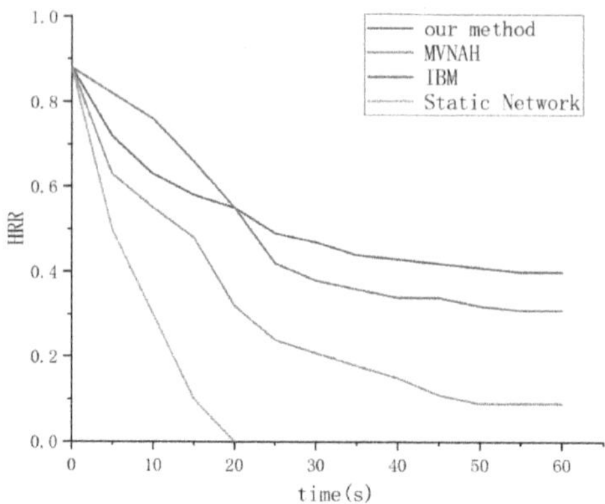

Fig. 4. *HRR* in different algorithms

measured by sending ICMP Request packets from legitimate clients every 10 s and calculating the mean and variance of Round-Trip Time (*RTT*) in milliseconds. Lower latency indicates higher service availability.

The baseline scenario is a network under no attack, used to test the upper limit of the original system's performance. The results are shown in Table 5. MVNAH performs the worst in terms of server response latency due to its relatively fixed, high-frequency virtual topology transformations, resulting in a low RTT variance, indicating consistently high latency. IBM has the best mean latency performance but suffers from high RTT variance due to frequent strategy triggers, causing system service jitter. Our method, while not achieving the best mean latency, has the lowest RTT variance, indicating stable, low-latency service provision, making it the best overall performer.

Table 5. Comparison of 4 algorithms in performance analysis

Methods	Mean RTT(ms)	RTT Variance	Latency Increase Factor
MVNAH	34.5	5.3	1.84x
IBM	25.6	10.1	1.36x
Our method	26.2	5.7	1.40x

Affordability Analysis. For affordability analysis, Honeypot Resource Waste Rate (*WR*) is used to measure the ineffective costs incurred by the algorithm [29]. The formula for this metric is:

$$WR = \frac{NH^M + NH^R}{NH} \tag{18}$$

where NH represents the number of created honeypot hosts,NH^M represents the number of misjudged honeypot hosts (legitimate traffic mistakenly identified as attacks), and NH^R represents the number of idle honeypot hosts (deployed but with no effective interaction sessions within the valid time frame). A lower WR indicates higher honeypot utilization and more valuable cost expenditure.

The results are shown in Fig. 5. In the static network, due to the fixed increasing number of honeypot hosts, attackers quickly identify them, avoiding traffic redirection to these hosts. By 20 s, WR reaches 1, indicating that attackers fully understand the virtual topology transformation patterns, rendering all subsequent honeypot deployments ineffective. MVNAH, after an initial period (0–25 s) of frequent honeypot failures, changes its virtual topology generation strategy but gradually reverts to its original pattern after 30 s, with WR approaching 0.9. This indicates that MVNAH incurs significant ineffective costs. Our algorithm performs similarly to IBM, with WR stabilizing at approximately 0.63 by 34 s. In summary, our method outperforms MVNAH and IBM in the BRSMG-based network attack and defense framework. We attribute this to (1) a more realistic game model that aligns with actual network attack and defense processes, (2) the decision-making adaptability of the PT-MAA2C algorithm tailored to the BRSMG model, and (3) a comprehensive reward function design that fully considers bounded rationality conditions to guide targeted strategy optimization.

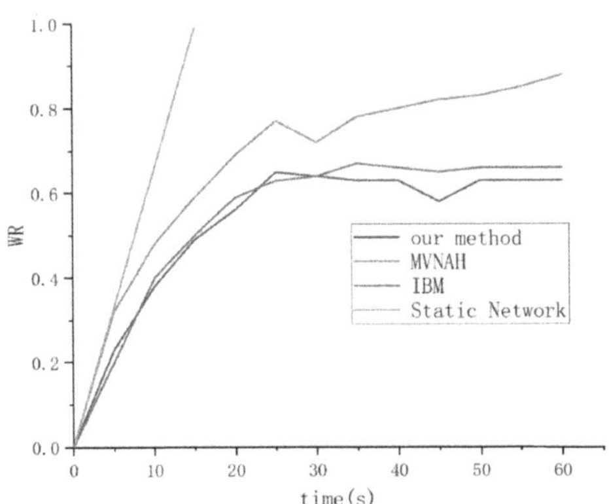

Fig. 5. HRR in different algorithms

5   Conclusion

This paper proposed a game model based on bounded rationality and supermodular games for MTD attack and defense scenarios, incorporating prospect theory to comprehensively account for the complexity of decision-makers' bounded rational behaviors and the complementary nature of network attack and defense strategies. To efficiently solve the proposed BRMSG model, the PT-MAA2C algorithm was proposed, integrating behavioral economic models with reinforcement learning frameworks to overcome the limitations of traditional methods in adversarial equilibrium solving and risk preference modeling. Theoretical analysis and experimental validation demonstrated that the combination of supermodular games and MARL provided an interpretable and adaptive solution for MTD decision-making under bounded rationality, helping defenders find optimal dynamic balances under relevant constraints.

Acknowledgments. Due to the nature of this research, participants of this study agree for their data to be shared publicly as demand. This work is funded by National Natural Science Foundation of China No.62302520.

Disclosure of Interests. The authors have no competing interests to declare that are relevant to the content of this article.

References

1. Cho, J.H., et al.: Toward proactive, adaptive defense: a survey on moving target defense. IEEE Commun. Surv. Tutorials **22**(1), 709–745 (2020)
2. Ma, D., Tang, Z., Sun, X., Guo, L., Wang, L., Chen, K.: Game theory approaches for evaluating the deception-based moving target defense. In: MTD 2022 - Proceedings of the 9th ACM Workshop on Moving Target Defense, Co-Located with CCS 2022, pp. 67–77 (2022)
3. Tan, J., et al.: A survey: When moving target defense meets game theory. In: Computer Science Review (Vol. 48). Elsevier Ireland Ltd. (2023)
4. Zheng, J., Namin, A.S.: A survey on the moving target defense strategies: an architectural perspective. J. Comput. Sci. Technol. **34**(1), 207–233 (2019)
5. Connell, W., Albanese, M., Venkatesan, S.: A framework for moving target defense quantification. IFIP Advances in Information and Communication Technology **502**, 124–138 (2017)
6. Xiong, X., Zhao, G., Wang, X.: A system attack surface based MTD effectiveness and cost quantification framework. ACM International Conference Proceeding Series, pp. 175–179 (2018)
7. Spyridopoulos, T., Karanikas, G., Tryfonas, T., Oikonomou, G.: A game theoretic defence framework against DoS/DDoS cyber attacks. Comput. Secur. **38**, 39–50 (2013)
8. Schlenker, A., et al.: Deceiving cyber adversaries: a game theoretic approach. In: IFAAMAS, vol. 9 (2018)
9. Xu, D., Li, Y., Xiao, L., Mandayam, N., Vincent, H.: prospect theoretic study of cloud storage defense against advanced persistent threats. 2016 IEEE Global Communications Conference (GLOBECOM): proceedings: Washington, DC USA, 4-8 December 2016 (2016)
10. Simon, H.A.: A behavioral model of rational choice. Q. J. Econ. **69**(1), 99 (1955)
11. Camerer, C.F.: Behavioral game theory: Experiments in strategic interaction. Russell Sage Foundation (2003)
12. McKelvey, R.D., Palfrey, T.R.: Quantal response equilibria for normal form games. Games Econom. Behav. **10**(1), 6–38 (1995)

13. Kulkarni, T.D., Narasimhan, K., Saeedi, A., Tenenbaum, J.B.: Hierarchical Deep Reinforcement Learning: Integrating Temporal Abstraction and Intrinsic Motivation. ArXiv, abs/1604.06057 (2016)
14. Topkis, D.M.: Supermodularity and Complementarity. Princeton University Press (1998)
15. Vives, X.: Nash equilibrium with strategic complementarities. J. Math. Econ. **19**(3), 305–321 (1990)
16. Milgrom, P.R., Roberts, J.E.: Rationalizability, learning, and equilibrium in games with strategic complementarities. Econometrica **58**, 1255–1277 (1990)
17. Narang, A., Sadeghi, O., Ratliff, L., Fazel, M., Bilmes, J.: Online SuBmodular + SuPermodular (BP) Maximization with Bandit Feedback (2024). arXiv:2207.03091
18. Lowe, R., Wu, Y., Tamar, A., Harb, J., Abbeel, P., Mordatch, I.: Multi-Agent Actor-Critic for Mixed Cooperative-Competitive Environments (2017). ArXiv, abs/1706.02275
19. Kahneman, D., Tversky, A.: Prospect theory: an analysis of decision under risk. In: P. Gärdenfors & N.-E. Sahlin (Eds.), Decision, probability, and utility: Selected readings, pp. 183–214 (1988). (Reprinted from "Econometrica," 47 (1979), pp. 263–291. Cambridge University Press
20. Gonzalez, C.: From individual decisions from experience to behavioral game theory: lessons for cybersecurity. In: Jajodia, S., Ghosh, A., Subrahmanian, V., Swarup, V., Wang, C., Wang, X. (eds.) Moving Target Defense II. Advances in Information Security, vol 100. Springer, New York (2013)
21. Achleitner, S., La Porta, T.F., McDaniel, P., Sugrim, S., Krishnamurthy, S.V., Chadha, R.: Deceiving network reconnaissance using SDN-based virtual topologies. IEEE Trans. Netw. Serv. Manage. **14**(4), 1098–1112 (2017)
22. Aron, L., Assane, G.: Network topology vulnerability/cost trade-off: model, application, and computational complexity. Internet Math. **11**, 588–626 (2015)
23. Zhu, M., Anwar, A. H., Wan, Z., Cho, J.-H., Kamhoua, C., Singh, M.P.: Game-Theoretic and Machine Learning-based Approaches for Defensive Deception: A Survey (2021). arXiv:2101.1012
24. Mnih, V., Kavukcuoglu, K., Silver, D., Graves, A., Antonoglou, I., Wierstra, D., Riedmiller, M.A.: Playing Atari with Deep Reinforcement Learning (2013). ArXiv, abs/1312.5602
25. Schulman, J., Wolski, F., Dhariwal, P., Radford, A., Klimov, O.: Proximal Policy Optimization Algorithms. ArXiv, abs/1707.06347 (2017)
26. Sutton, R.S., McAllester, D.A., Singh, S., Mansour, Y.: Policy Gradient Methods for Reinforcement Learning with Function Approximation. Neural Information Processing Systems (1999)
27. Zhou, B., Pan, G., Wu, C.: Multi-variant network address hopping to defend stealthy crossfire attack. Sci. China Inf. Sci. **63**, 169301 (2020)
28. Hyder, M.F., Fatima, T.: Towards crossfire distributed denial of service attack protection using intent-based moving target defense over software-defined networking. IEEE Access **9**, 112792–112804 (2021)
29. Xu, X., Zhu, X., Zhu, C.: GAN-based deep learning framework of network reconstruction. Complex Intell. Syst. **9**, 3131–3146 (2023)

Investigating How Trading Patterns and Twitter Impact the CryptoPunks NFT Market

Yuxiang Liu[1], Xinyu Feng[2], and Mingdong Tang[2(✉)]

[1] School of Computer Science and Engineering, Macau University of Science and Technology, Macau, China
[2] School of Computer Science and Engineering, Guangdong University of Foreign Studies, Guangzhou, China
mdtang@126.com

Abstract. A non-fungible token (NFT) is a unique digital asset stored on the blockchain. With growing interests from investors and collectors, understanding the factors influencing the NFT market is crucial. This study investigates the influence of Twitter social media and trading patterns on transaction volume in the CryptoPunks NFT market. We focus on the influencing factors such as trading behavior, Twitter sentiment, and Twitter features. Based on them, we employ machine learning to predict the CryptoPunks transaction volume. The results reveal a strong correlation between these features and transaction volumes. The proposed PSO-Voting model, which takes all features into consideration, can improve the predictive accuracy significantly, achieving an impressive model accuracy (R2) exceeding 96%. Each feature's contribution to the transaction volume prediction is also explained. By unveiling the influence of Twitter social media and trading patterns on the CryptoPunks market, this study provides novel insights into the dynamics of the NFT market.

Keywords: Non-Fungible Tokens · Explainable Artificial Intelligence · CryptoPunks · Feature Extraction

1 Introduction

Blockchain technology, renowned for its decentralized distributed ledger system, has permeated finance [9], supply chain management [12], and digital identity [2], offering secure information storage and transmission. This innovative amalgamation of cryptography and distributed networks ensures data integrity while circumventing control by centralized institutions. Within this context, Non-Fungible Tokens (NFTs), a manifestation of blockchain application, have emerged as a disruptive innovation, capturing escalating attention [4].

NFTs are digital assets on a blockchain representing unique manifestations of distinct digital or tangible items like art, music, and videos [3]. Their uniqueness,

W. Liang et al. (Eds.): SecureComm 2025, LNICST 690, pp. 410–429, 2026.
https://doi.org/10.1007/978-3-032-23456-8_22

inability to be divided, and traceability provide inherent value to each NFT, simplifying blockchain transactions. This intrinsic feature presents creators with a novel economic model, enabling them to convert their works into NFTs, facilitating market transactions for enhanced profits. This has significantly reshaped the digital economy, enabling direct monetization of digital creations [15].

With this rise in NFT popularity and adoption, social media platforms have become critical venues for driving the NFT discourse. Integrating NFT discussions on Twitter has positioned it as an influential player in the digital asset market [8]. Here, investors, traders, and analysts exchange insights on emerging trends, project potential, and strategies, fostering dynamic debates that profoundly influence NFT asset pricing and trading. In this way, Twitter provides a vital forum for collective engagement that drives the rapidly evolving NFT marketplace.

Furthermore, the dynamics of the NFT market are profoundly moulded by the conduct of its traders [19]. Amidst the intricate dynamics that delineate the NFT landscape, the behaviors of traders emerge as a commanding force. Third-party trading platforms, such as OpenSea, exemplify this influence by providing pivotal features like quoting and withdrawing. These platforms aspire to enhance trading flexibility and liquidity, enabling traders to promptly convey their interest and willingness to engage with specific NFT assets, aligning with market conditions and personal inclinations.

These platform features wield considerable influence over the market. The frequency of quoting reflects market interest depth and directly affects transaction volume. Conversely, bid withdrawals indicate caution and can anticipate market fluctuations. However, active traders are the heart of the NFT market's vitality. Their behaviors drive increased activity and engagement within the NFT market.

The burgeoning NFT market has drawn significant interest from new investors. However, the considerable fluctuation in the NFT market has also elicited apprehension regarding the risk-reward profile of investments in this nascent asset class. While active transaction volumes and participation frequently signal a thriving marketplace, the NFT market appears susceptible to speculative manias and social media trends. This makes it difficult for investors to assess risks and value NFTs sensibly.

Currently, academia has undertaken extensive research in the crypto art market [5], encompassing the overall correlation between NFTs, Ethereum, and Bitcoin markets [1]; NFT asset evaluation [6]; and the analysis of opportunities and challenges within the NFT market [20]. However, a knowledge gap persists concerning social media's precise role and trading behavior and how it influences the NFT market. Therefore, in this study, we take the CryptoPunks market as an example to delve into the influence of Twitter social media and trading behavior on the CryptoPunks NFT transaction volume.

In this study, we collected substantial Twitter and transaction data from the CryptoPunks market to achieve this objective. We extracted multiple features, including trading behavior, Twitter sentiment, and Twitter features. Subsequently, by analyzing these features, we explored their influence on the CryptoPunks market. We adopted some machine learning models to integrate the aforementioned diverse features, enhancing the predictive capability for the daily transaction volume of the CryptoPunks market. By experimentally comparing the performance of different models and evaluating the predictive results using multiple indicators, we unveiled the influence of individual features on the predictive task and the overall effect of feature combinations. Finally, the SHAP (Shapley Additive exPlanations) method from interpretable machine learning was employed to further the understanding of various features' contribution levels to the transaction volume prediction.

In summary, this article makes the following contributions:

- We comprehensively analyze trading behavior, Twitter sentiment, and Twitter features to provide a holistic perspective on their influence on the CryptoPunks NFT market.
- We utilize multiple machine learning models to assess the predictive power of different features on market transaction volume. Notably, our proposed PSO-Voting model demonstrates exceptional performance. When integrating all features, we observe significant improvements across multiple evaluation metrics.
- We explain how each feature contributes to the forecast results using the SHAP library. This method helps us to gain a deeper understanding of the influence of trading behavior, Twitter features, and Twitter sentiment on CryptoPunks market volumes.

The rest of the paper is organized as follows. Section 2 describes the data collection process and data processing procedures. In Sect. 3, we extract and analyze features grouped into three categories. Section 4 outlines the underlying principles of the models employed in our experimentation. Section 5 discusses the evaluation results. Section 6 reviews related work. Finally, Sect. 7 concludes this paper.

2   Data Collection and Processing

In this study, we gathered data from the official website of CryptoPunks and the Twitter platform. Specifically, we collected all transaction data and tweets related to the CryptoPunks topic on Twitter between January 2019 and November 2022. We performed preprocessing to ensure data quality and reliability, including handling empty values and outliers. Subsequently, the data was sorted and analyzed chronologically for further examination.

2.1   CryptoPunks Data

We accessed the official website of CryptoPunks[1] and crawled to collect all transaction data. The website provides detailed information about sold CryptoPunks, including the sale price, Bid, the addresses of buyers and sellers, as well as the

---

[1] https://www.larvalabs.com/CryptoPunks.

transaction time and ID. To efficiently obtain the data, we automated this process using a web scraper program and saved the data as a CSV file for subsequent analysis and processing.

After obtaining the data, we conducted a series of preprocessing steps to ensure data quality and consistency. Firstly, we performed data type conversion, converting specific data from strings or other formats to appropriate data types such as integers or dates. This step ensures the correct utilization of the data in subsequent analysis. Secondly, we conducted data cleaning by removing any missing or inaccurate data, such as non-existent addresses or data with incorrectly formatted timestamps. Following the above steps for data acquisition and preprocessing, we obtained an accurate, complete, and reliable dataset of CryptoPunks transactions.

Figure 1 visualizes the original and logarithmically transformed transaction volume data for the CryptoPunks market. It is evident that before 2021, the market exhibited relatively modest transaction volumes. However, a notable shift occurred in 2021, with a rapid ascent in trading activity. This upward trend reached its zenith in August 2021, giving way to a gradual decline, and ultimately stabilizing over time.

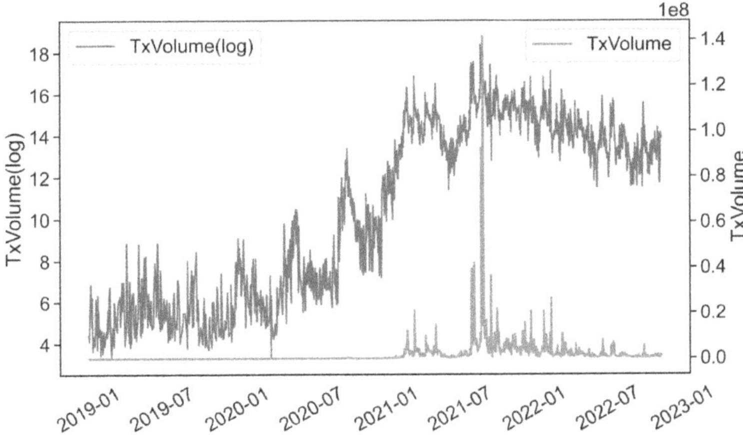

Fig. 1. This figure presents the trends in CryptoPunks market volume and its logarithmic counterpart.

2.2 Twitter Data

In this study, the open-source Twitter data collection tool Twint was employed for retrieving tweets. Twint, a shorthand for "Twitter intelligence," is a robust data scraping tool for Twitter content. It encompasses functionalities for tweet search and removal. Twint presents distinct advantages over the Twitter search API. Firstly, Twint operates without requiring authentication, enabling universal utilization for tweet acquisition. Secondly, Twint evades rate limitations, thereby accommodating the extraction of a larger corpus of tweet data.

In contrast, the Twitter search API exclusively offers access to the most recent 3200 tweets. Additionally, Twint encompasses nearly all features inherent to the Twitter search API, permitting users to formulate specific queries and apply filters related to language, region, geographical location, and temporal scope. Lastly, Twint facilitates the generation of output files in formats such as CSV, JSON, and Txt, streamlining data processing and analysis for users.

The prevalent keyword on Twitter, frequently associated with the context of this study, is "CryptoPunks." Employing the "#" symbol as a hashtag effectively categorizes content about CryptoPunks within tweets. This practice of hashtag utilization serves to filter out extraneous content, enhancing the ease of locating and discerning pertinent information. From June 2017 to November 2022, our data collection efforts yielded 33,412 tweets containing the CryptoPunks hashtag. Supplementary details regarding these tweets, including metrics such as likes, retweets, timestamps, and usernames of the tweet authors, were also amassed.

3   Feature Extraction and Analysis

In this section, we analyze how Twitter and trading behavior influence transaction volume in the CryptoPunks market. We use data-driven analysis to understand the impact of market dynamics. We extract Twitter features and Twitter sentiment from Twitter data to study the mechanisms through which social media affects the market. Table 2 presents the extracted features and their explanations. Table 1 shows the statistical information of the data set.

3.1   Twitter Features

In this section, we explore the influence of transaction volume on the CryptoPunks market through social media; we employ data-driven analysis in our discussions of the influences of market dynamics. We extract tweet features derived from Twitter data to understand the mechanisms through which this influence takes place. These features capture the interactive behaviors of market participants and the level of attention that CryptoPunks garners across social media platforms.

During feature extraction, we focus on tweet interactions, including comments, likes, and retweets. These interactions reflect user interest and sentiment towards CryptoPunks. We derive features like total comment count, total like count, and total retweet count. These features represent sentiment and can significantly influence market activity. We also calculate averages and maximum values for these features to reveal market participant behavior and distinguish short-term fluctuations from sustained trends.

User count and tweet count are essential features as well. User count reflects community participation, and tweet count indicates market attention and information dissemination intensity. Including these features helps us understand market activity, participant diversity, and sentiment trends, enhancing our understanding of the connection between tweet activity and transaction volume.

Table 1. The type and value range of the features.

Feature	Mean	Std	Min	Max
Bid_Count	23.64	30.55	0.00	374.00
Withdrawn_Count	16.12	19.01	0.00	141.00
Sold_Count	17.72	34.62	1.00	355.00
active_traders	26.25	31.59	1.00	306.00
Negative_Sum	0.62	0.64	0.00	3.72
Negative_Count	3.79	4.07	0.00	32.00
Neutral_Sum	24.99	20.86	0.00	94.62
Neutral_Count	10.22	8.20	0.00	41.00
Positive_Sum	1.98	1.81	0.00	10.00
Positive_Count	13.57	12.42	0.00	59.00
Compound_Sum	6.15	5.92	-1.56	33.33
Total_Comments	125.75	612.29	0.00	19907.00
Max_Comments	56.37	310.11	0.00	9581.00
Mean_Comments	2.95	17.90	0.00	603.24
Total_Likes	174.00	467.14	0.00	11114.00
Max_Likes	75.77	274.01	0.00	5217.00
Mean_Likes	4.18	12.04	0.00	336.79
Total_Retweets	576.51	1055.99	0.00	16496.00
Max_Retweets	181.74	472.41	0.00	6455.00
Mean_Retweets	13.59	22.36	0.00	402.30
User_Count	23.37	19.83	0.00	71.00
Twitter_Count	27.59	23.16	0.00	107.00
Transaction_Sum	11.05	4.02	3.30	18.77

We conducted visual analysis, and the data fluctuations led us to apply logarithmic transformation to highlight the relationships between tweet features and daily transaction volume. We found a strong correlation between tweet features and transaction volume. More tweets generate more attention and discussions about CryptoPunks, leading to increased trading activity. This, in turn, reflects market vibrancy and encourages engagement and discussions. Analyzing these relationships helps us understand how tweet activities quantitatively influence daily transaction volume.

The influence of daily tweet count on CryptoPunks market transaction volume is illustrated in Fig. 2(a). It shows that as the number of users engaging in CryptoPunks discussions on Twitter increases, the market transaction volume also grows. Notably, when the number of daily users is limited, transaction volume is more volatile. However, as the number of users participating in discussions increases, transaction volume fluctuations decrease, indicating a strong link between social media discussions and market stability.

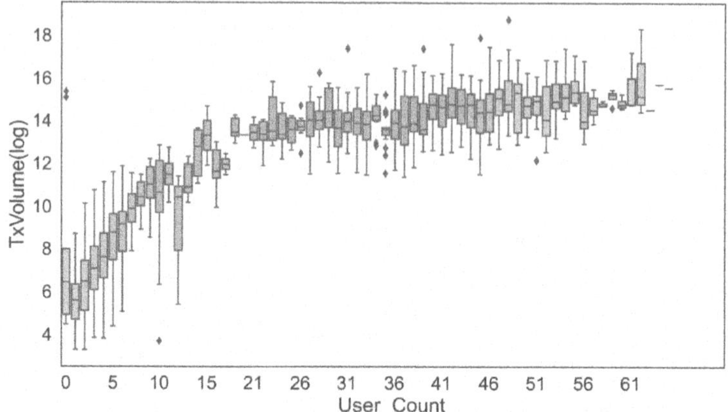

(a) This boxplot illustrates how transaction volumes (TxVolume) vary across different user counts (User_Count) using a logarithmic scale, revealing distribution and central tendencies.

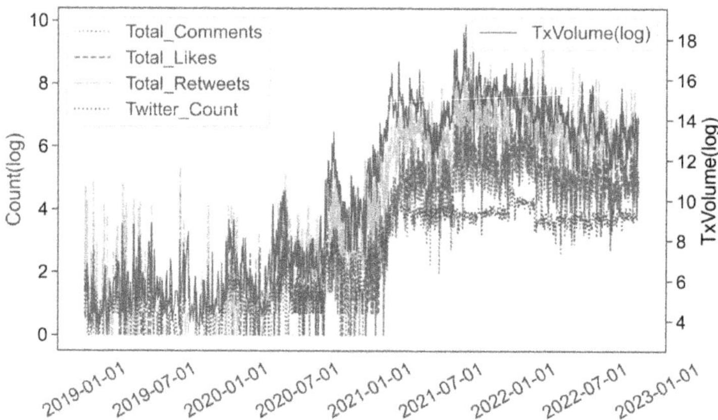

(b) This figure illustrates social media engagement (Comments, Likes, Retweets, Twitter Count) and transaction volume trends (TxVolume) using logarithmic scales, showcasing patterns and correlations over time.

Fig. 2. This figure visualizes transaction volume variations across user counts using a logarithmic scale, and it also showcases social media engagement and transaction volume trends over time with logarithmic scales.

3.2 Twitter Sentiment

In this section, we used the VADER[2] library for sentiment analysis of tweets to assess the sentiment of each tweet. VADER is known for its adaptability in ana-

---

[2] https://github.com/cjhutto/vaderSentiment.

lyzing sentiment in social media texts [11], providing positive, negative, neutral, and compound sentiment scores. We consider a composite score exceeding 0.05 as positive, falling below –0.05 as negative, and ranging between -0.05 and 0.05 as neutral. We computed the total scores and averages of positive, negative, and neutral sentiments, as well as the quantity of text for each sentiment category.

The constructed tweet sentiment features include the sum and quantity of sentiment scores obtained from daily tweets, along with the summary "Compound" score, providing a foundation for in-depth analysis of sentiment trends in Twitter data.

Figure 3(a) illustrates how positive and negative sentiment scores concentrate with increasing transaction volume, while neutral sentiment scores have a broader distribution. The scores for neutral sentiments gradually rise with higher transaction volume.

Figure 3(b) shows how the distribution of daily tweets for the three sentiment categories changes with transaction volume. When transaction volume is low, neutral sentiment tweets dominate, while positive and negative sentiment tweets are limited. As transaction volume rises, the quantity and values of tweets for all three sentiments increase. Positive sentiment tweets become highly concentrated with high transaction volume.

3.3 Trading Behavior

In this section, we establish a series of indicators that reflect the features of trading behavior. These indicators encompass bid count, withdrawal count, sold count, and the number of active traders.

The bid count serves as a gauge of market participant activity. Higher bid counts indicate more potential buyers and sellers, potentially driving increased transaction volume. On the other hand, the bid withdrawal count reflects market participants' hesitancy in their decision-making. Elevated withdrawal count may exert a negative influence on market transaction volume. Trade count directly mirrors the actual level of market trading activity, with a higher trade count signifying a more active market. The count of active traders can provide insights into the overall participation hunger in the market, with increased active trader engagement likely propelling an enhancement in transaction volume. The extraction of these indicators aids in a comprehensive analysis of market participant behavioral traits and the overall state of trading activity, thereby facilitating a deeper understanding of mechanisms influencing transaction volume.

Furthermore, we analyze the relationships between bid count, withdrawal count, trade count, and total transaction volume. The results are shown in Fig. 4(a). As the daily bid count rises, we can observe that the trade count exhibits a corresponding growth trend. Conversely, trade count and transaction volume experience varying degrees of decline under elevated bid withdrawal count. This suggests a potential connection between increased bid withdrawal count and heightened uncertainty among market participants, negatively affecting actual trade execution.

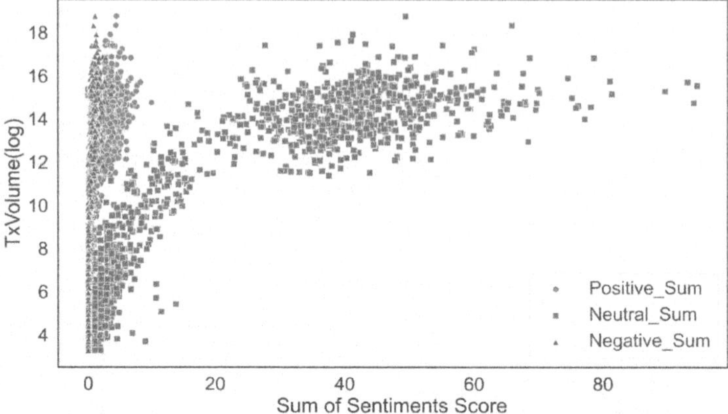

(a) This figure displays the relationship between the sum of sentiment scores and transaction volume (TxVolume) using logarithmic scales.

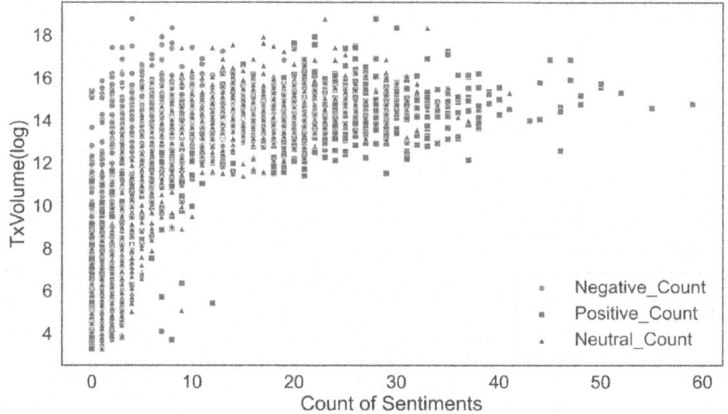

(b) This figure illustrates the relationship between tweets sentiment counts (Negative, Positive, Neutral) and transaction volumes (TxVolume) using scatter plots.

Fig. 3. This figure shows the correlation between sentiment scores and transaction volume (TxVolume) using logarithmic scales, as well as the relationship between tweet sentiment counts (Negative, Positive, Neutral) and transaction volumes using scatter plots.

Additionally, we investigate the relationship between the count of active traders and transaction volume, as illustrated in Fig. 4(b). The study reveals that with an augmentation in the count of active traders, trading amount demonstrates an upward trajectory. This underscores that an overall enhancement in market activity can positively influence transaction volume. The growth in active trader count likely reflects market participants' confidence in market prospects, prompting increased trading activity and thus propelling transaction volume higher.

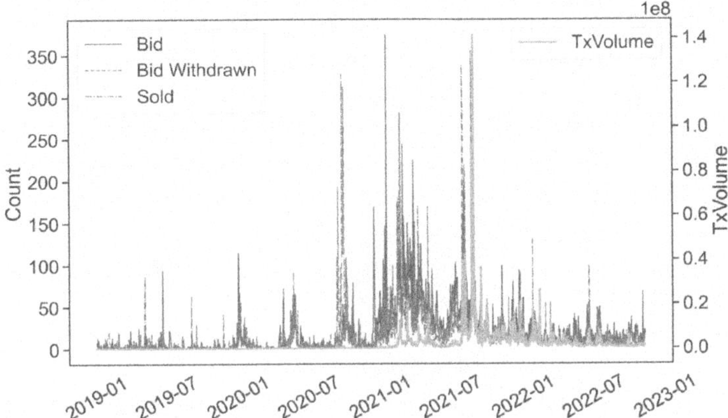

(a) This figure shows the daily bidding activity trends (Bids, Bid Withdrawals, Sold) and transaction volume over the specified date range, revealing the relationship between bid sentiment and transaction volume.

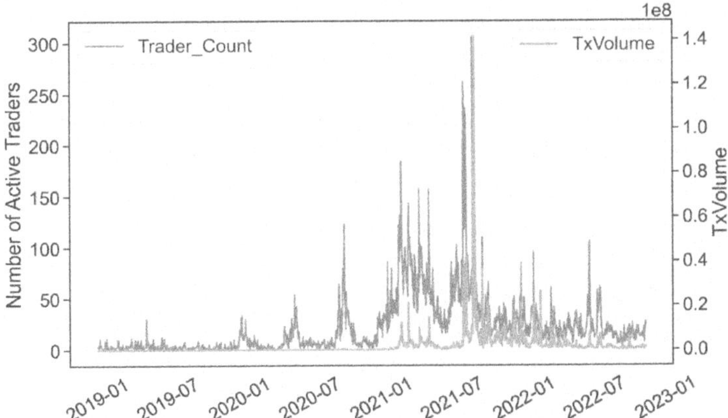

(b) This figure shows the number of active traders and transaction volume over time, revealing the relationship between trader activity and transaction volume.

Fig. 4. This figure shows activity trends and transaction volume, revealing the relationship between activity sentiment/engagement and transaction volume.

Table 2. Description of key features.

Feature	Type	Description
User_Count	Twitter	The daily count of users posting tweets.
Total_Likes	Twitter	The total number of likes received per day for all tweets
Total_Retweets	Twitter	The total number of retweets received per day for all tweets
Max_Comments	Twitter	The maximum number of comments among all daily tweets.
Negative_Count	Sentiment	The total number of daily tweets that are negative.
Positive_Count	Sentiment	The total number of daily tweets that are positive.
Neutral_Count	Sentiment	The total number of daily tweets that are neutral.
TxVolume	Transaction	The daily transaction volume.
Positive_Sum	Sentiment	The cumulative sum of positive sentiment scores for daily tweets.
Compound_Sum	Sentiment	The cumulative sum of compound sentiment scores for daily tweets.
Bid_Count	behaviors	The total count of bids placed by users daily.
Withdrawn_Count	behaviors	The total count of bids withdrawn by users daily.
Sold_Count	behaviors	The total count of NFTs sold by users daily.
active_traders	behaviors	The daily number of users engaged in active trading activities.

Table 3. Machine Learning Algorithms and Optimal Hyperparameters

Models	Optimal Hyperparameters
LightGBM	n_estimators: 80, min_child_samples: 7, max_depth: 8, learning_rate: 0.1
RF	n_estimators: 40, min_samples_split: 2, max_depth: 24
XGBoost	subsample: 0.9, min_child_weight: 1, max_depth: 6, learning_rate: 0.1
CatBoost	iterations: 100, depth: 6, learning_rate: 0.1
GBDT	n_estimators: 60, max_depth: 5, learning_rate: 0.2
AdaBoost	n_estimators: 50, learning_rate: 0.7
KNN	weights: distance, p: 1, n_neighbors: 3
DT	splitter: best, min_samples_split: 6, min_samples_leaf: 1, max_depth: 9
PSO	c_1: 2, c_2: 2, w: 0.8, r_1: 0.6, r_2: 0.3, N: 50, I: 40, d: 2, 3, ..., 7

4 Methodology

The algorithms utilized in this study include Random Forest (RF), Light Gradient Boosting Machine (LightGBM), eXtreme Gradient Boosting (XGBoost), Categorical Boosting (CatBoost), Gradient Boosting Decision Trees (GBDT), AdaBoost, k-Nearest Neighbors (KNN), and Decision Tree (DT). The overall

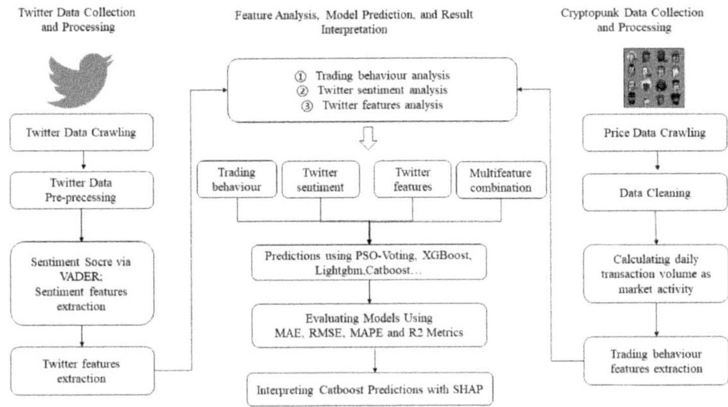

Fig. 5. The proposed model workflow for CryptoPunks transaction volume prediction using multiple categories of features.

experimental procedure is illustrated in Fig. 5. Table 3 shows the optimal hyperparameters of the machine learning algorithm.

4.1 PSO-Voting

In this study, we employ a Particle Swarm Optimization (PSO) method to configure the model for Voting. The PSO algorithm helps us select the best combination of base models and best voting weights for each model for the voting.

In the PSO algorithm, particles explore a pool of regressors, denoted as $\mathcal{R}$. These regressors can be thought of as different machine learning algorithms. Each particle, represented as $\mathbf{X}_i$, is assigned a specific combination of regressors. The performance of this combination, denoted as $f(\mathbf{X}_i)$, is evaluated using the Root Mean Square Error (RMSE) score of the forecasted data by the meta-model. The goal is to minimize $f(\mathbf{X}_i)$ by selecting the best combination of machine learning algorithms.

If $f(\mathbf{X}_i)$ for the current particle is better than $f(\mathbf{p}_i)$ (the best performance achieved by that particle so far), then $\mathbf{X}_i$ becomes the new $\mathbf{p}_i$, and $f(\mathbf{X}_i)$ becomes the new $f(\mathbf{p}_i)$. Similarly, if $f(\mathbf{p}_i)$ is better than $f(\mathbf{g})$ (the best performance across all particles), then $\mathbf{p}_i$ becomes the new $\mathbf{g}$, and $f(\mathbf{p}_i)$ becomes the new $f(\mathbf{g})$.

The regressor combination represented by the current particle $\mathbf{X}_i$ is added to the subset of chosen regressors $\mathcal{M}'$ if it improves the overall performance. Otherwise, $\mathcal{M}'$ remains unchanged. In the same way, use the above method to set different voting weights for each model, and add the optimal weight combination to a subset of weight $\mathcal{W}'$. If the solution provided by the particles does not improve after a predetermined number of iterations, the PSO algorithm adjusts the particle positions to explore new combinations.

This process continues iteratively until the optimal combination of regressors, denoted as $\mathcal{M}'$, and best voting weights for each model denoted as $\mathcal{W}'$ are found. The PSO-Voting algorithm is outlined in Algorithm 2 in pseudocode, and it helps us determine the best combination of machine learning algorithms and best voting weights for each model for our Voting model.

As shown in Fig. 6, within the two steps of the Voting algorithm, the first step comprises n distinct ML algorithms, while the second step involves each ML algorithm voting on prediction results. Initially, the PSO algorithm is employed to select the best k models from the base models. Subsequently, the PSO algorithm is used to determine the voting weights for each model concerning the prediction results of these k models, thereby yielding the final prediction results.

Algorithm 1. PSO-Voting Algorithm

Input: Fitness function f according to the data MAE scores
Output: Best combination of base models: M' and their weights: W'

1: PSO parameters: $I, N, d, w, c_1, c_2, r_1, r_2$
2: Position range: $[X_{\min}, X_{\max}]$
3: Velocity range: $[-V_{\max}, V_{\max}]$
4: Particles: X_i, V_i, p_i, g, W
5: Available base models: M and their weights: W
6: Initialize particles: X_i, V_i, p_i, g, and W
7: $t \leftarrow 1$
8: **while** $t \leq I$ **do**
9:     **for** $i = 1$ to N **do**
10:         **if** $f(X_i) < f(p_i)$ **then**
11:             $f(p_i) \leftarrow f(X_i)$, $p_i \leftarrow X_i$
12:         **end if**
13:     **end for**
14:     **if** $f(p_i) < f(g)$ **then**
15:         $f(g) \leftarrow f(p_i)$, $g \leftarrow p_i$
16:     **end if**
17:     **for** $i = 1$ to N **do**
18:         Update particle velocity: $V_i' \leftarrow wV_i + c_1 r_1 (p_i - X_i) + c_2 r_2 (g - X_i)$
19:         Update particle position: $X_i' \leftarrow X_i + V_i'$
20:     **end for**
21:     Update weights W based on g and M
22:     $t \leftarrow t + 1$
23: **end while**
24: $M' \leftarrow$ Base models corresponding to g
25: $W' \leftarrow$ Weights corresponding to g

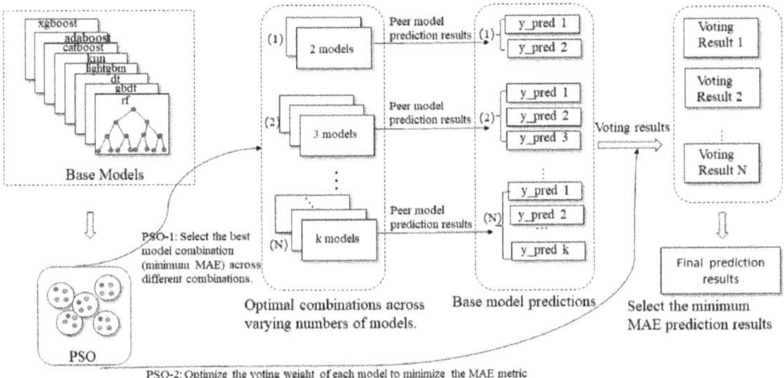

Fig. 6. The structure of the proposed PSO-Voting model.

4.2 Explainable Artificial Intelligence

This study introduces Explainable Artificial Intelligence to analyze multi-category characteristics to examine their influence on the CryptoPunks market. It aims to investigate the predictability of transaction volume in the underlying NFT market. Assessing the effects of various features on the CryptoPunks market is challenging due to the need for more relevant research.

Despite generating highly accurate forecasts, the predictive ensemble structures as opaque systems, offering limited interpretability [14]. This result highlights the practical necessity to explain the predictive influence of factors such as Twitter sentiment, Twitter features, and trading behavior. Such insights would prove advantageous to market participants at different levels, facilitating short-term and long-term strategic planning. To address this issue, we employ the emerging Shapley additive explanation (SHAP) technique [17] to expound on how different features influence the NFT market.

The SHAP measure, initially conceived by [13] to evaluate the contribution of individual entities in a collaborative game, has recently found new applications in the field of Explainable Artificial Intelligence. This development has led to utilizing the SHAP metric for feature evaluation, presenting novel opportunities. Mathematically, the SHAP measure is computed as follows:

$$\phi i = \sum_{S \subseteq Ni} \frac{|S|!(n - |S| - 1)!}{n!} [v(S \cup \{i\}) - v(S)] \tag{1}$$

where, ϕi denotes the contribution of ith feature, N is the set of all features with cardinality n, S is the subset of N with feature i, and $v(N)$ is the predicted outcome considering the ith feature.

The explanation is specified as follows:

$$g(z') = \phi_0 + \sum_{j=1}^{M} \phi_j z'_j \tag{2}$$

where, $z' \in \{0,1\}^M$, M denotes the number of features under consideration, and ϕ_i is determined using Eq. 2.

SHAP offers a different model explainer for accomplishing the task. The present research has utilized the SHAP utility to draw insights into relative importance features for building the CatBoost model.

5   Evaluation

In this section, we employ the PSO-Voting method alongside a collection of machine learning models to predict daily transaction volumes within the CryptoPunks market. The dataset is divided into 70% for training and 30% for testing to facilitate model evaluation. Grid search experiments are then conducted to identify the most suitable model parameters. Subsequently, we conducted a comprehensive performance comparison of four different feature sets, denoted as D1 to D4. D1 represents transactional behavior features, D2 represents Twitter sentiment features, D3 represents Twitter features, and D4 is the result of the integration of these three feature sets. It is worth noting that D1 to D3 represent the performance of individual feature sets, while D4 is the outcome of combining these three feature sets.

5.1   Evaluation Metrics

We employe four commonly used indicators to evaluate the proposed model, i.e., Mean Absolute Error (MAE), Root Mean Square Error (RMSE), Mean Absolute Percentage Error (MAPE), and the coefficient of determination (R2).

MAE gauges the average absolute difference between predicted and actual transaction volume, evaluating the model's accuracy in terms of magnitude. RMSE calculates the square root of the average squared differences between predicted and actual transaction volume, offering insights into the model's ability to capture small and large deviations. MAPE computes the average percentage difference between predicted and actual transaction volume, showcasing the model's performance in terms of relative errors. R2 measures the proportion of the variance in the dependent variable that is predictable from the independent variables, indicating the model's goodness of fit.

$$MAE = \frac{1}{n} \sum_{i=1}^{n} |y_i - \widehat{y_i}| \tag{3}$$

$$RMSE = \sqrt{\frac{1}{n} \sum_{i=1}^{n} (y_i - \widehat{y_i})^2} \tag{4}$$

$$MAPE = \frac{1}{n} \sum_{i=1}^{n} \frac{|y_i - \widehat{y_i}|}{y_i} \times 100\% \tag{5}$$

$$R^2 = 1 - \frac{SS_{res}}{SS_{tot}} \tag{6}$$

5.2   Results Analysis

We employ multiple different machine learning models, specifically LightGBM, XGBoost, Random Forest, CatBoost, DT, GBDT, KNN, Adaboost, and PSO-Voting, for experimental trials. Through a series of experiments, we assess the predictive performance of these models when exposed to different feature combinations. Evaluation metrics employed include Mean Absolute Error (MAE), Root Mean Square Error (RMSE), Mean Absolute Percentage Error (MAPE %), and R-squared (R2). This comprehensive analysis allows us to gain insights into the effectiveness of these models and feature combinations for predicting transaction volumes in the CryptoPunks market.

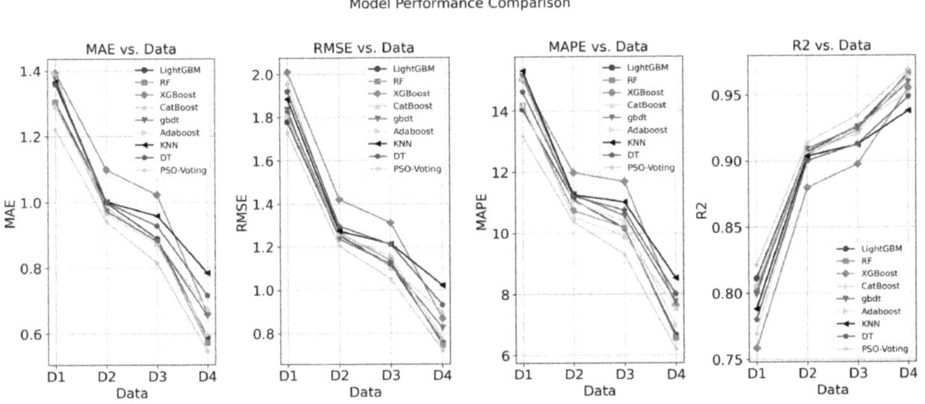

Fig. 7. This figure presents a comparison of model performance.

Table 4 shows the predictive capabilities of different models across distinct feature categories, and Fig. 7 visualizes these evaluation indicators. In Table 4, D1 represents trading behavior, D2 represents Twitter sentiment, D3 represents Twitter Features and D4 represents the combined use of Twitter Features, Twitter sentiment, and trading behavior. By comparing the performance of different feature sets, we can observe that the feature fusion in D4 excels in all evaluation metrics. In comparison to D1 through D3, D4 performs significantly better in terms of Mean Absolute Error (MAE), Root Mean Square Error (RMSE), Mean Absolute Percentage Error (MAPE), and Coefficient of Determination (R2). Specifically, in our experiments, D4, which incorporates Twitter sentiment, Twitter features, and trading behavior, improved approximately 55%, 41%, and 33% in MAE compared to the single feature sets D1 to D3. This indicates that the method of combining multiple feature sets, including Twitter sentiment, Twitter text, and transactional behavior, significantly enhances model performance.

Furthermore, we introduced a novel PSO-Voting model to compare the performance of the four feature sets (D1 to D4). Encouragingly, the PSO-Voting model excels across all feature sets, outperforming traditional machine learning

Table 4. Performance comparison of various methods.

Feature	Model	Evaluation Metrics			
		MAE	RMSE	MAPE(%)	R2
D1	LightGBM	1.3049	1.7793	14.0457	0.8111
	RF	1.3042	1.8192	14.179	0.8024
	XGBoost	1.3935	2.0106	15.0411	0.7587
	CatBoost	1.2924	1.9609	14.212	0.7705
	GBDT	1.3779	1.834	15.1505	0.7992
	Adaboost	1.3897	1.8069	15.0521	0.8051
	KNN	1.3652	1.8837	15.3216	0.7882
	DT	1.3579	1.9189	14.6297	0.7802
	PSO-Voting	**1.2208**	**1.7298**	**13.1641**	**0.8214**
D2	LightGBM	0.9989	1.2507	11.0912	0.9066
	RF	0.9748	1.2661	10.7387	0.9043
	XGBoost	1.099	1.4197	11.9749	0.8797
	CatBoost	0.9858	1.2727	10.5278	0.9033
	GBDT	0.9734	1.2356	11.2718	0.9089
	Adaboost	0.9632	1.2551	11.021	0.906
	KNN	1.0019	1.2716	11.2541	0.9035
	DT	1.0006	1.2947	11.2073	0.8999
	PSO-Voting	**0.9403**	**1.2026**	**10.3751**	**0.9137**
D3	LightGBM	0.8889	1.1148	10.1495	0.9258
	RF	0.8804	1.1345	10.1825	0.9232
	XGBoost	1.0224	1.3112	11.6837	0.8974
	CatBoost	0.8775	1.1013	9.8978	0.9276
	GBDT	0.8802	1.1179	10.5614	0.9254
	Adaboost	0.8711	1.1551	10.3757	0.9203
	KNN	0.9588	1.2122	11.0141	0.9123
	DT	0.9268	1.2095	10.7447	0.9127
	PSO-Voting	**0.8147**	**1.0496**	**9.2891**	**0.9342**
D4	LightGBM	0.5891	0.7563	6.6576	0.9659
	RF	0.5725	0.7437	6.5609	0.9671
	XGBoost	0.6602	0.8674	7.6304	0.9551
	CatBoost	0.6743	0.8973	7.5295	0.9519
	GBDT	0.6546	0.8234	7.7497	0.9595
	Adaboost	0.5962	0.774	6.9677	0.9642
	KNN	0.7842	1.0204	8.5207	0.9378
	DT	0.7159	0.9299	7.9943	0.9484
	PSO-Voting	**0.5467**	**0.7202**	**6.2006**	**0.9691**

models such as LightGBM, Random Forest (RF), and XGBoost. Specifically, the PSO-Voting model improved the MAE metric by approximately 7%, 6%, 8%, and 7%, respectively, compared to other traditional machine learning algorithms in D1 to D4. This indicates the exceptional performance of the PSO-Voting model provides an efficient and reliable approach for predicting CryptoPunks market transaction volume problems (Table 5).

Table 5. Comparison of performance metrics for PSO-Voting with different numbers of base models in D4.

Numbers	MAE	RMSE	MAPE	R2
2	0.5834	0.7616	6.5714	0.9653
3	0.6045	0.7888	6.9034	0.9628
4	**0.5467**	**0.7202**	**6.2006**	**0.9691**
5	0.5811	0.7560	6.4950	0.9658
6	0.5716	0.7495	6.4919	0.9664
7	0.5627	0.7402	6.3159	0.9672
8	0.5861	0.7666	6.6996	0.9649

6   Related Work

Research on Non-fungible Tokens (NFTs) has witnessed extensive exploration across various domains. [20] conducted a comprehensive overview, evaluation, and identification of opportunities and challenges within the NFT ecosystem, emphasizing persistent issues like privacy concerns and data accessibility within blockchain-based NFT systems. [16] delved into the statistical properties of the NFT market and its evolution, studying interaction networks among NFT traders and assets. [5] analyzed the emergence of NFTs in the crypto art space, examining adoption trends among artists and collectors to comprehend the evolving NFT ecosystem. Moreover, [1] explored the temporal development, cointegration, and interrelations of NFT markets on the Ethereum blockchain, shedding light on the interconnected submarkets within the NFT space.

Furthermore, [10] investigated the influence of social media, particularly Twitter, on NFT valuation, uncovering the impact of different platforms on the NFT market. [21] focused on the growing popularity of NFTs, explicitly highlighting the surge in attention toward NFTs in 2021. [18] explored NFT-driven networks in crypto art. [7] studied NFT market dynamics, trade networks, and visual features and utilized machine learning to predict NFT secondary sales prices.

7   Conclusion

This study delves into the factors influencing the CryptoPunks NFT market, including trading behavior, Twitter sentiment and Twitter data. We conducted extensive experiments using several machine learning models, including Light-GBM, XGBoost, Random Forest, and CatBoost, as well as our proposed PSO-Voting model. This paper reveals the varying impact of different feature sets on the CryptoPunks trading volume, with the performance of our proposed PSO-Voting model significantly outperforming other models on this dataset.

Although this study has demonstrated effectiveness in predicting daily transaction volume of the CryptoPunks NFT market, some limitations remain. Firstly, we only considered data from a specific timeframe, and future market dynamics could be influenced by more factors, necessitating the expansion of data scope to enhance model robustness. Secondly, despite integrating multiple feature categories, the possibility of other crucial influencing factors yet to be considered remains, and future research can further explore additional relevant features. Additionally, this study did not address the influence of external market factors on transaction volume, such as macroeconomic conditions. Incorporating these factors into the model could further enhance prediction accuracy in the future.

Acknowledgments. This work was supported by Guangdong Philosophy and Social Science Foundation Regular Project under grant No. GD24CXW05.

Disclosure of Interests. The authors declare that they have no known competing interests or personal relationships that could have appeared to influence the work reported in this article.

References

1. Ante, L.: The non-fungible token (nft) market and its relationship with bitcoin and ethereum. FinTech **1**(3), 216–224 (2022)
2. Ante, L., Fischer, C., Strehle, E.: A bibliometric review of research on digital identity: research streams, influential works and future research paths. J. Manuf. Syst. **62**, 523–538 (2022)
3. Fairfield, J.A.: Tokenized: the law of non-fungible tokens and unique digital property. Ind. LJ **97**, 1261 (2022)
4. Gunay, S., Kaskaloglu, K.: Does utilizing smart contracts induce a financial connectedness between ethereum and non-fungible tokens? Res. Int. Bus. Financ. **63**, 101773 (2022)
5. Horky, F., Rachel, C., Fidrmuc, J.: Price determinants of non-fungible tokens in the digital art market. Financ. Res. Lett. **48**, 103007 (2022)
6. Kapoor, A., Guhathakurta, D., Mathur, M., Yadav, R., Gupta, M., Kumaraguru, P.: Tweetboost: influence of social media on nft valuation. In: Companion Proceedings of the Web Conference 2022, pp. 621–629 (2022)
7. Nadini, M., Alessandretti, L., Di Giacinto, F., Martino, M., Aiello, L.M., Baronchelli, A.: Mapping the nft revolution: market trends, trade networks, and visual features. Sci. Rep. **11**(1), 20902 (2021)

8. Park, H., Ureta, I., Kim, B.: Trend analysis of decentralized autonomous organization using big data analytics. Information **14**(6), 326 (2023)
9. Patel, R., Migliavacca, M., Oriani, M.E.: Blockchain in banking and finance: a bibliometric review. Res. Int. Bus. Financ. **62**, 101718 (2022)
10. Qian, C., Mathur, N., Zakaria, N.H., Arora, R., Gupta, V., Ali, M.: Understanding public opinions on social media for financial sentiment analysis using ai-based techniques. Inform. Process. Manag. **59**(6), 103098 (2022)
11. Reshi, A.A., et al.: Covid-19 vaccination-related sentiments analysis: a case study using worldwide twitter dataset. In: Healthcare, vol. 10, p. 411. MDPI (2022)
12. Saberi, S., Kouhizadeh, M., Sarkis, J., Shen, L.: Blockchain technology and its relationships to sustainable supply chain management. Int. J. Prod. Res. **57**(7), 2117–2135 (2019)
13. Shapley, L.S., et al.: A value for n-person games (1953)
14. Stiglic, G., Kocbek, P., Fijacko, N., Zitnik, M., Verbert, K., Cilar, L.: Interpretability of machine learning-based prediction models in healthcare. Wiley Interdisciplinary Rev. Data Mining Knowl. Dis. **10**(5), e1379 (2020)
15. Tan, T.M., Saraniemi, S.: Trust in blockchain-enabled exchanges: Future directions in blockchain marketing. J. Academy marketing Sci., 1–26 (2022)
16. Tromp, J.G.: Extended reality & the backbone: towards a 3d mirrorworld. Roadmapping Extended Reality: Fundamentals and Applications, pp. 193–227 (2022)
17. Ullah, I., Liu, K., Yamamoto, T., Zahid, M., Jamal, A.: Prediction of electric vehicle charging duration time using ensemble machine learning algorithm and shapley additive explanations. Int. J. Energy Res. **46**(11), 15211–15230 (2022)
18. Vasan, K., Janosov, M., Barabási, A.L.: Quantifying nft-driven networks in crypto art. Sci. Rep. **12**(1), 2769 (2022)
19. Wang, C., Yu, C., Li, Y.: Toward understanding attention economy in metaverse: a case study of nft value. IEEE Trans. Comput. Soc. Syst. (2022)
20. Wang, Q., Li, R., Wang, Q., Chen, S.: Non-fungible token (nft): overview, evaluation, opportunities and challenges. arXiv preprint arXiv:2105.07447 (2021)
21. White, B., Mahanti, A., Passi, K.: Characterizing the opensea nft marketplace. In: Companion Proceedings of the Web Conference 2022, pp. 488–496 (2022)

A Cyber Threat Intelligence Entity Relation Extraction Method Based on Improved OneRel Model

Jing Luo, Yijiang Zhao[(⊠)] [ID], and Qiuwu Li

Hunan University of Science and Technology, Xiangtan, China
`zhaoyj@hnust.edu.cn`

Abstract. The current cybersecurity landscape is intricate and severe. Accurately extracting cybersecurity entities from threat intelligence and clarifying their relationships is of great significance for strengthening cybersecurity defense. However, the complexity of relation expressions and the prevalence of relation overlapping in natural language texts pose significant challenges to efficient and accurate information extraction. To tackle these challenges, this paper proposes an enhanced model based on the OneRel model. Specifically, the model incorporates a feature extraction module that combines IDCNN and BiGRU to capture local and global features effectively. It also integrates an Attention Mechanism to enhance the model's focus on critical relational information. Experimental results demonstrate that the improved model achieves F1 scores of 0.7794 and 0.6885 on the Baidu relation extraction dataset and our constructed cyber threat intelligence entity relation dataset, respectively, representing improvements of 2.22% and 2.95% over the original model. This study shows that the enhanced model significantly improves the learning of contextual information in Chinese text sentences, effectively boosting the accuracy and robustness of relation extraction.

Keywords: Entity Relation Extraction · Cyber Threat Intelligence · IDCNN · BiGRU · Attention Mechanism

1 Introduction

The rapid advancement of information technology and the continuous expansion of cyberspace have significantly escalated the complexity and severity of cybersecurity challenges. Cyberattacks are not only increasing in frequency but also evolving in sophistication, automation, and scale, which has rendered traditional defense approaches largely insufficient [1]. Against this backdrop, the critical importance of Cyber Threat Intelligence (CTI) has come to the forefront. CTI, comprising a wealth of information related to cyber threats, holds the potential to enable the early detection and proactive mitigation of potential cyberattacks. The process of extracting CTI from unstructured online sources such as articles and reports, and transforming it into a structured format, is of paramount significance. This approach is not only theoretically meaningful

© ICST Institute for Computer Sciences, Social Informatics and Telecommunications Engineering 2026
Published by Springer Nature Switzerland AG 2026. All Rights Reserved
W. Liang et al. (Eds.): SecureComm 2025, LNICST 690, pp. 430–445, 2026.
https://doi.org/10.1007/978-3-032-23456-8_23

but also practically valuable for bolstering cybersecurity research and strengthening defense capabilities. It represents an effective and innovative strategy for navigating the current intricate and challenging cybersecurity landscape [2].

The systematic extraction of entities and relationships within cyber threat intelligence is integral to constructing a nuanced presentation of a cyberattack. It encompasses the identification of the attacker, the target, the methods, and the attack pathways. This aids cybersecurity professionals in comprehensively understanding the threat's nature and characteristics, offering a basis for effective defense strategies. Knowledge graphs [3], as a structured method for knowledge representation and organization, have been widely applied in the field of artificial intelligence due to their ability to efficiently store and manage complex information structures [4]. By organizing entities, relationships, and events in a graph format, they provide robust support for machine understanding and reasoning. In the realm of cybersecurity, the extraction of entities and relationships from cyber threat intelligence constitutes the foundation for developing a cybersecurity knowledge graph [5]. This process integrates disparate pieces of threat intelligence into a cohesive and interconnected framework. It not only facilitates knowledge visualization but also enables in-depth correlation analysis. Furthermore, the extraction of entities and relationships promotes cross-organizational intelligence collaboration and sharing. This collective approach enhances the protective capabilities of the entire cybersecurity industry and fosters a more unified defense against cyber threats.

Network texts contain abundant explicit and implicit threat intelligence entities and relationships. However, the complexity, flexibility, and uncertainty of natural language texts present significant challenges for entity and relationship extraction from threat intelligence. Additionally, the presence of multiple overlapping relationship triplets within sentences further complicates this task. The scarcity of publicly available Chinese threat intelligence entities and relationship annotated datasets further restricts model performance improvement. To address these issues, this paper constructs a Chinese CTI entity relationship extraction dataset and proposes an efficient method based on an improved OneRel model for the automatic extraction of CTI entity relationships. Building on the OneRel model, the method introduces IDCNN (Iterated Dilated Convolutional Neural Network), BiGRU (Bidirectional Gated Recurrent Unit), and Attention Mechanism to enrich text feature representation and improve overall model performance. IDCNN extracts local and global features from the text, BiGRU captures long-distance dependencies in sequences, and the Attention Mechanism helps focus on key information, enhancing the modeling of complex relationships. These features, combined with contextual representations from the BERT model, provide richer feature representations, enabling the model to better understand entities and relationships in text. The proposed method significantly improves the joint extraction of CTI entity relations, thereby efficiently promoting the acquisition, inference, and application of CTI knowledge.

2 Related Work

In the research on entity relationship extraction, traditional rule-based matching methods were an important early approach. These methods primarily relied on rule matching and syntactic analysis to identify and extract entity relationship. For example, Aone et al.

[6] manually defined extraction rules, including lexical and syntactic features, matched them with corpus texts, and used fixed templates for relation extraction. Fundel et al. [7] proposed RelEx, a relation extraction method based on dependency parsing trees. It identifies relationships between entities by analyzing sentence dependencies. While these methods were effective to some extent, they heavily depended on manually crafted rules and dictionaries, making it difficult for them to adapt to large-scale, dynamic CTI texts.

With the continuous development of machine learning and deep learning technologies, corpus data based on manual annotation, combined with traditional machine learning methods such as Random Forest (RF) and Support Vector Machine (SVM), as well as deep learning methods like Convolutional Neural Network (CNN), Recurrent Neural Network (RNN), and Long Short-Term Memory network (LSTM), can automatically capture contextual features of text. As a statistical learning method, machine learning avoids the manual work of collecting dictionaries, patterns, or rules based on corpus and has the ability to identify new entity relationships. For example, Giuliano et al. [8] proposed the FBK-IRST method for semantic relation extraction using kernel methods. They combined five basic kernel functions as information sources, including context and WordNet semantic kernels. An SVM was used as the classifier to turn the relation extraction task into a classification problem.

With the continuous development of the field of information science, researchers have gradually realized the limitations of traditional machine learning methods in processing large-scale, dynamic text data. Although these methods perform well in certain specific tasks, they often struggle to adapt when faced with complex semantics and contextual changes. Therefore, researchers have begun to explore new technical approaches to overcome the limitations of traditional methods and improve the accuracy and efficiency of entity relationship extraction.

The rise of deep learning has brought new hope to this field. Unlike traditional machine learning methods, deep learning models can automatically learn complex feature representations from data, reducing the reliance on manual feature engineering. These models effectively capture contextual features of text by learning language patterns and structures in corpora, thereby improving the accuracy and efficiency of relationship extraction. For example, Gasmi et al. [9] explored LSTM for cybersecurity concept information extraction. They built an LSTM model to effectively identify and extract entities and relations in cybersecurity texts. This model offers a novel deep-learning solution for this domain's information extraction tasks. Pingle et al. [10] proposed the Relext method. It uses an FFNN classifier, combined with a Named Entity Recognition and Word2Vec model, to extract entity pair relations from cybersecurity texts and enhance cybersecurity knowledge graphs. Zhou et al. [11] utilized a BERT + BiLSTM + GRU + CRF deep-learning network to extract relations and entities from Chinese threat intelligence.

The implementation strategies for entity relation extraction are primarily divided into two categories: Pipeline Extraction and Joint Extraction. Pipeline extraction methods treat entity recognition and relation classification as two independent modules. First, the entity recognition model extracts entity information from text, and then the relation classification model determines the relationships between any two entities based on this information [12, 13]. However, research has gradually revealed significant drawbacks of the pipeline approach, such as error propagation, information redundancy, and failure to fully leverage the intrinsic connections between entities and relations. To address these issues, researchers proposed Joint Extraction methods. These methods use a unified encoder to generate contextualized representations for both entity recognition and relation classification tasks. Joint extraction enhances the interaction between the two tasks through multi-task learning, thereby improving the robustness of the model in both tasks. Examples include the tree-based model proposed by Miwa and Bansal [14] and the RNN model with Attention Mechanism proposed by Katiyar and Cardie [15]. Zeng et al. [16] introduced an end-to-end joint entity-relation extraction model based on sequence-to-sequence (Seq2Seq) learning. Wei et al. [17] proposed a novel cascaded binary tagging framework, CasRel, for extracting relation triplets from text. Jiang et al. [18] improved the CasRel model by integrating the ERNIE pre-trained model and BAB module, enabling joint extraction of geographical entities and overlapping spatial relations from geospatial text. Wang et al. [19] proposed a single-stage joint extraction model, TPLinker, which converts entity and relation extraction into a token-pair linking problem using a handshaking tagging scheme. In 2022, Shang et al. [20] introduced the OneRel model, which employs a scoring-based classifier and a Relation-Specific Horns Tagging strategy to transform entity-relation extraction into a fine-grained triplet classification problem. This approach effectively addresses issues of cascading errors and redundant information.

The phenomenon of overlapping relations is prevalent in Chinese cyber threat intelligence texts on the Internet. Furthermore, Research on using deep learning methods to extract entity relations from them is relatively limited, and the accuracy remains to be improved. To this end, this paper proposes an enhanced OneRel model for joint entity relation extraction in CTI. Through innovative model architecture and optimization strategies, the model demonstrates a significant boost in performance when grappling with complex Chinese CTI texts.

3   Methods

This paper improves the OneRel model by integrating an IDCNN-BiGRU-based feature extraction module with an Attention Mechanism, as shown in Fig. 1 This design enables the model to more effectively capture contextual information in Chinese text sentences.

The OneRel model conceptualizes the joint extraction task as a fine-grained triplet classification problem. It introduces Relation-Specific Horns Tagging, dynamically generating start/end tags for head and tail entities for each relation type to explicitly mark entity boundaries. This strategy naturally handles overlapping relations, including entity pair overlapping (EPO), single entity overlapping (SEO), and head/tail overlapping (HTO). However, while the BERT-based OneRel model is excellent at capturing contextual information, it lacks fine-grained feature extraction. This paper enhances the OneRel model by incorporating IDCNN, BiGRU, and an Attention Mechanism, enabling more effective learning of contextual information in Chinese text.

IDCNN. The IDCNN (Iterated Dilated Convolutional Neural Network) is a model that combines depth-wise convolutional layers with sequence data processing. It uses a

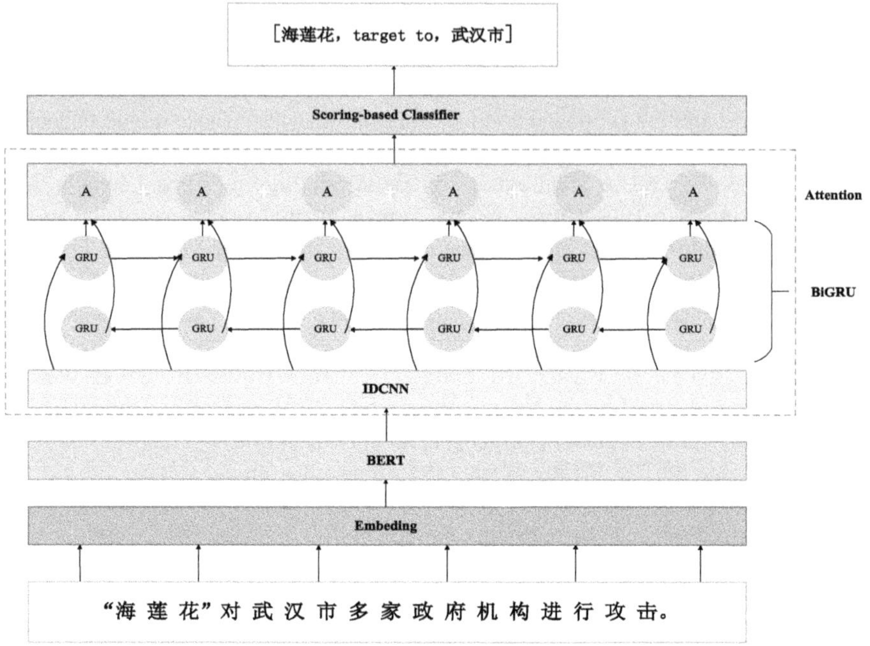

Fig. 1. Improved OneRel model. The improvements based on the OneRel model are indicated within the blue dashed-line box.

dilated convolution structure to capture long-range dependencies in sequences while maintaining computational efficiency. Unlike traditional CNNs, dilated convolutions operate on non-contiguous contexts, skipping inputs at intervals determined by the dilation width. This allows the effective receptive field to grow exponentially with depth, without losing resolution. As shown in Fig. 2, a dilated convolution with a kernel size of 3 and two layers has a context size of 7, compared to 5 for a traditional convolution. For a kernel size of 3, the context size for traditional convolution at layer L is $2L + 1$, while for dilated convolution, it is $2^{(L+1)} - 1$. Thus, dilated convolution achieves a larger context with fewer layers.

The IDCNN architecture is built by stacking convolutional layers with varying dilation rates and activation functions. Given the vector representation of a sentence sequence as x_t, the j-th dilated convolutional layer with dilation width d is denoted as $D_d^{(j)}$. The first layer with a dilation rate of 1 is expressed as:

$$i_t = D_1^{(0)} x_t \tag{1}$$

Subsequent layers use exponentially increasing dilation widths. Starting from $c_t^{(0)} = i_t$, the output of the j-th layer is:

$$c_t^{(j)} = r\left(D_{2^{j-1}}^{(j-1)} c_t^{(j-1)}\right) \tag{2}$$

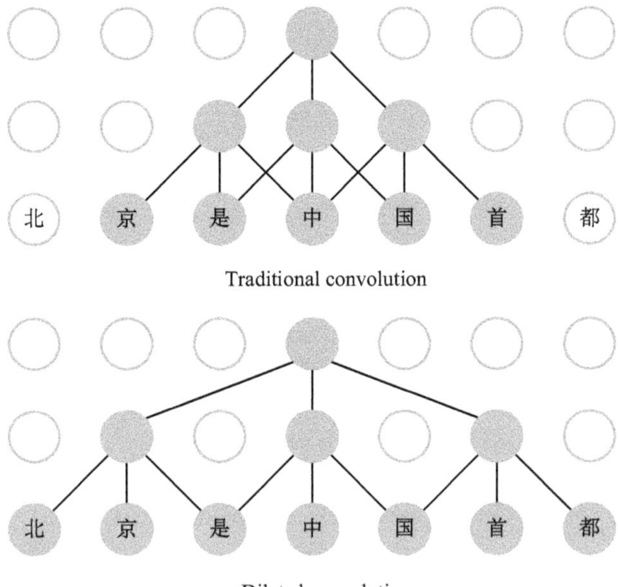

Fig. 2. Dilated convolution and traditional convolution context size.

where $r()$ is the activation function. An additional layer with a dilation width of 1 is added at the end:

$$c_t^{(j)} = r\left(D_{2^{j-1}}^{(j-1)} c_t^{(j-1)}\right) \tag{3}$$

These $j + 1$ layers form a block $B(\cdot)$ with equal input and output dimensions. To incorporate a broader context without deepening B, the block $B(\cdot)$ is reused Lb times. Starting with $b_t^{(1)} = B(i_t)$, the repeated application is:

$$b_t^{(k)} = B\left(b_t^{(k-1)}\right) \tag{4}$$

IDCNN extracts multi-scale features by stacking layers and expanding the receptive field, providing a multi-scale representation of the text sequence.

BiGRU. The BiGRU is an improved RNN structure. It has two independent GRU units, one processing the sequence forward and the other backward, capturing context from both directions for richer feature representation. As shown in Fig. 3, GRU is a simplified LSTM version with two key structural improvements. First, it merges the LSTM's forget and input gates into an update gate, relying on this and a reset gate to regulate information flow. Second, it combines the cell and hidden states, simplifying the network. These changes make GRU more efficient with fewer parameters. Formulas (5)–(8) describe the GRU unit's computation:

$$Updategate : z_t = \sigma\left(W_z \cdot \left[h_{t-1}, x_t\right] + b_z\right) \tag{5}$$

$$Resetgate : r_t = \sigma\left(W_r \cdot \left[h_{t-1}, x_t\right] + b_r\right) \tag{6}$$

$$Candidatestate : \tilde{h}_t = tanh\left(W_h \cdot \left[r_t \cdot h_{t-1}, x_t\right] + b_h\right) \tag{7}$$

$$Finalstate : h_t = (1 - z_t) \cdot h_{t-1} + z_t \cdot \tilde{h}_t \tag{8}$$

Here, σ represents the sigmoid function, which constrains values to the range [0,1]. A gate signal closer to 1 retains more information, while values closer to 0 indicate more forgetting. z controls updates. r controls resets, W_z, W_r, W_h are weight matrices, and b_z, b_r, b_h are biases. The operation $[\cdot, \cdot]$ denotes vector concatenation, combining reset-gated data with the tanh activation to constrain outputs to $[-1,1]$, yielding the hidden state $\tilde{h}$. The update gate selectively forgets prior states $(1 - z_t) \cdot h_{t-1}$ and retains new information $z_t \cdot \tilde{h}_t$.

The forward and backward computations in BiGRU are expressed as:

$$\overrightarrow{h} = GRU\left(x_t, \overrightarrow{h}_{t-1}\right) \tag{9}$$

$$\overleftarrow{h} = GRU\left(x_t, \overleftarrow{h}_{t-1}\right) \tag{10}$$

$$h_t = f\left(W_{\overrightarrow{h}_t} \overrightarrow{h}_t + W_{\overleftarrow{h}_t} \overleftarrow{h}_t + b_t\right) \tag{11}$$

Here, $\overrightarrow{h}$ and $\overleftarrow{h}$ are the forward and backward hidden states at time t, $W_{\overrightarrow{h}_t}$ and $W_{\overleftarrow{h}_t}$ are their respective weights, and b_t is the bias at time t.

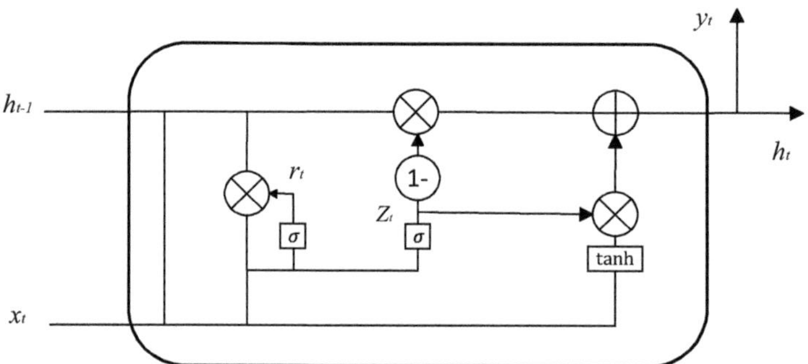

Fig. 3. GRU unit.

Attention Mechanism. The Attention module is added to further extract text features and highlight key information in the input sequence. Attention Mechanism assign weights based on information importance, known as attention values. The process involves: first calculating the attention score function by estimating the distribution of focus on input information, then transforming the score function using a softmax function to normalize it into a probability distribution where the sum of all weights equals 1. This emphasizes the weight of important elements. Let h_m represent the input information vector and h_t represent the query vector for identifying key information. The formula is shown in (12):

$$a_m = softmax(s(h_m, h_t)) = \frac{exp(s(h_m, h_t))}{\sum_{j=1}^{N} exp(s(h_m, h_t))} \tag{12}$$

Here, a_m denotes the probability of selecting the m-th input information, and the vector composed of all a_m forms the attention distribution. N represents the number of input information items. The attention function $s(h_m, h_t)$ uses an additive model, as shown in formula (13).

$$s(h_m, h_t) = v^T tanh(Wh_m + Uh_t) \tag{13}$$

where W, U, and v are learnable parameters in the neural network. This function calculates the similarity between two vectors. Finally, the probabilities of all input information are aggregated into a weighted sum to obtain the attention value V, as shown in formula (14):

$$V = \sum_{m=1}^{N} a_m h_m \tag{14}$$

Given a sentence $S = \{w_1, w_2, w_3, \cdots, w_L\}$ with L tokens and K predefined relations $R = \{r_1, r_2, r_3, \cdots, r_k\}$. The goal of the joint entity and relation extraction is to identify all possible triplets $T = \{(h_i, r_i, t_i)\}_{i=1}^{N}$ where N is the number of triplets, and h_i, t_i are head and tail entities composed of consecutive tokens. The encoding process is as follows: The input token sequence $\{x_1, x_2, x_3, \cdots, x_L\}$ is first encoded using a BERT model to generate an initial contextual representation H. The representation H is then processed by an IDCNN module to capture long-range contextual information and local and global features, resulting in an intermediate representation. A linear layer further transforms this intermediate representation into H_{IDCNN}.

H_{IDCNN} is input into a BiGRU module to capture bidirectional dependencies, generating a bidirectional contextual representation H_{BiGRU}. Finally, an Attention Mechanism is applied to H_{BiGRU} to produce a weighted contextual representation E. The specific formulas are shown in (15)–(18):

$$H = BERT(\{x_1, x_2, x_3, \cdots, x_L\}) \tag{15}$$

$$H_{IDCNN} = Liner(IDCNN(H)) \tag{16}$$

$$H_{BiGRU} = BiGRU(H_{IDCNN}) \tag{17}$$

$$E = Attention(H_{BiGRU}) \tag{18}$$

Here, x_i is the input representation of each token, which is the sum of the token embedding and position embedding. The initial contextual representation $H \epsilon R^{L \times d}$, where d is the hidden dimension of BERT. The intermediate representation $H_{IDCNN} \epsilon R^{L \times d_{IDCNN}}$ where d_{IDCNN} is the output dimension of IDCNN. The bidirectional contextual representation $H_{BiGRU} \epsilon R^{L \times 2d_{GRU}}$, where d_{GRU} is the hidden dimension of the GRU unit. $E = \{e_1, e_2, e_3, \cdots, e_L\}$, where each e_i is a weighted contextual token vector.

Scoring-based Classifier. A scoring function evaluates whether a token pair and a relation form a valid triplet. For a token pair (w_i, w_j) and a predefined relation r_k, the scoring function $f_r(h, t)$ calculates the validity score of the combination, as shown in formula (19):

$$f_r(h, t) = r^T \oslash \left([h; t]^T W + b \right) \tag{19}$$

Here, h and t are the embedding representations of the head and tail entities. $\oslash$ is the ReLU activation function. $[\cdot; \cdot]$ denotes the concatenation operation. W and b are trainable weights and biases. $W \epsilon R^{d_e \times 2d}$, where d_e is the dimension of the entity pair representation, and $2d$ is the dimension after concatenating the head and tail entity feature vectors.

For an input sentence, the model first generates embeddings for each token. It then enumerates all possible (e_i, r_k, e_j) combinations and calculates their scores using the scoring function in formula (20):

$$v_{(w_i, r_k, w_j)} = R^T \oslash \left(drop\left([e_i; e_j]^T \right) W + b \right) \tag{20}$$

Here, R is a matrix of all relation representations, $R \epsilon R^{d_e \times 4K}$, where 4 is the number of classification labels. Drop is the Dropout operation for preventing overfitting.

The scoring vector $v_{(w_i, r_k, w_j)}$ is fed into the softmax function to predict the corresponding label, as shown in formula (21):

$$P\left(y_{(w_i, r_k, w_j)} | S \right) = Softmax\left(v_{(w_i, r_k, w_j)} \right) \tag{21}$$

Here, $y_{(w_i, r_k, w_j)}$ is the annotated label, and S represents the contextual information.

The objective function is defined in formula (22):

$$\mathcal{L}_{triple} = -\frac{1}{L \times K \times L} \times \sum_{i=1}^{L} \sum_{k=1}^{K} \sum_{j=1}^{L} logP\left(y_{(w_i, r_k, w_j)} = g_{(w_i, r_k, w_j)} | S \right) \tag{22}$$

Here, $g_{(w_i, r_k, w_j)}$ is the gold-standard label from the annotations. $L \times K \times L$ represents the total number of possible triplets, forming a three-dimensional tensor.

4 Experiment

4.1 Dataset and Evaluation Metrics

Experiments were conducted on two datasets: the Baidu Relation Extraction Dataset and the dataset constructed in this study. The Baidu dataset, a large-scale Chinese information extraction dataset, is publicly released by Baidu and sourced from Baidu Encyclopedia,

News, and Tieba, covering news, entertainment, and user-generated content. It includes 9 entity types and 17 relation types. In this study, we constructed a CTI dataset with 30 entity types and 29 relationships. The data mainly came from open-source Chinese threat intelligence reports on the internet, with entity relationships related to regions supplemented by the "*Comprehensive Encyclopedia of Chinese Geography*". Our defined entity types include attackers, tools, industries, regions, and campaigns, fully encompassing all elements associated with cybersecurity threats In terms of relationship definition. In terms of relationship definition, we have clarified key relationships, such as "target at", "originated from", and "operating in", to precisely delineate the association patterns between entities. Notably, our detailed classification of the region entity. Breaking away from traditional vague description methods, we have subdivided regions into a hierarchical structure, including country, province, and city levels. Furthermore, we have accurately distinguished the directional and semantic relationships between regions. This approach to classification and relationship definition offers multiple advantages. It equips security researchers with the means to conduct precise analyses of threat sources, propagation paths, and attack targets. Thus, it provides robust support for the development of more targeted defense strategies. Additionally, this approach not only makes the dataset more enriched and multi-dimensional, but also equips it to meet the diverse requirements of different users in the fields of cybersecurity research, threat intelligence analysis, and security policy-making. The specific distribution of the training, validation, and test sets for both datasets is shown in Table 1.

Evaluation metrics include Precision (P), Recall (R), and F1-score, with F1 being the primary metric.

Table 1. Dataset details.

Baidu Relation Extraction Dataset		Dataset Constructed in This Paper	
Dataset	Quantity	Dataset	Quantity
Train	55959	Train	878
Test	13418	Test	216
Valid	11192	Valid	146

4.2 Experimental Environment and Parameter Configuration

The model was trained on a server with an RTX3090GPU, 24 GB VRAM, 45 GB RAM, and a 14-core Intel(R) Xeon(R) Platinum 8362 CPU @ 2.80 GHz. The deep learning framework used was PyTorch 1.8.1, with Python 3.8 (Ubuntu 18.04) and CUDA 11.1. The model, built on pre-trained BERT models for joint extraction of CTI entity relations, was developed using the PyTorch framework. Detailed parameters are listed in Table 2.

Table 2. Parameter configuration.

Parameter	Value
Maximum length of input sentences	100
Batch_size	8
Dilation widths	1,1,2,4
Maximum length of input sentences	4
Convolution kernel window size	3
Learning rate	1e−5
Optimizer	AdamW

4.3 Comparative Experimental Results and Analysis

The experimental results of our improved model, compared with the OneRel, CasRel, SpERT, and ETL-Span models, are shown in Table 3, Table 4, and Fig. 4, Fig. 5 on the Baidu and our constructed datasets.

SpERT [21]: This end-to-end framework uses a BERT-based span classification method to unify entity and relation extraction, reducing cascading errors.

ETL-Span [22]: This model decomposes the joint extraction task into two stages: head entity extraction and tail entity-relation extraction, addressing challenges in overlapping and complex relations.

CasRel [17]: By cascading subject extraction and relation-object pair extraction, this model models relations as functions from subjects to objects, effectively handling overlapping relations.

Table 3. Results on the Baidu dataset.

Model	P	R	F1
OneRel	0.7624	0.7521	0.7572
CasRel	0.7285	0.7829	0.7548
SpERT	0.6909	**0.7967**	0.7406
ETL-Span	0.7730	0.7022	0.7359
OneRel_IDCNN_BiGRU_Atten	**0.8012**	0.7589	**0.7794**

Table 4. Results on the dataset constructed in this article.

Model	P	R	F1
OneRel	0.6955	0.6261	0.6590
CasRel	0.6454	0.6447	0.6451
SpERT	0.6684	**0.6941**	0.6810
ETL-Span	0.7409	0.5693	0.6438
OneRel_IDCNN_BiGRU_Atten	**0.7483**	0.6375	**0.6885**

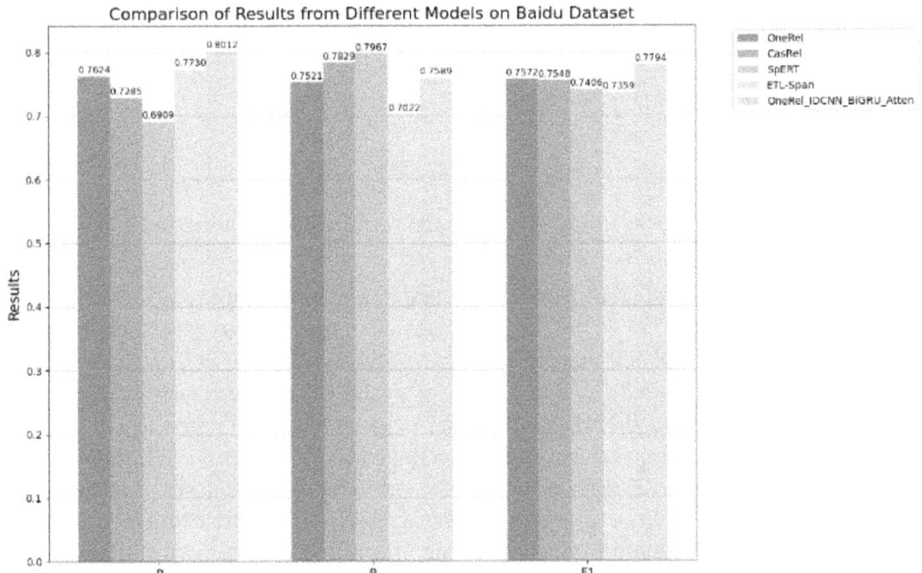

Fig. 4. Comparison of results from different models on the Baidu dataset.

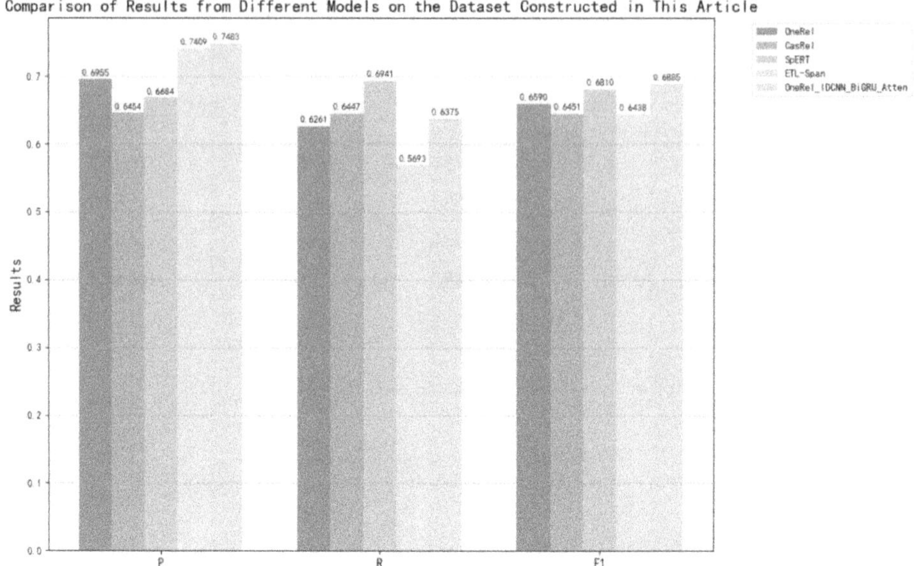

Fig. 5. Comparison of Results from Different Models on the dataset constructed in this article.

From the experimental results in Table 3, and Table 4, our improved OneRel model achieves F1 scores of 0.7794 on the Baidu dataset and 0.6885 on our constructed dataset. Compared to CasRel, SpERT, and ETL-Span: On the Baidu dataset, our model shows improvements of 2.46%, 3.88%, and 4.35%, respectively. On our constructed dataset, improvements are 4.34%, 0.75%, and 4.47%, respectively. Compared to the original OneRel model: On the Baidu dataset, our model improves Precision, Recall, and F1-score by 3.88%, 0.68%, and 2.22%, respectively. On our constructed dataset, improvements are 5.28%, 1.14%, and 2.95%, respectively. These results demonstrate that incorporating IDCNN, BiGRU, and Attention Mechanism significantly enhances the OneRel model's performance in CTI entity relation extraction. These modules improve the model's ability to capture contextual information and model complex relationships.

4.4   Results and Analysis of the Ablation Experiment

To verify the effectiveness of adding IDCNN, BiGRU, and Attention Mechanism to the OneRel model, ablation studies were conducted on two datasets, and the results are presented in Table 5 and Table 6.

Table 5. The ablation experiment results on the Baidu dataset.

Model	P	R	F1
OneRel	0.7624	0.7521	0.7572
OneRel_BiGRU	0.7962	0.7510	0.7729

(continued)

Table 5. (*continued*)

Model	P	R	F1
OneRel_BiGRU_Atten	0.7948	0.7555	0.7746
OneRel_IDCNN_BiGRU_Atten	**0.8012**	**0.7589**	**0.7794**

Table 6. The ablation experiment results on the dataset constructed in this article.

Model	P	R	F1
OneRel	0.6955	0.6261	0.6590
OneRel_BiGRU	0.7030	0.6228	0.6605
OneRel_BiGRU_Atten	0.7421	0.6151	0.6727
OneRel_IDCNN_BiGRU_Atten	**0.7483**	**0.6375**	**0.6885**

The experimental results show that adding a BiGRU module increased the F1 score by 1.57% and 0.15% on the Baidu and custom datasets, respectively. This is attributed to BiGRU's ability to process sequential data bidirectionally, leveraging both past and future information to capture long-range dependencies. This enables the model to excel in handling complex textual data, particularly in dealing with multiple and overlapping relationships. On the OneRel_BiGRU model, adding an Attention module further improved the F1 score by 0.17% and 1.22% on the two datasets. The Attention Mechanism dynamically weights the importance of each element in the input sequence, enabling the model to focus on key information and enhancing its ability to model complex relations. Furthermore, incorporating an IDCNN module into the OneRel_BiGRU_Atten model led to F1 score increases of 0.48% and 1.58%. IDCNN captures long-range dependencies and extracts local and global features through dilated convolutions, enriching the feature representation when combined with BERT's contextual information. These improvements highlight the positive impact of the added modules on the task of CTI entity relation extraction, as confirmed by ablation studies.

5   Discussion and Conclusion

The comparative experimental results indicate that this paper's model performs less effectively on our constructed dataset than on the publicly available Baidu dataset. We attribute this to two main factors. Firstly, the smaller size of our constructed dataset limits the model's ability to learn a sufficient number of features and patterns. This makes it difficult to accurately identify entities and relationships, especially complex ones. The lack of adequate positive and negative samples hinders the model's ability to distinguish between different relationships. Secondly, the small dataset has insufficient diversity and representativeness, which limits the model's exposure to various text patterns and relationship expressions during training. This limitation prevents the model from generalizing effectively to new and unseen text situations, leading to a subpar performance on the test set.

To address the scarcity of publicly available in the cybersecurity domain, this paper constructs a dataset, named Chinese CTI entity relation extraction datasets, to effectively extract CTI entity relation triplets from Chinese text. This study also improves the OneRel model by incorporating IDCNN, BiGRU, and Attention Mechanism, which significantly enrich the feature representation of the text and enhance the overall model performance. To validate the superiority of the proposed model, a series of comparative experiments are designed. The improved OneRel model is comprehensively compared with the original OneRel, CasRel, SpERT, and ETL-Span models on both the Baidu dataset and the constructed dataset. The results show that the proposed model achieves significant improvements in key evaluation metrics, demonstrating its effectiveness in CTI entity relation extraction. Finally, ablation studies are conducted to further verify the contributions of each added module and their synergistic effects on model performance.

Acknowledgement. This research was funded by the Humanities and Social Sciences Project of Ministry of Education of China (No. 24YJAZH237), Scientific Research Fund of Hunan Provincial Education Department of China (No. 22A0341), Science and Technology Innovation Program of Hunan Province (No. 2023SK2081).

References

1. Khaleel, Y.L., Habeeb, M.A., Albahri, A.S., Al-Quraishi, T., Albahri, O.S., Alamoodi, A.H.: Network and cybersecurity applications of defense in adversarial attacks: a state-of-the-art using machine learning and deep learning methods (2024). https://doi.org/10.1515/jisys-2024-0153

2. Conti, M., Dargahi, T., Dehghantanha, A.: Cyber threat intelligence: challenges and opportunities. In: Dehghantanha, A., Conti, M., and Dargahi, T. (eds.) Cyber Threat Intelligence, pp. 1–6. Springer, Cham (2018). https://doi.org/10.1007/978-3-319-73951-9_1

3. Hogan, A., et al.: Knowledge graphs. ACM Comput. Surv. **54**, 71:1–71:37 (2021). https://doi.org/10.1145/3447772

4. Peng, C., Xia, F., Naseriparsa, M., Osborne, F.: Knowledge graphs: opportunities and challenges. Artif. Intell. Rev. **56**, 13071–13102 (2023). https://doi.org/10.1007/s10462-023-104 65-9

5. Zhao, X., Jiang, R., Han, Y., Li, A., Peng, Z.: A survey on cybersecurity knowledge graph construction. Comput. Secur. **136**, 103524 (2024). https://doi.org/10.1016/j.cose.2023.103524

6. Aone, C., Halverson, L., Hampton, T., Ramos-Santacruz, M.: SRA: description of the IE2 system used for MUC-7. In: Seventh Message Understanding Conference (MUC-7): Proceedings of a Conference Held in Fairfax, Virginia, 29 April–1 May 1998 (1998)

7. Fundel, K., Küffner, R., Zimmer, R.: RelEx—relation extraction using dependency parse trees. Bioinformatics **23**, 365–371 (2007)

8. Giuliano, C., Lavelli, A., Pighin, D., Romano, L.: FBK-IRST: kernel methods for semantic relation extraction. In: Proceedings of the Fourth International Workshop on Semantic Evaluations (SemEval-2007), pp. 141–144 (2007)

9. Gasmi, H., Laval, J., Bouras, A.: Information extraction of cybersecurity concepts: an LSTM approach. Appl. Sci. **9**, 3945 (2019)

10. Pingle, A., Piplai, A., Mittal, S., Joshi, A., Holt, J., Zak, R.: Relext: relation extraction using deep learning approaches for cybersecurity knowledge graph improvement. In: Proceedings of the 2019 IEEE/ACM International Conference on Advances in Social Networks Analysis and Mining, pp. 879–886 (2019)
11. Zhou, Y., et al.: Cdtier: a Chinese dataset of threat intelligence entity relationships. IEEE Trans. Sustain. Comput. **8**, 627–638 (2023)
12. Zelenko, D., Aone, C., Richardella, A.: Kernel methods for relation extraction. J. Mach. Learn. Res. **3**, 1083–1106 (2003). https://doi.org/10.3115/1118693.1118703
13. Chan, Y.S., Roth, D.: Exploiting syntactico-semantic structures for relation extraction, Portland, Oregon, USA (2011)
14. Miwa, M., Bansal, M.: End-to-end relation extraction using LSTMs on sequences and tree structures (2016). https://aclanthology.org/P16-1105/, https://doi.org/10.18653/v1/P16-1105
15. Katiyar, A., Cardie, C.: Going out on a limb: joint extraction of entity mentions and relations without dependency trees (2017). https://aclanthology.org/P17-1085/, https://doi.org/10.18653/v1/P17-1085
16. Zeng, X., Zeng, D., He, S., Liu, K., Zhao, J.: Extracting relational facts by an end-to-end neural model with copy mechanism (2018). https://aclanthology.org/P18-1047/, https://doi.org/10.18653/v1/P18-1047
17. Wei, Z., Su, J., Wang, Y., Tian, Y., Chang, Y.: A novel cascade binary tagging framework for relational triple extraction (2020). https://aclanthology.org/2020.acl-main.136/, https://doi.org/10.18653/v1/2020.acl-main.136
18. Jiang, M., Yang, C., Shang, H., Qin, Z., Wang, Z.: Improved CasRel model for joint extraction of geographical entity and overlapping space relation. Acta Geodaetica et Cartographica Sinica. **52**, 1387–1397 (2023)
19. Wang, Y., Yu, B., Zhang, Y., Liu, T., Zhu, H., Sun, L.: TPLinker: single-stage joint extraction of entities and relations through token pair linking (2020). https://aclanthology.org/2020.coling-main.138/, https://doi.org/10.18653/v1/2020.coling-main.138
20. Shang, Y.-M., Huang, H., Mao, X.: OneRel: joint entity and relation extraction with one module in one step. Proc. AAAI Conf. Artif. Intell. **36**, 11285–11293 (2022). https://doi.org/10.1609/aaai.v36i10.21379
21. Markus, E., Adrian, U.: Span-based joint entity and relation extraction with transformer pre-training. Front. Artif. Intell. Appl. IOS Press (2020). https://doi.org/10.3233/FAIA200321
22. Yu, B., et al.: Joint extraction of entities and relations based on a novel decomposition strategy (2020)

Dependency Tree-Based Multi-task Learning for Extracting Process Models in Safety Management

Xiaoyang Su[(✉)] and Yiping Wen[(✉)]

School of Computer Science and Engineering, Hunan University of Science and Technology, Xiangtan, China
`xiaoyangsu99@gmail.com, ypwen81@gmail.com`

Abstract. In safety management, process models are widely adopted to guide the implementation of safety-critical protocols. Extracting process models from text can help to enhance tasks such as compliance verification and risk assessment in safety management. However, existing process model extraction (PME) methods do not fully exploit syntactic dependency information in text structures, leading to limited modeling of contextual semantic relations. In this paper, we propose a dependency tree-based multi-task learning method for process models extraction (DT-MPME). It can effectively capture structural information within dependency tree and extract multi-granular features. Besides, an attention-weighted feature fusion layer is designed for efficiently integrating global, local, and hierarchical text features. The experimental results show that the proposed method outperforms existing mainstream approaches in terms of classification accuracy on two widely used datasets.

Keywords: Process Model Extraction · Attention Mechanism · Multi-Task Learning · Dependency Tree

1 Introduction

In recent years, process model extraction (PME) has attracted growing attention due to its potential to enhance organizational efficiency [1]. For example, modeling in network security incident response can facilitate timely analysis, optimized resource allocation, and enhanced security management [2]. Extracting process models from text can also reduce manual effort, save time, and improve cyber threat detection effectiveness. However, traditional process mining methods that are designed for structured event log analysis, face significant limitations in managing the exponentially growing volume and inherent complexity of unstructured data (e.g., text, images, and videos) due to their lack of predefined schemas and contextual variability [3, 4].

W. Liang et al. (Eds.): SecureComm 2025, LNICST 690, pp. 446–459, 2026.
https://doi.org/10.1007/978-3-032-23456-8_24

Therefore, developing novel automated methods for extracting process models is urgently required to advance automation technologies. These methods would provide both theoretical frameworks and practical solutions for enhancing safety management and supporting data-driven decision-making processes, ultimately improving organizational competitiveness.

The core task of PME is to identify and extract structured process information from process text. Figure 1 illustrates an example of the PME, which has three main steps. The initial step is text segmentation, wherein the process text is divided into short sentences containing only a single activity or relation. For instance, the sentence "When a security alert is triggered?" is a result of text segmentation. The subsequent step involves process information extraction, wherein decision conditions, process activities, and their interrelationships are extracted from these short sentences. The final step is model construction, where the process model is built from the process information.

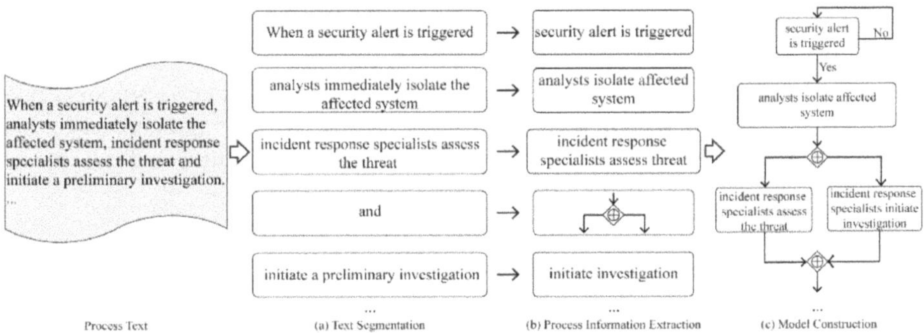

Fig. 1. An Example of extracting process model from text

Recent advances in deep learning-based studies indicate that neural network-based text classification effectively extracts process information without requiring manually defined features [5]. Another study developed automated methods for extracting UML activity diagrams by predicting time-activity relationships [6]. Additionally, Ordered Neurons Long Short-Term Memory (ON-LSTM) networks have been proposed to capture hierarchical text structures, thereby improving the identification of logical and hierarchical relationships among sentences [7]. However, the sequential learning design of ON-LSTM may constrain its ability to capture hierarchical relationships, thereby impacting the accuracy of latent hierarchy extraction. Furthermore, existing methods that integrate multi-source textual features often neglect balanced feature weighting, resulting in information redundancy or loss and consequently affecting model accuracy and robustness [5–7].

This study aims to optimize process model extraction by enhancing the representation and fusion of process information features, thereby improving extraction quality. It aims to accomplish two core objectives: (1) using dependency tree structures to enhance process information extraction accuracy; and (2) employing a multi-feature weighted fusion strategy to improve feature quality, thereby preventing information redundancy and the loss of key details.

Therefore, we propose a dependency tree-based multi-task learning method for PME. Our primary contributions include the following:

- We propose a dependency tree-based multi-task learning method for process models extraction (DT-MPME), which leverages dependency trees to capture hierarchical structures in texts. DT-MPME employs a multi-task learning module to classify key process elements, such as roles, activities, and conditions, and to extract their relationships, thereby improving extraction effectiveness.
- We design a multi-feature weighted fusion module based on a multi-head attention mechanism (MHA) to integrate process text features from multiple sources, thereby enhancing the quality of feature representation for process model extraction tasks.
- Experiments on the Cooking Recipes (COR) and Maintenance Manuals (MAM) datasets demonstrate that our model outbalance baseline methods in terms of classification accuracy.

2 Related Work

We review two related areas: (1) process model extraction, including traditional rule-based and pattern-based methods, as well as recent deep learning approaches; and (2) multi-task learning, emphasizing applications in text classification and information extraction.

2.1 Process Model Extraction Methods

Early research primarily adopted rule-based or pattern-matching approaches to extract process models from text [8–11]. These traditional methods typically rely on predefined syntactic rules and patterns and extract process elements by identifying keywords and syntactic structures in the text. Friedrich et al. [12] proposed an automated method that incorporates natural language processing tools, thereby enhancing the extraction quality of process models through improved co-reference resolution mechanisms. Ana et al. [13] developed the BPMN Sketch Miner tool, which further simplified the modeling process by enabling real-time extraction of BPMN diagrams from narrative descriptions. To enhance model robustness, Sholiq et al. [14] proposed a two-stage approach that integrates natural language processing with mapping rules, thereby improving the accuracy of converting text into BPMN diagrams through structured text analysis. Furthermore, some researchers have reexamined the process model extraction problem from a machine translation perspective. Sonbol et al. [15] proposed a translation method based on semantic transfer, which divides the process modeling task into two stages: knowledge extraction and model generation. This approach translates text into a model through semantic, syntactic, and morphological operations, achieving an 81% similarity between the extracted model and the manually crafted model.

Some researchers have focused on extracting structured data, such as spreadsheets [16, 17] and event logs [18], rather than directly extracting process models. Subsequently, they construct process models using traditional methods [19]. Geeganage et al. [18] innovatively designed the Text2EL method, which combines sentence embedding with context validation techniques to effectively transform unstructured text into structured data, thereby addressing the scarcity of log data in process mining. However, these methods generally rely on predefined transformation rules and extensive manual intervention, making it challenging to handle complex and variable natural language expressions and limiting their generalization across different domains [20].

In order to surmount the limitations of early conventional methodologies, researchers have begun to explore the application of deep learning techniques in PME. [21–24]. On one hand, researchers have not abandoned the use of rules and patterns but have instead proposed an integrated approach for extracting process information [25]. On the other hand, Chen et al. [5] were the first to establish a formalized framework for PME tasks, conceptualizing them as a multi-granularity text classification problem. They involved the development of a hierarchical neural network-based model architecture. This method employs a coarse-to-fine learning mechanism that improves the performance of fine-grained tasks through high-level knowledge sharing, thereby laying an important foundation for subsequent research. In addition, Zhu et al. [6] proposed the TAG method, which innovatively combines sequence labeling with graph neural networks. By leveraging multi-level semantic fusion, the approach improves the prediction accuracy of temporal activity relationships, thereby enabling the automatic extraction of UML activity diagrams. Experiments have shown that the approach achieved a prediction accuracy of 79.87% on standard datasets.

Recently, Han et al. [7] explored the BERT in process modeling and proposed an ON-LSTM-based text hierarchical structure retrieval method. This approach captures the hierarchical features of text by jointly performing language modeling and structural learning, and demonstrates strong performance on several public datasets. However, since ON-LSTM is essentially a sequential learning model, there is still room for improvement in its understanding of hierarchical structures. Furthermore, the adaptive balancing of feature weights when processing multi-source text features remains an unresolved challenge in existing deep learning methods. Recent analyses have indicated that deep learning techniques have been proven to be highly effective in enhancing the generalizability and adaptability of models; however, there remains substantial room for improvement in hierarchical structure learning and feature fusion. These observations provide both the research motivation and a theoretical foundation for the process model extraction method proposed in this paper.

2.2 Multi-task Learning Methods of PME

Multi-task learning (MTL) is a machine learning approach designed to improve the generalization of all tasks by learning them together and sharing relevant information between them. [26]. Compared to treating multiple classification tasks independently, multi-task learning methods can share knowledge more effectively across tasks and learn more robust and generalizable feature representations, thereby improving classification accuracy. By sharing features, parameters, or instances, MTL can more effectively capture latent relationships among tasks, modeling the common features of related tasks and making the classification models more efficient. Han et al. [7] proposed an ON-LSTM-based method that retrieves process text structures using a deep learning model and jointly extracts process activity attributes and relationships. Etikala et al. [12] introduced a parallel task framework for extracting business decision process models, which first classifies sentences and then extracts decision logic and dependency relationships based on sentence categories. However, this approach does not incorporate knowledge sharing among multiple tasks, thereby leading to ineffective modeling of task correlations. Chen et al. [5] introduced a multi-granularity text classification approach that was the first to incorporate a multi-task learning framework into the process model extraction task. Their method enables the sharing of coarse-grained knowledge captured by deep learning models with fine-grained tasks, thereby establishing correlations among multiple sub-tasks.

Although research on multi-task learning in process model extraction is limited, existing studies have confirmed its effectiveness, thereby providing theoretical support for our proposed approach. Furthermore, an analysis of the current situation research in PME and MTL reveals significant room for improvement in handling textual hierarchical structures and feature fusion. These findings provide both the theoretical basis and the innovative impetus for our proposed dependency tree-based MTL model.

3   Methodology

In this study, we propose a method for PME. It integrates dependency tree structures with multi-dimensional feature extraction, weighted multi-dimensional fusion, and multi-task learning mechanisms to enhance both extraction accuracy and efficiency. Section 3.1 defines the three sub-tasks of the process model extraction task, and Sect. 3.2 describes the modules and their implementation.

3.1   Task Definition

The PME task can be modeled as a text classification problem with multiple levels of granularity [5]. The process text was defined as $Text = (S_1, S_2, ..., S_n)$, where each sentence $Si = (W_{1i}, W_{2i}, ..., W_{ni})$ is a sequence of words. The sentence labels are described as:

$$sLabel = \{sType, sRel, sAttrs\} \tag{1}$$

The sType indicates the category of the individual sentence, sRel represents the relationship of sentences, and sAttrs indicate the attributes of the sentence that are useful for parsing the process model. Therefore, the PME task can be viewed as the following three sub-tasks:

- ST1: classification of the individual sentence.
- ST2: classification of the relationship of sentences.
- ST3: classification of the attribute of each activity within the sentences.

ST1: Sentence classification is critical for process information extraction, as it determines whether sentences participate in subsequent tasks, such as relationship recognition or activity attribute identification. To simplify text parsing, sentence categories are described as:

$$Labels\ of\ sType = \{Act, Rel\} \tag{2}$$

- Act: This type of sentence contains specific details of the action in the procedure, usually describing who carried out what task and to whom.
- Rel: This type of sentence defines the relationship between the previous and subsequent sentences, usually expressed by conjunctions or time-verbal.

ST2: Sentence relationship classification aims to identify semantic associations between sentences in process texts, constituting a key step in constructing complete process models. This task classifies sentences labeled Rel to establish logical sequences or associations between consecutive sentences. Sentence relationship categories are described as:

$$\text{Labels of sRel} = \{\text{Sequential, Exclusive, Parallel}\} \tag{3}$$

- Sequential: This type of relation indicates that the actions described in the preceding and following sentences occur in a temporal or logical sequence.
- Exclusive: This type of relation indicates that the actions described in two sentences are mutually exclusive events, with only one scenario occurring.
- Parallel: This type of relation indicates that the actions described in the preceding and following sentences occur simultaneously.

ST3: Activity attribute classification aims to determine the specific attributes of each activity within the sentences, serving as a crucial component in parsing process models. The activity attribute categories are described as:

$$\text{Labels of sAttrs} = \{\text{None, Role, Acrion, Object}\} \tag{4}$$

- None: Denotes the information is not relevant to the process model;
- Role: Denotes the executor in the process activity;
- Action: Denotes the behavior in the process activity;
- Object: Denotes the target object in the process activity acts.

3.2 Overall Framework

A process model normally consists of two fundamental elements: activity attributes and activity relationships. Existing extraction methods can be broadly categorized into independent and joint approaches. While independent methods achieve satisfactory performance on individual tasks, they often overlook task correlations, thereby limiting overall performance. We suggest an approach that utilizes a dependency tree for multi-task learning, adept at extracting both attributes and relationships of activities while employing shared features to improve the extraction's efficiency.

As shown in Fig. 2, initially, we encode the process text using a BERT model. Next, we employ a multi-granularity feature extraction module, consisting of parallel Bidirectional Long Short-Term Memory (Bi-LSTM) and Convolutional Neural Network (CNN), to extract both global and local features from the text. The Bi-LSTM network

452   X. Su and Y. Wen

captures the sentence's global features, while the CNN captures its n-gram features. In addition, we incorporate the dependency tree structure and semantic features into a Graph Convolutional Network (GCN) to model the text's hierarchical structure. Subsequently, we construct a multi-feature weighted fusion layer to process the global, n-gram, and hierarchical features to enhance the quality of the text representations. Finally, we adopt a multi-task deep learning framework and design three text classification sub-tasks, in which a multi-layer perceptron (MLP) maps the features to category probabilities.

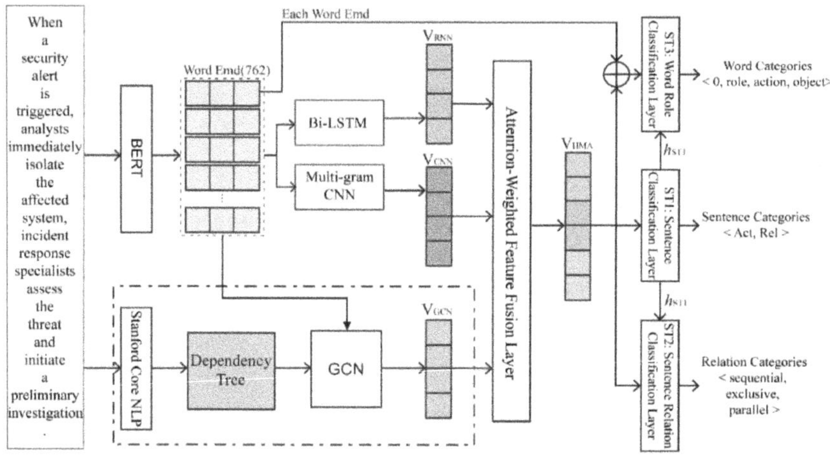

Fig. 2. Dependency Tree-based Multi-task Learning Method for Process Models Extraction

Multi-granular Feature Extraction Based on Bi-LSTM and CNN: In this work, the multi-granularity feature extraction layer comprises a Bi-LSTM and a CNN, fully leveraging the strengths of both architectures. Specifically, the Bi-LSTM captures long-term dependencies and extracts global contextual information (denoted as V_{RNN}) from both directions of a sentence, while the CNN focuses on extracting local n-gram features (denoted as V_{CNN}) to identify fine-grained local patterns in the text. The implementation of this fusion strategy facilitates the comprehension of the semantic structure of the entire sentence by the model and ensures the accurate capture of crucial local details, thereby providing a richer and more precise representation for sentence-level tasks. Thus, it establishes an efficient and robust feature foundation for downstream multi-task learning, significantly enhancing the overall performance in classification and semantic recognition [5]. V_{RNN} and V_{CNN} are formulated as:

$$V_{RNN} = \overrightarrow{LSTM(w_j^i)} + \overleftarrow{LSTM(w_j^i)} \tag{5}$$

$$V_{CNN} = [\max(v_1),\ \max(v_2),\ \max(v_3)] \tag{6}$$

where $\overrightarrow{LSTM(\cdot)}$ and $\overleftarrow{LSTM(\cdot)}$ denote the LSTM processing the text sequence in two-way orders, respectively. w_j^i Represents the feature vector of the word obtained through

BERT encoding. The function $max(\bullet)$ indicates a pooling operation, and v_1, v_2, v_3 correspond to the feature maps generated by convolution kernels of lengths 1, 2, and 3, respectively.

Structural Feature Extraction Based on Dependency Tree: We apply a dependency tree combined with a Graph Convolutional Network (GCN) to extract features from the text's hierarchical structure, improving the model's grasp of the textual framework. The GCN effectively captures complex relationships between words in the text, demonstrating a strong capability to capture dependencies among non-adjacent words. Within a GCN, information is effectively propagated between nodes, enabling the model to capture the text's hierarchical structure and semantic relationships more efficiently. This capability is crucial for improving performance on complex text tasks, particularly in processing procedural texts. In particular, the GCN significantly enhances the model's understanding on text structure and provides robust support for subsequent multi-task learning.

In addition, the dependency tree is stored in the form of matrices and vectors, where the enhanced adjacency matrix $\widehat{A}$ for a sentence is obtained by adding the original adjacency matrix to the identity matrix, and the tree nodes correspond to the word vectors w_j^i. The GCN process is formulated as:

$$h_{x_k}^{(L+1)} = \varphi(\Sigma_{j=1}^{n} c^{x_k} \widehat{A}_{x_k j}(W^{(L)} h_j^{(L)} + b^{(L)})) \tag{7}$$

$$V_{GCN} = [h_{z_1}^{(max)}, h_{z_2}^{(max)}, \cdots, h_z^{(max)}] \tag{8}$$

where $b^{(L)}$ represents the bias term, and $W^{(L)}$ is the parameter matrix that is learned during the training process. $h_{x_k}^{(L)}$ Represents the hidden feature of node x_k at L layer in the GCN, while c^{x_k} is a normalization constant, which we set as $c^{x_k} = 1/d^{x_k}$. The term d^{x_k} represents the graph degree of node and is computed as $d^{x_k} = \sum_{j=1}^{n} A_{x_k j}$. The function $\varphi(\bullet)$ denotes the ReLU non-linear activation function. After L layers of graph convolution, the feature output of node x_k is given by $h_{x_k}^{(L+1)}$. To distinguish the output layer, we denote its node as z_k, and $h_{z_k}^{(max)}$ represents the final output feature of the node.

The attention-weighted feature fusion layer, which is composed of MHA, is designed to integrate global, local, and hierarchical text features through a unified attention framework. It can capture multi-dimensional information and adaptively adjust the importance of various features within the task. Global features contribute to understanding the overall semantics of the text, local features capture lexical details, and hierarchical structural features reveal intrinsic connections within the text's organizational framework. Therefore, dynamically assigning different weights to these features is crucial. By adjusting feature weights with the MHA, the model not only prevents conflicts or loss of information but also improves its ability to capture semantics and enhance classification accuracy, thereby significantly boosting the overall effectiveness of process information extraction.

We split the different feature matrices extracted from the text and input them into MHA for weighted fusion.

$$[V_{RNN}, V_{CNN}, V_{GCN}] = [Z_1, Z_2, \cdots, Z_n] \tag{9}$$

where $Z_i(i \in [1, n])$ represents the text features of attention head input.

Subsequently, we map the input of each attention head to (Q_i, K_i, V_i) via a linear transformation as follows:

$$Q_i = X_i \bullet W_i^Q; K_i = X_i \bullet W_i^K; V_i = X_i \bullet W_i^V \tag{10}$$

where, W_i^Q, W_i^K and $W_i^V \in \mathbb{R}^{\frac{3d}{n} \times d_r}$ represent the parameter matrices for the i_{th} attention head in the MHA. Here, dd denotes the dim of the vector corresponding to each individual feature source of a word, and d_r is the dimension of the mapped (Q_i, K_i, V_i).

Next, we compute the attention weights of each attention head and splice the outputs of all heads. V_{HMA} is formulated as:

$$head_i = softmax(\frac{Q_i(K_i)^T}{\sqrt{d_n}})V_i \tag{11}$$

$$V_{HMA} = Concat(head_1, \cdots, head_n)W_o \tag{12}$$

where T denotes the transpose of a matrix. W_o is output weight

The output layer consists of multiple sub-task output modules that are designed to fuse the V_{HMA} features into the final prediction results. Since the output of ST1 determines the subsequent processing pathway for the sentence, we assign a higher priority to ST1 within the framework. ST1's output are formulated as:

$$h_{ST1} = W_{ST1}^1 \bullet V_{HMA} + b_{ST1}^1 \tag{13}$$

$$O_{ST1} = softmax(W_{ST1}^2 \bullet h_{ST1} + b_{ST1}^2) \tag{14}$$

$$softmax(\bullet) = \frac{\exp(\bullet)}{\sum_{i=1}^{T}\exp(\bullet)} \tag{15}$$

where h_{ST1} is the hidden layer output of the ST1 task, and the output O_{ST1} represents the probability distribution over the sentence categories. W_{ST1}^1, b_{ST1}^1, W_{ST1}^2 and b_{ST1}^2 are the parameters for the first and second layers of the MLP, respectively. The symbol T denotes the class number of each classification task.

Furthermore, the hidden features from ST1 are integrated into the input representation of ST2 to model the conditional relationship between two classification subtasks. ST1's output is formulated as:

$$O_{ST2} = softmax(W_{ST2}^2 \bullet (W_{ST2}^1 \bullet (V_{HMA} + h_{ST1}) + b_{ST2}^1) + b_{ST2}^2) \tag{16}$$

To satisfy the word-level feature requirements of the ST3 task, we extend the integration of ST1 hidden features by incorporating the corresponding word features w_j^i as supplementary training inputs. ST1's output is formulated as:

$$O_{ST3} = softmax(W_{ST3}^2 \bullet (W_{ST3}^1 \bullet (V_{HMA} + h_{ST1} + w_j^i) + b_{ST3}^1) + b_{ST3}^2) \tag{17}$$

Note that during the ST3 training phase, the parameters training of ST2 have been frozen, thereby preventing ST3's training from disrupting the parameters already learned by ST2 and maintaining the stability of ST2's performance.

The cross-entropy loss function is utilized in each training phase. The training data for the network model is designated as $\{x_k, y_k, e_k\}$, where x_k is the k_{th} training data to be predicted, y_k represents the ground-truth type in one-hot format, and e_k is the model's predicted outcome. The objective of the training phase is to minimize the loss function. Loss functions of ST1 and ST2 are formulated as:

$$L(\theta_1, \theta_2) = -\lambda_1 \sum_{i=1}^{M} \sum_{t_1=1}^{t_1=T_1} y_k^{t_1} \bullet \log(e_k^{t_1}) - \lambda_2 \sum_{i=1}^{M} \sum_{t_2=T_1+1}^{t_2=T_1+T_2} y_k^{t_2} \bullet \log(e_k^{t_2}) \tag{18}$$

$$\lambda_1 + \lambda_2 = 1(\lambda_1, \lambda_2 \geq 0) \tag{19}$$

where M is the volume of training samples, while T_1 and T_2 correspond to the number of classification categories for ST1 and ST2, respectively. λ_1, λ_2 are linear balancing parameters. The MTL stage can be subdivided into the sequential learning of two distinct tasks. ST3's loss function is formulated as:

$$L(\theta_3) = -\sum_{i} \sum_{t_3=1}^{t_3=T_3} y_k^{t_3} \bullet \log(e_k^{t_3}) \tag{20}$$

where M is the volume of training samples, while T3 corresponds to the number of classification categories for ST3.

4 Experiments

4.1 Datasets

We conducted experiments on two datasets: Cooking Recipes (COR) and Maintenance Manuals (MAM) [5]. These datasets comprise a sentence category annotation set SC, a relation category annotation set SSR, and an activity role annotation set SRL, all designed for multi-task learning. Details of the datasets are shown in Table 1.

Table 1. Datasets Statistics

	COR	MAM
# Annotated Sentences	2636	2172
# Annotated Words	14260	20612
# Sentence Categories	2	2
# Relationship Categories	3	3
# Word Categories	4	4

4.2 Baselines

We selected several representative baselines:

- A ON-LSTM based method (A-BPS) [7], which introduces an ordered neural network approach for joint language modeling.
- A language-rule based method (ARWE) [27], which uses a lexical strategy along with two other methods, derived from analyzing a workflow corpus through statistical methods to develop a set of association rules.
- A multi-granularity text categorization based methods (MGTC) [5], which introduces a knowledge-sharing training approach that considers the influence of high-level task knowledge on low-level tasks.

4.3 Overall Performance

We assessed the classification accuracy of DT-MPME against baseline methods and various alterations.

To validate the effectiveness of the text hierarchical feature extraction module and the text feature weighted fusion module, we conducted an ablation study on the DT-MPME model. The lower-part of Table 2 displays the experimental results of tasks on two datasets, where the symbol "\" is used to indicate the removal of the corresponding module from the model. The experimental results demonstrate that removing any module from the approach to a marked decrease in the precision and reliability of extracting information and models from processes. It substantiates the pivotal function of these two modules in augmenting model performance.

Table 2. Experimental results (Acc; %) of all baselines, DT-MPME and its variants. Gate, C2f, OPM, ARM, and FMS denote the mechanisms applied in references.

Method	Tasks & Datasets							
	ST1 (%)		ST2 (%)		ST3 (%)		PME	
	COR	MAM	COR	MAM	COR	MAM	COR	MAM
A-BPS + ON-LSTM	-	-	60.74	64.76	77.30	77.37	34.69	35.89
MGTC	93.34	91.74	91.53	86.49	82.39	80.44	**77.40**	**75.77**
MGTC\Gate	90.37	88.58	89.40	84.57	77.62	76.42	67.39	71.64
MGTC\C2F	91.55	89.45	88.31	84.53	79.44	76.22	74.46	72.29
ARWE + OPM	70.66	60.46	62.43	62.45	58.46	61.62	52.46	51.09
ARWE + OPM + ARM	76.39	69.51	56.52	72.53	71.38	77.62	65.21	59.50
ARWE + OPM + ARM + FMS	71.63	69.60	61.37	64.48	72.64	78.26	69.57	66.11
DT-MPME	**94.46**	**95.31**	**93.78**	**94.35**	**89.76**	**90.14**	82.59	87.43
DT-MPME\GCN	93.51	93.79	91.87	91.67	83.96	82.87	79.77	78.34

(continued)

Table 2. (*continued*)

Method	Tasks & Datasets							
	ST1 (%)		ST2 (%)		ST3 (%)		PME	
	COR	MAM	COR	MAM	COR	MAM	COR	MAM
DT-MPME\HMA	93.83	94.45	93.21	93.45	88.76	88.15	81.19	80.63

As shown in Table 2, the proposed DT-MPME model significantly outperformed the other comparative methods across all sub-tasks. In the ST1, DT-MPME improved classification accuracy by 1.12% on the COR and 3.57% on the MAM. In the ST2, accuracy increased by 2.25% and 7.86% on COR and MAM, respectively, while in the ST3, improvements of 7.37% and 9.70% were achieved on COR and MAM, respectively. We believe that because the dependency tree primarily provides relational information between words, it yields a more significant accuracy boost in the ST3 task. On the accuracy of PME [5, 28], DT-MPME outperformed COR and MAM by 5.19% and 11.66%, respectively. This further demonstrates that the proposed method extracts process models more accurately, thereby reducing labor and time costs and offering significant benefits for process management research.

4.4 Further Investigation

To investigate the effect of GCN layer on DT-MPME, we conducted comparative experiments with different layer configurations. Figure 3 shows the accuracy comparison for each sub-task under various GCN layer settings.

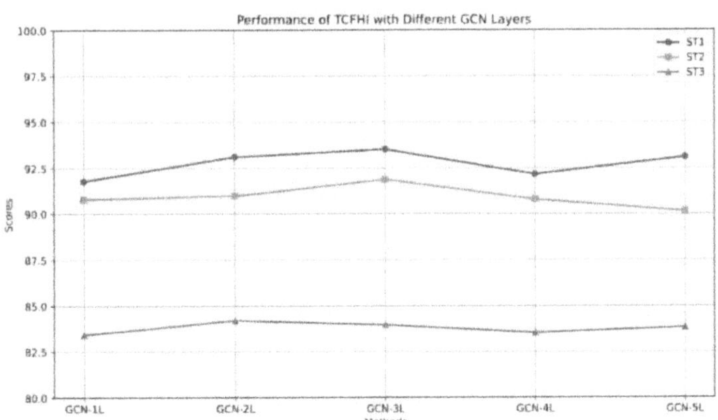

Fig. 3. The effect of number of GCN layers in the DT-MPME method

Experimental results indicate that a 3-layer GCN network yields the best performance in extracting hierarchical features. As shown in the line chart, the accuracy of the sub-tasks' peaks at $L = 3$ and declines thereafter. Thus, a 3-layer GCN network is optimal for feature extraction.

5 Discussion and Conclusion

In this paper, we propose a dependency tree-based multi-task learning method for automatically extracting process models from text. It integrates multi-granularity feature extraction, hierarchical structure modeling using dependency trees, and MHA. Experiment results on two datasets show that our proposed effectively enhances feature extraction and fusion, thereby improving classification method accuracy.

Acknowledgments. This work was supported by the National Natural Science Foundation of China (No. 62177014), and the Hunan University of Science and Technology Excellence Scholar Program (No. 402-SZ2408).

References

1. Text="CE: Unable to parse this reference. Kindly do manual structure" Schüler, S., Alpers, S.: State of the art: automatic generation of business process models. In: De Weerdt, J., Pufahl, L. (eds.) Business Process Management Workshops, pp. 161–173. Springer, Cham (2024)
2. Elkoumy, G., et al.: Privacy and confidentiality in process mining -- threats and research challenges. ACM Trans. Manag. Inf. Syst. **13**, 1–17 (2022)
3. Koschmider, A., et al.: Process Mining for Unstructured Data: Challenges and Research Directions (2024)
4. Adnan, K., Akbar, R.: An analytical study of information extraction from unstructured and multidimensional big data. J. Big Data **6**, 91 (2019)
5. Qian, C., Wen, L., Long, M., Li, Y., Kumar, A., Wang, J.: Process extraction from texts via multi-task architecture. arXiv. abs/1906.02127, null (2019)
6. Zhu, R., Li, W., Jin, C.: TAG: UML activity diagram deeply supervised generation from business textual specification. In: 2023 IEEE International Conference on Software Analysis, Evolution and Reengineering (SANER), pp. 956–961. IEEE, Taipa, Macao (2023)
7. Han, X., et al.: A-BPS: automatic business process discovery service using ordered neurons LSTM. In: 2020 IEEE International Conference on Web Services (ICWS), pp. 428–432. IEEE, Beijing, China (2020)
8. Wang, W., Chen, T., Indulska, M., Sadiq, S., Weber, B.: Business process and rule integration approaches—an empirical analysis of model understanding. Inf. Syst. **104**, 101901 (2022)
9. Robrecht, A., Kopp, S.: SNAPE: a sequential non-stationary decision process model for adaptive explanation generation: In: Proceedings of the 15th International Conference on Agents and Artificial Intelligence, pp. 48–58. SCITEPRESS - Science and Technology Publications, Lisbon, Portugal (2023)
10. Abbad Andaloussi, A., Buch-Lorentsen, J., López, H.A., Slaats, T., Weber, B.: Exploring the modeling of declarative processes using a hybrid approach. In: Laender, A.H.F., Pernici, B., Lim, E.-P., De Oliveira, J.P.M. (eds.) ER 2019. LNCS, vol. 11788, pp. 162–170. Springer, Cham (2019). https://doi.org/10.1007/978-3-030-33223-5_14
11. Ferreira, R.C.B., Thom, L.H., De Oliveira, J.P.M., Avila, D.T., Dos Santos, R.I., Fantinato, M.: Assisting process modeling by identifying business process elements in natural language texts. In: De Cesare, S., Frank, U. (eds.) ER 2017. LNCS, vol. 10651, pp. 154–163. Springer, Cham (2017). https://doi.org/10.1007/978-3-319-70625-2_15
12. Etikala, V.: Extracting Decision Model Components from Natural Language Text for Automated Business Decision Modelling

13. Ivanchikj, A., Serbout, S., Pautasso, C.: From text to visual BPMN process models: design and evaluation. In: Proceedings of the 23rd ACM/IEEE International Conference on Model Driven Engineering Languages and Systems, pp. 229–239. ACM, Virtual Event Canada (2020)
14. Sholiq, S., Sarno, R., Astuti, E.S.: Generating BPMN diagram from textual requirements. J. King Saud Univ. – Comput. Inf. Sci. **34**, 10079–10093 (2022)
15. Sonbol, R., Ghaida, R., Nada, G.: A machine translation like approach to generate business process model from textual description. SN Comput. Sci. (2022)
16. Ferreira, R.C.B., Thom, L.H., Fantinato, M.: A semi-automatic approach to identify business process elements in natural language texts: In: Proceedings of the 19th International Conference on Enterprise Information Systems, pp. 250–261. SCITEPRESS - Science and Technology Publications, Porto, Portugal (2017)
17. Honkisz, K., Kluza, K., Wisniewski, P.: A Concept for Generating Business Process Models from Natural Language Description (2018)
18. Geeganage, D.T.K., Wynn, M.T., Ter Hofstede, A.H.M.: Text2EL: exploiting unstructured text for event log enrichment. In: 2022 16th International Conference on Signal-Image Technology and Internet-Based Systems (SITIS), pp. 1–8. IEEE, Dijon, France (2022)
19. Bellan, P., Dragoni, M., Ghidini, C.: A Qualitative Analysis of the State of the Art in Process Extraction from Text
20. Vacareanu, R., Valenzuela-Escarcega, M.A., Barbosa, G.C.G., Sharp, R., Surdeanu, M.: From Examples to Rules: Neural Guided Rule Synthesis for Information Extraction (2022). http://arxiv.org/abs/2202.00475
21. Zhu, R., Liu, H., Xu, X., Lin, L., Chen, Y., Li, W.: A-PGRD: attention-based automatic business process model generation from RPA process description. Concurr. Comput. **36**, e7940 (2024)
22. Bombieri, M., Rospocher, M., Ponzetto, S.P., Fiorini, P.: Machine understanding surgical actions from intervention procedure textbooks. Comput. Biol. Med. **152**, 106415 (2023)
23. Licardo, J.T., Tanković, N., Etinger, D.: A method for extracting BPMN models from textual descriptions using natural language processing. Procedia Comput. Sci. **239**, 483–490 (2024)
24. Lin, L., Jin, Y., Zhou, Y., Chen, W., Qian, C.: MAO: A Framework for Process Model Generation with Multi-agent Orchestration (2024). http://arxiv.org/abs/2408.01916
25. Freyer, N., Thewes, D., Meinecke, M.: GUIDO: A Hybrid Approach to Guideline Discovery & Ordering from Natural Language Texts (2023)
26. Zhang, Y., Yang, Q.: A Survey on Multi-task Learning (2021). http://arxiv.org/abs/1707.08114
27. Schumacher, P., Minor, M., Schulte-Zurhausen, E.: On the use of anaphora resolution for workflow extraction. In: Bouabana-Tebibel, T., Rubin, S.H. (eds.) Integration of Reusable Systems, vol. 263, pp. 151–170. Springer, Cham (2014). https://doi.org/10.1007/978-3-319-04717-1_7
28. Weidlich, M., Mendling, J., Weske, M.: Efficient consistency measurement based on behavioral profiles of process models. IEEE Trans. Softw. Eng. **37**, 410–429 (2011)

Joint Beamforming and Reflection Design for Physical Layer Security in RIS-Assisted Integrated Sensing and Communication Systems

Sitong Guo[1,2], Hao Zheng[1,2(✉)], Yinghui Zhang[1,2], and Junkun Yan[3]

[1] College of Electronic Information Engineering, Inner Mongolia University, Hohhot, China
`zhenghao1994@imu.edu.cn`
[2] Inner Mongolia Key Laboratory of Intelligent Communication and Sensing and Signal Processing, Inner Mongolia University, Hohhot 010021, China
[3] National Laboratory of Radar Signal Processing, Xidian University, Xi'an 710071, China

Abstract. Integrated Sensing and Communication (ISAC) has been identified as a promising candidate for 6th Generation networks. However, one of the key challenges with ISAC systems is the potential for communication information to be intercepted by malicious sensing targets, which raises concerns about the security of the transmitted data. In this context, the concept of Reconfigurable Intelligent Surfaces (RIS) offers a novel solution, as it can dynamically manipulate the wireless environment, thereby assisting in improving the physical layer security of ISAC systems. This study focuses on the RIS-assisted ISAC system, which is responsible for both communicating with several legitimate users and detecting various malicious sensing targets. Maximizing the sum secrecy rate of the system is achieved through the optimization of both the transmitting beamforming matrix at the base station (BS) and the phase shift matrix of the RIS, subject to constraints on the gain of the sensing beampattern, the attainable sum-rate for communication users, power restrictions of BS, and the reflection coefficients of the RIS. To effectively address this intricate optimization task, an alternating optimization method is applied, which integrates semi-definite relaxation with successive convex approximation techniques. The results from simulations demonstrate that the approach based on RIS significantly enhances security performance in comparison to random RIS scheme and without RIS scheme.

This work was supported by the National Natural Science Foundation of China 62461047, 62071345, 62361046, 62371264, Natural Science Foundation of Inner Mongolia Autonomous Region of China 2023QN06003 and 2021JQ07, Young Talents of Science and Technology in Universities of Inner Mongolia Autonomous Region NJYT22109, Training Plan for Young Innovative of Grassland Talents Project in Inner Mongolia Autonomous Region Q2022003, Innovation Capability Support Program of Shaanxi 2023KJXX-015.

W. Liang et al. (Eds.): SecureComm 2025, LNICST 690, pp. 460–475, 2026.
https://doi.org/10.1007/978-3-032-23456-8_25

Keywords: Integrated Sensing and Communication · Reconfigurable
Intelligent Surfaces · Physical Layer Security · Secrecy Rate

1   Introduction

The issue of wireless spectrum scarcity is obviously solved by Integrated Sensing and Communication(ISAC) for 6th Generation networks [1]. ISAC system is defined as sharing spectrum bands by integration on a unified platform of communication and radar functions [2]. Such integration, though proven to be useful, also proves to be a security vulnerability. More specifically, the base station (BS) broadcasts critical information for both communication users (CUs) and sensing targets at the same, which may allow malicious sensing targets to know the sensitive information and leak to the outside. These issues all pose critical challenges for physical layer security (PLS) [3].

To address these key challenges, Reconfigurable Intelligent Surfaces (RIS) are integrated into ISAC systems [4]. By generating virtual Line-of-Sight (LoS) links for the Non Line of Sight (NLoS) targets, RIS dynamically manages the wireless environment and removes the signal obstructions which are typical of millimetre wave frequencies in ISAC systems [5]. Further, RIS provides quality of service (QoS) for legitimate users and restricts QoS to potential eavesdroppers. This approach significantly boosts the security capabilities of ISAC systems.

Given the significant advantages of RIS, its integration into ISAC systems has generated considerable interest in academic research. Many studies have primarily concentrated on optimizing communication performance while ensuring that the sensing requirements are met [6–10]. For example, some works have utilized RIS to enhance the total achievable sum-rate for CUs [6,7], improve the signal-to-noise ratios (SNR) of CUs [8,9], and reduce multi-user interference (MUI) among the CUs [10]. Despite these efforts, the issue of PLS has not been extensively addressed in most existing studies. Some researchers have acknowledged the potential threat posed by sensing targets, considering them as eavesdroppers and exploring initial solutions within a joint communication, sensing, and secrecy rate (C&S&S) optimization framework [11–13]. However, these studies primarily focused on scenarios where RIS is deployed solely near communication users, without facilitating the establishment of reflection links for the sensing targets. This limitation compromises the performance of the sensing aspect of the system. Moreover, the existing works typically assume a single sensing target, while in practical applications, multiple sensing targets often exist. The presence of several eavesdroppers significantly increases the risk of information leakage, making PLS concerns even more critical.

To the best of current knowledge, there is a lack of comprehensive studies that ensure the balanced performance of both sensing and communication while maintaining security in RIS-assisted ISAC systems, especially when multiple sensing targets are involved. Building on previous research, this paper presents a holistic joint optimization approach for C&S&S in RIS-assisted ISAC systems. In particular, the paper addresses PLS challenges in a system where communication occurs with several legitimate CUs, while detecting multiple malicious sensing targets located in the NLoS region of the BS. The optimization problem involves jointly designing the transmitting beamforming matrix at BS and the phase shift matrix of RIS to maximize the secrecy rate (SR), while adhering to several constraints: the sensing beampattern gain, the achievable sum-rate for CUs, the power budget of the system, and the RIS reflection coefficient. A novel alternative optimization (AO) algorithm improves RIS-assisted security performance.

The manuscript is organized in the subsequent sections. Section 2 elaborates on the signal model and delineates the optimization problem. In Sect. 3, the introduced algorithm is utilized to address the optimization challenge. Section 4 presents the simulation outcomes, and Sect. 5 concludes the study.

2 System Model and Problem Formulation

Referring to the Fig. 1, an RIS-assisted ISAC system is considered in this paper. The system is composed of a BS with M transmit/receive antennas in uniform linear array, an RIS with N reflecting elements, K single-antenna legitimate CUs, and L single-antenna sensing targets (Eves). The BS communicates with multiple CUs and detects multiple sensing targets (Eves), while the Eve can eavesdrop the message from BS to CUs. Assuming the sensing targets are in the blind zone of the BS, the LOS links between the targets and the BS are established through the RIS, while the direct links between the BS and targets are blocked. Moreover, additional LOS links for legitimate CUs are also created by the RIS. Besides, we assume that the transmission links between target and users are blocked.

2.1 Signal Model

The received signal at the user can be expressed as

$$y_k = \left(\mathbf{h}_k^{\mathrm{H}} + \mathbf{g}_k^{\mathrm{H}}\boldsymbol{\Theta}\mathbf{G}\right)\mathbf{W}\mathbf{s} + n_k, \tag{1}$$

where $n_k \sim \mathcal{CN}\left(0,\sigma_k^2\right)$ is the noise at the receiver of CUs. $\mathbf{W} = \left[\mathbf{w_1},\mathbf{w_2},...,\mathbf{w_k}\right] \in \mathbb{C}^{M\times K}$ is the beamforming matrix, with each column corresponding to the beamforming vector for each user. $\mathbf{s} \in \mathbb{C}^K$ is the desired symbol vector of users with $\mathrm{E}\left\{\mathbf{s}\mathbf{s}^{\mathrm{H}}\right\} = \mathbf{I}_K$.

$\boldsymbol{\Theta} = \mathrm{diag}\left(\beta_1 e^{j\theta_1}, \cdots, \beta_N e^{j\theta_N}\right) \in \mathbb{C}^{N\times N}$ represents the RIS diagonal phase shift matrix, where $\beta_n \in [0,1]$, $\theta_n \in [0,2\pi]$. $\mathbf{h}_k \in \mathbb{C}^{M\times 1}$, $\mathbf{g}_k \in \mathbb{C}^{N\times 1}$ and $\mathbf{G} \in \mathbb{C}^{N\times M}$ are channels of the BS-CUs, RIS-CUs, BS-RIS links. $\mathbf{h}_k = \sqrt{\beta d_{BC}{}^{-\alpha_{BC}}}\mathbf{f}_h$, $\mathbf{g}_k = \sqrt{\beta d_{RC}{}^{-\alpha_{RC}}}\mathbf{f}_g$ and $\mathbf{G} = \sqrt{\beta d_{BR}^{-\alpha_{BR}}}\mathbf{f}_G$. β is the channel power gain of unit distance. d_{BC}, d_{BR}, d_{RC} denote actual distance from BS to CUs, from BS to RIS, and from RIS to CUs respectively. The path loss exponent is α. $\mathbf{f}_h$ is Rayleigh fading vectors. $\mathbf{f}_g$ and $\mathbf{f}_G$ represent Rician fading vectors [14].

Likewise, the received signal at Eve(target) can be expressed as

$$y_{e,l} = \eta\mathbf{a}^{\mathrm{H}}(\theta_l)\boldsymbol{\Theta}\mathbf{G}\mathbf{W}\mathbf{s} + n_e, \tag{2}$$

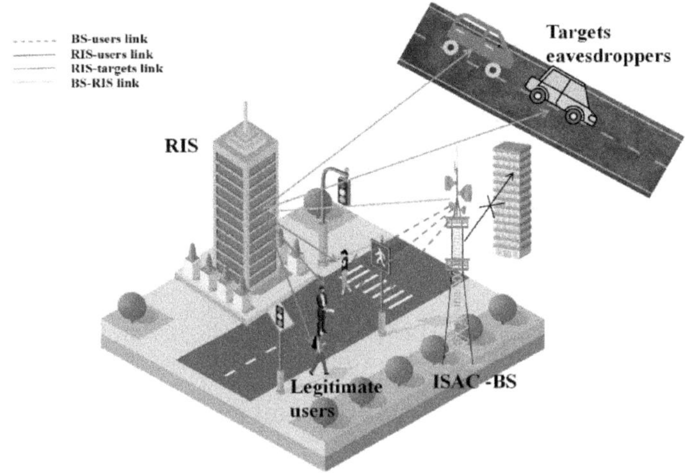

Fig. 1. System model.

where $n_e \sim \mathcal{CN}\left(0, \sigma_e^2\right)$ denotes the noise at the sensing target, η is the complex target amplitude. $\mathbf{a}(\theta_l) \triangleq \left[1, e^{j\Delta \sin(\theta_l)}, \ldots, e^{j(N-1)\Delta \sin(\theta_l)}\right]^{\mathrm{T}} \in \mathbb{C}^{N \times 1}$ denotes the steering vector of the RIS reflecting elements at direction θ_l, where θ_l and Δ represent the azimuth angle of the target and the normalized interval between adjacent antennas respectively.

2.2 Metrics

Based on the previously described system model, the SINR_k of the user k can be written as

$$\mathrm{SINR}_k = \frac{\left|\mathbf{t}_k^{\mathrm{H}} \mathbf{w}_k\right|^2}{\sum_{j \neq k, j \neq 1}^{K} \left|\mathbf{t}_k^{\mathrm{H}} \mathbf{w}_j\right|^2 + \sigma_k^2}, \tag{3}$$

where $\mathbf{t}_k = \left(\mathbf{h}_k^{\mathrm{H}} + \mathbf{g}_k^{\mathrm{H}} \boldsymbol{\Theta} \mathbf{G}\right)^{\mathrm{H}}$ is denoted for convenience.

The achievable transmission rate of legitimate user k is given as

$$\begin{aligned}
R_k &= \log_2\left(1 + \mathrm{SINR}_k\right) \\
&= \log_2(1 + \frac{\left|\mathbf{t}_k^{\mathrm{H}} \mathbf{w}_k\right|^2}{\sum_{j \neq k, j=1}^{K} \left|\mathbf{t}_k^{\mathrm{H}} \mathbf{w}_j\right|^2 + \sigma_k^2}).
\end{aligned} \tag{4}$$

Similarly, the $\mathrm{SINR}_{e,l,k}$ of the Eve l for decoding user k can be written as

$$\mathrm{SINR}_{\mathrm{e,l,k}} = \frac{\left|\eta \mathbf{a}^{\mathrm{H}}(\theta_l) \boldsymbol{\Theta} \mathbf{G} \mathbf{w}_k\right|^2}{\sum_{j \neq k, j=1}^{K} \left|\eta \mathbf{a}^{\mathrm{H}}(\theta_l) \boldsymbol{\Theta} \mathbf{G} \mathbf{w}_j\right|^2 + \sigma_e^2}, \tag{5}$$

The achievable transmission rate of eavesdropper Eve l is given as

$$R_{e,l,k} = \log_2\left(1 + \text{SINR}_{e,k}\right)$$

$$= \log_2\left(1 + \frac{\left|\eta \mathbf{a}^{\mathrm{H}}\left(\theta_l\right)\boldsymbol{\Theta}\mathbf{G}\mathbf{w}_k\right|^2}{\sum_{j\neq k, j=1}^{K}\left|\eta \mathbf{a}^{\mathrm{H}}\left(\theta_l\right)\boldsymbol{\Theta}\mathbf{G}\mathbf{w}_j\right|^2 + \sigma_e^2}\right). \tag{6}$$

Thus, the worst-case SR is expressed as [15]

$$\mathbf{SR}_k = \left[R_k - \max_{\forall l} R_{e,l,k}\right]^+. \tag{7}$$

The beampattern at angle θ_l of RIS is given by

$$P(\theta_l) = \sum_{k=1}^{K} \mathbf{a}^{\mathrm{H}}\left(\theta_l\right)\boldsymbol{\Theta}\mathbf{G}\mathbf{w}_k\mathbf{w}_k^{\mathrm{H}}\mathbf{G}^{\mathrm{H}}\boldsymbol{\Theta}^{\mathrm{H}}\mathbf{a}(\theta_l). \tag{8}$$

2.3   Problem Formulation

The goal of this work is to maximize the sum SR of system by jointly optimized the transmitting beamforming matrix of BS and the phase shift matrix of RIS. To ensure the system has adequate communication and sensing performance while meeting energy consumption requirements, we impose constraints on the beampattern gain of sensing, the achievable sum-rate of CUs, the power budget of system, and the RIS reflection coefficients in the optimization problem. The optimization problem is formulated as

$$\max_{\mathbf{w}_k\boldsymbol{\Theta}} \sum_{k=1}^{K}\left[R_k - \max_{\forall l} R_{e,l,k}\right]^+ \tag{9a}$$

$$s.t. P(\theta_l) \geq P_{th}, \forall l \tag{9b}$$

$$R_k \geq R_{min}, \forall k \tag{9c}$$

$$\sum_{j=1}^{K}\|\mathbf{w}_j\|^2 \leq P_{max} \tag{9d}$$

$$|\boldsymbol{\Theta}|_{n,n} = 1, \tag{9e}$$

where P_{th} and $P_{\max}$ represent the pre-defined threshold for the beampattern gain of sensing and the power budget of BS respectively. $R_{\min}$ is the pre-defined threshold for achievable rate of legitimate users.

The presence of the logarithmic fractions and multivariate couplings in the objective function (9a) and the constraints (9c) and (9d) make problem (9) highly non-convex. To address the non-convex problem (9), AO method is used to disassemble it into two sub-problems. Then the semi-definite relaxation (SDR) and successive convex approximation (SCA) algorithms are applied to solve the sub-problems iteratively.

3   Problem Transformation and Solution

In this section, the transmitting beamforming $\mathbf{W}$ and the phase shift matrix $\boldsymbol{\Theta}$ are alternately optimized with two subproblems. The iterative optimization of $\mathbf{W}$ and $\boldsymbol{\Theta}$ in the two sub-problems is carried out using an SDR-SCA based AO algorithm.

3.1   Optimizing W with Fixed $\boldsymbol{\Theta}$

In this section, with the fixed phase shift matrix $\boldsymbol{\Theta}$, the sub-problem for transmitting beamforming $\mathbf{W}$ is formulated as

$$
\begin{aligned}
\max_{\mathbf{w}_k} \ & \sum_{k=1}^{K}\left[R_k - \max_{\forall l} R_{e,l,k}\right]^{+} \\
\text{s.t.} \ & \sum_{k=1}^{K} \mathbf{a}^{H}\left(\theta_l\right)\boldsymbol{\Theta}\mathbf{G}\mathbf{w}_k\mathbf{w}_k^{H}\mathbf{G}^{H}\boldsymbol{\Theta}^{H}\mathbf{a}\left(\theta_l\right) \geq P_{th}, \forall l \\
& \log_2\!\left(1 + \frac{\mathbf{t}_k^{H}\mathbf{w}_k\mathbf{w}_k^{H}\mathbf{t}_k}{\sum_{j\neq k,j=1}^{K}\mathbf{t}_k^{H}\mathbf{w}_j\mathbf{w}_j^{H}\mathbf{t}_k + \sigma_k^{2}}\right) \geq R_{min}, \forall k \\
& \sum_{j=1}^{K}\mathbf{w}_j\mathbf{w}_j^{H} \leq P_{max}.
\end{aligned}
\tag{10}
$$

However, due to the presence of logarithmic fractions, the optimization problem (10) is non-convex in nature. The primary challenge in solving (10) lies in the quadratic terms related to the variable $\mathbf{w}_k$. The SDR approach is employed as an initial step to relax the problem [16]. We define $\mathbf{W}_k = \mathbf{w}_k\mathbf{w}_k^{H}$.

$$
\mathbf{W}_k = \mathbf{w}_k\mathbf{w}_k^{H} \iff \mathbf{W}_k \geq \mathbf{0}, rank\left(\mathbf{W}_k\right) = 1, \forall k.
\tag{11}
$$

The rank-one constraint is non-convex, so it is relaxed by using SDR. Subsequently, we define $\mathbf{T}_k = \mathbf{t}_k\mathbf{t}_k^{H}$, $A_l = |\boldsymbol{\eta}|^{2}\mathbf{G}^{H}\boldsymbol{\Theta}^{H}\mathbf{a}(\theta_l)\mathbf{a}^{H}(\theta_l)\boldsymbol{\Theta}\mathbf{G}$, and $r_k = 1/\sigma_k^2, r_e = 1/\sigma_e^2$. Then R_k and $R_{e,l,k}$ can be reformulated as

$$
R_k = \log_2\left(r_k\sum_{j=1}^{K} tr\left(\mathbf{T}_k\mathbf{W}_j\right) + 1\right) - \log_2\left(r_k\sum_{j\neq k,j=1}^{K} tr\left(\mathbf{T}_k\mathbf{W}_j\right) + 1\right),
\tag{12}
$$

$$
R_{e,l,k} = \log_2\left(r_e\sum_{j=1}^{K} tr\left(\mathbf{A}_l\mathbf{W}_j\right) + 1\right) - \log_2\left(r_e\sum_{j\neq k,j=1}^{K} tr\left(\mathbf{A}_l\mathbf{W}_j\right) + 1\right)
\tag{13}
$$

466   S. Guo et al.

Denoting $\mathbf{q}_w = [q_{w,1} \cdots q_{w,k}]^{\mathrm{T}}$, the problem (10) can be reformulated as

$$\max_{\mathbf{w}, q_w} \sum_{k=1}^{K} \left(R_k - q_{w,k} \right) \tag{14a}$$

$$\text{s.t.} \sum_{k=1}^{K} tr\left(\mathbf{A}_l \mathbf{W}_k \right) \geq P_{th} |\eta|^2, \forall l \tag{14b}$$

$$tr\left(\mathbf{T}_k \mathbf{W}_k \right) \geq \left(2^{R_{min}} - 1 \right) \cdot \left(\sum_{j \neq k, j=1}^{K} tr\left(\mathbf{T}_k \mathbf{W}_j \right) + \sigma_k^2 \right), \forall k \tag{14c}$$

$$\sum_{j=1}^{K} tr(\mathbf{W}_j) \leq P_{max} \tag{14d}$$

$$q_{w,,k} \geq R_{e,l,k}, \forall (l, k) \tag{14e}$$

$$\mathbf{W}_k \geq 0, \forall k. \tag{14f}$$

It can be observed that the non-convexity in above problem (14) is confined to the objective function (14a). By utilizing various linear iteration schemes, one can remain within the convex feasible region. Consequently, to address this problem, the objective function can be transformed into a linear approximation. A SCA method is proposed to solve problem (14a). The main approach involves performing a first-order Taylor expansion at a given point $\widetilde{\mathbf{W}}_j$ for the non-convex part.

Finally, R_k and $R_{e,l,k}$ can be equivalently reformulated into

$$\begin{aligned}
\widetilde{R}_k = {}& \log_2 \left(r_k \sum_{j=1}^{K} tr\left(\mathbf{T}_k \mathbf{W}_j \right) + 1 \right) - \log_2 \left(r_k \sum_{j \neq k, j=1}^{K} tr\left(\mathbf{T}_k \widetilde{\mathbf{W}}_j \right) + 1 \right) \\
& - \frac{r_k \sum_{j \neq k, j=1}^{K} tr\left(\mathbf{T}_k \left(\mathbf{W}_j - \widetilde{\mathbf{W}}_j \right) \right)}{\left(r_k \sum_{j \neq k, j=1}^{K} tr\left(\mathbf{T}_k \widetilde{\mathbf{W}}_j \right) + 1 \right) \ln 2},
\end{aligned} \tag{15}$$

$$\begin{aligned}
\widetilde{R}_{e,l,k} = {}& \log_2 \left(r_e \sum_{j=1}^{K} tr\left(\mathbf{A}_l \widetilde{\mathbf{W}}_j \right) + 1 \right) \\
& + \frac{r_e \sum_{j=1}^{K} \left(tr\left(\mathbf{A}_l \left(\mathbf{W}_j - \widetilde{\mathbf{W}}_j \right) \right) \right)}{\left(r_e \sum_{j=1}^{K} tr\left(\mathbf{A}_l \widetilde{\mathbf{W}}_j \right) + 1 \right) \ln 2} - \log_2 \left(r_e \sum_{j \neq k, j=1}^{K} tr\left(\mathbf{A}_l \mathbf{W}_j \right) + 1 \right)
\end{aligned} \tag{16}$$

where $r_k = 1/\sigma_k^2, r_e = 1/\sigma_e^2$. Then problem (14) can be reformulated as

$$\max_{\mathbf{w},q_w} \sum_{k=1}^{K} \left(\widetilde{R}_k - q_{w,k} \right)$$

$$s.t. q_{w,k} \geq \widetilde{R}_{e,l,k}, \forall (l,k)$$

$$(14b), (14c), (14d) \text{ and } (14f). \tag{17}$$

It's note that the problem above is convex and can be effectively solved using the CVX toolbox [17]. Due to the one-rank relaxation of SDR, the optimal solutions may have rank larger than 1. After obtaining $\mathbf{W}_k, \forall k$ if it satisfies the rank-one constraint, the optimal solution $\mathbf{W}_k, \forall k$ is typically derived using singular value decomposition (SVD). However, if the solution is of high rank, Gaussian randomization [16] can convert it into a feasible rank-one solution.

3.2   Optimizing $\boldsymbol{\Theta}$ with Fixed $\mathbf{W}$

In this section, with the given beamforming matrix $\mathbf{W}$, the sub-problem for phase shift matrix $\boldsymbol{\Theta}$ is formulated as

$$\max_{\boldsymbol{\Theta}} \sum_{k=1}^{K} \left[R_k - \max_{\forall l} R_{e,l,k} \right]^+$$

$$s.t. \sum_{k=1}^{K} tr\left(\mathbf{A}_l \mathbf{W}_k\right) \geq P_{th} |\eta|^2, \forall l$$

$$\log_2\left(1 + \frac{\mathbf{t}_k^{\mathrm{H}} \mathbf{w}_k \mathbf{w}_k^{\mathrm{H}} \mathbf{t}_k}{\sum_{j \neq k, j=1}^{K} \mathbf{t}_k^{\mathrm{H}} \mathbf{w}_j \mathbf{w}_j^{\mathrm{H}} \mathbf{t}_k + \sigma_k^2}\right) \geq R_{min}, \forall k$$

$$|\boldsymbol{\Theta}|_{n,n} = 1. \tag{18}$$

Same as in the previous subsection, SDR is used to address the quadratic terms related to the variable $\boldsymbol{\Theta}$. Firstly, $\mathbf{v} = \left[e^{j\theta_1}, \cdots, e^{j\theta_N}\right]^{\mathrm{H}}$ is denoted, so $\boldsymbol{\Theta} = diag(\mathbf{v})$. Then $\overline{\mathbf{v}} = \left[1, \mathbf{v}^{\mathrm{H}}\right]^{\mathrm{H}}$ and $\mathbf{V} = \overline{\mathbf{v}}\,\overline{\mathbf{v}}^{\mathrm{H}}$ are used for further operations. Similarly, since rank$(\mathbf{V})=1$ is non-convex, SDR is used to relax the rank-one constraint in subsequent operations. R_k and $R_{e,l,k}$ can be further reformulated as follows

$$R_k = \log_2\left(r_k tr\left(\mathbf{H}_k \mathbf{V}\right) + 1\right) - \log_2\left(r_k tr\left(\mathbf{D}_k \mathbf{V}\right) + 1\right), \tag{19}$$

$$R_{e,l,k} = \log_2\left(r_e tr\left(\mathbf{S}_l \mathbf{V}\right) + 1\right) - \log_2\left(r_e tr\left(\mathbf{U}_{l,k} \mathbf{V}\right) + 1\right), \tag{20}$$

where $\mathbf{H}_k$, $\mathbf{D}_k$, $\mathbf{S}_l$ and $\mathbf{U}_{l,k}$ can be expressed as

$$\mathbf{H}_k = \begin{bmatrix} \mathbf{h}_k^{\mathrm{H}} \\ diag(\mathbf{g}_k^{\mathrm{H}})\mathbf{G} \end{bmatrix} \sum_{j=1}^{K} \mathbf{w}_j \mathbf{w}_j^{\mathrm{H}} \begin{bmatrix} \mathbf{h}_k^{\mathrm{H}} \\ diag(\mathbf{g}_k^{\mathrm{H}})\mathbf{G} \end{bmatrix}^{\mathrm{H}}, \tag{21}$$

468   S. Guo et al.

$$\mathbf{D}_k = \begin{bmatrix} \mathbf{h}_k^{\mathrm{H}} \\ diag(\mathbf{g}_k^{\mathrm{H}})\mathbf{G} \end{bmatrix} \sum_{j \neq k, j=1}^{K} \mathbf{w}_j \mathbf{w}_j^{\mathrm{H}} \begin{bmatrix} \mathbf{h}_k^{\mathrm{H}} \\ diag(\mathbf{g}_k^{\mathrm{H}})\mathbf{G} \end{bmatrix}^{\mathrm{H}}, \tag{22}$$

$$\mathbf{S}_l = \begin{bmatrix} 0 & \mathbf{0}_{1 \times N} \\ \mathbf{0}_{N \times 1} & |\eta|^2 \, diag(\mathbf{a}^{\mathrm{H}}(\theta_l))\mathbf{G} \times \\ & \sum_{j=1}^{K} \mathbf{w}_j \mathbf{w}_j^{\mathrm{H}} \mathbf{G}^{\mathrm{H}} diag(\mathbf{a}(\theta_l)) \end{bmatrix}, \tag{23}$$

$$\mathbf{U}_{l,k} = \begin{bmatrix} 0 & \mathbf{0}_{1 \times N} \\ \mathbf{0}_{N \times 1} & |\eta|^2 \, diag\left(\mathbf{a}^{\mathrm{H}}(\theta_l)\right)\mathbf{G} \times \\ & \sum_{j \neq k, j=1}^{K} \mathbf{w}_j \mathbf{w}_j^{\mathrm{H}} \mathbf{G}^{\mathrm{H}} diag\left(\mathbf{a}(\theta_l)\right) \end{bmatrix}. \tag{24}$$

Then, we define variables $\mathbf{C}_k = \begin{bmatrix} \mathbf{h}_k^{\mathrm{H}} \\ diag(\mathbf{g}_k^{\mathrm{H}})\mathbf{G} \end{bmatrix} \mathbf{w}_k \mathbf{w}_k^{\mathrm{H}} \begin{bmatrix} \mathbf{h}_k^{\mathrm{H}} \\ diag(\mathbf{g}_k^{\mathrm{H}})\mathbf{G} \end{bmatrix}^{\mathrm{H}}, \mathbf{q}_v = \left[q_{v,1} \cdots q_{v,k} \right]^{\mathrm{T}}$, and the problem (18) can be reformulated as

$$\max_{\mathbf{V}, q_v} \sum_{k=1}^{K} (R_k - q_{v,k}) \tag{25a}$$

$$s.t. \; tr(\mathbf{S}_l \mathbf{V}) \geq P_{th} |\eta|^2, \forall l \tag{25b}$$

$$tr(\mathbf{C}_k \mathbf{V}) \geq \left(2^{R_{min}} - 1\right) \cdot \left(tr(\mathbf{D}_k \mathbf{V}) + \sigma_k^2\right), \forall k \tag{25c}$$

$$q_{v,k} \geq R_{e,l,k}, \forall(l, k) \tag{25d}$$

$$\mathbf{V}_{n,n} = 1, n = 1...N + 1. \tag{25e}$$

The objective function of the above optimization problem is still non-convex. As the previous subsection, the same method SCA is used to handle the objective function.

$$\widehat{R_k} = \log_2\left(r_k tr(\mathbf{H}_k \mathbf{V}) + 1\right) - \log_2\left(r_k tr\left(\mathbf{D}_k \widetilde{\mathbf{V}}\right) + 1\right)$$
$$- \frac{r_k tr\left(\mathbf{D}_k\left(\mathbf{V} - \widetilde{\mathbf{V}}\right)\right)}{\left(r_k tr\left(\mathbf{D}_k \widetilde{\mathbf{V}}\right) + 1\right) \ln 2}, \tag{26}$$

$$\widehat{R_{e,l,k}} = \log_2\left(r_e tr\left(\mathbf{S}_l \widetilde{\mathbf{V}}\right) + 1\right) + \frac{r_e tr\left(\mathbf{S}_l\left(\mathbf{V} - \widetilde{\mathbf{V}}\right)\right)}{\left(r_e tr\left(\mathbf{S}_l \widetilde{\mathbf{V}}\right) + 1\right) \ln 2} \tag{27}$$
$$- \log_2\left(r_e tr(\mathbf{U}_{l,k}\mathbf{V}) + 1\right).$$

Finally, problem (25) is reformulated as

$$\max_{\mathbf{V}, q_v} \sum_{k=1}^{K} \left(\widehat{R_k} - q_{v,k}\right)$$
$$s.t. q_{v,k} \geq \widehat{R_{e,l,k}}, \forall(l, k) \tag{28}$$
$$(25b), (25c), \text{ and } (25e).$$

This is a concave maximization problem that can be solved using CVX, and the rank-1 solution of $\mathbf{V}$ can be converted through SVD and Gaussian randomization.

Based on the analysis of the above algorithm, the specific process is summarized in Algorithm 1.

Algorithm 1 SDR-SCA-based AO algorithm

Input: $\mathbf{h}_k$, $\mathbf{a}(\theta_l)$, $\mathbf{g}_k$, $\mathbf{G}$, $\mathbf{M}$, $\mathbf{N}$, $\mathbf{K}$, R_{min}, P_{max}, P_{th}, σ_k^2, σ_e^2

1: Initialize $\mathbf{\Theta}$ in a feasible region,
2: Set iteration index $i = 1$, maximum iteration number $L_{\max}$ and termination threshold ε
3: **repeat**
4:     Set iteration $i_1 = 1$, initialize $\widetilde{\mathbf{W}} = \mathbf{w}\mathbf{w}^{\mathbf{H}}$.
5:     **repeat**
6:       For given $\mathbf{\Theta}$,$\widetilde{\mathbf{W}}$,obtain optimal $\mathbf{W}$ by solving (17).
7:         **Update** $\widetilde{\mathbf{W}} = \mathbf{W}$
8:         $i_1 = i_1 + 1$.
9:     **until** convergence or $i_1 = L_{\max}$.
10:    **Recover** $\mathbf{W}$ using SVD or Gaussian randomization.
11:    Set iteration $i_2 = 1$ and $\bar{\mathbf{v}} = \left[\mathbf{1}, \mathbf{v}^{\mathbf{H}}\right]^{\mathbf{H}}$, initialize $\widetilde{\mathbf{V}} = \mathbf{v}\mathbf{v}^{\mathbf{H}}$.
12:    **repeat**
13:      For given $\mathbf{W}$,$\widetilde{\mathbf{V}}$,obtain optimal $\mathbf{V}$ by solving (28).
14:        **Update** $\widetilde{\mathbf{V}} = \mathbf{V}$
15:        $i_2 = i_2 + 1$
16:    **until** convergence or $i_2 = L_{\max}$
17:    **Recover** $\mathbf{V}$ using SVD or Gaussian randomization.
18:    $i = i + 1$
19: **until** convergence or $i = L_{\max}$.
Output: $\mathbf{w}$, $\mathbf{\Theta}$.

---

4 Numerical Results

The performance analysis of the suggested algorithm is carried out using simulations based on the Monte Carlo method in this section. The maximum number of iterations is set to $L_{\max} = 20$, and the convergence threshold is chosen as $\varepsilon = 0.001$. For the simulation setup, the values are fixed as $M = 3$, $K = 3$, $\sigma_e^2 = \sigma_k^2 = -75\,\mathrm{dB}$, and the sensing target amplitude is set to $\eta = 0.001$. The positions of the BS and RIS are specified as $(-3\,\mathrm{m},\ 0\,\mathrm{m},\ 1\,\mathrm{m})$ and $(0\,\mathrm{m}, 3\,\mathrm{m}, 1\,\mathrm{m})$, respectively. The CUs are randomly distributed within a circle of $2\,\mathrm{m}$ radius, centered at $(50\,\mathrm{m},\ 0\,\mathrm{m})$. The angles of the point targets are defined at $\theta = 0°, -50°, 50°$. The path loss exponents are $\alpha_{BC} = 3.8$, $\alpha_{BR} = 2.2$, $\alpha_{RC} = 2.6$, with the path loss coefficient $\beta = -30\,\mathrm{dB}$.

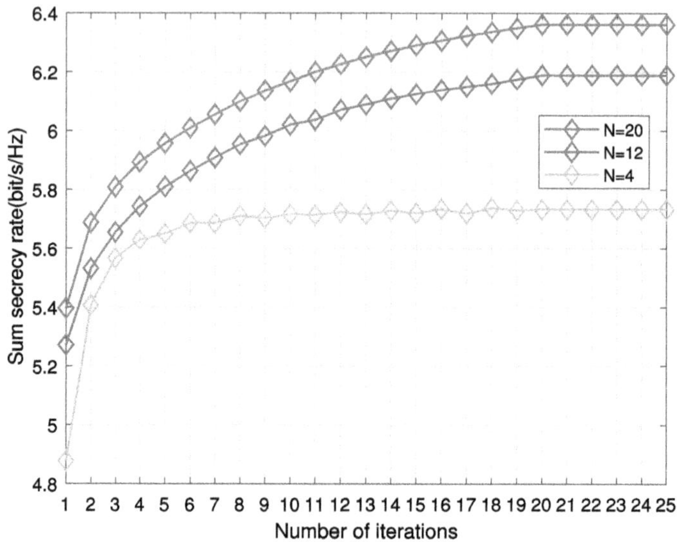

Fig. 2. The convergence of the objective function($P_{max} = -30\,\mathrm{dBm}$, $R_{min} = 1$, $P_{th} = -20\,\mathrm{dBm}$).

Figure 2 illustrates that the algorithm converges quickly within a few iterations. Generally, augmenting the number of RIS elements, leads to an enhancement in SR. A higher count of N results in an increased degrees of freedom (DoF), thereby significantly boosting the security performance. However, adding more N also raises computational complexity, resulting in slower convergence.

Figure 3 demonstrates how varying the number of RIS elements, represented by N, influences the SR. The results demonstrate that our algorithm significantly improves security performance compared to randomly deployed RIS configurations and scenarios without RIS. This highlights the importance of optimizing RIS phase shifts for enhancing ISAC system security. Additionally, the sum SR increases monotonically with the number of N. More RIS elements provide greater DoF, allowing precise control of the propagation environment and enhancing passive beamforming gain. This increased gain enables legitimate users to receive stronger signals, thereby reducing the risk of eavesdropping.

In addition, the security performance is also influenced by the number of eavesdroppers, denoted as L. Specifically, as the number of N increases, the SR at $L = 2$ generally remains higher than that at $L = 3$. This is because the presence of more eavesdroppers raises the likelihood of interception, leading to a potential reduction in SR.

Figure 4 illustrates the correlation between the overall SR and the maximum allowed transmit power budget P_{max} of the system. Consistently with expectations, the SR exhibits a steady increase as P_{max} is elevated. The phenomenon arises from allocating more transmit power, which enhances data transmission and reduces interference. The results show that the proposed scheme achieves sig-

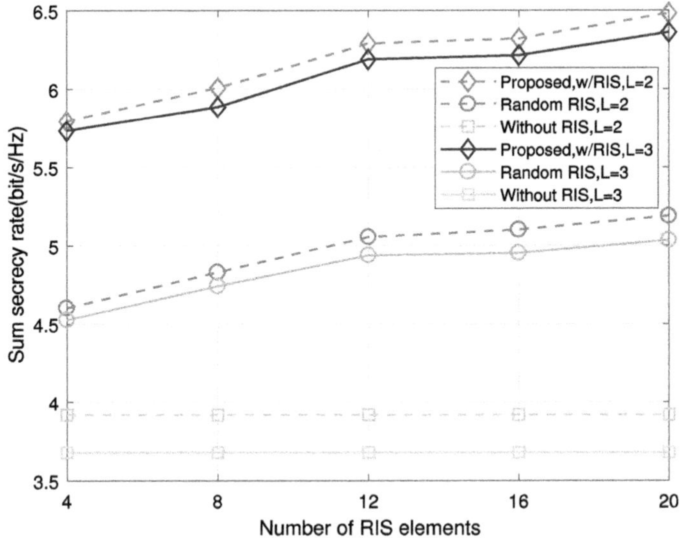

Fig. 3. Sum secrecy rate versus the number of N($P_{max} = -30\,\mathrm{dBm}$, $R_{min} = 1$, $P_{th} = -20\,\mathrm{dBm}$).

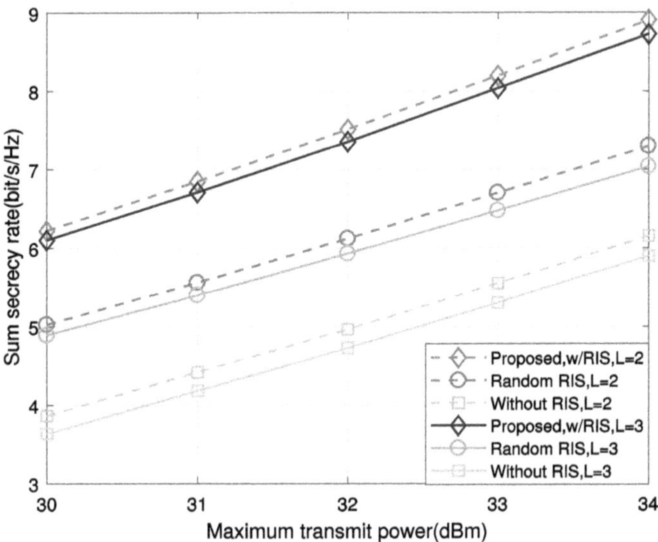

Fig. 4. Sum secrecy rate versus the transmitting power budget $P_{\max}$ ($N = 12$, $R_{min} = 1$, $P_{th} = -20\,\mathrm{dBm}$).

nificantly better SR performance than both random RIS deployment and without RIS scenarios, demonstrating its effectiveness.

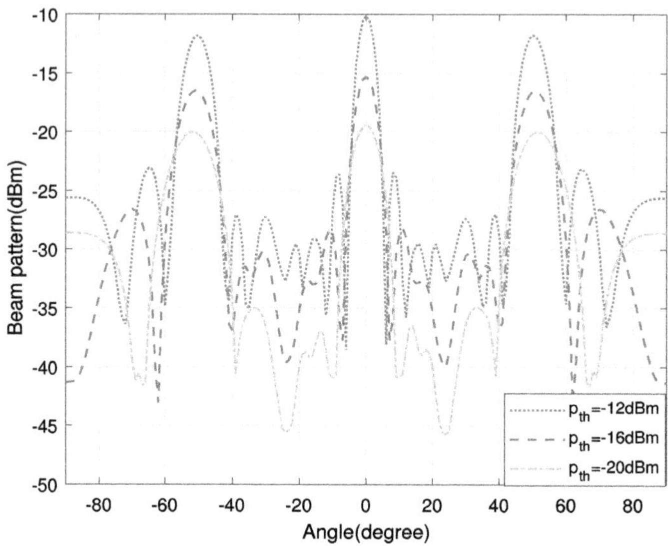

Fig. 5. Sensing beampattern on different threshold P_{th} ($P_{max} = -30\,\text{dBm}$, $N = 12$, $R_{min} = 1$).

Figure 5 presents the simplified sensing beampattern gain from the RIS towards the target as a function of the target angle for different sensing thresholds, denoted by P_{th}. From the graph, it is evident that the sensing constraints are satisfied at the target angles of $\theta = 0°, -50°, 50°$, ensuring that the proposed method meets the required sensing performance. Furthermore, a higher value of the sensing threshold P_{th}, results in more resources being allocated to the sensing task, which leads to an increased beampattern gain.

Figure 6 illustrates the sum SR versus the sensing beampattern threshold P_{th}. As both the P_{th} and L increase, a decline in SR is observed. It implies that a larger resources is allocated to the eavesdroppers, leading to an increased probability of information leakage, so the SR decreases. Furthermore, as P_{th} increases, the feasible region for optimization shrinks, which further leads to a reduction in the SR. This demonstrates the inherent trade-off between sensing and communication performance. Specifically, by sacrificing some sensing performance, the system can allocate more resources to enhance ISAC security, thereby improving secrecy performance. In contrast, the proposed scheme consistently outperforms both random RIS and without RIS configurations in sum SR.

Figure 7 illustrates the relationship between the sum SR and the threshold R_{min} of legitimate CUs. As the value of R_{min} increases, there is a noticeable decline in the SR. This decline is primarily due to the more stringent resource allocation required to meet the higher R_{min}, which places additional pressure on the ability to maximize the SR. In particular, the optimization problem becomes more challenging as the R_{min} rises, leading to a reduced feasible region within which the algorithm can operate efficiently. Notably, when the communication

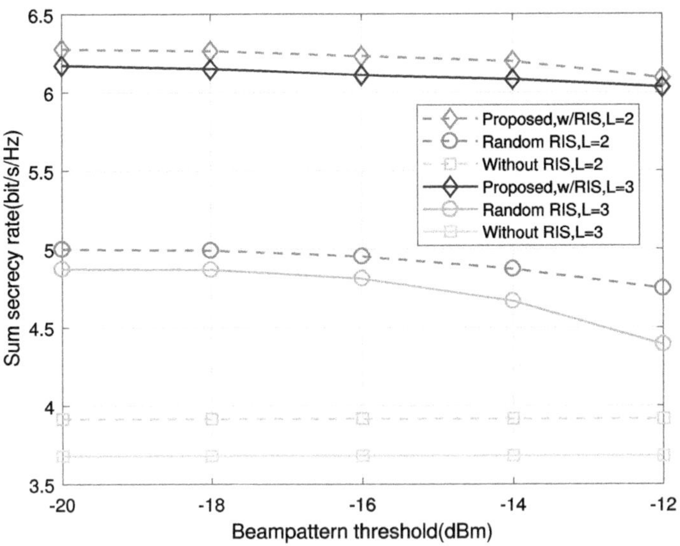

Fig. 6. Sum secrecy rate versus sensing beampattern threshold P_{th} ($P_{max} = -30\,\text{dBm}$, $N = 12$, $R_{min} = 1$).

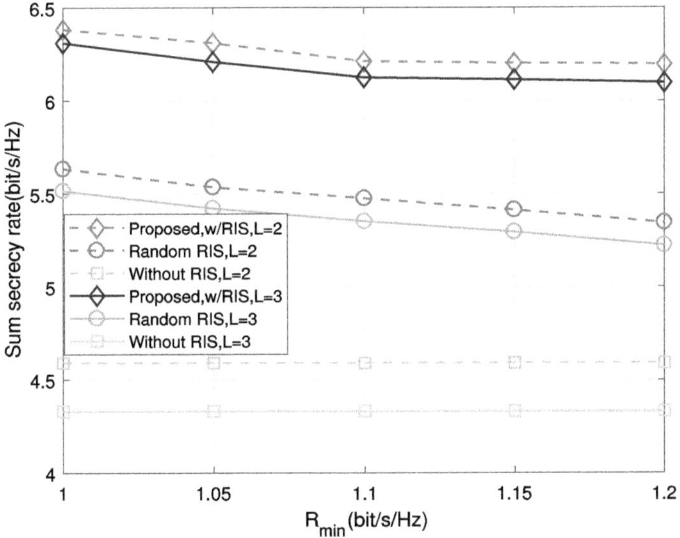

Fig. 7. Sum secrecy rate versus rate threshold R_{min} ($P_{max} = -30\,\text{dBm}$, $N = 12$, $P_{th} = -20dBm$).

threshold R_{min} is set to a high value, the proposed algorithm still demonstrates a notable advantage in terms of security performance. The reduction in SR is less pronounced compared to both the random RIS and without RIS schemes.

5   Conclusion

This research examines the integration of RIS within ISAC systems for improved PLS. The primary objective is to design a robust system that effectively optimizes the transmit beamforming and the RIS phase shifts to fortify security. An optimization problem aimed at maximize the SR under the constraints of sensing beampattern gain, the QoS of CUs, power budget of system and the RIS reflecting coefficients is formulated. Addressing the inherent non-convexity of this optimization problem, the study introduces an alternating optimization method that utilizes SDR and SCA techniques. Simulation results show that the proposed scheme significantly enhances security performance compared to random RIS scheme and without RIS scheme, thus underscoring the strategic benefit of RIS integration for security reinforcement in ISAC system.

References

1. Liu, F., et al.: Seventy years of radar and communications: the road from separation to integration. IEEE Sig. Process. Mag. **40**(5), 106–121 (2023)
2. Liu, A., et al.: A survey on fundamental limits of integrated sensing and communication. IEEE Commun. Surv. **24**(2), 994–1034 (2022)
3. Jameel, F., Wyne, S., Kaddoum, G., Duong, T.Q.:A comprehensive survey on cooperative relaying and jamming strategies for physical layer security. IEEE Commun. Surv. Tutor. **21**(3), 2734–2771 (2018)
4. Pan, C., et al.: An overview of signal processing techniques for RIS/IRS-aided wireless systems. IEEE J. Sel. Top. Sig. Process. **16**(5), 883–917 (2022)
5. Wu, Q., Zhang, R.: Towards smart and reconfigurable environment: intelligent reflecting surface aided wireless network. IEEE Commun. Mag. **58**(1), 106–112 (2019)
6. Chen, J., Wu, K., Niu, J., Li, Y., Xu, P., Zhang, J.A.: Spectral and energy efficient waveform design for RIS-assisted ISAC. IEEE Trans. Commun. (2024)
7. Saikia, P., Jee, A., Singh, K., Pan, C., Tsiftsis, T.A., Huang, W.-J.: RIS-aided integrated sensing and communications. In: GLOBECOM 2023–2023 IEEE Global Communications Conference, pp. 5080–5085. IEEE (2023)
8. Luo, H., Liu, R., Li, M., Liu, Y., Liu, Q.: Joint beamforming design for RIS-assisted integrated sensing and communication systems. IEEE Trans. Veh. Technol. **71**(12), 13393–13397 (2022)
9. Ismail, M.I., Shaheen, A.M., Fouda, M.M., Alwakeel, A.S.: RIS-assisted integrated sensing and communication systems: joint reflection and beamforming design. IEEE Open J. Commun. Soc. (2024)
10. Zhong, K., Hu, J., Pan, C., Deng, M., Fang, J.: Joint waveform and beamforming design for RIS-aided ISAC systems. IEEE Sig. Process. Lett. **30**, 165–169 (2023)
11. Liu, Q., Zhu, Y., Li, M., Liu, R., Liu, Y., Lu, Z.: DRL-based secrecy rate optimization for RIS-assisted secure ISAC systems. IEEE Trans. Veh. Technol. (2023)
12. Jiang, C., Zhang, C., Huang, C., Ge, J., He, J., Yuen, C.: Secure beamforming design for RIS-assisted integrated sensing and communication systems. IEEE Wirel. Commun. Lett. (2023)
13. Yang, Z., Zhang, S., Chen, G., Dong, Z., Wu, Y., da Costa, D.B.: Secure integrated sensing and communication systems assisted by active RIS. IEEE Trans. Veh. Technol. (2024)

14. Zhao, L., Geraci, G., Yang, T., Ng, D.W.K., Yuan, J.: A tone-based AoA estimation and multiuser precoding for millimeter wave massive MIMO. IEEE Trans. Commun. **65**(12), 5209–5225 (2017)
15. Su, N., Liu, F., Masouros, C.: Sensing-assisted eavesdropper estimation: an ISAC breakthrough in physical layer security. IEEE Trans. Wirel. Commun. (2023)
16. Luo, Z.Q., Ma, W.K., So, A.M.C., Ye, Y., Zhang, S.Z.: Semidefinite relaxation of quadratic optimization problems. IEEE Sig. Process. Mag. **27**(3), 20–34 (2010)
17. Grant, M., Boyd, S.: CVX: Matlab software for disciplined convex programming, version 2.1. (2014)

OptiGame: Game-Theoretic Enhancements for Optimistic Rollups Through Bayesian Strategies

Alvi Ataur Khalil[1(✉)], MGM Mehedi Hasan[2],
and Mohammad Ashiqur Rahman[3]

[1] Computer Science, Southern Illinois University Carbondale (SIUC), Carbondale,
IL, USA
a.khalil@siu.edu
[2] Computer Science, Iona University, New Rochelle, USA
mmehedihasan@iona.edu
[3] Knight Foundation School of Computing and Information Sciences, Florida
International University, Miami, FL, USA
marahman@fiu.edu

Abstract. Despite revolutionizing financial transactions, blockchain technology faces critical scalability challenges, impeding its global adoption. Optimistic rollup, a state-of-the-art Layer 2 (L2) scaling solution, addresses scalability issues by assuming transaction validity unless challenged. Through this work, we formally identify that interactions within optimistic rollup systems inherently constitute an inspection game between aggregators and verifiers, which is vulnerable to adversarial behaviors, as rational aggregators may act dishonestly for illicit gains, while verifiers often avoid challenges to prevent slashing penalties. To address these vulnerabilities, we propose OptiGame, an enhanced protocol incorporating a Bayesian game model and a reputation mechanism to strengthen optimistic rollup systems. Our approach incentivizes honest aggregator behavior and mitigates verifier losses (due to slashing) by aligning economic incentives with security requirements. The proposed model leverages symbolic mathematics to construct an initial mutable payoff matrix based on system parameters and dynamically updates it in response to players' interactions. To validate OptiGame's effectiveness in real-world scenarios, we deploy it on the Optimism Sepolia testnet and analyze various performance metrics.

Keywords: Blockchain · Rollup · Game theory · Nash equilibrium

1 Introduction

Blockchain technology and cryptocurrencies have transformed the financial sector, delivering significant efficiencies and innovative applications since their inception in 2009 [1,2]. However, widespread adoption remains elusive, as no current blockchain is capable of efficiently supporting global-scale operations [3,4].

© ICST Institute for Computer Sciences, Social Informatics and Telecommunications Engineering 2026
Published by Springer Nature Switzerland AG 2026. All Rights Reserved
W. Liang et al. (Eds.): SecureComm 2025, LNICST 690, pp. 476–499, 2026.
https://doi.org/10.1007/978-3-032-23456-8_26

Amid the fast-paced evolution of blockchain advancements, optimistic rollup has emerged as a cutting-edge innovation in Layer 2 (L2) scaling solutions. Like other L2 approaches such as sidechains [5], plasma [6], and payment channel networks [7–9], optimistic rollup offloads a substantial amount of transaction processing and smart contract execution from the main blockchain. This method enhances efficiency by batching transactions, reducing on-chain activities, and lowering transaction costs [10,11]. Importantly, optimistic rollup ensures high security by relying on the main chain's security model [12].

Optimistic rollups function under the assumption that transaction batches are valid unless challenged, thereby reducing computational overhead [13]. Thus, it is evident that the optimistic rollup system is modeled as an inspection game, which introduces vulnerabilities, as malicious aggregators may exploit the system for adversarial gains, while verifiers face potential slashing penalties for incorrect challenges [14]. The existing game aims to balance incentives and penalties for honesty and dishonesty; however, depends heavily on the integrity of aggregators, leaving it exposed to adversarial behavior. For instance, Ethereum Layer 2 solutions like Arbitrum [15] and Optimism [16] have documented attempts by dishonest aggregators to manipulate state roots for fraudulent gains [17]. Moreover, the verifiers bear significant financial risks when challenging batches; an incorrect challenge can result in slashing penalties. The fear of slashing penalties discourages many verifiers from actively participating in challenge activities [18,19]. Further, the lack of mechanisms to reward verifiers for consistent honesty or penalize aggregators for recurrent adversarial conduct undermines long-term trust and cooperative behavior in these systems. Finally, disputes and challenges often create bottlenecks that limit throughput, negating the scalability benefits of rollups. For example, disputes on Optimism have been observed to delay resolution by several hours [20,21]. Addressing these challenges is critical to ensure the robustness and scalability of optimistic rollups.

Recent research has explored various strategies to enhance the efficiency and security of rollup systems. Among the above-discussed issues, existing works strive to address the challenge of designing proper incentive mechanisms for verifiers, as highlighted in Luu et al. [22], where the issue is referred to as the verifier's dilemma. Game theory is also utilized by the literature to reform the strategic interactions between the aggregators and verifiers. Tas and Boneh propose an innovative game [23] where the verifiers are not explicitly rewarded for their contributions. Instead, the authors rely solely on punitive strategies to incentivize correct behavior and analyze pure strategy Nash equilibrium solutions. Another relevant contribution, by Brünjes et al. [24], explores blockchain security from a game-theoretic perspective, particularly in devising reward-sharing mechanisms for validation. This model incorporates varying the validation costs across verifiers. Similarly, Gersbach et al. [25] investigate scenarios with differential validation costs and examine delegated validation, a common strategy for earning rewards. However, these approaches fail to holistically address the interplay of throughput, trust, and verifier risks in optimistic rollup systems, leaving a critical gap in the literature.

Motivated by these limitations, this paper proposes a more robust and efficient game-theoretic framework for optimistic rollup systems. By modeling the

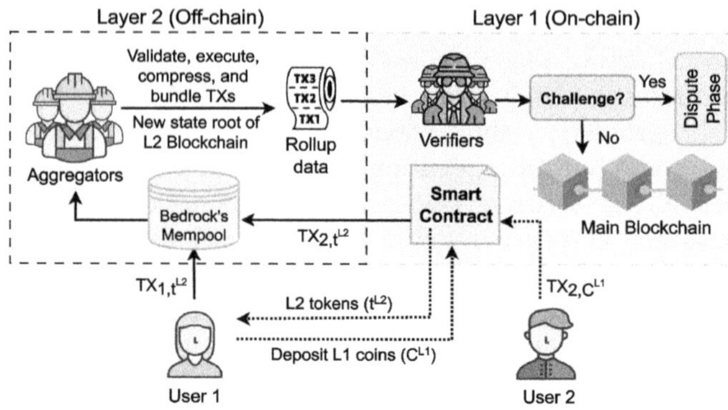

Fig. 1. Optimistic Rollup workflow.

strategic interactions between aggregators and verifiers, we determine the potential illicit gains and penalties associated with their actions. Building on these insights, we propose OptiGame, an enhanced protocol for the optimistic rollup, designed using the Bayesian game model and a reputation-based belief mechanism. OptiGame introduces a novel approach to incentivize honest behavior among aggregators and mitigate verifier losses from slashing mechanisms, thereby improving the robustness and efficiency of the system.

Our contributions to this work are four-fold:

- We formally model the game existent in the optimistic rollup system, defining utilities for rational aggregators and verifiers. To the best of our knowledge, this work is the first to identify that the interactions within optimistic rollup systems inherently constitute the inspection game. We explore how throughput, system integrity, adversarial gains, and verifier penalties influence strategic behavior in the existing protocol.
- To address the system's vulnerabilities, we propose a novel Bayesian game model that introduces a reputation mechanism for aggregators. The updated utility functions incentivize honest behavior, reducing adversarial gains and enhancing system integrity.
- We use symbolic mathematics to create a mutable pay-off matrix that adapts to system parameters and real-time player interactions, ensuring robust incentive alignment.
- To validate the theoretical contributions, we implement the proposed protocol on Optimism Sepolia [26] testnet. Experiments confirm the real-world effectiveness of the enhanced model in achieving its objectives.

We discuss necessary preliminary information in Sect. 2. The related works are discussed in Sect. 3. We analyze the exiting game in the optimistic rollup in Sect. 4. We introduce our proposed OptiGame and the technical details in Sect. 5. In Sect. 6, we explain the empirical analysis and findings. At last, we conclude the work in Sect. 7.

2 Background

This section introduces key concepts for understanding the proposed model.

Table 1. Related Work

Work	Game Model	Incentive Mechanism	Reputation System	TestNet Validate
Tas and Boneh [23]	Static	✓	✗	✗
Brunjes et al. [24]	Static	✓	✗	✗
Li et al. [32]	Static	✓	✗	✗
Zero-sum [33]	Static	✓	✗	✗
Dong et al. [34]	Static	✓	✗	✗
Liu et al. [35]	Static	Limited	✗	✗
OptiGame	Dynamic	✓	✓	✓

2.1 Optimistic Rollup

Blockchain systems currently face significant limitations in achieving a level of service quality comparable to centralized systems, particularly in terms of transactions per second [27,28]. Optimistic rollups have emerged as an L2 scaling solution for blockchain networks, which processes transactions off-chain while ensuring their validity through an optimistic framework supported by a dispute resolution mechanism [29]. Rollup systems operate via Layer 1 (L1) smart contracts, where entities such as aggregators and verifiers interact with the system. The workflow of optimistic rollups, as depicted in Fig. 1, comprises several sequential steps. Initially, users require L2 tokens (t^{L2}) to engage with the rollup system, which can be exchanged for other cryptocurrencies (C^{L1}) through the L1 smart contract. L2 transactions are then submitted to Bedrock's Mempool [30], where aggregators collect and process them. Users can either send their transactions directly to Bedrock's Mempool or route them via the L1 smart contract. Aggregators subsequently process these transactions, compute cryptographic aggregates, generate the Merkle state root of the L2 chain, and submit the results to the verifiers. Verifiers on L1 monitor these submissions and are responsible for identifying and disputing fraudulent or invalid transactions within a given batch. In the event of suspected fraud, a challenge period is initiated, allowing verifiers to provide fraud-proofs to contest the optimistic assumption. If the fraud is validated, the disputed transactions are reverted, and the malicious party forfeits their security deposit. Conversely, if no valid challenge arises within the dispute window, the transactions are finalized and incorporated into the blockchain [31].

2.2   Inspection Game

The inspection game is a foundational game theory model that examines the interaction between two opposing agents: the "inspector," who monitors compliance, and the "inspectee," who seeks to evade detection [36]. It highlights the conflicting objectives of inspection costs for the inspector and the risks and rewards of non-compliance for the inspectee. Framed as a non-cooperative, zero-sum game, both players use mixed strategies to maximize payoffs. The inspector optimizes resource allocation for efficiency and detection, while the inspectee adjusts compliance based on perceived inspection probability [37]. Equilibrium balances deterrence and monitoring costs. Advanced models incorporate repeated interactions, asymmetric information, and stochastic events, enabling analysis of trust, learning, strategic uncertainty, and optimal resource use under constraints.

2.3   Bayesian Game

A Bayesian game extends classical game theory to cases with incomplete information, where players use probabilistic beliefs to make decisions [38]. Each player has a "type," representing private information drawn from a known distribution [39]. Players form beliefs about others' types, leading to a **Bayesian Nash Equilibrium (BNE)**, where strategies are optimal given these beliefs [40]. Advances include dynamic models where players update beliefs over time [41,42].

2.4   Symbolic Mathematics Solver

Symbolic mathematics manipulates mathematical expressions in abstract form, enabling precise reasoning beyond numerical approximations [43]. It supports analytical solutions, identity verification, and parameter sensitivity analysis without fixed numerical inputs [44]. In the context of optimistic rollup, symbolic mathematics models dynamic variables like economic incentives, security thresholds, and penalties, allowing adaptive pay-off matrices that adjust to system changes.

3   Related Work

The application of game theory to blockchain systems, especially optimistic rollups, has garnered significant attention for aligning individual incentives with network security and efficiency. Li et al. analyzed the security of optimistic rollup mechanisms, using game theory to study validators' and aggregators' strategic behavior, highlighting vulnerabilities such as dishonest reporting and manipulation of transaction validity [32]. By examining the potential vulnerabilities, such as the risk of dishonest reporting or strategic manipulation of transaction validity, they emphasizes the need for robust mechanisms that ensure validator incentives align with network security. Building on this, Mamageishvili and Felten proposed reward schemes to incentivize honest validator behavior and align

Table 2. List of Notations for the Inspection Game

Symbol	Definition
A	Set of rollup aggregators
V	Set of rollup verifiers
s_A	Strategy set of the aggregators
s_V	Strategy set of the verifiers
$\mathcal{H}$	Aggregator's move when it sends valid Merkle state root proof
$\mathcal{D}$	Aggregator's move when it sends manipulated Merkle state root proof
$\mathcal{C}$	Verifier's move when it challenges a proof
$\mathcal{I}$	Verifier's move when it ignores challenging a proof
u_A^c	Aggregator's expected payoff when the proof is challenged
u_A^n	Aggregator's expected payoff when the proof is not challenged
u_V^c	Verifier's expected payoff when it challenges a proof
u_V^i	Verifier's expected payoff when it ignores challenging a proof
x	Monetary value of transactions in the rollup batch in consideration
C_A	Aggregator's cost for submitting a rollup batch
L_t	Throughput loss incurred due to dispute phase
B_A	Benefits of adversarial aggregator through fraudulent batches
P_A	Penalty for adversarial aggregator when fraudulent batches caught
B_t	Throughput benefit of Aggregator due to uninterrupted batches
S_V	Slashing of verifier collateral for the wrong challenge
T_V	Cost of verifier for damaging the system trust (ignoring fraud)
R_V	Verifier's reward for challenging fraudulent batch

actions with blockchain goals [33]. However, Landis et al. raised concerns about incentive misalignment, showing how individual motivations can diverge, leading to issues like verifiers' failing to challenge invalid transactions [45]. Gersbach et al. extended this work to staking pools, analyzing reward-sharing mechanisms to prevent free-riding and encourage optimal participation, a critical aspect for rollup validators pooling resources [25]. Similarly, Brünjes et al. studied staking pool dynamics, proposing fair reward-distribution mechanisms to maintain network integrity [24].

The intersection of game theory and the security of decentralized systems is broad, with extensive research bridging these areas. For instance, Asharov et al. [46] explore secure computation through a game-theoretic lens, providing insights into multi-party computational settings. Dong et al. addressed betrayal and collusion in decentralized systems, introducing smart counter-collusion contracts to enforce protocol adherence, which can mitigate risks in optimistic rollups [34]. Liu and Zeng proposed a game-theoretic model to optimize public announcements, reducing inefficiencies and enhancing validators' decision-making processes [35]. Nabi et al. examined incentivized verifiable computation systems, offering models to ensure correctness in outsourced computations, a concept directly relevant to optimistic rollups where off-chain computations must be reliably verified [47]. Similarly, Gersbach et al. [48] address the optimal design of bug-searching committees, investigating the ideal number of searchers and reward schemes under a fixed budget. Collectively, these studies provide a comprehensive view of how game theory can enhance the scalability, efficiency, and security of optimistic rollups by addressing key behavioral challenges.

Previous studies discussed above largely focus on static game-theoretic models for incentive alignment and countering dishonesty. However, they do not fully address the dynamic nature of strategic interactions between aggregators and verifiers in an optimistic rollup environment. They also overlook reputation mechanisms, which are critical for fostering trust and encouraging consistent honesty over repeated interactions. This work addresses these gaps by introducing a more advanced framework combining Bayesian game theory and a reputation mechanism. The proposed utility functions balance system throughput, verifier risks, and adversarial gains. The Bayesian model adds depth to modeling uncertainty in validator behavior, while the reputation mechanism incentivizes long-term trustworthy behavior, addressing key limitations of prior studies. A comparative analysis of the existing games is presented in Table 1.

4   Conventional Optimistic Rollup Game

In this section, we discuss the existing game in the conventional optimistic rollup setup – the inspection game. It involves two players: the Aggregator (A), who submits batches of transactions to the rollup, and the Verifier (V), who monitors batches and decides whether to challenge the aggregator's submitted state root. We discuss the strategy sets of each player, the payoff functions, the extensive form of the game, and the algorithm in the current optimistic rollup setup. Table 2 presents all the notations used in modeling the game.

4.1   Strategies

Each player of the game has a unique set of strategies. The Aggregator can behave **honestly** (submitting valid state roots) or **dishonestly** (submitting tampered state roots). Thus, strategies for the Aggregator are:

$$s_A = \{\mathcal{H}, \mathcal{D}\}$$

where $\mathcal{H}$ denotes A submitting valid batch state roots, and $\mathcal{D}$ denotes submitting tampered transaction batches or invalid state roots. The verifier must decide to **challenge** or **ignore** based on their belief about the Aggregator's behavior. The strategies for the Verifiers are:

$$s_V = \{\mathcal{C}, \mathcal{I}\}$$

where $\mathcal{C}$ denotes V challenging the batch at a validation cost, and $\mathcal{I}$ denotes not challenging, allowing the batch to pass.

4.2 Payoff Functions

Each player's payoff depends on the action it takes and the action the other player takes. We present an extensive form of the game in Fig. 3, where the aggregator first plays one of its strategies, and then the verifier plays a strategy without being able to observe the action the aggregator took (being on the same information set, shown through the dotted line). Each leaf of the extensive form shows the final payoff in pairs, the first element being the payoff for the aggregator and the second for the verifier. The payoffs are explained in the following sections.

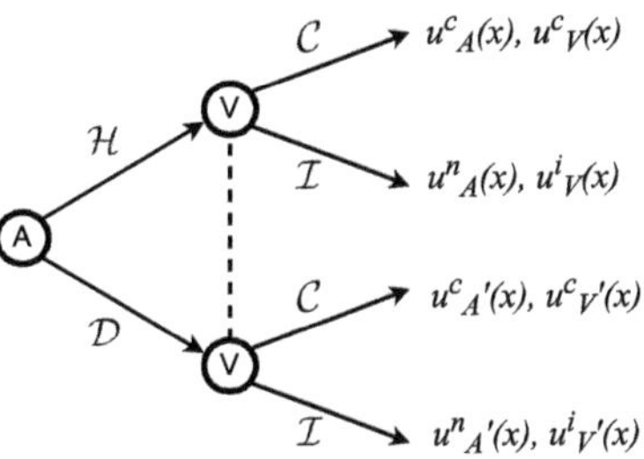

Fig. 2. Existing Inspection game in Optimistic Rollup.

Aggregator Payoff. The Aggregator's payoff $u_A(x)$ balances the reward for submitting valid batches against the penalty for being challenged when found dishonest. If the Aggregator acts honestly, then its payoff could be calculated using the following equation, given that the verifier doesn't challenge:

$$u_A^n(x) = R_A - C_A(x) \tag{1}$$

where R_A is the aggregator's reward if the batch is accepted, and $C_A(x)$ is the submission cost, dependent on the batch's transactions' monetary value x. If the aggregator acts honestly, however, the verifier decides to challenge, then its payoff could be calculated using the following equation:

$$u_A^c(x) = u_A^n(x) - L_t(x) \tag{2}$$

where $L_t(x)$ refers to the transaction throughput loss due to the dispute phase, which delays the processing of the valid rollup batch.

On the other hand, if the Aggregator acts dishonestly, then its payoff could be calculated using the following equation, given that the verifier doesn't challenge:

$$u_A^{n'}(x) = B_A(x) - C_A(x) \tag{3}$$

where $B_A(x)$ refers to the adversarial benefits aggregator achievers by getting the fraudulent batches into the L1 chain (where, $B_A(x) \gg R_A$). Conversely, if the Aggregator acts dishonestly and the verifier challenges, then its payoff:

$$u_A^{c'}(x) = -C_A(x) - L_t(x) - P_A \tag{4}$$

where P_A refers to the penalty for adversarial aggregator for submitting fraudulent batches.

Verifier Payoff. The verifier's payoff $u_V(x)$ balances the cost of challenging fraudulent batches against the cost of ignoring valid or fraudulent batches. If the verifier ignores challenging a valid batch, then its payoff:

$$u_V^i(x) = B_t(x) \tag{5}$$

where $B_t(x)$ refers to the transaction throughput benefit for the verifier for facilitating uninterrupted batch addition to the L1 chain, however, if the verifier challenges a valid batch, then its payoff:

$$u_V^c(x) = -S_V - L_t(x) \tag{6}$$

where S_V refers to the slashing of verifier collateral for the wrong dispute phase initiation (challenging a valid proof).

Again, if the verifier ignores challenging a fraudulent batch, then its payoff:

$$u_V^{i'}(x) = -T_V(x) \tag{7}$$

where $T_V(x)$ is the cost of ignoring a fraudulent batch, undermining system trust. If the verifier challenges a fraudulent batch, then its payoff:

$$u_V^{c'}(x) = R_V(x) - L_t(x) \tag{8}$$

where $R_V(x)$ is the verifier's reward for detecting a fraudulent batch.

4.3   Inspection Game Algorithm in Optimistic Rollup

In this system, the set of aggregators ($\mathbb{A}$) batch and submit transactions to the rollup chain, while the set of verifiers ($\mathbb{V}$) ensure the integrity of these submissions. The interaction between these two types of operators is inherently strategic, as both parties aim to maximize their utilities while navigating potential risks. Honest aggregators incur standard costs (C_A) for submitting batches and may face throughput losses (L_t) if verifiers challenge their proofs. However, they also gain rewards (R_A) when a valid batch is accepted. Dishonest aggregators, in contrast, risk significant penalties (P_A) and dispute-related costs if their fraud is detected; however, they stand to gain adversarial benefits (B_A) if their manipulation goes unnoticed. Verifiers act as the system's watchdogs. Challenging potentially fraudulent submissions carries both risks and rewards: verifiers can earn rewards (R_V) for successfully identifying fraud, thus maintaining system integrity; however, they also risk collateral slashing (S_V) for incorrectly challenging a valid proof. Ignoring fraud to avoid disputes results in costs (T_V) as it undermines system trust; however, verifiers may gain throughput benefits (B_t) when no disputes arise.

Algorithm 1 iteratively processes each rollup batch ($r \in RollupBatches$), computing transactions' monetary value (x) and evaluating operator utilities. Aggregator utility (u_A) depends on whether their proofs are challenged, while verifier utility (u_V) is based on their actions and aggregator behavior. Honest

---

Algorithm 1: Conventional Game in Optimistic Rollup

```
 1  Function InspectionGame(𝔸, 𝕍):
 2      (C_A, L_t, B_A, P_A, B_t, S_V, T_V, R_V) ← Set
 3      for r ∈ RollupBatches do
 4          x ← Amount(r)
 5          for A ∈ 𝔸 do
 6              if A plays ℋ then
 7                  if ∃_{V∈𝕍} s_V == 𝒞 then
 8                      │  u_A ← R_A(x) − C_A(x) − L_t(x)
 9                  else
10                      │  u_A ← R_A(x) − C_A(x)
11                  end
12              else
13                  if ∃_{V∈𝕍} s_V == 𝒞 then
14                      │  u_A ← −C_A(x) − L_t(x) − P_A(x)
15                  else
16                      │  u_A ← B_A(x) − C_A(x)
17                  end
18              end
19              u_𝔸[r, A] ← u_A
20          end
21          for V ∈ 𝕍 do
22              if V plays ℐ then
23                  if ∃_{A∈𝔸} s_A == 𝒟 then
24                      │  u_V ← −T_V(x)
25                  else
26                      │  u_V ← Bt(x)
27                  end
28              else
29                  if ∃_{A∈𝔸} s_A == 𝒟 then
30                      │  u_V ← R_V(x) − L_t(x)
31                  else
32                      │  u_V ← −S_V(x) − L_t(x)
33                  end
34              end
35              u_𝕍[r, V] ← u_V
36          end
37      end
38  return u_𝔸, u_𝕍;
```

---

aggregators face throughput losses (L_t) if challenged but no penalties, whereas dishonest ones either gain if unchallenged or incur heavy penalties (P_A) and dispute costs (C_A, L_t). The system ensures integrity by penalizing dishonest aggregators when at least one verifier $(V \in \mathbb{V})$ challenges fraud. If no verifier acts against a bad proof, verifiers face penalties (T_V) for neglecting their responsibility to uphold system trust (T_V).

5   Technical Details of OptiGame

In this section, we discuss the proposed OptiGame in detail. First, we introduce the modules of the framework. Then, we discuss the Bayesian game modeling. Afterward, we explain the symbolic solver technique we devised to synthesize the initial payoff matrix. Later, we present the belief function which is based on the reputation mechanism. Finally, we discuss OptiGame algorithm.

Table 3. List of Additional Notations for OptiGame

Symbol	Definition
$\mathbb{E}$	Expected value
β_k	Reputation value of the k-th aggregator
θ	Probability of aggregator being malicious
λ	Probability of malicious aggregator providing valid proof
γ	Probability of regular aggregator providing invalid proof
π	Probability of verifier challenging a valid proof
ω	Probability of verifier challenging a invalid proof
α	Aggregator's payoff
ν	Verifier's payoff
ϕ	Accumulated 'risk indicators' observed in batches submitted
t	Time instance
η_{max}	Threshold of reputation above which is defined 'Good'
η_{min}	Threshold of reputation below which is defined 'Bad'
$\rho_{A,r}^{c}$	Regular aggregator's utility when challenged
$\rho_{A,r}^{n}$	Regular aggregator's utility when not challenged
$\rho_{A,m}^{c}$	Malicious aggregator's utility when challenged
$\rho_{A,m}^{n}$	Malicious aggregator's utility when not challenged
$\rho_{V,c}^{r}$	Verifier's utility when challenges regular aggregator
$\rho_{V,n}^{r}$	Verifier's utility when does not challenge regular aggregator
$\rho_{V,c}^{m}$	Verifier's utility when challenges malicious aggregator
$\rho_{V,n}^{m}$	Verifier's utility when does not challenge malicious aggregator

5.1 OptiGame Framework

The proposed framework, as presented in Fig. 3, integrates symbolic mathematics, dynamic Bayesian game theory, and a reputation mechanism to model and analyze the interactions within the rollup system.

At its core, the framework employs a '*Symbolic Mathematics Solver*' to compute initial payoff matrices based on two considerations: (i) the rollup system's parameters, such as rewards, penalties, and submission costs, and (ii) a set of desired behavior property (i.e., probability of players taking specific actions). These matrices are dynamically updated during the game, based on real-time interactions between players, enabling adaptive recalibration of incentives as the sys-

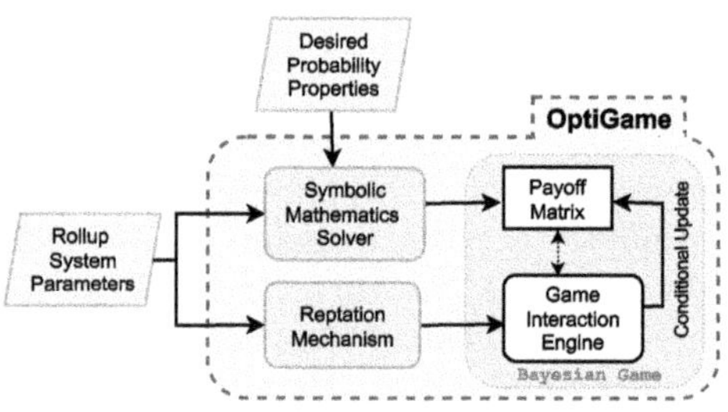

Fig. 3. System diagram of OptiGame.

tem evolves. This adaptability ensures that the payoff structure remains robust against strategic adversarial behavior. The Bayesian '*Game Interaction Engine*' drives the interaction between aggregators and verifiers, leveraging belief functions to estimate probabilities of variable behaviors. The '*Reputation Mechanism*' tracks the performance of both types of players, conditionally updating their reputation scores after each interaction. Honest behavior is rewarded with enhanced reputational standing, reducing submission costs and penalties, while dishonest or incorrect challenges result in reputational penalties, influencing future payoffs. This mechanism introduces a feedback loop to the payoff matrix, embedding long-term incentives for honesty and diligence, creating an evolving system where participants adapt their strategies for optimal performance. The framework only updates the payoff matrix values (low-weight) whenever a player diverges from its expected behavior.

5.2   Bayesian Game Modeling

In this section, we elaborate on the modeling of the Bayesian game. All the notations used to model the game are presented in Table 3. Unlike the existing inspection game, where the players have no belief system, the proposed game utilizes a reputation-based belief system (discussed later in this section) to model the likelihood of different behaviors. As shown in Fig. 4, there is a belief formed about the aggregator, which is presented by θ. This value ($0 \leq \theta \leq 1$) refers to the probability that the aggregator is malicious. When a new aggregator joins the L2 optimistic rollup, the initial belief is calculated using the belief function (having a temporary initial reputation value), and this value gets updated each batch submission, indicating the accumulated "risk indicators" of that aggregator.

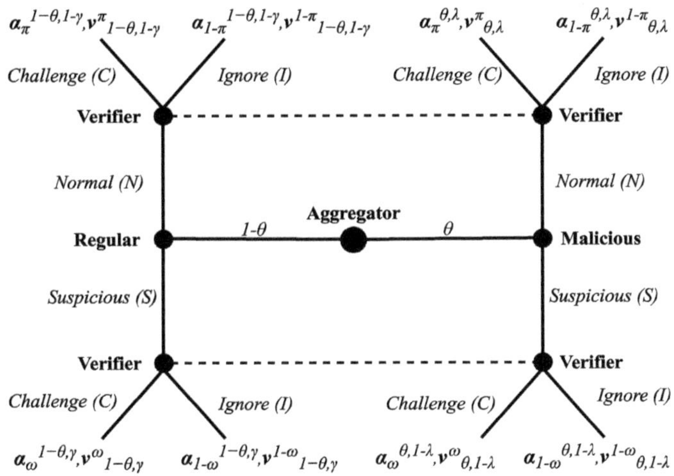

Fig. 4. Proposed Bayesian game in Optimistic Rollup.

Moreover, the inspection game assumes that the honest aggregator will always be able to provide valid state-root proof, which might not hold in real-world scenarios. Thus, we consider the cases when the honest aggregator acts suspiciously (i.e., unintentional mistake of invalid proof) and present the probability with γ where $0 \leq \gamma \leq 1$. Again, the inspection game assumes that the malicious aggregator will always attack by formulating fake state-root proof, which might not hold in real-world scenarios. Thus, we consider the cases when the malicious aggregator acts normally (i.e., sends valid proofs) and present the probability with λ where $0 \leq \lambda \leq 1$. Consequently, we set behavioral patterns for the verifier for challenging rollup batches since only belief about the aggregator is insufficient (i.e., honest aggregator sending invalid batch or malicious aggregator sending valid batch). We present the probability of a verifier challenging a valid batch by π and the probability of a verifier challenging an invalid batch by ω, where $0 \leq \pi, \omega \leq 1$. If an honest (regular) aggregator is challenged, then its expected utility could be calculated using the following equation:

$$\mathbb{E}(\rho_{A,r}^{c}) = (1 - \gamma) \cdot \alpha_{\pi}^{1-\theta,1-\gamma} + \gamma \cdot \alpha_{\omega}^{1-\theta,\gamma} \tag{9}$$

where $\alpha_{\pi}^{1-\theta,1-\gamma}$ presents the regular aggregator's payoff when it acts normally, however gets challenged by the verifier and $\alpha_{\omega}^{1-\theta,\gamma}$ presents the regular aggregator's payoff when it acts suspiciously and gets challenged by the verifier. If a regular aggregator is not challenged, then its expected utility could be calculated using the following equation:

$$\mathbb{E}(\rho_{A,r}^{n}) = (1 - \gamma) \cdot \alpha_{1-\pi}^{1-\theta,1-\gamma} + \gamma \cdot \alpha_{1-\omega}^{1-\theta,\gamma} \tag{10}$$

where $\alpha_{1-\pi}^{1-\theta,1-\gamma}$ presents the aggregator's payoff when it acts normally and does not get challenged by the verifier and $\alpha_{1-\omega}^{1-\theta,\gamma}$ presents the aggregator's payoff when it acts suspiciously, however the verifier ignores to challenge it. If a malicious aggregator is challenged, then its expected utility could be calculated using the following equation:

$$\mathbb{E}(\rho_{A,m}^{c}) = \lambda \cdot \alpha_{\pi}^{\theta,\lambda} + (1 - \lambda) \cdot \alpha_{\omega}^{\theta,1-\lambda} \tag{11}$$

where $\alpha_{\pi}^{\theta,\lambda}$ presents the malicious aggregator's payoff when it acts normally, however gets challenged by the verifier and $\alpha_{\omega}^{\theta,1-\lambda}$ presents the malicious aggregator's payoff when it acts suspiciously and gets challenged by the verifier. If a malicious aggregator is not challenged, then its expected utility could be calculated using the following equation:

$$\mathbb{E}(\rho_{A,m}^{n}) = \lambda \cdot \alpha_{1-\pi}^{\theta,\lambda} + (1 - \lambda) \cdot \alpha_{1-\omega}^{\theta,1-\lambda} \tag{12}$$

where $\alpha_{1-\pi}^{\theta,\lambda}$ presents the malicious aggregator's payoff when it acts normally and does not get challenged by the verifier and $\alpha_{1-\omega}^{\theta,1-\lambda}$ presents the malicious aggregator's payoff when it acts suspiciously, however the verifier still ignores to challenge it.

Again, the expected utility for a verifier for challenging a rollup batch from an aggregator believed to be regular could be calculated using the following equation:

$$\mathbb{E}(\rho_{V,c}^{r}) = (1 - \gamma) \cdot \nu_{1-\theta,1-\gamma}^{\pi} + \gamma \cdot \nu_{1-\theta,\gamma}^{\omega} \tag{13}$$

where $\nu_{1-\theta,1-\gamma}^{\pi}$ presents the verifiers' payoff when it challenges a regular aggregator who provided valid proof (negative payoff or penalty for a wrong challenge) and $\nu^\omega_{1-\theta,\gamma}$ presents verifiers' payoff when it challenges a regular aggregator who provided an invalid proof (positive payoff or reward for correct challenge). If a verifier challenges a rollup batch from an aggregator believed to be malicious, then its expected utility could be calculated using the following equation:

$$\mathbb{E}(\rho^m_{V,c}) = \lambda \cdot \nu^\pi_{\theta,\lambda} + (1 - \lambda) \cdot \nu^\omega_{\theta,1-\lambda} \tag{14}$$

where $\nu^\pi_{\theta,\lambda}$ presents the verifiers' payoff when it challenges a malicious aggregator who provided valid proof (negative payoff or penalty for a wrong challenge) and $\nu^\omega_{\theta,1-\lambda}$ presents verifiers' payoff when it challenges a malicious aggregator who provided an invalid proof (positive payoff or reward for correct challenge). Again, the expected utility for a verifier for not challenging a rollup batch from an aggregator believed to be regular could be calculated using the following equation:

$$\mathbb{E}(\rho^r_{V,n}) = (1 - \gamma) \cdot \nu^{1-\pi}_{1-\theta,1-\gamma} + \gamma \cdot \nu^{1-\omega}_{1-\theta,\gamma} \tag{15}$$

where $\nu^{1-\pi}_{1-\theta,1-\gamma}$ presents the verifiers' payoff when it does not challenge a regular aggregator who provided valid proof and $\nu^{1-\omega}_{1-\theta,\gamma}$ presents verifiers' payoff when it does not challenge a regular aggregator who provided an invalid proof (negative payoff or penalty for a wrong challenge). If a verifier does not challenge a rollup batch from an aggregator believed to be malicious, then its expected utility could be calculated using the following equation:

$$\mathbb{E}(\rho^m_{V,n}) = \lambda \cdot \nu^{1-\pi}_{\theta,\lambda} + (1 - \lambda) \cdot \nu^{1-\omega}_{\theta,1-\lambda} \tag{16}$$

where $\nu^{1-\pi}_{\theta,\lambda}$ presents the verifiers' payoff when it does not challenge a malicious aggregator who provided valid proof and $\nu^{1-\omega}_{\theta,1-\lambda}$ presents verifiers' payoff when it does not challenge a malicious aggregator who provided an invalid proof (negative payoff or penalty for a wrong challenge).

5.3   Symbolic Solver-Based Initial Payoff Matrix

Using symbolic mathematics, we construct an initial mutable pay-off matrix that captures aggregators' and verifiers' economic and strategic interactions. This matrix is specifically tailored to reflect the system's parameters, such as reward, cost, penalty, etc. structures, and desired security thresholds (e.g., low γ value, high λ value, etc.). By encoding these factors symbolically, the matrix offers flexibility in representing varying configurations of the rollup ecosystem. In the last section, we presented the expected utility calculations for various cases, which leads to the calculation of the BNE. When each player maximizes their expected utility, given the other players' strategies, BNE is reached. Equation (9) presents a regular aggregator's expected utility if the verifier challenges it, while Eq. (10) presents its expected utility if the verifier does not challenge it. Thus, the regular aggregator will choose to send valid proofs if:

$$\mathbb{E}(\rho^c_{A,r}) \geq \mathbb{E}(\rho^n_{A,r}) \tag{17}$$

Algorithm 2: OptiGame Framework

---

1 **Function** OPTIGAME($\mathbb{A}, \mathbb{V}, \pi, \omega, \gamma, \lambda$):
2     $\beta_k \leftarrow 0.5, \ \forall A_k \in \mathbb{A}$
3     $\theta \leftarrow \theta_k(\beta_k, \phi_k(0)), \ \forall A_k \in \mathbb{A}$
4     $(\alpha_-^{-,-}, \nu_{-,-}^-) \leftarrow \text{Symbolic-Solver}(\pi, \omega, \gamma, \lambda, \theta)$
5   **for** $t \in TimeInstance$ **do**
6   **for** $A_k \in \mathbb{A}$ **do**
7   **if** $\beta_k > \eta_{\max}$ **then**
8              $A_k \sim$ Regular
9              $\text{Proof}_{k,t} \leftarrow Valid$ with probability $(1 - \gamma) \vee Invalid$ with probability (γ)
10   **else if** $\beta_k < \eta_{\min}$ **then**
11              $A_k \sim$ Malicious
12              $\text{Proof}_{k,t} \leftarrow Valid$ with probability $\lambda \vee Invalid$ with probability $(1 - \lambda)$
13   **else**
14              $\text{Proof}_{k,t} \leftarrow Valid$ with probability $(1 - \gamma + \lambda)/2 \vee Invalid$ with probability $(1 - \lambda + \gamma)/2$
15   **end**
16           $\theta_k(t) \leftarrow \min\left(1, \dfrac{e^{(\phi_k(t)/\beta_k)} - 1}{e - 1}\right)$
17           $MemPool \leftarrow \text{Proof}_{k,t}$
18   **end**
19   **for** $V \in \mathbb{V}$ **do**
20   **if** $Proof_{k,t} \in MemPool\ seems\ Valid$ **then**
21   **if** $\theta_k(t)$ $suggests\ A_k\ is\ Malicious$ **then**
22   **Challenge** with probability $\theta_k(t) \cdot \pi \vee$ **Ignore** with probability $\theta_k(t) \cdot (1 - \pi)$
23   **else**
24   **Challenge** with probability $(1 - \theta_k(t)) \cdot \pi \vee$ **Ignore** with probability $(1 - \theta_k(t)) \cdot (1 - \pi)$
25   **end**
26   **else**
27   **if** $\theta_k(t)$ $suggests\ A_k\ is\ Malicious$ **then**
28   **Challenge** with probability $\theta_k(t) \cdot \omega \vee$ **Ignore** with probability $\theta_k(t) \cdot (1 - \omega)$
29   **else**
30   **Challenge** with probability $(1 - \theta_k(t)) \cdot \omega \vee$ **Ignore** with probability $(1 - \theta_k(t)) \cdot (1 - \omega)$
31   **end**
32   **end**
33   **if** $Challenge$ **then**
34   **if** $DisputePhase(A_k) == Honest$ **then**
35                $\beta_k \leftarrow \beta_k + \Delta\beta_k$
36   **else**
37                $\beta_k \leftarrow \beta_k - \Delta\beta_k$
38   **end**
39              $\phi_k(t) \leftarrow \phi_k(t - 1) + \text{RiskIndicators}(A_k)$
40              $(\alpha_-^{-,-}, \nu_{-,-}^-) \leftarrow \text{Update}(\theta)$
41   **end**
42   **end**
43   **end**
44 **return** $\alpha_-^{-,-}, \ \nu_{-,-}^-$

If the expected utility of a regular aggregator, when not challenged (i.e., $\mathbb{E}(\rho_{A,r}^n)$), is greater than its utility when it is challenged (i.e., $\mathbb{E}(\rho_{A,r}^c)$) than the regular aggregator will always send invalid proof. Thus, to ensure that the regular aggregator sends valid rollup batches, Eq. (17) must hold. Again, Eq. (11) presents a malicious aggregator's expected utility if the verifier challenges it, while Eq. (12) presents its expected utility if the verifier does not challenge it. Thus, the malicious aggregator will choose to send valid proofs if:

$$\mathbb{E}(\rho_{A,m}^c) \geq \mathbb{E}(\rho_{A,m}^n) \tag{18}$$

If the expected utility of a malicious aggregator, when not challenged (i.e., $\mathbb{E}(\rho_{A,m}^n)$), is greater than its utility when it is challenged (i.e., $\mathbb{E}(\rho_{A,m}^c)$) than the malicious aggregator will always send invalid proof. Thus, to ensure that the malicious aggregator sends valid rollup batches, Eq. (18) must hold.

For the verifier, Eq. (13) and Eq. (14) present the expected utilitys for challenging regular aggregators and malicious aggregators, respectively. Thus, the expected utility of the verifier for challenging, given the belief θ, could be calculated using the following equation:

$$\mathbb{E}(\rho_{V,c}) = (1-\theta) \cdot \mathbb{E}(\rho_{V,c}^r) + \theta \cdot \mathbb{E}(\rho_{V,c}^m) \tag{19}$$

Similarly, Eq. (15) and Eq. (16) present the verifier's expected utilitys for not challenging regular aggregators and malicious aggregators, respectively. Thus, the expected utility of the verifier for not challenging, given the belief θ, could be calculated using the following equation:

$$\mathbb{E}(\rho_{V,n}) = (1-\theta) \cdot \mathbb{E}(\rho_{V,n}^r) + \theta \cdot \mathbb{E}(\rho_{V,n}^m) \tag{20}$$

If the verifier's expected utility for not challenging (i.e., $\mathbb{E}(\rho_{V,n})$) is greater than its utility for challenging (i.e., $\mathbb{E}(\rho_{V,c})$), then the verifier will always choose to ignore challenging the batches, irrespective of the belief about the aggregator. Thus, to make sure the verifiers continue to play the role of watchdogs, the following inequalities must hold:

$$\mathbb{E}(\rho_{V,c}) \geq \mathbb{E}(\rho_{V,n}) \tag{21}$$

Therefore, the BNE strategies are obtained by solving the inequalities presented in Eqs. (17), (18), and (21). We leverage the symbolic mathematics solver to synthesize the initial payoff matrix values and determine the equilibrium strategies based on the input values.

5.4   Reputation-Based Belief Function

Proposed Reputation Mechanism. The reputation system is fundamental in the OptiGame framework, promoting honest behavior among aggregators while penalizing dishonest actions. The reputation value is presented by β (i.e., $0 \leq \beta \leq 1$), and each aggregator is assigned an initial reputation score of 0.5. These reputation scores evolve dynamically based on the aggregator's actions and interactions within the system, allowing the protocol to distinguish between different aggregators. Aggregators are categorized into three types based on their reputation scores:

- **Good aggregators**, defined as those with a reputation above a designated threshold (e.g., η_{max}), are inherently more trustworthy and have a high likelihood of submitting honest proofs. Their reputation increases further when they perform as expected, creating a reinforcing feedback loop incentivizing continued honest behavior.

Table 4. Interaction with OptiGame in OP Sepolia

TX Type	TX Hash	Block Number	L1 Gas Limit	Gas usage	TX fees (Gwei)
OptiGame Contract	0x8..8b7	20738073	26,100	99.05%	678
Valid batch submission	0x8..fce	20738218	1,600	15.63%	111
False batch submission	0xd..94f	20738285	1,600	13.28%	91
Valid batch to L1	0x7..d59	20738332	1,600	13.28%	94
False batch reverted	0xf..b6a	20738300	1,600	3.01%	21

- **Bad aggregators**, with reputations below a lower threshold (e.g., η_{min}), are characterized by a tendency to engage in fraudulent activities, such as submitting malicious proofs to gain undue benefits. Such aggregators face frequent challenges from verifiers and significant penalties for dishonest behavior, further eroding their reputation over time.
- **Grey aggregators**, with intermediate reputations, falling between the thresholds for good and bad actors. These entities exhibit mixed behavior, with no clear inclination toward honesty or dishonesty.

Reputation updates occur dynamically after each interaction based on the aggregator's actions and the verifiers' responses. Honest actions, such as submitting valid proofs, contribute positively to an aggregator's reputation. In contrast, malicious activities cause reputation decline, particularly if their actions are successfully challenged by verifiers. Grey aggregators receive reputation adjustments depending on whether their behavior aligns with honesty or dishonesty.

Belief Functions. The verifiers use a belief function, $\theta(t)$, to estimate the likelihood that an aggregator is dishonest based on prior observations and the characteristics of the batch. The belief function $\theta(t)$ represents the probability that the aggregator is acting dishonestly at time t. It is updated dynamically as the verifier observes the aggregator's behavior:

$$\theta_k(t) = \min\left(1, \frac{e^{(\phi_k(t)/\beta_k)} - 1}{e - 1}\right) \tag{22}$$

where $\phi_k(t)$ refers to the accumulated "risk indicators" of aggregator k observed in the submitted batches up to time t, e.g., anomalies in state root computation, transaction patterns, or inconsistencies in proofs. β_k refers to aggregator k's reputation at time t and e is the exponential scaling factor. Higher $\phi(t)$ increases the belief that the aggregator is dishonest, prompting more challenges.

5.5 Proposed Algorithm Using Bayesian Game

The OptiGame framework, as presented in Algorithm 2, models aggregators-verifiers' interactions using a Bayesian game. The algorithm begins by initializing

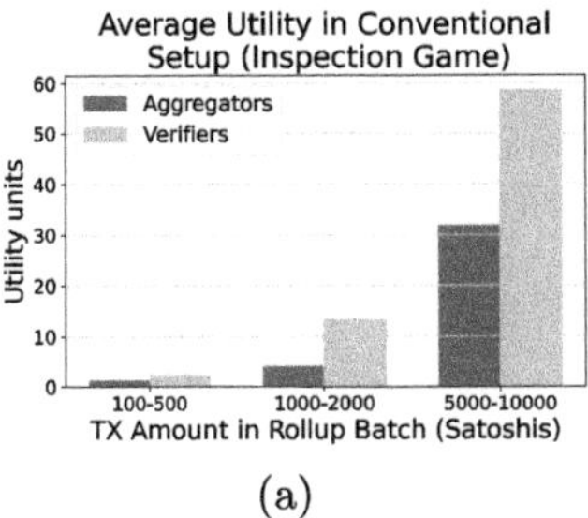

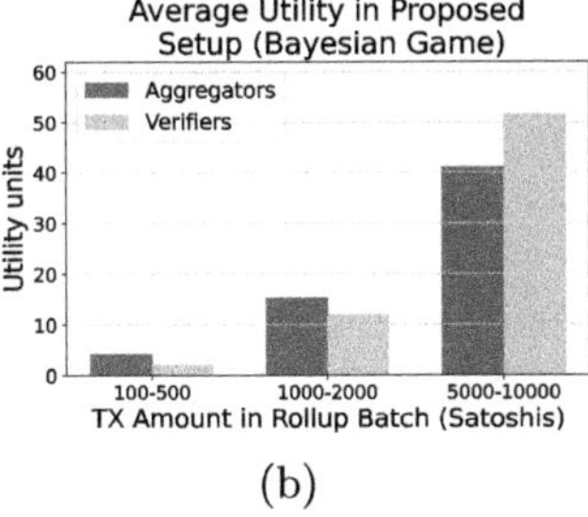

Fig. 5. Contrasting the average expected utilities of the aggregators and verifiers with different valued rollup batches when playing (a) the conventional inspection game and (b) the proposed Bayesian game.

key parameters, including the reputation (β_k) for each aggregator, thresholds for action probabilities, and symbolic solvers for payoff calculations. Aggregators are classified as good, bad, or grey based on the reputation threshold. At each time instance, the framework determines the aggregator's type and assigns a probability of producing valid or invalid proofs ($\text{Proof}_{k,t}$) based on their behavioral tendencies. These probabilities are influenced by different behavioral parameters (i.e., $\gamma, \lambda, \pi, \omega$). Verifiers assess actions via a belief metric $\theta_k(t)$, influenced by reputation and contextual factors (ϕ_k). If suspicious, verifiers challenge or ignore probabilistically using π and ω. Dispute outcomes update reputations: honest actions increasing it, while malicious ones do reduction ($\Delta\beta_k$). The algorithm monitors Bedrock's Mempool for rollup batches, recalibrates belief metrics, updates payoffs, and ensures BNE adherence, maintaining rollup integrity.

6   Evaluations

In this section, we conduct experimental analysis by deploying the OptiGame protocol on the Optimism Sepolia testnet chain [26]. We present one example of each type of interaction with our deployed contract in Table 4. We first calculate the expected utility achieved by each player, playing both the conventional and proposed games. Then, we calculate the throughput achieved when the system incorporating each type of game with a variable ratio of aggregators and verifiers. Afterward, we compute the incorrect dispute phase initiations with respect to the slashing of the verifier under different system considerations. Finally, we analyze the impact of the verifier's challenge probabilities on aggregators' behavioral dynamics. All the experiments were performed on a computer with an 11th Gen Intel(R) Core (TM) i7-1195G7 @2.90 GHz processor and 16 GB of memory.

6.1   Expected Utilities with Incremental Valued Batches

This section computes the expected utility for aggregators and verifiers in the conventional inspection game and the proposed Bayesian game with a reputation mechanism (Fig. 5). In the conventional model (Fig. 5a), aggregators' utilities depend on rewards from processing rollup batches and adversarial gains when verifiers overlook malicious proofs. Verifiers achieve modest utility due to their reactive role, leading to frequent disputes and delays. In contrast, the Bayesian model (Fig. 5b) incentivizes aggregators to submit valid proofs, offering higher and more stable utility for honest behavior, as invalid proofs risk reputational and monetary penalties. Verifiers experience slightly lower utility due to fewer challenges but benefit from reduced adversarial actions and minimized wrong challenges. The proposed model significantly increases aggregator utility for valid proofs, reducing malicious behavior and enhancing system robustness and throughput.

6.2   Throughput with Variable Aggregator-Verifier Proportions

This section analyzes system throughput based on transactions processed per unit time under different aggregator-to-verifier ratios (Fig. 6) and evaluates the modified game's impact on performance. Figure 6a shows that throughput increases with batch size across all ratios, but aggregator-heavy configurations (e.g., 3:1, 5:2) achieve higher throughput at the cost of increased vulnerability, while balanced or verifier-heavy ratios (e.g., 3:2, 1:1) ensure greater scrutiny at lower throughput. In the Bayesian game, throughput also rises with batch size but reaches higher overall levels across all ratios (Fig. 6b). Aggregators are incentivized to submit valid proofs, reducing verifier workload and accelerating processing. The gap between aggregator-heavy and verifier-heavy setups narrows, with balanced ratios (e.g., 3:2, 1:1) approaching aggregator-heavy throughput levels (e.g., 3:1). This suggests that the reputation mechanism and Bayesian decision-making improve scalability while preserving integrity. Overall, the proposed game enhances throughput by aligning incentives and mitigating adversarial actions.

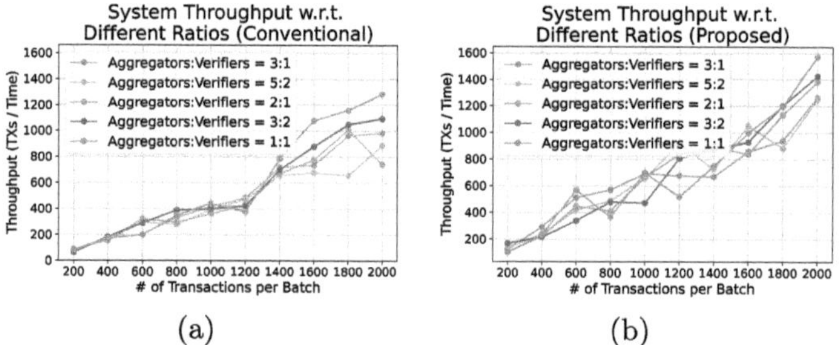

Fig. 6. The transaction throughput of the system w.r.t. the number of transactions processed per unit of time with different proportions of aggregators and verifiers when playing (a) the inspection game and (b) the Bayesian game.

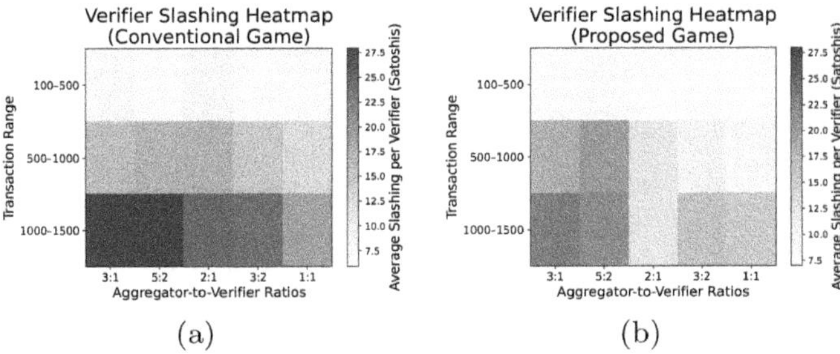

Fig. 7. Contrasting the verifier slashing amounts due to incorrect challenge with (a) the inspection game and (b) the Bayesian game with different valued rollup batch and variable aggregator-verifier ratios.

6.3 Analysis of Verifier Slashing

This section examines verifier slashing due to incorrect challenges under different aggregator-to-verifier ratios and transaction ranges (Fig. 7), comparing the inspection and Bayesian games. In the inspection game (Fig. 7a), slashing levels are higher across all configurations, increasing significantly in aggregator-heavy ratios (e.g., 3:1, 5:2) due to limited monitoring and rushed disputes. Larger batch sizes further amplify slashing as verifiers struggle with accurate assessments. Balanced or verifier-heavy ratios (e.g., 3:2, 1:1) see lower slashing but still experience notable penalties due to adversarial incentives. In the Bayesian game (Fig. 7b), slashing is uniformly lower across all setups, as reputation mechanisms and Bayesian decision-making improve verifier accuracy and reduce wrongful challenges. While aggregator-heavy setups (e.g., 3:1, 5:2) still show slightly higher slashing, the gap is narrower than in the inspection game. Larger transaction ranges have less impact, indicating the Bayesian framework's robustness to batch size variations.

6.4 Analysis of Transaction Integrity

This section analyzes transaction integrity in optimistic rollups (Fig. 8) and highlights the Bayesian game's improvements over the inspection game. In the inspection game (Fig. 8a), integrity losses are highest in aggregator-heavy setups (e.g., 3:1) with low honesty probabilities, as fewer verifiers enable dishonest aggregators to exploit the system. Even in balanced setups (e.g., 1:1), integrity hampering remains moderate when honesty is below 50%, revealing the inspection game's weakness in relying solely on verifiers to detect fraud. In contrast, the Bayesian game (Fig. 8b) mitigates integrity losses through reputation mechanisms and probabilistic decision-making. Even in aggregator-heavy setups, dishonest aggregators face reputational penalties, reducing incentives for fraud. As honesty probabilities rise, integrity hampering drops to negligible levels across all configurations, demonstrating the Bayesian game's effectiveness in promoting valid proof submissions.

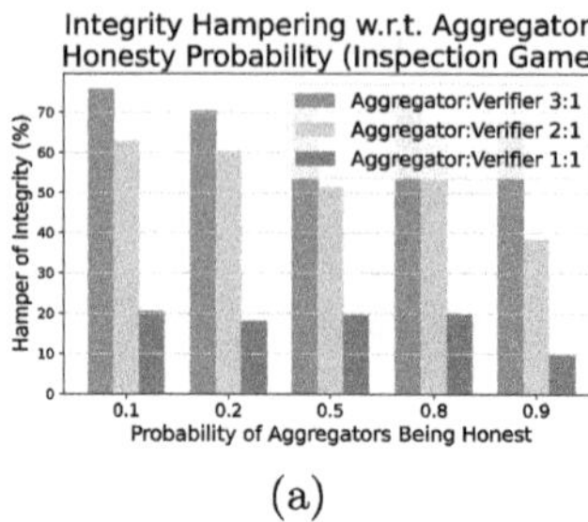

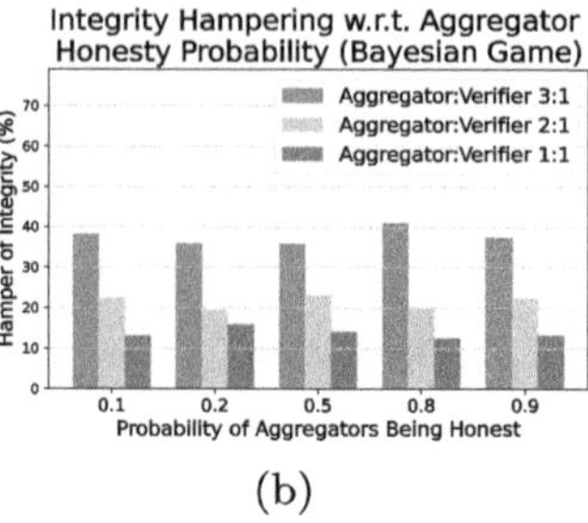

(a)   (b)

Fig. 8. Analyzing the integrity of the transactions processed by optimistic rollup when playing (a) the inspection game and (b) the Bayesian game, with variable aggregator-verifier ratios.

6.5   Trend of Aggregators' Behavior

This section examines how verifier challenge probabilities influence the distribution of aggregators as "Good," "Grey," or "Bad" (Fig. 9). First, we analyze varying invalid batch challenge probabilities (ω) while keeping valid batch challenges fixed ($\pi = 0.25$) (Fig. 9a). At moderate $\omega = 0.7$, the number of "Bad" aggregators is lowest, as higher scrutiny deters malicious behavior. However, increased verifier strictness ($\omega = 0.9$) further reduces "Bad" aggregators while stabilizing or slightly increasing "Good" aggregators. "Grey" aggregators decline as stricter verification limits occasional protocol violations. Higher values of ω not only minimize the presence of "Bad" aggregators, it also create conditions that reinforce adherence to protocol by "Good" and "Grey" participants. Next, we analyze different values of λ (likelihood of bad aggregators submitting valid proofs) with $\omega = 0.7$ (Fig. 9b). At low $\lambda = 0.15$, "Bad" aggregators are most prevalent, as frequent detection classifies them accordingly. As λ increases to 0.25, "Bad" aggregators decline, with some shifting to "Grey" status due to partial compliance. At $\lambda = 0.35$, "Bad" aggregators reach their lowest level, with more shifting to "Grey." Throughout, "Good" aggregators remain stable. A moderate λ (0.25) balances reducing bad actors while encouraging grey aggregators to adapt, fostering system stability.

7   Conclusion

Scalability and security are crucial for any L2 solution. This work introduces OPTIGAME, an enhanced optimistic rollup protocol using a Bayesian game model and a reputation mechanism to address security flaws in inspection game frameworks. By aligning incentives, OPTIGAME encourages valid proof submissions, increasing honest behavior's utility. While verifiers may experience lower utility due to fewer fraudulent proofs, this trade-off is outweighed by overall improvements in system integrity and efficiency. The reduction in erroneous challenges and adversarial actions strengthens security and scalability. By employing symbolic mathematics to construct a dynamic and adaptive pay-off matrix,

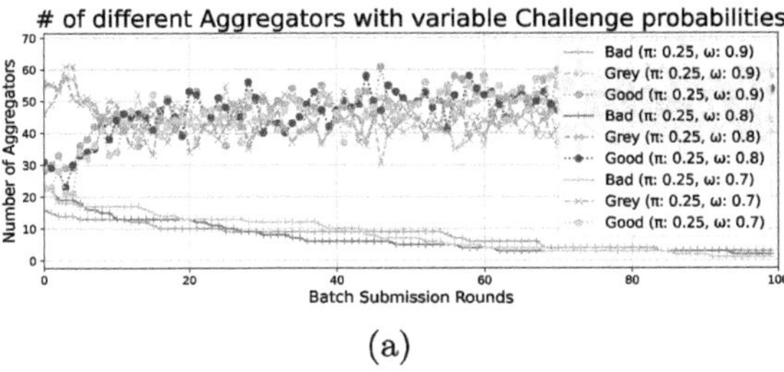

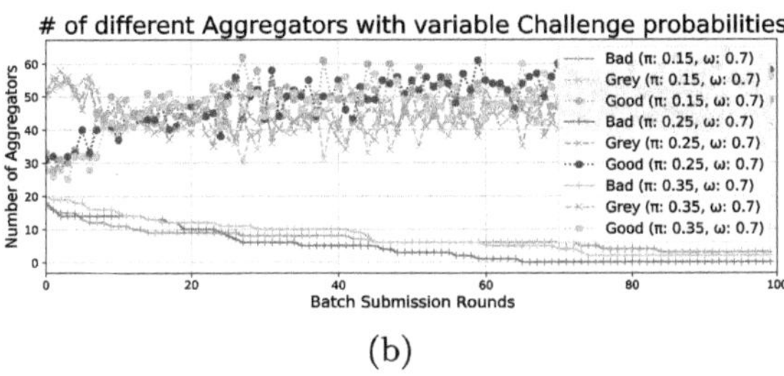

Fig. 9. Count of aggregator types across batch submission rounds in the OP Sepolia testnet with: (a) varying verifier challenge probabilities for invalid batches (fixed 25% for valid batches) and (b) varying verifier challenge probabilities for valid batches (fixed 70% for invalid batches).

OptiGame provides a flexible foundation for further optimization of L2 protocols. Our experimental results on the Optimism Sepolia testnet validate the practical efficacy of the proposed model in the real world, highlighting its potential to enhance the overall robustness and performance of optimistic rollup.

References

1. Nakamoto, S.: Bitcoin whitepaper. URL: https://bitcoin.org/bitcoin.pdf-(:17.07. 2019) (2008)
2. Khalil, A.A., Franco, J., Parvez, I., Uluagac, S., Shahriar, H., Rahman, M.A.: A literature review on blockchain-enabled security and operation of cyber-physical systems. In: 2022 IEEE 46th annual computers, software, and applications conference (COMPSAC), pp. 1774–1779. IEEE (2022)
3. Yang, D., Long, C., Xu, H., Peng, S.: A review on scalability of blockchain. In: Proceedings of the 2020 the 2nd International Conference on Blockchain Technology, pp. 1–6 (2020)
4. Rajabi, T., et al.: Feasibility analysis for sybil attacks in shard-based permissionless blockchains. Distributed Ledger Technol. Res. Practice **2**(4), 1–21 (2023)
5. Singh, A., et al.: Sidechain technologies in blockchain networks: an examination and state-of-the-art review. J. Network Comput. Appl
6. Poon, J., Buterin, V.: Plasma: Scalable autonomous smart contracts. White paper, pp. 1–47 (2017)
7. Malavolta, G., Moreno-Sanchez, P., Kate, A., Maffei, M., Ravi, S.: Concurrency and privacy with payment-channel networks. In: Proceedings of the 2017 ACM SIGSAC Conference on Computer and Communications Security, pp. 455–471 (2017)

8. Khalil, A.A., Rahman, M.A.: Ship: securing hashed timelock contracts in payment channel networks. In: 2023 IEEE Conference on Communications and Network Security (CNS), pp. 1–2. IEEE (2023)
9. Khalil, A.A., Rahman, M.A., Kholidy, H.A.: Fakey: fake hashed key attack on payment channel networks. In: 2023 IEEE Conference on Communications and Network Security (CNS), pp. 1–9. IEEE (2023)
10. Khalil, A.A., Rahman, M.A.: Parole: profitable arbitrage in optimistic rollup with erc-721 token transactions. In: 2024 54th Annual IEEE/IFIP International Conference on Dependable Systems and Networks (DSN), pp. 129–141. IEEE (2024)
11. Khalil, A.A., Rahman, M.A.: Rollguard: Defending rpc manipulation attacks in optimistic rollups with graph ml. In: 2025 26th International Symposium on Quality Electronic Design (ISQED), pp. 1–8. IEEE (2025)
12. Thibault, L.T., Sarry, T., Hafid, A.S.: A comprehensive survey. IEEE Access, Blockchain scaling using rollups (2022)
13. Donno, L.: Optimistic and validity rollups: Analysis and comparison between optimism and starknet. *arXiv preprint* arXiv:2210.16610 (2022)
14. Armstrong, M.: Ethereum, smart contracts and the optimistic roll-up (2021)
15. Arbitrum. L2 rollup: Arbitrum. https://arbitrum.io/
16. Optimism. L2 rollup: Optimism. https://www.optimism.io/
17. Medium. Offchainlabs: Security disclosure. https://medium.com/offchainlabs/security-disclosure-289a4ad50709
18. Ethresear. Reducing challenge times in rollups. https://ethresear.ch/t/reducing-challenge-times-in-rollups/14997
19. Medium. Or not secure enough. https://medium.com/tokamak-network/optimistic-rollup_is-not-secure-enough-than-you-think-cb23e6e6f11c
20. Delphidigital. A look at dispute resolution protocols in optimistic rollups. https://members.delphidigital.io/reports/a-look-at-dispute-resolution-protocols-in-optimistic-rollups#delay-attacks-a76c
21. Insights. Making sense of rollups, part 2: Dispute resolution on arbitrum and optimism. https://insights.deribit.com/market-research/making-sense-of-rollups-part-2-dispute-resolution-on-arbitrum-and-optimism/
22. Luu, L., Teutsch, J., Kulkarni, R., Saxena, P.: Demystifying incentives in the consensus computer. In: Proceedings of the 22nd ACM SIGSAC Conference on Computer and Communications Security, pp. 706–719. ACM (2015)
23. Tas, E.N., Boneh, D.: Cryptoeconomic security for data availability committees. Forthcoming at Financial Cryptography (2023)
24. Brünjes, L., Kiayias, A., Koutsoupias, E., Stouka, A.-P.: Reward sharing schemes for stake pools. In: 2020 IEEE European Symposium on Security and Privacy (EuroS&p), pp. 256–275. IEEE (2020)
25. Gersbach, H., Mamageishvili, A., Schneider, M.: Staking pools on blockchains. CoRR, abs/2203.05838 (2022)
26. Ethereum. Op sepolia. https://docs.optimism.io/chain/addresses#op-sepolia-l2
27. Croman, K., et al.: On scaling decentralized blockchains: (a position paper). Springer, In International conference on financial cryptography and data security (2016)
28. Buterin, V., et al.: A next-generation smart contract and decentralized application platform. white paper **3**(37), 2–1 (2014)
29. Yu, T., et al.: Dual-blockchain-based p2p energy trading system with an improved optimistic rollup mechanism. IET Smart Grid (2022)
30. Optimism-Documentation. Mempool. https://community.optimism.io/docs/developers/bedrock/differences-mempool

31. Schaffner, T.: Scaling public blockchains. University of Basel, A comprehensive analysis of optimistic and zero-knowledge rollups (2021)
32. Li, J.: On the security of optimistic blockchain mechanisms. Available at SSRN 4499357 (2023)
33. Mamageishvili, A., Felten, E.W.: Incentive schemes for rollup validators. In: The International Conference on Mathematical Research for Blockchain Economy, pp. 48–61. Springer (2023)
34. Dong, C., Wang, Y., Aldweesh, A., McCorry, P., Van Moorsel, A.: Betrayal, distrust, and rationality: smart counter-collusion contracts for verifiable cloud computing. In *Proceedings of the 2017 ACM SIGSAC Conference on Computer and Communications Security*, pp. 211–227 (2017)
35. Siyuan Liu and Yulong Zeng. Games in public announcement: How to reduce system losses in optimistic blockchain mechanisms. *arXiv preprint* arXiv:2407.21413, 2024
36. Avenhaus, R., Von Stengel, B., Zamir, S.: Inspection games. Handbook of game theory with economic applications **3**, 1947–1987 (2002)
37. Hohzaki, R., Kudoh, D., Komiya, T.: An inspection game: Taking account of fulfillment probabilities of players' aims. Naval Research Logistics (NRL) **53**(8), 761–771 (2006)
38. Dekel, E., Fudenberg, D., Levine, D.K.: Learning to play bayesian games. Games Econ. Behav. **46**(2), 282–303 (2004)
39. Emami-Taba, M., Tahvildari, L.: A bayesian game decision-making model for uncertain adversary types. In: Proceedings of the 26th Annual International Conference on Computer Science and Software Engineering, pp. 39–49 (2016)
40. Sadzik, T.: Beliefs revealed in bayesian-nash equilibrium. Unpublished paper.[484] (2011)
41. Nurmi, P.: Modelling routing in wireless ad hoc networks with dynamic bayesian games. In: 2004 First Annual IEEE Communications Society Conference on Sensor and Ad Hoc Communications and Networks, 2004. IEEE SECON 2004., pp. 63–70. IEEE (2004)
42. McDonald, K.R., Broderick, W.F., Huettel, S.A., Pearson, J.M.: Bayesian nonparametric models characterize instantaneous strategies in a competitive dynamic game. Nature Commun. **10**(1), 1808 (2019)
43. Hopkins, B.C.: The origin of the logic of symbolic mathematics: Edmund Husserl and Jacob Klein. Indiana University Press (2011)
44. Li, Y., Albarghouthi, A., Kincaid, Z., Gurfinkel, A., Chechik, M.: Symbolic optimization with smt solvers. ACM SIGPLAN Notices **49**(1), 607–618 (2014)
45. Landis, D.: Incentive non-compatibility of optimistic rollups. arXiv preprint arXiv:2312.01549 (2023)
46. Asharov, G., Canetti, R., Hazay, C.: Towards a game theoretic view of secure computation. In: Advances in Cryptology–EUROCRYPT 2011, pp. 426–445. Springer (2011)
47. Nabi, M., Avizheh, S., Kumaramangalam, M.V., Safavi-Naini, R.: Game-theoretic analysis of an incentivized verifiable computation system. In: Financial Cryptography and Data Security: FC 2019 International Workshops, VOTING and WTSC, St. Kitts, St. Kitts and Nevis, February 18–22, 2019, Revised Selected Papers 23, pp. 50–66. Springer (2020)
48. Gersbach, H., Mamageishvili, A., Pitsuwan, F.: Decentralized attack search and the design of bug bounty schemes. CoRR, abs/2304.00077 (2023)

CCGCRN: Cluster and Completion Graph Convolution Recurrent Network for Incomplete Traffic Flow Forecasting

Ruotian Xie[1,2], Jigang Wen[3], Caiping Liu[1,2]($\boxtimes$), Yani Jin[1,2], Kun Xie[1,2]($\boxtimes$), Shiming He[4], and Kuanching Li[3,5]

[1] Hunan University, Changsha, China
{liucaiping,liucaiping,xiekun}@hnu.edu.cn
[2] Ministry of Education Key Laboratory of Fusion Computing of Supercomputing and Artificial Intelligence, Changsha, China
[3] Hunan University of Science and Technology, Xiangtan, China
[4] Changsha University of Science and Technology, Changsha, China
[5] Hunan Key Laboratory for Service computing and Novel Software Technology, Changsha, China

Abstract. The spatial-temporal forecasting has attracted remarkable attention due to the increasing number of widespread applications with electricity, finance, climate, environment, and traffic. Although various studies on spatial-temporal forecasting exist, these algorithms leverage the same neural network to model all traffic series, which unreasonably and incapably learn spatial-temporal correlations from traffic series with different patterns using common parameters, and unfortunately, none of these algorithms considers data loss of time series, which greatly affects forecasting performance. Due to such, we propose a novel Cluster and Completion Graph Convolution Recurrent Network (CCGCRN) for incomplete traffic flow forecasting. To learn the spatial-temporal correlations better, we utilize CCGCRN to learn the common parameters within the cluster with strong relevance among traffic flows. Three techniques are proposed: (1) To learn the common parameters for traffic series sharing the same patterns, we propose the Cluster Parameter Learning module (CPL) to cluster traffic series based on the orthogonal non-negative matrix factorization algorithm, (2) To complete the missing values of traffic series by utilizing the commonality of series within a cluster, we propose the Completion Learning Network (CLN) to learn the spatial-temporal interaction relationships, and (3) To accurately forecast traffic series, we propose the Graph Convolution Recurrent Neural Network (GCRNN) that learns the graph construction adaptively and captures spatial-temporal correlations in each cluster. Extensive experimentations on two real-world datasets with 10% and 30% missing rates demonstrate that the proposed model achieves superior forecasting performance than the other eight baselines.

Keywords: Traffic series forecasting · Cluster-specific parameter learning · Traffic data completion · Graph neural networks

W. Liang et al. (Eds.): SecureComm 2025, LNICST 690, pp. 500–523, 2026.
https://doi.org/10.1007/978-3-032-23456-8_27

1   Introduction

With the collection of large-scale data by sensors and monitoring systems, forecasting tasks have been widely studied in various fields, such as climate [4,32,33], finance [1,15], and traffic [2,7,17,22,26,27,39]. As a canonical application, traffic forecasting is an indispensable component of Intelligent Transportation Systems (ITS), significantly improving urban transportation services' quality. Given historical traffic flows and existing road information, predicting future traffic conditions is critical. However, each future variable of a traffic flow depends on its historical values and other traffic flows, which is an intractable challenge. Furthermore, there are commonalities and characteristics between traffic flows, which provides favorable conditions for fine-grained traffic prediction that the loss of traffic series is not accidental due to network jitter, or device failures, if otherwise.

The tasks of traffic forecasting essentially belong to the category of time series forecasting. Most traditional methods, such as Auto-regressive Integrated Moving Average (ARIMA) [30] and Gaussian Process (GP) [23], assume that each traffic flow is a stationary sequence. These algorithms cannot deal with nonlinear long-term correlations and complicated spatial dependencies in traffic flows. As the amount of data increases, the complexity of the algorithms also rises sharply.

In recent decades, the deep neural network has achieved great success, especially in the fields of computational vision, natural language processing, and traffic forecasting. For traffic flow prediction, spatial-temporal correlations are captured by Convolution Neural Networks (CNN) and Recurrent Neural Networks (RNN), including their variants respectively. For example, both LSTNet [24] and STCNN [20] adopt CNN and RNN to extract local dependency patterns among variables and discover long-term patterns for time series trends. However, it is limited to regular grid structures rather than non-Euclidean correlations dominated by irregular road networks.

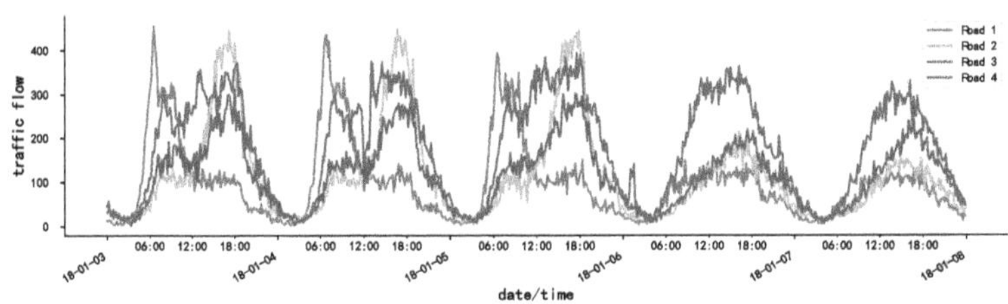

Fig. 1. Different traffic flows with diverse patterns. (2018-1-3   2018-1-5: weekdays, and 2018-1-6   2018-1-7: weekends).

Graph Convolution Networks (GCN) are proposed to present the spatial feature of traffic networks via constructing graphs to process the irregular graph information of traffic data. The tremendous amount of work such as ASTGCN

[17], MTGNN [39], and HGCN [16] achieves the performance in the aspect of capturing spatial-temporal dependencies dynamically. They consider each road segment or sensor point as a node and characterize spatial correlations through the neighbor relationships between nodes. Even though there has been lots of work, the following challenges remain.

- Most traffic forecasting models [6,27,39,40,44,47] prefer learning common parameters (as example in Sect. 4.3) for all traffic series to capture features. That is, they claim all traffic flows have common patterns. Nevertheless, as shown in Fig. 1, there are similar, dissimilar, and even completely opposite patterns in traffic flow. The traffic flow of road 1 shows a morning peak pattern but flows of road 2 and road 4 show an evening peak pattern. The flow on road 3 presents a relatively stable pattern that differs from flows on the other three highways, so it is unreasonable that the features of all traffic flows are learned by sharing the common parameters in a neural network model.
- Most traffic forecasting models [2,6,40,44] ignore the missing values for traffic flows due to poor network conditions or equipment failures and remain highly susceptible to these gaps. Traditional completion methods, such as SVT [5], MF, and interpolation filling, perform poorly as the missing rate of traffic data increases. Although a few models [47] consider these missing values, they typically do not account for the significant differences in traffic flow patterns, as shown in Fig. 1, which can impact prediction accuracy.
- Graph neural networks have been applied in some existing research to capture complex spatial correlations that are not restricted to regular grid structures. However, most of them are implemented by a given graph structure that cannot reflect the dynamic dependencies among traffic nodes. Moreover, the predefined graph structure constrains the generality of the forecasting model.

In this work, we propose a novel graph-based neural network spatial-temporal forecasting model, called Cluster and Completion Graph Convolution Recurrent Network (CCGCRN), for forecasting traffic flows with missing values. Several components are elaborately designed to cope with the abovementioned problems, and the following technical contributions are made in CCGCRN.

- To learn the common parameters for similar traffic flows, we design the Cluster Parameter Learning (CPL) module to cluster traffic data based on the orthogonal non-negative matrix factorization algorithm. Unlike traditional clustering methods such as K-means and DBSCAN which cannot cluster data with missing values, our algorithm can divide traffic flows into several clusters even when it suffers from missing data. This way, the traffic flows in the same cluster have commonalities, while the traffic data in different clusters have specificities.
- To complete the missing values of the traffic series, we propose the Completion Learning Network (CLN) to learn the spatial-temporal interaction function by the element-wise product instead of the inner product. We complete traffic data within each cluster by effectively utilizing commonalities among traffic

flows of the same cluster. Moreover, as the missing rate rises, our completion module can still maintain good completion performance for better traffic forecasting.

- To forecast the future status of traffic series, we elaborately design the Graph Convolution Recurrent Neural Network (GCRNN) to learn spatial-temporal correlations in each cluster. We propose a recurrent neural network based on gate mechanisms to capture the long-term temporal dependencies. To fully extract the dynamic and complex spatial features, we also propose a graph convolution neural network based on a data-driven approach instead of the predefined graphs method to acquire graph structures, enabling the proposed model to more generally handle other forecasting problems for incomplete spatial-temporal data.

- The proposed method CCGCRN learns cluster-specific patterns within each cluster to forecast incomplete traffic flows in a fine-grain way. Traffic flows from the same cluster share a common parameter space, while those from different clusters learn completely independent parameter spaces. In summary, our method combines the advantages of common parameter learning methods and node-specific parameter learning methods. Compared with the former, we capture spatial-temporal features more fine-grained. Compared with the latter, we learn fewer parameters and avoid the overfitting problem.

- We have conducted extensive experiments on two real-world traffic datasets, PeMS04 and PeMS08 with missing rates of 10% and 30%. The results demonstrate that the proposed model CCGCRN outperforms the other eight baselines. For example, when the missing rate on the PeMS04 dataset is 30%, the RMSE under our method is 71% lower than that under the best baseline.

The remainder of this paper is organized as follows. Section 2 presents related work, the problem definition and model overview are shown in Sect. 3, the details of three components of CPL, CLN, and GCRNN modules are discussed in Sect. 4, and finally, experimental evaluation and analysis of the proposed model CCGCRN are depicted in Sect. 5, and finally, concluding remarks and future directions in Sect. 6.

2   Related Work

2.1   Traffic Flow Forecasting

In recent decades, research on traffic flow forecasting—an essential part of intelligent transportation systems—has grown significantly. This problem uses multivariate time series from sensors to predict future conditions. Early statistical methods, such as ARIMA, SVM, and GP [23,30,46], rely on stationarity and focus solely on temporal information. With the rise of deep learning, researchers shift to deep neural networks like RNN and CNN to capture non-linear temporal correlations and complex spatial patterns by splitting the city into grids [14,20,24,31,42]. However, assuming urban road networks are Euclidean is often inaccurate. Therefore, several methods combining graph neural networks and sequential learning models are proposed to measure spatial and temporal dependencies simultaneously [2,7,10,11,17,26,28,36,39]. The predefined graph is a worthwhile scrupulosity among the above graph learning methods, although it achieves better performance.

2.2   Graph Convolution Network

Graph convolution networks, commonly applied in graph tasks such as classification [35,38,43], representation learning [13,45], and prediction [37,41], have been widely employed in traffic forecasting to model spatial dependencies in non-Euclidean spaces along with long-term temporal relations. For instance, DCRNN [27] models traffic flow as a diffusion process on a bidirectional graph, while transformer-inspired approaches like DSAN [29] and GMAN [44] use self-attention mechanisms to capture dependencies. These methods could measure dependencies aggregating features of neighbors, but their graphs are predetermined, relying on a large amount of prior knowledge. Consequently, recent studies have focused on adaptively generating graphs from data; MTGNN [39] extracts uni-directed relations without an explicit graph, and AGCRN [2] learns inherent characteristics through simple modules.

On the one hand, except for AGCRN, the above-mentioned methods capture the common pattern between traffic nodes to learn spatial-temporal features. Although common parameter learning approaches reduce the number of parameters and decrease the computational cost, they are inferior in forecasting traffic flows since not all traffic nodes have commonalities. On the other hand, utilizing the node-specific parameter learning method such as AGCRN learns specific correlations for each traffic time series while they are not entirely different from each other. Worse yet, it easily brings about overfitting and generates a large number of parameters. To capture the common pattern among similar traffic nodes, our proposed model leverages a cluster-specific parameter learning method that combines the advantages of the common and node-specific parameters while avoiding their disadvantages.

2.3   Missing Values Completion

Traffic data, gathered via various sensors, frequently suffer from missing values, which disrupt monitoring and hinder further analysis. Despite increasing efforts on this issue in recent years, some inadequacies remain. Statistical methods (e.g., SVT [5], MF, and zero filling) ignore the stochastic variations and the relationship between traffic series, resulting in poor performance. DSMI [8], a decision tree-based method, uses both within- and between-record correlations to impute numerical or categorical values but is more suitable for discrete data than for sequential traffic data. Similarly, MVLM [25] combines several existing algorithms at a high computational cost. Motivated by [19], we extend matrix factorization to neural network mining multi-dimensional inherent information to impute traffic series. To the best of our knowledge, there is no specific work on missing value completion in spatial-temporal forecasting.

3   Methodology

3.1   Problem Definition

As shown in Fig. 2, there are multiple sensors on the road. Each sensor collects flow data at all times to form a traffic flow. Therefore, each sensor is regarded as a node in this investigation. We represent N incomplete traffic flows by $X = \{\boldsymbol{x}_{:,1}, \boldsymbol{x}_{:,2}, \ldots, \boldsymbol{x}_{:,n}, \ldots, \boldsymbol{x}_{:,N}\} \in R_+^{T \times N}$ where $\boldsymbol{x}_{:,n} \in R_+^T$ denotes a traffic flow with T time steps of node n. The flow values of a node are denoted as R_+ since they are always non-negative at all times.

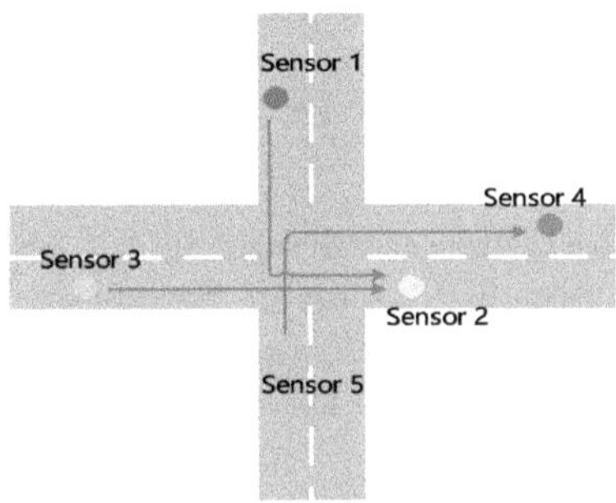

Fig. 2. Sensors collect traffic flows on the roads.

In the research, traffic flows X are incomplete because some entry values are missing. The reasons can be summarized into two aspects. On the one hand, the transportation system suffers some faults due to equipment malfunctions, environmental changes, and others. On the other hand, the traffic flows can be lost in server communications and system conditions. As such, we use $\bar{X}$ to denote the observed values set of all nodes. Correspondingly, $\bar{\boldsymbol{x}}_{:,n} \in R_+^T$ constitutes observed values of node n at all time points. In this study, we define the completion problem as $\bar{X} \to \hat{X}$ where $\hat{X} \in R_+^{T \times N}$ represents traffic flows after completion.

Assuming the current time is t_0, our forecasting task based on graph neural network for incomplete traffic flows can be defined as: $\{\boldsymbol{x}_{t_0+1}, \boldsymbol{x}_{t_0+2}, \ldots, \boldsymbol{x}_{t_0+\tau}\} = f(\boldsymbol{x}_{t_0-T+1}, \boldsymbol{x}_{t_0-T+2}, \ldots, \boldsymbol{x}_{t_0}; \mathcal{G})$, which will be addressed by traffic series X and the graph $\mathcal{G}$ in this study. Here, $X = \{\boldsymbol{x}_{t_0-T+1}, \boldsymbol{x}_{t_0-T+2}, \ldots, \boldsymbol{x}_{t_0}\} \in R_+^{T \times N}$ is N traffic flows with missing values over the historical T time steps and $Y = \{\boldsymbol{x}_{t_0+1}, \boldsymbol{x}_{t_0+2}, \ldots, \boldsymbol{x}_{t_0+\tau}\} \in R_+^{\tau \times N}$ is complete forecasting results for N nodes with τ future time steps. The function $f(\cdot)$ maps X into Y by minimizing the absolute loss between complete forecasting results Y and ground truth Y'. Additionally, the undirected graph $\mathcal{G} = (V, E, A)$ represents a topological connection of the road network. At this point, V is the set of $|V| = N$ nodes on the road network, E is the set of edges to denote the connectivity among nodes, and $A \in R^{N \times N}$ is the weighted adjacency matrix with $A_{ij} > 0$ if $(v_i, v_j) \in E$ and $A_{ij} = 0$ if $(v_i, v_j) \notin E$ where $v \in V$. The larger A_{ij} is, the closer the relationship between nodes v_i and v_j is.

3.2 Model Overview

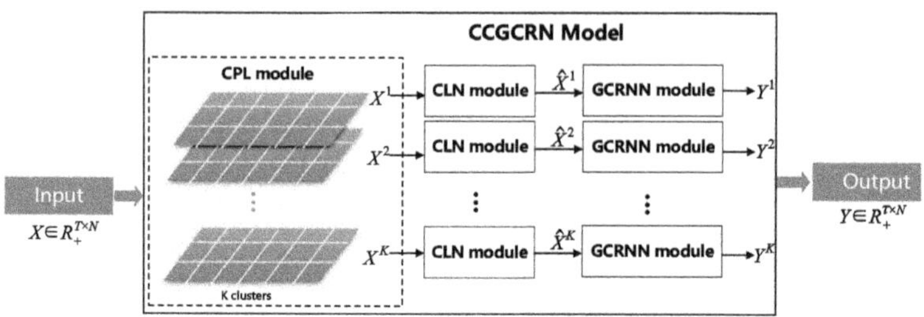

Fig. 3. The framework of CCGCRN.

Figure 3 demonstrates the overall framework of our proposed model CCGCRN, which includes three components: a Cluster Parameter Learning module (CPL), a Completion Learning Network (CLN), and a Graph Convolution Recurrent Neural Network (GCRNN). Details of the three modules are depicted as follows:

CPL Module. In Sect. 4.1, we propose the CPL module based on the nonnegative matrix factorization algorithm constrained by orthogonality to cluster traffic nodes even if there are missing data. Compared to other clustering methods, our algorithm adapts to the missing values of traffic flows. As shown in Fig. 3, the input of CPL can be expressed as:

$$X = \{\boldsymbol{x}_{:,1}, \boldsymbol{x}_{:,2}, \ldots, \boldsymbol{x}_{:,n}, \ldots, \boldsymbol{x}_{:,N}\} \in R_+^{T \times N} \tag{1}$$

where X is N incomplete traffic flows over the T moments. Then the output of CPL is illustrated as follows:

$$\{ X^1, X^2, \ldots, X^K\}. \tag{2}$$

We aggregate traffic flows X into K clusters $\{C_1, C_2, \ldots, C_K\}$. All traffic nodes in the cluster C_K compose the K-th traffic matrix X^K.

CLN. In Sect. 4.2, we propose CLN, a concise neural network, for imputing missing traffic flow entries to obtain the complete traffic data. To improve completion performance, we complete within the cluster with close dependencies among traffic flows. Figure 3 illustrates the input of CLN in the cluster C_K expressed as:

$$X^K = \{\boldsymbol{x}_{:,1}^K, \boldsymbol{x}_{:,2}^K, \ldots, \boldsymbol{x}_{:,n_K}^K\} \in R_+^{T \times n_K} \tag{3}$$

where the incomplete traffic node $\boldsymbol{x}_{:,n_K}^K \in R_+^T$ exists in X^K and n_K is the number of nodes from X^K. Correspondingly, n_1 and n_2 are the number of nodes from X^1 and X^2, respectively, and then $n_1 + n_2 + \cdots + n_K = N$. Processed by CLN, the output is completion traffic flows expressed as:

$$\{\hat{X}^1, \hat{X}^2, \ldots, \hat{X}^K\} \tag{4}$$

where $\hat{X}^K = \{\hat{x}_{:,1}^K, \hat{x}_{:,2}^K, \ldots, \hat{x}_{:,n_K}^K\} \in R_+^{T \times n_K}$ is traffic flows after completing and $\hat{x}_{:,n_K}^K \in R_+^T$ is a complete traffic node now.

GCRNN. In this module, we discuss spatial-temporal features to accurately forecast traffic flows. The traffic flow at a certain time is not only determined by the past time but also influenced by other traffic flows, especially highly correlated traffic series. To this end, GCRNN captures each cluster's complex spatial correlation and long-term temporal dependency. The cluster-specific pattern means that our module learns common parameters for traffic nodes in the same cluster. Meanwhile, our graphs are learned from traffic data adaptively to capture hidden and dynamic correlations among nodes. The input of this module is the output of CLN, i.e. $\{\hat{X}^1, \hat{X}^2, \ldots, \hat{X}^K\}$. Then the output of GCRNN can be expressed as:

$$\{Y^1, Y^2, \ldots, Y^K\} \tag{5}$$

where Y^K is the forecasting results in the cluster C_K.

4   Model Design

4.1   Cluster Parameter Learning Module

Traditional clustering approaches like K-means and DBSCAN clustering usually calculate the Euclidean distance among nodes to cluster data. Nodes closer to each other form the same cluster, and nodes farther away form different clusters. But the traffic nodes we clustered contain missing values with a high missing rate. The above clustering algorithms do not apply to incomplete traffic flows.

Based on the above analysis, we propose the G-orthogonal non-negative matrix factorization (ONMF) algorithm in this module to cluster traffic nodes, as:

$$\min_{F \geq 0, G \geq 0} \|X - FG^T\|^2, s.t. G^T G = I. \tag{6}$$

ONMF factorizes input non-negative traffic matrix X into two non-negative matrices: $X \approx FG^T$ under the orthogonal constraint $G^T G = I$. Here, $X \in R_+^{T \times N}$ is an incomplete matrix of traffic series. $F \in R_+^{T \times K}$ and $G \in R_+^{N \times K}$ are factor matrices of X. Generally, the rank of matrices F and G is much lower than the rank of X (i.e., $K \ll \min(N, T)$).

Theorem 1. *ONMF Eq. (6) is equivalent to K-means clustering*

$$\min \sum_{k=1}^K \sum_{i \in C_k} \|x_i - c_k\|^2. \tag{7}$$

Proof. We denote minimizing ONMF as $J = \|X - FG^T\|^2 = Tr(XX^T - 2F^T XG + F^T F)$. The zero gradient condition $\partial J / \partial F = -2XG + 2F = 0$ gives $F = XG$. Then $J = Tr(XX^T - G^T X^T XG)$. Since $Tr(XX^T)$ is a constant, the optimization problem of ONMF becomes

$$\max_{G \geq 0} Tr(G^T X^T XG), s.t. G^T G = I. \tag{8}$$

Then, the K-means clustering can be expressed as $\min \sum_{k=1}^K \sum_{i \in C_k} \|x_i - c_k\|^2 = \min \sum_{k=1}^K \sum_{i=1}^N g_{ik} \|x_i - c_k\|^2$ where c_k is the cluster centroid of the k-th cluster

C_k, x_i is a traffic node clustering into C_k and $G \in R_+^{N \times K}$ is regarded as a cluster indicator matrix: $g_{ik} = 1$ if $x_i \in C_k$ and $g_{ik} = 0$ otherwise. Let the normalized $\tilde{G} = G(G^T G)^{-1/2}$. Similarly, the optimization problem of K-means clustering can be expressed as:

$$\max_{\tilde{G}^T \tilde{G}=I, \tilde{G} \geq 0} Tr(\tilde{G}^T W \tilde{G}), \tag{9}$$

where $W_{ij} = x_i^T x_j$ is the value of the i-th row and the j-th column of the matrix W.

According to the optimization problem Eq. (8) and Eq. (9), ONMF Eq. (6) is equivalent to K-means clustering Eq. (7). Furthermore, we cluster traffic nodes according to the decomposition factor G in ONMF, whose iterative update rules are as follows:

$$G_{IK} \leftarrow G_{IK} \sqrt{\frac{(X^T F)_{IK}}{(GG^T X^T F)_{IK}}} \tag{10}$$

$$F_{JK} \leftarrow F_{JK} \frac{(XG)_{JK}}{(FG^T G)_{JK}}.$$

Specifically, the K-th probability variable is the maximum value of the node x_i in G, which means that the traffic node x_i belongs to the cluster C_K. For example, Fig. 4 illustrates that the incomplete traffic matrix $X \in R_+^{5 \times 4}$ is factorized into factor matrices $F \in R_+^{5 \times 3}$ and $G \in R_+^{4 \times 3}$. According to the iterative results of matrix G in Fig. 4, four nodes $\{x_1, x_2, x_3, x_4\}$ will be clustered into 3 clusters $\{C_1, C_2, C_3\}$. In Fig. 4, x_1 will be clustered into C_2. Because the probability that x_1 belongs to C_2 is greater than the probability that it belongs to C_1 and to C_3. In this work, the orthogonal non-negative matrix factorization algorithm of the CPL module clusters incomplete traffic series X into K clusters $\{C_1, C_2, \ldots, C_K\}$ to compose K traffic matrices $\{X^1, X^2, \ldots, X^K\}$.

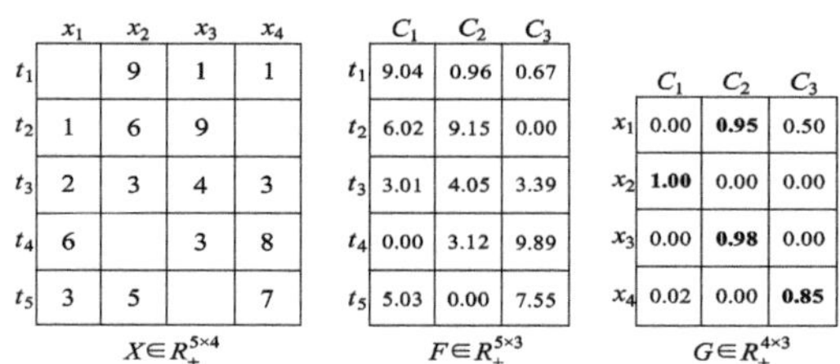

	x_1	x_2	x_3	x_4
t_1		9	1	1
t_2	1	6	9	
t_3	2	3	4	3
t_4	6		3	8
t_5	3	5		7

$X \in R_+^{5 \times 4}$

	C_1	C_2	C_3
t_1	9.04	0.96	0.67
t_2	6.02	9.15	0.00
t_3	3.01	4.05	3.39
t_4	0.00	3.12	9.89
t_5	5.03	0.00	7.55

$F \in R_+^{5 \times 3}$

	C_1	C_2	C_3
x_1	0.00	**0.95**	0.50
x_2	**1.00**	0.00	0.00
x_3	0.00	**0.98**	0.00
x_4	0.02	0.00	**0.85**

$G \in R_+^{4 \times 3}$

Fig. 4. The decomposition results F and G of incomplete traffic flows X.

In this investigation, our module CPL based on ONMF avoids the impact of missing data by only iteratively updating observables, which is not possible with other clustering algorithms. After clustering, the relationships among traffic nodes in the same cluster are close, while the relationships among nodes in different clusters are weak.

4.2 Completion Learning Network

To eliminate the influence of missing values, we propose a Completion Learning Network (CLN) impute these values to construct complete traffic data. The traffic flows within the same cluster are more closely related than other clusters. Therefore, completing missing entries in the same cluster with close relationships among traffic nodes can improve the accuracy of completion.

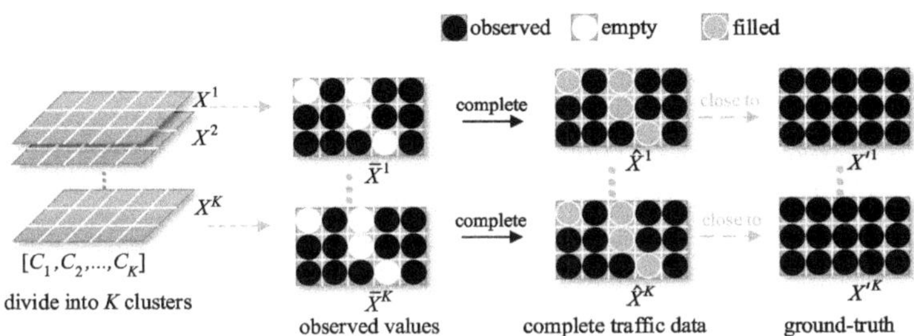

Fig. 5. Completion notation.

As shown in Fig. 5, this is the completion notation of traffic data. Taking the cluster C_K as an example, we train observed values of traffic flows $\bar{X}^K$ to impute the missing entries to constitute complete traffic data $\hat{X}^K$. In other words, the complete data $\hat{X}^K$ obtained by CLN is as close to the ground-truth traffic values X'^K as possible.

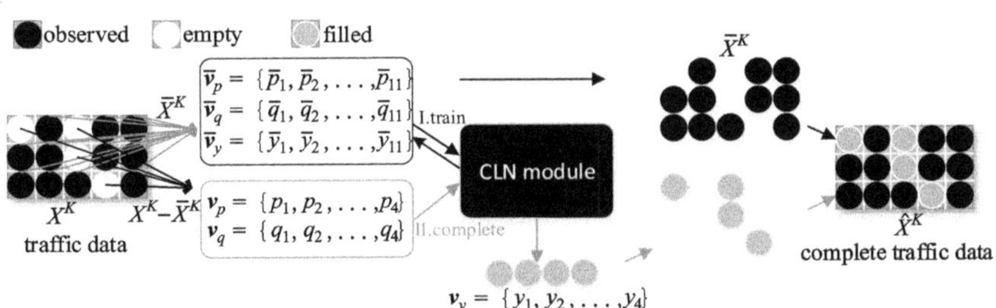

Fig. 6. Completing processing via CLN module in the cluster C_K.

Specifically, we divide the observable data $\bar{X}^K$ into three vectors: time vector $\bar{v}_p = \{\bar{p}_1, \bar{p}_2, \ldots, \bar{p}_{\bar{m}}\} \in R_+^{\bar{m}}$, node vector $\bar{v}_q = \{\bar{q}_1, \bar{q}_2, \ldots, \bar{q}_{\bar{m}}\} \in R_+^{\bar{m}}$ and traffic flow vector $\bar{v}_y = \{\bar{y}_1, \bar{y}_2, \ldots, \bar{y}_{\bar{m}}\} \in R_+^{\bar{m}}$, where $\bar{m}$ is the number of observables. As shown in Fig. 6, the number of observables is 11, i.e. $\bar{m} = 11$. The vector $\bar{v}_y$ consists of all observed flow values $\{\bar{y}_1, \bar{y}_2, \ldots, \bar{y}_{11}\}$ from the observable data $\bar{X}^K$. Then the time vector $\bar{v}_p$ and node vector $\bar{v}_q$ are the abscissa and ordinate of all observed flow values, respectively. Correspondingly, the time vector

$v_p = \{p_1, p_2, \ldots, p_m\} \in R_+^m$ and node vector $v_q = \{q_1, q_2, \ldots, q_m\} \in R_+^m$ are got from unobservable data $X^K - \bar{X}^K$. v_p and v_q are the abscissa and ordinate of all unobserved flow values, respectively. CLN trains $\bar{v}_p$, $\bar{v}_q$ and $\bar{v}_y$ to learn the spatial-temporal interaction function and then utilizes v_p and v_q to impute the missing values v_y. Figure 7 demonstrates that the CLN module includes an embedding layer, an MF learning layer, and a completion layer. The embedding layer projects one-dimensional representation to multidimensional representation, which is formulated as:

$$P = e_1(\bar{v}_p) \tag{11}$$

$$Q = e_2(\bar{v}_q) \tag{12}$$

where time latent matrix $P \in R^{\bar{m} \times f}$ and node latent matrix $Q \in R^{\bar{m} \times f}$ are embedding matrices, $e(\cdot)$ is the embedding function and f is the latent factor of embedding. The obtained time (node) embedding P or Q can be seen as the latent matrix for time (node) in the context of the latent factor model.

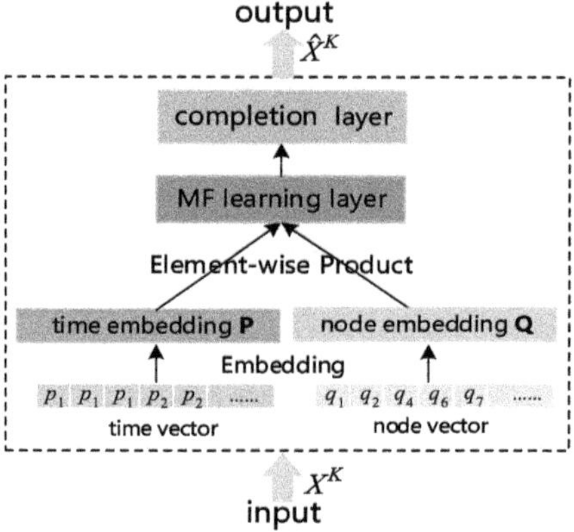

Fig. 7. the CLN module in the cluster C_K.

Traditional matrix factorization usually utilizes the inner product, a linear combination of latent features with the same weight, to complete data that can't capture the complex structure of spatial-temporal interaction data. In this module, we replace the inner product with the element-wise product to combine different weights for learning the interaction function. We capture the complicated correlations of spatial-temporal interaction through the MF learning layer as:

$$f(P, Q) = P \odot Q \tag{13}$$

where $\odot$ donates the Hadamard product. Ultimately, a fully connected layer is utilized as the completion layer to impute traffic data:

$$\bar{v}_y' = g(P, Q) = \sigma(W^T(P \odot Q) + b). \tag{14}$$

Here, W and b denote the learnable weight and bias, respectively, and σ denotes the activation function. The module utilizes the Rectified Linear Unit $\phi(x) =$

$\max(0, x)$ as σ and learns W and b from observed data with $L2$ loss, which is expressed as:

$$L2 = \frac{1}{\bar{m}} \sum_{i=1}^{\bar{m}} (\bar{v}_y - \bar{v}'_y)^2. \tag{15}$$

Once the training has been finished, we will get the imputation values v_y. Then the complete traffic flows $\hat{X}^K$ can be reconstructed according to v_p, v_q and v_y.

In this work, we elaborate that CLN learns complicated spatial-temporal interaction correlations to accurately complete traffic flows. Furthermore, even with high missing rates, CLN can still accurately complete the values of traffic flows, as shown in the experiments below.

4.3 Graph Convolution Recurrent Neural Network

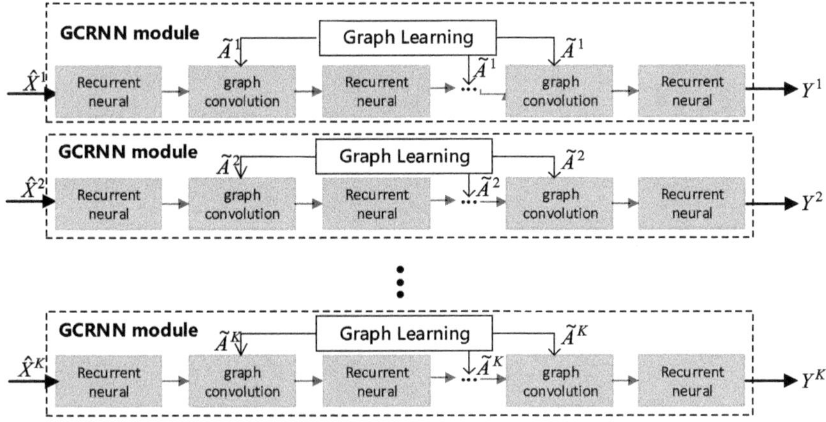

Fig. 8. The GCRNN overview of all clusters.

In this research, we propose a Graph Convolution Recurrent Neural Network (GCRNN) to capture each cluster's spatial correlations and temporal dependencies. The module learns common parameters among complete traffic flows within the cluster that contains commonalities. As shown in Fig. 8, in every cluster, there is a graph learning layer, a graph convolution network, and a recurrent neural network in GCRNN. The graph learning layer learns a graph based on traffic flows. Then the graph convolution network and recurrent network capture spatial and temporal correlations, respectively. The following elaboration still takes a module in the cluster C_K as an example.

Most methods empirically exploit a predefined graph for spatial correlation to learn spatial relationships, which restricts the forecasting model to specific occasions. Instead of the predefined graph, GCRNN learns the topological construction adaptively between the traffic nodes within the cluster. The formulation of learning an adjacency matrix is:

$$\tilde{A}^K = SoftMax(ReLU(E'^K \cdot (E^K)^T)) \tag{16}$$

where $\tilde{A}^K \in R^{n_K \times n_K}$ presents the processed adjacency matrix with n_K traffic nodes in the cluster C_K and $E^K \in R^{n_K \times e}$ is the node embedding (e is the dimension of node embedding) which is randomly initialized and updated automatically during training. Here, $ReLU$ function makes the matrix of multiplying E^K and $(E^K)^T$ sparse while reducing the computation cost for the following graph convolution. Then $SoftMax$ activation function regularizes the adjacency matrix resulting from the node embedding E^K. Furthermore, when the graph or the number of nodes is very large, learning the graph within every cluster can operate as usual and stabilize at better local optima.

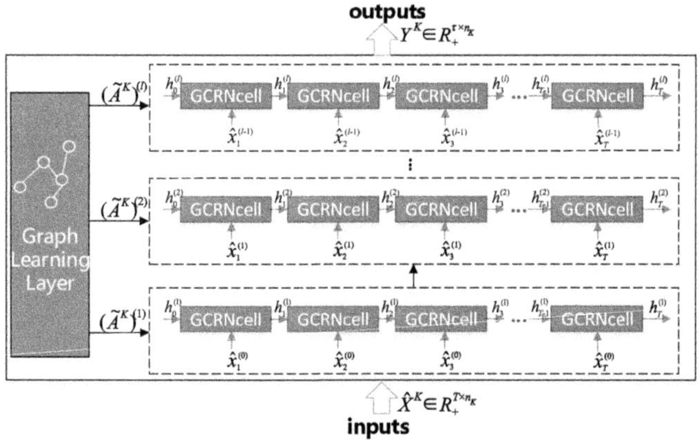

Fig. 9. The GCRNN module in the cluster C_K.

Next, our module exploits a spectral theory-based GCN to capture spatial dependencies. To characterize high-dimensional features with lower computational cost, we approximate GCN via Chebyshev polynomial expansion [9]

$$G(\tilde{A}^K) = \sum_{d=0}^{D-1} T_d(\tilde{A}^K) X^K \theta \tag{17}$$

of order d computed by the stable recursion $T_d(\tilde{A}^K) = 2\tilde{A}^K T_{d-1}(\tilde{A}^K) - T_{d-2}(\tilde{A}^K)$ with $T_0 = 1$ and $T_1 = \tilde{A}^K$. Except for the spatial correlations, the long-term temporal correlations are also significant for the traffic forecasting problem. In this module, we introduce Gated Recurrent Unit (GRU), a recurrent neural network, to capture temporal dependencies between the traffic flows under each cluster [21]. GRU is superior to traditional recurrent neural networks and Hidden Markov Model in long-term memory performance. The performance of GRU is similar to other RNNs, but it requires fewer parameters to train with cheaper computational costs. As shown in Fig. 9, we replace the fully-connected layer with the graph convolution layer in GRU to form GCRNcell. In the cluster C_K, one of the layers from the GCRNN module at t moment can be expressed as follows.

$$z_t = \sigma(\sum_{d=0}^{D-1} T_d(\tilde{A}^K)[\hat{\boldsymbol{x}}_t^K, h_{t-1}]\theta_z + b_z) \tag{18}$$

$$r_t = \sigma(\sum_{d=0}^{D-1} T_d(\tilde{A}^K)[\hat{\boldsymbol{x}}_t^K, h_{t-1}]\theta_r + b_r) \tag{19}$$

$$\hat{h}_t = tanh(\sum_{d=0}^{D-1} T_d(\tilde{A}^K)[\hat{\boldsymbol{x}}_t^K, r_t \odot h_{t-1}]\theta_h + b_h)$$

$$h_t = z_t \odot h_{t-1} + (1 - z_t) \odot \hat{h}_t \tag{20}$$

Combining Fig. 9 to illustrate the formulas, $\hat{\boldsymbol{x}}_t^K$ and h_t are the filled input and output of GCRNcell at time step t. The graph learning $\sum_{d=0}^{D-1} T_d(\tilde{A}^K)$ obtained by the node embedding is abbreviated as $(\tilde{A}^K)$ in the figure. As we can see from the formulas, the adjacency matrix $(\tilde{A}^K)$ keeps consistent between all GCRNN blocks in each cluster, which is in accord with our common logic. The gate status z_t and r_t are update grate and reset gate obtained by a learnable matrix $(\tilde{A}^K)$, transmission status h_{t-1} at the last moment and the input of the node $\hat{\boldsymbol{x}}_t^K$ at the current moment. The sigmoid activation function $\sigma(\cdot)$ is the core that z_t and r_t become the gates. Then the operation $[\cdot]$ concatenates multiple components and $\odot$ is also the Hadamard product. The series parameters of θ and b are learnable.

We take the parameter θ_z as an example to illustrate the differences between common parameter learning, node-specific parameter learning, and cluster-specific parameter learning. Common parameter learning assigns parameters for all nodes leading to $\theta_z \in R^{T \times h}$, which is unsuitable for nodes with different patterns sharing common parameters. h represents hidden dimensions. For node-specific parameter learning, assigning parameters for each node will result in $\theta_z \in R^{N \times T \times h}$, which is too huge to optimize. In our study, we assign parameters for each cluster leading to $\theta_z \in R^{K \times T \times h}$. Here, K (seeing Sect. 5.6 Parameter Analysis for details) is much smaller than N. Therefore, θ_z learned in a cluster-specific manner is much less than θ_z learned in a node-specific manner and more fine-grained than θ_z learned in a common manner. Likewise, the series parameters of θ and b are the same comparison results.

GCRNN captures spatial-temporal correlations from each cluster, a cluster-specific parameter learning method that can learn commonalities among traffic flows. Compared with common parameter learning methods, our model learns spatial-temporal features more fined-grained. Compared with node-specific parameter learning methods, we learn much fewer parameters. Moreover, our module learns graph structures based on data-driven, which makes the model more general for spatial-temporal forecasting problems. Besides, due to the existence of clustering, we still learn graph structures easily, even when the number of nodes is very large.

4.4   Traffic Flows Forecasting

Our model forecasts traffic flows $Y = \{Y^1, Y^2, \ldots, Y^K\} \in R^{\tau \times N}$ of all clusters at τ time steps with a convolution layer through the output of feature learning h_t. The output of all clusters from the Conv2d layer is collectively expressed as

$$Y = h_t \star f_{1 \times h} \tag{21}$$

where $f_{1 \times h}$ is the filter, h represents hidden dimensions and $\star$ denotes the convolution operation. In the training process, we adopt the mean absolute error (L1-loss), and the objective function is expressed as follows

$$O(Y, Y^{'}) = \frac{1}{N} \sum_{j=1}^{N} \sum_{i=1}^{\tau} |Y_i^j - Y_i^{'j}| \tag{22}$$

where Y is the forecasting value, $Y^{'}$ is the ground truth, N is the number of nodes and τ is the time steps of target data. All neural models of CCGCRN are trained using the Adam optimizer.

5   Experimental Results

In this section, we conduct extensive comparison experiments with eight baselines and ablation studies on two real-world datasets for traffic flow forecasting. We randomly discard some traffic flow values with two specific missing rates to demonstrate the advantages of our methods in completing missing values.

5.1   Datasets

We perform experiments on two real traffic datasets. In Table 1, we summarize statistics of benchmark datasets, PeMS04 and PeMS08, which are collected by the Caltrans Performance Measurement System (PeMS) in real-time every 30 s [34]. The traffic data is aggregated into 5-min intervals, which means there are 12-time steps in the traffic series for each hour. The raw data contains traffic flow, average speed, and occupancy measured by over 39, 000 detectors in California at different periods.

Table 1. Dataset description and statistics

Datasets	#Nodes	Time Steps	Time Span
PeMS04	307	16992	59
PeMS08	170	17856	62

Specifically,   PeMS04   contains   307 loop detectors in the period January~February 2018, and PeMS08 collected in the period July~August 2016 contained 170 sensors, as depicted in Table 1. Besides, we set missing rates to 10% and 30% with which original datasets are abandoned. After completing the missing values, we normalize input datasets by the standard normalization method to remove the mean and scale-to-unit variance.

5.2   Baselines

To validate the performance of the proposed model, we select eight baselines to compare, including statistic methods, predefined graph-based methods, and adaptive graph-based methods. The description of these baselines is as follows:

- **HA**: Considering the periodicity of traffic, this method exploits the average traffic value at the same time of day in the training datasets as the prediction.
- **ARIMA** [3]: A prominent statistical method consists of autoregressive term, integrated term, and moving average term.
- **LR**: A regression model is used to capture linear correlations between input and output.
- **LSTM**: A powerful recurrent neural network is mainly designed to solve the problem of gradient vanishing and gradient explosion during the training process of long sequence data.
- **DCRNN** [27]: A diffusion convolution recurrent network combines diffusion graph convolutions with recurrent neural networks.
- **MTGNN** [39]: A spatial-temporal graph convolution network utilizes external features to generate a unidirectional adaptive graph.
- **DMSTGCN** [18]: A spatial-temporal graph convolution model captures spatial-temporal dependencies with multi-faceted characteristics.
- **STGODE** [12]: A deep neural network considers spatial correlations with spatial neighbors and semantical neighbors comprehensively.

5.3   Experimental Settings

In this cluster module, we select matrix factor G instead of F to keep orthogonal. According to the datasets $X \in R_+^{T \times N}$, this proposed model clusters matrix columns (i.e., nodes) into K, and the best choice of the parameter K is set from $\{2, 3\}$ verified by experiments (see Sect. 5.6 for details). The factor size of embedding layers in CLN is 16, the max depth of graph convolution layers is 2, and the Chebyshev factor d is set to 2. The model is optimized by Adam optimizer with learning rate decay for a maximum of 100 epochs, and an early stop strategy is used with patience of 15. Considering the fairness of comparison experiments, all baseline methods are configured to achieve the best possible performance following the parameters selected by the original papers. The experiments are implemented and conducted on a Linux server, composed of one Intel Xeon Silver 4216 2.10 GHz CPU, and one NVIDIA GeForce RTX 3090 24 GB GPU card.

For multi-step traffic forecasting, we utilize 12 steps' historical data as input and the following 12 steps' data as output. In addition, all datasets are split into a training set (60%), a validation set (20%), and a test set (20%) in chronological order. During the experimentation, we use three conventional evaluation metrics, namely, Mean Absolute Error (MAE), Root Mean Squared Error (RMSE), and Mean Absolute Percentage Error (MAPE), and defined as:

$$MAE = \frac{1}{N} \sum_{(i,j) \in \Omega_{Test}} \left| Y_{ij} - Y'_{ij} \right| \tag{23}$$

$$RMSE = \sqrt{\frac{1}{N} \sum_{(i,j) \in \Omega_{Test}} \left(Y_{ij} - Y_{ij}'\right)^2} \tag{24}$$

$$MAPE = \left(\frac{1}{N} \sum_{(i,j) \in \Omega_{Test}} \left| \frac{Y_{ij} - Y_{ij}'}{Y_{ij}'} \right| \right) \times 100\% \tag{25}$$

where Ω_{Test} denotes the test set for evaluation. Y and Y' are prediction traffic flows and ground true values, respectively.

5.4 Comparison with Existing Models

Table 2. Performance comparison of baseline models and CCGCRN on PeMS datasets

Missing Ratio	Dataset	Metric	HA	ARIMA	LR	LSTM	DCRNN	MTGNN	DMSTGCN	STGODE	Ours
MR = 10%	PeMS04	MAE	99.98	60.95	54.46	54.00	38.89	127.56	40.49	45.77	**20.29**
		RMSE	125.00	100.03	96.40	95.94	86.39	160.20	87.48	85.21	**32.86**
		MAPE	61.67%	17.92%	16.47%	16.69%	**13.92%**	198.38%	15.88%	18.47%	14.51%
	PeMS08	MAE	101.90	66.22	74.94	55.27	36.71	120.75	36.98	43.12	**16.89**
		RMSE	136.82	111.43	142.15	109.21	86.80	147.88	87.67	84.28	**26.81**
		MAPE	40.54%	14.07%	17.96%	10.49%	11.49%	223.50%	10.68%	15.02%	**10.36%**
MR = 30%	PeMS04	MAE	125.42	103.28	98.16	90.86	69.70	130.60	71.67	81.68	**20.05**
		RMSE	148.21	137.21	152.62	141.09	131.95	170.19	133.22	123.10	**32.60**
		MAPE	59.42%	27.55%	25.58%	18.95%	14.21%	163.61%	15.39%	31.37%	**13.68%**
	PeMS08	MAE	146.78	126.42	116.85	105.09	70.99	125.16	71.70	87.67	**16.73**
		RMSE	172.25	162.25	186.14	172.47	136.12	158.24	136.74	123.10	**26.65**
		MAPE	42.65%	25.63%	20.06%	12.20%	**10.34%**	186.07%	11.50%	26.43%	12.73%

To demonstrate the effectiveness of the CCGCRN, we compare the proposed model with eight benchmark methods mentioned above on the datasets PeMS04 and PeMS08 with different missing rates (MR) in all metrics, and comparative results for incomplete traffic flow forecasting are shown in Table 2. In our experiments, the horizon is set to 12, which means we predict the flow for the next hour over PeMS0 datasets. The best result for each setting (data, MR, metric) is highlighted in boldface in this table. From the results, we have the following observations.

- **Overview results** Our proposed model is superior to the baselines in most scenarios. Specifically, the CCGCRN model shows greater advantages in the dataset with a higher missing rate. Furthermore, our model yields the best performance regarding all datasets' MAE and RMSE metrics, demonstrating that our framework mitigates the effect of incomplete traffic data and captures the complex and long-range spatial-temporal correlations. As for the metric MAPE, the results of our model are best on the datasets of PeMS04 (MR = 10%) and PeMS08 (MR = 30%). In addition, CCGCRN still performs excellently and even better when the missing rate increases.

- **Comparing neural networks with the traditional statistical algorithms** Neural networks (i.e., LR, LSTM, DCRNN, DMSTGCN, and STGODE) achieve better results than traditional statistical algorithms (i.e., HA and ARIMA), which also has been confirmed in many studies. Statistical methods only consider temporal correlations and ignore spatial dependencies whereas deep learning models (i.e., DCRNN, DMSTGCN, and STGODE) can take advantage of spatial-temporal information. Additionally, it can be seen from experiment results that MTGNN is unexpectedly poor, facing incomplete traffic data because its extraction of uni-directed relations strongly depends on data integrity.
- **Comparing adaptive graph-based models with predefined graph-based methods** DCRNN and STGODE models capture spatial dependencies with predefined graph constructions, whereas MTGNN and DMSTGCN models generate graphs adaptively. Their prediction performances are heavily influenced by missing data and, even worse, as the missing rate increases. In contrast to baseline models, CCGCRN has robust performance due to its CPL and CLN modules, which we will discuss further in the next part.

5.5 Ablation Experiments

To verify the capabilities of different modules from CCGCRN, we elaborately conduct the following ablation experiments, and the results are shown in Fig. 10. Specifically, we design four variants: CCGCRN w/o Ada, CCGCRN w/o CPL, CCGCRN w/o Com and CCGCRN w/o CC:

- **CCGCRN w/o Ada**: In this variant, instead of learning graph adaptive graph, we directly utilize a predefined adjacency matrix generated from distance to demonstrate the effectiveness of adaptive graph construction.
- **CCGCRN w/o CPL**: In this variant, we remove Cluster Parameter Learning to demonstrate the importance of the cluster-specific pattern. Instead of learning within each cluster, the model learns common parameters among all traffic flows.
- **CCGCRN w/o Com**: In this variant, Completion Learning Network in our proposed model is removed and we don't make special treatment for missing data to indicate the effectiveness of the data completion module in our proposed model.
- **CCGCRN w/o CC**: In this variant, we remove components of CPL and CLN, which integrates conventional GCN with GRU to capture spatial-temporal correlations for incomplete traffic data.

Results of ablation experiments are shown in Fig. 10 where it can be seen that critical components contribute to the improvement of the proposed model. The introduction of CLN significantly improves the results as it imputes traffic data well to guarantee data integrity. CPL's effectiveness is also evident: it captures cluster-specific patterns while learning the spatial-temporal features. The performance is significant in terms of MAE and RMSE. Eventually, adaptive

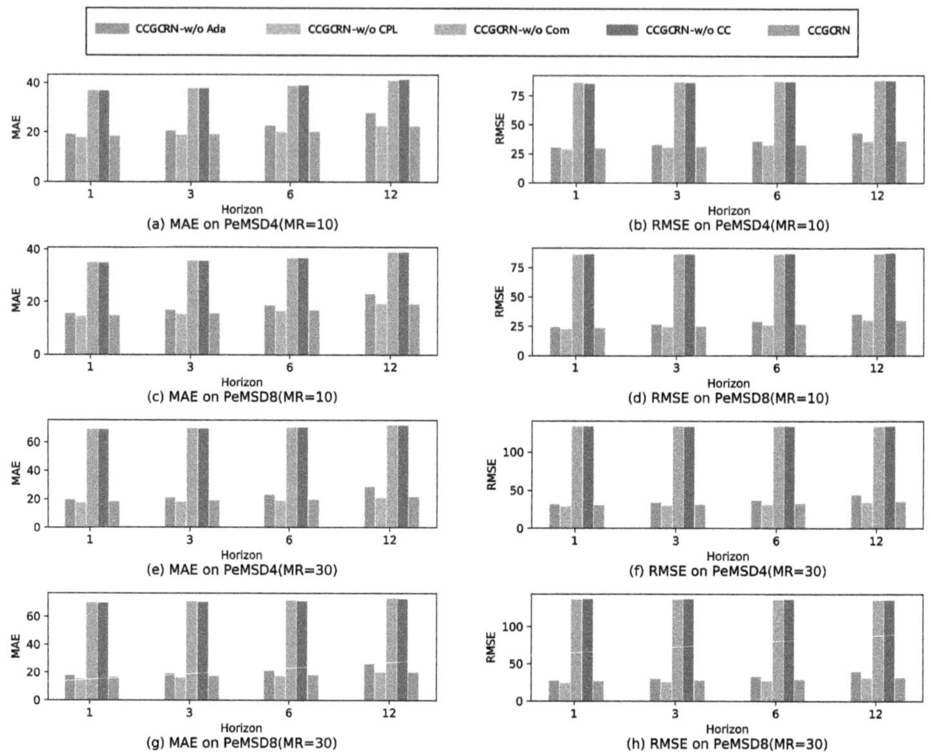

Fig. 10. Ablation experiments of CCGCRN.

graph learning is proved effective and can potentially be applied to more general forecasting tasks about time series. From the results, it also can be seen the powerful ability of the proposed model to make long-term predictions.

Figure 11 demonstrates comparison experiments on the PeMS04 (MR=30%) dataset, showing the effectiveness of our completion module CLN. Compared with traditional completion algorithms (zero fill, MF, and SVT), the results of CLN are the smallest among these completion results in terms of relative error and MAE. Here, the relative error is defined as $\frac{\|\Lambda \odot \hat{X} - \Lambda \odot X\|}{\|\Lambda \odot X\|}$ where Λ is a mask matrix: $\Lambda_{ij} = 1$ if the flow matrix X_{ij} is observed and $\Lambda_{ij} = 0$ otherwise.

5.6   Parameter Analysis

The number of clusters is the key parameter in our model, which decides the diversity of parameters in the CPL module and affects the performance of parameter learning. To evaluate how the number of clusters impacts forecasting performance, we implement experiments over different parameters for four datasets. As we can see from Fig. 12, results demonstrate the robustness of CCGCRN that our model obtains relatively good performance for all the tested number of clusters. Furthermore, setting the number of clusters to 2 or 3 is the best choice for

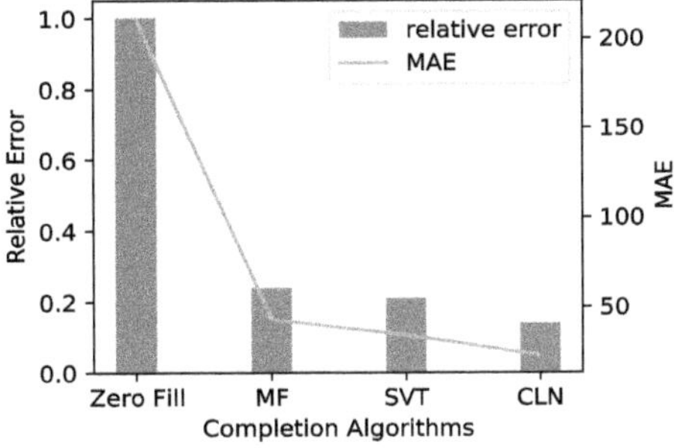

Fig. 11. Comparison of completion algorithms.

CCGCRN. In this parameter setting, the CPL module learns specific parameters for 2 or 3 clusters and learns the common pattern within a cluster. Specifically, the results are in line with the conjecture that there are 2 or 3 patterns for traffic flows, which may be morning rush hour, evening rush hour, or both rush hours. Nevertheless, the larger number of clusters leads to over-learning, leading to performance degradation and an increase in the parameters and time consumption. To summarize, choosing an appropriate cluster parameter will benefit the performance of forecasting.

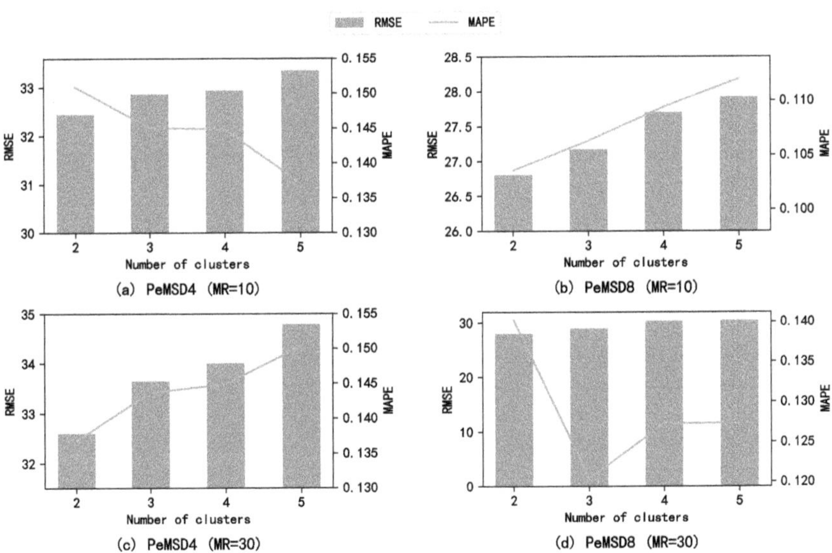

Fig. 12. Influence of the number of clusters.

6   Conclusions

In this paper, we propose a novel deep learning model CCGCRN to effectively address the traffic forecasting problem. Compared to these models with common parameter learning for all nodes, CCGCRN learns cluster-specific parameters to capture spatial-temporal correlations from incomplete traffic flows that share commonalities within the same cluster. Furthermore, to improve forecasting accuracy effectively, we propose a Cluster Parameter Learning module, a Completion Learning Network, and a Graph Convolution Recurrent Neural Network in our model. Comparison and ablation experiments are conducted on two real-world datasets with different missing rates to demonstrate the superiority of our proposed model. Additionally, the mechanism of cluster-specific parameter learning can be extended to other deep learning models which could capture features among similar data.

Acknowledgment. We would like to thank the anonymous reviewers for their feedback. This work is supported by the National Natural Science Foundation of China under Grants 62025201 and 62472167, the Hunan Provincial Natural Science Foundation of China under Grants 2024JJ3014 and 2024JJ5165, and in part by the Hunan Provincial Innovation Foundation for Postgraduates under Grant CX20230437.

References

1. Alonso, M.N., Batres-Estrada, G., Moulin, A.: Deep learning in finance: Prediction of stock returns with long short-term memory networks. Big data and machine learning in quantitative investment **1**, 251–277 (2018)
2. Bai, L., Yao, L., Li, C., Wang, X., Wang, C.: Adaptive graph convolutional recurrent network for traffic forecasting. Adv. Neural. Inf. Process. Syst. **33**, 17804–17815 (2020)
3. Box, G.E.P., Pierce, D.A.: Distribution of residual autocorrelations in autoregressive-integrated moving average time series models. J. Am. Stat. Assoc. **65**(332), 1509–1526 (1970)
4. Buizer, J., Jacobs, K., Cash, D.: Making short-term climate forecasts useful: linking science and action. Proc. Natl. Acad. Sci. **113**(17), 4597–4602 (2016)
5. Cai, J.-F., Candès, E.J., Shen, Z.: A singular value thresholding algorithm for matrix completion. SIAM J. Optim. **20**(4), 1956–1982 (2010)
6. Chen, L., Shao, W., Lv, M., Chen, W., Zhang, Y., Yang, C.: Aargnn: an attentive attributed recurrent graph neural network for traffic flow prediction considering multiple dynamic factors. IEEE Trans. Intell. Transp. Syst. **23**(10), 17201–17211 (2022)
7. Chen, W., Ling Chen, Yu., Xie, W.C., Gao, Y., Feng, X.: Multi-range attentive bicomponent graph convolutional network for traffic forecasting. In: Proceedings of the AAAI Conference on Artificial Intelligence **34**, 3529–3536 (2020)
8. Deb, R., Wee-Chung, A.: Liew: missing value imputation for the analysis of incomplete traffic accident data. Inf. Sci. **339**, 274–289 (2016)
9. Defferrard, M., Bresson, X., Vandergheynst, P.: Convolutional neural networks on graphs with fast localized spectral filtering. Advances in neural information processing systems, 29 (2016)

10. Diao, C., Zhang, D., et al.: A novel spatial-temporal multi-scale alignment graph neural network security model for vehicles prediction. IEEE Trans. Intell. Transp. Syst

11. Duan, W., He, X., Zhou, Z., Thiele, L., Rao, H.: Localised adaptive spatial-temporal graph neural network. In: Proceedings of the 29th ACM SIGKDD Conference on Knowledge Discovery and Data Mining, KDD '23, pp. 448–458 (2023)

12. Fang, Z., Long, Q., Song, G., Xie, K.: Spatial-temporal graph ode networks for traffic flow forecasting. In: Proceedings of the 27th ACM SIGKDD Conference on Knowledge Discovery & Data Mining, pp. 364–373 (2021)

13. Gao, C., Zhu, J., Zhang, F., Wang, Z., Li, X.: A novel representation learning for dynamic graphs based on graph convolutional networks. IEEE Trans. Cybern. **53**(6), 3599–3612 (2022)

14. Gao, K., et al.: Incorporating intra-flow dependencies and inter-flow correlations for traffic matrix prediction. In: 2020 IEEE/ACM 28th International Symposium on Quality of Service (IWQoS), pp. 1–10 (2020)

15. Gu, Y., Yan, D., Yan, S., Jiang, Z.: Price forecast with high-frequency finance data: An autoregressive recurrent neural network model with technical indicators. In: Proceedings of the 29th ACM International Conference on Information & Knowledge Management, pp. 2485–2492 (2020)

16. Guo, K., Yongli, H., Sun, Y., Qian, S., Gao, J., Yin, B.: Hierarchical graph convolution network for traffic forecasting. In: Proceedings of the AAAI Conference on Artificial Intelligence 35, pp. 151–159 (2021)

17. Guo, S., Lin, Y., Feng, N., Song, C., Wan, H.: Attention-based spatial-temporal graph convolutional networks for traffic flow forecasting. In: Proceedings of the AAAI Conference on Artificial Intelligence 33, pp. 922–929 (2019)

18. Han, L., Du, B., Sun, L., Fu, Y., Lv, Y., Xiong, H.: Dynamic and multi-faceted spatio-temporal deep learning for traffic speed forecasting. In: Proceedings of the 27th ACM SIGKDD Conference on Knowledge Discovery & Data Mining, pp. 547–555 (2021)

19. He, X., Liao, L., Zhang, H., Nie, L., Hu, X., Chua, T.-S.: Neural collaborative filtering. In: Proceedings of the 26th International Conference on World Wide Web, pp. 173–182 (2017)

20. He, Z., Chow, C.-Y., Zhang, J.-D.: Stcnn: a spatio-temporal convolutional neural network for long-term traffic prediction. In: 2019 20th IEEE International Conference on Mobile Data Management (MDM), pp. 226–233. IEEE (2019)

21. Hu, N., Zhang, D., Xie, K., et al.: Multi-range bidirectional mask graph convolution based gru networks for traffic prediction. J. Syst. Architect. **133**, 102775 (2022)

22. Hu, N., Zhang, D., Xie, K., Liang, W., Li, K.-C., Zomaya, A.Y.: Dynamic multi-scale spatial–temporal graph convolutional network for traffic flow prediction. Future Gener. Comput. Syst. **158**, 323–332 (2024)

23. Huang, S.-J., Shih, K.-R.: Short-term load forecasting via arma model identification including non-gaussian process considerations. IEEE Trans. Power Syst. **18**(2), 673–679 (2003)

24. Lai, G., Chang, W.-C., Yang, Y., Liu, H.: Modeling long-and short-term temporal patterns with deep neural networks. In: The 41st International ACM SIGIR Conference on Research & Development in Information Retrieval, pp. 95–104 (2018)

25. Li, L., Zhang, J., Wang, Y., Ran, B.: Missing value imputation for traffic-related time series data based on a multi-view learning method. IEEE Trans. Intell. Transp. Syst. **20**(8), 2933–2943 (2018)

26. Li, M., Zhu, Z.: Spatial-temporal fusion graph neural networks for traffic flow forecasting. In: Proceedings of the AAAI Conference on Artificial Intelligence 35, pp. 4189–4196 (2021)
27. Li, Y., Yu, R., Shahabi, C., Liu, Y.: Diffusion convolutional recurrent neural network: Data-driven traffic forecasting. arXiv preprint arXiv:1707.01926 (2017)
28. Liang, W., Li, Y., et al.: Spatial-temporal aware inductive graph neural network for c-its data recovery. IEEE Trans. Intell. Transp. Syst
29. Lin, H., Bai, R., Jia, W., Yang, X., You, Y.: Preserving dynamic attention for long-term spatial-temporal prediction. In: Proceedings of the 26th ACM SIGKDD International Conference on Knowledge Discovery & Data Mining, pp. 36–46 (2020)
30. Liu, C., Hoi, S.C.H., Zhao, P., Sun, J.: Online arima algorithms for time series prediction. In: Thirtieth AAAI Conference on Artificial Intelligence (2016)
31. Ma, X., Dai, Z., He, Z., Ma, J., Wang, Y., Wang, Y.: Learning traffic as images: a deep convolutional neural network for large-scale transportation network speed prediction. Sensors **17**(4), 818 (2017)
32. Nyadzi, E., Werners, S.E., Biesbroek, R., Ludwig, F.: Techniques and skills of indigenous weather and seasonal climate forecast in northern ghana. Climate Dev. **13**(6), 551–562 (2021)
33. Scher, S.: Toward data-driven weather and climate forecasting: Approximating a simple general circulation model with deep learning. Geophys. Res. Lett. **45**(22), 12–616 (2018)
34. Song, C., Lin, Y., Guo, S., Wan, H.: Spatial-temporal synchronous graph convolutional networks: A new framework for spatial-temporal network data forecasting. In: Proceedings of the AAAI Conference on Artificial Intelligence 34, pp. 914–921 (2020)
35. Wang, H., et al.: Gdi: a novel iot device identification framework via graph neural network-based tensor completion. IEEE Trans. Services Comput. (2024)
36. Wang, H., et al.: Easy begun is half done: Spatial-temporal graph modeling with st-curriculum dropout. In: Proceedings of the AAAI Conference on Artificial Intelligence **37**(4), pp. 4668–4675 (2023)
37. Wang, Z., et al.: A weighted symmetric graph embedding approach for link prediction in undirected graphs. IEEE Trans. Cybern. **54**(2), 1037–1047 (2022)
38. Man, W., Pan, S., Zhou, C., Chang, X., Zhu, X.: Unsupervised domain adaptive graph convolutional networks. In: Proceedings of The Web Conference 2020, pp. 1457–1467 (2020)
39. Wu, Z., Pan, S., Long, G., Jiang, J., Chang, X., Zhang, C.: Connecting the dots: Multivariate time series forecasting with graph neural networks. In: Proceedings of the 26th ACM SIGKDD International Conference on Knowledge Discovery & Data Mining, pp. 753–763 (2020)
40. Wu, Z., Pan, S., Long, G., Jiang, J., Zhang, C.: Graph wavenet for deep spatial-temporal graph modeling. arXiv preprint arXiv:1906.00121 (2019)
41. Xie, R., et al.: M2stl: Multi-range multi-level spatial-temporal learning model for network traffic prediction. IEEE Trans. Network Sci. Eng. (2024)
42. Yan, Z., et al.: Multivariate time series forecasting exploiting tensor projection embedding and gated memory network. In: 2021 IEEE/ACM 29th International Symposium on Quality of Service (IWQOS), pp. 1–6 (2021)
43. Yin, Y., et al.: Graphiot: lightweight iot device detection based on graph classifiers and incremental learning. IEEE Trans. Serv. Comput. (2024)
44. Zheng, C., Fan, X., Wang, C., Qi, J.: Gman: a graph multi-attention network for traffic prediction. In: Proceedings of the AAAI Conference on Artificial Intelligence 34, pp. 1234–1241 (2020)

45. Zhichao Zhou, Y.H., Zhang, Y., Chen, J., Cai, H.: Multiview deep graph infomax to achieve unsupervised graph embedding. IEEE Trans. Cybern. **53**(10), 6329–6339 (2022)
46. Zivot, E., Wang, J.: Vector autoregressive models for multivariate time series. Modeling financial time series with S-PLUS®, pp. 385–429 (2006)
47. Zuo, J., Zeitouni, K., Taher, Y., Garcia-Rodriguez, S.: Graph convolutional networks for traffic forecasting with missing values. Data Min. Knowl. Disc. **37**(2), 913–947 (2023)

A Secure Underwater Image Segmentation Method Combining Differential Privacy and Cross-Granularity Fusion

Linshu Chen$^{(\boxtimes)}$, Anxing Hu, Naixue Xiong, Yuxiang Chen, and Wei Liang

Hunan University of Science and Technology, Xiangtan 411201, Hunan, China
`linshuchen@hnust.edu.cn`

Abstract. Underwater image segmentation is crucial for applications such as marine resource exploration and biological research. However, the training process of segmentation models typically requires a large number of images and substantial computational resources. As a result, third-party service resources are often utilized, which poses the risk of image privacy leakage. To address this issue, this paper proposes a privacy-preserving algorithm for underwater images called AFGIPP (Adaptive Fuzzy Gaussian Image Privacy Protection) based on differential privacy. By adding adaptive noise to the luminance channel in the YUV color space, the algorithm effectively protects image information security while retaining the usability of the images. Additionally, to improve the accuracy of underwater image segmentation, we introduce AquaCrossNet, an underwater image segmentation network that innovatively incorporates a Cross-Granularity Complementary Fusion Module (CGCFM). This module enhances the complementarity of multi-granularity features through Transformer. Experiments demonstrate that AFGIPP exhibits superior privacy protection performance. Moreover, AquaCrossNet outperforms eight other methods in multiple objective evaluation metrics and also achieves good segmentation results on images processed by AFGIPP.

Keywords: Underwater image segmentation · Privacy Protection · Differential Privacy · Multi-scale features · Image Visual Security

1 Introduction

Underwater image segmentation technology is increasingly attracting attention and plays a vital role in numerous underwater practical applications [1,2]. For instance, in marine resource exploration, image segmentation can accurately identify the distribution of seafloor minerals and the characteristics of fish populations [3]. In marine biological research, it supports the observation of biodiversity [4], the recognition of archaeological relics [5,6], and the monitoring of

N. Xiong—Supported by the Joint Key Project of the National Natural Science Foundation of China under Grant U2468205, the National Key Research and Development Program of China under Grant 2022YFA1602200 and 2021YFA1000600, the National Natural Science Foundation of China under Grant 62072170 and 62202156, the international partnership program of the Chinese Academy of Sciences under Grant 211134KYSB20200057, and the Key Research and Development Program of Hunan Province under grant 2022GK2015.

W. Liang et al. (Eds.): SecureComm 2025, LNICST 690, pp. 524–540, 2026.
https://doi.org/10.1007/978-3-032-23456-8_28

ecosystems [7,8]. However, deep learning-based image segmentation techniques require a substantial amount of images and computational resources during the training process. The traditional approach is centralized training, which involves uploading a large number of image training samples to a third-party entity with abundant computational resources (such as cloud computing servers) to train the model, as shown in Fig. 1. This method can lead to serious privacy issues, as third-party services may potentially abuse and leak the sensitive data uploaded by users. For example, underwater images contain important information about different types of objects, such as minerals, metals, and endangered animals.

To address the aforementioned security issues, researchers have proposed two methods: homomorphic encryption [38]and federated learning [39]. Homomorphic encryption allows direct computation on encrypted data, eliminating the need for decryption during model training. However, due to its high computational complexity, it is limited in practical applications of deep learning. Federated learning, on the other hand, enables users to train models locally and only transmit model training parameters (such as gradients) rather than the data itself. Although this approach reduces privacy risks, attackers may still infer sample attributes from the shared gradients. In response to these challenges, this paper proposes an adaptive feature-guided image privacy protection algorithm (AFGIPP) based on differential privacy. This algorithm leverages differential privacy to add adaptive noise to the luminance channel in the YUV space, based on feature scores and local sensitivity. It effectively balances privacy and usability by protecting privacy while preserving the main information of the image.

Additionally, we have identified shortcomings in previous underwater image segmentation methods. Early approaches relied on traditional image segmentation techniques, such as graph theory [11], thresholding, and clustering algorithms [12]. Although these methods do not require extensive training with labeled data, their segmentation accuracy is limited due to the complex underwater environment. The advent of deep learning has brought high-precision, end-to-end processing to image segmentation through Convolutional Neural Networks (CNNs) [13,14]. However, these networks have limitations in handling long-range dependencies and global context information. Attempts to transfer methods used in terrestrial environments, such as COS [15,16], to underwater image segmentation tasks have been made, but these methods do not fully consider the spectral attenuation, scattering noise, and low-contrast degradation issues specific to underwater images, thus their adaptability is limited. This study proposes a cross-granularity complementary segmentation network (AquaCrossNet) for complex underwater scenes. It constructs a hybrid backbone network composed of ResNet50 and FPN, utilizing FPN's multi-scale top-down feature fusion mechanism to achieve progressive integration of deep high-semantic features and shallow detail features. The innovative cross-granularity complementary fusion module (CGCFM) is designed to coordinate the global semantic reasoning of deep coarse-grained features with the detail localization of shallow fine-grained features. By leveraging the Transformer attention mechanism, it establishes long-range dependencies and global context associations, thereby enhancing the accuracy of underwater image segmentation in complex scenes.

The main contributions of this paper are summarized as follows:

1. We have implemented an image privacy protection algorithm named AFGIPP and experimentally verified its privacy protection performance.

2. We propose an underwater image segmentation network, AquaCrossNet, which effectively enhances the fusion of multi-scale features. Experiments demonstrate that this network achieves satisfactory segmentation performance on RMAS masked images processed by AFGIPP.
3. We introduce a Cross-Granularity Complementary Fusion Module (CGCFM), which leverages Transformer to enhance the complementarity of multi-granularity features, effectively addressing issues of biological camouflage and blurred boundaries.
4. Experiments conducted on the RMAS and MASK benchmark datasets show that our proposed method outperforms eight other methods in multiple objective evaluation metrics.

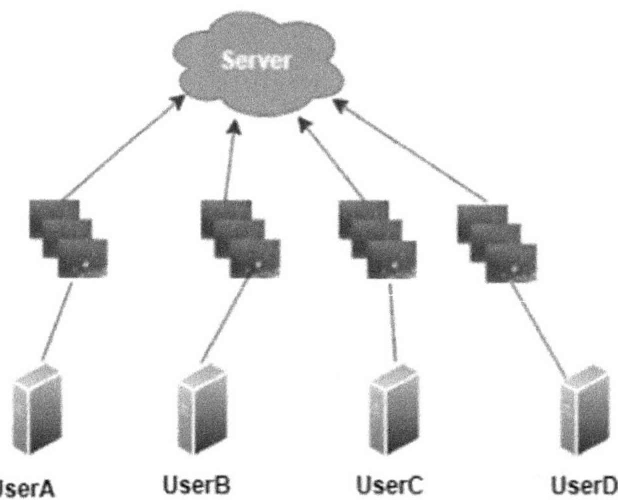

Fig. 1. Centralized training: It depicts a model in which users upload their respective training samples to a third-party entity (typically a cloud server with powerful computational resources), and this entity is responsible for generating the final model.

2 Related Work

2.1 Image Privacy Protection

With the widespread adoption of mobile devices and cloud services, people are increasingly reliant on third-party platforms for storing and processing personal data related to images. However, the potential security vulnerabilities of these third-party platforms may lead to data leakage, making image privacy protection a crucial research topic in the field of mobile computing and cloud services. The current mainstream protection schemes can be categorized into two types: those based on homomorphic encryption and those based on federated learning.

Homomorphic Encryption. Homomorphic encryption [38] allows neural networks to directly train on encrypted data without the need for prior decryption. CryptoNet [38], proposed by Gilad-Bachrach et al., attempts to apply homomorphic encryption to the inference of neural networks. Jia et al. [40] proposed a method that combines multi-layer homomorphic encryption with image tiling technology. This method not only significantly reduces the computational cost of homomorphic encryption but also maintains high accuracy in image classification. Challa et al. [41] introduced a homomorphic encryption algorithm based on LWE (Learning With Errors), which is used to encrypt images stored in the cloud or transmitted over insecure channels, ensuring the privacy and security of images during transmission. Yang et al. [42] proposed a privacy-preserving mechanism based on vector homomorphic encryption, which for the first time completes HOG feature extraction and SVM model training in the encrypted domain. This approach achieves high-precision pedestrian detection while reducing computational and communication overheads and ensuring privacy.

Federated Learning. Federated Learning (FL) allows collaborative distributed training of neural networks without sharing the data itself [39]. In this approach, what is transmitted is not the data, but the parameters generated by the model during training (such as weights and gradients). Wang et al. [43] proposed a privacy-preserving method for pathological image segmentation based on federated learning and differential privacy, named FedDP. This method effectively prevents data leakage and addresses the risk of gradient leakage in traditional federated learning. Li et al. [39] applied federated learning to brain tumor segmentation and proposed combining selective parameter sharing and Sparse Vector Technique (SVT) in federated learning to provide strong privacy protection for medical image analysis. Shi et al. [44] proposed personalized quantum federated learning for privacy-preserving image classification, which uses quantum channels to securely aggregate model parameters and protects the privacy of client image data during the interaction between the server and clients.

2.2 Underwater Image Enhancement

Underwater environments suffer from insufficient and complex lighting conditions, leading to prevalent image quality degradation. For instance, light with different wavelengths exhibits significant differences in attenuation rates underwater (e.g., red light, which has the longest wavelength, attenuates the fastest), resulting in color distortion that shifts the overall image tone towards blue-green hues [18,19]. Furthermore, suspended particles and plankton in water induce light scattering, resulting in blurred object contours and detail loss (e.g., coral textures or fish scale features become difficult to distinguish). To address the degradation issues (e.g., color distortion, detail blurring), underwater image enhancement technology has emerged. It is now an essential preprocessing tool for visual tasks like underwater object detection and semantic segmentation.

Underwater image enhancement (UIE) methods fall into three categories: model - free, physics - based, and deep - learning - based [20]. Model - free underwater image enhancement methods directly improve visual effects through spatial or frequency - domain processing without physical imaging models. For example, Zhang et al. [21] proposed a weighted wavelet - based visual perception fusion method. Physics - based methods restore images by modeling and inversely solving underwater optical degradation. Song et al. [22] used diffusion priors (UIEDP) for enhancement. Deep - learning - based methods enhance images via data - driven end - to - end mapping. Jiang et al. [23] proposed combining CLIP - aware loss with curriculum contrastive regularization.

2.3   Underwater Image Segmentation Model

Underwater image segmentation faces serious challenges due to the complex optical properties of water and the diverse degradation of targets. To boost underwater image segmentation accuracy, Li et al. [4] innovatively used an interactive feature enhancement module. It integrated multi - scale features to strengthen feature representation, and combined a cascaded decoder module to merge cross - layer features, achieving more comprehensive information extraction. Chen et al. [24] proposed a robust underwater object segmentation network. It uses a random style adaptation module and a siamese structure to mitigate diverse underwater degradations. Also, it adopts receptive field blocks to enhance multi - scale features and attention fusion blocks to integrate multi - level features, thus strengthening global context awareness. Xu et al. [25] first applied the Segment Anything Model (SAM) to underwater image segmentation. Through optimizing the bounding box prompt mode, fine - tuning specific components, extracting label categories, and using phased training strategies, they significantly improved underwater object segmentation performance. Fu et al. [26] designed a novel data augmentation strategy to randomly change the degradation and camouflage attributes of underwater objects. Combined with a siamese network architecture for learning shared semantic features, it effectively improves the model's adaptability to complex underwater scenes. Hong et al. [27], inspired by Low-Rank Adaptation (LoRA), integrated trainable rank-decomposition matrices into the Transformer layers of SAM's image encoder. This approach not only significantly boosts underwater object segmentation performance but also reduces the model's computational cost.

3   Details of AFGIPP

We propose the AFGIPP algorithm, which aims to protect the visual content privacy of image data while preserving the usability of images in image segmentation networks. The algorithm consists of four steps. The processing procedure for a single image is shown in Algorithm 1.

1. Feature Analysis: By calculating the gradient features (reflecting edge information) and local difference features (reflecting texture information) of the image, a fused feature score is obtained to measure the sensitivity of different regions in the image.
2. Adaptive Noise Generation: The noise intensity is dynamically adjusted based on local sensitivity and feature scores. More noise is added to privacy-sensitive regions, while relatively less noise is added to less sensitive regions. This approach protects privacy while retaining the main information of the image.
3. Differential Privacy Guarantee: Based on the given differential privacy parameter ϵ, noise is generated through the Laplace mechanism to ensure that the added noise satisfies the differential privacy requirements, thereby providing privacy protection for image data.

4. Color Space Optimization: Processing is conducted only on the luminance channel in the YUV color space. This method protects privacy while minimizing the impact on image color information and maintaining visual quality.

Algorithm 1. AFGIPP Image Privacy Protection Algorithm

linenosep=1pt,itemsep=1pt

Require: Image X, privacy budget ϵ, matrix size k
Ensure: Noised image $\tilde{X}$
1: Convert image X to YUV color space: $X_{\mathrm{YUV}} = \mathrm{ConvertToYUV}(X)$
2: **Feature Analysis:**
3: **for** $X_e \in \{X_R, X_G, X_B\}$ **do**
4:     **for** $i = 1, \ldots, h$ **do**
5:         **for** $j = 1, \ldots, w$ **do**
6:             Compute gradient magnitude G: $G_x = \mathrm{Sobel}(X_e, 1, 0), \quad G_y = \mathrm{Sobel}(X_e, 0, 1)$
7:             Compute gradient magnitude G: $G = \sqrt{G_x^2 + G_y^2}$
8:             Compute local mean difference D: $L = \mathrm{filter2D}(X_e, \mathrm{kernel}), \quad D = |X_e - L|$
9:             Compute feature score F: $F = 0.7 \cdot \frac{G}{\max(G)} + 0.3 \cdot \frac{D}{\max(D)}$
10:            Add F to set $\mathcal{F}$
11:         **end for**
12:     **end for**
13: **end for**
14: Compute local sensitivity S: $S = \mathrm{dilate}(X_e) - \mathrm{erode}(X_e)$
15: Compute adaptive β map: $\beta_{\mathrm{map}} = \frac{S}{\epsilon} \cdot \left(1 + 9 \cdot \frac{F}{\max(F)}\right)$
16: Generate Laplace noise N: $N \sim \mathrm{Lap}(0, \beta_{\mathrm{map}})$
17: **Color Space Optimization:**
18: Add noise to the luminance channel: $X_{\mathrm{YUV}}.Y = X_{\mathrm{YUV}}.Y + N$
19: Normalize noisy pixel values: $X_{\mathrm{YUV}}.Y = \mathrm{Clip}(X_{\mathrm{YUV}}.Y, 0, 255)$
20: Convert back to BGR color space: $\tilde{X} = \mathrm{ConvertToBGR}(X_{\mathrm{YUV}})$
21: **return** $\tilde{X}$

---

4   Details of AquaCrossNet

Figure 2 illustrates the overall architecture of the AquaCrossNet segmentation network. The network adopts an encoder-decoder structure, with ResNet50 as the encoder backbone. It combines Feature Pyramid Networks (FPN) to construct a multi - scale feature pyramid as the backbone network. The multi - scale features from different levels of the backbone network are fed into the cross - granularity complementary fusion module. This module enhances the model's representation ability in underwater degraded scenes through the interaction and fusion of coarse - grained semantic information and fine - grained local features. The network is trained with a hybrid loss function combining binary cross - entropy loss and intersection over union loss.

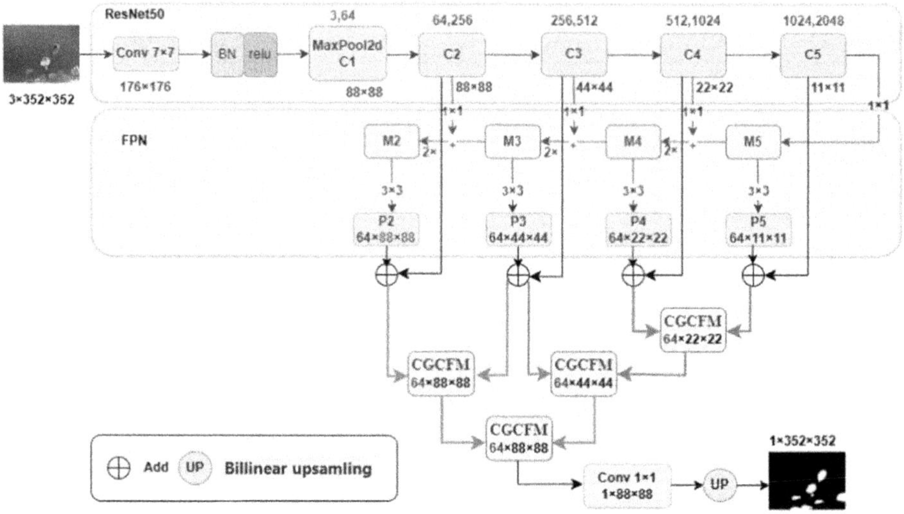

Fig. 2. shows the segmentation network architecture. It consists of a ResNet50 and Feature Pyramid Network (FPN) based backbone network (P2 - P5) and a cross - granularity complementary fusion module. Specifically, we integrate coarse - grained features (shown by blue lines) and fine - grained features (shown by purple lines) to achieve finer - boundary segmentation. (Color figure online)

4.1   Backbone Network

In semantic segmentation models, the backbone network is the foundation. It extracts key visual features (e.g., object contours, surface textures, and region shapes) by gradually analyzing the image and establishes semantic relationships between targets. A strong backbone network improves the model's generalization across datasets, enabling it to handle various semantic segmentation tasks. The model proposed in this paper uses a ResNet50 architecture with an integrated Feature Pyramid Network (FPN) as the backbone network, which has significant advantages in coping with the unique challenges of underwater image segmentation. Underwater environments have light absorption, scattering, and suspended particle interference. These factors lead to low - contrast, color - distorted, and unevenly illuminated underwater images, making segmentation tasks highly complex. ResNet50, with its deep residual structure and weights pre - trained on ImageNet - 1K, accelerates model convergence and enhances generalization. It can effectively reduce color deviation and extract robust multi - level semantic features, thus alleviating the boundary blurring caused by underwater image degradation. Meanwhile, FPN improves multi - scale perception via cross - scale feature fusion. It dynamically combines high - semantic deep features with high - resolution shallow details through lateral connections and upsampling, significantly boosting the model's ability to segment targets of different scales. The integration of ResNet50 and FPN not only strengthens the model's adaptation to underwater degradation factors but also creates a hierarchical feature pyramid that balances global semantics and local details. This synergy forms the core foundation for enhancing segmentation accuracy and robustness.

4.2 Cross-Granularity Complementary Fusion Module

Suspended particles in water, like plankton and silt, cause light scattering, reducing image contrast and blurring object edges. Meanwhile, marine organisms' camouflage, such as color/texture mimicry, creates target-background semantic confusion, further increasing image segmentation difficulty. To tackle the above dual challenges, we propose the Cross-granularity Complementary Fusion Module (CGCFM). It uses a multi-scale feature collaboration mechanism to jointly solve two key issues: 1. For edge blurring: Deep-network extracted coarse-grained semantic features (object categories, scene context) have large receptive fields. They can predict the main mask area via high-level semantic reasoning, but are prone to boundary errors due to low resolution. In this case, shallow-network derived fine-grained detail features (edges/textures) from high-resolution feature maps provide pixel-level positioning cues, enabling sub-pixel correction of coarse-grained prediction boundaries. 2. For camouflage interference: Shallow fine-grained features can capture local discriminative features of targets (e.g., special textures), but are easily affected by background in camouflage scenarios. Deep coarse-grained features, through global context modeling, can identify semantic associations between targets and environments (e.g., biological behavior patterns), offering a basis for fine-grained feature discrimination, thus breaking through the visual deception of local camouflage.

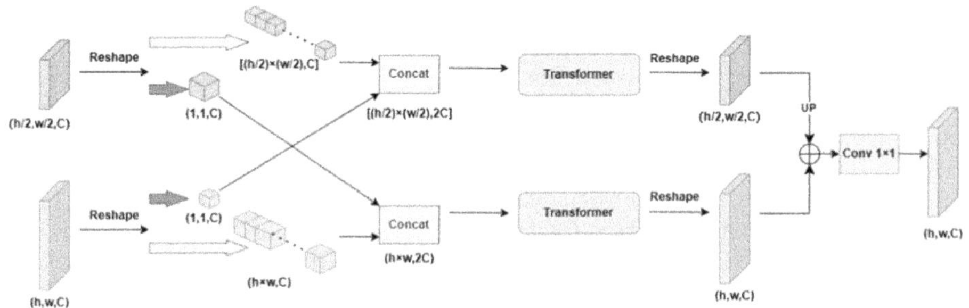

Fig. 3. Structure of the Cross-granularity Complementary Fusion Module.

As shown in Fig. 3, the proposed CGCFM module integrates multi - scale features via a dual - branch interaction mechanism. Input features are defined as.

Coarse - grained branch:

$$F_c \in \mathbb{R}^{\frac{H}{2} \times \frac{W}{2} \times C} \tag{1}$$

Fine - grained branch:

$$F_f \in \mathbb{R}^{H \times W \times C} \tag{2}$$

First, F_c and F_f are reshaped in the feature dimension as follows. The main branch is formed by flattening the spatial dimension into a sequence.

$$F_c^m \in \mathbb{R}^{(\frac{H}{2} \times \frac{W}{2}) \times C} = \text{Reshape}(F_c) \tag{3}$$

$$F_f^m \in \mathbb{R}^{(H \times W) \times C} = \text{Reshape}(F_f) \tag{4}$$

The auxiliary branch is generated through global average pooling to extract channel - level context.

$$F_c^s = \text{AvgPool}(F_c) \in \mathbb{R}^{1 \times 1 \times C} \tag{5}$$

$$F_f^s = \text{AvgPool}(F_f) \in \mathbb{R}^{1 \times 1 \times C} \tag{6}$$

Next, we perform cross - branch concatenation. First, the coarse - to - fine path concatenates the coarse - grained main branch with the fine - grained auxiliary branch. Then, the fine - to - coarse path concatenates the fine - grained main branch with the coarse - grained auxiliary branch. The concatenation process can be represented by the following formula:

$$F_c^{\text{fused}} = \text{Concat}(F_c^m, \text{Repeat}(F_f^s, N = \frac{H}{2} \times \frac{W}{2})) \in \mathbb{R}^{(\frac{H}{2} \times \frac{W}{2}) \times 2C} \tag{7}$$

$$F_f^{\text{fused}} = \text{Concat}(F_f^m, \text{Repeat}(F_c^s, N = H \times W)) \in \mathbb{R}^{(H \times W) \times 2C} \tag{8}$$

Next, the fused features F_c^{fused} and F_f^{fused} are input into the Transformer for global attention computation. (Taking the coarse to fine path as an example)

$$F_c^{\text{out}} = \text{Transformer}(F_c^{\text{fused}}) \in \mathbb{R}^{(\frac{H}{2} \times \frac{W}{2}) \times C} \tag{9}$$

The Transformer can capture long - range dependencies and global context connections between multi - scale features through its multi - head attention mechanism [28]. Its key advantage is that coarse - grained features (low - resolution, large receptive field) provide semantic priors (e.g., overall object shape) to the fine - grained branch, compensating for the lack of global information in the latter due to its local receptive field. Fine - grained features (high - resolution, rich details) inject boundary - location cues (e.g., edge gradient direction) into the coarse - grained branch. This corrects the spatial - information loss in the latter caused by downsampling. The final output features can be represented by the following formula:

$$Z_{\text{out}} = \text{Conv}_{1 \times 1}(\text{up}(F_c^{\text{out}}) \oplus F_f^{\text{out}}) \in \mathbb{R}^{H \times W \times C} \tag{10}$$

Here, $Conv_{1 \times 1}(\cdot)$ denotes a 1×1 convolutional layer, $\text{up}(\cdot)$ represents the $2\times$ bilinear upsampling process, and $\oplus$ indicates the fusion of the two features through element-wise addition. Through cross - branch global attention modeling and multi - scale feature complementarity, the CGCFM module effectively overcomes the dual challenges of edge blurring and camouflage interference in underwater scenes. It provides robust feature representation for subsequent segmentation tasks.

4.3   Hybrid Loss Function

Accurate object segmentation is crucial for understanding underwater scenes and marine life in underwater image segmentation tasks. Here, our model uses a hybrid loss function combining Binary Cross - Entropy (BCE) and Intersection over Union (IoU) loss functions [29].

The binary cross - entropy (BCE) loss function performs well in binary - classification tasks. It measures the per - pixel differences between model predictions and true labels. For binary tasks, given the true label $y \in \{0, 1\}$ and the model - predicted probability $p \in [0, 1]$ (obtained via the Sigmoid function), the BCE loss is defined as:

$$\mathcal{L}_{BCE} = -\frac{1}{N} \sum_{i=1}^{N} [y_i \log(p_i) + (1 - y_i) \log(1 - p_i)] \tag{11}$$

Here, N represents the total number of pixels. The loss function amplifies the penalty for incorrect predictions by taking the logarithm of the predicted probability for each pixel, thus enabling the model to focus more on accurately classifying each pixel.

The Intersection over Union (IoU) loss function evaluates the similarity between predicted and true labels from the perspective of region overlap. In underwater image segmentation, it intuitively reflects the model's performance in object localization and segmentation. Its formula is:

$$L_{IoU} = 1 - \frac{\sum_{i=1}^{N} (y_i \cap p_i)}{\sum_{i=1}^{N} (y_i \cup p_i)} \tag{12}$$

A smaller IoU loss value indicates a higher overlap ratio between the predicted region and the true label. Combining these two loss functions can fully utilize their complementary advantages: BCE loss ensures pixel - level classification accuracy, and IoU loss optimizes the overall region matching degree. The final loss function is:

$$L = L_{BCE} + L_{IoU} \tag{13}$$

5   Experiments and Results

5.1   Dataset and Evaluation Metrics

In this work, we evaluate our model on two public Marine Animal (MAS) benchmark datasets. For the MAS3K dataset [30], following the default split, we use 1,769 images for training and 1,141 for testing. The RMAS dataset [26]consists of 3,014 marine animal images in total, with 2,514 used for training and 500 for testing.

To comprehensively evaluate our proposed model, we use five metrics. They are mean Intersection over Union (mIoU), Structural Similarity (S_α) [31], weighted F value (F_β^w) [32], mean Enhanced Alignment Measure (mE_ϕ) [33], and mean Absolute Error (MAE) [34].

5.2 Implementation Details

We train our network using PyTorch. During training, images in the dataset are normalized and augmented (via random cropping and flipping), then resized to 352×352. The Adam optimizer [35] is adopted, with a learning rate of 1×10^{-4}. The network is trained on two NVIDIA RTX 2080 Ti GPUs for 200 epochs with a batch size of 4.

5.3 Privacy Protection Capability Evaluation

To verify the effectiveness of AFGIPP in protecting image privacy, we conducted analyses from the perspectives of SSIM (Structural Similarity Index) and visualization.

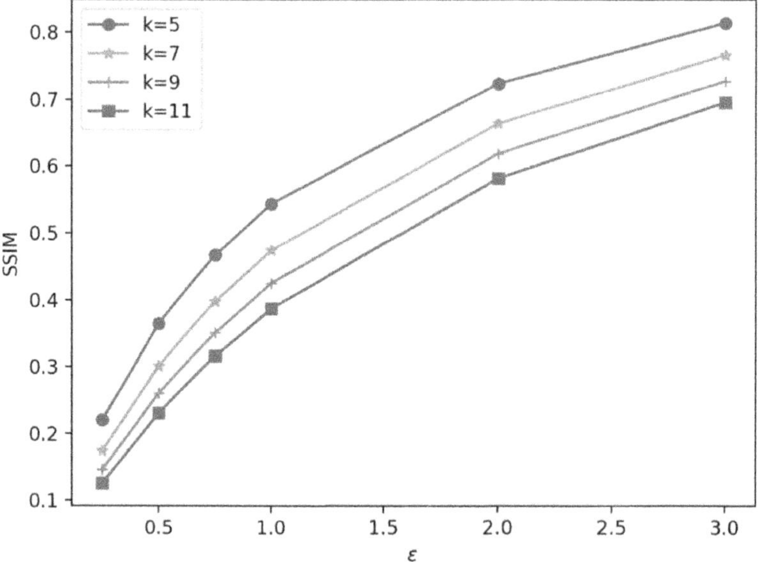

Fig. 4. SSIM under different values of ϵ and k

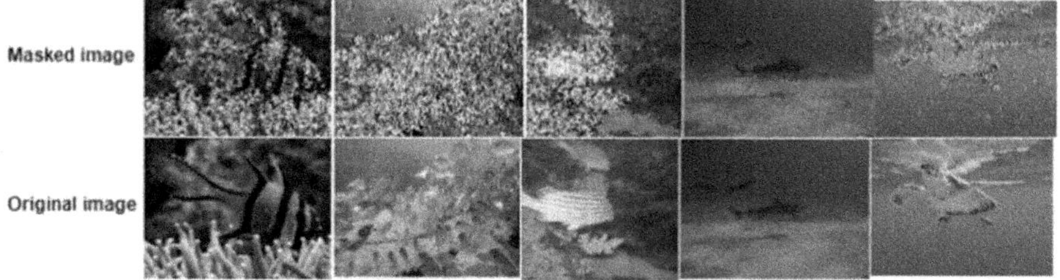

Fig. 5. Visual comparison between the original image and the masked image processed by AFGIPP.

- SSIM: The Structural Similarity Index (SSIM) is a quality evaluation metric that measures the similarity between two images. It is based on the comparison of structure, luminance, and contrast, and combines these factors into a single score. The range of SSIM values is between -1 and 1, where 1 indicates that the two images are identical, 0 indicates no similarity, and -1 indicates complete dissimilarity. Generally, when the SSIM value is greater than 0.9, the two images are considered to be very similar. As shown in Fig. 4, when $0 < \epsilon < 3$, the SSIM values are all less than 0.9, indicating that our algorithm can effectively disrupt the structure of the original image.
- Visualization Analysis: As can be intuitively observed from Fig. 5, there is a significant difference between the masked image processed by AFGIPP and the original image.

5.4   Image Segmentation Results

We compare our method with eight others on two public marine animal (MAS) datasets. These include saliency object segmentation models (SCRN [36], BASNet [29]), camouflage object segmentation model (PF-Net [17]), general object segmentation model (C2FNet [16]), and underwater image segmentation - specific models (ECD-Net [4], WaterSNet [24], MASNet [26], UISS-Net [37]).

- Quantitative Comparison: Tables 1 and 2 present quantitative comparison results on the typical Marine Animal Segmentation (MAS) dataset. Our model achieves the best performance in the RMAS dataset comparison, with all indicators reaching the highest values. Specifically, its mIoU value is on average 3.2% higher than existing saliency object segmentation models, and 1.9%, 2.6%, and 4.3% higher than general segmentation models, camouflage segmentation models, and underwater image segmentation models, respectively. Moreover, our model outperforms other methods in the S_α, F_β^w, and

Table 1. Performance comparison on the RMAS dataset. Note: The best and second - best results are highlighted in red and blue, respectively. As the source code of ECD-Net is not publicly accessible, the metrics are represented by '——'.

Method	Year	$mIoU \uparrow$	$S_\alpha \uparrow$	$F_\beta^w \uparrow$	$mE_\phi \uparrow$	$MAE \downarrow$
SCRN [36]	2019	0.690	0.842	0.770	0.895	0.026
BASNet [29]	2019	0.704	0.845	0.766	0.910	0.031
PF-Net [17]	2021	0.703	0.846	0.779	0.906	0.028
C2FNet [16]	2021	0.710	0.852	0.777	0.915	0.027
ECD-Net [4]	2021	——	——	——	——	——
WaterSNet [24]	2022	0.711	0.851	0.783	0.912	0.027
MASNet [26]	2023	0.725	0.856	0.800	0.918	0.025
UISS-Net [37]	2024	0.617	0.793	0.696	0.869	0.037
Ours	2025	0.729	0.861	0.801	0.923	0.024

mE_ϕ metrics. Additionally, our model achieves a lower MAE value, indicating smaller deviations between predicted and true values, enabling more precise target segmentation in practical applications. On the MAS3K dataset, our model exceeds other methods by 3.6%, 2.7%, 1.7%, and 3.1% in the mIoU, S_α, mE_ϕ, and F_β^w metrics, respectively, and ranks second in the MAE metric. Experiments show that the model has stronger robustness and segmentation accuracy in complex underwater scenes.

- Qualitative Comparison: As shown in some visualization results in Fig. 6, the effectiveness of our method is further verified. It can be observed that our model is more accurate in object boundary segmentation than other methods and has less uncertainty on boundaries. For challenging samples with camouflage characteristics (rows 1, 5, and 7), the model can still maintain accurate positioning ability. This is due to the design of the cross - granularity complementary fusion module, which effectively enhances the expression ability of subtle boundary features through multi - scale feature interaction.

Table 2. Performance comparison on the MAS3K dataset. Note: The best and second - best results are highlighted in red and blue, respectively. Since ECD-Net's source code is not publicly available, the original paper's data is directly used for comparison.

Method	Year	$mIoU$ ↑	S_α ↑	F_β^w ↑	mE_ϕ ↑	MAE ↓
SCRN [36]	2019	0.730	0.861	0.774	0.892	0.032
BASNet [29]	2019	0.739	0.865	0.781	0.898	0.031
PF-Net [17]	2021	0.728	0.861	0.773	0.897	0.031
C2FNet [16]	2021	0.742	0.866	0.787	0.906	0.027
ECD-Net [4]	2021	0.711	0.850	0.766	0.901	0.036
WaterSNet [24]	2022	0.741	0.866	0.786	0.900	0.030
MASNet [26]	2023	0.751	0.862	0.784	0.901	0.029
UISS-Net [37]	2024	0.629	0.802	0.684	0.845	0.045
Ours	2025	0.758	0.871	0.798	0.910	0.029

Table 3. Ablation Study of the CGCFM Module.

Method	$mIoU$ ↑	S_α ↑	F_β^w ↑	mE_ϕ ↑	MAE ↓
Base	0.708	0.851	0.782	0.911	0.026
Base+CGCFM	0.729	0.861	0.801	0.923	0.024

Table 4. Ablation Study of Backbone Network.

Method	$mIoU \uparrow$	$S_\alpha \uparrow$	$F_\beta^\omega \uparrow$	$mE_\phi \uparrow$	$MAE \downarrow$
Resnet50	0.717	0.855	0.791	0.917	0.026
Resnet50+FPN	0.729	0.861	0.801	0.923	0.024

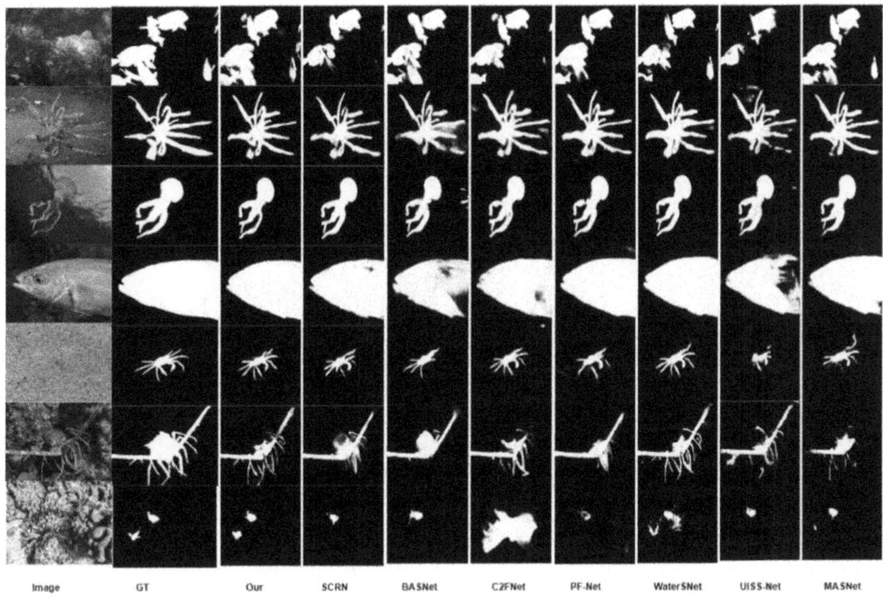

Fig. 6. visualizes the comparison of our method with several state - of - the - art methods on the MAS3K and RMAS datasets. The first four images are from the RMAS dataset, and the last three are from the MAS3K dataset.

5.5 AquaCrossNet Ablation Study

On the RMAS dataset, we conducted ablation studies on the cross - granularity complementary fusion module and the backbone network. As shown in Table 3, adding the CGCFM module to the Resnet50 + FPN - based backbone network (Base) improves multiple evaluation metrics and reduces error metrics, indicating the module's effectiveness in enhancing model performance in ablation study tasks. Also, the backbone network comparison in Table 4 shows ResNet50 + FPN outperforms single ResNet50 by 1.2%, 0.6%, 1%, and 0.6% in mIoU, S_α, F_β^w, and mE_ϕ. The MAE metric drops by 0.2%, confirming FPN's key role in multi - level feature extraction.

6 Conclusion

In this paper, we propose an adaptive feature-guided image privacy protection algorithm based on differential privacy. This algorithm leverages differential privacy to add adaptive noise to the luminance channel in the YUV space, based on feature scores and local sensitivity, to protect image privacy. Additionally, we introduce AquaCrossNet, an underwater cross-granularity complementary segmentation network, designed to address the issues of blurred edges in underwater images and the camouflage of certain marine organisms. We also designed the Cross-Granularity Complementary Fusion Module (CGCFM), which integrates multi-scale features through a dual-branch interaction mechanism. Experimental results demonstrate that our network achieves excellent performance on two widely used MAS datasets.

References

1. Li, C., et al.: An underwater image enhancement benchmark dataset and beyond. IEEE Trans. Image Process. **29**, 4376–4389 (2020). https://doi.org/10.1109/TIP.2019.2955241
2. Peng, L., Zhu, C., Bian, L.: U-shape transformer for underwater image enhancement. IEEE Trans. Image Process. **32**, 3066–3079 (2023). https://doi.org/10.1109/TIP.2023.3276332
3. Garcia-D'Urso, N.E., Galan-Cuenca, A., Climent-Pérez, P., Saval-Calvo, M., Azorin-Lopez, J., Fuster-Guillo, A.: Efficient instance segmentation using deep learning for species identification in fish markets. In: 2022 International Joint Conference on Neural Networks (IJCNN), pp. 1–8 (2022). https://doi.org/10.1109/IJCNN55064.2022.9892945
4. Li, L., Dong, B., Rigall, E., Zhou, T., Dong, J., Chen, G.: Marine animal segmentation. IEEE Trans. Circuits Syst. Video Technol. **32**(4), 2303–2314 (2022). https://doi.org/10.1109/TCSVT.2021.3093890
5. Arnaubec, A., Ferrera, M., Escartín, J., Matabos, M., Gracias, N., Opderbecke, J.: Underwater 3D reconstruction from video or still imagery: matisse and 3dmetrics processing and exploitation software. J. Marine Sci. Eng. **11**(5) (2023). https://doi.org/10.3390/jmse11050985
6. Calantropio, A., Chiabrando, F.: Underwater cultural heritage documentation using photogrammetry. J. Marine Sci. Eng. **12**(3) (2024). https://doi.org/10.3390/jmse12030413
7. Strachan, N.J.C.: Recognition of fish species by colour and shape. Image Vision Comput. **11**(1), 2–10 (1993). https://doi.org/10.1016/0262-8856(93)90027-E
8. Catalán, I.A., et al.: Automatic detection and classification of coastal mediterranean fish from underwater images: good practices for robust training. Front. Marine Sci. **10** (2023) https://doi.org/10.3389/fmars.2023.1151758
9. Xue, B., Green, R., Zhang, M.: Artificial intelligence in New Zealand: applications and innovation. J. R. Soc. N. Z. **53**(1), 1–5 (2023). https://doi.org/10.1080/03036758.2023.2170165
10. Hong, H., Yang, X., You, Z., Cheng, F.: Visual quality detection of aquatic products using machine vision. Aquacult. Eng. **63**, 62–71 (2014). https://doi.org/10.1016/j.aquaeng.2014.10.003
11. Pal, N.R., Pal, S.K.: A review on image segmentation techniques. Pattern Recogn. **26**(9), 1277–1294 (1993). https://doi.org/10.1016/0031-3203(93)90135-J
12. Liu, F., Fang, M.: Semantic segmentation of underwater images based on improved deeplab. J. Mar. Sci. Eng. **8**(3) (2020). https://doi.org/10.3390/jmse8030188
13. He, K., Zhang, X., Ren, S., Sun, J.: Deep residual learning for image recognition. In: 2016 IEEE Conference on Computer Vision and Pattern Recognition (CVPR), pp. 770–778 (2016). https://doi.org/10.1109/CVPR.2016.90
14. Huang, G., Liu, Z., Van Der Maaten, L., Weinberger, K.Q.: Densely connected convolutional networks. In: 2017 IEEE Conference on Computer Vision and Pattern Recognition (CVPR), pp. 2261–2269 (2017). https://doi.org/10.1109/CVPR.2017.243

15. Lv, Y., et al.: Simultaneously localize, segment and rank the camouflaged objects. In: 2021 IEEE/CVF Conference on Computer Vision and Pattern Recognition (CVPR), pp. 11586–11596 (2021). https://doi.org/10.1109/CVPR46437.2021.01142
16. Chen, G., Liu, S.-J., Sun, Y.-J., Ji, G.-P., Wu, Y.-F., Zhou, T.: Camouflaged object detection via context-aware cross-level fusion. IEEE Trans. Circuits Syst. Video Technol. **32**(10), 6981–6993 (2022). https://doi.org/10.1109/TCSVT.2022.3178173
17. Mei, H., Ji, G.-P., Wei, Z., Yang, X., Wei, X., Fan, D.-P.: camouflaged object segmentation with distraction mining . In: 2021 IEEE/CVF Conference on Computer Vision and Pattern Recognition (CVPR), Los Alamitos, CA, USA, pp. 8768–8777. IEEE Computer Society (2021). https://doi.org/10.1109/CVPR46437.2021.00866. https://doi.ieeecomputersociety.org/10.1109/CVPR46437.2021.00866
18. Li, C., Anwar, S., Porikli, F.: Underwater scene prior inspired deep underwater image and video enhancement. Pattern Recogn. **98**, 107038 (2020). https://doi.org/10.1016/j.patcog.2019.107038
19. Ancuti, C., Ancuti, C.O., Haber, T., Bekaert, P.: Enhancing underwater images and videos by fusion. In: 2012 IEEE Conference on Computer Vision and Pattern Recognition, pp. 81–88 (2012). https://doi.org/10.1109/CVPR.2012.6247661
20. Liu, R., Fan, X., Zhu, M., Hou, M., Luo, Z.: Real-world underwater enhancement: challenges, benchmarks, and solutions under natural light. IEEE Trans. Circuits Syst. Video Technol. **30**(12), 4861–4875 (2020). https://doi.org/10.1109/TCSVT.2019.2963772
21. Zhang, W., et al.: Underwater image enhancement via weighted wavelet visual perception fusion. IEEE Trans. Circuits Syst. Video Technol. **34**(4), 2469–2483 (2024). https://doi.org/10.1109/TCSVT.2023.3299314
22. Du, D., et al.: UIEDP: boosting under- water image enhancement with diffusion prior. Expert Syst. Appl. **259**, 125271 (2025). https://doi.org/10.1016/j.eswa.2024.125271
23. Cao, J., et al.: Unveiling the underwater world: clip perception model-guided underwater image enhancement. Pattern Recogn. **162**, 111395 (2025). https://doi.org/10.1016/j.patcog.2025
24. Chen, R., Fu, Z., Huang, Y., Cheng, E., Ding, X.: A robust object segmentation network for underwater scenes. In: ICASSP 2022 - 2022 IEEE International Conference on Acoustics, Speech and Signal Processing (ICASSP), pp. 2629–2633 (2022). https://doi.org/10.1109/ICASSP43922.2022.9746176
25. Xu, M., Su, J., Liu, Y.: AquaSAM: underwater image foreground segmentation. In: Zhai, G., Zhou, J., Ye, L., Yang, H., An, P., Yang, X. (eds.) Digital Multimedia Communications, pp. 3–14. Springer, Singapore (2024)
26. Fu, Z., Chen, R., Huang, Y., Cheng, E., Ding, X., Ma, K.-K.: MASNet: a robust deep marine animal segmentation network. IEEE J. Oceanic Eng. **49**(3), 1104–1115 (2024). https://doi.org/10.1109/JOE.2023.3252760
27. Hong, Y., Zhou, X., Hua, R., Lv, Q., Dong, J.: WaterSAM: adapting SAM for underwater object segmentation. J. Mar. Sci. Eng. **12**(9) (2024). https://doi.org/10.3390/jmse12091616
28. Vaswani, A., et al.: Attention is all you need. In: Proceedings of the 31st International Conference on Neural Information Processing Systems. NIPS'17, Red Hook, NY, USA, pp. 6000–6010. Curran Associates Inc. (2017)
29. Qin, X., Zhang, Z., Huang, C., Gao, C., Dehghan, M., Jagersand, M.: Basnet: Boundary-aware salient object detection. In: 2019 IEEE/CVF Conference on Computer Vision and Pattern Recognition (CVPR), pp. 7471–7481 (2019). https://doi.org/10.1109/CVPR.2019.00766
30. Li, L., Rigall, E., Dong, J., Chen, G.: Mas3k: an open dataset for marine animal segmentation. In: Wolf, F., Gao, W. (eds.) Benchmarking, Measuring, and Optimizing, pp. 194–212. Springer, Cham (2021)
31. Fan, D.-P., Cheng, M.-M., Liu, Y., Li, T., Borji, A.: Structure-measure: a new way to evaluate foreground maps. In: 2017 IEEE International Conference on Computer Vision (ICCV), pp. 4558–4567 (2017). https://doi.org/10.1109/ICCV.2017.487

32. Margolin, R., Zelnik-Manor, L., Tal, A.: How to evaluate foreground maps. In: 2014 IEEE Conference on Computer Vision and Pattern Recognition, pp. 248–255 (2014). https://doi.org/10.1109/CVPR.2014.39
33. Fan, D.-P., Gong, C., Cao, Y., Ren, B., Cheng, M.-M., Borji, A.: Enhanced-alignment measure for binary foreground map evaluation. In: International Joint Conference on Artificial Intelligence (2018). https://api.semanticscholar.org/CorpusID:44072899
34. Perazzi, F., Krahenbuhl, P., Pritch, Y., Hornung, A.: Saliency filters: contrast based filtering for salient region detection. In: 2012 IEEE Conference on Computer Vision and Pattern Recognition, pp. 733–740 (2012). https://doi.org/10.1109/CVPR.2012.6247743
35. Kingma, D.P., Ba, J.: Adam: a method for stochastic optimization. CoRR abs/1412.6980 (2014)
36. Wu, Z., Su, L., Huang, Q.: Stacked cross refinement network for edge-aware salient object detection. In: 2019 IEEE/CVF International Conference on Computer Vision (ICCV), pp. 7263–7272 (2019). https://doi.org/10.1109/ICCV.2019.00736
37. He, Z., et al.: UISS-Net: underwater image semantic segmentation network for improving boundary segmentation accuracy of underwater images. Aquacult. Int. 5625–5638 (2024). https://doi.org/10.1007/s10499-024-01439-x
38. Gilad-Bachrach, R., Dowlin, N., Laine, K., Lauter, K., Naehrig, M., Wernsing, J.: Cryptonets: applying neural networks to encrypted data with high throughput and accuracy. In: International Conference on Machine Learning, PMLR, pp. 201–210 (2016)
39. Li, W., et al., Privacy-preserving federated brain tumor segmentation. In: Suk, HI., Liu, M., Yan, P., Lian, C. (eds.) MLMI 2019. LNCS, vol. 11861, pp. 133–141. Springer, Cham (2019). https://doi.org/10.1007/978-3-030-32692-0-16
40. Jia, H., Cai, D., Yang, J., et al.: Efficient and privacy-preserving image classification using homomorphic encryption and chunk-based convolutional neural network. J. Cloud Comp. **12**, 175 (2023). https://doi.org/10.1186/s13677-023-00537-0
41. Challa, R., VijayaKumari, G., Sunny, B.: Secure Image processing using LWE based Homomorphic encryption. In: 2015 IEEE International Conference on Electrical, Computer and Communication Technologies (ICECCT), Coimbatore, India, pp. 1–6 (2015). https://doi.org/10.1109/ICECCT.2015.7226064
42. Yang, H., Zhou, Q., Ni, J., Li, H., Shen, X.: Accurate image-based pedestrian detection with privacy preservation. IEEE Trans. Veh. Technol. **69**(12), 14494–14509 (2020). https://doi.org/10.1109/TVT.2020.3043203
43. Wang, J., Jin, Y., Stoyanov, D., Wang, L.: FedDP: dual personalization in federated medical image segmentation. IEEE Trans. Med. Imaging **43**(1), 297–308 (2024). https://doi.org/10.1109/TMI.2023.3299206
44. Gurung, D., Pokhrel, S.R.: Performance analysis and design of a weighted personalized quantum federated learning. IEEE Trans. Artif. Intell. https://doi.org/10.1109/TAI.2025.3545393.

When VR is Not Just for Gaming: Unmasking GPU Resource Misuse on VR Headset

Dianshi Yang$^{(\boxtimes)}$ and Xing Gao

University of Delaware, Newark, DE 19716, USA
{cyberfox,xgao}@udel.edu

Abstract. Security issues related to hardware resource misusage have been a major challenge for the graphics processing unit (GPU) on smart devices. Recent research mainly focuses on hijacking the GPU resources on smartphones or personal computers. However, unethical developers can also target Virtual Reality (VR) headsets with sufficient GPU resources for graphic rendering. We present two proof-of-concept attacks targeting GPU computing resources for cryptomining and machine learning model training by standalone VR and WebXR applications. The evaluation shows that the cryptomining scripts injected into the standalone VR application can nearly fully exploit GPU resources, with utilization reaching up to 97.57%. Additionally, these scripts can negatively impact user experience when the frame rate falls below 72 FPS. The machine learning model training scripts used by the WebXR application can utilize GPU resources by over 67%, which is 11% more than the baseline, and it does not influence the overall user experience.

Keywords: Virtual Reality · Hardware Abuse · GPU · Cryptojacking

1 Introduction

Virtual Reality (VR) has emerged as a transformative technology, offering users an immersive experience that blurs the boundaries between the virtual and real worlds. As VR becomes integrated with applications on headsets on users' end, new challenges arise with pressing security concerns [57]. Considering the similar system components and frameworks between VR devices and ordinary portable or IoT devices [48], some security concerns existing in ordinary Android smart phone [41] and IoT system [42] can also be found in VR devics. One security concern among these is the potential threat of hardware misuse of VR devices without users' awareness, which exposes new attack surfaces for unethical malicious developers and attackers. Due to the high performance of hardware capabilities and computing resources provided by the graphics processing unit (GPU) for graphic rendering, VR devices' hardware resources are always the target of unethical developers who misuse them for profit. One form of hardware misuse is cryptojacking, which involves illicitly harnessing the computational power of

W. Liang et al. (Eds.): SecureComm 2025, LNICST 690, pp. 541–564, 2026.
https://doi.org/10.1007/978-3-032-23456-8_29

a victim's device to mine cryptocurrency without the user's consent. Malicious VR applications with cryptojacking scripts can leverage substantial hardware computing resources of VR headsets, especially GPUs that can provide strong computing capabilities. This secret mining operation not only leads to an additional burden on electricity consumption but also inflicts a substantial impediment on the computational efficiency of the host device. The average cost to build a standard home rig for cryptomining is about $1,000 to $2,000, which is extremely high for a benign home miner [58]. Driven by profit, unethical miners intend to steal resources from others for cryptomining. According to the statistics [51], *cryptojackers make $1 for every $53 their victim is billed*. This is sufficient to demonstrate that the vulnerabilities related to cryptojacking, as an example of hardware resource misuse, lead to significant losses for victims and enormous costs for attackers with almost no expense. Considering that the operating systems of most VR headsets on the market belong to the same OS family as common smartphones (e.g., Android for Meta Quest VR headsets), similar cryptojacking attacks targeting mobile devices [38] are believed to be capable of migrating to VR devices.

Another potential form of hardware resource misuse on VR devices is training machine learning (ML) models in a decentralized manner on the user end. Although large-scale machine learning model training requires substantial computing resources, decentralization techniques can distribute the training work across multiple decentralized edge devices or servers [36]. In this case, the training data are distributed on mobile devices, and a shared model by aggregating locally-computed updates is learned [54]. By stealing computing resources, the malicious developer can save costs on renting computing resources online and reduce the gaming experiences of VR users.

In this paper, we present two proof-of-concept attacks by VR applications targeting GPU computing resources with the implementation on Meta Quest 3 VR headset [11]. Two attack scenarios to leverage GPU computing capabilities in cryptojacking and machine learning model training are designed and implemented separately by an Android VR application and a WebXR [9] application. In designing attack scenarios, we overcome the challenge of how a VR application calls the graphic rendering functions for computing. To overcome this challenge, the High-Level Shader Language (HLSL) [30], a C-like high-level shader language defining the behavior of the GPU in graphics rendering pipeline, is used for VR application development for GPU general-purpose computing. Another challenge is that the victims should remain unaware of the misuse of hardware resources. The additional computing tasks must not interfere with the overall graphic rendering in VR scenes. To find out the critical point where hardware computing resources can be most effectively utilized without significantly impacting user experience, we recruit actual VR users to engage in our research and provide feedback on VR scenes.

To the best of our knowledge, this is the first work that implements GPU resource hijacking on VR headset for cryptomining and machine learning model training by Android VR application and WebXR application. To evaluate the performance of the attacks and the impact on the VR headset, a simple VR immersive scene is established for both resource misuse scenarios with the injected attack scripts running in multiple threads. We have measured GPU performance and frame rate while the attacks are running at different levels. To evaluate the impact of attacks on user experience, we invited 10 volunteers to wear the VR headset and give feedback on the smoothness of object movement inside the immersive scene while the attack scripts are running with different threads. The evaluation results show that for the Android VR app, there is not much impact on the user's VR experience when the frame rate exceeds 72 and GPU utilization is below 58% with fewer than 2^{14} computing threads for cryptomining. Also, for the WebXR app with ML model training, practical users are not affected much even when the threads reach 2^{13}.

Main Contributions. The contributions of this paper are as follows:

- We analyze the Android VR application development pipeline by Unity [23] and utilize the compute shader of HLSL for the hash computing of cryptomining.
- We analyze the WebXR application framework and utilize WebGL [26] techniques for GPU general-purpose computing for ML model training.
- GPU resources hijacked by a VR standalone application for cryptomining can increase GPU utilization up to 97.5% at most and up to 58% without much user experience effect. For the ML model training misuse by WebXR application, the GPU utilization can be increased from 55% up to 67%.

2   Background

2.1   VR Device and Applications

VR devices provide users with immersive interactive experience through head-mounted displays (HMDs), motion controllers, and spatial tracking technology. These devices typically include Oculus Quest, HTC Vive, PlayStation VR, etc., which can enhance immersion through visual, auditory, and even tactile feedback. According to the statistics by Statista[1], Meta occupies the majority of the VR headset shipment share worldwide from 2023 to 2024, especially 70.8% in Q3 2024 [50]. Also, by September 2024, 60.4% of Steam users have been using Meta Quest and Oculus VR devices for game playing [61]. Therefore, considering the proportion of users on VR devices, our research focuses on the Meta Quest VR headset.

The Meta Quest 3 VR headset [11] is one of the most popular VR devices on the market. The Quest 3 can operate completely wirelessly or connect to a PC with a wired connection. It runs on Meta Horizon OS [10] (formerly known as Meta Quest Platform), an extended reality operating system developed by Meta Platforms. Specifically, Horizon OS is a modified version of Android that

---

[1] Statista: an online platform that specializes in data gathering and visualization. https://www.statista.com.

has been optimized for running VR environments and applications. The Meta Quest 3 utilizes the Qualcomm Snapdragon XR2 Gen 2 system-on-chip made by Qualcomm [21], paired with Adreno 740 GPU [1], delivering 1.84 TFLOPS[2] of computing performance.

SideQuest [20] is a popular third-party app store featuring Android VR applications, mostly developed by Unity [23] or Unreal [24]. These applications are known as *standalone applications*, meaning they can run on VR headsets independently without needing to connect to a PC. Additionally, the *WebXR* application[3], which provides an immersive environment on a VR headset with support from browser [14], is also compatible with Meta Quest headsets.

Our research focuses solely on the attack scenarios for the standalone Android VR application and the WebXR application on Meta Quest 3.

2.2 Resource Hijacking

Resource hijacking refers to the unauthorized and malicious use of a victim's computing resources, including CPU, GPU, or other hardware capable of computing, to perform harmful or unintended activities [67]. Adversaries may engage in illicit cryptocurrency mining, distributing spam, consuming network bandwidth, and any other activities requiring substantial computing power [33]. One potential example involves embedding JavaScript in websites for cryptomining. Platforms like CoinHive [66] (now defunct but previously widely used) permitted site owners to insert scripts that exploited visitors' hardware resources to mine Monero (XMR) without their knowledge or consent. Cryptojacking malware is also possible in Android [34,38]. This type of cryptojacking has remained undetected for long periods, resulting in poorer user experiences and substantial computational overhead.

VR devices normally equip GPU with strong capabilities for computation for graphic rendering. This exposes the attack surface for those who plan to steal computing resources from others for profit at zero cost. Similar to cryptomining, GPU computing resource is also the target for training machine learning models. Cloud services that provide ML training often cost a lot. For example, according to Google Cloud Price Calculator [45], the price to rent an NVIDIA V4 GPU for one month is about $116.80 with the basic configuration. Through decentralized and collaborative machine learning technologies [44], malicious developers may attempt to hijack the computing resources of unsuspecting victims, pooling the benefits from thousands of individuals. A VR user's hardware resources can potentially be exploited simply by visiting a VR game website in a browser if the online browser-based VR game has been compromised with malicious scripts for ML model training, similar to the methods of cryptojacking by webpages.

---

[2] TFLOPS: tera (10^{12}) floating point operations per second.

[3] The WebVR [27] has now been deprecated and replaced by WebXR [9]. However, this paper does not focus on augmented reality (AR) or mixed reality (MR) outside of the VR concept.

2.3 VR Application Development by Unity

The Unity game engine [23] offers a strong ecosystem for immersive VR application development across various platforms. Android VR development usually focuses on standalone devices like the Meta Quest series. The Meta XR plugin [13] provides developers with device- and platform-specific capabilities, including camera rig configurations, VR motion control, and hand tracking. With the plugin's support, Unity can be utilized for Android VR applications designed for Meta VR devices.

The High-Level Shader Language (HLSL) [30], which was developed by Microsoft for the DirectX framework, serves as the foundation for numerous custom shader implementations within Unity. While Unity encapsulates HLSL within its ShaderLab framework [19], the fundamental syntax and methodology remain strongly aligned with HLSL standards. It describes how the GPU operates within the graphics rendering pipeline and can be utilized to create vertex shaders and pixel shaders, as well as implement the renderer in applications that use these shaders.

The Open Graphics Library (OpenGL) [17] is an API that renders both 2D and 3D vector graphics and is compatible with various languages and platforms. OpenGL for Embedded Systems (OpenGL ES) [16] is a lightweight subset of the OpenGL specification, specifically designed for mobile and embedded platforms. It provides a broadly compatible, hardware-accelerated graphics API that is widely supported across smartphones, tablets, and standalone VR headsets. OpenGL ES can serve as the primary rendering backend in Unity VR application development. In practice, OpenGL ES cannot directly read or execute HLSL code. Instead, Unity and other engines that support multiple rendering backends first translate the HLSL source code into a shader language suitable for the target platform during the compilation or build phase [29]. The shader compiler of OpenGL ES then compiles the shader language into machine instructions that can be executed by the target GPU at runtime.

WebGL [26] is a cutting-edge web graphics API that enables low-overhead access to GPU functionalities within browsers. It features a native shading language called OpenGL Shading Language (GLSL) [6], which serves as an alternative for writing shaders directly in a web context. Developers can convert their existing HLSL shaders to GLSL using toolchains provided by Unity, facilitating the reuse of essential shader logic across both native and web platforms [40]. Although Unity does not officially support direct WebXR development via WebGL, various WebXR plugins and extensions enable WebGL-based WebXR app development within Unity [9].

3 Threat Model

In this study, we consider two attack vectors that malicious developers may exploit for resource misuse: cryptomining and training machine learning models. Figure 1 shows an overview of the misuse of computing resources on the VR device of the victim. Adversaries can inject exploitative scripts into VR apps

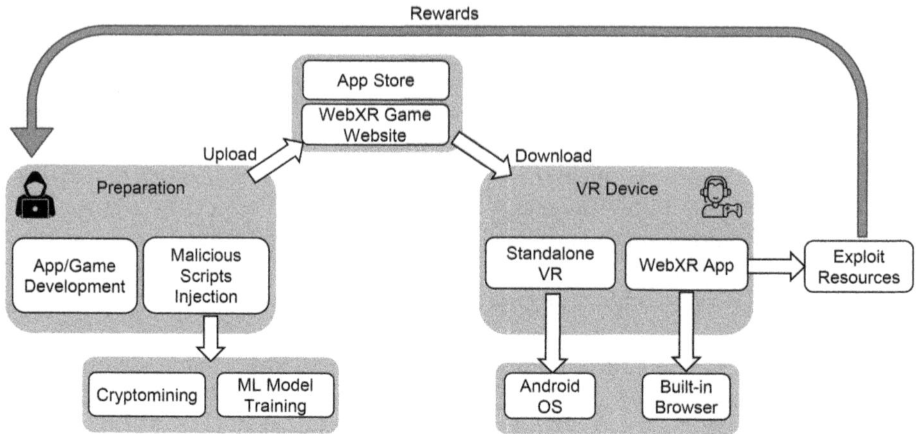

Fig. 1. Overview of the misuse of computing resources on VR device.

and publish these malicious applications to app stores or online gaming websites to lure victims into downloading or playing online.

We demonstrate that adversaries can inject malicious scripts to hijack GPU computing resources into VR applications or games during development. These scripts should not be easily detectable and can execute silently without affecting the common functionality of applications. The adversaries then register a developer account at app stores or online WebXR game websites, and upload malicious applications to the app store or websites to attract victims to download them. The platforms cannot detect the malicious scripts attached to the application. The victims either download the standalone VR app and install it on the local VR device, or launch the WebXR app online using an immersive browser. After the victims launch the application and experience its immersive environment, the malicious scripts begin exploiting GPU computing resources to generate profits for the adversaries. The victims should not be aware of the unusual operations of VR hardware, nor any unusual stuttering or delays in motion within the immersive environment. The malicious app should then send back the rewards to adversaries. This step involves either sending hashing results to the mining pool in cryptomining abuse cases, or transmitting ML model training results to adversaries or an online database. As time passes, the energy consumption and hardware depreciation of victims gradually turn into profits for adversaries.

Cryptojacking by Android VR App. The malicious developer may inject cryptojacking scripts into an Android standalone VR app and publish it to a third-party app store to attract victims for download. The hash computing process is programmed using shading language to utilize GPU capability. After the app is downloaded and run on a local VR headset, the victim will enjoy the immersive VR environment provided by the app. At the same time, the malicious scripts are launched to leverage GPU computing resources silently, without the victim's awareness. Any rewards created by mining will be sent back for the attacker's profit.

ML Model Training by WebXR App. The GPU computing resources can be misused for training ML models. In this situation, the attacker could inject scripts for ML model training within a WebXR app and host it on a third-party WebXR app website. If a victim navigates to the corresponding webpage and engages with the immersive environment offered by this malicious WebXR app, the scripts will utilize the browser to access graphics rendering APIs (e.g. WebGL) for GPU computing tasks. The results of the training will then be sent back to the attacker, all while the victim remains oblivious to the ongoing process as they interact with the immersive VR scenes.

4   System Design

In this section, we outline our development frameworks and attack models. In Sect. 4.1, we introduce the Android VR application development framework. Next, in Sect. 4.2, we describe the WebXR application development framework with WebGL [22].

4.1   Unity Development Framework for Android VR Application

The development pipeline for standalone VR Android applications in Unity involves multiple stages, as Fig. 2a shows. In the Unity Editor, developers create scenes by importing assets such as 3D models, textures, and scenes, and configuring lighting and materials. Application logic and interactions are controlled through MonoScripts written in C#. MonoScript [15] in Unity refers to the script used to define the behavior, logic, and interactions of game objects within a Unity project. For rendering, the graphics shading language, e.g. HLSL, defines the behavior of the GPU in graphics rendering pipeline (e.g. vertex shader, fragment shader, geometry shader, computer shader for non-graphic general computing tasks, etc.) and provides complex visual effects. Once development is complete, Unity's IL2CPP (Intermediate Language To C++) [8] backend converts C# scripts into C++ for improved performance, and the Android Native Development Kit (NDK) [2] compiles these into native binaries. Graphics shading language scripts are also compiled into bytecode by Microsoft's FXC HLSL compiler, followed by translation into OpenGL Shading Language (GLSL) [6] using HLSLcc[4] [18]. OpenGL ES API [16] then compiles GLSL into GPU instructions for execution at GPU rendering pipeline. The final build is packaged into an APK package and deployed to the Meta Quest VR headset. At runtime, the application manages VR components, user interactions, and real-time rendering, with OpenGL ES facilitating communication between the app and GPU.

---

[4] HLSLcc: DirectX shader bytecode cross compiler. https://github.com/Unity-Technologies/HLSLcc.

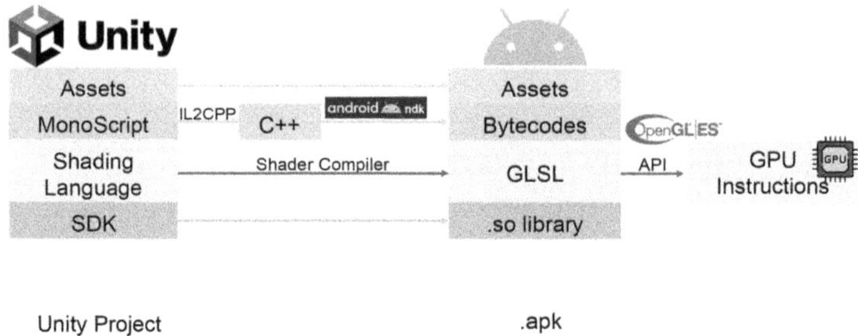

(a) Normal Unity development pipeline for Android VR applications.

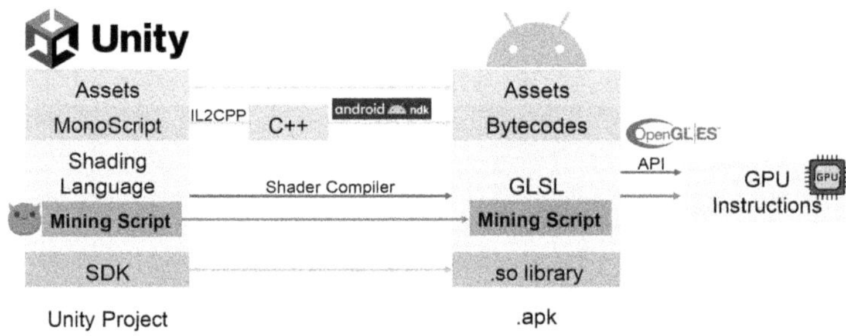

(b) Unity development pipeline for Android VR applications with cryptomining scripts.

Fig. 2. The Unity development pipeline for Android VR applications. (a) shows the normal development pipeline. (b) shows that an unethical developer can inject cryptomining scripts into the shading language to leverage GPU computing resources.

Figure 2b shows the development framework where hash computing functions of cryptojacking attack scripts are injected into graphic shader language. By leveraging the GPU's parallel computing capabilities, hash computations, which are coded as compute shader by graphics shading language and interface with GPU by OpenGL ES API, can be executed simultaneously with graphical rendering tasks. Since shaders operate concurrently across a large number of threads, this approach makes hash computation highly efficient.

4.2   Unity Development Framework for WebXR Application

An example of a common WebXR application integrated with WebGL is shown in Fig. 3a. The structure of a WebXR application consists of several interconnected layers. At the top layer, the WebXR app handles the core application logic and user interactions. The app interacts with the browser to provide access to spatial web features through the WebXR Device API [28] that allows developers to retrieve real-time poses of the user's head, hands, or controllers and to display the resulting images on XR devices. To render 3D environments, browsers rely on web-based graphics APIs such as WebGL [26]. These APIs serve as a

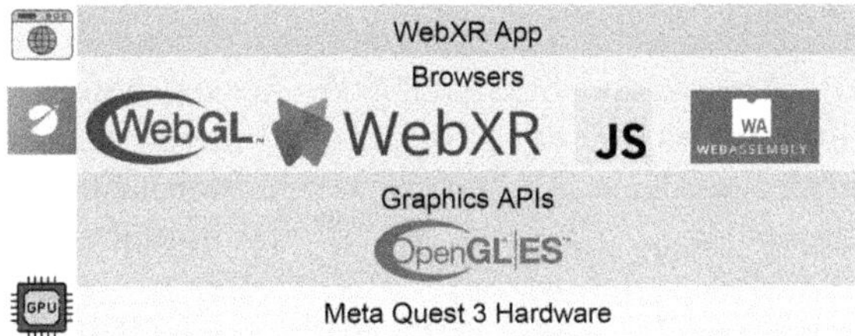

(a) The framework of WebXR applications with WebGL.

(b) WebXR application development pipeline with WebGL integration and machine learning script injected.

Fig. 3. The structure of WebXR applications. As (a) shows, browsers provide access to spatial web app features through the WebXR Device API. (b) indicates that an unethical developer might inject ML model training scripts as a variant of shading language (e.g., HLSL).

bridge between the browser and the graphic hardware. At a lower level, graphics APIs such as OpenGL ES [16] handle direct communication with GPU. The browser implements these APIs natively, depending on the specific hardware and platform it's running on [3].

Figure 3b illustrates the development framework where an unethical WebXR developer injects ML model training scripts in form of shading language (e.g. HLSL) to exploit GPU resources. In contrast to the Android VR application, WebXR development involves converting MonoScript with game functionalities into C++ scripts by IL2CPP, which are then compiled into WebAssembly (Wasm) [22] by Emscripten [7], a complete compiler toolchain. The shading language is converted into GLSL, the WebGL-specific shading language used for graphics rendering. The graphical rendering is handled through OpenGL ES as the primary graphics API, which interfaces with the GPU on Meta Quest 3. This attack scenario ensures the parallel processing power of intensive ML model training tasks while maintaining the appearance of a standard VR immersive user experience.

5   Implementation and Evaluation

In this section, we implement two practical attack scenarios, **Attack 1:** Cryptojacking by Android VR App, and **Attack 2:** ML Model Training by WebXR

App. The implementation is on a Meta Quest 3 VR headset with Runtime version 69.0.0.403 and OS version SQ3A.220605. As a proof-of-concept work, we only implement attacks locally without connecting the headset to the mining pool or remote server. Multiple tests are conducted for each scenario with different computing threads or data volume levels. The implementation was done in the indoor room where the temperature is kept constant at 23.89°C. The GPU measurement results, which include GPU utilization, GPU temperature, GPU level, and frame rate[5], are recorded. Each test lasts seven minutes. Appendix 8 provides explanations of GPU-level concepts. There are seven thermal sensors at the GPU of the headset. The average value of these seven sensors for each timestamp is recorded for GPU temperature metrics. To evaluate the effectiveness of attacks as a background process, we evaluate cryptojacking on the Android VR app for both screen-on and screen-off conditions. We only evaluate the WebXR ML training attacks when the screen is on because we consider Attack 2 scenario in which the victims are immersed in a virtual environment with the browser's support. The WebXR app will exit when victims close the browser and remove the headset.

The metrics tools provided by Meta are used for data collection. The OVR Metrics Tool [32] can monitor and store performance metrics in real time. Also, the real-time metrics of GPU utilization and GPU temperature measurements can be accessed directly from the device's system directory. For the convenience of performance metrics recording, the headset is connected to a PC by cable during implementation and monitored via the Meta Quest Developer Hub (MQDH) [12], an application that provides statistical data and tracks device metrics over time. As a baseline of performance metrics, we record the idle performance of the headset with the average frame rate 90 FPS (frames per second), GPU level 2, and GPU utilization 7%.

In addition to evaluating the impact of attacks on user experience, we invite volunteers to wear the VR headset during the implementation, stare at the moving object in the scene, and give feedback about the smoothness of object movement and image quality of the immersive environment. There are 10 participants involving our experiment for two attack scenarios, with ages over 18 but less than 30. Among these participants, 7 are graduate students majoring in computer science, 1 is working in a job related to computer science, and 2 are employed in other fields. For each participant, all the scenes with different attack levels are shown in random sequence. Several questions about the image quality are raised, including whether the movement of the object is laggy or choppy, whether it moves at a steady speed, whether there is a shadow beside the object, and whether the edges of the object are jagged. The details of the survey questions refer to Appendix 8.

---

[5] Frame rate stands for the measurement of how quickly a number of frames appear within a second.

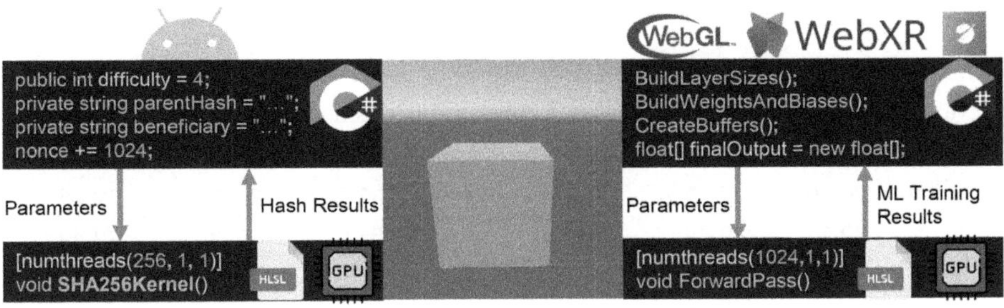

Fig. 4. The program structure and scene of Unity project for two attacks

5.1 Cryptojacking by Android VR App

We implement the cryptojacking VR application on a Meta Quest 3 VR headset. The application with hash computing scripts for cryptomining is developed and built by Unity version 2022.3.16f1 with the support of Meta XR All-in-One SDK [13]. The hash computation uses the HLSL shading language to initiate GPU execution, while other VR functionalities are developed using MonoScript, as shown on the left in Fig. 4. To demonstrate, a sample scene features a cube that exhibits reciprocating motion at a consistent speed of $2\,\text{m/s}$. The miner script is attached to the object and runs continuously. As our research is a local demonstration, block parameters used for mining, such as timestamp, parent hash, difficulty level, etc., are all assigned locally, and the nonce is increased by 1024 for each iteration. The miner defined in the MonoScript calls the SHA256 hash functions in the HLSL compute shader for multi-thread hash computing.

As the Table 1 shows, we set up 10 groups of experiments to evaluate the performance of the cryptojacking attack at different numbers of computing threads. These included one baseline without an attack and nine attacks with different levels of hash threads.

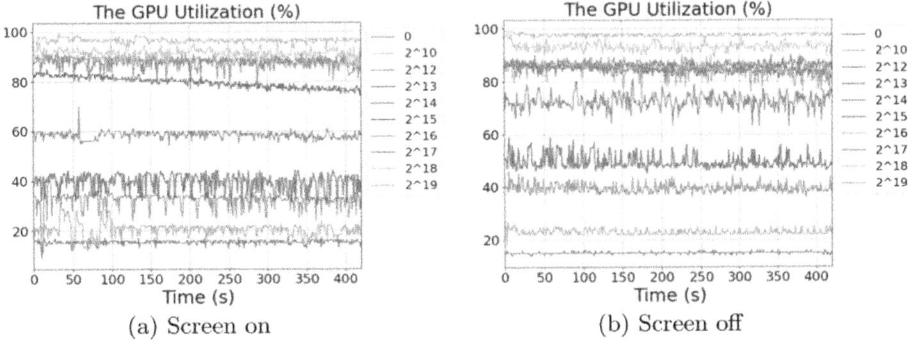

(a) Screen on (b) Screen off

Fig. 5. The GPU utilization for cryptojacking VR application with different threads of hash computing

Table 1. Average metrics of cryptojacking VR app

Threads Num.	GPU Util. (%)		GPU Level		GPU Temp. (°C)		Frame Rate (FPS)
	Screen on	Screen off	Screen on	Screen off	Screen on	Screen off	
0	15.33	15.01	3	3	52.57	55.09	72.54
2^{10}	20.40	22.85	3	3	55.12	54.81	72.45
2^{12}	32.17	39.34	3	3	55.91	55.38	72.49
2^{13}	39.40	49.46	3	3	57.68	55.96	72.44
2^{14}	58.30	72.41	3	3–4	61.14	59.46	72.42
2^{15}	79.58	84.42	4	4	60.81	55.07	60.90
2^{16}	87.52	84.84	4	4	61.14	63.94	35.01
2^{17}	88.40	86.01	4–5	4	61.68	63.02	17.80
2^{18}	91.40	93.02	4–5	4–5	61.59	59.13	9.55
2^{19}	96.47	97.57	4–5	4–5	61.49	62.95	5.01

GPU Performance Evaluation. Figure 5 presents the GPU utilization measurement results at various levels, all with the screen on and off. The data indicates that when there is no attack, GPU utilization hovers around 15%. In contrast, when the number of hash computing threads reaches 2^{19}, GPU utilization can soar to approximately 97%. Interestingly, the results reveal that for the same thread number of hash computing, GPU utilization can be higher when the screen is off than when it is on when the threads are over 2^{10}. This is particularly evident in Fig. 5 for 2^{12}, 2^{13}, and 2^{14} hash threads, where a significant difference can be observed. This observation will be addressed in Sect. 6.1.

The GPU level remains 3 when the multi-thread number is less than 2^{14}. As the thread number increases to 2^{14} for screen-on cases and 2^{15} for screen-off cases, the GPU level skips to 4. The GPU level can reach 5 during certain periods when the thread number reaches 2^{17} with average GPU utilization above 88%.

We also assess the thermal metrics of the cryptojacking VR application summarized in Fig. 6. The headset has been operational for a duration, and we introduce a time interval between each experiment to minimize the influence of thermal effects from other sources. When there is no attack from the VR application, the GPU temperature is between 50–55 °C. As the thread number increases, the temperature has the trend to grow. Even when the GPU utilization gets to 97%, the temperature is lower than 65 °C.

In summary, the standalone VR application experiencing cryptojacking attack can greatly enhance GPU utilization while also increasing power consumption. Nonetheless, the effect on GPU temperature remains minimal.

Frame Rate and User Experience Evaluation. Figure 7 shows the frame rate of the VR headset when the Android VR application with cryptomining scripts operates with different hash computing threads. The frame rate keeps around 72 FPS when the thread number is lower than 2^{14} or the average GPU

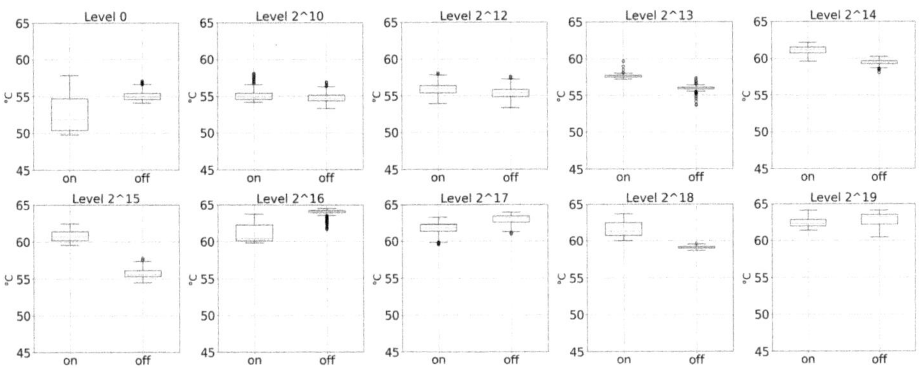

Fig. 6. The thermal measurement (°C) for cryptojacking VR application with different threads of hash computing with screen-on and screen-off

utilization is lower than 58%. With the thread number increases, the frame rate drastically drops until 5.01 FPS on average when the GPU utilization is over 96%.

In order to further investigate the impact of cryptojacking on user experience, we invite 10 volunteers to wear the headset, remain still, and look at the moving object in the VR scene while the cryptojacking attacks of different levels are launched in a random sequence. From the feedback listed in Table 2, when the frame rate is at 72 FPS during the cryptomining script running, the impact of cryptojacking on user experience in the VR scene is not significant. Only three participants reported that the moving object gets stuck for only a very few moments, and one participant mentioned that the movement becomes laggy or choppy only when it is directly in front of the user or in the front-left position. However, as the attack level rises and the frame rate drops, the laggy or choppy movement along with the jagged edges of the object becomes apparent, showing zigzagging borders, pixelation, and afterimages. The blurred edges are also more

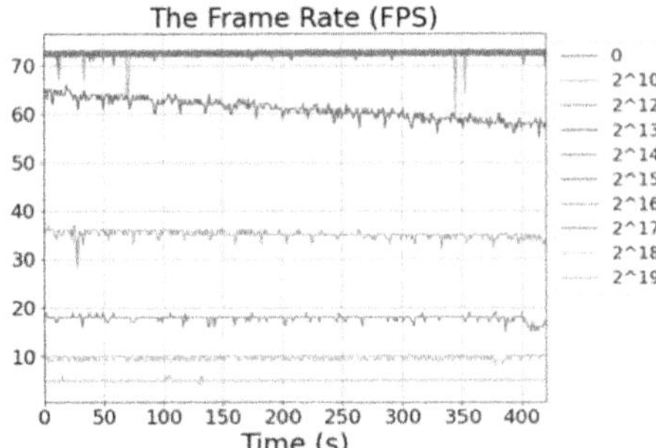

Fig. 7. The frame rate for cryptojacking VR application with different threads of hash computing

Table 2. The number of users reported negative feedback regarding image quality in Android VR scenes.

Level	FPS	Laggy or Choppy?	Jagged Edges?	Shadow?
0	72.54	0	0	0
2^{10}	72.45	1	0	0
2^{12}	72.49	3	0	0
2^{13}	72.44	3	1	0
2^{14}	72.42	1	2	0
2^{15}	60.90	10	6	0
2^{16}	35.01	10	8	2
2^{17}	17.80	10	7	2
2^{18}	9.55	10	10	6
2^{19}	5.01	10	10	5

noticeable if the frame rate drops below 35. When the frame rate drops below 10, all the participants state that the moving speed of the object appears to slow down, and two participants even assert that the movement is completely halted when the thread number reaches 2^{19}.

In summary, the cryptojacking attack via standalone VR application on headset can significantly reduce the frame rate when the number of hash threads exceeds 2^{14}. However, the user may not notice any issues with the image quality as long as the frame rate stays above 72.

5.2   ML Model Training by WebXR Application

The WebXR application, with ML model training scripts, is built by Unity version 6000.2.0a1 (alpha) with WebGL support and the unofficial WebXR extension *WebXR Export* [69]. Similar to the cryptojacking attack scenario, there is also an object in the scene for reciprocating motion at a steady speed of 2 m/s. The structure of the simple neural network for training contains three hidden layers, each hidden layer with 100 neurons. The input layer has 100 neurons, and the output layer has 10 neurons. As shown on the right in Fig. 4, the training work is implemented using the HLSL shading language, while other functionalities are developed through MonoScript. We established seven experimental groups to evaluate the impact on GPU performance and frame rate. Group 0 served as the baseline for comparison, consisting of no ML training scripts and only a VR scene featuring a moving cube. For the other groups, we set different numbers of threads for training. The training dataset consists of random data generated by the program. Similar to the cryptojacking attack, the GPU performance and frame rate data collection lasts for seven minutes, with ML training iterating for an infinite number of epochs.

Table 3. Average metrics of WebXR app

Threads Num.	GPU Util. (%)	SD of GPU Util.	GPU Temp. (°C)	SD of Temp.	Frame Rate (FPS)	SD of FPS
0	55.47	2.34	71.19	2.06	63.75	2.49
2^8	62.56	3.93	73.68	2.94	49.52	4.76
2^9	61.21	3.03	72.38	2.63	54.86	4.27
2^{10}	64.54	2.97	73.28	3.17	50.52	7.76
2^{11}	66.41	1.86	74.75	4.29	53.12	9.63
2^{12}	65.85	2.32	70.54	2.27	58.38	5.76
2^{13}	67.67	2.47	71.75	2.56	55.80	3.34

GPU Performance Evaluation. Figure 8 presents the GPU utilization measurement results of three experimental groups with both the screen on and off. With the results in Table 3, we can conclude that the ML model training scripts do not significantly improve GPU utilization but rather make it more unstable from the high value of variances compared to the baseline group for most situations. Compared to the baseline, the ML training increases GPU utilization by no more than 11%, and the GPU utilization across all cases remains unstable. The Standard Deviation (SD) is used to illustrate and compare the dispersion of the measurement results. In addition, the GPU level for all experiments of the three groups stays at 3.

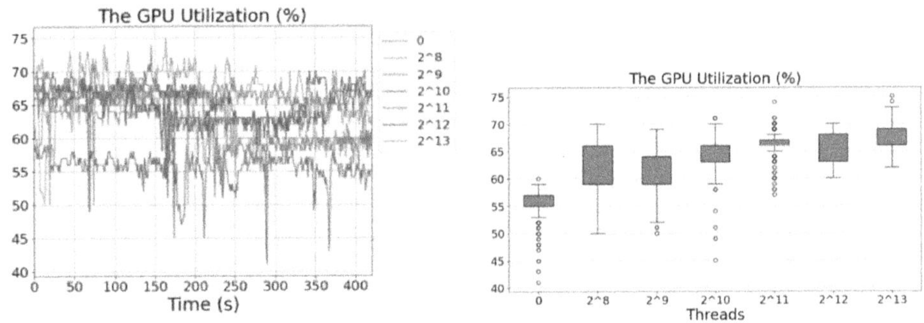

Fig. 8. The GPU utilization for WebXR application for ML model training with different threads.

The thermal metrics of the ML model training WebXR application in Fig. 9 and Table 3 indicate that during the training of the ML model, the temperature becomes noticeably more unstable. All the Standard Deviation (SD) values for GPU temperature exceed the baseline value. We can speculate that the combined impact of ML model training, graphical display, and browser functionality contributes to these unstable thermal fluctuations.

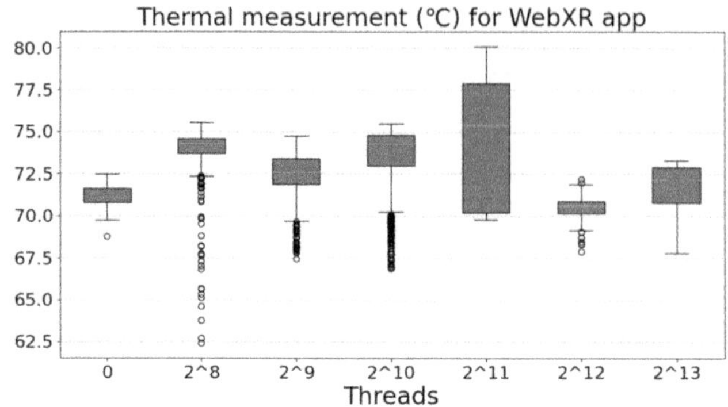

Fig. 9. The thermal measurement (°C) for ML model training WebXR application.

In summary, the superposition effect of machine learning model training and graphic display increases variations in GPU utilization and temperature to some extend.

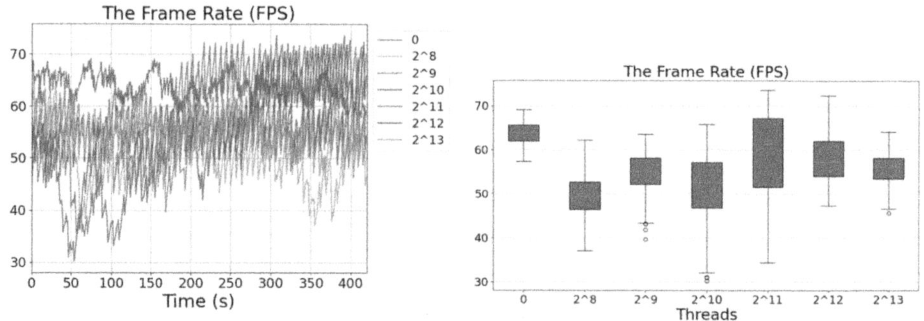

Fig. 10. The frame rate for ML model training WebXR application.

Frame Rate Evaluation. The internal functions of Unity record the frame rate for the WebXR application. Figure 10 shows the frame rate results of all experiment cases. We can get the result that the frame rate keeps unstable for all cases with huge fluctuations. In cases involving ML training scripts, the average frame rate decreases as the degrees of dispersion increase.

To further investigate the impact of training ML models in WebXR apps on user experience, we invite 10 volunteers to wear the headset and launch WebXR apps in the built-in web browser of the Meta Quest 3. Similar to the previously mentioned Android VR app experiment, participants are asked to observe the moving object in the VR scene while the ML model training script runs at different thread levels launched in a random sequence. From the feedback listed in Table 4, For each thread level, there are always participants claiming that they can see the object movement is laggy or choppy at certain times. However, all the participants claim that this kind of laggy or choppy movement only lasts for a moment (less than 1 s) and then disappears immediately. Based on participant feedback, the movement is generally smooth across all thread levels, and the impact of lagging movement under one second does not affect the overall experience. Additionally, the participants assert that they can see jagged edges or shadows on the edges of the object only in specific situations when the object changes direction.

Table 4. The number of users reported negative feedback regarding image quality in Android VR scenes.

Level	FPS	Laggy or Choppy?	Jagged Edges?	Shadow?
0	63.75	0	0	0
2^8	49.52	3	1	0
2^9	54.86	4	2	1
2^{10}	50.52	4	5	1
2^{11}	53.12	6	7	2
2^{12}	58.38	6	8	4
2^{13}	55.80	8	5	7

In summary, training the ML model using a WebXR application on a headset can significantly increase fluctuations in the frame rate, and users may notice minor changes in image quality. However, these minor negative impacts generally do not affect the user experience.

6 Discussion

6.1 Thermal Throttling

The GPU utilization evaluation of the cryptojacking VR standalone application in Sect. 5.1 and the comparison in Fig. 5 reveal that when the number of hash threads is between 2^{12} and 2^{15}, the average GPU utilization with the screen off is significantly higher than under the same conditions with the screen on. This result may be due to the GPU optimization and thermal throttling mechanisms of the VR headset. Thermal throttling techniques involve capping the maximum frequency at which a system-on-chip (SoC) may operate [35]. When an SoC device executes any application that requires sustained higher performance than normal, thermal throttling is available to limit thermal diffusion to avoid reduced device reliability and increased leakage power consumption [70]. Considering that the screen of the VR headset releases more heat while displaying, the thermal throttling mechanism may limit GPU performance to prevent a dramatic increase in heat. In comparison, if the screen is off, the heat source from graphic display disappears, allowing the GPU to allocate more resources for hash computing as optimization, which leads to higher GPU utilization.

6.2 Detection of GPU Resource Hijacking Shading Language Scripts

Currently, the detection mechanisms for cryptojacking malware on Android devices are based on system event monitoring, identification of existing mining libraries, network monitoring, and the identification of mining credentials and keywords, etc. [38,64]. However, these approaches may not apply to self-programmed miners programming with shading languages (e.g., HLSL, GLSL, etc.). We uploaded both our malicious standalone Android VR application and WebXR application to VirusTotal [25], an online service that integrates antivirus engines and website scanners to analyze suspicious files for malware and malicious content. After being scanned by more than 60 antivirus engines and scanners, the results show that there is no malicious content in our applications. Additionally, we attempt to extract our self-programmed malicious shading scripts using AssetRipper [4], a tool for extracting and converting assets from the Unity engine. The extraction results indicate that our self-programmed shading scripts can only be extracted as bytecode, which complicates the detection of malicious shading scripts.

6.3 Limitations in WebXR Attack Cases

When implementing the ML model training features in the WebXR application, we set the maximum thread count to 2^{13}. This is because the browser would freeze or crash when we tried to increase the thread number further. Therefore we only limited the number of threads up to 2^{13}. This might be related to the unofficial WebXR extension's compatibility with Unity when attempting to enable support for custom shading scripts. To the best of my knowledge, this is the first work that attempts to implement self-programmed shading scripts in a WebXR app for non-graphic purposes. The detailed issues in implementation are still awaiting discovery and resolution.

7   Related Work

Security and Privacy in Virtual Environments. Several recent studies illustrate security and privacy issues in virtual environments. For example, potential hidden operations threat in mobile AR systems [52] can be leveraged by malicious developers to conduct additional operations behind the scenes without alerting the users. Additionally, users in virtual environments face potential risks from attack surfaces introduced by applications [39], such as runtime data flow analysis [65] or motion detection [55] for user identification inferring, as well as potentially malicious libraries [53] used during the application development process. Also, some potential mechanisms are talked about to mitigate potential attacks and risks in content monitoring, access control, output control [46], and data anonymization by differential privacy [56]. The previous work lacks research on hardware resource misuse in virtual environments due to the abuse of the graphics rendering process. In this work, we focus on the hijacking of hardware resources on VR devices by leveraging GPU graphics rendering.

Cryptojacking Malware. A number of current research in cryptojacking has been done for both attacking and defending. The fundamental systematization of knowledge in cryptojacking malware is introduced [64], featuring practical exploitation examples in online web applications and gaming platforms. It covers malware types, including in-browser and host-based cryptojacking, as well as sources, infection methods, and victim characteristics. However, there is still a blank in cryptojacking malware on VR applications and VR hardware. Our work will fill in the gap. There are other works about cryptojacking malware implementation and detection in Android platforms or applications [34,37,43], web browsers, web applications [47,60,62], and IoT networks [63]. Given that almost no VR devices currently have detection mechanisms for cryptojacking malware scripts or actions like those used by PC antivirus software, malicious developers can easily lure naïve users into downloading or browsing injected applications online, taking device resources without users' awareness.

Resource Hijacking. Attackers might exploit a compromised resource offered by computing hardware to perform tasks. Previous research has addressed hardware resource hijacking, highlighting the extensive connectivity features of modern computing systems and providing examples of attacks and countermeasures at both the physical and data levels [49]. Similar research has been conducted on protection mechanisms to secure GPU execution in cyber-physical systems [68] and on detecting GPU resource misuse in HPC-based systems [59]. However, there are currently insufficient methods for detecting and defending against the misappropriation and hijacking of hardware computing resources, particularly on commercial-off-the-shelf VR devices, which exposes potential attack surfaces for malicious developers.

8   Conclusion and Future Work

Summary. We present a comprehensive study and implementation of GPU resource hijacking on the Meta Quest 3 VR headset. We also developed a standalone VR application for cryptojacking and a WebXR application for ML model training using GPU computing resources. The evaluation results show that by using cryptojacking scripts in the standalone VR application, GPU utilization can increase up to about 58% with frame rate 72FPS and almost unnoticeable impact to use experience, and increase up to 97.57% with 2^{19} hash computing threads with user experience totally negatively impacted. The WebXR application with ML training scripts has a greater impact on volatility than the numerical changes in GPU and frame metrics, and the effect on user experience is minimal.

Limitations and Future Directions. Further research and development are necessary to determine how the WebXR application can utilize GPU resources for ML training further. The feasibility of using Wasm for multi-threaded functions by browsers can be further investigated. From the attackers' perspective, further study on how to reduce the impact of hardware resource abuse on user experience is worthwhile. Additionally, future efforts will focus on detecting malicious scripts or functions in shading languages.

Acknowledgments. We would like to thank the anonymous reviewers for their insightful comments. This work was partially supported by the National Science Foundation (NSF) grants CNS-2317830 and CNS-2338837.

Appendix

A Ethics

During our research on the impact of cryptomining and machine learning scripts on user experience, we invited volunteers to wear our Meta Quest 3 VR headset and describe their feelings about object movement and image quality in VR scenes. The University of Delaware Institutional Review Board (UD IRB) has approved our research with human subjects, with the approval number 2271335-1. We have taken adequate cleaning measures to ensure that each VR headset is thoroughly cleaned before each participant uses it. We also informed each participant of the risks related to VR sickness before participating. No participants reported physical or mental discomfort during and after the experiment.

B The Concept of GPU Level

According to the Meta Quest documentation [31], the clock speed of the headset's GPU can be changed when running apps. High clock speed means high power consumption and costly features in applications. If possible, GPU level will increase when GPU utilization is 87% or greater, and decrease when GPU utilization is 81% or lesser. GPU level 5 can only be granted when the headset has sufficient thermal headroom [5]. For the GPU level of Meta Quest 3 headset from 0 to 5, the clock speed is 285 MHz, 350 MHz, 456 MHz, 492 MHz, 545 MHz, 599 MHz, separately. GPU level 0–2 is always available. GPU level 3–4 is available if the application does not enable passthrough features. GPU level 5 is available if GPU level 4 is available, and CPU and GPU level trading is set to +1, or dynamic resolution is enabled.

C Survey Questions for User Experience

- Can you see a cube is moving?
- Is this cube moving at a steady speed?
- Do you feel that the movement of this cube is laggy or choppy?
- Do you think the border of this cube is with jagged edges?

– Do you see any shadow beside the cube?
– Do you have any other comments, including the moving speed of the cube, the image quality, and so on?

D Device Directories for GPU Metrics

GPU utilization: /sys/class/kgsl/kgsl-3d0/gpu_busy_percentage.
GPU temperature at different thermal zones: /sys/class/thermal/tz-by-name/gpuss-N/temp ($1 \leq N \leq 7$).

References

1. Adreno gpu on mobile: Best practices. https://docs.qualcomm.com/bundle/publicresource/topics/80-78185-2/best_practices.html?product=1601111740035277
2. Android ndk. https://developer.android.com/ndk
3. Angle project. https://chromium.googlesource.com/angle/angle
4. Assetripper. https://assetripper.github.io/AssetRipper
5. Boosting cpu and gpu levels. https://developers.meta.com/horizon/documentation/native/android/po-quest-boost
6. Core language (glsl). https://www.khronos.org/opengl/wiki/Core_Language_(GLSL)
7. Emscripten. https://emscripten.org
8. Il2cpp overview. https://docs.unity3d.com/Manual/scripting-backends-il2cpp.html
9. Immersive web developer home. https://immersiveweb.dev
10. Meta horizon os developers. https://developers.meta.com/horizon
11. Meta quest 3: Mixed reality vr headset. https://www.meta.com/quest/quest-3
12. Meta quest developer hub. https://developers.meta.com/horizon/documentation/native/android/ts-odh
13. Meta xr all-in-one sdk. https://developers.meta.com/horizon/downloads/package/meta-xr-sdk-all-in-one-upm
14. Mixed reality support in browser. https://developers.meta.com/horizon/documentation/web/webxr-mixed-reality
15. Monoscript. https://docs.unity3d.com/ScriptReference/MonoScript.html
16. Opengl es overview. https://www.khronos.org/opengles
17. Opengl overview - the khronos group inc. https://www.khronos.org/opengl
18. Shader compilation. https://docs.unity3d.com/6000.2/Documentation/Manual/shader-compilation.html
19. Shaderlab language reference. https://docs.unity3d.com/Manual/SL-Reference.html
20. Sidequest. https://sidequestvr.com
21. Snapdragon xr2 gen 2 platform. https://www.qualcomm.com/products/mobile/snapdragon/xr-vr-ar/snapdragon-xr2-gen-2-platform
22. Unity - manual getting started with webgl development. https://docs.unity3d.com/2020.1/Documentation/Manual/webgl-gettingstarted.html
23. Unity real-time development platform. https://unity.com

24. Unreal engine. https://www.unrealengine.com
25. Virustotal. https://www.virustotal.com
26. Webgl - low-level 3d graphics api based on opengl es. https://www.khronos.org/webgl
27. Webvr - bringing virtual reality to the web. https://webvr.info
28. Webxr device api. https://www.w3.org/TR/webxr
29. Writing hlsl shader programs. https://docs.unity3d.com/6000.0/Documentation/Manual/writing-shader-writing-shader-programs-hlsl.html
30. High-level Shader language (HLSL). https://learn.microsoft.com/en-us/windows/win32/direct3dhlsl/dx-graphics-hlsl (2021)
31. CPU and GPU levels. https://developers.meta.com/horizon/documentation/unity/os-cpu-gpu-levels (2024)
32. Monitor performance with OVR metrics tool. https://developers.meta.com/horizon/documentation/native/android/ts-ovrmetricstool (2024)
33. Resource hijacking technique t1496 - enterprise. https://attack.mitre.org/techniques/T1496 (2024)
34. Adjibi, B.V., Mbodji, F.N., Bissyandé, T.F., Allix, K., Klein, J.: The devil is in the details: unwrapping the cryptojacking malware ecosystem on android. In: 2022 IEEE 22nd International Working Conference on Source Code Analysis and Manipulation (SCAM), pp. 153–163. IEEE (2022)
35. Bantock, J.R., Al-Hashimi, B.M., Merrett, G.V.: Mitigating interactive performance degradation from mobile device thermal throttling. IEEE Embed. Syst. Lett. **13**(1), 5–8 (2020)
36. Beltrán, E.T.M., et al.: Decentralized federated learning: fundamentals, state of the art, frameworks, trends, and challenges. IEEE Commun. Surv. Tutor. (2023)
37. Chen, Y., Ding, Z., Wagner, D.: Continuous learning for android malware detection. In: 32nd USENIX Security Symposium (USENIX Security 23), pp. 1127–1144 (2023)
38. Dashevskyi, S., Zhauniarovich, Y., Gadyatskaya, O., Pilgun, A., Ouhssain, H.: Dissecting android cryptocurrency miners. In: Proceedings of the Tenth ACM Conference on Data and Application Security and Privacy, pp. 191–202 (2020)
39. De Guzman, J.A., Thilakarathna, K., Seneviratne, A.: Security and privacy approaches in mixed reality: a literature survey. ACM Comput. Surv. (CSUR) **52**(6), 1–37 (2019)
40. Duncan, B.: Implementing WebGPU for unity (2024). https://www.khronos.org/assets/uploads/developers/presentations/Implementing_WebGPU_For_Unity_Khronos_GDC_2024.pdf
41. Enck, W., Octeau, D., McDaniel, P., Chaudhuri, S.: A study of android application security. In: Proceedings of the 20th USENIX conference on Security, pp. 21–21 (2011)
42. Fernandes, E., Jung, J., Prakash, A.: Security analysis of emerging smart home applications. In: 2016 IEEE Symposium on Security and Privacy (SP), pp. 636–654. IEEE (2016)
43. Gao, J., Kong, P., Li, L., Bissyandé, T.F., Klein, J.: Negative results on mining crypto-API usage rules in android apps. In: 2019 IEEE/ACM 16th International Conference on Mining Software Repositories (MSR), pp. 388–398. IEEE (2019)
44. González-Soto, M., Díaz-Redondo, R.P., Fernández-Veiga, M., Fernández-Castro, B., Fernández-Vilas, A.: Decentralized and collaborative machine learning framework for IoT. Comput. Netw. **239**, 110137 (2024)
45. Google: Google cloud pricing calculator. https://cloud.google.com/products/calculator

46. Guzman, J.A.D., Thilakarathna, K., Seneviratne, A.: Privacy and security issues and solutions for mixed reality applications. In: Nee, A.Y.C., Ong, S.K. (eds.) Springer Handbook of Augmented Reality, pp. 157–183. Springer, Cham (2023). https://doi.org/10.1007/978-3-030-67822-7_7

47. Hong, G., et al.: How you get shot in the back: a systematical study about cryptojacking in the real world. In: Proceedings of the 2018 ACM SIGSAC Conference on Computer and Communications Security, pp. 1701–1713 (2018)

48. Hu, M., Luo, X., Chen, J., Lee, Y.C., Zhou, Y., Wu, D.: Virtual reality: a survey of enabling technologies and its applications in IoT. J. Netw. Comput. Appl. **178**, 102970 (2021)

49. Hu, W., Chang, C.H., Sengupta, A., Bhunia, S., Kastner, R., Li, H.: An overview of hardware security and trust: threats, countermeasures, and design tools. IEEE Trans. Comput. Aided Des. Integr. Circuits Syst. **40**(6), 1010–1038 (2020)

50. IDC: Augmented reality (AR) and virtual reality (VR) headset companies shipment share worldwide from 2023 to 2024, by quarter (2024). https://www.statista.com/statistics/1407105/ar-vr-headset-companies-shipment-share

51. Lang, N., Belak, A.: Cryptojacking: free money for attackers, huge cloud bill for you (2022). https://thenewstack.io/cryptojacking-free-money-for-attackers-huge-cloud-bill-for-you

52. Lehman, S.M., Alrumayh, A.S., Kolhe, K., Ling, H., Tan, C.C.: Hidden in plain sight: exploring privacy risks of mobile augmented reality applications. ACM Trans. Priv. Secur. **25**(4), 1–35 (2022)

53. Li, M., et al.: Large-scale third-party library detection in android markets. IEEE Trans. Software Eng. **46**(9), 981–1003 (2018)

54. McMahan, B., Moore, E., Ramage, D., Hampson, S., Arcas, B.A.: Communication-efficient learning of deep networks from decentralized data. In: Artificial Intelligence and Statistics, pp. 1273–1282. PMLR (2017)

55. Nair, V., et al.: Unique identification of 50,000+ virtual reality users from head & hand motion data. In: 32nd USENIX Security Symposium (USENIX Security 23), pp. 895–910 (2023)

56. Nair, V.C., Munilla-Garrido, G., Song, D.: Going incognito in the metaverse: Achieving theoretically optimal privacy-usability tradeoffs in VR. In: Proceedings of the 36th Annual ACM Symposium on User Interface Software and Technology, pp. 1–16 (2023)

57. Odeleye, B., Loukas, G., Heartfield, R., Sakellari, G., Panaousis, E., Spyridonis, F.: Virtually secure: a taxonomic assessment of cybersecurity challenges in virtual reality environments. Comput. Secur. **124**, 102951 (2023)

58. Perez, E.: How much does it cost to build a crypto mining rig at home? (2024). https://cointelegraph.com/news/cost-home-crypto-mining-bitcoin

59. Pott, C., Gulmezoglu, B., Eisenbarth, T.: Overcoming the pitfalls of HPC-based cryptojacking detection in presence of GPUs. In: Proceedings of the Thirteenth ACM Conference on Data and Application Security and Privacy, pp. 177–188 (2023)

60. Saad, M., Khormali, A., Mohaisen, A.: Dine and dash: Static, dynamic, and economic analysis of in-browser cryptojacking. In: 2019 APWG Symposium on Electronic Crime Research (eCrime), pp. 1–12. IEEE (2019)

61. Steam: Share of steam users with a virtual reality (VR) headset worldwide as of September 2024, by device (2024). https://www.statista.com/statistics/265018/proportion-of-directx-versions-on-the-platform-steam

62. Tahir, R., Durrani, S., Ahmed, F., Saeed, H., Zaffar, F., Ilyas, S.: The browsers strike back: countering cryptojacking and parasitic miners on the web. In: IEEE INFOCOM 2019-IEEE Conference on Computer Communications, pp. 703–711. IEEE (2019)
63. Tekiner, E., Acar, A., Uluagac, A.S.: A lightweight IoT cryptojacking detection mechanism in heterogeneous smart home networks. In: NDSS (2022)
64. Tekiner, E., Acar, A., Uluagac, A.S., Kirda, E., Selcuk, A.A.: SoK: Cryptojacking malware. In: 2021 IEEE European Symposium on Security and Privacy (EuroS&P), pp. 120–139. IEEE (2021)
65. Trimananda, R., Le, H., Cui, H., Ho, J.T., Shuba, A., Markopoulou, A.: {OVRseen}: auditing network traffic and privacy policies in oculus {VR}. In: 31st USENIX Security Symposium (USENIX security 22), pp. 3789–3806 (2022)
66. Truță, F.: Coinhive crypto-mining service announces shutdown (2019). https://www.bitdefender.com/en-us/blog/hotforsecurity/coinhive-crypto-mining-service-announces-shutdown
67. Twingate: What is resource hijacking? how it works & examples (2024). https://www.twingate.com/blog/glossary/resource%20hijacking
68. Wang, J., Wang, Y., Zhang, N.: Secure and timely GPU execution in cyber-physical systems. In: Proceedings of the 2023 ACM SIGSAC Conference on Computer and Communications Security, pp. 2591–2605 (2023)
69. Weizman, O.: WebXR export - develop and export webXR experiences using unity webGL (2020). https://de-panther.github.io/unity-webxr-export
70. Xie, Q., Kim, J., Wang, Y., Shin, D., Chang, N., Pedram, M.: Dynamic thermal management in mobile devices considering the thermal coupling between battery and application processor. In: 2013 IEEE/ACM International Conference on Computer-Aided Design (ICCAD), pp. 242–247. IEEE (2013)

Author Index